Law, Bubbles, and Fina
Regulation

Financial regulation can fail when it is needed the most. The dynamics of asset price bubbles weaken financial regulation just as financial markets begin to overheat and the risk of crisis spikes. At the same time, the failure of financial regulations adds further fuel to a bubble.

This book examines the interaction of bubbles and financial regulation. It explores the ways in which bubbles lead to the failure of financial regulation by outlining five dynamics, which it collectively labels the "Regulatory Instability Hypothesis." These five dynamics include:

The regulatory stimulus cycle. As bubbles form and markets boom, policymakers face increasing pressure to provide regulatory stimulus for financial markets. Policymakers provide this stimulus not only by deregulating financial markets and repealing statutes and regulations, but also by lowering enforcement, providing exemptions to legal rules, and choosing not to apply legal rules to new contexts. In many cases, governments intervene in markets by providing legal preferences, monopolies, and other subsidies to select market participants.

Compliance rot. Bubbles undermine the compliance by market participants with antifraud and other financial rules.

Regulatory arbitrage frenzies. Bubbles foster increased gamesmanship of financial regulations by market participants. Bubbles sharpen the creativity of these parties and their appetite for legal risk.

Procyclical regulation. Certain regulations exacerbate boom and bust cycles in financial markets, without policymakers changing legal rules or market participants varying their level of compliance.

Promoting of investment herding. Other legal rules encourage investors and financial institutions to engage in dangerous herding into particular investments.

The book concludes by outlining approaches to make financial regulation more resilient to these dynamics that undermine law.

Erik F. Gerding is Associate Professor at the University of Colorado Law School.

The Economics of Legal Relationships
Sponsored by Michigan State University College of Law
Series Editors:
Nicholas Mercuro
Michigan State University College of Law
and
Michael D. Kaplowitz
Michigan State University

*The first three volumes listed above are published by and available from Elsevier

Law, Bubbles, and Financial Regulation

Erik F. Gerding

Routledge
Taylor & Francis Group

LONDON AND NEW YORK

First published 2014
by Routledge
2 Park Square, Milton Park, Abingdon, Oxfordshire OX14 4RN

and by Routledge
711 Third Avenue, New York, NY 10017, USA

First issued in paperback 2016

Routledge is an imprint of the Taylor & Francis Group, an informa business

British Library Cataloguing in Publication Data
A catalogue record for this book is available from the British Library

Library of Congress Cataloging in Publication Data
Gerding, Erik F., 1973–
   Law, bubbles and financial regulation / Erik F. Gerding.
   pages cm
   ISBN 978-0-415-77939-5 (hbk) – ISBN 978-1-315-88504-9 (ebk)
   1. Finance–Government policy. 2. Finance–Law and legislation.
   3. Capital markets–Government policy. 4. Stocks–Prices. 5. Financial
   crises. 6. Financial institutions–Law and legislation. I. Title.
   HG173.G44 2013
   332–dc23
                                                         2013014203

ISBN 13: 978-1-138-67439-4 (pbk)
ISBN 13: 978-0-415-77939-5 (hbk)

Typeset in Times New Roman
by Wearset Ltd, Boldon, Tyne and Wear

For Andrea

Contents

Figures

Tables

Acknowledgments

Chapters 2 and 3 were inspired by my article, "The Next Epidemic: Bubbles and the Growth and Decay of Securities Regulation," which appeared in Volume 38 of the *Connecticut Law Review*.

Chapter 6 builds off my article, "Deregulation Pas De Deux: Dual Regulatory Classes of Financial Institutions and the Path to Financial Crisis in Sweden and the United States," which appeared in Volume 15 of the journal *Nexus*.

I began my research for Chapter 8 when writing "Laws Against Bubbles: An Experimental Asset Market Approach to Analyzing Financial Regulation," which was published in the 2007 volume of the *Wisconsin Law Review*.

A portion of Chapter 9 builds off my article, "Credit Derivatives, Leverage, and Financial Regulation's Missing Macroeconomic Dimension," which appeared in Volume 8 of the *Berkeley Business Law Journal*.

In writing this book, I accumulated a long list of debts to family, friends, and colleagues. The following acknowledgments represent a meager and incomplete down payment.

Margaret Blair, Jim Cox, and Gordon Smith have been generous mentors throughout my career. Margaret's research and counsel shaped Chapter 9 in particular. Don Langevoort provided encouragement early in my career. It would be hard to isolate Anna Gelpern's influence on this book. Barak Orbach provided guidance from the moment I started my first law review article until the end of this book. Thank you to my friend and colleague Vic Fleischer. Thank you also to Jay Livingstone for first suggesting that I read Edward Chancellor's excellent *Devil Take the Hindmost*.

Several chapters of this book benefitted mightily from participants at workshops or the audience at presentations, including at the following: the Southwest/West Junior Law Faculty Workshop at the Arizona State University O'Connor College of Law, the University of Arizona James E. Rogers College of Law, the University of Colorado Law School, the University of Georgia School of Law, the University of Illinois College of Law, Loyola Law School in Los Angeles, Marquette University Law School, the University of New Mexico Department of Economics, the University of New Mexico School of Public Administration, and the Seattle University School of Law.

I presented chapters at a financial regulation workshop at the 2009 Law and Society Annual Meeting organized by Matt Bodie and David Zaring, the 2009 Canadian Law and Economics Association Annual Meeting, the 2009 *Nexus* Symposium on "The 80th Anniversary of the Great Crash of 1929: Law, Markets, and the Role of the State" organized by Tim Canova, the 2009 Rocky Mountain Junior Legal Scholars Workshop organized by Gordon Smith at BYU, the 2010 Conference on International Financial and Monetary Law organized by Eric Pan at Cardozo Law School, the Law and Entrepreneurship Workshops organized by Gordon Smith and Brian Broughman at the 2010 and 2011 Law and Society Annual Meetings, the 2011 University of Pennsylvania Wharton School of Business International Financial Regulation Conference organized by David Zaring, the 2011 American University Business Law Review Symposium, the 2011 University of Colorado Junior Corporate Law Scholars Workshop organized by Andrew Schwartz, the 2011 conference on "Bridging Theory and Practice in Finance, Macroeconomics, and Regulation" at the Vanderbilt University Law School/Owen Graduate School of Management that was organized by Margaret Blair, the 2012 Clearinghouse Annual Meeting, the 2013 International Financial Regulation Conference organized by Stavros Gadinis at the University of California, Berkeley, School of Law and a symposium on bubbles and group-think organized by Barak Orbach at the 2013 Law and Society Annual Meeting. Thank you to the organizers and participants at those workshops.

I am also grateful to the following scholars for inviting me to present at their institutions: Russell Munk, who organizes the U.S. Department of Treasury Speakers Series; Steven Schwarcz, who organized a panel on Shadow Banking at the 2012 American Bar Association Annual Meeting; Eric Talley at the University of California, Berkeley's Center for Law, Business, and the Economy; and Randall Thomas, who leads the Vanderbilt University Law School Law and Business Colloquium.

Large portions of Chapter 2 and other segments of the book were written while I was a Deutsche Akademische Austauschdienst fellow at the law faculty at Humboldt University in Berlin during the summer of 2010. That research was also financed by the University of New Mexico Research Allocations Committee. I am grateful for Professor Dr. Stefan Grundmann for hosting me in Berlin and for the research advice provided by Professor Dr. Jan Thiessen, now at the University of Tübingen.

A large number of scholars gave me valued feedback on several of the chapters of this book (or the law review articles that served as construction material for those chapters). These scholars include Matt Bodie, Larry Cunningham, Matias Fontenla, Peter Huang, John P. Hunt, Howell Jackson, Rob Jackson, Kim Krawiec, Kate Judge, Pat McCoy, Frank Partnoy, Carol Rose, Christine Sauer, John Schlegel, and Lynn Stout.

I am particularly indebted to the following scholars who provided comments on multiple sections of the book: Onnig Dombalagian, Adam Feibelman, Cristie Ford, Bob Hockett, Adam Levitin, Brett McDonnell, Saule Omarova, David Reiss, Heidi Schooner, Dan Schwarcz, Arthur Wilmarth, and David Zaring.

I appreciate the patience and support of my co-bloggers at *The Conglomerate*, including Lisa Fairfax, Christine Hurt, and Usha Rodrigues. Thank you to my international "agents" Eleanor Sebastian and Karina Bacalu.

I am indebted to the deans who have supported me over the years including Suellyn Scarnecchia, Leo Romero, and Kevin Washburn at New Mexico and Phil Weiser at Colorado.

I owe much to the patient and diligent librarians at both the University of New Mexico and University of Colorado Law Schools. At the former, Eileen Cohen, Ernesto Longa, Michelle Rigual, and Sherri Thomas deserve special thanks. At the latter, Jane Thompson and Matt Zafiratos worked research miracles as I finished the manuscript. Sally Quinn worked expertly to copy edit this manuscript.

My colleagues at the University of New Mexico School of Law took a huge risk in hiring me out of practice and provided a home for five wonderful years. Their support gave me the confidence to start this book before I had tenure. They also heard multiple presentations of early versions of many chapters of this book. Thank you to Norman Bay, Reed Benson, Barbara Bergman, Kip Bobroff, Sherri Burr, Camille Carey, Barbara Creel, Chris Fritz, Eileen Gauna, Laura Gomez, April Land, Alfred Mathewson, Max Minzner, Margaret Montoya, Jenny Moore, Sergio Pareja, Ted Parnall, Liz Rapaport, Rob Schwartz, Gloria Valencia-Weber, Peter Winograd, and Christine Zuni-Cruz. Michael Browde, Ruth Singer, Nathalie Martin, and Stewart Paley welcomed my family to New Mexico and made us feel at home. Carol Suzuki's friendship and close and careful reading of various manuscripts deserves special mention. Fred Hart provided wise counsel throughout.

Thank you to my colleagues at my new home at the University of Colorado Law School.

Most importantly, I would like to thank my family. My parents and my uncle provided moral support. Lucas and Violeta provided inspiration. I would not have finished this book but for Andrea.

Introduction
The Regulatory Instability Hypothesis

We move through the economic and social wreckage of the global financial crisis. Sifting through the debris field, we encounter the once shiny and still strange detritus of financial market failure: option adjustable rate mortgages (ARMs), synthetic collateralized debt obligations, credit default swaps, trust preferred securities. All this devastation, examined at great length in other books, seems hypermodern, bewildering, and even alien.

Unless our eyes shift their focus. We have been here before. With a changed focus and on a different level of abstraction, contours begin to emerge of a landscape that would have been familiar to our grandparents and to their grandparents as well. After three centuries of financial market history – from stock jobbers in London in the 1690s to NASDAQ in the 1990s – we face once again the bitter aftermath of a collapsed asset price bubble, the most destructive one since the Great Depression.

The postmortem confronts us with thorny questions. How did this happen? Who is to blame? How could this disaster have been averted? Why did the vast apparatus of national and international financial regulation, first erected in the wake of the Great Depression, fail to prevent the Panic of 2007–2008? (Admittedly this moniker is a misnomer, as the financial crisis continues to reverberate in Europe if it does not threaten to spread to Asia and other continents.) These questions are not merely academic; lawmakers face enormous pressure to find ways to avert a recurrence of the crisis. After all, less than a decade lapsed from the implosion of the U.S. technology stock boom until the first tremors of what started as the "subprime crisis."

Strangely, even though the landscape should be familiar, financial reform has emphasized fixing immediate symptoms, i.e., the particular financial products and markets that broke apart in the Panic: central clearing for derivatives, new rules for securitizations, and "living wills" for complex financial institutions. Legislators have grafted new regulatory structures on top of the existing architecture of financial law. Financial regulation has seen no revolutionary change. This has led some to wonder if financial reform is preparing only to re-fight the last war. Are policymakers constructing high-tech Maginot lines against an enemy that will not wield the same weapons or invade by the same route again? We have been here before. The causes of this crisis resemble the causes of many past crises, but only if we examine them with the right lens and proper degree of abstraction.

With the proper historical focus, a disturbing insight emerges, one that should gnaw at any faith placed in this round – or perhaps any incarnation – of financial reform. In past bubbles throughout three centuries of history, financial laws buckled over and again. They failed to prevent bubbles. Moreover, law did too little to mitigate the economic destruction after asset price bubbles popped. Most troubling, financial law appears, in many cases, to have contributed to the growth of bubbles and to the severity of their implosion.

After each crisis, lawmakers responded with a regulatory backlash, launching flotillas of new legal rules. Yet many of these laws ultimately faded or failed when the next bubble emerged. Financial regulation has been caught in a series of long historical cycles, which were propelled not by iron laws, but by political and economic undercurrents that are powerful nonetheless. These currents swirl as booming markets and failing financial laws feed one another.

This book explores the interactions of financial regulation and asset price bubbles. Scholars have written rich tomes on the economics and history of asset price bubbles. Yet the role that law and financial regulation has played in bubbles and the effects that bubbles have on financial laws has remained largely in the background. The chapters that follow examine the interactions among bubbles and laws. The book argues that these interactions generated formidable and recurrent feedback loops. This feedback damaged financial markets and deteriorated the effectiveness of financial regulations, whether in banking, securities, or corporate law. This book explains how bubbles trigger the deterioration and decay of financial laws by introducing a set of theories called the Regulatory Instability Hypothesis.[1] This Regulatory Instability Hypothesis posits that strong forces act to decay financial regulations at the precise moment when they are most needed – when markets boom, investors and financial institutions exercise less care and take on more risk and leverage, and financial crisis looms. The Regulatory Instability Hypothesis argues that the following five dynamics cause the effective deterioration of financial regulation during bubbles:

1   *The regulatory stimulus cycle*: bubbles create strong pressure on governments to make regulatory changes to stimulate booming financial markets. Regulatory stimuli often take the form of deregulation (i.e., the repeal or roll back of legal rules). Yet deregulation is but one example; other forms of regulatory stimulus include lower enforcement and looser interpretations of existing rules by public officials. Furthermore, lawmakers and regulators create regulatory subsidies when they grant legal preferences to, or direct the government to make investments in, particular financial markets.

2   *Compliance rot*: bubbles skew the incentives of financial market participants against obeying financial laws. Deteriorating legal compliance by some players undermines compliance by others in the marketplace and financial fraud and other law-breaking can reach epidemic proportions.

3 *Regulatory arbitrage frenzies*: asset price bubbles likewise increase the incentives of market participants to game financial laws short of breaking them altogether. Eager to participate in surging financial markets, investors and financial institutions become more aggressive in seeking or devising economic substitutes for heavily regulated or prohibited transactions. Again, rising levels of regulatory arbitrage can generate cascades and contagion effects in the marketplace.

4 *Procyclical regulations*: some financial regulations interact with economic cycles to exacerbate market booms and busts. This occurs in the normal operation of these regulations. It requires neither changes in regulator behavior nor deteriorating compliance by market participants with financial laws.

5 *Herd-promoting regulations*: financial regulation does too little to counteract the herd behavior that drives asset price bubbles. Moreover, many financial regulations, by creating preferences for certain asset classes, actively encourage this herding. These regulations thus perversely increase the correlations of risk among financial institutions with destructive market-wide consequences.

Together, these five dynamics weaken financial regulations just as the storm clouds of a financial crisis gather.

What are bubbles, when they matter, and why they matter

To understand this ominous warning, a little context is necessary. It is important to understand what asset price bubbles are, when and how they threaten financial markets, and which types of bubbles pose the greatest dangers. The answers to these questions illuminate the cases in which the dynamics of the Regulatory Instability Hypothesis pose the greatest danger. These answers can help identify those most crucial financial regulations that, when undermined, would cause the most economic damage.

Bubbles are unfortunately not an alien concept to the public today. The global economy still struggles with a massive financial crisis (which this book calls the Panic of 2007–2008)[2] with roots in real estate investment bubbles. The tale of how the crisis began has now been told many times over: subprime and exotic mortgages and complex financial instruments based on those mortgages fueled a dramatic and prolonged boom in U.S. housing prices.[3] However, the U.S. real estate bubble of the last decade is not the only story. The financial crisis gathered strength in Europe because of severe losses incurred by European financial institutions. These firms suffered not only because of their mortgage-related investments in the United States,[4] but also from the collapse of a string of European real estate bubbles that stretched along an arc from Iceland to Ireland to the Iberian peninsula to the Black Sea.[5] Now, after financial markets have crashed, media stories find financial bubbles in every corner of the global economy – Chinese stocks,[6] Chinese real estate,[7] gold,[8] U.S. Treasury Bonds,[9] and even higher education in the United States funded by student loans.[10] Perhaps bubble thinking is experiencing a bubble of its own. Although this intellectual epidemic of anxiety over overvalued financial markets would have been far more useful while real estate markets were overheating in the years before the Panic of 2007–2008.

The Panic of 2007–2008 reawakened interest in a rich lode of scholarship on the economic history of financial bubbles.[11] One problem with the widespread use of the term bubble is that it seems to take on any number of meanings. To prevent this intellectual coin from being debased, it is important to turn to economists, who have been, as should be expected, more rigorous than the public in defining what they mean by an asset price bubble. The most widely used definition of a bubble, and the one adopted by this book, is when current market prices for a class of assets, such as stocks or real estate, diverge from the fundamental value of those assets.[12] An asset's fundamental value is, in turn, defined as the present value of all future cash streams from that asset.[13] This definition, as Chapter 1 of this book discusses in more depth, presents numerous analytic challenges. In particular, figuring out whether a bubble exists at the present time requires forecasting future cash flows, and determining whether a forecast is reasonable is inescapably subjective. Identifying historical bubbles by comparing past prices to whether the projected cash flows of assets actually materialized runs the intellectual risk of hindsight bias. So, indentifying bubbles for either descriptive or prescriptive purposes involves a significant degree of uncertainty. As this introduction underscores later, this uncertainty poses insurmountable obstacles for neither the descriptive nor the prescriptive aims of this book.

This renewed public interest in bubbles should be welcomed as financial history demonstrates that asset price bubbles bear responsibility for some of the most profound financial crises in terms of the destruction of national wealth, damages to the real economy (unemployment, loss of productivity), extreme social dislocation, and even political upheaval and violence. The worst of these effects strike after the implosion of a particular kind of bubble, namely one fueled by borrowed money and leveraged financial institutions. Alone, an asset price bubble or a banking crisis can cause serious economic damage; when coupled together, they generate catastrophe.[14] Of course, even asset price bubbles *not* financed with borrowed money (sometimes called equity bubbles) can inflict economic devastation by destroying investor wealth, spawning epidemics of financial fraud and lawbreaking, and damaging investor confidence in financial markets. This book will explore these consequences as well. Yet the most gripping concern are those bubbles in which credit and leverage play a central role, for reasons which this chapter previews and the book later explains in more detail.

Renewed public and political concern with bubbles can benefit from over two decades of path-breaking economic research on how bubbles form in financial markets and the role that they play in financial crises. Chapter 1 will examine some of this research, but several threads are worth unspooling here. First, much of this research represents a synthesis of the behavioral finance movement that emerged in the last twenty years, on the one hand, and earlier, less quantitative economic scholarship that posited that financial markets suffer from cyclical instability, on the other. Behavioral finance itself builds off evidence from psychological experiments that document how individuals suffer from various behavioral biases and cognitive limitations. These biases and limitations cause individuals to make decisions that deviate from the predictions of economic models that assume individuals are rational actors who maximize their self-interest.[15] If asset prices spike, behavioral biases can cause investors to chase price trends and engage in herd behavior.

Behavioral finance connects experimental evidence and theory on the cognitive limitations of individuals to market phenomena. It argues that these biases and cognitive limitations help explain empirical evidence that prices in financial markets have at times diverged significantly from what neoclassical economics, generally, and the Efficient Markets Hypothesis, in particular, would predict.[16] The work of behavioral finance scholars has strong affinities with the work of an older generation of economists, including Charles Kindleberger and Hyman Minsky, who presented historical evidence and theoretical models that explained how financial markets suffer from periodic bouts of bubbles and crashes.[17]

Although "irrational behavior" is central to many of the current models of how bubbles initially form, it is important to underscore that rational behavior also can play a crucial role. Indeed, a great deal of research on individual decisions made in the crowd of a financial market focuses on how individually rational responses can contribute to the folly of the collective destruction of wealth. Rationality can drive a decision by an investor to buy stocks in a boom even if she thinks prices are unsustainably high.[18] Rationality can also undergird a decision by a depositor who withdraws money from a bank during a run even if he thinks the bank is currently solvent.[19] Indeed, it would be often be *irrational* for many investors, even those who think market prices are unsustainable, to bet against the bubble.[20]

This odd cohabitation of irrational and rational decision-making will be explored throughout this book. It will inform the models this book uses to explain the behavior of lawmakers, regulators, and market participants (investors, company promoters, financial intermediaries) as they create, demolish, interpret, enforce, obey, bend, and break legal rules.

Another strand of economic scholarship looks at the importance of expanding credit and increasing leverage in fueling asset price bubbles. This scholarship, surveyed in Chapter 9, includes cutting-edge research on the workings of a leverage cycle in which the leverage in the economy dramatically expands as markets boom and radically contracts when markets crash.[21] Consistent with this model, other economists have presented empirical evidence that financial institutions increased their leverage during the boom years preceding the Panic of 2007–2008 and then shed leverage once the crisis took hold and financial markets plummeted.[22] This research sheds more light on why bubbles fueled by credit and leverage pose greater dangers. When financial institutions, businesses, and households increase leverage during asset booms, they magnify the losses to equity holders should markets fall.[23] However, collective increases in leverage have the pernicious effect of masking this risk, by driving asset prices higher.

Increases in financial institution leverage effectively increase the total amount of money (or "liquidity") that can be invested in financial markets.[24] When financial institutions collectively deleverage (for example, because of losses when asset prices fall), the supply of money contracts. A perfect economic storm then brews: falling prices generate losses for leveraged financial firms who deleverage, causing prices to sink further. This dynamic can cause financial institutions, already rendered more fragile by higher leverage, to fail and credit markets to seize.[25] The widespread failure of financial institutions, in turn, can devastate economies.[26] As financial institutions deleverage or even fail, credit contracts and chokes off economic growth. Systematic bank failure can cause disruption of financial intermediation in the economy, as banks lose the capacity (including the human capital of loan officers) to distinguish "good" borrowers from "bad."[27] It cannot be understated: bubbles fueled by debt and linked to financial institutions pose the most severe risk.

The leverage cycle points to a recurrent theme in economic research on bubbles – the role that feedback loops play in generating bubbles and crashes and in destabilizing financial markets. When leverage increases during an economic boom and decreases during a crash, it also exacerbates the boom and crash.[28] Furthermore, behavioral finance models claim that bubbles form because of positive feedback investment strategies; when investors chase price trends, rising prices spur more investors to buy assets, leading to higher prices.[29] These feedback loops foster the formation of boom/bust cycles in financial markets.[30]

Feedback mechanisms serve as a recurrent theme of this book. Economic research focuses on how feedback mechanisms can make markets behave in nonlinear ways – suffering spectacular booms, busts, and moments of profound disequilibrium. This book argues that feedback mechanisms also cause financial laws to experience severe bouts of instability and disequilibrium of their own.

Impoverished legal responses to bubbles

Despite the richness of economic research on bubbles, the legal response to economic crises has often been less than fully informed by economic insight. That is not to say that law does not react to bubbles. Legal scholars have demonstrated quite the opposite: the most profound historical changes in banking and securities regulations have tended to emerge from the frothy political wake of collapsed bubbles.[31] Often, however, these regulatory changes bear little connection to the causes and effects of financial bubbles. Curiously, for all the media talk about bubbles, statutes passed in response to a financial crisis seldom treat bubbles as a cause or contributing factor to financial crisis.[32]

Instead, legislation in the wake of crises typically addresses symptoms specific to that historical period. For example, in the United States, the Dodd-Frank Act of 2010[33] tackles a long list of suspected culprits of the Panic of 2007–2008. It addresses, among other things, subprime mortgages sold to unsophisticated households,[34] over-the-counter derivatives threatening the solvency of large financial institutions,[35] and executive compensation.[36]

The problem with this kind of ahistorical and particularized legislative response is that it ignores the larger context – historical, economic, and political. This context would reveal deep connections between the Panic of 2007–2008 and past financial crises that struck when financial booms imploded. This lack of context explains why legislatures and financial regulators are at risk of preparing to re-fight the last war, which is never a good military strategy.

Unfortunately, that missing historical context would also reveal that vast legal responses in the wake of crises are part of a larger regulatory cycle. Financial laws passed in the wake of many historical bubbles have been repealed, re-interpreted, under-enforced, and ignored when financial markets later boomed again. Ahistorical, highly particularized responses to crises fail to provide a sustainable long-term approach to mitigating the effects of asset price bubbles. One of the overarching aims of this book is to integrate economic research on the causes and effects of asset price bubbles with legal scholarship on the fragility of financial regulation. It adds a much needed legal perspective on the causes and consequences of bubbles and the policy responses to the crises that ensue.

Another aim of the book is to bring the insights from legal scholarship to bear on economic thought on bubbles. Although many cutting edge economists who have studied asset price bubbles look at specific legal rules (for example, legal constraints on arbitrage), the role of financial regulation in the development of bubbles is often not the centerpiece of the inquiry. This book will examine the role that both laws and legal change – including change through regulatory stimulus and regulatory arbitrage – plays in the formation of bubbles.

However, this book focuses much of its energy on the more novel question about the reverse effects: namely, what impacts do the dynamics of asset price bubbles have on financial regulation? How do bubbles change the content, interpretation, and enforcement of legal rules? How do they affect compliance with legal rules? A failure to look at how bubbles change the content, application, and effectiveness of financial laws can have dire consequences.

Even reform proposals based on sound economic research and data must eventually be translated into concrete legal rules. These rules are subject to repeal; as memories of the Panic of 2007–2008 fade, the current round of financial reform will be subject to deregulatory pressures. This may strike the contemporary reader as unsurprising. Indeed, there is a widespread, popular, yet inchoate notion that deregulation caused the current financial crisis.[37] As with "bubbles," popular thought may find the correct target in a very general sense, yet fail to achieve a nuanced understanding of what "deregulation" means and how it contributes to bubbles and financial crises. Legal thought can help policymakers and the public understand how regulation, deregulation, and legal change more generally can take different forms and be measured in different ways. Legal scholarship can thus help move the public debate beyond cartoonish, binary questions of "more" or "less" regulation. It is not just the quantity or even the substance of regulation that should concern us, but also how regulators, judges, and market participants interpret, apply, and comply with legal rules.

Because legal rules are not self-executing computer codes, they are subject to heavier or lighter enforcement, as well as to creative interpretation, gamesmanship, and violation by human agents.

The Regulatory Instability Hypothesis

The problem is that bubbles radically alter both the content and application of legal rules. Market booms can interact with political markets, psychological dynamics, ideologies and social norms, and legal institutions to trigger dramatic deterioration and decay in the effectiveness of financial regulation. To see how this occurs, the five elements of the Regulatory Instability Hypothesis deserve further elaboration. Each of these elements is summarized below.

The regulatory stimulus cycle: deregulation and beyond

An examination of financial history reveals a clear pattern of governments changing legal rules to stimulate markets before or during the inflation of numerous asset price bubbles. I call these changes "regulatory stimulus." Then, after markets crash, policymakers respond with a regulatory backlash of new rules to constrain investment and risk-taking in financial markets. This *regulatory stimulus cycle* leads to a perverse result. There is less regulation and less effective regulation just as markets begin to overheat and the risk of crisis and of financial fraud and law-breaking spikes. Then re-regulation takes hold only after the bubble has burst, the economic damage has been done, and investors and markets have been chastened by a crash.

Regulatory stimulus includes deregulation – i.e., the repeal or substantive alteration and dilution of financial rules – that promotes investment in particular financial markets. However, regulatory stimulus covers quite a bit more too. It would be a mistake to focus on the repeal of statutes and regulations to the exclusion of other modes by which governments change legal rules to promote investment in particular asset markets. Consider the following analysis. Financial regulation can operate as a "tax" on investment or lending, whether in general or in a particular market.[38] The economic opposite of a government tax is of course a government subsidy; a subsidy for a particular investment can have the same net economic effect as repealing a tax on that investment. Regulatory subsidies or stimuli can take a wide number of forms, including granting business ventures a legal monopoly to encourage them to develop new investment markets. Governments can also create various legal preferences for certain investments, such as by crafting exemptions to financial regulations. Similarly, policymakers can choose not to collect a regulatory tax by lowering enforcement efforts or by not applying an existing regulation to emerging, but economically equivalent activities.

The term "regulatory stimulus" as used in this book thus encompasses the following legal changes to the extent they promote or unleash greater investment or lending in particular asset markets:

- *the repeal or roll back of statutes, regulations, or legal rules*;
- *exemptions or waivers* from particular rules granted by lawmakers or regulators;
- *looser interpretations of financial laws and regulations* either by courts or regulatory agencies;
- *reduced enforcement of existing statutes and regulations* by regulatory authorities; and
- *active government stimulation of financial markets* through various legal devices, including via

  - *granting of charters or legal monopolies*,
  - *government guarantees of, or investments in, particular markets or ventures*, or
  - *the creation of other legal preferences for certain investments*, such as exemptions from rules applicable to a broad range of other financial instruments or markets.

If one takes an even broader definition, regulatory stimulus might also include a failure to exercise existing legal authority or to adapt existing authority to new, but economically equivalent investment contexts. In many historical episodes surveyed, regulatory stimulus took the form of creating, authorizing, or facilitating a particular financial innovation – such as a new financial instrument. Indeed, the legal history of bubbles provided in Chapter 1 includes a long list of examples of lawmakers endorsing, subsidizing, or even midwifing the birth of new financial technologies.

Moving from deregulation to a broader conception of regulatory stimulus runs some risk of looseness in evaluating historical evidence. Yet the risk of cherry-picking is outweighed by a broader and more nuanced understanding of what "law" means. "Law in action" rather than merely "law in the books" helps focus on the concrete effects of legal rules and the actual behavior of legal actors rather than simply counting whether there are more or fewer pages in the statute books. This book therefore builds on the foundation of the Legal Realism and Law and Society movements, which pushed legal scholars to look beyond statutes and cases.[39] Understanding the real world effects of laws requires studying how lawmakers interpret and enforce legal rules. It also requires considering a broad range of legal actors, including legislators, heads of government, regulators at various agencies, judges and courts, international organizations, and even private actors to whom regulatory functions have been delegated. Moreover, understanding the effects and effectiveness of legal rules requires looking at the behavior of individuals and firms subject to the law's command.

Chapter 3 of this book provides three models to explain the historical pattern of regulatory stimulus as markets boom and regulatory backlash after they crash. The first model looks at how bubbles radically alter the rational calculus of competing interest groups in demanding (or opposing) regulatory stimulus, as well as the rational calculus of lawmakers in supplying it. This analysis, heavily influenced by public choice theory, is supplemented with a second model that examines how bubbles interact with the behavioral biases of regulators and interest groups to promote regulatory stimulus. Again, the interaction of rational and "irrational" decision-making serves as a recurrent motif in the book. For example, central bankers or bank regulators may be unwilling to suffer the career ramifications of taking actions that might cause financial markets to drop.[40] Meanwhile, they may also suffer from "disaster myopia," that is the tendency to underestimate the probability of an economic crisis when one has not occurred for a long period.[41] Yet, economic or psychological explanations may not provide a complete account of the decisions of the regulators and regulated. Accordingly, the third model examines how bubbles interact with ideological currents and changing social norms to encourage regulatory stimulus.

No matter the model used, the regulatory stimulus cycle and asset price bubbles generate powerful feedback loops; less and looser restrictions on investment or borrowing – particularly regulations that govern the provision of credit and the leverage of financial institutions – can stimulate financial markets. Booming markets, in turn, promote further pruning and slackening of those legal restrictions.

Compliance rot: deteriorating obedience to financial laws

Even those financial regulations that survive the regulatory stimulus cycle intact – i.e., those that are not repealed or more loosely interpreted or enforced – may, nonetheless, be rendered ineffective by the dynamics of a bubble. The prospect of sustained rising prices in financial markets can undermine obedience with financial laws by investors, financial institutions and intermediaries, and other market participants. Laws on the books have less meaning when compliance rot sets in.

Chapter 4 uses the same three-part template described above to create models – based on rational calculations, behavioral biases, and ideologies and norms – to explain how legal compliance deteriorates radically during boom times. Under the rational model, booms provide immediate benefits yet delay legal liability and other costs for breaking the law. Those who would engage in financial misconduct understand that the budgets and capacities of regulatory watchdogs may not keep pace with mushrooming volume of transactions during bubble times. If compliance deteriorates widely, there can be a jailbreak effect; firms and individuals may conclude that, "they can't catch us all." Second, bubbles exacerbate the behavioral biases of market participants, which can cause them to systematically underestimate the legal and other consequences to violating the law. Third, bubbles often coincide with broader social shifts in which norms of legal compliance and the perceived legitimacy of laws erodes.

Chapter 4 focuses much of the analysis on deteriorating compliance with antifraud rules during bubbles. Yet it also applies these same three models to prudential banking rules, including laws designed to protect the safety and soundness of financial institutions and mitigate systemic risk. Lower compliance with financial laws causes the deterioration in the effectiveness of those rules. Here too feedback loops form. Deteriorating compliance with laws that combat fraud or restrain investment and lending can add further fuel to a bubble, which, in turn, can further vitiate obedience to financial law.

Regulatory arbitrage frenzies

The same dynamics that encourage market participants to break laws also lead them to bend laws using techniques of "regulatory arbitrage." Regulatory arbitrage is a new bottle for old wine. It describes how firms and individuals will seek to lower the "regulatory tax" on a transaction (that is, when financial regulations either prohibit or render a transaction extremely costly). They accomplish this by seeking or devising close economic substitutes that are less regulated or completely unregulated. Chapter 5 explains how regulatory arbitrage is more complex than simple evasion or finding loopholes. Investors and financial institutions seek to exploit the "incompleteness" and jurisdictional limitations inherent in all legal rules by engaging in one or both of two strategies. First, they can move capital to less regulated markets subject to other jurisdictions. Chapter 5 labels this "investment switching." Alternatively, they can hire lawyers, investment bankers, accountants, and other advisors to construct elaborate transactional structures to provide the same economics as a heavily regulated or prohibited investment but subject to a much lower regulatory tax. Chapter 5 labels this "investment structuring."

Just as they cause the deterioration of legal compliance, asset price bubbles increase the immediate benefits to regulatory arbitrage and delay the potential legal costs; booms increase the incentives to game legal rules that might otherwise shut institutions and individuals out of increased profit opportunities. Bubbles also can exacerbate behavioral biases that cause market actors to discount excessively the risks to regulatory arbitrage. Finally, bubbles affect the norms in financial and legal communities in ways that make aggressive use of regulatory arbitrage more acceptable.

Regulatory arbitrage can thus become contagious. Widespread use of investment switching and structuring encourages more market participants to partake. Those investors and institutions that do not will face the marketplace's punishment for failing to enjoy the returns of a booming market. Regulatory arbitrage frenzies begin.

To demonstrate the complexity of the techniques of regulatory arbitrage, Chapter 5 examines in detail an important species, regulatory capital arbitrage, which describes the gaming of bank capital rules. Regulatory capital arbitrage allows financial institutions to increase and cloak their leverage. As mentioned above, increased financial institution leverage has rippling and reverberating effects. It renders financial institutions more vulnerable to downturns. It increases the supply of credit to financial markets, which can fuel asset prices and the growth of bubbles. By inflating asset prices, increased leverage masks the risks it poses both to individual firms and markets as a whole. Once again, particularly insidious feedback loops between bubbles and regulatory dynamics can form.

Regulatory arbitrage can also prevent policymakers from seeing new forms of risk that materialize in financial markets. Moreover (as Part IV of the book argues) regulatory arbitrage has also obscured the emergence of new channels in the economy for providing credit and increasing leverage. As noted above (and analyzed further in Chapters 2 and 9), credit and leverage can inflate bubbles. Thus, new, by fostering new channels for credit and leverage, regulatory arbitrage enlarges a dangerous regulatory blind spot.

Procyclical regulations

Bubbles and financial regulations can have perverse interactions even if regulations are not rolled back and remain fully enforced and obeyed. Economists have pointed to evidence that some financial regulations exacerbate boom and bust cycles in the economy in their normal modes, without any misconduct by financial firms or regulators. Through their mechanical operation, these *procyclical regulations* interact with market cycles to spur financial firms to make more investments and increased lending during booms and to throttle back after a crash.

To explain this, a simple example suffices for now.[42] Loan loss reserves require banks to set aside money to cover the probability of defaults on their mortgages or other loans. If the amount of the reserve required by legal rule is based on the previous year's losses on mortgages or other loans, then a real estate or other bubble that lasts several years can lead to troubling results.

Consider how rising market prices can lead to fewer loan defaults. When real estate prices surge for a protracted period, mortgage borrowers can exit loans they can no longer afford by selling their homes for a higher price (or by refinancing, if credit is cheap). Under the regulation, lower defaults allow banks to lower reserves. This frees a bank to lend more money. More credit can drive housing prices higher and a feedback loop develops.

However, the feedback loop jumps into reverse should real estate prices falter. Defaults rise. Lower prices narrow the exit options for borrowers to resell or "flip" assets. Higher default rates leads to higher reserve rates, which throttles back bank lending. Less bank credit further depresses asset prices, prevents more borrowers from reselling or refinancing, and increases the default rate.

This type of poorly designed (but unfortunately not uncommon) loan loss reserve requirements amplifies market cycles. Economists label these regulations "procyclical." Note that this procyclicality has both macroeconomic and microeconomic dimensions. Procyclical regulations have macroeconomic effects by inflating market booms and deepening market crashes. They also have microeconomic effects: lower loan loss reserves mean banks are more exposed to market downturns. Procyclical regulations thus run counter to regulations that aim to mitigate the risk of individual financial institutions failing. The systematic failure of financial institutions, in turn, can have macroeconomic consequences of their own.

Herd-promoting regulations

Financial regulations can also promote dangerous collective behavior by financial institutions. As noted briefly above (and as analyzed in more detail in Chapter 1), bubbles arise because of the herding of investors into particular asset classes. The economic logic behind this destructive behavior has a close analogue in the investor decision-making that drives bank runs.[43]

Financial regulation not only does too little to prevent these two forms of herding, it can actually promote them. Legal rules, such as bank capital regulations, encourage financial institutions to invest in asset classes that theoretically involve lower risk and seem more liquid. Investment grade asset-backed securities and Greek sovereign debt serve as two examples. Collective investment in these asset classes can reinforce their apparent safety and liquidity. Even if this collective investment does not create an asset price bubble, a bubble can further enhance these appearances.

Yet the herd can turn. The riskiness of these assets can spike and their liquidity can evaporate when collapsing bubbles (or even the mere fear of a bubble's collapse) trigger a stampede by financial institutions out of these market segments. Chapter 7 looks at the various facets of this herd behavior during crises, including the economics of bank runs and liquidity spirals.

Regulations can also encourage herding into liquidity – a kind of bank-run-in-reverse – by creating various legal preferences for certain asset classes. Chapter 7 analyzes how regulations, including exemptions to the U.S. Bankruptcy Code, fostered liquidity in the markets for novel financial instruments. By promoting herding into liquidity, these regulatory changes set the stage for post-modern bank runs. Chapter 7 also looks at how government bailouts – or even market-wide expectations of government bailouts – encourage herding by financial institutions. These firms understand that if they congregate into certain asset classes, the government may be unwilling to let them fail collectively because of the severe economic fallout that would result. The government may have few or no legally, politically, or economically principled ways to bail out only part of the herd and leave the rest to their fate.

This "too-correlated-to-fail" problem highlights the severe consequences of herd-promoting regulations. These regulations can exacerbate asset price bubbles and set the stage for bank runs and liquidity crises. Moreover, by prompting financial institutions to take correlated risks, they increase the susceptibility of these firms to common economic shocks and thus elevate systemic risk.[44]

In outlining and examining these five elements of the Regulatory Instability Hypothesis, the book relies heavily on models, economic and otherwise. This runs some risk of presenting the messiness of politics, markets, and laws as operating in too mechanical a manner. This risk is worth running to the extent that creating those models and stripping out some of the details leads to either testable hypotheses or at least a clearer understanding of the tectonic forces that stress financial regulation during crucial market periods.

Creating models and theories should not, however, minimize the importance of context, nuance, and deep institutional knowledge. Indeed, regulatory changes during various historical bubble periods are alike, but only when viewed at a sufficient degree of abstraction. The forms of regulatory stimulus and backlash, the problems of deteriorating legal compliance ("compliance rot"), and the strategies of regulatory arbitrage were not the same in early nineteenth century Britain and late twentieth century Japan. Rather the legal dynamics of a bubble in a given country at a given historical moment are shaped by the nature of laws, the structure of legal institutions, the roles of lawyers, and the sociopolitical and cultural environment. These contextual factors provide form to the abstract forces at work behind regulatory subsidies, regulatory backlash, non-compliance with legal rules, regulatory arbitrage...

The consequences of regulatory instability

Together and apart, the five elements of the Regulatory Instability Hypothesis paint a bleak and unnerving picture for regulating financial markets. They suggest that the risk of financial regulation failure increases at precisely the moment those regulations are most needed. These four dynamics may not be present to an equal extent in every booming market, and this book does not argue that there are iron laws to financial history. Nevertheless, the dynamics of asset booms and bubbles create powerful undercurrents with which financial regulation must contend.

The dynamics may affect legal rules in different domains of financial law: banking regulation, securities regulation, and even corporate law. However, when the Regulatory Instability Hypothesis applies to certain categories of financial regulation, concerns should be elevated. When these dynamics undermine regulations that govern the credit extended by, and the leverage of, financial regulations, they attack two critical regulatory functions. As noted above, these regulations both mitigate the magnitude of bubbles and promote the resiliency of financial institutions and markets to popped bubbles. When these regulations weaken and leverage increases, asset prices climb, as does the fragility of financial institutions and entire markets. Bubbles fed by credit and marked by highly leveraged financial institutions generate the worst crises.

Many of these same credit and leverage regulations also have a role in protecting the "safety and soundness" of financial institutions. These regulations serve a heightened purpose of mitigating systemic risk – or the risk of losses to entire markets, from which investment diversification offers little shelter.[45] Regulations governing bank liquidity and deposit insurance are also intended to mitigate systemic risk, by protecting financial institutions from liquidity shocks and the classic problem of bank runs.[46] Policymakers should then be concerned when any of the elements of the Regulatory Instability Hypothesis – regulatory subsidies (particularly deregulation and under-enforcement), compliance rot, frenzies of regulatory arbitrage, and procyclical or herd-promoting regulations – threaten to subvert systemic risk regulations. When these regulations buckle, bursting bubbles threaten to create economic chaos.

   The Regulatory Instability Hypothesis therefore provides a framing device for a series of recurrent and even cyclical threats to what should be considered the overriding *ur*-purpose of financial laws: mitigating the damage to financial markets and to the "real" economy from financial crises. Asset price bubbles, which have been a persistent feature of financial history, can both spawn financial crises and subvert financial laws. The collapse of bubbles has tended to generate the most significant changes in financial laws.[47] It is not that large a leap then to say that the animating purpose of financial regulation born of crisis and bubble is – or should be – to ensure that future crises do not become severe enough to melt down capital markets and the economy, if not to prevent crises altogether.

   However, lawmakers can lose sight of the forest in the trees. Attempts to address what are perceived to be the immediate causes of the last crisis or to solve particular market failures may distract from the original and overarching objective: reducing the likelihood that a financial crisis will generate widespread economic and social devastation. This *ur*-purpose of financial regulation tends to be forgotten slowly during long intermissions between financial crises. Efforts to fine-tune various securities and banking laws may lead focus to shift towards subsidiary policy goals. This change in focus, together with a tendency to exult in the ability of markets to govern themselves during prosperous economic periods, obscures the most important purpose of regulation: to protect markets and societies from the worst-of-the-worst market meltdowns. These factors may also obscure the recurrent dynamics that cause the deterioration and decay of financial laws and undermine their ability to serve this fundamental objective.

The descriptive tools and aims of this book: a preview of shadow banking

The primary objective of this book is not to generate a simple list of policy proposals. Instead, the boom aims to describe in broad brush and fine grain the challenges to financial regulation during bubbles. It looks to elaborate on the Regulatory Instability Hypothesis as a construct to organize and understand those problems. Although the focus is on law, the book looks heavily to insights from history and economics. The longest chapter of the book, Chapter 2, provides a historical background to financial regulation and fraud before, during, and after over a dozen bubble periods. The book also surveys economic research (both microeconomic and macroeconomic) on asset price bubbles and financial regulation. Still the overall focus remains on describing and examining the Regulatory Instability Hypothesis. Thus the book does not seek to match a historian's thick or comprehensive description of financial history or the econometrician's intense quantitative analysis.

   In setting forth the Regulatory Instability Hypothesis, this book of course discusses the Panic of 2007–2008. However, it does not seek to provide a soup-to-nuts account of that crisis; bookstores are already crowded with texts that attempt to do just that.[48] Rather it situates the Panic in a larger historical and economic context and uses elements of the current crisis to illustrate the components of the Regulatory Instability Hypothesis.

One facet of the current crisis bears particular mention now. In various places, the book analyzes the growth over the last two decades of the so-called "shadow banking system" and how that system contributed to the Panic of 2007–2008." Part IV of the book describes the shadow banking system in great detail. However, a simple definition should suffice for this introduction: the shadow banking system describes a web of complex financial instruments that connected household and corporate borrowers to investors in capital markets.[49] These instruments included asset-backed securities (securitization), asset-backed commercial paper, money market mutual funds, repurchase agreements, and credit derivatives.

Securitization created one of the most important arteries in this system. It funneled credit from capital markets to households and businesses and transferred credit risk in the opposite direction. Securitization describes a transaction in which mortgages or other loans are pooled together and sold to an investment vehicle. The vehicle purchases these assets with the proceeds of securities it issues to investors (called "asset-backed securities"). The future cash payments on the underlying mortgages and loans fund (and provide collateral for) the payments to investors on those securities.[50]

This system or network of financial instruments is called "shadow banking" because it constructs a bypass around the traditional banking system, in which banks borrow money from depositors and lend to consumers and businesses. Like banks, the shadow banking system provided an important source of credit in the economy, but it offered some theoretical advantages to the model of traditional deposit-taking banks. Traditional banks face the problem of having highly illiquid and long-term assets (mortgages and loans with maturities far in the future), but short-term liabilities (given that depositors often have the right to withdraw their funds on demand). This mismatch, combined with the fact that banks earn profits by lending out most of the money they take in from depositors, leaves banks vulnerable to bank runs. In a run, depositors flock to withdraw their funds, fearing either that the bank will suffer huge losses or that other depositors will withdraw first and leave the cupboard bare.[51] Highly illiquid assets like loans means that banks also can suffer from heavy and long-lasting concentrations of risk to certain types of borrowers or certain geographic areas.[52]

Securitization offered to solve these problems for banks and other lenders by allowing them to make loans and then sell them to an investment vehicle in a securitization. Banks thus offload illiquid assets and risk, and receive cash, which they can redeploy in making new loans. Investors purchasing asset-backed securities gain because they can participate, indirectly, in lucrative loan markets, while limiting their exposure to just a sliver of the risk from a pool of loans. The pooling of loans provides further diversification. Moreover, the investment vehicle often issues multiple classes or categories of securities to customize the level of risk and reward for individual investors. Different classes of securities would have different rights (or priorities on payment) to the cash streams from the underlying assets.[53] By linking capital markets to borrowers, shadow banking allowed the credit risk of loans to be spread widely and efficiently (at least theoretically). This lowered the borrowing costs for households and businesses.[54]

Note how often the paragraph above makes the "theoretically" qualification. As this book will sketch out in Part IV, the shadow banking system broke down in the Panic of 2007–2008. Its failure demonstrated that this system was actually subject to many of the same economic risks as traditional banking, while subject to far fewer regulatory safeguards. Perversely, a system designed to solve banking risks and evade banking laws came to suffer from a banking crisis. Even more perversely, the crisis prompted the government to use many of the same tools it uses to address banking crises to save the shadow banking system. Shadow markets thus enjoyed the cake – being free from bank regulations – and got to eat it too – enjoying the benefits of bank-style government rescue.

The analysis of the shadow banking system in Part IV provides a master class in the Regulatory Instability Hypothesis. This system has its origins in deregulation and regulatory subsidies granted to particular financial markets and institutions.[55] It flourished and its individual constituent financial markets fused together because of regulatory arbitrage.[56] Indeed, in the later years of the U.S. real estate bubble, just before the Panic of 2007–2008 struck, some economists argue that the explosive growth of shadow banking markets was propelled primarily by financial institutions purchasing financial instruments to game bank capital regulations and dramatically increase and camouflage their leverage.[57]

In these late stages, an epidemic of law-bending and law-breaking erupted throughout the system – from abuses by subprime mortgage lenders to the aggressive masking of leverage by financial institutions such as Lehman Brothers.[58] During this period, regulators failed to aggressively enforce consumer laws.[59] Moreover, policymakers actively encouraged institutions to invest more in the riskiest sectors of the shadow banking system. For example, legislators and regulators pushed mortgage giants Freddie Mac and Fannie Mae (and those giants lobbied hard to be allowed) to purchase subprime mortgages and subprime-related mortgage-backed securities.[60] Regulations encouraged U.S. and European financial institutions to herd into the same supposedly safe and liquid financial markets, including investment grade asset-backed securities and asset-backed commercial paper, repos, and money market mutual funds.[61] Moreover, economic studies indicate that financial institutions used the shadow banking system to increase their leverage at the same time, putting in motion a dangerously procyclical leverage cycle.[62]

All the dynamics of the Regulatory Instability Hypothesis were thus at work in the shadow banking system. Ominously, these dynamics worked against the most crucial kinds of financial regulations: legal rules governing financial institution lending, leverage, and systemic risk. These dynamics fueled the growth of shadow banking and the inflation of the real estate bubble. They also set the stage for economic catastrophe.

Disconcertingly, in the years leading up to the Panic of 2007–2008, regulators and the Federal Reserve seem to have missed the larger implications of the rise of the shadow banking system. They realized that individual markets for shadow instruments were flourishing, but they failed to see how the pieces fit together to create a system that rivaled the size of the traditional banking sector. They missed the monetary effects of shadow banking. In fact, the Federal Reserve chose to stop monitoring a broader measure of the money supply just when it would have signaled the alarm (perhaps not coincidentally this was approximately the same moment when economists believe regulatory arbitrage via shadow banking skyrocketed).[63]

They of course, also failed to perceive the way financial laws governing financial institutions and markets were deteriorating. They paid little heed to the dangers framed by the Regulatory Instability Hypothesis: cycles of regulatory stimulus, compliance rot, regulatory arbitrage, and procyclical and herd-promoting regulations.

The prescriptive aims: towards robust financial regulation

The bulk of this book is descriptive, on the theory that "a problem well put is half-solved."[64] However, Part IV and the conclusion venture into the realm of policy prescription. They consider what architects of financial regulation could and should do in light of bubbles and the Regulatory Instability Hypothesis. Recommending regulatory changes after arguing that very ancient, powerful, and recurrent phenomena undermine regulation is, to understate the case massively, a daunting task.

The prescriptive elements of this book attempt to navigate between twin myths: a Scylla that law can do nothing about asset price bubbles and the Charybdis that law can abolish bubbles. The first myth may have several variants. One version sees bubbles as simple products of irrational investors. The moral of this myth is that there is little law can do to remedy human folly and that attempts to do after the fact may only provide insurance to gamblers.[65]

If it would be error to say there is nothing that law can do about asset price bubbles, it would also be a grave mistake to assume they can do too much. Financial regulation can neither abolish nor prevent financial crises altogether; history has shown that both bubbles[66] and financial crises[67] more generally are remarkably robust phenomenon. They have formed with regularity throughout financial history in countries with different cultures, forms of government, and regulatory architectures. Bubbles have also proven remarkably resilient in economic experiments conducted in simulated bond markets.[68] Thus the objective of financial regulation should not be to eradicate bubbles, let alone to eliminate business cycles.

Instead, the objectives should be more modest: to reduce the incidence and severity of bubbles or, moreover, to mitigate their effects of financial markets. A regulatory redesign would focus on shoring up financial laws against fraud and law-breaking. It would aim to make households, financial institutions, and markets more resilient to the bursting of bubbles.

To meet these objectives, the book's conclusion explores ways to make financial regulation more robust in the face of asset price bubbles and to contribute less to the development of those speculative booms. This means confronting the five elements of the Regulatory Instability Hypothesis head-on by designing regulations and institutions that:

- *withstand political pressures* as the regulatory stimulus cycle turns and the tide rolls against policymakers preserving and vigorously interpreting and enforcing financial laws;
- *promote and reinforce compliance* in the face of bubble pressures that undermine obedience by market participants with critical legal rules;
- *manage and adapt to regulatory arbitrage* and ensure that policymakers keep pace with financial innovations and evolving markets and treat similar economic risks similarly;
- *reduce procyclicality and promote counter cyclicality in regulations*; and
- *reduce incentives for financial institutions to engage in dangerous herding* and mitigate correlated risk-taking among financial institutions.

Economists often debate whether central banks can address potential asset price bubbles as they develop by adjusting monetary policy to "lean into" the economic wind.[69] The final chapters ask whether legal rules can do the same. Can policymakers adjust financial regulations – or create regulations that adjust automatically – to adapt when the climate for financial law harshens as financial markets begin to bubble? A very loose analogy might be drawn between creating adaptive regulations that adjust to bubbles and the economic objectives of Keynesianism. The comparison is, however, inexact. This book does not propose using financial regulations to smooth business cycles, nor does it examine the right and wrong ways to manage financial crises.

The concluding chapter emphasizes not so much changing the substance of financial regulation, as it does rethinking the design of regulatory institutions. How can institutions be redesigned to make them resilient to economic and political pressures that thwart effective financial regulation? How can regulators be given the capacities and incentives to adapt legal rules to bubble periods? Here the tension between the different models that explain regulatory failure – rational, behavioral, and norms/ideologies – comes to the fore. For example, rational models may call for increasing carrots and sticks to market participants and policymakers. Yet this approach may undermine efforts to cultivate norms and the intrinsic motivations of legal actors.

The concluding chapter also returns to another of the book's core themes: the regulatory problems created by various powerful feedback loops. It examines whether this feedback could be dampened by decoupling political, regulatory, and economic cycles. The linkages among these cycles pose the greatest dangers when they affect regulations that govern the lending and leverage of financial institutions. Part IV and the conclusion of this book therefore examine how financial regulation and monetary policy might be better integrated. One of the core lessons of those parts is that simply knowing and communicating the extent to which regulations deteriorate during bubbles and the microeconomic and macroeconomic impact of that deterioration would represent significant advances.

Achieving simpler and more modest goals may be challenging enough. Indeed, the Regulatory Instability Hypothesis may inject the reader with a strong dose of fatalism. It may leave her or him skeptical that any laws that attempt to ameliorate bubbles or their effects will be counterproductive, rolled back, or rendered ineffective. If most of the book bears witness to the cyclical failings of financial regulation, the conclusion looks to provide at least some balm from Gilead.

The Regulatory Instability Hypothesis and fundamental value

Both the prescriptive and descriptive aims of this book must confront a standard objection to scholarship on asset price bubbles, namely that it is difficult to identify bubbles in hindsight, let alone to identify them *in media res*. Indeed, several prominent economists have questioned whether some of the more prominent historical episodes identified as bubbles could in fact be explained by the fundamental values of assets.[70] Identifying bubbles as they develop requires determining that prices cannot be justified by future cash flows. The inherent uncertainty of this determination has led many macroeconomists, including Ben Bernanke (while he was still an economist at Princeton and before his apotheosis to the U.S. Federal Reserve Chairmanship) to argue against using monetary policy to curb inflation in financial markets.[71]

As the work of a legal scholar, this book will add little to the ability of economists to measure the fundamental value of assets. However, the problem of measuring fundamental value with precision poses a serious threat to neither the descriptive nor the prescriptive parts of this book for several reasons. First, many macroeconomists and central bankers are more comfortable than Chairman Bernanke that central banks can and should use monetary policy to curb the threat of inflation in asset markets affecting the macro economy.[72] The Panic of 2007–2008 may have tipped the scales in the debate towards this more activist, anti-bubble view, as heads of central banks in Europe[73] and Canada[74] have warmed to using monetary policy in this way.[75] These economists believe central bankers can exercise judgment as to whether prices in a particular market constitute a bubble or are otherwise justified by economic fundamentals.[76]

To be sure, exercising judgment in determining whether a bubble has formed presents its own set of challenges both for central bankers, as well as for the banking and securities regulators who are more the focus of this book. Judgment as to when markets are overheating – and when the elements of the Financial Instability Hypothesis pose particular dangers – requires that regulators have considerable capacities. They would need among other things, new training, sophisticated economic data and models, and financial resources. Moreover, regulators must be able to withstand the political pressure that would work against strenuous regulation during boom times. Modern macroeconomics also provides the insight that market expectations of future economic conditions and future policy changes matter.[77] Regulatory changes may be frustrated when they fly in the face of those expectations and markets doubt the resoluteness of policy-makers. None of these challenges to the exercise of judgment by regulators are, however, insurmountable.

Second, a lack of certainty as to when bubbles form may not pose the dire economic consequences that the Bernanke camp fears should financial regulators attempt to adjust to market bubbles. Chairman Bernanke argued that using tradi-tional monetary policy to raise or lower overall market interest rates to curb potential asset price bubbles created significant spillover costs.[78] For example, raising interest rates to dampen what may be a bubbly stock market would also act to dampen investment in real estate markets that might not be overheating. Higher interest rates might also impact labor markets, currency exchange rates, foreign trade, and a host of other sectors. Bernanke famously labeled this use of monetary policy as "surgery with a sledgehammer."[79]

However vivid this metaphor may be, it should not obscure that many finan-cial regulations can target credit and leverage flowing into asset markets (which Bernanke concedes can feed bubbles) more surgically than broad brush monetary policy tools. Chapter 9 will explain how various financial regulations can restrict credit flowing into particular asset markets. Moreover, even if financial regula-tions are not used as monetary policy levers, it is important to understand how regulatory changes can have unintended monetary effects. The roll back, under-enforcement, compliance rot, or other weakening of these regulations may have significant macroeconomic consequences and contribute to asset price inflation. Chapter 9 and Part IV examine more closely the nexus between regulations gov-erning financial institution lending and leverage and monetary conditions.

Furthermore, this sledgehammer critique does not strike at the prescriptive aims of this book. Again, this book is principally engaged with the effectiveness of financial regulations. It does not focus on using regulations to eradicate or pop bubbles. Accordingly, the spillover effects that rightly trouble Bernanke pose less of a concern when policymakers look to fix microeconomic regulations rather than to set macroeconomic policy. More modest goals and less dire spill-over costs require less certainty as to whether a bubble exists.

Third, many of the most important dynamics of the Regulatory Instability Hypothesis do not strictly depend on whether asset prices have risen above fundamental value. Therefore, it is not necessary to determine fundamental value to determine when these dynamics are at work in a booming market. Measuring fundamental value does not present a prerequisite to developing policies that address the Regulatory Instability Hypothesis. Indeed, the models outlined in the following chapters explain the dynamics of the Regulatory Instability Hypo-thesis not by reference to fundamental values, but rather to other factors at work during prolonged market booms. A combination of booming prices, investor herding, behavioral biases, and shifting norms and ideologies cause the deterio-ration and decay of financial regulation. For example, deteriorating enforcement by regulatory agencies during booms can stem from regulators becoming over-whelmed as transaction volumes rise while their budgets remain flat. Booms may change regulator behavior by exacerbating disaster myopia and other behavioral biases or by reinforcing shifts in social norms, in each case, *regardless of whether or not market prices exceeded fundamental value.*

In many cases, the same causal factors that may contribute to the formation of a bubble may also drive regulatory failures. It is more important to draw a causal connection between these factors and regulatory failure than to find a causal rela-tionship between a bubble (and the relationship between asset prices and funda-mental value) and regulation. Consider deregulation and the regulatory stimulus cycle during a period of surging prices in the financial markets. Surging markets may give financial institutions more resources to lobby for deregulation, con-tribute to the disaster myopia of regulators, and overwhelm the resources of even vigilant regulators. Similarly, compliance with financial regulations may deteriorate, as sustained price booms undermine the deterrent effect of liability rules and weaken norms of compliance. All of these regulatory failures can occur even if there is a debate among economists on whether a bubble has formed according to a strict economic definition.

Even if it is at times difficult to see the precise mechanisms that subvert fin-ancial regulation during booms, it is easier to see many of the troubling con-sequences. Policymakers can measure increased financial institution leverage (even though financial institutions make efforts to cloak this). Policymakers can track (albeit imperfectly) alleged violations of the law and the development of regulatory arbitrage structures (although care must be taken in attempting to measure law-breaking and compare it across historical periods). Policymakers can use historical market data to see when financial institutions are engaging in procyclical behavior and when they are herding into particular asset classes.

If describing the problem does not require certainty as to fundamental value, neither would prescribing and analyzing remedies for the dynamics of the Regu-latory Instability Hypothesis. For example, addressing the decreased incentives and resources of financial regulators to regulate during prolonged booms would not require a determination of fundamental value. Even simple solutions, such as increasing regulator budgets during boom times, might advance the cause.

None of this suggests that rethinking regulatory design in the face of the Reg-ulatory Instability Hypothesis does not require empirical data or good economic modeling. Yet neither does it suggest that mending and reinvigorating regulatory institutions requires answering one of economics' most contentious questions, namely "how do we measure the fundamental value of assets."

A roadmap to the chapters that follow

The following provides a brief overview of the structure of this book.

Part I provides background for the remainder of the book by discussing the economics and legal history of asset price bubbles. Chapter 1 discusses how asset price bubbles have been defined in the economic literature and the problems with those definitions. The first chapter outlines the most influential economic research on how bubbles form. Chapter 2 examines the legal history of over a dozen asset price bubbles over 300 years and across several continents. This chapter does not aim to provide a comprehensive or colorful history of each episode – other books have already done that – but, instead, focus on certain aspects in each of these bubbles. The chapter looks at the regulatory stimulus cycle at work in each of these historical episodes, i.e., how governments provided regulatory stimulus as bubbles inflated, as well as the regulatory backlash after they popped. Chapter 2 also describes the prevalence of financial fraud and other law-breaking during each bubble studied.

Part II of the book then unpacks the Regulatory Instability Hypothesis. Chapter 3 provides three models – one rational, one behavioral, and one based on shifting ideologies and social norms – to explain the political economy of this regulatory stimulus cycle. Chapter 4 examines the causes of outbreaks of fraud epidemics during bubbles. It uses three similar models to explain first how bubbles undermine compliance with antifraud rules and then how they subvert obedience by financial institutions with prudential banking regulations. Chapter 5 extends this analysis to explain increasing regulatory arbitrage during bubbles. Chapter 5 also provides a case study of regulatory capital arbitrage.

If previous chapters attempted to isolate elements of the Regulatory Instability Hypothesis, Chapter 6 argues that they can also provide virulent feedback for one another. That chapter provides a model of how deregulation/regulatory subsidies and regulatory arbitrage can trigger or reinforce one another. It then looks at how this model explains the legal dynamics during the real estate bubbles in Sweden and Japan in the 1980s. It also considers whether this model sheds light on certain aspects of the U.S. subprime bubble, particularly the interactions between Freddie Mac and Fannie Mae on the one hand, and "private label" securitization, on the other.

Chapter 7 explores the final two elements of the Regulatory Instability Hypothesis. It analyzes procyclical regulations. It then looks in greater depth at the problem of herd behavior during asset price bubbles, and examines the connections between the economics of bubbles and bank runs. Chapter 7 then investigates how certain regulations and government interventions promote herding by financial institutions.

Part III of the book analyzes whether regulations can be used to fight asset price bubbles. Chapter 8 examines evidence of the effectiveness of various legal rules and policies in preventing or pricking bubbles or dampening their magnitude. This chapter sifts through evidence from experimental economics, particularly experimental asset markets (a kind of simulated bond market used to conduct economic experiments).

Chapter 9 evaluates one category of anti-bubble laws that appears to be the most effective in preventing, pricking, and dampening bubbles: those that constrict the flow of credit to financial markets. In doing so, this chapter also outlines the deep connections between certain regulations of financial institutions and markets, on the one hand, and monetary policy, on the other. Regulations that affect financial institution leverage and regulatory preferences that allow certain financial instruments to take on more of the economic characteristics of money can have enormous monetary and macroeconomic effects.

Part IV then fits the pieces of the book together to show how they help explain one pivotal factor behind the Panic of 2007–2008, the rise of the shadow banking system. Chapter 10 provides a primer on the shadow banking system and its component markets for financial instruments. Chapter 11 then describes how the Regulatory Instability Hypothesis helps explain the origins and phenomenal growth of shadow banking. It also examines how this burgeoning parallel credit sector facilitated regulatory arbitrage, law-breaking, and procyclical and herd behavior by financial institutions.

As there are no precise cookbooks for financial regulation in light of bubbles, the concluding chapter examines the cooks. It proposes ways in which to give regulators and policymakers the capacities and incentives to resist the political pressure of the regulatory cycle to deregulate and dial down enforcement during boom times. It recommends measures to ensure that regulators keep pace with law-breaking and regulatory arbitrage. It examines fixes for procyclical and herd-promoting regulations. The last chapter thus addresses one of the least-explored questions in the wake of the Panic of 2007–2008 – not whether regulators need new tools, but how should we design legal institutions to ensure that regulators appropriately use the powers at their disposal. More broadly: how should legal institutions be designed so that law retains its force when it is most needed?

Notes

1 I chose this label to harken back to Hyman Minsky's Financial Instability Hypothesis, which models how financial markets are prone to booms and crashes. Hyman P. Minsky, *Can "It" Happen Again? Essays on Instability and Finance* (1982, M.E. Sharpe).

2 This colorful term reflects the fact that the crisis assumed full force over these two years as credit markets started to seize up and mammoth financial institutions began to founder. This term should not, however, distract from the fact that the crisis had roots far earlier than that year and, unfortunately, has continuing effects that will last long after.

3 For short versions of this story told by economists in popular books, see, e.g., Raghuram G. Rajan, *Fault Lines: How Hidden Fractures Still Threaten the World Economy*, 32–45 (2010, Princeton University Press) (describing expansion of subprime mortgage market in the United States); Nouriel Roubini and Stephen Mihm, *Crisis Economics: A Crash Course in the Future of Finance*, 18–19 (2010, Penguin).

4 For an account of the impact of the collapse of the U.S. mortgage-backed securities markets on European financial institutions, see Dalvinder Singh, U.K. Approach to Financial Crisis Management, 19 *Transnational Law and Contemporary Problems* 872 (2012).

5 Mark Landler, Housing Woes in U.S. Spread Around Globe, *New York Times*, April 14, 2008, at A1.

6 Cesar Bacani, Is a China Stock Bubble Forming? *Time*, July 1, 2009 (online edition) available at www.time.com/time/world/article/0,8599,1908032,00.html (last visited July 12, 2013).

7 Chris Isidore, Is China Another Real Estate Bubble? *CNN Money*, April 15, 2010 available at http://money.cnn.com/2010/04/15/news/economy/china_bubble/ (last visited July 12, 2013).

8 Robert Lenzner, Gold is the Ultimate Asset Bubble, Forbes.com, March 12, 2010 available at www.forbes.com/2010/03/12/soros-paulson-novagold-markets-gold-bubble.html (last visited July 12, 2013).

9 Katrina Nicholas, "Man on Street" Bond Buyers Signal Bubble, Credit Agricole Says, *Bloomberg Businessweek*, September 10, 2010 (online edition) available at www. bloomberg.com/news/2010-08-27/-man-on-street-buying-bonds-may-signal-price-bubble-credit-agricole-says.html (last visited July 12, 2013).

10 Joseph Marr Cronin and Howard E. Horton, Will Higher Education Be the Next Bubble to Burst? *Chronicle of Higher Education*, May 22, 2009, at 56.

11 Some of the classics in the economics field include: Charles P. Kindleberger, *Manias, Panics, and Crashes* (4th ed. 2000, John Wiley & Sons) (providing a non-quantitative, narrative economic analysis of historical bubbles); Minsky, *supra* note 1 (presenting non-quantitative theoretical models of the formation of bubbles and financial crises). For a more modern, quantitative analysis of bubbles that builds on this older generation of work, see Andrei Shleifer, *Inefficient Markets: An Introduction to Behavioral Finance*, 154–74 (2000, Oxford University Press). For another technical economic work, see Markus K. Brunnermeier, *Asset Pricing under Asymmetric Information* (2001, Oxford University Press). For a more accessible, popular book on bubbles by a prominent economist, see Robert J. Shiller, *Irrational Exuberance* (2000, Princeton University Press). For one older, non-scholarly collection of bubble histories, see Charles MacKay, *Extraordinary Popular Delusions and the Madness of Crowds* (1980 [1841], Crown Trade Paperbacks).

12 See, e.g., Robert P. Flood and Peter M. Garber, Market Fundamentals Versus Price-Level Bubbles: The First Tests, 88 *Journal of Political Economy* 745, 746 (1980); Henry T.C. Hu, Faith and Magic: Investor Beliefs and Government Neutrality, 78 *Texas Law Review* 777, 794 (2000). At times, economists have expanded this basic definition to include a proposed reason that asset prices diverge from their fundamental values. Markus K. Brunnermeier, Bubbles, in *The New Palgrave Dictionary of Economics*, 578 (Steven N. Durlauf and Lawrence E. Blume eds., 2nd ed. 2008, Palgrave Macmillan) ("Bubbles refer to asset prices that exceed an asset's fundamental value because current owners believe that they can resell the asset at an even higher price in the future").

The definition of a bubble as a divergence in market prices from fundamental value has several advantages over a simpler definition used by other historians and economists. For example, one study defined a bubble as "an upward price movement over an extended range that then implodes." Kindleberger, *supra* note 11, at 16. Although this simpler definition captures the intuitive shape of a bubble, it fails to single out any causal explanation for the rise and crash of prices and thus cannot generate any testable hypotheses or predictions.

Of course, defining bubbles as a deviation in asset prices from fundamental value leads to secondary questions of whether *any* divergence constitutes a bubble or whether prices must diverge to a pronounced extent and for a prolonged period.

13 See, e.g., Ellen R. McGrattan and Edward C. Prescott, Testing for Stock Market Over-valuation/Undervaluation, in *Asset-Price Bubbles: The Implications for Monetary, Regulatory, and International Policies*, 271 (William C. Hunter, George G. Kaufman, and Michael Pomerleano eds., 2003, MIT Press). One alternative to defining fundamental value in terms of future cash flows is to say that the best guess as to fundamental value is whatever the market price is. That tautology would make it impossible for prices ever to be "wrong."

14 Chapters 1, 7, and 9 and Part IV of this book examine the links between asset price bubbles and banking in greater detail.

15 For an overview of behavioral finance, see Nicholas Barberis and Richard Thaler, A Survey of Behavioral Finance, in *1B Handbook of the Economics of Finance*, 1054 (George M. Constantinides, Milton Harris, and René M. Stulz, eds., 2003, Elsevier North Holland).

16 E.g., Shleifer, *supra* note 11, at 10–12. The Efficient Market Hypothesis is described in Chapter 1, notes 18, 34–5 and accompanying text.

17 Kindleberger, *supra* note 11; Minsky, *supra* note 1.

18 Shleifer, *supra* note 11, at 154–74.

19 For the classic economic article that models bank runs, see Douglas W. Diamond and Philip H. Dybvig, Bank Runs, Deposit Insurance, and Liquidity, 91 *Journal of Political Economy* 401 (1983).

20 The dangers for money managers when they bet against a bubble are discussed in greater detail in Chapter 1. See also Markus K. Brunnermeier and Stefan Nagel, Hedge Funds and the Technology Bubble, 59 *Journal of Finance* 2013, 2030–2 (2004) (providing an example of a hedge fund that was forced to liquidate after refusing to invest in technology stocks during the late 1990s technology stock bubble and consequently losing investors).

21 See e.g., Ana Fostel and John Geanakoplos, Leverage Cycles and the Anxious Economy, 98 *American Economic Review* 1211 (2008); John Geanakoplos, The Leverage Cycle, Cowles Found, *Discussion Paper No. 1715* (July 31, 2009) available at http://papers.ssrn.com/sol3/papers.cfm?abstract_id=1441943 (last visited July 12, 2013).

22 Tobias Adrian and Hyun Song Shin, The Changing Nature of Financial Intermediation and the Financial Crisis, *Federal Reserve Bank of New York Staff Report No. 439* (March 2010).

23 Credit, leverage, and their contributions to bubbles are the subjects of Chapter 9 of this book. Leverage entices investors because of its near magical ability to magnify returns to equity holders. Of course, leverage also magnifies their potential losses. Investors can lose far more than their initial investment should market prices stagnate and asset returns cannot keep pace with the interest rate payments they owe to their lenders.

24 For an explanation of how leverage can increase liquidity in markets and the effective money supply in the economy, see Tobias Adrian and Hyun Song Shin, Liquidity and Leverage, 19 *Journal of Financial Intermediation* 418 (2009) [hereinafter, Adrian and Shin, Liquidity and Leverage]; Tobias Adrian and Hyun Song Shin, Money, Liquidity and Monetary Policy, 99 *American Economic Review* 600 (2009) [hereinafter, Adrian and Shin, Money, Liquidity and Monetary Policy]; Margaret M. Blair, Financial Innovation, Leverage, Bubbles, and the Distribution of Income, 30 *Review of Banking and Financial Law* 225 (2010).

   To understand the basics, consider that financial institutions are in the business of borrowing money and then re-lending it at higher rates. These firms only keep a fraction of their total assets in reserve to cover their obligations to their creditors. They lend the remainder (a business model commonly known as "fractional reserve banking"). A financial institution may re-lend a portion of any money it borrows to another financial institution. That recipient financial institution may, in turn, re-lend again. This process creates a multiplier effect in which the initial dollar loaned may turn into many dollars.

   Similarly, any investor or financial institution increasing leverage can increase the total amount of liquidity (or the supply of money) available to purchase assets. Liquidity also increases to the extent that the leverage of one financial institution is layered on top of the leverage of another. Greater liquidity chasing the same assets tends to push the prices of those assets higher. This mechanism clangs sharply into reverse and liquidity contracts when leverage is reduced. See Blair, *supra* this note. Chapter 9 of this book analyzes the economic links between credit, leverage, and asset price bubbles in greater detail. Chapters 9, 10, and 11 explain how various financial regulations that directly and indirectly regulate credit and leverage by financial institutions play vital, if overlooked, roles in exacerbating or mitigating asset price bubbles.

25 See Geanakoplos, *supra* note 21; sources *supra* note 24; see also Chapter 9, "Dangerous feedback: when the Regulatory Instability Hypothesis matters most," Chapter 10, "Banking risks," and Chapter 11, "The Regulatory Instability Hypothesis and a perfect storm."

26 Asli Demirgüç, Enrica Detragiache, and Poonam Gupta, Inside the Crisis: An Empirical Analysis of Banking Systems in Distress, *World Bank Policy Research Paper 2431* (2000) available at http://papers.ssrn.com/sol3/papers.cfm?abstract_id=237651 (last visited July 12, 2013); Vasudevan Sundararajan and J.T. Tomás Baliño eds., *Banking Crises: Cases and Issues* (1991, IMF). See also Carmen M. Reinhart and Kenneth S. Rogoff, *This Time is Different: Eight Centuries of Financial Folly*, 141–73 (2009, Princeton University Press) (providing data on historical banking crises).

27 Ben S. Bernanke, *Essays on the Great Depression*, 41–69 (2004, Princeton University Press).

28 See Geanakoplos, *supra* note 21; sources, *supra* note 24.

29 Shleifer, *supra* note 11, at 154–74.

30 These various strands of economic research should not be understood as attempting to demolish the Efficient Markets Hypothesis or neoclassical macroeconomics. The thrust of behavioral economics is not to demonstrate that markets fail to work efficiently all the time, but instead to understand the instances when they do not. It is those instances, when markets experience profound bouts of disequilibrium, which should concern financial regulators the most.

31 See generally Stuart Banner, What Causes New Securities Regulation? 300 Years of Evidence, 75 *Washington University Law Quarterly* 849, 850 (1997); Joseph A. Grundfest, Commentary: Punctuated Equilibria in the Evolution of United States Securities Regulation, 8 *Stanford Journal of Law, Business and Finance* 1 (2002) (describing how capital market events stimulate regulation "between relatively tranquil periods of common law interpretation"); Larry E. Ribstein, Commentary: Bubble Laws, 40 *Houston Law Review* 77, 77–8 (2003) (describing a historic cycle of stock market bubbles inflating then bursting, followed by increased regulation).

32 There is, however, one obscure recent exception. Section 946 of the Dodd-Frank Act requires the Financial Stability Oversight Council to conduct a study on new rules in that statute that require the originators of loans in asset-backed securities transactions to retain part of the risk of those loans. The study must address whether these rules might have "macroeconomic effects" including "minimizing real estate price bubbles."

33 Dodd-Frank Wall Street Reform and Consumer Protection Act (Public Law No. 111–205) [Hereinafter "Dodd-Frank Act"].

34 The desire to protect consumers after the subprime crisis animated Dodd-Frank Act's controversial creation of a new Bureau of Consumer Financial Protection within the Federal Reserve Board. Dodd-Frank Act, §§ 1001 et seq. The following law review article is widely considered to have created the intellectual foundations for this consumer financial regulator: Oren Bar-Gill and Elizabeth Warren, Making Credit Safer, 157 *University of Pennsylvania Law Review* 1 (2008). See also Dodd-Frank Act, §§ 1400 et seq. (creating new regime for regulation of residential mortgage loans).

35 Dodd-Frank Act, Title VII, Subtitle A.

36 Dodd-Frank Act, §§ 951–7.

37 For a critical view of the notion that deregulation caused the current financial crisis, see Mark A. Calabria, Did Deregulation Cause the Financial Crisis? 31 *Cato Policy Report* 1 (July/August 2009).

38 Chapter 5 argues that financial institutions view regulatory capital requirements as form of tax. Higher taxes encourage these institutions to devise structures (regulatory arbitrage) to minimize their tax rates. Chapter 5, "Capital requirements as regulatory tax." See also David Jones, Emerging Problems with the Basel Capital Accord: Regulatory Capital Arbitrage and Related Issues, 24 *Journal of Banking and Finance* 35, 38–9 (2000).

39 Fostering a more expansive, nuanced, and sociological view of law and legal system is one of the central objectives of the law and society movement. See Lawrence M. Friedman, The Law and Society Movement, 38 *Stanford Law Review* 763 (1986). For an early, contemporaneous introduction to the much earlier Legal Realism school, see Lon L. Fuller, American Legal Realism, 82 *University of Pennsylvania Law Review* 429 (1934).

40 See Geoffrey P. Miller, The Role of a Central Bank in a Bubble Economy, 18 *Cardozo Law Review* 1053, 1076–7 (1996) (describing political pressures operating against a central bank taking active measures against a bubble).

41 Jack M. Guttentag and Richard J. Herring, Disaster Myopia in International Banking, 3–4 *Working Paper*, Princeton University International Finance Section (1986).

42 The following example and discussion borrows from the following: Jaime Caruana, Banking Provisions and Asset Price Bubbles, in *Asset-Price Bubbles: The Implications for Monetary, Regulatory, and International Policies*, 537 (William C. Hunter, George G. Kaufman, and Michael Pomerleano eds., 2003, MIT Press); see also Jeffrey Carmichael and Neil Esho, Asset Price Bubbles and Prudential Regulation, in *Asset-Price Bubbles: The Implications for Monetary, Regulatory, and International Policies*, 481, 495–7 (William C. Hunter, George G. Kaufman, and Michael Pomerleano eds., 2003, MIT Press).

43 Diamond and Dybvig, *supra* note 19.

44 See Chapter 7, "Financial institution herding and homogeneity."

45 George G. Kaufman and Kenneth E. Scott, What is Systemic Risk, and Do Bank Regulators Retard or Contribute to It? 7 *Independent Review* 371, 371 (2003); see also Steven L. Schwarcz, Systemic Risk, 97 *Georgetown Law Journal* 193 (2008).

46 Chapter 7 "Legal preferences for financial instruments and trading liquidity."

47 *Supra* note 31, and accompanying text.

48 See e.g., Roubini and Mihm, *supra* note 3.

49 Gary Gorton and Andrew Metrick, Regulating the Shadow Banking System, *Brookings Papers Economic Activity*, 261 (Fall 2010).

50 Erik F. Gerding, Code, Crash, and Open Source: The Outsourcing of Financial Regulation to Risk Models and the Global Financial Crisis, 84 *Washington Law Review* 127, 147–9 (2009).

51 See Diamond and Dybvig, *supra* note 19.

52 See generally Frank J. Fabozzi, *Bond Portolio Management*, 491 (2nd ed. 2001, John Wiley & Sons) (describing concentration risk).

53 Gerding, *supra* note 50, at 149.

54 See generally Ronald J. Gilson and Charles K. Whitehead, Deconstructing Equity: Public Ownership, Agency Costs, and Complete Capital Markets, 108 *Columbia Law Review* 231 (2008).

55 Chapter 11, "Regulatory stimulus and the legal origins of the shadow banking system."

56 Chapter 11, "Regulatory capital arbitrage revisited."

57 Chapter 11, notes 95–102 and accompanying text.

58 Chapter 11, "Law-bending and breaking along the securitization pipeline."

59 Chapter 11, notes 92–3 and accompanying text.

60 Chapter 6, "Securitization and the U.S. subprime crisis."

61 Chapter 7, "How financial regulation contributes to investment herding."

62 Chapter 11, "Money: the emergence of a shadow monetary transmission belt, financial regulation, and herding."

63 Chapter 9, "The gathering storm," and Chapter 11, "A shadow monetary transmission belt."

64 John Dewey, The Pattern of Inquiry, in *Logic: Theory of Inquiry*, reprinted in John Dewey, *The Later Works: 1925–1953, Vol. 12: 1938*, 112 (Jo Ann Boydston ed., 1st ed. 1986, Southern Illinois University).

65 This view seems to have animated some judicial opinions during the wave of securities litigation after the 1990s technology stock bubble. As a case in point, see the opinion of Lewis Pollack, one of the more respected securities law experts then on the federal bench, in the following case: *In re Merrill Lynch & Co., Inc.: Research Reports Securities Litigation*, 273 F. Supp. 2d 351 (S.D.N.Y. 2003).

The flip side of the current media obsession with bubbles is to view the current crisis as a historical aberration, a 100-year storm, or a "black swan" event. This last metaphor has suffered a rhetorical hijacking and has been used to justify the impossibility of the private and public sectors to perceive the growing risk of financial meltdown. It is worthy of note that 100-year storms tend to occur much more often than once a century.

66 Kindleberger, *supra* note 11.

67 Reinhart and Rogoff, *supra* note 26.

68 Erik F. Gerding, Laws Against Bubbles: An Experimental-Asset-Market Approach to Analyzing Financial Regulation, 2007 *Wisconsin Law Review* 977 (2007).

69 See Chapter 9 of this book.

70 Peter M. Garber, *Famous First Bubbles* (2000, MIT Press) (arguing that price rises and crashes in the Tulipomania in Holland in 1637 and the Mississippi and South Sea bubbles in early eighteenth century France and England, respectively, can be explained by fundamental value of the assets that were traded). For a critique of Garber's analysis, see Edward Chancellor, *Devil take the Hindmost: A History of Financial Speculation*, 23–6 (1999, Plume Books).

See also McGrattan and Prescott, *supra* note 13, at 273 (arguing that the stock market was undervalued in 1929); Lubos Pástor and Pietro Veronesi, Was There a Nasdaq Bubble in the Late 1990s? University of Chicago Center for Research in Security Prices, *Working Paper No. 557* (2004) available at http://papers.ssrn.com/sol3/papers.cfm?abstract_id=557061 (last visited July 12, 2013) (arguing that bubbles may not have existed in the 1920s and 1990s).

71 E.g., Ben Bernanke and Mark Gertler, Monetary Policy and Asset Price Volatility, in *New Challenges for Monetary Policy: Proceedings of the Federal Reserve Bank of Kansas City*, 77 (1999, Federal Reserve Bank of Kansas City).

72 See, e.g., Stephen G. Cecchetti, Hans Genberg, and Sushil Wadhwani, Asset Prices in a Flexible Inflation Targeting Framework, in *Asset-Price Bubbles: The Implications for Monetary, Regulatory, and International Policies*, 427 (William C. Hunter, George G. Kaufman, and Michael Pomerleano eds., 2003, MIT Press) (arguing that monetary policy should take into account asset price "misalignments").

73 Andrew Mountford, Leaning into the Wind: A Structural VAR Investigation of UK Monetary Policy, 67 *Oxford Bulletin of Economics and Statistics* 597 (2005).

74 Mark Carney, Governor of the Bank of Canada, Some Considerations on Using Monetary Policy to Stabilize Economic Activity, Remarks for Federal Reserve Bank of Kansas City Symposium, Jackson Hole, Wyoming (August 22, 2009) available at www.kansascityfed.org/publicat/sympos/2009/papers/carney.08.22.09.pdf (last visited July 12, 2013).

75 Chapter 9 outlines the arguments of the anti-bubble camp in more detail. The arguments of macroeconomists in favor of using monetary policy to target bubbles breaks into several parts. First, booming prices in a particular asset class may send a warning signal about the risk of inflation in the entire economy. Steven G. Cecchetti, Hans Genberg, John Lipsky, and Sushil Wadhwani, *Asset Prices and Central Bank Policy*, 8–9 (2001, International Center for Monetary and Banking Studies/Centre for

Economic Policy Research). Second, the risk that a collapsed bubble poses to a country's financial stability justifies taking action even in the face of spillover costs and potential uncertainty as to whether booming prices represent a bubble. Claudio E.V. Borio and Phillip W. Lowe, Asset Prices, Financial and Monetary Stability: Exploring the Nexus, *BIS Working Paper No. 114* (July 2002) available at http://papers.ssrn.com/sol3/papers.cfm?abstract_id=846305 (last visited July 12, 2013).

76 William C. Dudley, President, Federal Reserve Bank of New York, Remarks at the Eighth Annual BIS Conference, Basel, Switzerland (July 3, 2009) available at www.newyorkfed.org/newsevents/speeches/2009/dud090702.html (last visited July 12, 2013).

77 See generally George W. Evans and Sepp Honkapohia, *Learning and Expectations in Macroeconomics*, 5–18 (2001, Princeton University Press) (discussing role of expectations and learning in macroeconomics).

78 Bernanke and Gertler, *supra* note 71.

79 Governor Ben S. Bernanke, Asset Price "Bubbles" and Monetary Policy, Remarks at the New York Chapter of the National Association for Business Economics, New York, New York (October 15, 2002) available at www.federalreserve.gov/BoardDocs/Speeches/2002/20021015/default.htm (last visited July 12, 2013).

Part I

The economics and legal history of bubbles

1 The economics of bubbles

Everyone and their uncle has an intuitive sense of what a bubble is. In folk wisdom, a bubble is a meteoric rise in prices of an asset followed by a calamitous crash. Everyone and their uncle blame the bubble on speculators who look to flip assets – selling to a "greater fool," and pocketing a profit before prices crash to earth. After a crash, everyone and their uncle claim to have known all along that the boom times were a bubble bound to burst. (That is not to say that everyone and their uncle did not try to ride the boom themselves.) Once a boom and bust cycle has ended, everyone and their uncle see fresh bubbles forming everywhere. Indeed, the wake of the Panic of 2008 has been no different; as the Introduction to this book noted, journalists now spot bubbles everywhere.

Too bad that too few voiced concerns (let alone acted on them) during the boom times just ended. Wisdom in hindsight is cold comfort to those who lost mightily in the last crash. Although the folk wisdom of bubbles is not necessarily wrong, its lack of rigor offers little aid in identifying with any precision when a bubble has formed, how it formed, and whether past financial crises involved a bubble. Without a more rigorous definition and theory of bubbles, policymakers have little to guide them in seeking to guard against the economic and social damage caused by recurrent financial boom and busts.

The Potter Stewart approach to bubbles – "we know it when we see it" – only works in hindsight. A meteoric rise in prices in a financial market just might be justified by some transformational shift in the economy (a new technology, a new market, a new political order). Moreover, the financial lightning of an investment mania seldom strikes twice in the same asset class with the same group of investors. The burghers of Holland were unlikely to have participated in another Tulipomania, but severe losses in flower bulbs (or technology stocks) may do little to chasten investors from investing in booming real estate markets. And a new generation of greater fools is born every minute. The "new era" or "this time is different" logic takes hold because no two financial manias are quite the same.

How then can policymakers or scholars identify what constitutes a bubble and which financial crises involve bubbles? This chapter will examine the economic theories of bubbles and how they form. The chapter begins by looking at the thorny definitional issues of what is a bubble and what is "fundamental value."

It then turns to the principal sets of theories on how bubbles form. Behavioral finance offers a compelling account of bubble formation that informs much of the rest of this book. It argues that bubbles have their genesis in the behavioral biases and cognitive limitations of investors. These same limitations can afflict lawmakers and market participants in their decisions to make, enforce, or obey financial regulation.

The chapter also considers other theories of bubbles that offer crucial insights that will reappear throughout the book. In contrast with the cognitive limitations of behavioral finance, the "rational-bubble" literature contends that asset price bubbles can form when investors have rational expectations. Although this research has its limitations, which are outlined below, it offers two powerful lessons. First, once bubbles form and prices begin to skyrocket, it can be completely rational for investors to buy into a booming market. Indeed, it may be irrational for them to attempt to swim against the tide, as the marketplace may punish them for doing so. The complex interplay between "irrational" and rational decision-making reverberates as a theme in later chapters. Second, a subset of the rational-bubble literature explains how credit can fuel the growth of bubbles. This nexus between credit and bubbles is another thread that runs through the book. This chapter also considers other theories of bubbles that have, until recently, lain outside mainstream economic scholarship. For example, Hyman Minsky's "Financial Instability Hypothesis" offers a powerful account of how cycles can destabilize financial markets. His work provides a template, not only for how bubbles form, but for cycles in financial regulation as well.

After considering economic theories of bubbles, the chapter returns to the difficulties of identifying bubbles, and discusses research in experimental economics that demonstrates the prevalence and robustness of bubbles in experimental asset markets. The chapter concludes with a discussion that introduces the tradeoff between achieving absolute certainty that a bubble exists with learning and applying pragmatic lessons about the risks and dynamics of bubbles. It bears repeating that the dynamics of the Regulatory Instability Hypothesis described in the ensuing chapters – the regulatory stimulus cycle, compliance rot, regulatory frenzies, and procyclical and herd-promoting regulations – do not strictly depend on asset prices diverging from fundamental value. Rather, the same dynamics that mark and inflate bubbles, as described in this chapter, also cause the deterioration in financial laws. Among these dynamics are rising prices, behavioral biases, rational and irrational herd behavior, short horizon investment, an influx of first time investors, and cheap credit and rising leverage. This chapter thus plays a key role in this book not because it suggests a foolproof answer to the riddle of when a bubble has formed, but rather because it unpacks the economic forces at work during bubbles that also affect and afflict financial laws during bubble periods.

Definitional problems: bubbles and fundamental value

The basic definition: price deviation from fundamental value

Earlier, economic research into bubbles had a less quantitative and more narrative methodology. This early literature (particularly the work of Charles
Kindleberger) defined bubbles in terms of an extended rise in the price of a particular asset and a subsequent price crash.[1] This straightforward definition has
numerous drawbacks. Although it captures the intuitive shape of a bubble, the
definition fails to single out any causal explanation for the rise and crash of
prices. It thus cannot generate any testable hypotheses or predictions.

So economists have searched for definitions with more explanatory power.
The consensus definition on which many economists have settled defines an
asset price bubble as a deviation in the price of a certain financial asset (or class
of assets) from its fundamental value.[2] Fundamental value, according to most
definitions in the economic literature, represents the present value of all future
cash flows from that asset.[3] As an example, the fundamental value of a bond
equals the present value of future payments of interest and principal on the bond
with some discount for credit risk.[4] A bubble forms when the price rises above
this present value. (Implicit in most bubble definitions is an assumption that only
pronounced and prolonged deviations from fundamental value are of interest.)

This tidy example masks practical difficulties and several logical shortcuts.
Three problems stand out. First, economists have calculated fundamental value for
stocks and real estate by estimating future dividends and rental payments.[5] But
many companies have adopted policies of retaining earnings rather than paying
dividends,[6] and many real estate owners cannot rent their property due to legal or
practical restrictions.[7] For these assets, the only future cash flow is whatever price
a buyer will pay on sale. This makes defining fundamental value not only a speculative endeavor (double entendre intended) but potentially a circular one as well.[8]

Second, defining bubbles by reference to fundamental value requires not only
a calculation of future cash flows, but also a determination of the correct discount rate. The presence of two variables in this equation raises the "joint hypothesis problem" that has also plagued efforts to prove (or disprove) the Efficient
Markets Hypothesis.[9]

Third, even measuring fundamental value solely on the basis of expected dividends or rental payments requires forecasting. It would be inappropriate to
judge the decisions of investors with the benefit of hindsight. Just because prices
later crashed, does not mean that investors were making decisions based on
something other than forecasts of fundamental value. It is difficult to know in the
middle of a price boom when the flavor of reasonable risk-taking becomes the
poison of wild optimism. Whether a forecast is reasonable is inescapably subjective. To evaluate the reasonableness of future-cash-flow estimations, economists resort to a host of different metrics that usually involve looking at
historical patterns of the relationship between an asset's price and measures of
an asset's income (e.g., company earnings).[10]

However, reliance on historical patterns leads to the standard objection of securities disclosure boilerplate: past performance does not guarantee future results.[11] Transformational economic changes – the introduction of a new technology or the opening of a new market – may create historically aberrant growth.[12] These transformational changes generate fantastic early market returns and lead investors to believe that historical ratios between an asset's price and measures of its income might be obsolete. The question is, how much of a price rise is justified?

Conflation of risk and uncertainty

The difference between the economic concepts of risk and uncertainty helps frame the dilemma faced by economists in determining whether prices have exceeded fundamental value. These two concepts were first distinguished by economist Frank Knight towards the beginning of the twentieth century.[13] Risk describes potential losses or gains when the probabilities are known beforehand. Playing a game of dice involves risk. Uncertainty describes potential future gains or losses in which the probabilities are not known. Since historical prices of assets do not necessarily predict future prices (it is possible that economies can undergo transformation), investing involves uncertainty.[14]

Yet is difficult to measure and model uncertainty. By using historical benchmarks to judge whether or not bubbles have formed, economists essentially use historical data to turn risk into a proxy for uncertainty. These economists assume that the fundamental value of an asset will track historical measurements of income from that asset class. If prices of an asset diverge from historical patterns, one explanation is that a bubble has formed because investors are miscalculating historical probabilities and thus miscalculating risk.[15] Indeed, the behavioral finance theories of bubbles, described below, build on empirical and experimental research that documents the bounded rationality of investors and their inability to calculate and make decisions under risk.

If investors face uncertainty not risk, it is critical to remind ourselves that scholars use mistakes made by investors with respect to financial risk as a proxy to predict investor mistakes under conditions of uncertainty. There is always the possibility that investors participating in a price boom are justified in believing that a new era has dawned or that this time is indeed different. Of course, financial history is replete with price crashes that betrayed this faith in historical exceptionalism.[16]

Refinements: asset prices and fundamental information

To get around the bramble bush of measuring fundamental value, some economists define a bubble in terms of the information that investors use to trade; if investors trade on information that cannot be related to fundamental value, a bubble may have formed. This could be rephrased into a more formal definition: bubbles represent "unsustainable increases" in asset prices caused by investors trading on a pattern of price increases, rather than information on fundamental values.[17] The economists who use this definition challenge the Efficient Markets Hypothesis (EMH), which, even in its weak form, holds that investors cannot earn superior risk-adjusted returns by trading off the past prices of assets.[18]

The difficulties with defining fundamental value outlined above also plague efforts to define what constitutes information on fundamental value. To prove the existence of a bubble under this definition requires economists to preclude that information relied on by investors was related to fundamental value.[19] As described below, behavioral finance has identified several examples of stock-price movements that cannot readily be explained by investors acting on information on fundamentals.[20]

A more nuanced definition

The thorniness of defining fundamental value in terms of future cash flows has led a few economists to adopt a more nuanced definition. They define funda-mental value as the price a rational investor would pay for an asset if she held that asset "to horizon." Accordingly, a bubble forms when asset prices rise for a prolonged period above what investors would be willing to pay if they were to hold those assets for the long term.[21] It is, however, difficult to discern the price investors would pay holding an asset over the long term. Futures prices provide one gauge to measure the difference between immediate and long-run prices.

Disputes on historical bubbles

Using any of these definitions, economists have made careers out of disputing whether or not historical financial manias and crashes constituted bubbles. Even canonical bubbles, such as the seventeenth century Dutch Tulipomania,[22] the U.S. stock market circa 1929,[23] and the NASDAQ technology stock bubble in the late 1990s,[24] have been the subject of contrarian interpretations that market prices during these financial frenzies were indeed justified by fundamentals.

These debates illuminate the definitional problems outlined above and tend to break down along the lines of whether economists believe that investors are rational actors and the EMH holds or if they believe that the rationality of investors is bounded and the stock market is less than efficient. This schism has generated two different models for how bubbles form – rational-bubble models, and behavioral-finance models of bubbles, both of which will be dis-cussed below.

This schism also highlights both sides of a logical trap. On one side, finding that a bubble existed in the past (only after "future" cash flows have become historical fact) because past price increases did not pan out, creates the risk of hindsight bias.[25] On the other side, there is the risk of tautology. Unless theoret-ical conditions of irrationality in the marketplace can be identified, rational expectations and efficient markets may revert to unfalsifiable articles of faith rather than hypotheses that can be tested. Claims of market efficiency would also have to respond to any patterns of asset price movements that would violate the keystone of the EMH that asset prices exhibit a random walk.[26] In fact, as we will see, behavioral finance has offered evidence of systematic patterns in the marketplace that do not accord with a random walk. It has identified examples of market mispricings that indicate investors were not trading on fundamental information.

Experimental evidence of bubbles

The various difficulties identifying bubbles in historical markets – including the uncertainty surrounding fundamental value and appropriate discount rates and the difficulty of untangling causal effects in complex markets – creates a strong demand for an alternative means to test whether or not bubbles exist and, if so, what causes, exacerbates, and suppresses them.

Experimental economics offers an attractive alternative. A laboratory setting allows economists to specify fundamental value and set up controls for various economic factors. Experimental economists have conducted sets of experiments in which subjects trade a fixed-income security with each other on a computer trading system over a set number of trading periods.[27] In these experiments, traders knew that the security would mature at the end of the last trading period and were informed of the probabilities that a fixed dividend would be paid at the end of every trading period. In plain English, this means that there was a true fundamental value to the security (i.e., there was no Knightian uncertainty)[28] and that traders could calculate this value as of each trading period.[29]

Yet traders in these experiments repeatedly engaged in bidding wars that drove the prices of securities higher than fundamental values. Prices returned to fundamental value, often via a dramatic crash, only in the last trading period.[30] Bubbles in these experimental markets have proven remarkably robust under various conditions.[31] These experimental markets buttress much of the theoretical and empirical work of behavioral finance by demonstrating how even relatively financially sophisticated investors can behave like noise traders in simulated stock markets.[32]

Chapter 8 explains the design and results of these experiments in further detail and looks at how one can carefully infer lessons from them for real markets. In particular, Chapter 8 considers what experimental results mean for the effectiveness of "anti-bubble laws," that is, various policies and legal interventions designed to prevent, prick, or dampen asset price bubbles.

Microeconomic models of bubbles

Behavioral finance models of bubbles

Behavioral finance explains that bubbles form because of the herd behavior, or positive-feedback behavior, of investors. However, behavioral finance departs from the view of neoclassical economic finance that investors are rational actors.

Instead, behavioral finance describes the rationality of investors as "bounded," and behavioral-finance models of bubbles argue that it is this departure from perfect rationality that sparks the initial inflation of a bubble.[33]

According to the logic of neoclassical finance that undergirds the EMH,[34] the mispricings of a bubble cannot occur for the following three reasons: (1) investors invest and trade in the capital markets in a rational manner; (2) any irrational trades are random and cancel each other out; and (3) arbitrage corrects any remaining irrational trading not canceled out.[35] Behavioral finance counters each of these assumptions in turn.

Bounded rationality and noise traders

Behavioral finance's first line of attack on neoclassical finance and the foundation for its explanation of how asset price bubbles form is that many investors do not exhibit perfect rationality in making investment decisions.[36] Behavioral finance argues that many investors do not: (1) gather optimal information to evaluate the fundamentals of assets; (2) carefully calculate probabilities and risk; and (3) make decisions that maximize their self-interest.[37] Instead, behavioral finance argues that many unsophisticated investors trade on "noise" – information not related to assessing the fundamental value of assets.[38] These "noise traders" evaluate whether to buy or sell assets based on price trends,[39] emotions,[40] or estimations about what other investors in the market will do.[41]

Unsophisticated investors trade on noise, according to behavioral finance, because their decision-making is marred by behavioral biases.[42] Behavioral finance draws on extensive experimental literature from the fields of psychology and other cognitive sciences, now well explored by the legal academy,[43] that shows individuals use mental shortcuts, called "heuristics," to process information and make complex economic decisions.[44] These heuristics lead to systematic behavioral biases in the perception of risk. The following are some of the common biases that may contribute to bubbles:

- *Overoptimism* describes how individuals possess an overly optimistic view of their own fortunes. Overoptimism means investors have too rosy a view of future stock prices in their portfolio.[45]
- *Overconfidence* describes the tendency of individuals to overestimate their own abilities. In bubbles, this may equate with investors being overconfident in their ability to pick investments and to exit before prices crash.[46]
- *The availability bias* describes how more recent or salient events exert excessive influence over an individual's estimate of probabilities.[47] For example, a neighbor's grisly car crash yesterday can cause an individual to calculate the risk of suffering a car accident herself as being much higher than statistics suggest. Conversely, the remoteness of the last market crash causes investors to discount the possibility of incurring heavy losses. The availability bias thus contributes to *disaster myopia* or underestimating the likelihood of catastrophe.[48]

Other biases, such as framing,[49] belief perseverance,[50] and anchoring,[51] further contribute to the suggestibility of investors and their stubborn reluctance to abandon optimism over their own prospects in the stock market despite mounting evidence to the contrary.[52] According to behavioral finance scholarship, during an extended market boom with conspicuous gains by early investors, these and other biases cause investors to conclude that rising prices will continue.[53] Moreover, investors conclude that they will profit handsomely from flipping assets and that they will be able to sell before a price downturn due to their self-perceived superior skill.[54]

Herding and positive-feedback investment loops

Second, behavioral finance presents evidence that refutes the second contention of neoclassical scholars. Instead of canceling each other out, noise traders reinforce each other because bounded rationality and behavioral biases cause highly correlated and mutually reinforcing – rather than random – investment decisions.[55] Behavioral finance presents evidence that investors are influenced by social dynamics. Investors thus engage in herd behavior, follow fads, and chase trends.[56]

Behavioral finance places this behavior in a larger rubric of "positive-feedback investment strategies."[57] If prices of an asset rise, investors who pursue these strategies bid prices higher as they base their analysis on the asset price trend.[58] The resulting rise in prices further increases demand among these noise traders, and a feedback loop develops.[59] Later chapters explore how both herd behavior and feedback mechanisms apply to financial regulation.

Limited arbitrage

Betting against noise traders in the middle of a positive-feedback loop can prove perilous. The risk faced by arbitrageurs points to the third response of behavioral finance to neoclassical economics: arbitrage may not correct deviations from fundamental value because arbitrageurs face severe limitations in attempting to exploit the mispricings caused by noise traders.[60] Many legal and economic scholars focus on legal limitations on arbitrage, notably short sale restrictions.[61]

Arbitrageurs also face various forms of economic risks. First, arbitrageurs face a "fundamental risk," which is the risk that future news about a company may drive the prices against the arbitrageur's position.[62] Arbitrageurs may not be able to find perfect substitutes to hedge investments that "short" a bubble.[63] Second, arbitrageurs face "noise-trader risk," which is the risk that noise traders will drive the prices further away from fundamental values.[64] This risk becomes pronounced if a period of prolonged investor irrationality begins.[65]

Arbitrageurs who aim to exploit (and thus correct) mispricings may be unable to outlast noise traders. Economists have shown that, contrary to the assumptions of the EMH, noise traders can persist in financial markets for extended periods.[66] On the other hand, arbitrageurs enjoy neither unlimited resources nor infinite time horizons.[67] Most arbitrageurs have short horizons because they are managing the money of other investors; this creates a classic agency problem. If an arbitrageur loses considerable money in the short-run trading against noise, investors and creditors may view this as a sign of the arbitrageur's incompetence and threaten to withdraw funds or loans, forcing the arbitrageur to liquidate positions prematurely.[68]

The risks arbitrageurs face in betting against irrational investors are not just theoretical. The Tiger Fund – perhaps the most prominent fund that refused to invest in technology stocks in the late 1990s – suffered heavy losses and was forced to close in March 2000, mere months before the peak of the NASDAQ.[69] Furthermore, even if a market crash wipes out noise traders, a new generation of noise traders could enter the market in time for a new bubble. This real possibility counters the argument of some proponents of the EMH that the bursting of one bubble precludes future episodes of irrationality.[70] Noise trading could be countered by the combined resources of several arbitrageurs, but arbitrageurs face a final risk – collective-action failure.[71]

In contrast to neoclassical theory, arbitrageurs with superior information may have a strong incentive to trade ahead of, not against, noise traders.[72] Arbitrageurs who adopt this strategy can reap enormous profits and then liquidate their positions before noise traders reverse course. Strong empirical evidence indicates that arbitrageurs in fact behave in this manner, exacerbating the severity of mispricing caused by noise trading.[73]

A behavioral-finance model of asset price bubbles

One behavioral-finance scholar connects these elements of behavioral finance in a simple model of how bubbles form.[74] First, a "displacement" – either an external macroeconomic or political event or good news about a specific industry – causes corporate profits to rise. Changes in legal rules can cause or accentuate displacement. For example, Chapter 3 describes how regulatory stimulus, including deregulation, changing levels of legal enforcement, and government subsidies of investment markets, can contribute to bubble formation.

After displacement, investors with superior information make conspicuous gains as share prices rise. Noise traders, attracted by rising prices, enter the market and bid prices even higher, adopting positive-feedback investment strategies. Informed investors and arbitrageurs (known as "smart money") anticipate noise-trader demand and bid-up prices in advance of noise traders, further stimulating demand. When smart money senses the market overheating, it sells. Ultimately, noise traders follow and, once a tipping point is reached, prices crash.[75]

Evidence: anomalies and mispricings

Behavioral-finance scholars back up their theoretical challenge to neoclassical finance and the EMH with empirical evidence of stock-market mispricings, that is, examples of various pricing anomalies in capital markets that violate the tenets of investor rationality and the EMH.[76] Phenomena, such as the closed-end fund puzzle,[77] the twin-share anomaly,[78] the initial public offering (IPO) carve out,[79] and internet-name anomalies,[80] represent instances in which either certain stock prices could not have reflected fundamental value or investors could not have been trading on fundamental information. Economists consider these anomalies evidence of "investor sentiment."[81]

These anomalies may serve as indicia of the existence of stock-market bubbles and add to the set of imperfect tools for detecting bubbles.[82] But serious questions remain as to whether anomalies indicate broader market mispricings or are merely isolated curiosities.[83] Phrased differently, does evidence of investor sentiment equate with evidence of asset price bubbles?[84] Economists are working to develop other tools for detecting bubbles, such as investor surveys.[85] Yet evidence from anomalies and other tools often points in contrary directions. Identifying historical bubbles, let alone determining whether markets are *currently* experiencing a bubble, remains more art than science.

Criticism of behavioral finance: open questions

Critics of behavioral finance charge that behavioral finance offers a laundry list of cognitive biases but does not adequately specify the particular biases (or the relative role among biases) that lead to mispricings and bubbles.[86] Other scholars note that certain behavioral biases, such as the hot-hand[87] and gambler's[88] fallacies, run counter to one another.[89] Other biases, such as conservatism,[90] would work against positive-feedback loops by causing investors to discount recent price trends and overemphasize long-term price probabilities.

Moreover, behavioral finance has yet fully to flesh out an explanation of seller behavior during the rise of a bubble.[91] At least two explanations are possible. The first is a model with two groups: noise traders that buy and smart money that sells.[92] The second explanation involves noise traders rapidly flipping stocks among each other, with each trader overconfident that he or she knows better than his or her counterpart when a stock is under- or overvalued.[93]

These critiques of behavioral finance indicate open research questions, including the need to articulate which behavioral biases cause investor sentiment and asset mispricings, which types of investors suffer from which biases and to what degree, and when certain biases come to dominate opposing biases.[94]

Rational bubbles

Scholars working within neoclassical economics have long attempted to create models of asset price bubbles that assume investors have rational expectations.[95] Many of these efforts predated behavioral finance. Rational bubbles are generally defined as self-fulfilling prophecies created by rational expectations of higher prices.[96] Often, rational-bubble models have been used to argue that asset price bubbles cannot exist because either investor rationality would prevent prices from ever departing from fundamentals[97] or bubbles would grow ad infinitum.[98]

Other scholars have used the circularity in this logic to launch trenchant critiques of rational-bubble models. These critics claim that rational-bubble models offer no explanation of how bubbles could ever begin,[99] are extremely un-robust to small changes in model assumptions,[100] and generate mathematically indeterminate solutions.[101] Most devastatingly, these scholars argue that rational-bubble theorists have failed to offer any empirical evidence of rational bubbles occurring in the real world.[102]

The rationality of herding

Even if rational-bubble theories have severe limitations, they offer one crucial insight that can contribute to more robust models of bubbles: once a bubble has formed and the expectations of investors drive asset prices higher, it may be perfectly rational for other investors to join in bidding prices higher. In some cases, it may prove costly and irrational *not* to join the herd. Indeed, behavioral finance work on bubbles builds on this insight.[103]

The rationality of herd behavior has other analogues in economic literature. For example, the most influential economic models of bank runs are built on the rational behavior of depositors. Banks have illiquid, long-term assets (such as thirty-year mortgages to homebuyers) but liquid, short-term liabilities (such as deposits that can be withdrawn upon demand by depositors). This leaves a bank vulnerable to runs should depositors begin to withdraw their deposits. A depositor might do so if she fears other depositors will begin withdrawing funds, leaving the bank's cupboard bare. Bank runs have thus been modeled as self-fulfilling prophecies.[104] Depositors may be sparked to withdraw funds if they anticipate a downturn in a business cycle that might cause other depositors to need cash and withdraw bank funds.[105]

"Information cascades" represent another example and explanation of rational herding. Information cascades form when individuals must make a similar decision in sequence. Individuals can see the decisions made by earlier counterparts, but do not have access to the information underlying those choices. It may be optimal for those later decision-makers simply to mimic the behavior of the earlier individuals rather than gather costly information themselves.[106] This logic is not all that different from Keynes' description of the stock market as a "beauty contest," in which an investor wins not by picking the stocks that she thinks are likely to produce gains, but by buying those she thinks others are likely to pick.[107]

Together, this literature on rational herding demystifies phenomena such as investment mania and panics that have been described in purely psychological terms. Seemingly irrational behavior may have completely rational logic. The question remains over what triggered the herd behavior. However, the behavioral finance models of bubbles present a nuanced synthesis of irrational and rational behavior. This interaction between behavioral and rational decisions will inform later chapters that discuss decisions to make, enforce, and obey regulation.

Agency costs and the role of credit

A subset of the rational-bubble literature makes a second valuable contribution by tying bubble formation to credit. Franklin Allen and Douglas Gale contend that bank credit can fuel bubbles. In their model, lenders face information asymmetries when they lend to speculators. The lenders cannot fully monitor the speculators, and speculators enjoy limited liability. This skews the incentives of speculators to make higher risk investments given that they are betting with other people's money. Allen and Gale posit that this can drive asset prices above fundamental value.[108]

Even though this model has limiting assumptions,[109] it provides a microeconomic foundation to macroeconomic and experimental research on the role of credit and monetary policy in generating bubbles (previewed below in this chapter and discussed in more detail in Chapter 9).

Outside the mainstream: Minsky, leverage, and cycles

Other theories that developed outside the mainstream of economic scholarship yield valuable insights of their own. The work of Hyman Minsky provides a case in point. He argued that financial crises are not an aberration but a recurrent feature of financial markets. Minsky articulated a "Financial Instability Hypothesis," in which three distinct kinds of finance cycle through the economy. In "hedge finance," borrowers who repay loans from cash flow dominate. As the economy has a long run of growth, "speculative finance" – in which borrowers have sufficient cash flow to repay the interest on their debt but not principal – comes to replace hedge finance. In order to stay afloat, speculative borrowers must continuously roll-over and refinance loans. If the economy continues to grow or accelerate, a third class of borrowers enters and begins to dominate. These borrowers engage in "ponzi finance," meaning they can repay neither principal nor interest from cash flows. Instead, these investors must rely on being able to flip assets or borrow more. This behavior may stimulate the economy even further, but cannot be sustained as cash flows will not be able to catch up with debt loads. Thus, if an economy shifts from hedge finance to speculative and ponzi finance, it will also shift from stability to instability.

Minsky's work illustrates the power of cycles in asset markets. Financial cycles and their interaction with regulatory and political cycles represent another thread that runs through this book. As noted in the Introduction, Minsky's Financial Instability Hypothesis serves as an inspiration for the Regulatory Instability Hypothesis developed in this book.

The role of credit in bubbles: the dangers of debt-fueled bubbles

Both the rational- and behavioral-finance models of bubbles are constructs of microeconomics. But there is also a long history of macroeconomic scholarship regarding bubbles that focuses on the role of credit in driving mispricings. This line of inquiry could be considered as a complement to microeconomic models. Macroeconomists have studied the effects of monetary policy and noted a historic pattern: rising interest rates tend to prick asset price bubbles and lead to price downturns.[110] Even macroeconomists who disagree about the wisdom of using monetary policy to control asset prices agree that raising interest rates in many cases could have the effect of pricking a bubble.[111] Moreover, evidence from experimental economics suggests that the availability of credit can fuel bubbles.[112]

Economists disagree on how expansions of credit can cause asset mispricing. This chapter has already described the Allen and Gale agency cost explanation. An alternative theory posits that lower interest rates may fuel speculation through provision of cheap credit to investors purchasing assets, and rising interest rates make borrowing these funds too expensive.[113] But this theory is problematic, as lower costs of borrowing could stimulate investing in assets without necessarily causing prices to deviate from fundamental value. Rational actors should factor anticipated changes in interest rates into their bid and asking prices for assets.

This necessitates consideration of alternative theories. One controversial theory holds that asset price bubbles might be spurred by investor anticipation of fluctuations in interest rates due to inconsistent and changing monetary policy (which has the technical label of "process switching").[114] Other economists fault the presence of government guarantees (whether explicit guarantees, such as deposit insurance, or implicit guarantees) for creating moral hazard, spurring excessive risk-taking by lenders, and, in turn, exacerbating bubbles.[115]

Behavioral finance provides other explanations. Lower interest rates and the resulting lower inflation may cause investors to suffer from "money illusion," or mistakenly believing that fundamental value and not inflation represents the cause of rising asset prices.[116] (Money illusion describes confusing the nominal value of an asset with its real value.)[117] Even if lower costs of borrowing stimulate asset prices without deviating from fundamental value, the price boom may encourage noise traders to chase a price trend, perhaps in the mistaken belief that the boom stems from a change in fundamental value.

Instead of looking at how credit affects asset pricing on a microeconomic level, macroeconomists often consider the aggregate effects of credit expansion on the economy. Some of the most influential macroeconomic research of the past two decades looks at how the procyclical nature of bank lending – that is expanding in boom times and contracting after a downturn – can amplify the magnitude of business cycles.[118] John Geanakoplos argues that economies experience leverage cycles. During boom times, lenders allow borrowers to increase leverage by demanding less collateral for loans. However, after a bust, lenders demand more collateral, which results in deleveraging and curtails the supply of credit.[119] Economists Tobias Adrian and Hyun Song Shin provide empirical evidence of a cyclical pattern in financial institution leverage before and after the Panic of 2008.[120]

Together this macroeconomic research explains the potentially destructive feedback loops that can form between procyclical credit, on one hand, and boom and bust cycles in financial markets and the macroeconomy, on the other. Massive leveraging and deleveraging explains both why debt-fueled bubbles can be both larger in magnitude and can have much more destructive macroeconomic effects.[121]

The nexus between credit and bubbles is therefore explored in much more detail in several later chapters of this book. Chapter 7 will discuss how certain prudential banking regulations operate procyclically; they expand the supply of credit to asset markets during booms and choke credit after a bust. Chapter 9 explores the role of credit in bubbles more broadly. It examines the empirical and experimental evidence that greater credit can fuel a bubble and restrictions on credit can prick one. It outlines the debate among macroeconomists on whether monetary policy should target bubbles. That chapter also examines how changes to financial regulation can – intentionally or unintentionally – have the same effect on bubbles as traditional tools of monetary policy. That is, when certain credit and leverage regulations experience roll back, under-enforcement, deteriorating compliance, or heavy regulatory arbitrage, then the lowered effectiveness of these regulations alters the monetary environment in often dramatic but subsurface ways. Chapter 9 also discusses the potentially dangerous feedback loops that form when bubbles are driven by financial institution lending; collapsed bubbles and banking crises, when conjoined, produce particularly destructive economic storms.

Real estate bubbles

Much of behavioral-finance literature has focused on stock-market bubbles, which leads to the question of whether the same logic of irrational investors driving market mispricing applies to other asset classes, particularly real estate. Real estate assets possess economic characteristics such as immobility,[122] durability,[123] heterogeneity,[124] and consumability[125] that differ materially from securities. Because of these factors, real estate assets are not fungible and real estate markets are both fragmented – there are no central national markets for trading real estate properties as there are for securities[126] – and prone to inefficiencies.[127]

Although the connections to behavioral-finance theory remain underexplored, real estate economists have begun to map out how heuristics, behavioral biases, herd behavior, and positive-feedback loops can drive mispricing in real estate markets.[128] In some models, overoptimism by groups of real estate investors may drive prices above fundamental value.[129] As with asset prices generally, bank credit can contribute to a bubble's growth.[130]

Once mispricings begin, the unique properties of real estate markets may prolong them. For example, because real estate is not a common-value good and is not traded on a market, it is impossible to short sell individual real estate properties. This means arbitrage cannot correct mispricings.[131] In addition, because of their unique economic characteristics, real estate prices also exhibit rigidity or inflexibility ("stickiness"), particularly downward stickiness.[132] The long lag time in construction prevents supply from quickly responding to lower demand.[133] Downward stickiness has led some economists to analyze whether crashes may be delayed or whether certain real estate bubbles do not burst but persist or slowly deflate.[134]

Moreover, empirical research indicates that the EMH does not apply to real estate markets.[135] Real estate prices exhibit positive serial correlation, which, in lay terms, means that when prices rise, they continue to rise and, when they fall, they continue to fall.[136] Positive serial correlation can translate into boom and bust cycles in real estate markets.[137] Extended boom times in financial markets can mask mispricing of risk by market participants. For example, if the models used to price real estate based financial instruments (like mortgage-backed securities) use historical data that do not reach before the boom, the models may underestimate risk.[138] Furthermore, long cycles – and a long period since the last real estate crisis – may induce "disaster myopia" in both market participants and regulators.[139]

Historical studies reveal that the bursting of real estate bubbles, particularly those involving residential real estate, can inflict more severe economic damage than other bubbles. The collapse of real estate bubbles can destroy household wealth and show a high degree of historical correlation with banking crises.[140]

Rigor and pragmatism in identifying bubbles

Despite the advances made by behavioral finance, there is still no consensus among economists about how asset price bubbles form or whether particular historical episodes constituted bubbles.[141] Some economists doubt the possibility of asset price bubbles. Yet this lack of absolute consensus does not mean that policymakers should ignore the possibility of future bubbles forming. True, if bubbles are hard to identify after the fact, they are even harder to detect prospectively or *in media res*.

Even so, economic research does point to a list of warning signs that booming prices in asset markets may be unsustainable. These early warning alarms include more than skyrocketing asset prices and ratios of prices to earnings. They also include the following:

- historically cheap credit (measured by, among other things, low interest rates and a growing money supply);[142]
- higher leverage of households, financial institutions, and governments;[143]
- a surge of external capital flowing into a country (measured by trade or current account balances);[144] and
- an influx of inexperienced investors into a market.[145]

Prices in futures markets may also provide warning signs that bubble prices are unsustainable.[146]

In considering these warning signs, policymakers must factor the potential both for false positives and false negatives and the inherent messiness in interpreting data from complex markets. In fashioning policy responses to potential bubbles, policymakers must balance the expected costs of a given intervention (including dampening capital formation) against the very real costs of bubbles and crashes. Again, debt-fueled bubbles pose particularly dire risks.

Opponents of interventions against bubbles (and those who want boom times to continue) enjoy several advantages. They can offer "hard" data of the costs of restricting investment or credit. By contrast, the benefits of fighting bubbles are squishier given the inevitable uncertainty of whether a bubble exists. Opponents of bubble interventions can proffer "this time is different" explanations for booming prices. They can play off behavioral biases that cause investors and regulators to give excessive weight to recent booming prices.

Yet requiring absolute certainty on whether a bubble exists before a government takes any action to mitigate risk stacks the deck in favor of letting markets boom and crash no matter the economic or social consequences. Policymakers must make decisions under uncertainty all the time. The question is how policymakers can take pragmatic steps given the limitations of economic knowledge and conflicting data, and amid political pressure. This book will turn to policy prescriptions for dealing with the risk of bubbles only in Parts IV and V. Until then, this book will focus largely on describing the problems that bubbles cause for financial laws and regulations and how laws and regulations can fuel bubbles. As John Dewey once wrote, "a problem well put is half-solved."[147]

Even describing the historical relationships between bubbles and law raises the question of how to identify whether a particular boom and crash period was a bubble. The next chapter discusses the legal history of almost a dozen or so boom and bust periods in financial markets spread over four centuries and several continents. I chose these episodes based on two considerations. First, I looked for a rich literature on the economic and legal history of each period. Second, I wanted to compare and contrast the legal environments in which different boom and busts developed, choosing episodes in different time periods, economies, and cultures.

I rely on economists for the task of identifying the particular economic causes of each of these boom/bust episodes and debating whether each episode constituted a "bubble" according to the definitions explored in this chapter. Even lingering uncertainty as to whether prices diverged from fundamental value does not detract from the core lessons of the remainder of the book.

Indeed, whether prices exceeded fundamental value is less of a driving factor behind the components of the Regulatory Instability Hypothesis than the particular mechanisms at work in a boom/bust period. The combination of rising prices, the effects of rising prices on the incentives and capabilities of market actors and public officials, the behavioral biases of those same individuals, their herd behavior (whether rational or irrational), and the interaction of a wave first-time investors with sophisticated players, all help explain the feedback mechanisms between financial markets and legal rules explored throughout the remainder of the book.

Notes

1 See, e.g., Charles P. Kindleberger, *Manias, Panics and Crashes: A History of Financial Crises*, 16 (4th ed. 2000, Wiley Investment Classics) (defining a bubble as "an upward price movement over an extended range that then implodes").

2 See, e.g., Robert P. Flood and Peter M. Garber, Market Fundamentals Versus Price-Level Bubbles: The First Tests, 88 *Journal of Political Economy* 745, 746 (1980); Henry T. C. Hu, Faith and Magic: Investor Beliefs and Government Neutrality, 78 *Texas Law Review* 777, 794 (2000). At times, economists have expanded this basic definition to include the reason that asset prices diverge from their fundamental values. Markus K. Brunnermeier, Bubbles, in *The New Palgrave Dictionary of Economics* (Steven Durlauf and Lawrence Blume eds., 2008, Palgrave Macmillan) ("Bubbles refer to asset prices that exceed an asset's fundamental value because current owners believe that they can resell the asset at an even higher price in the future.").

3 See, e.g., Ellen R. McGrattan and Edward C. Prescott, Testing for Stock Market Overvaluation/Undervaluation, in *Asset-Price Bubbles: The Implications for Monetary, Regulatory, and International Policies*, 271 (William C. Hunter, George G. Kaufman, and Michael Pomerleano, eds., 2003, MIT Press) [hereinafter *Asset Price Bubbles*]. One alternative to defining fundamental value in terms of future cash flows is to say that the best guess as to fundamental value is whatever the market price is. That tautology would make it impossible for prices ever to be "wrong."

4 For a primer on bond valuation, see A. A. Groppelli and Ehsan Nikbakht, *Finance*, 119–22 (5th ed. 2006, Barron's Educational Series).

5 See, e.g., Kenneth A. Froot and Maurice Obstfeld, Intrinsic Bubbles: The Case of Stock Prices, 81 *American Economic Review* 1189 (1991) (developing a "rational-bubble" model for stocks using dividend payments as determinant of fundamental value); Charles Himmelberg, Christopher Mayer, and Todd Sinai, Assessing High House Prices: Bubbles, Fundamentals, and Misperceptions, National Bureau of Economic Research, *Working Paper No. 11643*, 1–2 (2005) (using the "imputed annual rental cost" of owning property to determine the presence of a real estate bubble).

6 Franklin Allen and Roni Michaely, Payout Policy, in *1A Handbook of the Economics of Finance*, 408 (George M. Constantinides, Milton Harris, and René M. Stulz, eds., 2003, Elsevier North Holland) (describing the recent historic shift from corporations making payouts to stock investors in dividends to payouts in share repurchases).

7 For example, condominium-association governing documents often prohibit or restrict leasing. See *Woodside Village Condominium Ass'n* v. *Jahren*, 806 So. 2d 452, 453 (Fla. 2002) (upholding agreement restricting leases).

8 Logically, the greater the proportion of the income (either expected or possible) from the sale of an asset to the income from dividend or rental streams, the more speculative (in every sense of that word) the fundamental value of the asset becomes (unless the variance in the sales price is less than the variance of dividend and rental income from the assets).

9 See Nicholas Barberis and Richard Thaler, A Survey of Behavioral Finance, in *1B Handbook of the Economics of Finance*, 1054, 1061 (George M. Constantinides, Milton Harris, and René M. Stulz, eds., 2003, Elsevier North Holland).

10 Robert J. Shiller, *Irrational Exuberance*, 180–3 (2001, Broadway Books) (investigating the link between stock dividends, prices, and bubble theories).

11 SEC regulations require this disclosure on advertising by investment companies that include performance data. 17 C.F.R. § 230.482(b)(3)(i) (2007).

12 In fact, many scholars trace the formation of bubbles to widespread adoption of new technologies (e.g., the first financial exchanges in the seventeenth century, railroads in the nineteenth century, radios and airplanes in the 1920s, and the internet in the

1990s), social changes (e.g., the end of wars), or the opening of new geographical markets. Kindleberger, *supra* note 1, at 38–41.

13 Frank H. Knight, *Risk, Uncertainty and Profit*, 19–20 (1921, Houghton Mifflin).

14 Allan H. Meltzer, Rational and Nonrational Bubbles, in *Asset Price Bubbles*, *supra* note 3, at 28–9.

15 Ibid. at 28–9.

16 These beliefs represent what economist Robert Shiller calls "new era thinking." Shiller, *supra* note 10, at 96. Many adherents to new era thinking, such as investors in technology stocks in the late 1990s, could justify their decisions only with what one economist labels "wildly optimistic expectations of sustained profit growth rates." See Meltzer, *supra* note 14, at 23, 27–8. Carmen M. Reinhart and Kenneth S. Rogoff, *This Time is Different: Eight Centuries of Financial Folly*, 15–20 (2009, Princeton University Press) (describing "this time is different" syndrome).

17 Andrei Shleifer, *Inefficient Markets: An Introduction to Behavioral Finance*, 154 (2000, Oxford University Press).

18 For an overview of the EMH and the challenge it faces from behavioral finance, see ibid. at 5–23. For a seminal work in legal literature on the implications of this challenge for those securities regulations and doctrines based on the EMH, see Donald C. Langevoort, Theories, Assumptions, and Securities Regulation: Market Efficiency Revisited, 140 *University of Pennsylvania Law Review* 851 (1992). For the seminal article introducing the EMH to legal literature, see Ronald J. Gilson and Reinier H. Kraakman, The Mechanisms of Market Efficiency, 70 *Virginia Law Review* 549 (1984).

19 E.g., Burton G. Malkiel, The Efficient Market Hypothesis and its Critics, 17 *Journal of Economic Perspectives* (Winter 2003), at 59 (questioning whether behavioral finance meets this standard).

20 Furthermore, legal scholars have noted that, in its strict sense, the EMH only contends that market prices reflect all available information regarding an asset and not that prices necessarily reflect that asset's fundamental value. See, e.g., Jeffrey N. Gordon and Lewis A. Kornhauser, *Efficient Markets, Costly Information, and Securities Research*, 60 *New York University Law Review* 761, 766–71 (1985) (drawing a distinction between arguments that markets are characterized by speculative (i.e., informational) efficiency and those discussing allocational efficiency). Despite this distinction, the economic literature on bubbles often appears to conflate informational and allocational efficiency. See, e.g., Barberis and Thaler, *supra* note 9, at 1054, 1056 (defining "fundamental value" as "the discounted sum of expected future cash flows" where investors are operating with all available information).

21 Franklin Allen and Gary Gorton, Churning Bubbles, 60 *Review of Economic Studies* 813, 815 (1993).

22 Compare Peter M. Garber, Tulipomania, 97 *Journal of Political Economy* 535 (1989) (arguing that prices of tulip bulbs during Dutch Tulipomania in the 1630s may have been justified by fundamentals), with Edward Chancellor, *Devil Take the Hindmost: A History of Financial Speculation*, 23–6 (1999, Plume Books) (disputing Garber's facts and analysis).

23 Compare McGrattan and Prescott, *supra* note 3, at 271–5 (presenting evidence that the 1929 U.S. stock market was not overvalued), with Peter Rappoport and Eugene N. White, Was There a Bubble in the 1929 Stock Market? 53 *Journal of Economic History* 549 (1993) (finding evidence that a bubble contributed to the 1920s stock-market boom and crash despite certain econometric tests that suggest no bubble existed).

24 Compare Lubos Pastor and Pietro Veronesi, Was There a NASDAQ Bubble in the Late 1990's? 81 *Journal of Financial Economics* 61 (2006) (presenting evidence that there was not a NASDAQ bubble), with Shiller, *supra* note 10, at 3–4 (arguing that the late 1990s market for technology stocks was overvalued).

25 Scholars often look back and see risk, but investors of the past looked forward into uncertainty. Robert J. Shiller, Bubbles, Human Judgment, and Expert Opinion, Yale Cowles Foundation, *Discussion Paper No. 1303*, 12–13 (2001) available at http://papers.ssrn.com/sol3/papers.cfm?abstract_id=275515 (last visited July 12, 2013). Only examples of investor behavior that, *at the time*, could not be squared with rational expectations or fundamental information on the value of assets would support findings of investor irrationality. See Kenneth L. Fisher and Meir Statman, Cognitive Biases in Market Forecasts, 27 *Journal of Portfolio Management* 72, 78–9 (2000) (evaluating behavioral finance and other research for hindsight bias in market forecasts). Only comparisons of ultimate cash flows to historical price changes that show that investors make *systematic* errors (under- or overestimating cash flows or under- or overreacting to information) weaken support for market efficiency. Many behavioral-finance scholars recognize this and produce evidence of systematic errors. See, e.g., Josef Lakonishok, Contrarian Investment, Extrapolation and Risk, in *Advances in Behavioral Finance Vol. II*, 273, 312–13 (Richard H. Thaler ed., 2005, Princeton University Press) (responding to criticisms of "data snooping" with evidence of a "systematic pattern of expectational errors" by investors).

26 See Eugene F. Fama, Random Walks in Stock Market Prices, 21 *Financial Analysts Journal* 55 (1965) (early articulation of the hypothesis that stock prices follow random walk).

27 See, e.g., Gunduz Caginalp, David Porter, and Vernon L. Smith, Overreactions, Momentum, Liquidity, and Price Bubbles in Laboratory and Field Asset Markets, 1 *Journal of Psychology and Financial Markets* 24 (2000); Ronald R. King, Vernon L. Smith, Arlington W. Williams, and Mark Van Boening, The Robustness of Bubbles and Crashes in Experimental Stock Markets, in *Nonlinear Dynamics and Evolutionary Economics*, 183 (Richard H. Day and Ping Chen eds., 1993, Oxford University Press); David P. Porter and Vernon L. Smith, Stock Market Bubbles in the Laboratory, 1 *Applied Mathematical Finance* 111 (1994); Vernon L. Smith, Gerry L. Suchanek, and Arlington W. Williams, Bubbles, Crashes, and Endogenous Expectations in Experimental Spot Asset Markets, 56 *Econometrica* 1119 (1988).

28 Porter and Smith, *supra* note 27, at 121–2.

29 See Caginalp *et al.*, *supra* note 27, at 24–5; David P. Porter and Vernon L. Smith, Futures Contracting and Dividend Uncertainty in Experimental Asset Markets, 68 *Journal of Business* 509, 509–10 (1995); Smith *et al.*, *supra* note 27, at 1124.

30 Caginalp *et al.*, *supra* note 27, at 26; King *et al.*, *supra* note 27, at 199–200; Porter and Smith, *supra* note 27, at 121–2; Smith *et al.*, *supra* note 27, at 1148–50.

31 See Caginalp *et al.*, *supra* note 27, at 26–32 (surveying experiments where bubbles occurred despite various changes in experimental market conditions). For samples of experiments testing for the occurrence of bubbles under various economic conditions and policies, see King *et al.*, *supra* note 27, at 185–200; Vivian Lei, Charles N. Noussair, and Charles R. Plott, Nonspeculative Bubbles in Experimental Asset Markets: Lack of Common Knowledge of Rationality vs. Actual Irrationality, 69 *Econometrica* 831 (2001); Smith *et al.*, *supra* note 27.

32 E.g., Caginalp *et al.*, *supra* note 27 (using experimental-asset-market results to create a "momentum model" explaining trader behavior).

33 See Brunnermeier, *supra* note 2, at 10.

34 See Shleifer, *supra* note 17, at 2–10.

35 Ronald J. Gilson and Reinier H. Kraakman, The Mechanisms of Market Efficiency, 70 *Virginia Law Review* 549, 579–88 (1984).

36 Shleifer, *supra* note 17, at 10–12 (summarizing principal behavioral finance research that investors are not "fully rational"); Barberis and Thaler, *supra* note 9, at 1065–9.

37 Barberis and Thaler, *supra* note 9, at 1065–74.

38 See Donald C. Langevoort, Taming the Animal Spirits of the Stock Markets:

A Behavioral Approach to Securities Regulation, 97 *Northwestern University Law Review* 135, 139–52 (2002) (surveying noise-trader research in economic literature).

39 Robert J. Shiller, Stock Prices and Social Dynamics, 2 *Brookings Papers on Economic Activity* 457 (1984).

40 For an analysis of how emotions affect the decisions of investors, see Peter H. Huang, Regulating Irrational Exuberance and Anxiety in Securities Markets, in *The Law and Economics of Irrational Behavior*, 501, 505–18 (Francesco Parisi and Vernon L. Smith eds., 2005, Stanford University Press).

41 See generally Robert J. Shiller, Fashions, Fads, and Bubbles in Financial Markets, in *Knights, Raiders and Targets*, 56 (John C. Coffee, Jr., Louis Lowenstein, and Susan Rose-Ackerman eds., 1988, Oxford University Press).

42 Behavioral finance builds off evidence that individuals often exhibit preferences that skew how investors evaluate risky gambles. Barberis and Thaler, *supra* note 9, at 1069–75.

43 For an introduction to the now-extensive literature on behavioral law and economics, see Christine Jolls, Cass R. Sunstein, and Richard Thaler, A Behavioral Approach to Law and Economics, 50 *Stanford Law Review* 1471 (1998). For a discussion of behavioral biases leading to the formation of stock-market bubbles, see Werner De Bondt, Bubble Psychology, in *Asset Price Bubbles*, *supra* note 3, at 205, 210–12.

44 Amos Tversky and Daniel Kahneman, Judgment Under Uncertainty: Heuristics and Biases, 185 *Science* 1124 (1974).

45 See, e.g., J. Bradford De Long and Andrei Shleifer, The Stock Market Bubble of 1929: Evidence from Closed-end Mutual Funds, 51 *Journal of Economic History* 675, 697 (1991) (concluding that overoptimism of investors contributed to the 1929 stock-market bubble).

46 See J. Bradford De Long, Andrei Shleifer, Lawrence H. Summers, and Robert J. Waldmann, The Survival of Noise Traders in Financial Markets, 64 *Journal of Business* 1, 5 (1991) (arguing that the overconfidence bias leads noise traders to remain in the market despite a risk of severe losses). Behavioral economists have presented substantial empirical evidence that individuals exhibit overoptimism in judging the probability of good outcomes and are overconfident in their own abilities, including their ability to estimate probabilities. See Barberis and Thaler, *supra* note 9, at 1065–6.

47 See Tversky and Kahneman, *supra* note 44, at 1127–8.

48 Richard J. Herring and Susan Wachter, Real Estate Booms and Banking Busts: An International Perspective, Wharton Financial Institutions Center, *Working Paper No. 99–27* (1999) available at http://fic.wharton.upenn.edu/fic/papers/99/9927.pdf (last visited July 12, 2013).

49 Empirical research demonstrates that individuals often reach different conclusions about the same problems depending on how problems are described or framed. Faced with difficult problems, individuals frame problems for themselves often in less than rational ways and engage in what has been labeled "mental accounting." See generally Richard S. Thaler, Mental Accounting Matters, in *Choices, Values and Frames*, 241 (Daniel Kahneman and Amos Tversky eds., 2000, Cambridge University Press).

50 Belief perseverance describes the tendency of individuals to maintain longstanding opinions even in the face of mounting contradictory evidence. Barberis and Thaler, *supra* note 9, at 1068 (citing Charles G. Lord, Lee Ross, and Mark R. Lepper, Biased Assimilation and Attitude Polarization: The Effects of Prior Theories on Subsequently Considered Evidence, 37 *Journal of Personality and Social Psychology* 2098, 2099 (1979)).

51 Anchoring describes the tendency of individuals to give undue weight to their initial estimates of a probability or other measurement. See Tversky and Kahneman, *supra* note 44, at 1128.

52 See De Bondt, *supra* note 43, at 208–9.
53 See J. Bradford De Long, Andrei Shleifer, Lawrence H. Summers, and Robert J. Waldmann, Positive Feedback Investment Strategies and Destabilizing Rational Speculation, 45 *Journal of Finance* 379, 383 (1990) (questioning why noise traders do not learn from previous bubbles).
54 See De Bondt, *supra* note 43, at 208–9.
55 See Shleifer, *supra* note 17, at 11–12.
56 Ibid. at 12. See Shiller, *supra* note 10, at 135–68 (outlining the psychological basis for investment decisions and the effect of herd behavior on capital markets); Shiller, *supra* note 39, at 457 (arguing that investors make decisions because of social and behavioral factors rather than through rational, self-interested calculations).
57 See Shleifer, *supra* note 17, at 154–5.
58 Ibid. at 155–6. Again, economists consider price-trend-information noise rather than information about the fundamental value of the asset.
59 For a model of this feedback loop, see ibid. at 158–68.
60 See Barberis and Thaler, *supra* note 9, at 1058–9.
61 See, e.g., Michael R. Powers, David M. Schizer, and Martin Shubik, Market Bubbles and Wasteful Avoidance: Tax and Regulatory Constraints on Short Sales, 57 *Tax Law Review* 233 (2004).
62 See Barberis and Thaler, *supra* note 9, at 1058–9.
63 Hedging by buying or selling substitute stocks cannot completely remove this risk given the rarity of perfect substitutes. Ibid.; Shleifer, *supra* note 17, at 14. In addition, substitute stocks may themselves be mispriced, which is more likely in periods of systematic mispricing, such as bubbles. Barberis and Thaler, *supra* note 9, at 1058 n.4. No substitutes exist for stocks or bonds as a whole, making arbitrage against market-wide mispricing impossible. Shleifer, *supra* note 17, at 13. Andrei Shleifer describes the huge losses that would have threatened an arbitrageur attempting to sell short during the apparent stock-market-wide overvaluation of the late 1990s. Ibid. at 15–16.
64 J. Bradford De Long, Andrei Shleifer, Lawrence H. Summers, and Robert J. Waldmann, Noise Trader Risk in Financial Markets, 98 *Journal of Political Economy* 703, 705 (1990).
65 See Shleifer, *supra* note 17, at 15–16 (describing the noise-trader risk faced by arbitrageurs attacking apparent overvaluation during the technology bubble).
66 See generally De Long and Shleifer, *supra* note 45 (arguing that the overconfidence bias leads noise traders to remain in the market despite a risk of severe losses).
67 Andrei Shleifer and Robert W. Vishny, The Limits of Arbitrage, 52 *Journal of Finance* 35, 38–43 (1997).
68 Ibid.
69 Markus K. Brunnermeier and Stefan Nagel, Hedge Funds and the Technology Bubble, 59 *Journal of Finance* 2013, 2030–2 (2004).
70 See Lynn A. Stout, The Mechanisms of Market Inefficiency: An Introduction to the New Finance, 28 *Journal of Corporation Law* 635, 666 (2003).
71 Other arbitrageurs may not similarly trade against noise because of different information. See Dilip Abreu and Markus K. Brunnermeier, Synchronization Risk and Delayed Arbitrage, 66 *Journal of Financial Economics* 341, 343 (2002) (labeling this risk of collective action failure as "synchronization risk"). Coordinated action is limited by the threat of defection and legal constraints. See ibid. See also Dilip Abreu and Markus K. Brunnermeier, Bubbles and Crashes, 71 *Econometrica* 173 (2003).
72 Shleifer, *supra* note 17, at 169, 172. See also Abreu and Brunnermeier, Bubbles and Crashes, *supra* note 71.
73 See Brunnermeier and Nagel, *supra* note 69, at 2014–16.
74 Shleifer, *supra* note 17, at 169–75.

75 Ibid. at 169–75. Economists José Scheinkman and Wei Xiong developed an alternative behavioral finance model of bubble formation, in which bubbles have their genesis in investor overconfidence. Investors believe they can profit by selling assets to others who are more optimistic about price increases. Arbitrage is also limited in this model. José A. Scheinkman and Wei Xiong, Overconfidence and Speculative Bubbles, 111 *Journal of Political Economy* 1183 (2003).

A number of economists working outside behavioral finance have created another set of theories for how bubbles develop that nonetheless resembles the work of behavioral finance. This third set of models posits that bubbles form due to the fact that investors have heterogeneous beliefs about the future market prices (compared to the homogeneous beliefs assumed by neoclassical economics). Lynn A. Stout, Why the Law Hates Speculators, 48 *Duke Law Journal* 701, 755–62 (1999) (describing this set of models). Under many of the models in this family, the divergence of investor beliefs stems from psychological biases, but all of these models include limitations on short selling. Brunnermeier, *supra* note 2. Heterogeneity of investor beliefs or expectations can lead to price inflation as optimistic investors bid prices up while more pessimistic investors cannot sell short because of arbitrage limitations. Ibid.

See also Harrison Hong, José Scheinkman, and Wei Xiong, Asset Float and Speculative Bubbles, 61 *Journal of Finance* 1073 (2006) (modeling bubble formation based on heterogeneous beliefs of investors, short sale constraints, and stock with limited float); Harrison Hong, José Scheinkman, and Wei Xiong, Advisors and Asset Prices: A Model of the Origins of Bubbles, 89 *Journal of Financial Economics* 268 (2008) (bubbles stem from heterogeneity among investment advisors, who have differing beliefs and sophistication regarding prospects of new technology).

76 Barberis and Thaler, *supra* note 9, at 1061–4; Shiller, *supra* note 10, at 179–80.

77 The prices of certain mutual funds have occasionally risen far above the net asset value of the fund, even after adjusting for tax and other considerations. This means that investors are paying more for shares in a fund than they would pay if they purchased the proportionate share of the stocks in that fund's portfolio. See De Long and Shleifer, *supra* note 45, at 697 (recognizing that this phenomenon existed in the late 1920s).

78 This anomaly occurs when a given security is traded on two different markets, but the prices in those markets diverge over an extended period of time. See Barberis and Thaler, *supra* note 9, at 1061–3 (explaining the twin-share anomaly and noting how arbitrageurs theoretically could exploit it).

79 After 3Com sold 5 percent of its shares of Palm in an initial public offering, Palm's stock price paradoxically rose above the implicit price of its parent, 3Com. This implied that, apart from its shareholdings in Palm, 3Com had a negative value. Owen A. Lamont and Richard H. Thaler, Can the Market Add and Subtract? Mispricing in Tech Stock Carve-Outs, 111 *Journal of Political Economy* 227, 230–1 (2003) (documenting multiple examples of this anomaly).

80 During the recent technology stock boom, researchers noted that shares of companies with ".com" in their name sold in public offerings for significantly higher prices statistically than those of comparable companies. Also, market news about certain companies would irrationally affect the prices of different companies with similar names or stock-market-ticker symbols. Yaron Brooks and Robert J. Hendershott, Hype and Internet Stocks, 10 *Journal of Investing* 53 (2001); Michael J. Cooper, Orlin Dimitrov, and P. Raghavendra Rau, A Rose.com by Any Other Name, 56 *Journal of Finance* 2371, 2371–2 (2001).

81 Malcolm Baker and Jeffrey Wurgler, Investor Sentiment in the Stock Market, 21 *Journal of Economic Perspectives* 129 (2007) (defining sentiment as "belief about future cash flows and investment risks that is not justified by the facts at hand").

Baker and Wurgler advocate a "top-down" approach to behavioral finance. Rather than attempting to draw a causal connection between individual behavioral biases and market mispricings, Baker and Wurgler argue that behavioral finance should start from empirical evidence of investor sentiment in financial markets. According to this approach, economists should then try to develop tests to predict when and which stocks are most susceptible to investor sentiment. Ibid.

82 See Robert J. Shiller, From Efficient Markets Theory to Behavioral Finance, 17 *Journal of Economic Perspectives* 83, 101–2 (2003).

83 See, e.g., Malkiel, *supra* note 19.

84 E.g., ibid.

85 See, e.g., Robert J. Shiller, Measuring Bubble Expectations and Investor Confidence, National Bureau of Economic Research, *Working Paper No. 7008* (1999). Cf. Ravi Dhar and William N. Goetzmann, Bubble Investors: What Were They Thinking, *Yale ICF Working Paper No. 06-22* (August 17, 2006) available at http://papers.ssrn.com/sol3/papers.cfm?abstract_id=683366 (last visited July 12, 2013) (retrospective survey of investor beliefs during tech stock bubble).

86 Robert S. Chirinko, Comments on: "Stocks as Money…" and "Bubble Psychology," in *Asset Price Bubbles*, *supra* note 3, at 231, 234–5 ("While reading the behavioral finance literature, one gets the feeling of being in a well-stocked supermarket with a multitude of psychological tendencies waiting to be plucked from the shelf to explain the NASDAQ decline and other financial market outcomes…. With a surplus of explanations, it is difficult to know how to evaluate and discriminate among behavioral theories.").

87 The hot-hand fallacy translates a phenomenon from the sports world where coaches and athletes believe that an individual's shooting streak will continue, despite the statistical evidence that the shooter is enjoying a streak of luck and his or her performance will revert to its long-term mean. Thomas Gilovich, Robert Vallone, and Amos Tversky, The Hot-Hand in Basketball: On the Misperception of Random Sequences, 17 *Cognitive Psychology* 295 (1985). The hot-hand fallacy could lead to investors bidding up assets based on the erroneous belief that rising prices indicate a streak of their personal investing skill rather than chance or the development of a positive-feedback loop.

88 This fallacy refers to a common mistake that one random event can affect or be used to predict another random event. The canonical example is the erroneous belief that if a coin is flipped four times and lands "heads" each of those times, it has a greater than 50 percent probability of landing "tails" on the next flip. Amos Tversky and Daniel Kahnemann, Belief in the Law of Small Numbers, 76 *Psychological Bulletin* 105, 106 (1971). In asset prices, the gambler's fallacy might lead an investor to conclude that a lucky streak of rising prices is about to end and cause him or her to sell, thus short circuiting a positive-feedback loop.

89 Gregory La Blanc and Jeffrey J. Rachlinski, In Praise of Investor Irrationality, in *The Law and Economics of Irrational Behavior*, 18 (Francesco Parisi and Vernon L. Smith eds., 2005, Stanford University Press).

90 Conservatism describes mistakes in calculating probability due to the overweighting of base-rate probabilities and the underweighting of sample probabilities. Ward Edwards, Conservatism in Human Information Processing, in *Formal Representation of Human Judgment*, 17–18 (Benjamin Kleinmutz ed., 1968, John Wiley & Sons).

91 See Meltzer, *supra* note 14, at 28.

92 See, e.g., Shleifer, *supra* note 17, at 169–74; Weihong Huang and Richard H. Day, Chaotically Switching Bear and Bull Markets: The Derivation of Stock Market Distributions from Behavioral Rules, in *Nonlinear Dynamics and Evolutionary Economics*, 169–81 (Richard H. Day and Ping Chen eds., 1993, Oxford University Press) (modeling stock-market cycles as nonlinear results of the interaction of noise

traders, investors trading on fundamental information, and market makers). This explanation would benefit greatly from further precision regarding the profiles of the investors who fall in each category and from an investigation into whether stocks become increasingly concentrated in the hands of noise traders. See Meltzer, *supra* note 14, at 26–8 (critiquing irrational-bubble models for failing to answer these questions).

93 In both explanations, further research is required to understand the mechanics of the tipping point between bubble and crash.

94 Gregory Mitchell argues that behavioral-law-and-economics scholarship has been impeded by its focus on "behavioral tendencies" and its failure to articulate the "boundary conditions" for those tendencies. Gregory Mitchell, Tendencies versus Boundaries: Levels of Generality in Behavioral Law and Economics, 56 *Vanderbilt Law Review* 1781 (2003). The difficulty in linking behavioral biases to mispricings (a "bottom-up approach") has led other economists to take a "top-down approach" and use clear statistical evidence of investor sentiment to identify types of securities more likely to suffer from sentiment. See, e.g., Baker and Wurgler, *supra* note 81, at 130.

95 See, e.g., Oliver Jean Blanchard, Speculative Bubbles, Crashes and Rational Expectations, 3 *Economics Letters* 387, 387 (1979). For more recent rational models of bubbles, see Peter M. DeMarzo, Ron Kaniel, and Ilan Kremer, Relative Wealth Concerns and Financial Bubbles, 21 *Review of Financial Studies* 19 (2007) (bubbles result from investors' relative wealth concerns or attempting to "catch up with the Joneses"); Kevin J. Lansing, Rational and Near-Rational Bubbles Without Drift, 120 *Economic Journal* 1149 (2010).

96 See Robert P. Flood and Robert J. Hodrick, On Testing for Speculative Bubbles, 4 *Journal of Economic Perspectives* 85, 86 (1990).

97 See, e.g., Jean Tirole, On the Possibility of Speculation Under Rational Expectations, 50 *Econometrica* 1163, 1179–80 (1982). Tirole bases this argument on the logic of general equilibrium that, if an initial price is efficient and everyone in the market is informed of that efficiency, no rational buyer would pay more than that price. Ibid.

98 Brunnermeier, *supra* note 2.

99 Meltzer, *supra* note 14, at 24.

100 Small changes in the assumptions of the rational-bubble models cause them to fail to generate bubbles. M. C. Adam and A. Szafarz, Speculative Bubbles and Financial Markets, 44 *Oxford Economic Papers* 626, 634 (1992).

101 Equations underlying rational-bubble models have mathematically indeterminate solutions. Ibid. at 636. This theoretical indeterminacy, in turn, leads to inconsistent empirical analysis. One pair of critics notes that "researchers working with the same data base and identical models will not necessarily detect the 'same' bubbles," ibid. at 638. Moreover, rational-bubble models can generate an infinite number of price patterns, which bear no resemblance to the intuitive "shapes" of bubbles – either the prolonged rise in asset prices or the subsequent sharp crash. Ibid.

102 Meltzer, *supra* note 14, at 24.

103 Shleifer, *supra* note 17, at 156–68 (creating a model of positive feedback investment strategies).

104 The classic economic model of a bank run can be found in Douglas W. Diamond and Philip H. Dybvig, Bank Runs, Deposit Insurance, and Liquidity, 91 *Journal of Political Economy* 401 (1983).

105 Franklin Allen and Douglas Gale, Optimal Financial Crises, 53 *Journal of Finance* 1245 (1998).

106 Sushil Bikchandani, David Hirshleifer, and Ivo Welch, A Theory of Fads, Fashion, Custom, and Cultural Change as Informational Cascades, 100 *Journal of Political Economy* 992 (1992).

107 John Maynard Keynes, *The General Theory of Employment, Interest, and Money*, 156 (1936, Palgrave Macmillan).

108 See, e.g., Franklin Allen and Gary Gorton, Churning Bubbles, 60 *Review of Economic Studies* 813 (1993); Franklin Allen and Douglas Gale, Bubbles and Crises, 110 *Economic Journal* 236, 236 (2000); Franklin Allen and Douglas Gale, Asset Price Bubbles and Stock Market Interlinkages, in *Asset Price Bubbles, supra* note 3, at 323, 325–9.

109 Asymmetric rational bubbles have several limiting assumptions, most notably that arbitrage – and specifically short selling – must face constraints. Franklin Allen, Stephen Morris, and Andrew Postlewaite, Finite Bubbles with Short Sale Constraints and Asymmetric Information, 61 *Journal of Economic Theory* 206 (1993). Asymmetric rational bubbles also depend on two additional assumptions. First, before a bubble forms, an asset's price equals its fundamental value, and initial purchasers cannot be aware that the price equals fundamental value. See Brunnermeier, *supra* note 2, at 9–10. Second, for the bubble to persist, this information asymmetry must also persist; subsequent trading cannot reveal to purchasers that prices have exceeded fundamental value. Allen *et al., supra* this note.

110 See Shiller *supra* note 10, at 222–3.

111 Compare Ben S. Bernanke and Mark Gertler, Should Central Banks Respond to Movements in Asset Prices, 91 *American Economic Review* 253 (2001) (arguing that monetary policy should not be used to prick asset price bubbles), with Stephen G. Cecchetti, Hans Genberg, and Sushil Wadhwani, Asset Prices in a Flexible Inflation Targeting Framework, in *Asset Price Bubbles, supra* note 3, at 427, 438–41 (arguing that monetary policy can and should respond to "asset price misalignments").

112 Ronald R. King, Vernon L. Smith, Arlington W. Williams, and Mark Van Boening, The Robustness of Bubbles and Crashes in Experimental Stock Markets, in *Nonlinear Dynamics and Evolutionary Economics*, 183, 188–89 (Richard H. Day and Ping Chen eds., 1993, Oxford University Press).

113 See Stephen Malpezzi and Susan M. Wachter, The Role of Speculation in Real Estate Cycles, 13 *Journal of Real Estate Literature* 143 (2005).

114 Robert P. Flood and Robert J. Hodrick, Asset Price Volatility, Bubbles and Process Switching, in *Speculative Bubbles, Speculative Attacks, and Policy Switching*, 135, 136 (Robert P. Flood and Peter M. Garber eds., 1994, MIT Press). In many macroeconomic models that examine the effects of interest rates on asset price bubbles, asset price bubbles are exogenous and their formation need not be explained. See, e.g., Ben Bernanke and Mark Gertler, Monetary Policy and Asset Price Volatility National Bureau of Economics Research, *Working Paper No. 7559*, 7, 15–25 (2000).

115 Charles Collyns and Abdelhak Senhadji, Lending Booms, Real Estate Bubbles, and the Asian Crisis, in *Asset Price Bubbles, supra* note 3, at 101, 103.

116 See Markus K. Brunnermeier and Christian Julliard, Money Illusion and Housing Frenzies, 21 *Review of Financial Studies* 135 (2008).

117 Ibid. Eldar Shafir, Peter Diamond, and Amos Tversky, Money Illusion, 112 *Quarterly Journal of Economics* 341 (1997).

118 The Kiyotaki-Moore model represents a forerunner of economic models that examine how credit restrictions can amplify business cycles. See Nobuhiro Kiyotaki and John Moore, Credit Cycles, 105 *Journal of Political Economy* 211 (1997); Ben Bernanke and Mark Gertler, Inside of a Black Box: The Credit Channel of Monetary Policy Transmission, 9 *Journal of Economic Perspectives* 27 (1995); Collyns and Senhadji, *supra* note 115, at 101.

119 See John Geanakoplos, The Leverage Cycle, Cowles Foundation, *Discussion Paper No. 1715* (2009) available at http://papers.ssrn.com/sol3/papers.cfm?abstract_id=1441943 (last visited July 12, 2013). See also Ana Fostel and John Geanakoplos, Leverage Cycles and the Anxious Economy, 98 *American Economic Review* 1211 (2008).

120 Tobias Adrian and Hyun Song Shin, Money, Liquidity, and Monetary Policy, 99 *American Economic Review* 600, 602 (2009).
121 Reinhart and Rogoff, *supra* note 16, at xlv, 7–8.
122 Real estate, by definition, cannot be moved from one location to another, which, in turn, influences the other economic properties of real estate discussed in this section. Michael Ball, Colin Lizieri, and Bryan D. MacGregor, *The Economics of Commercial Property Markets*, 273 (1998, Routledge) ("Partly because the investment is heterogeneous and immobile, no central trading market, equivalent to the stock market, has developed for property.").
123 Securities and the companies that issue them can terminate, but, barring cataclysm, land cannot be destroyed and buildings tend to have long lives. Thomas W. Shafer, *Real Estate and Economics*, 29–30 (1975, Reston Publishing) ("The possibility of the market making necessary adjustments in the short run to take advantage of temporary and short-lived demand is reduced by the long life of real estate assets.").
124 The uniqueness of each piece of real estate generates information costs for purchasers, complicates pricing, and limits the availability of substitutes. Ball *et al.*, *supra* note 122, at 273.
125 Real estate represents not only an investment good that can be leased or sold for a return, but also a consumption good used for work or living space; and investors often purchase a real estate asset for both investment and consumption functions. Ibid. at 14.
126 See *supra* note 122.
127 Immobility means that supply of real estate in one physical location cannot be moved to meet greater demand in another area; people and businesses must move to real estate, which involves high transaction costs. See Shafer, *supra* note 123, at 29–30. Durability means that the stock of housing cannot contract easily in periods of lower demand, creating the potential for gluts. See ibid. at 29. Heterogeneity contributes to higher information costs and information asymmetries. See Ball *et al.*, *supra* note 122, at 273–4. Heterogeneity also makes hedging difficult by limiting the availability of close substitutes and increasing the transaction costs of purchasing real estate. Ibid. at 273. The high transaction costs of purchasing and selling real estate slow market corrections. In turn, the high costs of development delays the entry of new real estate stock to meet demand. Ibid. at 15. Finally, the dual use of real estate for investment and consumption often leads individuals to "overinvest" in real estate by investing more money in a particular asset than can be recouped when selling the asset in the market. See Jan K. Brueckner, Consumption and Investment Motives and the Portfolio Choices of Homeowners, 15 *Journal of Real Estate Finance and Economics* 159 (1997) (evaluating evidence of overinvestment due to the consumption value of real estate).
128 E.g., Brunnermeier and Julliard, *supra* note 116; Robert J. Shiller, Historic Turning Points in Real Estate, Cowles Foundation, *Discussion Paper No. 1610* (2007) available at http://cowles.econ.yale.edu/P/cd/d16a/d1610.pdf (last visited July 12, 2013); Grace Wong Bucchianeri, The Anatomy of a Housing Bubble: Overconfidence, Media and Politics, Unpublished manuscript (April 2011) available at http://papers.ssrn.com/sol3/papers.cfm?abstract_id=1877204 (last visited July 12, 2013).
129 Richard Herring and Susan Wachter, Bubbles in Real Estate Markets, in *Asset Price Bubbles*, *supra* note 3, at 217, 218–20 citing Mark S. Carey, Feeding the Fad: The Federal Land Banks, Land Market Efficiency, and the Farm Credit Crisis, PhD dissertation, University of California, Berkeley (1990).
130 Herring and Wachter, *supra* note 129, at 220–1. For an empirical study of the role of bank lending in Asian real estate bubbles in the 1990s, see Collyns and Senhadji, *supra* note 115.
131 Collyns and Senhadji, *supra note* 115, at 103. Due to the innovations of economists, it is also now possible to invest in real estate futures contracts sold on the

Chicago Mercantile Exchange. These futures contracts allow property owners and investors to hedge against potential increases or decreases in property values in various regional markets. Economists also believe that by providing information to investors on expectations of long-run price trends these futures may also signal when real estate is overpriced and thus deter the formation of bubbles. Noam Scheiber, The Pork-Bellies Approach to Housing, *New York Times Magazine*, September 10, 2006, at 90.

132 Karl E. Case and Robert J. Shiller, The Behavior of Home Buyers in Boom and Post-Boom Markets, *New England Economic Review* 29, 44–5 (November–December 1988).

133 Collyns and Senhadji, *supra* note 115, at 103.

134 Karl E. Case and Robert J. Shiller, Is There a Bubble in the Housing Market? 2 *Brookings Papers Economic Activity* 299 (2003).

135 Man Cho, House Price Dynamics: A Survey of Theoretical and Empirical Issues, 7 *Journal of Housing Research* 145 (1996); Dean H. Gatzlaff and Doğan Tirtiroğlu, Real Estate Market Efficiency: Issues and Evidence, 3 *Journal of Real Estate Literature* 157 (1995).

136 For studies that show this positive serial correlation, See Karl E. Case and Robert J. Shiller, The Efficiency of the Market for Single-Family Homes, 79 *American Economic Review* 125 (1989); Peter Englund and Yannis M. Ioannides, House Price Dynamics: An International Empirical Perspective, 6 *Journal of Housing Economics* 119 (1997) (finding correlation of house prices within fifteen OECD countries); Peter Englund, John M. Quigley, and Christian L. Redfearn, Improved Price Indexes for Real Estate: Measuring the Course of Swedish Housing Prices, 44 *Journal of Urban Economics* 171, 195 (1998) (finding positive serial correlation in Swedish residential real estate); Edward L. Glaeser and Joseph Gyourko, Housing Dynamics, *Harvard Institute of Economic Research Discussion Paper No. 2137* (2007) available at http://papers.ssrn.com/sol3/papers.cfm?abstract_id=986604 (last visited July 12, 2013).

137 Franklin Allen and Elena Carletti, Systemic Risk from Real Estate and Macroprudential Regulation, Unpublished manuscript (August 22, 2011) available at www.federalreserve.gov/events/conferences/2011/rsr/papers/AllenCarletti.pdf (last visited July 12, 2013).

138 Erik F. Gerding, Code, Crash, and Open Source: The Outsourcing of Financial Regulation to Risk Models and the Global Financial Crisis, 84 *Washington Law Review* 127, 170–1 (2009).

139 Richard J. Herring and Susan Wachter, Real Estate Booms and Banking Busts: An International Perspective, Wharton Financial Institutions Center, *Working Paper No. 99-27* (1999) available at http://fic.wharton.upenn.edu/fic/papers/99/9927.pdf (last visited July 12, 2013).

140 Ibid. Carmen Reinhart and Kenneth Rogoff document a post-World War II pattern of real estate prices booming before major banking crises then declining in the year a banking crisis hit and continuing to decline for a period of several years afterwards. Their dataset shows that this pattern holds both in developed and in emerging market countries. Reinhart and Rogoff, *supra* note 16, at 159–61. See also Carmen M. Reinhart and Kenneth S. Rogoff, Is the 2007 U.S. Subprime Crisis So Different? An International Historical Comparison, 98 *American Economic Review* 339 (2008). In looking at developed countries in the period from 1970 to 2001, Michael Bordo and Olivier Jeanne found a pattern of many banking crises occurring either at the height of a real estate boom or immediately following a crash. Michael Bordo and Olivier Jeanne, Boom-Busts in Asset Prices, Economic Instability, and Monetary Policy, National Bureau of Economic Research, *Working Paper No. 8966*, 9–10 (2002) available at www.nber.org/papers/w8966 (last visited July 12, 2013). In another study that looked at housing price data before forty-six banking crises, a

boom and bust in real estate prices preceded over two-thirds of those crises. In that same study, banking crises followed thirty-five out of fifty-one real estate boom and bust cycles. Christopher Crowe, Giovanni Dell'Ariccia, Deniz Igan, and Pau Rabanal, How to Deal with Real Estate Booms: Lessons from Country Experiences, *IMF Working Paper 11/91* (April 2011) available at www.imf.org/external/pubs/cat/longres.aspx?sk=24812 (last visited July 12, 2013). See also Allen and Carletti, *supra* note 137. Other economists have documented links between specific banking crises (or series of banking crises in specific countries) and real estate boom and bust periods. Herring and Wachter, *supra* note 139. For a discussion of the links between the three banking crises in Norway from the 1890s to the 1990s and real estate booms and busts in that country, see Karsten Gerdrup, Three Episodes of Financial Fragility in Norway since the 1890's, Bank for International Settlements, *Working Paper 142* (October 2003) available at www.bis.org/publ/work142.htm (last visited July 12, 2013).

141 See, e.g., Lubos Pastor and Pietro Veronesi, Technological Revolutions and Stock Prices, National Bureau of Economic Research, *Working Paper No. 11876* (February 2008) available at www.nber.org/papers/w11876 (last visited July 12, 2013) (arguing "bubbles" stem from investors adapting to technological revolutions not investor irrationality; this prevents predictions of "bubble" periods occurring).

142 See, e.g. Reinhart and Rogoff, *supra* note 16, at 208–22 (discussing how policymakers before the current crisis ignored historical warning signs of crisis, particularly the influx of foreign capital, build-up of debt, and rising housing prices).

143 Ibid. Chapter 9 examines the role of leverage and credit in fueling asset price bubbles.

144 Reinhart and Rogoff, *supra* note 16, at 208–22 (faulting policymakers and economists for rationalizing the U.S. current account deficit and failing to recognize it as historic warning sign of impending crisis).

145 The noise trader literature in behavioral finance argues that bubbles grow out of the trades of irrational investors. See *supra* notes 36–59, 74–5. This literature, however, has yet to develop a detailed demographic profile that identifies noise traders and distinguishes them from other investors.

Nevertheless, experimental and empirical studies have identified one consistent trait that seems to make investors more prone to participating in a bubble: inexperience. Evidence from experimental asset markets indicates that inexperienced investors are more likely to bid prices above fundamental value. See Chapter 8, "Evaluating the evidence," and accompanying text; Erik F. Gerding, Laws Against Bubbles: An Experimental-Asset-Market Approach to Analyzing Financial Regulation, 2007 *Wisconsin Law Review* 977, 1022–5 (summarizing results from experimental studies).

See also Ernan Haruvy, Yaron Lahav, and Charles N. Noussair, Traders' Expectations in Asset Markets: Experimental Evidence, 97 *American Economic Review* 1901 (2007) (traders have adaptive expectations of prices in experimental markets; inexperienced traders generate bubbles). Cf. Martin Dufwenberg, Tobias Lindqvist, and Evan Moore, Bubbles and Experience: An Experiment, 95 *American Economic Review* 1731 (2005) (sufficient percentage of experienced traders counters inexperienced traders and eliminates bubbles in experimental markets). However, these results come with a number of caveats. Even financially sophisticated investors bid prices higher than fundamental value in these experiments. It is the experience of a crash in a previous experiment, not financial expertise, which appears to be one of the most effective factors in mitigating the development of a bubble. Gerding, *supra* at 1022–5.

Empirical studies also indicate that younger and more inexperienced traders in financial markets are more likely to invest in asset bubbles. E.g., Robin Greenwood and Stefan Nagel, Inexperienced Investors and Bubbles, 93 *Journal of Financial*

Economics 239 (2009) (finding young fund managers invested more heavily in technology stocks during 1990s technology stock bubble than older managers); Annette Vissing-Jorgensen, Perspectives on Behavioral Finance: Does "Irrationality" Disappear with Wealth? Evidence from Expectations and Actions, 18 *NBER Macroeconomics Annual* 139 (2003) (finding younger investors with less investment experience had higher expectations of investment returns during tech stock bubble).

Some scholars have argued that the participation of individual or retail investors in financial markets worsened historical bubbles. Compare Michael J. Brennan, How Did It Happen? 33 *Economic Notes* 3 (2004) (arguing that greater responsibility of retail investors for investment decisions contributed to technology stock bubble) with Mike Dash, *Tulipomania: The Story of the World's Most Coveted Flower and the Extraordinary Passions it Aroused*, 132, 140 (1999, Crown Publishing Group) (describing how investments by countryside residents and poorer investors drove Dutch tulip bubble).

In examining various histories of asset price bubbles, Eugene White concludes that the "appearance of new, apparently inexperienced investors" represents one of only two factors common to a number of historical bubbles surveyed (with the other factor being that underlying fundamentals of assets "cease to be well-identified"). Eugene N. White, Are There Any Lessons From History? in *Crashes and Panics: The Lessons from History*, 235, 238 (Eugene N. White ed. 1990, Dow Jones-Irwin).

146 See Gerding, *supra* note 145, at 1008, 1022 (describing proposals to use futures prices to mitigate bubbles and experimental evidence that futures markets dampen bubble formation).

147 John Dewey, The Pattern of Inquiry, in *Logic: Theory of Inquiry*, reprinted in *John Dewey, The Later Works: 1925–1953, Vol. 12: 1938*, 112 (Jo Ann Boydston ed., 1st ed. 1986, Southern Illinois University).

2   A legal history of bubbles

> The past does not repeat itself, but it sure does rhyme.
> – attributed to Mark Twain

Introduction

Economics has dominated the study of asset price bubbles and produced the rich literature described in the previous chapter. Yet this dominance has also obscured the legal and political dimensions of bubbles. With a few notable exceptions,[1] economists have focused scant attention either on the legal environment in which bubbles develop or on the legal aftermath after they burst. The legal dimensions of bubbles and the complex feedback mechanisms between legal rules and market booms and busts represent the central concerns of this book. This chapter begins to explore these legal aspects of bubbles and feedback mechanisms by selecting and examining the legal history of several bubble periods:[2]

1   the *1690 English stock market boom*, which represented arguably the first stock market bubble and crash in history;
2   the *French Mississippi bubble* that imploded in 1720;
3   the *South Seas bubble of 1719–1920*, a "copycat" bubble in England inspired by the Mississippi episode;
4   the *Panic of 1825*, arguably the first cross-border and emerging market bubble, which was stoked by English investments in South American companies;
5   *a subsequent cycle of nineteenth century English stock manias* that struck in ten year intervals after the Panic of 1825 and gave rise to the Panic of 1837, the Crisis of 1847, the Crisis of 1857, and the Overend, Gurney Crisis in 1866, respectively;
6   the *Panics of 1869 and 1873*, in which railway booms in the United States ended in stock market crashes;
7   the *Panic of 1873* in Germany and Austria, in which a railway mania (*Gründerboom* or "Founder's boom") and crash (*Gründerkrach* or "Founder's crash) paralleled the 1873 boom and bust in the United States;

8 the *1920s stock market and real estate booms* in the United States, including a largely overlooked bubble in Florida real estate, which ended in the Great Depression;

9 the *1980s Japanese real estate bubble* (which is summarized in this chapter and discussed in more detail in Chapters 5 and 6); and

10 the *1990s U.S. technology stock bubble.*

This book examines several additional bubbles in later chapters. Chapter 6 analyzes Sweden's real estate bubble in the 1980s in the context of a model that explains how financial deregulation and regulatory arbitrage can generate feedback for one another. That chapter also looks at how well that same model describes both the 1980s Japanese real estate bubble (first described in this chapter) and aspects of the U.S. "subprime" bubble. Chapters 10 and 11 then revisit this U.S. bubble. It describes the evolution and collapse of a "shadow banking system" that occupied the eye of the storm in the Panic of 2007–2008.

The legal histories in this chapter focus on the legal, regulatory, and political events during the rise of a particular bubble and in the wake of its collapse. That may sound rather ambitious. Accordingly, it is important to underscore what this chapter does not attempt. These histories do not endeavor to provide a complete account of the economic, social, or cultural forces at work during a particular boom and bust. Other authors in various eras have made admirable attempts to accomplish one or more of those objectives.[3] Nor, for the reasons outlined at the end of the last chapter, do these legal histories attempt to offer econometric proof that asset prices diverged from fundamental value.

Instead, this chapter focuses on two clear patterns that recur and reverberate throughout the history of bubbles in financial markets. First, these separate histories detail a pattern of "regulatory stimulus" as a bubble inflates, followed by a substantial legal backlash and regulatory reaction after the bubble collapses. In the stimulus phase, governments undertake a range of legal actions that spur investment in particular asset markets. In the backlash stage, governments impose new rules either to curb investment (or "speculation") in financial markets or restrain public officials from subsidizing that investment. Second, these histories reveal a tight correlation between the rise of bubbles and epidemics of massive fraud, corruption, and law-breaking. Indeed, the epidemics of financial fraud in the Enron and Subprime eras have precursors in historical asset price bubbles. The histories below detail these two patterns in the bubbles listed above. Table 2.a.1 in the Appendix to this chapter provides a chart summary of these histories, which includes several additional bubbles beyond those discussed in the text of this chapter.

Before delving into the historical data, these two patterns deserve to be unpacked a bit more.

Regulatory stimulus and legal backlash: beyond deregulation and re-regulation

The introductory chapter to this book defined the term "regulatory stimulus" and gave a preview of why this book uses that term. To elaborate on that discussion, policymakers may deploy many different kinds of government actions or legal interventions to stimulate financial markets. Financial "deregulation," which usually is shorthand for the repeal of statutes or regulations, represents one, but only one, such stimulus. Deregulation has been one of many potential causes of the Panic of 2007–2008 mentioned in public debates.[4] It would be a mistake to focus on the repeal of statutes and regulations to the exclusion of other modes by which governments promote investment in particular asset markets. The full range of regulatory stimuli can be understood with the following analysis. Financial regulation often acts as a "tax" on investment or lending.[5] The opposite of a tax is of course a subsidy, and providing a regulatory subsidy for a particular investment can have the same net effect of increasing investment as repealing a regulatory tax. Regulatory subsidies can take a wide number of forms, including granting business ventures a legal monopoly over particular investment markets. Policymakers can also stimulate investment and lower the effective regulatory tax rate by granting investors exemptions to financial regulation. Similarly, policymakers can fail to collect a tax by lowering enforcement efforts or by not applying a tax to emerging, but economically equivalent activities.

Accordingly, the term "regulatory stimulus" as used in this book and this chapter encompasses the following legal changes to the extent they encourage or unleash greater investment or lending in asset markets:

- *the repeal of statutes, regulations, or legal rules*;
- *exemptions or waivers from particular rules* granted by lawmakers or regulators;
- *looser interpretations of financial laws and regulations* by either courts or regulatory agencies;
- *lower enforcement of existing statutes and regulations* by regulatory authorities; and
- *active government stimulation of financial markets* through various legal devices, including the granting of charters, legal monopolies, or other subsidies or preferences.

In many historical episodes surveyed, regulatory stimulus took the form of creating, authorizing, or facilitating a particular financial innovation – such as a new financial instrument – that fueled the investment boom. Table 2.a.2 in the Appendix to this chapter provides a list of financial innovations in various bubbles that benefitted from regulatory stimuli.

To be certain, there are deep legal and practical differences among these various forms of regulatory stimulus. These differences translate into differences in the political economy – that is, the supply and demand in the political marketplace – for each type of regulatory stimulus. Indeed, the next chapter will unravel and examine these political differences in detail. These differences do not detract from the fact that different kinds of regulatory stimuli can have similar effects on the level of investment in particular assets or financial markets.

After bubbles collapse, the legal or regulatory backlash can also take an array of forms. The eleven histories below provide examples of governments responding with new statutes or regulations that attempt to levy new regulatory taxes on financial investment. In some cases, these statutes represented the re-imposition of legal rules repealed during a bubble's rise. Other typical responses include systematic prosecutions of the promoters of speculative ventures. After several historical bubbles collapsed and crisis ensued, lawmakers reacted by writing legal restrictions on the government's ability to provide subsidies to the private sector. Regulatory backlash often puts "speculators" in the cross-hairs. What policymakers might have called productive investment or healthy trading during boom times is deemed destructive speculation in the harsh light of a bust.

In describing regulatory backlash, this chapter does not focus on short-term crisis management by governments, such as attempts to resolve failing firms. It is admittedly not easy to disentangle crisis resolution from regulation. Yet, other scholars have focused recently on the legal history of financial crisis management.[6] As a general matter, this chapter also does not focus on changes in monetary policy by central banks, whether pre- or post-bubble. This topic has been the subject of volumes of economic research.[7] However, this chapter does examine cases in which policymakers created new institutions or legal architecture for monetary policy, whether in the lead up to a bubble (as in the Mississippi and South Seas bubbles) or in a bubble's wake (for example, the bitter legal and political battles over monetary institutions in the United States following the Panic of 1873). Chapter 9 delves in greater detail into the deep and under-explored connection between financial regulation and monetary conditions.

Casting a wider net to describe regulatory stimuli and regulatory responses yields several benefits. First, looking beyond the mere repeal and passage of statutes allows for a more insightful comparison of different historical periods. The histories in this chapter span a period of over three centuries and reach back well before the rise of the modern regulatory state. The first bubbles in the seventeenth and eighteenth centuries arose when financial markets were in their infancy and extensive financial regulations did not exist, at least in the modern sense.

Second, these broader definitions allow for a close examination of the ways in which lawmakers use corporate law as a tool to stimulate or regulate financial markets. Starting with the first bubble episode surveyed, the English stock market in the 1690s, governments used the power to grant corporate charters to create *de jure* monopolies in certain investment markets. Later governments, like Germany's in the early 1870s, liberalized the law of incorporations to stimulate investment. After bubbles collapsed, lawmakers reformed corporate law to curb speculation. These episodes underscore that corporate law has historically represented much more than a means to enable the private ordering of economic relationships. Indeed, corporate law has also served as a powerful tool by which lawmakers marshal and channel massive private sector investment into particular financial markets. In this sense, corporate law represents a branch of financial regulation.

Third, this broad view of regulatory stimulus and response allows for a more nuanced view of what "law" is. The Legal Realism and Law and Society movements taught legal scholars to look beyond the "law in the books" to the "law in action."[8] Laws in the books mean little outside of the ways lawmakers interpret and enforce them and the way individuals and organizations interpret and comply with those rules. The fact that law is not self-executing computer code requires us to look at a broad set of actors, including legislators, heads of government, regulators at various agencies, judges and courts, international organizations, and even private actors to whom regulatory functions have been delegated. It also requires us to look at a broader array of sources of laws beyond statutes, including at court decisions, regulations, international treaties and accords, and even the private ordering of market participants. The focus is on the effect of legal rules on the behavior of individuals and institutions in societies and markets. The conception of regulatory stimulus and backlash in this book echoes a movement by legal historians – particularly those working in a critical tradition – to analyze how changes in the common law subsidized economic development.[9]

This broad conception of regulatory stimulus and backlash does raise some risk of data-snooping or cherry-picking historical evidence to find a recurrent pattern. Care needs to be taken to show that a particular regulatory stimulus or backlash was tightly connected to the respective rise or fall of a bubble. The cherry-picking risk means that this book does examine another potential form of regulatory stimulus. Governments can also stimulate markets by failing to exercise legal authority or to adapt existing authority to new investment contexts despite warnings of increased risk of overheating markets, potential financial crises, and widespread fraud and law-breaking. The regulatory tax concept proves useful here too; government can decide not to apply an existing tax to an activity that is economically equivalent to a regulated one. This potential form of regulatory stimulus, however, may prove too difficult to discern and measure.

Furthermore, all the details of financial history do not always fit neatly into this pattern of regulatory stimulus and backlash, and the histories below describe counterexamples and countercurrents. Still, the pattern and the definitional rubric of regulatory stimulus and backlash strikes a useful balance between creating workable theory on the one hand and, on the other, reflecting the nuances of what "law" means and the multiple ways in which legal rules can affect (and be affected by) market booms and busts.

Fraud and law-breaking

The pattern of increased financial fraud and law-breaking as bubbles inflate is also more nuanced than the label suggests. In looking at instances of fraud uncovered after a bubble collapses, there is a risk of a peculiar kind of hindsight bias. There is a strong potential for "loser's history," as the individuals invested in highly risky ventures have incentives to claim fraud after their investments implode. In the wake of booms, governments may take their cue from the many who lost and place legal responsibility on the few, particularly those who sponsored speculative ventures. Whether fraud actually occurred according to the Anglo-American common law definition is often not easy to divine based on historical record.[10] In some cases, as in the French Mississippi bubble, there are indications that the promoters of disastrous ventures actually believed that the investment scheme was bona fide and sustainable.[11] Allegations of fraud must therefore be carefully weighed. Even so, the historical record in each of the bubbles surveyed below includes extensive accounts of market manipulation and financial shams.

It is similarly difficult to quantify the extent of law-breaking – that is violations of laws designed to restrict investment, limit firm risk-taking, protect investors, borrowers or consumers, or prevent public corruption – during bubbles compared to other periods in financial history. This chapter uses narrative description rather than quantitative study. As with first pattern of regulatory stimulus and backlash, this creates some risk of cherry-picking. Again, the chapter attempts to strike a balance and present the historical evidence of fraud and law-breaking with a large degree of nuance.

Correlation and causation

Later chapters will attempt to explain both patterns and not necessarily to explain cause and effect. Theory and evidence of causal links are left to later parts of the book. Chapter 3 will discuss the interaction of market booms and regulatory stimuli by examining theories of political economy and regulatory cycles. Chapter 4 will explain the second pattern, namely why fraud and law-breaking appear to increase during bubble periods. For now, it is important to recall the trite but true observation that correlation does not imply causation. The patterns of regulatory stimuli, fraud, and law-breaking during market booms does not lead inexorably to a conclusion that these phenomena caused a bubble, or that a bubble triggered these phenomena.

Looking at deregulation and other regulatory stimuli during the rise of a bubble, it often appears that something else sparked both. A new technology, the opening of a new trade route, or seismic social or political changes have stimulated strong investment demand for various assets (some models of asset price bubbles label this a "displacement").[12] These same technological, social, or political changes may also render legal rules obsolete and increase demands for legal modernization.

No matter what triggers a market boom or legal change, once these two wheels have been set into motion, they can generate powerful feedback effects on one another. The same is true for market booms and law-breaking. Although correlation does not imply causation, it is fair to say (as a preview of later chapters) that market booms and deregulation or market booms and law-breaking can be mutually reinforcing.

Let us now put this chapter's prologue in the past, and turn forward to history...

Histories

The 1690s English stock market boom

One of the first stock markets in history generated the first stock bubble. England in the 1690s gave birth to one of the first regular markets for trading shares in joint-stock companies. That market then experienced one of history's first recorded speculative bubbles.[13] The English government was deeply involved in the creation of this market and in the promotion of the speculative frenzy of the bubble. Regulatory stimulus took a number of forms in an era before regulation of financial markets in the modern sense. The stock market first took flight when the government created the Bank of England to borrow money from the public in small denomination loans that could be traded on a secondary market.[14] The government did more than spur the creation of the capital market; many of the speculative and fraudulent ventures of the decade operated under royal charters or government patents. This bestowed both a measure of authoritative blessing and a legal monopoly to the companies created under charter or patent.[15]

The shares of these joint-stock companies were then traded in the City of London. Crown and Parliament were reluctant to regulate the new stock market despite growing public outcry from politicians and pamphleteers over speculation, fraud, and market manipulation.[16] Official objections to the speculative frenzy and fraudulent schemes were muted as many company promoters distributed company shares to government figures to buy their support.[17] Parliament considered bills to regulate the markets in 1694 and the spring of 1696, but this legislative response stalled.[18] The bubble burst in the summer of 1696 when stock prices plummeted, investors lost fortunes, and financial crisis took hold.[19]

As the bubble inflated, an unsophisticated, newly minted investor class became easy prey for financial deceit. This ensured that the nascent stock market would serve as perhaps the first venue for widespread securities fraud. Fraud in the 1690s English stock market took many forms, including the creation of "sham companies ... launched for the enrichment of projectors," the manipulation of share prices, and the circulation of false rumors about company prospects.[20] The 1690s bubble sired perhaps the first incarnations of price manipulation by groups of stock brokers,[21] including what is now known as the "pump and dump" scam. This involved a group of stockholders publicly touting the baseless prospects of a company and then secretly selling their shares after the stock rose.[22] A new class of market professionals, known as "stock-jobbers," who would later be known as brokers, invented other market manipulating schemes that would be repeated in bubbles of later centuries, including efforts to "corner" markets of particular stocks.[23]

The bursting of the bubble led both to virulent public outcry against stock speculators and brokers and to England's first securities laws.[24] In 1697, Parliament reacted to the manipulation of stock prices during the bubble by cadres of brokers by passing an act that limited the number of brokers in London to 100, all of whom were to be licensed by the Aldermen of the City of London.[25] The lord mayor used his new licensing powers to institute quotas that capped the number of Jewish brokers and the number of foreign brokers to twelve each.[26] This legislation required that brokers pay an annual fee for their license and prohibited them from dealing for their own account or from charging commissions above a statutory limit.[27] The law also imposed tight restrictions on futures transactions by mandating that no more than three days elapse between contract formation and transfer of the securities. However, courts narrowly interpreted this restriction.[28] The strong political reaction against the bubble culminated in a 1695 parliamentary investigation into official corruption, leading to "the expulsion of the Speaker of the Commons, the impeachment of the Lord President of the Council, and the imprisonment of the Governor of the East India Company."[29]

After this initial, sharp legal backlash, the regulatory impulse subsided with the passage of time. In 1708, the 1697 statute expired.[30] In 1711, Parliament considered, but failed to pass a bill to revive all but a portion of that statute.[31] After 1711, Parliament passed no new major securities laws until it was forced to respond to the next bubble in 1720.[32]

The Mississippi bubble

Before turning to that next English bubble, it is useful to consider its inspiration; almost two decades after the English bubble burst in 1696, France suffered one of the most notorious bubbles in history. In this episode, the state became deeply involved in promoting the investment frenzy. In this absolute monarchy, the regulatory stimulus was almost absolute. The story in short: France got drunk on Scotch finance. Scottish financier John Law persuaded the crown in 1716 to establish a bank under his direction. This *Banque Générale* issued notes payable in gold or silver over a twenty year term. A year later, the crown required that taxes be payable in these notes. France had begun the move to a paper currency.[33]

The ambitious Law married his dreams of personal empire to the imperial visions of France. In 1717, Law founded a company (originally called the *Compagnie d'Occident*). The monarchy granted this company control over the commerce and governance of the undeveloped Louisiana Territory (including the Mississippi delta, which gave the bubble its name). Law sold shares in the company to the public. The government encouraged investors to purchase shares by exchanging their holdings of France's sovereign debt. In 1718, facing the prospective launch of a competing stock company, the monarchy granted the *Compagnie d'Occident* new monopolies, including all rights to tax revenue from tobacco and the rights to France's slave trade held by the Senegal Company.

Law's *Banque Générale* was granted a royal charter and renamed the *Banque Royale*. The bank assumed the functions of a central bank. Its notes were effectively decoupled from a silver standard and became true paper money.[34]

Law's *Compagnie d'Occident* grew by acquiring the French companies that controlled trade with the East Indies and China. The company, renamed *Compagnie des Indes*, increased its economic and political power by assuming control of both the sovereign right to collect taxes and the national mints. By 1719, when Law was appointed the nation's Controller General, he controlled much of France's tax collection, its mints, and currency, as well as the nation's important colonies and the trade revenue from them. He had privatized and securitized the national debt. Shareholders in his company stood to gain if France's colonial trade boomed. Law's company founded the city of New Orleans to spur this trade and sent thousands of settlers to colonize the city. Within a year of arriving, over 80 percent had died of starvation or tropical disease.[35]

To finance acquisitions of new assets, the *Compagnie des Indes* conducted several new rounds of share issuances, which diluted existing shareholders. The *Banque Royale* issued loans to investors to purchase new shares. The new paper currency gave Law an additional tool; he radically increased the nation's supply of money to bolster share prices further.[36]

By 1720, many investors became concerned that the rising share prices could not be sustained by future revenue. To create a floor price for *Compagnie* shares, the *Banque Royale* (which was taken over by the *Compagnie*) offered to buy shares at a set price and Law issued options allowing investors to purchase *Compagnie* shares in the future. These efforts did not have lasting effects. Individuals became fearful that share prices would collapse and the *Banque* notes would be devalued. They began to insist on using gold and silver in their transactions. Law reacted to the threat by making banknotes legal tender, banning the export of gold and silver, prohibiting the manufacture of gold and silver objects, and outlawing the possession of more than a set amount of coin.[37]

These measures could not stop the bubble from bursting. When share prices crashed and the paper currency became devalued, riots broke out and Law fled the country.[38] The massive deflation and crisis of confidence had lasting effects. The public distrust of paper currency stalled any future attempts at reforming public finances and left the nation tottering on the brink of bankruptcy well into the late 1780s. By that time, political revolution already had taken root.[39]

The traumatic collapse of the Mississippi bubble also stunted the development of private finance and financial innovation in France for over a century. It caused a regression in private credit and banking.[40] In France, "re-regulation" took the form of a resurgence of usury laws and religious restrictions on lending. Antoin Murphy explains how, in the wake of the Mississippi bubble, usury laws forced private credit to retreat into a very restricted, medieval proto-banking system:

> The failure of Law's System produced a very strong reaction against banks, credit, and financial innovation. It also heralded a *retour en arrière* for the French financial system to the old one dominated by religious directives

controlling the methods of borrowing and lending and the state constituting the main borrower of funds through the creation of *rentes* (annuities). In this strange financial no-man's-land where interest could not be explicitly charged, contracts had to be drawn up separating the ownership of savings from the streams of revenue it generated. The *notaires* (notaries) were at the center of this system. Indeed, their role was so central, in the absence of traditional-style bankers, that they became surrogate bankers.... The usury laws, allied with the failure of Law's Royal Bank, created an environment in which the standard evolution of banking from goldsmiths to credit-creating deposit banks did not take place in France in the eighteenth century.[41]

This return to more primitive forms of finance could be characterized, pardon the French, thus: *plus ça change...*

Murphy also describes how the Mississippi bubble stunted French corporate law. After 1721, companies faced enormous legal difficulties in obtaining limited liability. Entrepreneurs seeking to form joint-stock companies needed to obtain approval of the government through convoluted legal proceedings. Well into the nineteenth century, French law limited most new business entities to two forms of partnerships (the rough equivalent of general partnerships and limited partnerships in U.S. law).[42] In a fascinating example of cross-pollination and path dependence in corporate law, the restrictive French system came to influence the incorporation rules of various German states.[43] As this chapter will explain below, as Germany unified in the 1870s, the new nation jettisoned this restrictive set of legal rules on incorporation. This set the stage for a massive bubble in that country. Law's shadow has been long indeed.

The South Seas bubble

As the Mississippi bubble inflated, the envious English quickly moved to copy it. Two decades after England's first bubble, memories had faded enough to permit an even larger speculative stock market frenzy in the country, what is now known as the South Sea bubble. This bubble received its name from a scheme to privatize English sovereign debt via an entity known as the South Sea Company. This complex scheme resulted in sales of South Sea shares for many times the value of the only assets of the Company, the right to receive debt payments from the English crown.[44] As with the Mississippi bubble, regulatory stimulus by the government was clear and powerful. This British scheme was conducted through the South Sea Company, a stock corporation created by an Act of Parliament.[45] A second act (its passage lubricated by gifts of shares to members of Parliament) approved the terms of the scheme: the company assumed the national debt and then issued additional stock into the market.[46]

Promoters of this English scheme copied not only the French strategy of securitizing national debt, but the tactics of thoroughly co-opting the government as well.[47] The government fended off measures introduced by some members of

Parliament to regulate the terms of converting the debt in a manner less favorable to South Sea shareholders. These proposals ran against the interest of prominent ministers who held company stock granted to them by company insiders.[48] Indeed, the South Sea Company engaged in systematic bribery through overt distributions of stock and covert, illegal share options granted to courtiers, ministers, and members of Parliament.[49] (South Sea insiders themselves held secret shareholdings and stock options.[50]) The King and the Bank of England were also prominent, albeit publicly known, shareholders in the South Sea Company.[51] Government officials had less corrupt reasons to back the scheme, particularly a desire to reduce the national debt.[52]

The rocketing share price of the South Sea Company stock ignited a wider financial market boom. Just as in the 1690s, early fantastic capital gains by investors spawned wild speculation and a rash of newly incorporated stock companies. Many (but not all) of these companies were formed under royal charters. Fraudulent schemes proliferated; promoters again sold stock in companies with nonexistent assets and fictitious prospects.[53]

The South Sea promoters responded to competition from the proliferation of other stock company schemes by persuading the government to pass the Bubble Act.[54] This statute is often incorrectly described as arising in response to the collapse of the South Sea Company. Instead, it represented an attempt by the company to use the law to stifle completion.[55] The Bubble Act had two effects. It prohibited the formation of new companies without authorization by an act of Parliament. It also prevented existing companies from engaging in activities not specified in their charter.[56] The South Sea directors also pushed the Attorney General to issue writs of prosecution, called *Scire Facias*, against three companies for engaging in activities not authorized by their respective charters.[57]

The collapse of the South Sea bubble led to a passionate political reaction, including the formation of an extraordinary secret committee of Parliament to investigate the South Sea Company's directors. This committee uncovered widespread corruption.[58] Its findings provoked street protests and unprecedented trials in the House of Commons, sanctions, and even imprisonment in the Tower of London for some of the Company's promoters and corrupted members of Parliament.[59] Parliament ultimately passed *ex post facto* laws to seize the profits of directors of the South Sea Company.[60] The crash also prompted Parliament to pass Sir John Barnard's Act several years later, which prohibited short sales and trading in futures and options.[61] The South Sea bubble had such a profound effect on the English political and legal landscape that the Sir John Barnard's Act and the Bubble Act – which together stifled the formation of companies and financial innovation – remained in effect for over a century.[62]

The Panic of 1825: the first emerging markets crisis

Over a century later, the repeal of the Bubble Act coincided with the rise of England's next significant bubble in the 1820s.[63] This bubble, which culminated in the Panic of 1825, is sometimes called the first emerging markets bubble and the first Latin American financial crisis. A speculative frenzy in England resulted in massive investments in South American companies, particularly mining ventures, some of which were entirely fictional.[64]

The investment boom started when newly independent Latin American nations – such as Peru, Chile, and Columbia – began floating sovereign bond issuances in London.[65] In an early example of regulatory arbitrage, many of the underlying contracts for the sovereign bonds were signed in France, as interest rates on these bonds would have violated English usury laws.[66] Interest on the bonds was paid by newly raised capital, an early form of Ponzi finance.[67] The South American nations received little money from these bond issuances; English promoters recycled the funds to pay off early investors and took their own cut.[68] Surging demand by English investors for these sovereign bonds soon ignited a boom in stock offerings by private mining companies in South America as well as by ventures within England.[69]

Other government actions, in addition to issuing sovereign debt, stimulated the boom. After gaining independence, the Latin American republics repealed old Spanish laws that restricted foreign ownership of mines.[70] Meanwhile, in England, the formation of a joint-stock company still required an Act of Parliament. The speculative frenzy thus ignited a political frenzy; between March and April of 1824, the total number of private bills to form joint-stock companies introduced in Parliament increased from 30 to 250.[71] As in previous English bubbles, promoters of new ventures named members of Parliament to boards as "guinea pig" or "decoy" directors.[72] Some ventures flouted the law and formed without Parliamentary action.[73]

The rocketing demand for new bills to authorize joint-stock companies led to fierce debates in Parliament and ultimately to the repeal of the Bubble Act in 1825.[74] Members of Parliament believed that the century-old statute imposed draconian penalties, but also was also easily circumvented and did little to hinder excessive speculation or fraud.[75] Promoters of new ventures and other interest groups drove for repeal of the Act.[76] At the same time, the economic liberalism of Adam Smith, permeating the political and legal environment of the time, contributed to the demise of the statute.[77] The economic liberalism of influential members of Parliament also helped scuttle proposed legislation to curb stock speculation.[78]

During the boom, stock speculators received loans from largely unregulated country banks that operated outside London.[79] The legal restrictions that did govern these small banks served to limit their ability to compete with the Bank of England and made them more fragile: English law prevented banks outside London from organizing as joint-stock companies, limited the number of partners of country banks to six, and forbade these banks from branching.[80] After the bubble collapsed, the Bank of England and London merchant banks faulted the country banks for causing the crisis. They alleged that country bank partners invested in risky South American mining companies.[81]

Many of the South American and English ventures spawned during the boom were not only highly risky, but fraudulent to boot.[82] In the most colorful and extreme case of fraud, Gregor Macgregor, a Scotsman who had served as a general under Simon Bolivar, passed himself off in London as a senior official of the Central American Republic of Poyais. The reader will have a most difficult time locating this republic in a nineteenth century atlas due to the peculiar fact that it never existed. Macgregor conducted a sovereign debt issuance for Poyais on the London stock exchange and promptly absconded with the proceeds.[83]

Even inside England's shores, fraudulent companies abounded.[84] To sell shares, promoters of new companies employed budding writers to draft fanciful prospectuses and pamphlets that extolled invented business profits, prospects, and assets. The ranks of these ad men included a teenaged Benjamin Disraeli, future British Prime Minister.[85]

In 1825, panic struck. The bubble collapsed amidst serial default by Latin American republics on their bonds, widespread collapse of the new stock corporations, and massive failures of English country banks.[86] Debate in Parliament rang out with bitter accusations of widespread financial fraud and official corruption.[87] The regulatory backlash after the Panic of 1825, however, departs somewhat from historical form. The crash's most lasting imprint on English law was not re-regulation of financial markets, but changes in banking laws. Rather than aiming to curb speculation, the government focused on reforming the structure of the bank system.[88] Statutory changes allowed banks to form as joint-stock companies outside London (but their shareholders still did not enjoy limited liability) and compete with the Bank of England.[89] Political compromise resulted in the Bank of England retaining a legal monopoly on joint-stock banking within a sixty-five mile radius of London and gaining the power to establish branches.[90]

Cycles of corporate law and crises in nineteenth century Britain

The Panic of 1825 ushered in an era of bubbles and banking crises that struck England and the United States every ten years as both nations industrialized. This almost rhythmic recurrence of booms and busts gave rise to early economic theories on business cycles.[91] Even a brief look at these crises reveals that the patterns described in this chapter held over this period. Regulatory stimulus followed by regulatory backlash and epidemics of financial fraud and law-breaking marked the prominent crises in England in the mid-nineteenth century. The following paragraphs provide a brief summary of cycles of legal reform, crisis, and fraud in Britain from 1826 through the end of the 1860s. Table 2.a.3 in the Appendix to this chapter provides an overview of the regulatory cycles over this period in chart format. Its serpentine layout starkly depicts the cycles of regulatory stimulus, crash, and regulatory backlash.

The 1830s railway boom to the Panic of 1837. A decade after the Panic of 1826, English stock markets again experienced a mania. As in the run-up to the Panic of 1825, company promoters and lawyers incorporated a rash of new joint-stock railway companies in the early to mid-1830s. As before, to found a joint-stock company, the promoters needed to obtain a private Act of Parliament. The sale of stock in these new ventures was marred by rampant fraud, often orchestrated by corporate lawyers. A Parliamentary Committee formed in the wake of the British stock market crash of 1836 and chaired by future Prime Minister William Gladstone detailed the "modes of deception" employed by stock promoters during the boom. These modes included the following:

- using the names of prominent members of Parliament and lawyers as directors of a company without consent to make the company appear safe and legitimate to investors;
- misleading statements in company prospectuses;
- falsified accounting;
- the creation of sham companies; and
- payments to brokers to create markets for the stock of these sham companies.

Testimony from lawyers and promoters to Gladstone's committee revealed that many of them felt insulated from any civil or criminal liability for fraud. The London stock market could not bear the continued issuance of railway company stock and crashed in 1836.[92] Economic crisis deepened a year later when the Panic of 1837 struck the United States.[93]

The 1840s railway mania to the crisis of 1847. The Gladstone Committee that investigated fraud during the railway mania of the early 1830s recommended changes to English corporation laws to move away from laissez faire regulation of joint-stock companies and simultaneously to facilitate the incorporation process.[94] These recommendations shaped the Joint Stock Companies Act 1844, by which Parliament dramatically liberalized the incorporation process.[95] After the statute passed, entrepreneurs no longer needed a private bill of Parliament to form a joint-stock company. The 1844 law established a two-step registration process for incorporating a joint-stock company.[96] The registration process imposed new public disclosure and accounting requirements on joint-stock companies.[97] Under the Act, the formation of railway companies still required an Act of Parliament. However, promoters exploited particular exceptions in the statute for railways that allowed for provisional incorporation before Parliament passed a private bill.[98] Another legal response to the crash took shape in 1845, when Parliament passed a law that imposed rudimentary accounting requirements on joint-stock companies. However, this statute provided little clarity or common standards as to basic accounting terms or principles.[99]

This liberalization of incorporation – particularly provisional incorporation – facilitated yet another boom in the foundation of railway companies in the mid-1840s.[100] Parliament further contributed to the "railway mania" by authorizing hundreds of new rail lines.[101] A select committee of Parliament took charge of reviewing applications for new railway bills, but conflicts of interest abounded. Members of Parliament were accused of having sold their support for railway bills.[102] Members of the Board of Ordinance, which examined railway ventures, speculated in railway shares.[103] Pressure from railway companies combined with a laissez faire political mindset to prevent the government from taking effective action against the tidal wave of investment in railway shares.[104]

Rampant fraud also marred this railway mania. Promoters of railway companies engaged in an array of schemes, including selling forged shares (scrip) in railways, selling more shares in a company than had been actually issued by a company, embezzlement, and insider trading.[105] Investigations after the mania crashed focused on the practice of some railway companies of paying dividends out of capital.[106] Lawyers were intimately involved not only in setting up railway companies, but in devising schemes to defraud investors as well.[107]

The Panic of 1847 ended the mania but triggered an uneven regulatory backlash. The House of Lords issued a standing order, which remained in force for several decades, that inserted into every future railway bill a clause prohibiting the company from paying dividends or "interest" out of capital.[108] In the wake of the crash, Parliamentary committees looked at regulating the practice of private lawyers who lobbied Parliament for private bills. The Parliamentary bar fought vigorously against external regulation and pushed successfully for self-regulation by the profession.[109]

Rules also took shape outside government. Perhaps the most significant legal reaction to the crisis was a "hurricane" of private litigation in which investors sued railway directors and promoters.[110] The collapse of the railway mania generated two "accounting revolutions" in Britain. Shareholder committees of investigation, set up to examine accounting fraud, relied on outside accountants. The accounting profession increasingly came to audit companies and saw a substantial increase in its power and prestige. Parliamentary investigations into accounting seemed to have resulted in less regulation than "private ordering" in the marketplace.[111]

The 1850s boom to the crisis of 1857. Parliament returned to its liberalizing ways in 1855, when the Limited Liability Act[112] introduced limited liability for shareholders for certain joint-stock companies.[113] The Joint Stock Companies Act 1856[114] consolidated English company law and further cemented the concept of limited liability of shareholders.[115] This 1856 statute also removed many of the accounting, audit, and disclosure requirements imposed on joint-stock companies by the 1844 statute. In the place of these older rules, the 1856 statute set forth model articles of association.[116] The 1856 law's expansion of limited liability led to yet another surge in hundreds of incorporations.[117]

During the boom, three spectacular bank failures involved notorious fraud and mismanagement of customer assets: Strahan Paul and Bates (which failed in 1855), Tipperary Joint Stock Bank (failed in 1856), and the Royal British Bank (1856).[118] Economist Geoffrey Williams calculates that each of these three bank failures caused losses that, when compared to the country's GDP at the time, rivaled the magnitude of the Bernie Madoff Ponzi scheme that collapsed in the United States in 2008.[119] Williams further notes that five additional banks failed during the Crisis of 1857, each because of fraud or mismanagement concealed by falsified reports.

Parliamentary committees later investigated a number of these banks.[120] The immediate regulatory backlash to this crisis was muted. But the crisis' long-term historical effects were profound. The crisis fueled the rise of trade unionism.[121]

The crisis also pushed Karl Marx to develop further his historical critique of capitalism, inspiring his *Grundrisse* book.[122]

The 1860s boom in limited liability companies to the Overend, Gurney Crisis of 1866. The political cycle turned once again back to regulatory stimulus in the early 1860s. Parliament again amended English companies law to facilitate incorporation. The Companies Act 1862[123] allowed more joint-stock companies to afford limited liability protections to shareholders. As before, this corporate law change stimulated an investment boom as new joint-stock companies formed.[124] The boom in new joint-stock company banks was particularly pronounced.[125] Moreover, many established companies switched to the joint-stock form to take advantage of limited liability.[126] Commentators of the time decried what they saw as a wave of financial fraud.[127]

In keeping with historical pattern, the boom ended in a market crash when the Overend, Gurney Crisis erupted in 1866.[128] After the crisis, Parliament investigated misleading disclosure by company promoters and the devastating losses of shareholders who made investments on margin.[129] Although the directors of Overend and Gurney, the most prominent bank that failed in the crisis, were acquitted on criminal fraud charges, scholars underscore the extent to which the bank's books deceived investors by hiding debts and impaired assets.[130]

Committees of Parliament considered imposing more stringent restrictions on the formation of limited liability companies. However, stiff resistance from business interest groups led to a milder set of corporate law reforms. These reforms allowed companies to retain the option of unlimited liability for shareholders, but required greater disclosure in a company prospectus on its material contracts.[131] Parliament did impose stricter accounting rules on railway companies, including requiring double entry accounting and the auditing of railway financial statements.[132] However, the most significant economic and political result of the Crisis of 1866 occurred in monetary policy. After decades of debate and false starts, the Bank of England assumed the role of lender-of-last-resort during a crisis. The government and Parliament acquiesced to this during the crisis by suspending legal restrictions on the Bank's issuance of notes.[133]

The Panics of 1869 and 1873 in the United States

The rapid industrialization and growth of railroads and mining that spurred England's series of financial booms and busts during the mid-nineteenth century arrived later in the United States. When it did come, the United States experienced financial bubbles and crises of its own in quick succession. Among the most important crises was a bubble ending in the Panic of 1869 and then a second, more massive and destructive bubble leading to the Panic of 1873. As in England, these railway and mining manias in America's Gilded Age benefitted from regulatory stimulus, fueled financial fraud, and triggered a regulatory shockwave in response. Yet, if U.S. bubbles replayed English tunes, they also reinvented them; regulatory stimulus, regulatory backlash, and financial fraud took on distinctively American features.

U.S. railway companies extracted huge subsidies from states and municipalities eager to ensure that the railroad ran through their town and economic development along with it. Federal, state, and local governments donated property outright to railroad companies. Between 1862 and 1871, railroads received 100 million acres of government-donated land. By the end of the 1870s, federal, state, and local governments contributed $700 million to railroads and donated 155 million acres of public land.[134] States and municipalities financed loans and investments in railroads by issuing a tidal wave of government bonds. Often, the proceeds of these issuances were funneled directly to a railway corporation.[135]

Railway companies competed for subsidies by bribing public officials and purchasing the support of entire legislatures.[136] The state judicial system enjoyed no immunity from corruption. Railway companies waged war in courtrooms and aimed to use lawsuits as weapons to thwart competitors and protect their economic interests. To win, they bought the support of judges and juries.[137] Charles Francis Adams denounced this judicial corruption in 1871 as, "a monstrous parody of the forms of law; some saturnalia of bench and bar."[138] Rampant political corruption led to this period in U.S. political history being nicknamed the "Great Barbecue."[139] Corruption involving railroad stocks enriched Boss Tweed and Tammany Hall, the Democratic Party machine that controlled New York City politics.[140]

Railroad tycoons also used political connections to engage in insider trading and complex schemes to manipulate stock prices and corner markets. Jay Gould and financial "robber barons," such as Jim Fisk, Daniel Drew, and Cornelius Vanderbilt, manipulated capital markets with the acquiescence and, at times, the participation of lawmakers.[141] The role of government officials in fraudulent schemes grew out of a confluence of laissez faire philosophy and improper influence, including bribery.[142] One of the most egregious examples of public graft abetting private fraud came when Jay Gould attempted to corner the gold market in 1869 by exploiting inside information on monetary policy procured from members of the corrupt Grant administration.[143] Gould's failure in this attempt triggered the Panic of 1869.[144] Greatly enriched by his market manipulation, Gould shielded himself from creditors and lawsuits for breach of contract through twelve injunctions and court orders issued by judges whom he controlled.[145]

These American bubbles also spawned more garden variety frauds that replayed many of the fraudulent schemes in Britain. Promoters sold shares in non-existent companies and drafted fraudulent prospectuses. Officers and directors of companies engaged in massive insider trading and self-dealing.[146] Mine company frauds proliferated and culminated in the Great Diamond Hoax of 1872. In this fraud, two confidence men lured investors to purchase shares in a bogus Colorado mining venture by leading out-of-state investors to a field outside Denver that the fraudsters had seeded with uncut diamonds purchased in London.[147]

News of a series of scandals involving massive securities fraud and political corruption – most notably the Crédit Mobilier[148] and Pacific Mail Steamship Company[149] scandals – shook the confidence of investors, and contributed to the crash of 1873.[150] This market implosion resulted not only in a collapse in stock prices, but also the failure of prominent brokerage houses, runs on banks, and the worst depression the nation had faced to that time.[151]

In the two panics, the regulatory backlash matched the intensity of the crisis. The Panic of 1869 prompted a congressional investigation that exposed Gould's machinations.[152] By contrast, the Panic of 1873 triggered a sea change in American law and politics. The Grant administration became mired in corruption scandals and the Democratic Party made large gains in the congressional elections of 1874.[153] The gold standard and tighter monetary policy returned with the enactment by the U.S. Congress of the Resumption of Specie Act in 1875.[154] The country became gripped by what would become a decades-long conflict over the extent to whether the dollar would be backed by silver or gold.[155] Robert Sobel argues that, beyond these specific and immediate reactions, the bursting of the 1873 economic bubble resulted in a substantial shift in the focus of American politics and law:

> The 1873 panic was not merely a severe jolt to the economy; it marked the end of the era dominated by problems of slavery and secession (despite the fact that Reconstruction would continue for another four years) and the beginning of one in which monetary and class issues would occupy center stage.[156]

The U.S. Supreme Court was also swept up in this transformation.[157] The Court reacted to financial crises in the post-Civil War era by sanctioning the federal government's ability to print paper money.[158] The Court thus "broadened substantially the terms of the government's involvement in the economy, particularly with respect to the effect economic legislation might have on individual rights."[159]

Within this sea change, political and legal cross-currents swirled. This growth (however modest according to twentieth century yardsticks) of federal powers coincided with a movement in the states to limit severely the power of state and local governments. The Panic of 1873 and the state and local subsidies to railroads that preceded the Panic left state and local governments with crippling debt. This led to the inclusion in many state constitutions of numerous new restrictions on the powers of state legislatures and municipal governments. These constitutions revived and strengthened a tradition in U.S. state constitutions that aimed to prevent legislatures from granting special benefits to corporations and other persons. As one example, the Missouri Constitution of 1875 included a battery of provisions that sharply delimited the authority of both state and local governments.[160] That constitution included restrictions on the legislature and municipal governments from incurring debt, raising taxes, and extending credit to private corporations.[161] Other Missouri constitutional provisions curbed the ability of the legislature to pass special legislation that would benefit particular individuals or corporations.[162] Missouri's Constitution also prohibited counties and municipalities from "subscribing to the capital of any railroad or other corporation or association, or to make appropriations or donations or lend their credit to or in aid of any corporation or association."[163]

This Missouri Constitution served as a model for the Texas Constitution of 1876, which included a similarly extensive battery of restrictions on the legislature of that state.[164] The agrarian Grange movement heavily influenced the drafting of the Texas Constitution. That constitution prohibited the Texas legislature from offering grants or extending credit to corporations or municipalities, making appropriations for private persons, subscribing to the capital of private corporations, incurring indebtedness beyond $100,000, raising taxes for non-public purposes, and incorporating state banks.[165] Commentators have found a link between the Panic of 1873 and similar restrictions in the constitutions of other states.[166] For example, the railway mania and the Panic of 1873 shaped Colorado's first constitution in 1876. In particular, lingering memories of the Panic contributed to provisions in that state's constitution that both enabled state regulation of railroads and other corporations and restricted the ability of the state and local governments to subsidize corporations and incur indebtedness.[167]

It is important to place these state constitutional provisions in the wake of the Panic of 1873 in context. These anti-subsidy provisions have reappeared in state constitutions at various historical moments. Indeed, an 1837 wave of anti-subsidy provisions in state constitutions also followed a bubble and financial crisis.[168] Taking a step back, the regulatory backlash to the Panic of 1873 had a particularly American cast to it; it focused on limiting government power and government support of finance, and thus harkened back to the politics of Jefferson and Jackson.

Gründerboom *and* Gründerkrach: *the Panic of 1873 in Germany and Austria*

The regulatory response to the same Panic of 1873 in Germany presents a sharp contrast to the course of American law and politics in that same era. If the 1825 crisis represents the first emerging markets and Latin America crisis, the period from 1869 to 1873 serves as the harbinger of cross-border crises among more developed nations. Comparing the American history with that of Germany and Austria demonstrates that the pattern of regulatory stimulus and backlash holds even in different legal and political cultures. At the same time, the Panic of 1873 in Germany reveals how different legal, political, and institutional environments can generate radically different forms of regulatory backlash.

Germany and Austria experienced a boom and crash that both paralleled and helped inflate the railway bubble in the United States at the beginning of the 1870s. By one estimate, one-third of capital invested in U.S. railways in the early 1870s came from German investors.[169] This German and Austrian boom (called the *Gründerboom* or "Founders' boom") was stoked by Prussia's victory in the Franco-Prussian War of 1870–1871, its receipt of war reparations from France, and its success in creating a unified German nation.[170] Both Germany and Austria enjoyed rapid industrialization during this *Gründerzeit* ("Founders' period").[171]

Unification ushered in not only a boom in railroad and other stocks, but also an era of ascendant political and economic liberalism in both Germany and Austria.[172] A belief in the power of free markets captured support among the political and intellectual elite and resulted in the National Liberal party gaining strength in Germany's Parliament.[173] Liberalism drove the new German nation's economic policies. Bismarck, the first German Chancellor, embraced *Gewerbefreiheit* (translated either as "economic freedom" or "free enterprise"), not because of personal conviction. Rather, he saw in liberalism the means to advance his political aims for rapid development of the new nation's economy and military.[174]

Economic liberalism manifested itself in numerous laws and in particular in the reform of corporate law.[175] In 1870, the German Parliament enacted a new law governing *Aktiengesellschaften* (joint-stock companies).[176] The drafters of the law saw the liberalization of the legal process for incorporating these companies as vital; it would facilitate the growth of capital-intensive industries and thus spur national economic development.[177] The drafters of the German law were also influenced by recent changes to English and French corporate law that liberalized incorporation in those countries.[178]

The 1870 statute demolished the old *Konzessionssytem* in German corporate law, which had imposed onerous restrictions on incorporation.[179] Under this old system, joint-stock companies could only be formed with the approval of state officials, after they had conducted an intensive inquiry into the finances and proposed business of the company.[180] This old system borrowed from older French corporate law, which, in turn, was heavily influenced by the collapse of the Mississippi bubble in the early eighteenth century.[181] Under the German *Konzessionssytem*, public officials had to determine that the business purposes of the proposed company met the public interest, which was often a daunting standard.[182] Approval of railroad companies, for example, required not only an examination of the proposed company's finances, but also extensive consultation with military officials on the implications of new railroad lines for military objectives.[183] In reviewing applications for new incorporations, officials looked to prevent "excessive" competition.[184] Given that Germany before unification consisted of numerous fragmented states, the potential for protectionism was high.[185]

In the place of this *Konzessionssytem*, the 1870 law introduced a *Normativsystem*, which allowed joint-stock companies to be formed without official examination so long as the company met certain conditions in the statute.[186] Removal of these restrictions led to an explosion of new companies. Over 850 *Aktiengesellschaften* were founded in Germany during the *Gründerzeit* (from 1870–1874) compared to fewer than 300 of these companies being formed in German states in the previous twenty years.[187] Commentators credited the change in corporate law and the subsequent rise in bank formation for the significant economic growth during the *Gründerboom*.[188]

The *Gründerzeit* also witnessed the founding of a wave of new banks in Germany, including future international titans such as Deutsche Bank,

Commerzbank, and Dresdner Bank.[189] These lightly regulated banks extended credit to new and expanding railroad and industrial companies and thus fueled the boom in Germany and Austria.[190] The explosion of stock issuances from banks and other companies ignited stock market speculation in both nations.[191] Stock markets in Germany and Vienna enjoyed light to little regulation, and investors were allowed to purchase shares on margin.[192]

Capital from German investors also helped spark a stock bubble in Austria that fueled the creation of new railroad companies in that empire as well. New rail lines crisscrossed the Hapsburg Empire.[193] The Austro-Hungarian government promoted this by providing guarantees and tax subsidies to largely unregulated private railway companies.[194] Austria and Hungary also experienced an unprecedented boom in bank formation of their own during this period. In Vienna alone, seventy new banks formed between 1868 and 1873.[195] Banks benefitted from the almost complete repeal of laws prohibiting usury (called the *Wucherpatent*) in Austria in 1868.[196] The partial legal integration of the Austrian and Hungarian states in 1867 (the *Ausgleich*) allowed joint-stock companies and other business entities to operate in both territories.[197]

The stock market bubble also stoked feverish real estate speculation in Germany and Austria.[198] Real estate investment in Austria received additional stimulus through legal reforms. Austria changed its law of succession to allow for unrestricted divisibility of estate. It also removed special legal restrictions on the inheritance of rural property.[199]

Flush with cash, German investors also invested in U.S. railway stock, fueling the parallel bubble across the Atlantic.[200] Traces of the connection between the two booms can still be found on U.S. maps. Promoters of a railroad in North Dakota named the capital of that territory Bismarck in a bid to attract German capital.[201]

In 1873, *Gründerboom* turned into *Gründerkrach* (Founder's crash). Scholars attribute the immediate causes of the ensuing panic in Germany to several events. These include the end of war reparations from France and the failure of U.S. railroads, which led to substantial losses to German investors.[202] The *Gründerkrach* began with the Vienna stock market crashing in May 1873, followed by the implosion of prices on the New York Stock Exchange in September of that year and then a second crash in Vienna later in November.[203] Widespread bank failures in Germany and Austria deepened the crisis.[204] In Germany, a large number of the companies formed during the boom times ended in insolvency.[205] Every third joint-stock company ended in liquidation, causing losses of over one billion marks.[206]

Politicians and scholars later blamed much of this wave of failures on *Schwindelgründungen*, a colorful term that conveys that the founders of companies had fraudulent intent.[207] Later investigations enumerated a number of different maneuvers that unscrupulous founders used to take advantage of shareholders in the new companies. Policymakers and scholars cited a range of deceptive practices by founders, including the following: misstating the value of their non-cash contributions upon a company's formation, secretly withdrawing cash contributions or otherwise looting the company treasury just as shares were being issued to new investors, pocketing the capital provided by new investors without using it for corporate purposes, and founding companies with no intention of running them for the business purposes stated in the organizational documents.[208]

The economic carnage of widespread corporate bankruptcies produced a sea change in German economic policy. The imperial government turned from a policy of *Gewerbefreiheit* to strong state control of industry.[209] The government promoted the formation of economic cartels among large firms and trade unions to dampen the risks of excessive competition, industrial over-production, and social conflict.[210] These policies resulted in significant market concentration in industry and banking.[211] The state nationalized railroads and other companies.[212] At the same time, the government implemented a wide system of tariffs to protect German industry.[213] All of these policies would mark German economic development well into the twentieth century. More ominously, the 1873 crash also triggered a rise in anti-Semitism, as many blamed the Jewish community for the crisis.[214]

Curiously, despite outcry over *Schwindelgründungen*, the German corporate law was not rewritten until 1884.[215] The 1884 corporate reform focused on creating new corporate governance mechanisms for *Aktiengesellschaften* and requiring public disclosure when a company is founded – regulatory tools that would be familiar to modern corporate and securities lawyers.[216] Regulation of stock exchanges was similarly delayed until 1881 and 1884, when new laws both restricted brokers from trading for their own account and set standards for stock exchange listings.[217] In 1881, another new law imposed taxes on securities issuances and transfers.[218]

This eleven year lag between crisis and corporate law reform stemmed in part from laborious investigation and debate in Parliament, on the one hand, and interest group politics, on the other.[219] However, Dr. Jan Thiessen lays out a more provocative thesis: this long delay may have occurred by German Chancellor Bismarck's design. According to Thiessen, the Chancellor reckoned that allowing corporate law reform to twist in the wind would increase political support for his efforts to bring the economy under greater state control.[220]

Austria-Hungary also abandoned laissez faire economic policies after the Panic of 1873. Like Germany, Austria-Hungary moved to strong state intervention in the economy.[221] Yet financial reform occurred more swiftly in the Hapsburg Empire than in its neighbor. The Austro-Hungarian government passed a new statute regulating joint-stock companies in 1874 and a new stock exchange law in 1875. These two statutes resulted in greater government control and taxation of joint-stock companies.[222] In the wake of the crisis, the government also encouraged mergers of joint-stock companies and nationalized certain railway companies.[223]

The rise of state interventionism in Austria in the wake of the Panic of 1873 triggered a profound shift in popular beliefs regarding the proper role of government. The public increasingly viewed the state as an administrator responsible for caring for all citizens.[224] The rising interventionist political movement resulted in reforms to Austria's trading and industrial code and tariffs and other protectionist measures to promote small industry. The Austrian government looked to promote political and social stability by encouraging industry consolidation and the organization of trade and guild associations. This coincided with both rising public suspicion of various social classes perceived to have prospered during the boom years. It also fostered the growth of anti-capitalist, anti-Semitic, and anti-liberal movements.[225]

The regulatory backlash in Germany and Austria-Hungary to the Panic of 1873 provides a stark contrast to the experience in the United States. While the United States saw greater legal controls imposed on the powers of state and local governments, Germany and Austria-Hungary moved towards massive state intervention in the economy. These different responses underscore that, while the general pattern of regulatory stimulus and backlash in bubble periods may be found in different types of economies and political systems, the exact forms that stimulus and backlash assume vary greatly. In the shaping of stimulus and backlash, the legal, political, and institutional contexts matter intensely.

The 1920s stock market and real estate booms

The most catastrophic bubble and financial crisis in history has also been perhaps the most examined. The U.S. stock market boom in the roaring 1920s represents one of the most studied bubbles in history because of the way in which it ended. However, the Great Depression has overshadowed many of the legal facets of the decade-long boom that preceded the Crash.[226] Largely unregulated and highly leveraged, utility holding companies became the subject of a bubble of their own in the 1920s.[227] Over those ten years, the nation also experienced a real estate boom, now generally forgotten.[228] From 1920 through 1926, a particularly intense frenzy of land speculation occurred in Florida, fueled by bank lending.[229] Regulatory stimulus contributed to each of these stock market and real estate bubbles in powerful, but largely overlooked, ways. Furthermore, both the stock and real estate booms of 1920 generated epidemics of financial market fraud, manipulation, and misconduct that seared the national psyche. Fraud and massive investor losses, in turn, provided the impetus for the erection of the New Deal's massive financial regulatory architecture.

Regulatory stimulus during a decade of laissez faire politics

The investment frenzy of the 1920s flourished in a political climate that disfavored government regulation and in which progressivism was in retreat.[230] Wall Street came to dominate the politics of the nation. The financial industry shaped public policy in what some scholars have decried as "crony capitalism."[231] The corruption of the era reached its apogee in the Teapot Dome scandal.[232]

The nation elected Presidents Coolidge and Hoover on laissez faire platforms. This belief in free markets was encapsulated in Coolidge's famous dictum that, "the business of America is business."[233] Coolidge dramatically reduced taxes on the wealthy, corporations, and capital gains, which fueled investment in stocks.[234] In addition, the 1920s witnessed a relaxation of antitrust laws, deregulation of the banking industry, and a laissez faire attitude towards securities markets, including burgeoning margin loans for stock speculation.

LAX ANTITRUST ENFORCEMENT AND THE RISE OF UTILITY HOLDING
COMPANIES

In the 1920s, the robust enforcement of antitrust laws of the Progressive era gave way to a much more permissive approach. Antitrust scholar Frederick Rowe explains how the "antitrust fervor faded and ultimately died." He writes:

> The alliance of government and business for World War I's industrial mobilization created a climate of collaboration that lasted for years. The rise of the trade association movement, dedicated to self-regulation by business and to civilized competition with government blessing, tamed antitrust's adversarial thrust with a spirit of cooperation and harmony.[235]

Those antitrust enforcement cases that were brought by the government resulted in a string of prominent defeats in the U.S. Supreme Court.[236] Historian Steve Fraser notes that the federal government successfully blocked only one out of 1268 mergers during the tenure of Andrew Mellon as U.S. Secretary of the Treasury (which ran from 1921–1932).[237] Looser antitrust enforcement led to a merger wave in the railroad, financial, and utility sectors.[238]

Electricity companies consolidated, forming complex, sprawling interstate conglomerates.[239] One conglomerate alone, the United Corporation, owned electric utilities in twelve states and generated one-fifth of the nation's electricity. To gain political influence, this trust sold shares at low prices to prominent politicians, including former President Coolidge, former cabinet members, and the Democratic Party's chair and presidential candidate.[240]

Electricity magnates, such as Samuel Insull, structured these conglomerates in pyramid form. Operating subsidiaries in numerous states sat at the bottom of the pyramid. They were owned by several layers of affiliated companies, with a public utility holding company at the top of the pyramid. These conglomerates used high degrees of leverage; the capital structures of the various entities in the pyramid were heavily weighted towards bonds and preferred stock. This meant that the owners of the holding company at the apex contributed only a razor thin level of equity. Leverage magnified their returns (and ultimately their losses). These conglomerates made money in two ways. First, they provided power to a public thirsty for the still new innovation of electricity. Second, the conglomerates fed an almost insatiable investor appetite by issuing waves of new securities.[241]

Regulation made public utility holding securities particularly attractive for investors. The operating utilities at the bottom of the pyramid were subject to state regulation. Indeed, industry leaders, like Insull, actively sought state regulation of these subsidiaries to limit competition, ensure that the utilities enjoyed a guaranteed return, and stave off more radical policy proposals such as government ownership of utilities.[242] At the same time, the interstate holding companies were largely unregulated.[243] This lack of regulation owes much to the 1927 U.S. Supreme Court decision in *Public Utilities Commission of Rhode Island* v. *Attleboro Steam & Electric Co.*[244] In *Attleboro*, the Court prevented states from regulating interstate transactions by utility companies in the wholesale electricity market.[245]

Holding companies exploited this disparity between state-granted oligopoly and absence of interstate regulation. They entered into complex contracts that allocated charges and expenses to their state operating subsidiaries.[246] This allowed the operating companies to hike consumer rates and led to accusations that holding companies were artificially inflating electricity prices.[247] Utility holding companies thus had their cake – guaranteed returns from state regulators at the bottom the pyramid – and could eat it too – enjoying the lack of regulation at the top of the pyramid.

Utility companies paid to maintain this favorable political environment. Samuel Insull, for example, spent lavishly on campaign contributions in the 1920s. Insull's contributions in the 1926 U.S. Senate race in Illinois produced one of the decade's most explosive political scandals. Insull's candidate, Frank L. Smith, served as chair of that state's utility regulator. Thus, the largest utility in Illinois became the largest campaign contributor to the principal utility regulator in the state. Insull's actions led to an investigation by a newly created U.S. Senate Special Committee that was examining corruption in Senate election campaigns. When Smith won the election, the U.S. Senate refused to allow him to take his seat. The scandal triggered a wider backlash against the electric industry, as the Senate passed a resolution in 1928 directing the Federal Trade Commission (FTC) to investigate gas and electric utilities.[248]

The FTC took seven years to complete its study. By the time it finished, the Great Crash had triggered the collapse of numerous utilities under staggering losses that were magnified by their excessive leverage.[249] The FTC report became the basis for the Public Utility Holding Company Act (discussed below), passed by the U.S. Congress in 1935.[250] The FTC report focused on financial abuses by utility holding companies, including overstating holding company assets, acquisitions of properties at inflated values, and excessive dividends.[251]

CHANGES IN BANKING LAWS FACILITATE REAL ESTATE LENDING AND SECURITIES ACTIVITIES

Changes in the regulatory environment stimulated more established industries, as well, and fueled the national build-up of leverage during the 1920s in more direct ways. Law professor Arthur Wilmarth details how an expansion of national bank powers in the first two decades of the twentieth century set the stage for a surge in bank real estate lending and securities activities. In turn, increased bank lending, investment, and securities underwriting contributed to booming real estate and capital markets in the 1920s.[252]

Bank deregulation began in the previous decade. The Federal Reserve Act of 1913 allowed national banks in small cities and rural areas to make loans secured by farm land.[253] A 1916 federal law allowed national banks to make loans secured by any type of real estate with terms of up to one year.[254] In 1927, the McFadden Act gave national banks the power to make loans secured by real estate with terms up to five years, subject to certain quantitative limits.[255]

Over the same time period, national banks also received new powers to underwrite, deal, and invest in, securities. Wilmarth explains how in the early years of the century, the Office of Comptroller of the Currency (OCC) permitted national banks to open bond departments that could underwrite, deal, and purchase federal, state, and municipal securities. The McFadden Act formally ratified this OCC policy. Although the Act did not allow national banks to underwrite or invest in corporate bonds or stocks, national banks easily circumvented statutory restrictions on these activities by creating affiliates to conduct them. Before the Great Depression, federal bank regulators did not take action to stop this end-run around regulation.[256]

Wilmarth describes how Congress and regulators expanded the real estate and securities powers of national banks to allow these banks to compete with state-chartered banks which had already been allowed to enter these business lines. Both national and state banks were responding to a transformed competitive landscape. Before the Great War, banks served as the primary sources of financing for large corporations. Afterwards, however, larger corporations turned away from bank loans and sought financing in the capital markets. Real estate lending and capital markets activities thus offered national banks a source of profits to replace their lost business.[257]

National banks took advantage of their new powers to enter real estate and securities markets in dramatic fashion. Between the Great War and the Great Depression, national bank real estate loans grew tenfold. Much of this growth concentrated in booming urban real estate markets.[258] Bank securities activities also grew explosively. Total bank loans on securities grew in the period from 1919 to 1930 from $5.2 billion to $13 billion and from 24 to 38 percent of total bank loans. Total securities investments by commercial banks increased from $8.4 billion to $13.7 billion from 1921 to 1930. Commercial banks also increased their securities underwriting business to compete with investment banks. The number of commercial banks with securities underwriting departments or affiliates increased from 277 to 591 between 1922 and 1929. In the latter years, participation in underwriting by banks accelerated; banks originated 22 percent and participated in 37 percent of U.S. bond issues in 1927. Two years later, these numbers increased to 45 and 51 percent, respectively. Several banks, notably National City Bank and Chase, built nationwide securities distribution networks.[259]

Expansion into real estate lending and securities activities radically altered the overall composition of bank balance sheets. Real estate loans and loans on securities increased from 30 percent to one-half of all commercial bank loans from 1919 to 1929. In the 1920s, the investment portfolios of commercial banks swelled by over $5 billion, with 80 percent of this growth in more risky, less liquid securities. Over this decade, the asset side of bank balance sheets shifted from primarily liquid assets, such as commercial paper and U.S. government bonds, to primarily real estate loans and non-government securities.[260]

Scholars have also documented a decline in supervisory standards by federal bank regulators in the 1920s. Eugene White notes that banking regulation of the time rested on three pillars: disclosure, examination of banks by bank regulators, and enforcement.[261] He presents data showing how each of these pillars weakened over the decade. Before the decade started, banks complained about the aggressive disclosure requirements imposed on them by the OCC. The OCC had the authority to require banks to issue public reports, or "call reports," at moments of the regulator's choosing. As a result of these complaints, the Federal Reserve Act of 1917 transferred the authority to require disclosure of state banks to the Federal Reserve. More importantly, the number of required call reports dropped in the 1920s.[262] Chapter 4 looks in detail at how the boom in banking business spread thin the flat examination and enforcement resources of federal bank regulators over the decade.[263]

REGULATING BANKS IN THE SUNSHINE STATE

The Florida real estate boom of the 1920s merits a closer examination of bank regulation in that state. One scholar calls this boom, "the greatest speculative frenzy in history," overshadowing the California gold rush of 1849 and the Klondike gold rush of 1898.[264] A number of commentators have documented lax supervision of banks in Florida in this period and the capture and corruption of state and federal bank regulators.[265] Banking in Florida in the decade was originally constrained by an OCC policy from 1907 to 1921 not to grant new national bank charters. However, a pair of Florida banker/real estate developers, Wesley D. Manley and James R. Anthony, Jr., lobbied their U.S. Senator to intercede on their behalf and convince the OCC to reverse its policy. By 1925, the duo had created a chain of sixty-one national and state banks in Florida.[266]

Anthony had also developed close ties with state bank regulators in Florida. In return for giving regulators campaign donations and unsecured bank loans for real estate speculation, Anthony received state charters for new banks, lax supervision of his banks, and control of receiverships. Regulators intentionally overlooked widespread and often illegal bank loans to insiders. State bank regulators also engaged in forbearance, which describes when regulators fail to close, or take action against, banks facing imminent risk of insolvency. State bank regulator reports in 1926 concealed the deteriorating condition of many banks, including the insolvency of one institution controlled by Anthony and his brother.[267] Federal regulators themselves engaged in forbearance. In early 1926, when a federal bank examiner found that a national bank controlled by a politically influential real estate developer had become insolvent, his superiors blocked its closure.[268] Simultaneously, the Federal Reserve Bank of Atlanta (whose Governor was a friend of Manley and Anthony) extended a large loan to that same bank.[269] These incidents were just the tip of the iceberg of fraud and public corruption in Florida banking and real estate.[270]

BUILDING AND LOAN ASSOCIATIONS, MORTGAGE-BACKED SECURITIES, AND THE REAL ESTATE BOOM

Real estate booms occurred in other U.S. states during the 1920s fed by bank lending and innovative capital market products. Real estate lending flourished due to several market and regulatory developments, including the rapid growth of mortgage lending by Building & Loan Associations (a forerunner of Savings & Loans in the United States). Under state law, entrepreneurs could incorporate a Building & Loan association far more easily than they could charter a regulated deposit-taking institution. This allowed Building & Loan Associations to enjoy phenomenal growth in the 1920s. Their customer base rose from four million to twelve million members and their assets ballooned from $2.5 to $8 billion over the decade. The number of these associations rose from 8000 in 1919 to 13,000 in 1927. Low barriers to entry allowed Building & Loan Associations to expand rapidly in the South and West. Low barriers also allowed real estate developers to found associations to finance their own suburban real estate developments. State regulators later investigated abuses and conflicts of interest by developer-owned associations.[271]

Over the 1920s, Building & Loan Associations dramatically increased their mortgage lending. By the end of the decade, their mortgage loan volume exceeded that of commercial banks, life insurance companies, and mutual savings banks combined. These associations enjoyed a special edge in affordable housing loans and pioneered innovative long-term and second lien mortgages that made credit available to a wider range of home buyers.[272]

In an eerie parallel of the subprime crisis of the twenty-first century, an early form of mortgage-backed securities featured prominently in the nationwide real estate boom of the Roaring Twenties. These securities, called mortgage bonds, fueled the growth of mortgage lending in the decade. Mortgage bonds were collateralized by pools of mortgages and sold to investors, including non-institutional investors. The bonds benefitted from mortgage guarantees, under which mortgage guarantee companies insured the payments due under either the bonds or the underlying mortgages.[273] Mortgage guarantee companies, the ancestors of monoline bond insurers, began issuing these policies after the legislature in New York State (where the most important of these companies were based) amended the law governing these companies in 1904.[274] The ranks of mortgage insurers in that state subsequently swelled from twelve in 1920 to fifty in 1930. Over that same period, the amount of mortgages guaranteed by mortgage guaranteed companies in New York rose from $0.5 billion to $3 billion, with $0.8 billion guaranteeing mortgages underlying mortgage-backed securities.[275]

Unfortunately, the New York law governing mortgage insurance contained numerous holes. It required insurance companies to maintain a reserve fund based on the amount of a company's capital rather than the volume of insurance policies it had underwritten or the credit risk it assumed. The growth of mortgage lending, insurance, and bonds overwhelmed the state regulators responsible for overseeing these markets. Regulators did not examine whether the loan to value ratio for the mortgages underlying insured mortgage bonds met the legally mandated standard of 50 percent. Instead, they merely accepted the appraisals presented by the mortgage guarantee companies.[276]

A New York gubernatorial commission investigating mortgage guarantee companies after the Great Crash found that regulatory failures enabled the companies to engage in abusive practices. For example, the insurance companies insured mortgages and issued bonds on properties with inflated appraisals and even on foreclosed properties. While 30 percent of the guaranteed mortgages went into default, almost 60 percent of mortgage bonds defaulted.[277] In another harbinger of the recent financial crisis, credit rating agencies, such as Moody's, which rated mortgage bonds did not impose stringent standards in their review of the creditworthiness of mortgage bonds.[278]

When the Great Depression hit, defaults on residential mortgages and mortgage bonds soared. This triggered runs on, and the serial failures of, Building & Loan Associations. Over half of the Building & Loan Associations operating in 1929 foundered by 1941. The national foreclosure crisis, liquidation of Building & Loan Associations, and work out of payments under mortgage bonds and guarantees took years to sort out.[279]

Government investigations of New York's mortgage guarantee industry uncovered that firms violated underwriting standards, substituted non-performing mortgages for performing mortgages in their pools, and maintained inadequate reserves. Government investigations also ferreted out abuses by the unregulated real estate bond houses that sold mortgage bonds. These abuses included over-appraising properties in the mortgage bond pools, improper management of the trust accounts for the bonds, and improper practices in selling bonds to investors.[280]

STOCK MARKET: MARGIN LOANS AND MANIPULATION

The U.S. stock market boomed in parallel to the real estate market frenzy. As with real estate investment, credit – in the form of margin loans – fueled stock market investment in the second half of the 1920s. Loans to stock market investors by brokers and banks alone reached $16 billion by October 1929. This equaled roughly 18 percent of the market capitalization of all listed stocks. In the previous year, President Coolidge stated that margin loans were not a cause for concern. The Federal Reserve disagreed. In February 1929, it warned member banks against making these loans. Yet this warning did not curb the practice. Even if the Federal Reserve had regulated margin loans, these loans were increasingly being provided in the 1920s by corporations and foreign banks outside the Federal Reserve's legal reach.[281]

The stock market boom was not only fueled by borrowing, it also provided fertile ground for stock market manipulation and fraud. Wall Street firms formed large investment trusts or pools that engaged in market manipulation and insider trading.[282] The extent of securities fraud during the 1920s, however, has become the subject of debate by historians.[283] After the Great Crash, investigators – most notably the Pecora Commission – documented an array of stock market schemes.[284] The perception of widespread securities fraud during the decade seared the national psyche. Historian Steve Fraser writes:

> "Reloaders" and "dynamiters," high pressure stock promoters, roamed the land pumping up and deflating expectations, often on the flimsiest, even fabricated pretexts, and on rare occasions, as in the case of "the Wall Street Iconoclast," one Graham Rice, ending up in Sing Sing. This whole three-ring circus of frenzied finance – investment trusts, pools, financial department stores, boiler rooms and bucket shops, insider traders and felonious stock tipsters – was ballasted by the weight of the underlying economy, empowered by the subservience of the political order, and infused with the élan of Wall Street's global supremacy.[285]

This era, of course, ended in economic and social ruin.[286]

Regulatory backlash in the New Deal

The collapse of the 1920s stock market and the onset of the Great Depression led to the election of Franklin Roosevelt and greatest expansion of federal government power in U.S. history. The New Deal included not only various programs to stimulate the economy but also waves of new financial regulation. Between Roosevelt's first election and the outbreak of World War II, Congress erected a vast new regulatory architecture in stages. Reform legislation governed each of the financial markets that had boomed and crashed in the previous decade.[287]

The New Deal introduced the modern U.S. federal securities law regime. This regime created the U.S Securities and Exchange Commission (SEC) and imposed vast new disclosure and registration requirements on securities issuers, broker dealers, investment companies, and investment advisors. Congress enacted in series the Securities Act of 1933,[288] the Securities Exchange Act of 1934,[289] the Trust Indenture Act of 1939,[290] the Investment Company Act of 1940,[291] and the Investment Advisers Act of 1940.[292] As sweeping as federal securities legislation was, it still reflected deep political compromises. The Roosevelt administration and Congress rejected calls for more intrusive reforms in which regulators would review and approve individual securities based on substantive merits in favor of a disclosure based regime.[293] The compromise, however, did not result in toothless rules; the Securities Act and Securities Exchange backed up disclosure requirements with a powerful regime of anti-fraud liability.[294]

At the same time, Congress extended the ambit of federal securities regulation to electricity companies. The collapse of highly leveraged utility holding companies led Congress to pass the Public Utility Holding Company Act of 1935.[295] This statute charged the SEC with the responsibility to regulate the capital raising and structure of utilities in two respects. First, the act mandated that utilities simplify their corporate structures and engage in geographic integration. Second, the statute gave the SEC the power to regulate the financing and continued operation of holding companies, including their transactions with affiliates.[296] The Federal Power Commission received authority to regulate interstate electricity transmission. Moreover, the statute barred bankers and investment bankers from serving as officers of public utility companies.[297]

In addition to establishing a regulatory regime to govern securities markets, the New Deal also erected a wall separating the securities business from depository banking. In the 1933 Glass-Steagall Act, Congress prevented depository banks from engaging in securities and investment banking activities.[298] That same statute also revolutionized banking law by creating the federal deposit insurance system.[299] The Glass-Steagall Act, together with the Banking Act of 1935, overhauled the governance of the Federal Reserve System and gave the Federal Open Market Committee the power to set monetary policy.[300] Congress further added to the architecture of federal banking law, when it passed the Federal Credit Union Act in 1934 to promote the growth of federally chartered non-profit, cooperative lending institutions.[301]

In addition to laying these cornerstones of federal securities and banking law, the New Deal Congress created a phalanx of new federal authorities charged with promoting residential mortgage lending in the wake of the collapse of U.S. real estate markets. The National Housing Act of 1934 created both the Federal Housing Administration and a separate deposit insurance system for savings and loan institutions, which were important mortgage lenders.[302] The various real estate-related New Deal statutes followed earlier initiatives by the Hoover administration to jumpstart the residential housing market, such as the creation of the Federal Home Loan Banks in 1932.[303]

Other markets that had boomed during the previous decade became the subject of other major pieces of New Deal legislation. For example, the Communications Act of 1934 created the Federal Communications Commission to serve as the single federal regulator of the broadcasting industry.[304] Many of the major legislative pieces of the New Deal regulatory state outlined above endured for decades. Yet many of them were significantly scaled back or repealed six decades later in the 1990s. The turning of this very long regulatory cycle becomes evident in Table 2.a.4 in the Appendix at the end of this chapter, which outlines some of the principal statutes passed in the New Deal in the securities, banking, and energy sectors, and their repeal or significant dilution in the 1990s.[305]

Japan's real estate bubble

The pattern of regulatory stimulus, regulatory backlash, and fraud during bubble periods holds even in the modern era and even in countries with vastly different legal, political, and institutional environments. Japan and its massive real estate and stock market bubbles in the 1980s provide a fascinating contemporary case study and counterpoint to the older European and American examples already detailed in this chapter.

The culture, institutions, and structure of Japanese financial regulation differ in marked respects from Anglo-American examples.[306] Law professors Curtis Milhaupt and Geoffrey Miller describe the informal, yet complex manner in which regulation was made in Japan in the 1970s and 1980s.[307] They portray several distinct features of Japanese financial regulation, including limits on competition. Legal rules restricted competition and compartmentalized financial services into narrow and distinct sectors, including commercial banking, trust banking, long-term credit banking, and regional banking. Initially, each sector served a distinct market.[308] Another category of financial institution, called *jusen*, originally provided residential home loans. *Jusen*, as we will see in Chapter 6, came to play a pivotal role in Japan's real estate and stock market bubbles and in its financial crisis.[309] Professors Milhaupt and Miller detail how Japanese financial regulators exerted influence less by imposing rules on these various institutions and more by negotiating with organized groups of financial firms. This process created what these scholars call "regulatory cartels."[310]

Chapter 6 details how several economic and political shocks hit Japanese financial markets in waves throughout the late 1970s and 1980s. These shocks upset the carefully calibrated competitive and political equilibrium in Japan's financial services sector by triggering a deregulatory cascade. This cascade liberalized financial markets in that country in waves. Chapter 6 describes how early deregulation of Japanese financial markets enabled Japanese corporations to raise more capital by issuing bonds. This afforded firms a new alternative to borrowing from banks. Deregulation also benefitted investors in Japan, who could obtain better rates of return on bonds and other capital market products than on the bank deposits to which they were historically limited. This new competition, fostered by financial liberalization, spurred Japanese banks to call for deregulation of their own sector. Deregulation of both capital markets and banking fueled a credit boom and twin asset price bubbles in the Japanese real estate and stock markets in the 1980s.[311]

Law-breaking was also pervasive during these Japanese bubbles. Chapter 5 describes how these bubbles stimulated and were stimulated by regulatory arbitrage of Japanese financial regulations. It outlines how Japanese financial firms designed complex financial engineering (called *zaitech*) to enable Japanese corporations to engage in stock speculation. Some of this financial engineering not only gamed Japan's financial laws, it broke them outright. For example, Japanese brokerage firms offered their clients illegal *eigyo-tokkin* accounts to engage in tax-free stock speculation with guaranteed returns, as Japanese regulators looked the other way.[312]

As in bubbles in other times and other climes, Japan's bubble spawned pervasive financial fraud and stock manipulation, including stock corners and insider trading.[313] Prominent politicians joined the wave of insider trading.[314] Companies purchased the support of other politicians with gifts of shares. This set the stage for some of the largest political scandals in the country in Japan's post-war era.[315] Lured by the scent of illicit profits, the *Yakuza*, or Japanese mafia, became clients of brokerage houses. The gangsters joined insider trading and stock manipulation schemes and added extortion and murder to the already lurid story of the bubble.[316] Regulators knew and even boasted of the manipulation on the Tokyo Stock Exchange.[317] Banks involved in real estate lending also engaged in deceptive practices to evade the law. They ignored loan-to-value regulations or evaded them by either transferring loans to non-bank affiliates or ginning up property appraisals.[318]

Japan's colossal bubble finally burst in 1991. It left in its wake the detritus of bad loans worth billions of U.S. dollars. The collapse ruined *jusen* and crippled banks and other financial institutions. The regulatory backlash in Japan took two forms. The first response, the government's anemic attempt to resolve bad loans, resulted in "zombie banks" and what has come to be known as Japan's "Lost Decade" of stagnant economic growth.[319] Japan also responded with several rafts of financial reform legislation. One series of reforms required bank regulators to take "prompt corrective action" against failing financial institutions and to place them in bankruptcy.[320] Another reform overhauled Japan's deposit insurance system.[321] Later legislation stripped the Ministry of Finance of responsibility for financial institution supervision and transferred and consolidated that authority in a new agency.[322] A separate law attempted to make the Bank of Japan more independent to remedy the political pressure that led to easy monetary policy that fueled Japan's bubble.[323]

When economic growth failed to return, Japan introduced further financial reforms. These reforms changed the structure of the Japanese central bank, strengthened the government supervision of Japanese financial institutions, aimed to remove government safety nets that prevented the failure of financial institutions, *and* further broke down some of the restrictions that kept financial institutions into separate segments.[324] Part of Japanese financial reform should thus be seen as *liberalizing* the regulation of financial institutions and markets in order to spur investment and make Japanese firms more competitive. These moves reveal that the regulatory backlash in the wake of bubbles can take complex forms as policymakers and politicians attempt to resuscitate damaged financial markets and respond to public outcry.

The 1990s bubble: from a decade of deregulation to Sarbanes-Oxley

The long legal history of bubbles that begins at the cusp of the eighteenth century continued through the turn of the twenty-first. The "technology stock bubble" of the late 1990s closes out this chapter and demonstrates again the pattern of regulatory stimulus, fraud, and regulatory backlash. Deregulation contributed to the inflation of this bubble in a number of different ways. Federal deregulation of the telecommunications industry and state deregulation of the energy sector sparked investment booms in those markets. Moreover, federal legislation and judicial decisions throughout the decade dramatically lowered securities law liability. Together, these three waves of deregulation fueled a bubble in internet, telecommunications, and energy company stocks. Massive financial fraud took root in each of these sectors, with the Enron and WorldCom scandals serving as the worst examples.

Telecommunications deregulation

The Telecommunications Act of 1996[325] deregulated the U.S. telecommunications markets and opened what one senator correctly predicted would be a "land rush" in investment in this sector.[326] The statute transformed the U.S. telecommunications industry in the most sweeping legal reform since the Communications Act of 1934.[327] Congress deregulated the industry to remove what it perceived to be regulatory barriers to entry. To accomplish this objective, the statute, among other things, preempted state and local laws, required carriers to connect their networks to each other, required incumbent carriers to allow new market entrants to access to their networks, and allowed the regional Bell companies (the successors to the breakup of Bell Telephone) to offer long distance service.[328]

When the statute forced existing telephone companies to open their networks, it gave birth to a menagerie of new competitors. These included companies that offered digital subscriber lines (DSL) and competitive local exchange carriers (CLECs), which offered local, long distance, and internet services primarily to businesses.[329] Capital investments in broadband telecommunications skyrocketed, peaking at U.S.$6.7 billion in 2000.[330] The fees earned by investment banks from the telecommunications industry rose from U.S.$1.06 billion in 1996 to U.S.$4.14 billion in 2000.[331] The deregulated industry fed the increased demand for bandwidth by the mushrooming internet industry.

Yet even this growing demand could not keep pace with the skyrocketing leverage of telecommunications companies. Unable to service their burgeoning debt (amassed through high-yield junk bond and convertible debt offerings), telecommunications companies suffered a wave of bankruptcies when the bubble burst in 2001.[332] The market capitalization of the CLEC companies alone plummeted from a high of U.S.$86.5 billion in 1999 to only U.S.$3 billion two years later.[333]

The collapse of telecommunications companies uncovered an epidemic of securities fraud. WorldCom became the largest Chapter 11 bankruptcy history in the United States.[334] The company admitted to approximately U.S.$11 billion in financial misstatements.[335] Its chief executive, Bernie Ebbers, was convicted of securities fraud and sentenced to twenty-five years in prison.[336] A long roster of other prominent telecommunications companies and their executives also became ensnared in securities fraud litigation.[337]

Energy deregulation

While the U.S. Congress was overhauling federal telecommunications law, Congress and federal agencies deregulated wholesale electricity markets in the 1990s. Various states followed suit and deregulated their retail electricity markets. As with telecommunications markets, deregulation of the energy sector spawned new companies, such as Enron, and fueled their spectacular growth.

Federal energy deregulation began in the 1970s and gained steam in the 1990s.[338] In 1992, the U.S. Congress passed the Energy Power Act,[339] which established the foundation for deregulation of the wholesale electricity market in the United States.[340] The legislation gave the Federal Energy Regulatory Commission the power to require power transmission line owners to carry power from wholesale generators for a fee.[341] The act also created a new regulatory category of companies (called "EWGs") that could generate wholesale electricity. It exempted these generators from various federal laws and regulations, including the Depression-era Public Utility Holding Company Act.[342]

The Federal Energy Regulatory Commission exercised its new statutory authority two years after the passage of the Energy Power Act. The Commission required transmission line owners to give companies generating power access to their lines without discriminating on price.[343] It also required utilities to "unbundle" various services, including separating transmission from power generation.[344] This caused many existing utilities to divest many of their generating assets.[345]

This opened the door for new entrants into power markets. It spawned new companies that generated electricity. It also gave birth to new firms engaged in the marketing and trading of both energy and financial derivatives based on energy. Enron stepped into these two breaches and enjoyed spectacular growth.[346] Enron benefitted from the weak enforcement of the Public Utility Holding Company Act. The company lobbied actively for repeal of this statute (as well as for enactment of the Energy Power Act).[347] The Federal Energy Regulatory Commission chose to interpret the restrictions of the Depression-era statute liberally and to permit many holding companies to own EWGs.[348] Enron also successfully lobbied the Commission to permit it to trade and broker power.[349]

With wholesale electricity markets deregulated on the federal level, Enron and other growing energy conglomerates engaged in a lobbying and public relations blitz to deregulate state retail markets for electricity.[350] In the deregulation of these markets, California blazed the trail and other states followed suit. Nevertheless, as Professor Richard Pierce explains, the state engaged not so much in "deregulation," as in handcuffing its local electric utilities. In 1998, the state gave consumers the option of purchasing electricity from providers other than their traditional utility. More importantly, California forced the three electric utilities in the state to sell many of their generators to third parties. Without their previous capacity to generate power, the utilities became market intermediaries that had to buy electricity on the wholesale market (which itself was newly deregulated by the Federal Energy Regulatory Commission). At the same time, the state prevented the utilities from entering into long-term supply contracts, leaving them to buy electricity on the spot market. Finally, the state "temporarily" froze the rates that retail customers had to pay for electricity.[351] Together, these regulatory changes left California's electric utilities at the mercy of sudden extreme spikes in the price of wholesale electricity. These spikes led many politicians to criticize what they saw as manipulation of California's deregulated electricity markets, although multiple factors may have contributed to skyrocketing prices.[352]

Federal and state deregulation of electricity and energy markets allowed companies like Enron to form large, highly leveraged conglomerates that owned power generators and pioneered the trading of power and novel energy derivatives. Deregulation thus allowed Enron to mimic Samuel Insull's complex, highly leveraged electricity trusts of the Roaring Twenties.[353] When Enron's earnings could not keep pace with its skyrocketing stock price and the expectations of the marketplace, its executives – like those of many boom companies of the decade – resorted to securities fraud.

Securities deregulation

Indeed, the decade spawned an epidemic of securities fraud. This outbreak of law-breaking came on the heels of a series of major federal statutes and judicial opinions that lowered securities law liability in private litigation.[354] Deregulation occurred through both congressional action and prominent judicial rulings. First, in 1995 and 1998, Congress passed two laws that placed high hurdles in the way of private securities litigation against securities issuers and financial intermediaries. In passing these statutes, legislators responded to pressure from Wall Street interest groups, including large securities issuers, investment banks, accounting firms, and law firms.[355] One of these statutes, the Private Securities Litigation Reform Act of 1995 (PSLRA)[356] included the following reforms:

- raising the pleading standards for securities class actions;[357]
- replacing the "joint and several liability" previously imposed on defendants in private securities litigation with proportional liability (unless the defendant is found to have knowingly violated the law);[358]
- precluding RICO laws from being used by plaintiffs to obtain treble damages in securities fraud cases;[359] and
- adopting an expansive safe-harbor for "forward-looking" information provided in securities disclosure.[360]

Three years after enacting PSLRA, Congress acted again to narrow the forms of relief available to plaintiffs in securities fraud litigation. Among other things, the Securities Litigation Uniform Standards Act of 1998 (SLUSA) precluded class actions alleging securities fraud from being brought in state courts.[361] At the end of the decade, Congress acted again: this time not to lower securities law liability, but instead to change the entire landscape of the securities industry. In 1999, Congress repealed one of the centerpieces of the New Deal era securities laws, the Glass-Steagall Act. It thus dismantled six-decade-old legal barriers between commercial banking, investment banking, and insurance activities.[362]

Second, some of the interest groups that pushed for the passage of these statutes also successfully beat back or diluted attempts to impose new obligations on securities market intermediaries. The most glaring example: the accounting industry's successful campaign at the end of the Clinton administration to thwart SEC Chairman Arthur Levitt's attempts to regulate it. Levitt sought to restrict the scope of non-audit services that accountants could provide to clients whose financial statements they audited.[363] Levitt ultimately proved to be a Cassandra, as these non-audit relationships compromised the objectivity of auditors. Policy-makers and scholars blamed these relationships for the failure of auditors to adequately police the financial accounting of securities issuers.[364]

Third, prominent court rulings during the 1990s placed new restrictions on securities lawsuits and thus lowered the potential liability of securities issuers and their representatives. Two Supreme Court decisions epitomized this trend. In 1991, *Lampf, Pleva, Lipkind, Prupis & Petigrow* v. *Gilbertson* shortened the statute of limitations for certain securities fraud actions.[365] The Court's 1994 ruling in *Central Bank of Denver* v. *First Interstate Bank of Denver* eliminated certain secondary liability causes of action against defendants for "aiding and abetting" violations of securities laws.[366] Beyond these high profile cases, the 1990s witnessed judges developing a number of different doctrines – including, the "bespeaks caution" doctrine[367] and the "no fraud by hindsight" doctrine[368] – that cumulatively curtailed the remedies available to plaintiffs in securities fraud cases.[369]

Finally, not only did the risk of private enforcement abate in the 1990s, but the risk of public enforcement actions brought by the SEC against gatekeepers also dropped, as the SEC changed its enforcement priorities.[370]

An epidemic of fraud

The collapse of the technology stock bubble revealed an epidemic of financial fraud epitomized by the Enron. That scandal, however, represented the tip of an iceberg. Chapter 4 presents data on the scope of securities fraud during the technology stock bubble. It also presents a theory of why financial fraud increased during this period as in previous bubble episodes.

The regulatory backlash

The fall of the NASDAQ in 2000 and the subsequent exposure of widespread corporate fraud prompted a dramatic legislative and regulative response, albeit one whose long-term effectiveness is still being hotly debated.[371] The Sarbanes-Oxley Act and its follow-on SEC regulations instituted a broad array of securities law and corporate governance reforms. These included:

- requirements that executive officers of public companies certify both the accuracy of their company's quarterly and annual SEC filings and the existence of internal controls to ensure the integrity of company disclosure;[372]
- a mandate that every public company create an audit committee;[373]
- the establishment of the Public Company Accounting Oversight Board to oversee the accounting industry and its auditing of public company financial statements;[374]
- a limit on the services that auditors can perform for the companies whose public financial statements they audit;[375] and
- regulation of the conduct of private securities lawyers in advising public corporations.[376]

The Sarbanes-Oxley Act represented only the first act. New regulations addressing security analyst conflicts of interest were passed by the SEC, the National Association of Securities Dealers, and the New York Stock Exchange.[377] These rules followed in the wake of a widely publicized investigation into analyst practices during the 1990s by the New York State Attorney General and a legal settlement between the Attorney General and securities firms.[378] SEC enforcement actions and private litigation regarding the Enron scandals also heralded substantial increases in the liability of investment banks, auditors, and law firms.[379]

Conclusion

The U.S. technology stock boom provides one coda to three centuries of asset price bubbles and legal history. Throughout this history, bubbles have occurred in radically different financial markets and societies. In each of the bubbles surveyed above, the pattern of regulatory stimulus, financial fraud, and regulatory backlash can be found.

But, why? What explains these patterns? The following two chapters look to provide answers. The next chapter analyzes the pattern of regulatory stimulus and backlash. In so doing, it also looks to explain why regulatory stimulus and backlash assumed different forms in different environments. The differences between historical episodes can reveal as much as the similarities. Chapter 4 then aims to explain why financial fraud and law-breaking increase during bubble times. If this chapter provided historical data and context for the legal dimensions of asset price bubbles, the next two chapters represent the beginnings of an outline of the Regulatory Instability Hypothesis and a description of the mechanisms by which bubbles shape law and vice versa.

Appendix

Table 2.a.1 Fraud, regulation, and bubbles

Time period	Country and focus of investment	Prevalence of fraud, law-breaking, corruption	Regulatory stimulus	Regulatory backlash
1690s	England, stocks	Widespread; stock issuances of sham companies; early "pump and dump" scams and "corners." Promoters give government figures stock to buy support for ventures.	Royal charters and patents granted towards numerous speculative or fraudulent ventures. Parliamentary bills to regulate capital markets fail.	England's first securities laws, including limits on number of brokers in London. Restrictions on futures contracts. (Laws wane over two subsequent decades.)
1719 *Mississippi bubble*	France, shares in the Mississippi Company	The bubble resembled a Ponzi scheme (but promoter may have believed in bona fide prospects of company).	Mississippi Company assumes national debt and exclusive right to revenue from Louisiana and other French colonies. Promoter of bubble given right to create central bank, collect taxes, and print money to support scheme.	Reform of public finance in France stalled until 1787. Usury laws regain force and stifle private credit. Legal restrictions on incorporation of new companies.
1720 *South Sea bubble*	Britain, shares in the South Sea Company and other ventures	Widespread; stock issuances in fraudulent companies. Massive insider trading in South Sea shares. Bribery of Members of Parliament, courtiers, and ministers. Company promoters give government figures stock to buy support for ventures.	South Sea Company and the privatization and securitization of national debt authorized by separate acts of Parliament. Government resisted measures to control conversion of national debt into shares of South Sea Company. The Bubble Act is passed to eliminate competition for South Sea Company.	The Bubble Act endures for a century. Sir John Barnard's Act. Unprecedented prosecutions.

1820s Panic of 1825	Britain, stock in new companies, particularly South American mines and South American sovereign debt	Widespread; stock issuances in fraudulent companies. Bond issuance by fictional Republic of Poyais. Misleading prospectuses for sovereign bonds. (Use of offshore contracts to evade British usury laws.) "Ponzi finance": payment of foreign loans out of capital, instead of out of earnings.	Repeal of the Bubble Act. Wave of parliamentary charters granted to English companies. Members of Parliament act as directors of companies. Cabinet refuses to intervene in bubble.	Reforms of regulations governing Bank of England.
1830s Panic of 1837	Britain, railroad stocks	Rampant financial fraud orchestrated by lawyers, including sham companies, misleading prospectuses, falsified accounting, and misappropriating names for boards of directors.	Companies formed by Acts of Parliament.	Formation of Gladstone Committee, which led to Joint Stock Companies Act of 1844, which regulated (but also liberalized) incorporation process. Statute imposing rudimentary accounting requirements for joint-stock companies.
1845–1846 Crisis of 1847	Britain, railroad stocks	Companies sell more shares than authorized. Company insiders sell forged shares. Accounting fraud, embezzlement and insider trading.	Joint Stock Companies Act of 1844 liberalizes incorporation. Parliamentary bills authorize dozens of competing railway lines. Prime Minister dilutes regulations that would have curbed new railway development to avert a glut.	Suspension of the Bank Act. Parliament prohibits dividends being paid out of capital. "Accounting revolutions."

continued

Table 2.a.1 Continued

Time period	Country and focus of investment	Prevalence of fraud, law-breaking, corruption	Regulatory stimulus	Regulatory backlash
1850s *Crisis of 1857*	Britain, joint stock companies	Widespread fraud at banks, including Strahan Paul and Bates, Tipperary and Royal British Bank (losses when these three banks failed rivaled magnitude of investor losses in Madoff Ponzi scheme of 2000s).	Limited liability for shareholders introduced and furthered by Limited Liability Act of 1855 and Joint Stock Companies Act 1856; repeal of earlier accounting and disclosure requirements for joint stock companies imposed in 1844 Act.	Unclear. Short term: muted, Parliamentary inquiries. Long term: fueled trade unionism.
1860s *Overend, Gurney crisis of 1866*	Britain, limited liability companies	Securities fraud, misleading disclosure by company promoters.	Companies Act 1862 extended limited liability protection.	Mild corporate law reforms, but major accounting rules. Bank of England permanently assumes "lender of last resort" role.
Late 1860s *Panic of 1869*	United States, stocks	Widespread market manipulation; Jay Gould attempts to corner gold market. "Great Barbecue": widespread graft and bribery of public officials.	State loans to, investments in, and grants to railroads. Gould uses inside information from corrupt Grant administration.	Congressional investigation into Gould. Supreme Court broadens economic powers of federal government in *Knox v. Lee*.

Early 1870s *Panic of 1873*	United States, railroad stocks	"Great Barbecue" continues. Massive insider trading and securities fraud. Great Diamond Hoax of 1872. Crédit Mobilier and Pacific Mail Steamship scandals.	State loans to, investments in, and grants to railroads. Federal land grants to railroads, many of which obtained through bribes.	Sea change in American politics as monetary and class issue take precedence. State constitutional provisions restricting ability of states and municipalities to incur public debt or extend credit or give subsidies/donations to railroads and other private companies. Democrats gain in 1874 congressional elections. 1875 Resumption of Specie Act. *Julliard v. Greenman.*
Early 1870s *Gründerboom,* *Gründerkrach*	Germany, Austria	*Schwindelgründungen* (fraudulent incorporations, misleading company disclosures, and misappropriation of shareholder funds by insiders of new companies).	Liberalization of incorporation law in Germany. Austria subsidizes railroads, repeals usury laws, reforms real property laws.	Era of massive state intervention in economy in both countries: nationalization of some companies, imposition of tariffs and trade protectionism, encouragement of formation of cartels and trade unions. Corporate law reform.
1880s *Argentina boom*	Britain, investment company stocks and loans to South America	Alleged fraud by Argentine government. Collusion between investment company officers and South American governments.	Active involvement of Argentine and other South American governments in soliciting, structuring, and guaranteeing investments in infrastructure. Alleged fraud by Argentine government.	Bank of England leads bailout of Baring Brothers. *Coup d'état* in Argentina followed by laws restricting foreign investment.

continued

Table 2.a.1 Continued

Time period	Country and focus of investment	Prevalence of fraud, law-breaking, corruption	Regulatory stimulus	Regulatory backlash
1920s *Roaring Twenties* to Great Depression	United States, stocks, real estate	Widespread fraud and market manipulation alleged in stock market. Fraud, graft in Florida real estate market. Abuses by mortgage lenders and insurers.	"The business of America is business"; end of the Progressive era of regulation. Lax antitrust enforcement. Favorable state regulation of utility operating companies, *while* Supreme Court strikes down state regulation of utility holding companies. Federal deregulation of bank real estate and securities activities. Decline of federal bank supervision. Capture of Florida bank regulators. New York allows mortgage insurance.	New Deal. Passage of major securities and banking laws including: • Securities Act of 1933; • Securities Exchange Act of 1934; • Public Utilities Holding Company Act; • Glass-Steagall Act; and • federal deposit insurance. Creation of federal programs for residential mortgage lending.

1960s *Conglomerate stock boom*	United States, "growth stocks," and "new-issues," stocks of conglomerates, "concept stocks"	Deceptive and fraudulent accounting practices. Insider trading and market manipulation by brokers and underwriters. Scandals at AMEX.	Lax enforcement of securities and antitrust laws.	1968 FTC investigation of conglomerates. Williams Act. SEC attacks deceptive accounting practices. New broker–dealer regulations. SEC investigation of AMEX. SEC fraud investigations of securities issuers.
1980s *Japanese bubble*	Japan, real estate, stocks	Stock speculation enabled by unlawful brokerage accounts. Pervasive financial fraud and stock manipulation. Stock corners and insider trading. Banks evade law in real estate lending practices	Cascading waves of liberalization of Japanese financial services sector starting with securities firms and bond markets and later banks.	Reform of Japanese banking law.

continued

Table 2.a.1 Continued

Time period	Country and focus of investment	Prevalence of fraud, law-breaking, corruption	Regulatory stimulus	Regulatory backlash
Late 1990s	United States, technology stocks	Major securities fraud scandals particularly in energy and telecom sectors, including at Enron, WorldCom, and Tyco.	Securities laws lowering liability: • Private Securities Litigation Reform Act of 1995; • Securities Litigation and Uniform Standards Act of 1998. Supreme Court cases lowering securities law liability or restricting scope of securities laws: • *Lampf, Pleva;* • *Central Bank of Denver.* Development of other judicial doctrines raising bar for securities litigation claims. Repeal of Glass-Steagall Act. Resistance to proposed SEC reforms, particularly by accounting industry. Telecommunications Act of 1996. Federal deregulation of energy markets (Energy Power Act of 1992). Deregulation of California state energy markets.	Sarbanes-Oxley Act. SEC Enforcement actions and settlements; New York State Attorney General investigates securities practices; prosecution of officers of prominent companies; wave of private securities litigation with record verdicts and settlements.

Table 2.a.2 Financial/legal innovations and instruments

Bubble period or ensuing crisis	Financial/legal innovation (e.g., financial instruments invented or improved)	Enabling legal development; active regulatory stimulus (or passive government acquiescence)
1690s *English joint-stock boom*	Joint-stock companies. Development of option contracts.	Joint-stock companies chartered by Parliament.
1719 *French Mississippi bubble*	Complex scheme to privatize and securitize national debt and trade revenues. Creation of French central bank and introduction of paper currency.	Royal charters and various grants of legal authority to key companies: Mississippi Company and *Banque Royale*.
1720 *South Sea bubble*	Complex scheme to privatize and securitize national debt and trade revenues. Development of futures and option contracts.	Parliament privatizes national debt and grants South Sea Company trade monopoly. Private joint-stock companies chartered by Parliament.
1820s *Latin American investment boom; Panic of 1825*	Expansion and innovative contracting in sovereign debt issuances.	Newly independent Latin American republics float bonds.
1840s *British railway mania; Crisis of 1847*	Expansion and innovation in preferred share issuances.	Railway companies chartered by Parliament.
1850s *British stock market boom; Crisis of 1857*	Limited liability for shareholders of joint-stock companies.	Limited Liability Act 1855; Joint Stock Companies Act 1856.
1860s *Overend, Gurney crisis*	Limited liability extended to more types of joint-stock companies.	Companies Act 1862.

continued

Table 2.a.2 Continued

Bubble period or ensuing crisis	Financial/legal innovation (e.g., financial instruments invented or improved)	Enabling legal development; active regulatory stimulus (or passive government acquiescence)
1860s-1873 U.S. Panic of 1869; U.S. Panic of 1873	Creative state and municipal financing and subsidization of railroads.	State and municipal governments competing for railroads.
1870s Gründerboom and Gründerkrach in Germany and Austria	Liberalization of joint-stock company form.	German corporate law reform.
1920s U.S. stock market and Florida real estate bubbles	Mortgage guarantees, mortgage-backed securities; highly leveraged utility holding company structures; investment trusts and stock pools. Ivar Kreuger introduces financial innovations including dual class shares (one class holding more voting rights); forerunner of American Depository Receipts; off-balance sheet financings, certain foreign exchange options, convertible debt instruments, and other derivatives.[1]	New York state enables mortgage guarantees. Mortgage bond houses left unregulated. Utility holding companies successfully seek favorable state regulation (and monopolies) for *operating* companies and fight state regulation of *holding* companies. Government acquiescence to investment trusts and pools.
1960s U.S. conglomerate stock boom	Horizontally integrated conglomerates.	(Government acquiescence; lax enforcement of antitrust laws.)

1980s *Japanese real estate bubble*	Corporate warrant bonds. Complex brokerage accounts for speculation by corporate investors (*tokkin* and *eigyo tokkin*). Complex real estate finance mechanisms.	(Deregulation of capital markets; government acquiescence.)
1990s *U.S. tech stock bubble*	Enron off-balance sheet financing (illegal). Development of complex energy derivatives and trading markets (legal). (Spread of venture capital financing: convertible preferred stock for investing in companies and limited partnerships to pool investor resources (legal).)	Favorable and manipulable accounting rules facilitated off-balance sheet financing. Federal and state deregulation of electricity sector spurred used of energy derivatives and markets. (Venture capital use of convertible preferred stock as investment mechanism largely resulted from private ordering. Growing use of limited partnership form for venture capital funds had legal origins that predated bubble.)

Note
1 See Chapter 5, notes 75–8 and accompanying text.

Table 2.a.3 Nineteenth century British corporate law and crises

Year	Law liberalizing incorporation or investment	Financial crisis	Regulatory backlash
1820s	Hundreds of new companies formed by Acts of Parliament.	—	—
1825	*Bubble Companies Act*: repeals Bubble Act of 1720 (July 5).	Panic of 1825 (begins in November).	—
1826	—	—	*Country Bankers Act of 1826*: statutory reform of banking sector and corporate governance of banks.
1835–1836	Rash of new companies formed by Acts of Parliament.	—	—
1836–1837	—	British stock markets crash in 1836.	
1837		Panic of 1837 (in United States; spills over to Britain).	
1841–1844	—	—	Gladstone Commission: recommends corporate law reforms to move away from laissez faire regulation but also to facilitate formation of joint stock companies.
1844–1845	*Joint Stock Companies Act 1844*: influenced by Gladstone Commission, the Act expanded access to incorporation by removing requirement for Act of Parliament *but also* imposed accounting, audit, and disclosure requirements on joint-stock companies; still no limitation on liability of shareholders. Joint Stock Company Act facilitates formation of hundreds of joint-stock railway companies from 1884–1845.	—	*Bank Charter Act*: prohibits banks from issuing notes, giving exclusive power to Bank of England.
1845–1847	—	Stock market crash led by collapse of railway stocks leads to Crisis of 1847.	—

Period	Financial crisis	Corporate/accounting legislation	Regulatory and institutional response
Late 1840s	—	—	Parliament prohibits companies from paying dividends out of capital. "Accounting revolutions," as shareholders force outside accountants to audit companies.
1855, 1856	—	*Limited Liability Act 1855*: first established limited liability for shareholders, but limited to certain categories of companies; repealed accounting, audit, and disclosure requirements of 1844 Act; replaced with model articles of association. *Joint Stock Companies Act 1856*: expands companies that can take advantage of limited liability for shareholders. Both lead to boom in incorporation of joint-stock railway companies.	—
1857	Crisis of 1857	—	—
Late 1850s	—	—	Muted regulatory backlash (parliamentary inquiries), but rise of trade unionism.
1862–1866	—	*Companies Act 1862*: expands companies that can take advantage of limited liability for shareholders; boom in limited liability companies.	—
1866	Overend, Gurney crisis	—	—
Late 1860s	—	—	Mild corporate law reforms but significant accounting law reforms. Bank of England accepts "lender of last resort role."

Table 2.a.4 Regulatory cycle: the 1920s, New Deal, 1990s, and beyond

1920s development	Depression-era regulatory response	Major deregulation in the 1990s (and 2000s)	Market reaction	Regulatory response
Allegations of widespread securities fraud and manipulation (investigated by Pecora Commission).	Securities Act of 1933. Securities Exchange Act of 1934.	Restrictions on private rights of action under federal securities laws via: Public Securities Litigation Reform Act of 1995, Securities Litigation Uniform Standards Act of 1998, and *Central Bank* and other judicial decisions.	Lower expected securities law liability contributed to epidemic of securities fraud.	Sarbanes-Oxley Act.
Financial conglomerates (e.g., National City Bank) combining banking and securities business. Office of the Comptroller of the Currency facilitates.	Glass-Steagall Act.	1999 repeal of Glass-Steagall; weakening of statute before repeal via agency interpretations.	Formation of financial conglomerates placing commercial banking, investment banking, and insurance under one corporate umbrella.	Volcker Rule and other Dodd-Frank Act provisions impose investment restrictions on financial conglomerates (albeit after Panic of 2007–2008).

Bank runs after Great Crash.	Federal Deposit Insurance Corporation.	Under-charging banks for deposit insurance premia.	FDIC under-funded during epidemic of bank failures in Panic of 2007–2008.	Dodd-Frank Act imposes new capital requirements on banks; Volcker Rule restricts bank investments.
Public utility holding companies form (e.g., Samuel Insull's trusts); operating companies receive monopoly status, guaranteed returns under state regulation. But, interstate holding companies. In 1927, Supreme Court precludes states from regulating interstate wholesale electricity transactions.	Public Utility Holding Company Act.	Lax enforcement and exemptions from PUHCA in 1990s. (Repeal of statute in 2005.) Federal Energy Power Act deregulated electricity markets in 1992. State deregulation of electricity markets, particularly in California.	Formation and rapid expansion of Enron and other energy conglomerates.	Re-regulation of state retail electricity markets.
No comprehensive regulatory scheme for emerging broadcast industry.	Communications Act of 1934.	Telecommunications Act of 1996.	Investment boom in an array of different telecommunications companies.	–

Notes

1 Among these exceptions are the narrative economic history of Charles Kindleberger and the more recent behavioral finance scholarship of Andrei Shleifer. Charles P. Kindleberger, *Manias, Panics and Crashes: A History of Financial Crises*, 16 (4th ed. 2000, Wiley Investment Classics); Andrei Shleifer, *Inefficient Markets: An Introduction to Behavioral Finance*, 169–74 (2000, Oxford University Press).

2 For a historical account of speculation and fraud in the early years of the Dutch stock market, see Joseph de la Vega, *Confusión de Confusiones* (Hermann Kellenbenz trans., 1957, Baker Library, Harvard Graduate School of Business Administration) (1688, José Félix Botella Lillo). Speculation in the Dutch stock market also spilled over into the earliest known bubble, the Dutch Tulipomania of the 1630s. See Edward Chancellor, *Devil Take the Hindmost: A History of Financial Speculation*, 14–20 (1999, Plume Books).

3 For very old, entertaining, but not always scholarly accounts of various financial manias, see de la Vega, *supra* note 2; and Charles Mackay, *Memoirs of Extraordinary Popular Delusions* (1841, Richard Bentley). Both of these are reprinted in Martin S. Fridson ed. *Extraordinary Popular Delusions and the Madness of Crowds and Confusión de Confusiones* (1996, John Wiley & Sons). For an encyclopedic and largely narrative economic account of bubbles and other financial crises, see Kindleberger, *supra* note 1. For a more contemporary and accessible series of histories, see Chancellor, *supra* note 2. For a comprehensive dataset of various financial crises, bubbles and otherwise, see Carmen M. Reinhart and Kenneth S. Rogoff, *This Time is Different: Eight Centuries of Financial Folly* (2009, Princeton University Press).

4 E.g., U.S. Financial Crisis Inquiry Commission, Financial Crisis Inquiry Report 52–66 (2011, U.S. Government Printing Office). For an insightful study of how Western nations have been stuck in cycles of deregulation leading to booms leading to financial crises since the 1970s, see James Crotty, Structural Causes of the Global Financial Crisis: A Critical Assessment of the "New Financial Architecture," 33 *Cambridge Journal of Economics* 563 (2009).

   Some scholars with a free market orientation have criticized effort to blame deregulation. E.g., Peter J. Wallison, Deregulation and the Financial Crisis: Another Urban Myth, American Enterprise Institute Financial Services Outlook (October 2009). Wallison's arguments take a fairly narrow view of deregulation. He argues that the repeal of Glass Steagall could not have played a role in causing the financial crisis, because U.S. law still restricted banks from engaging in the securities business. This ignores the other ways in which financial conglomerates may have transferred government subsidies from banks to less regulated affiliates. See Chapter 11, "The demise of Glass-Steagall and subsidy leakage." Wallison also argues that there is no evidence that any failure to regulate credit derivatives contributed to the crisis. This minimizes the role that credit derivatives played in the downfall of AIG. Markus K. Brunnermeier, Deciphering the Liquidity and Credit Crunch 2007–2008, 23 *Journal of Economic Perspectives* 77, 89, 96–7 (2009). For analysis of how credit derivatives contributed to monetary expansion, see Chapter 9, "Margin, embedded leverage and financial instruments."

5 Chapter 5 argues that financial institutions view regulatory capital requirements as form of tax. Higher taxes encourage these institutions to devise structures (regulatory arbitrage) to minimize their tax rates. Chapter 5, "Capital requirements as regulatory tax." See also David Jones, Emerging Problems with the Basel Capital Accord: Regulatory Capital Arbitrage and Related Issues, 24 *Journal of Banking and Finance* 35, 38–9 (2000).

6 For one of the best examples of this line of scholarship, see Anna Gelpern, Financial Crisis Containment, 41 *Connecticut Law Review* 493 (2009).

7 For a small sample, see Franklin Allen and Douglas Gale, Asset Price Bubbles and

Monetary Policy, in *Global Governance and Financial Crises*, 19 (Meghnad Desai and Yahi Said eds. 2004, Routledge); Ben Bernanke and Mark Gertler, Monetary Policy and Asset Price Volatility, in *New Challenges for Monetary Policy: Proceedings of the Federal Reserve Bank of Kansas City*, 77 (1999, Federal Reserve Bank of Kansas City); Ben Bernanke and Mark Gertler, Should Central Banks Respond to Movements in Asset Prices? 91 *American Economic Review* 253 (2001); Stephen G. Cecchetti, Hans Genberg, and Sushil Wadhwani, Asset Prices in a Flexible Inflation Targeting Framework, in *Asset-Price Bubbles: The Implications for Monetary, Regulatory, and International Policies*, 427 (William C. Hunter, George G. Kaufman, and Michael Pomerleano eds., 2003, MIT Press); Robert P. Flood and Peter M. Garber, *Speculative Bubbles, Speculative Attacks, and Policy Switching* (1994, MIT Press).

Chapter 9 discusses this literature in more depth when it examines the connections among financial regulation, monetary policy, and asset price bubbles.

8 Fostering a more expansive, nuanced, and sociological view of law and legal system is one of the central objectives of the law and society movement. See Lawrence M. Friedman, The Law and Society Movement, 38 *Stanford Law Review* 763 (1986). For an early, contemporaneous introduction to the much earlier Legal Realism school, see Lon L. Fuller, American Legal Realism, 82 *University of Pennsylvania Law Review* 429 (1934).

9 E.g., Morton J. Horwitz, *The Transformation of American Law: 1780–1860*, 63–108 (1977, Harvard University Press). Earlier legal historians found evidence that U.S. law developed during the nineteenth century in ways that promoted development. James Willard Hurst, for example, developed the famous "release of energy" theory to describe the course of American law during this period. By contrast with Horwitz, however, Hurst focused on the way law promoted individual freedom and growth, rather than serving powerful economic interest groups. See James Willard Hurst, *Law and the Conditions of Freedom in the Nineteenth Century United States* (1956, University of Wisconsin Press).

10 For an overview of American common law rules on fraud and misrepresentation, see, e.g., Restatement (Second) of Torts § 525 (defining tort of fraudulent misrepresentation); E. Allan Farnsworth, *Contracts*, §§ 4.9, 4.10 (4th ed. 2004, Aspen Law and Business) (discussing elements of misrepresentation under contract law).

11 For a nuanced account of John Law's machinations in creating the Mississippi bubble and an examination of where Law's schemes fell in the spectrum from unsound and overoptimistic economics to fraud see Niall Ferguson, *The Ascent of Money: A Financial History of the World*, 137–55 (2008, Penguin).

12 See Kindleberger, *supra* note 1, at 14.

13 See Chancellor, *supra* note 2, at 31–2, 47–8, 52.

14 See ibid. at 23.

15 The boom began with the spectacular success of royally chartered trading companies and was further fueled by the spectacular success of diving companies that received public "patents" to recover shipwrecks or that obtained technological patents for diving equipment. Chancellor, *supra* note 2, at 34–6. Other companies soon floated shares touting patents for a wide array of other inventions. See ibid. at 37–9. See generally Christine MacLeod, The 1690s Patent Boom: Invention or Stock-Jobbing? 39 *Economic History Review* 549 (1986) (summarizing patents enrolled during the time period 1691–1693).

16 See Stuart Banner, *Anglo-American Securities Regulation*, 39 (1998, Cambridge University Press) (describing how the "government's growing dependence on the credit market posed an obstacle to regulation").

17 See Chancellor, *supra* note 2, at 48–9.

18 See Banner, *supra* note 16, at 39.

19 See Chancellor, *supra* note 2, at 51–2.

20 Ibid. at 48; See also Banner, *supra* note 16, at 30–1. Daniel Defoe, author of

Robinson Crusoe, fell victim to one such scam and thereafter authored numerous pamphlets denouncing stock speculators and calling for government regulation of the market. See Banner, *supra* note 16, at 29–30, 32–6 (citing Daniel Defoe, *Essays Upon Several Subjects* (1702, Booksellers of London and Westminster); Daniel Defoe, *The Villainy of Stock-Jobbers Detected* (1701, Anne Baldwin); Daniel Defoe, *The Anatomy of Exchange-Alley: Or, a System of Stock-Jobbing* (1719, E. Smith)).

21 See Banner, *supra* note 16, at 30–1; Chancellor, *supra* note 2, at 52.

22 See Chancellor, *supra* note 2, at 48 (discussing the practice of "stockjobbing"); SEC, Pump and Dump Schemes, available at www.sec.gov/answers/pumpdump.htm (last visited October 30, 2005). Early entrepreneurs of fraud took full advantage of the new technologies of the printing press and the media. Economist Robert Shiller theorizes that the history of bubbles begins with the history of newspapers, as newspapers (and later television) facilitated the spread of investor beliefs about the market, especially manias and rumors. See Robert J. Shiller, *Irrational Exuberance*, 71, 73 and 267 n.1 (2001, Broadway Books).

23 See Banner, *supra* note 16, at 25–7, 30–1.

24 See ibid.

25 An Act to Restrain the Number and Ill Practice of Brokers and Stock Jobbers, 1697, 8 and 9 Will. 3, c. 32; accord Banner, *supra* note 16, at 39; Chancellor, *supra* note 2, at 52.

26 Banner, *supra* note 16, at 39.

27 Banner, *supra* note 16, at 39–40; Chancellor, *supra* note 2, at 52–3.

28 Banner, *supra* note 16, at 40.

29 Chancellor, *supra* note 2, at 49.

30 Banner, *supra* note 16, at 39–40. Stuart Banner writes that when the act expired, Parliament did authorize the city of London to license brokers and impose a fee, but that this new legislation was a shadow of its predecessor. "[T]he new statute placed no limit on the number of brokers, and appears to have been intended primarily as a means of raising revenue for the city rather than curbing securities trading." Ibid. at 40.

31 Banner, *supra* note 16, at 40. The only aspect of the 1697 act that was revived in 1711 was the reestablishment of limits on broker commissions. See ibid. at 40 (citing 1711, 10 Ann. c. 19, § 121).

32 Banner, *supra* note 16, at 40.

33 Ferguson, *supra* note 11, at 139–49. For another history of John Law's Mississippi "System," see Pierre Des Essars, Banking in France: Chapter II: The Bank and "System" of Law: France at the Close of the Reign of Louis XIV, in *A History of Banking in All the Leading Nations Vol. III*, 11 (William Graham Sumner ed. 1896, Journal of Commerce).

34 Ferguson, *supra* note 11, at 140–2.

35 Ibid. at 142–7.

36 Ibid. at 142–5.

37 Ibid. at 149–50.

38 Ibid. at 151–2.

39 Ibid. at 154.

40 Pierre Des Essars, Banking in France: Chapter III: the Discount Bank – La Caisse D'Escompte, in *A History of Banking in All the Leading Nations Vol. III*, 31, 31 (William Graham Sumner ed. 1896, Journal of Commerce). Des Essars wrote:

> The failure of Law's "System" left such a lasting impression that the creation of any new bank of issue was impossible in France for many years. These establishments, having no other earnest of success save the confidence of the people from whom they borrow by means of the bills they issue, cannot thrive in a country where the very name of bank arouses the most intense aversion.

The next bank to issue notes was not founded in France until 1867. Ibid.

41 Antoin Murphy, Corporate Ownership in France: The Importance of History, in *A History of Corporate Governance around the World: Family Business Groups to Professional Managers*, 185, 195 (Randall K. Morck ed., 2005, University of Chicago Press).

42 Ibid. at 201–2.

43 *Infra* notes 179–82 and accompanying text.

44 Chancellor, *supra* note 2, at 62. For the history of the South Sea bubble, see John Carswell, *The South Sea Bubble* (1960, Cresset Press); see also Chancellor, *supra* note 2, at 58–95. For a more dated account of the bubble, see Charles MacKay, *Extraordinary Popular Delusions and the Madness of Crowds*, 49–91 (1980 [1841], Crown Trade Paperbacks).

For one economic analysis of the South Sea financial structure and the resultant bubbles, see Larry D. Neal, How the South Sea Bubble was Blown Up and Burst: A New Look at Old Data, in *Crashes and Panics: The Lessons from History*, 33 (Eugene N. White ed., 1990, Dow Jones-Irwin). For an account by an economist who argues that the South Sea episode does not meet the economist definition of a bubble because stock prices in the period could be explained by fundamental values, see Peter M. Garber, *Famous First Bubbles*, 91–93, 105–07 (2000, MIT Press).

For an in-depth analysis of the legal response to this bubble, see Banner, *supra* note 16, at 41, 75–87.

45 Carswell, *supra* note 44, at 54.

46 See Banner, *supra* note 16, at 43.

47 For an account of the political maneuverings of the South Sea promoters to curry favor with the king and the governing party, see Balen, *supra* note 53, at 41–4, 72, 76–7.

48 See Chancellor, *supra* note 2, at 64–5.

49 Chancellor, *supra* note 2, at 91; See also Malcolm Balen, *The Secret History of the South Sea Bubble*, at 76, 81–2, 89, 169, 205 (2003, Fourth Estate).

50 E.g., Chancellor, *supra* note 2, at 75 (describing the activities of company co-founder John Blunt).

51 See Balen, *supra* note 49, at 40; Chancellor, *supra* note 2, at 68.

52 See Balen, *supra* note 49, at 69–76.

53 See Malcolm Balen, *The Secret History of the South Sea Bubble*, 89–90, 97 (2003, Fourth Estate); Chancellor, *supra* note 2, at 70–71.

54 The official name of the Bubble Act was "An Act to Restrain the Extravagant and Unwarrantable Practice of Raising Money by Voluntary Subscription for Carrying on Projects Dangerous to the Trade and Subjects of the United Kingdom," 1720, 6 Geo. c. 18.

55 One popular misconception is that the Bubble Act was passed in reaction to the collapse of the South Sea Bubble. In fact it was passed before the collapse at the urging of directors of the South Sea Company. Carswell, *supra* note 44, at 139. These directors sought to protect their stock offerings from competition in the capital markets from other speculative ventures. Chancellor, *supra* note 2, at 82.

It was only later that commentators erroneously recast the Bubble Act as a response to the collapse of the bubble. Banner, *supra* note 16, at 75 n.129. Nevertheless, this misconception contains a kernel of insight, as the century-long duration of the Bubble Act stems from the lasting public memory of both the fraud during the bubble and the severe economic fallout from the bubble's ultimate collapse. See ibid. at 75–79; Chancellor, *supra* note 2, at 88–90. The Bubble Act therefore represents both an example of government intervention to support a bubble *and* a government response to the perceived evils of the bubble after the crash.

56 Chancellor, *supra* note 2, at 82.

57 Ibid at 82. Ultimately, this tactic backfired, as these writs caused the price of these three companies to plummet, which, in turn, instigated a general market panic that quickly engulfed the South Sea Company. Ibid. at 83. South Sea share prices

nose-dived and the complex Ponzi scheme created by the Company directors unraveled. See ibid. at 83–4.

58 See Balen, *supra* note 49, at 169, 175–6, 181.
59 See ibid. at 207–10.
60 Balen, *supra* note 49, at 216–20.
61 1734, 7 Geo. 2, c. 8; Chancellor, *supra* note 2, at 88.
62 Ibid. at 88, 90. The bubble also prompted more drastic proposals to outlaw specula-tion and securities brokering that never passed. See ibid. at 88.
63 Banner, *supra* note 16, at 79 (citing 1825, 6 Geo. 4, c. 91).
64 For a comprehensive history of this bubble, see Frank Griffith Dawson, *The First Latin American Debt Crisis: The City of London and the 1822–25 Loan Bubble* (1990, Yale University Press). For a description of some of the fraudulent ventures during this period, see ibid. at 40–2; Chancellor, *supra* note 2, at 100–9.
65 Dawson, *supra* note 64, at 22–46.
66 Ibid. at 28; Chancellor, *supra* note 2, at 100.
67 Chancellor, *supra* note 2, at 100.
68 Ibid.
69 Ibid. at 100–6; Bishop Carleton Hunt, *The Development of the Business Corporation in England 1800–1867*, 32 (1936, Harvard University Press).
70 Dawson, *supra* note 64, at 88.
71 Hunt, *supra* note 69, at 32.
72 Ibid. at 36–7; Chancellor, *supra* note 2, at 106–7.
73 Hunt, *supra* note 69, at 34–5.
74 Ibid. at 37–41. Bubble Companies Act, 6 Geo. IV, c. 91 1825.
75 Hunt, *supra* note 69, at 37–41.
76 Ron Harris has authored a nuanced study of the political economy of the Bubble Act repeal that looks at the relative contributions of interest group pressure, ideology, and a changing English legal institutions and judicial culture to the death of the statute. Ron Harris, Political Economy, Interest Groups, Legal Institutions, and the Repeal of the Bubble Act in 1825, 4 *Economic History Review* 675 (1997).
77 See Chancellor, *supra* note 2, at 108–9. B. Mark Smith, *A History of the Global Stock Market from Ancient Rome to Silicon Valley*, 49, 54 (2004, University of Chicago Press).
78 Chancellor, *supra* note 2, at 109.
79 Ibid. at 111.
80 Michael D. Bordo, Commentary, *Federal Reserve Bank St. Louis Review* 77, 78 (May/June 1998).
81 Larry Neal, The Financial Crisis of 1825 and the Restructuring of the British Finan-cial System, *Federal Reserve Bank St. Louis Review* 53, 65 (May/June 1998). Pro-fessor Neal challenges the view, however, that country banks expanding note issuances contributed to the inflation of asset prices. Ibid. at 65–7.
82 Chancellor, *supra* note 2, at 100–6.
83 Dawson, *supra* note 64, at 41–2, 59–61; Chancellor, *supra* note 2, at 96–7. See also David Sinclair, *The Land That Never Was: Sir Gregor MacGregor and the Most Audacious Fraud in History* (2004, Da Capo Press Inc.).
84 Chancellor, *supra* note 2, at 106.
85 Dawson, *supra* note 64, at 105; Chancellor, *supra* note 2, at 101–4.
86 Chancellor, *supra* note 2, at 110–15.
87 Hunt, *supra* note 69, at 49.
88 Neal, *supra* note 81.
89 Neal, *supra* note 81, at 69–73 (describing these changes and the political process that led to them). Michael Haupert, Panic of 1825, in *Business Cycles and Depres-sions: An Encyclopedia*, 511, 513 (David Glasner ed. 1997, Routledge). Country Bankers Act of 1826, 7 Geo. IV. c. 46, Sec. I.

90 Haupert, *supra* note 89, at 513; Neal, *supra* note 81, at 72. Country Bankers Act of 1826, 7 Geo. IV. c. 46, Sec. II–III.

91 Chancellor, *supra* note 2, at 121. For a capsule historical survey of economic theories on business cycles, see Victor Zarnowitz, Business Cycles, in *Business Cycles and Depressions: An Encyclopedia*, 62 (David Glasner ed. 1997, Routledge).

92 Rande W. Kostal, *Law and English Railway Capitalism 1825–1875*, 19–25 (1994, Oxford University Press).

93 Richard H. Timberlake, Jr., The Panic of 1837, in *Business Cycles and Depressions: An Encyclopedia*, 514, 514–16 (David Glasner ed. 1997, Routledge).

94 Gladstone was persuaded of the benefits of joint-stock companies, but believed a laissez faire approach to incorporation was responsible for the bubble. The statute "was thus drafted with facilitative and regulatory goals in mind." Kostal, *supra* note 92, at 25.

95 See 7 and 8 Vict. c.110.

96 Kostal, *supra* note 92, at 27.

97 In particular, names of promoters, investors, and capital needed to be filed with a central register office. Ibid. citing 7 and 8 Vict. c. 110, s. 4, 7.

   The act also imposed responsibility for ensuring that this public disclosure was made on a company's lawyers. It imposed monetary penalties and loss of license on lawyers who failed to perform these functions or who were found responsible for fraudulent omissions or misrepresentations in the disclosure. Kostal, *supra* note 92, at 26, citing 7 and 8 Vict. c. 110, s. 4, 6, 10, 11, 14, 24.

   For a summary of the accounting requirements placed on joint-stock companies by the statute, see Christopher Napier, The History of Financial Reporting in the United Kingdom, in *European Financial Reporting: A History*, 259, 262 (Peter Walton ed. 1995, Academic Press). Parliament passed the Companies Clauses Consolidation Act a year later, which imposed additional accounting rules on joint-stock companies and set out model regulations. The accounting rules, however did not apply to companies that had already been formed. Ibid. at 262–3.

98 Kostal, *supra* note 92, at 27.

99 John J. Glynn, The Development of British Railway Accounting, 11 *Accounting Historians Journal* 103, 108–11 (1984) (discussing Companies Clauses Consolidation Act 1845).

100 Ibid.

101 Chancellor, *supra* note 2, at 129–34, 140–1. Deluged by increasing applications for bills and recognizing that railway lines created natural monopolies, Parliament passed the Railway Act of 1844. Ibid. at 129; Railway Regulation Act 1844, 7 and 8 Vict. 85; Iain McLean and Christopher Foster, The Political Economy of Regulation: Interests, Ideology, Votes, and the UK Regulation of Railways Act 1844, 70 *Public Administration* 313 (1992) (testing political economy explanations of what led to passage of act). This statute imposed rate caps and required a minimum amount and quality of train services. Ibid. 313–14 (summarizing provisions of bill). Yet, under pressure from prominent railroad promoters, Parliament watered the final version of the act down. Chancellor, *supra* note 2, at 130.

   The Act created a new Railway Department to make non-binding recommendations to Parliament on the authorization of new lines, but this institution proved weak and ineffective, and was disbanded in 1845. Ibid. at 130–5.

102 Chancellor, *supra* note 2, at 133. For a description of the role private lawyers played in lobbying for private bills, see Kostal, *supra* note 92, at 110–27.

103 Chancellor, *supra* note 2, at 139.

104 Chancellor, *supra* note 2, at 130–3. Parliament did attempt to restrain speculation, inflation, and tighter monetary policy by passing the Bank Charter Act 1844, 7 and 8 Vict. c. 32. Chancellor, *supra* note 2, at 132–3. To dampen inflation and speculation, this statute removed the legal authority of private banks (banks other than the Bank

of England) to issue notes. The Bank Charter Act, §§ X–XII. The Act also restricted the note issuances by the Bank of England. See Chancellor, *supra* note 2, at 132–3. This action did not succeed in preventing the rampant speculation during the railway mania. Ibid. at 133–4. H.M. Hyndman, *Commercial Crises of the Nineteenth Century*, 59 (2nd ed. 1902, Charles Scribner's Sons).

105 Ibid. at 139, 144–7.
106 Ibid. at 144–5.
107 For a detailed account, see Kostal, *supra* note 92, at 31–52.
108 Ching Chun Wang, Legislative Regulation of Railway Finance in England, VII *University of Illinois Studies in the Social Sciences* 123 (March 1918); Edwin Guthrie, Payment of Interest on Capital during Construction of Works, *The Accountant*, 98, 99 (February 13, 1886).
109 Kostal, *supra* note 92, at 127–34.
110 Ibid. at 53–109 (giving history of this litigation wave).
111 See Andrew Odlyzko, The Collapse of the Railway Mania, the Development of Capital Markets, and the Forgotten Role of Robert Lucas Nash, 21 *Accounting History Review* 309 (2011).
112 See 18 and 19 Vict. c.133.
113 For a history of the debate surrounding limited liability for shareholders that led to the act, see Hunt, *supra* note 69, at 116–33.
114 See 9 and 20 Vict. c.47.
115 Hunt, *supra* note 69, at 134–5.
116 Napier, *supra* note 97, at 265.
117 Hunt, *supra* note 69, at 143.
118 Geoffrey Williams, Trust but Verify: Fraud in Victorian Banking and Its Diminishment, 10–11, Unpublished manuscript (January 11, 2012) available at http://papers.ssrn.com/sol3/papers.cfm?abstract_id=1983633 (last visited July 12, 2013). In the case of Strahan Paul and Bates, bankers improperly used client securities to cover large bank losses. The failure of Tipperary Joint Stock Bank represented a case of "undiluted fraud," as the director of the bank used almost all of that bank's funds to speculate in German and California mining companies, loaned a large sum of bank funds to himself, and forged bank documents. The director took his own life before the full extent of his fraud could be uncovered. In the third scandal, a manager and two directors of the bank loaned bank funds to themselves and friends and falsified records to hide those loans. All three individuals received prison sentences for this fraud. Ibid.
119 Ibid. at 10.
120 Ibid. at 11.
121 Simon Clarke, *Marx, Marginalism and Modern Sociology: From Adam Smith to Max Weber*, 115 (1982, Macmillan).
122 Michael R. Krätke, Marx's "Books of Crisis" of 1857–8, in *Karl Marx's* Grundrisse*: Foundations of the Critique of Political Economy 150 Years Later*, 169 (Marcello Musto ed. 2008, Routledge).
123 See 25 and 26 Vict. c.89.
124 Richard S. Grossman, Overend, Gurney Crisis (1866), in *Business Cycles and Depressions: An Encyclopedia*, 502, 503 (David Glasner ed. 1997, Routledge). See also Napier, *supra* note 97, at 265 (noting "steady (indeed accelerating) stream of incorporations under the 1862 Act"). Hunt, *supra* note 69, at 145–53.
125 Hunt, *supra* note 69, at 146–50.
126 Ibid. at 151–3.
127 For an account of financial fraud, actual and alleged, during this historical period, see George Robb, *White-Collar Crime in Modern England: Financial Fraud and Business Morality, 1845–1929*, 69–72 (2002, Cambridge University Press). See also Hunt, *supra* note 69, at 153.

128 Grossman, *supra* note 124.
129 Hunt, *supra* note 69, at 155–6.
130 Williams, *supra* note 118, at 12.
131 Ibid. at 149–50; The Companies Act 1867, 30 and 31 Vict. c.131. See also Hunt, *supra* note 69, at 156.
132 Regulation of Railways Act 1868, 31 and 32 Vict. c.119. See Napier, *supra* note 97, at 263. See also Glynn, *supra* note 99, 113–15.
133 See Grossman, *supra* note 124 at 505–6; Richard J. Herring and Reinhard H. Schmidt, The Economic Rationale for Financial Regulation Reconsidered: An Essay in Honour of David Llewellyn, in *The Financial Crisis and the Regulation of Finance*, 68, 69–72 (Christopher J. Green, Eric J. Pentecost, and Tom Weyman-Jones eds., 2011, Edward Elgar).
134 Steve Fraser, *Every Man a Speculator: A History of Wall Street in American Life*, 119 (2005, Harper).
135 David M. Gold, Redfield, Railroads, and the Roots of Laissez-Faire Constitutionalism, 27 *American Journal of Legal History* 254, 260 (1983).
136 Chancellor, *supra* note 2, at 175, 183; Robert Sobel, *Panic on Wall Street*, 168 (1988, Truman Talley/E.P. Dutton) Fraser, *supra* note 134, at 113–26.
137 Fraser, *supra* note 134, at 113–22 (describing corruption in this era).
138 Charles Francis Adams and Henry Adams, Chapters of Erie (1886) cited in Steve Fraser, *Wall Street: America's Dream Palace*, 33 (2008, Yale University Press).
139 Fraser, *supra* note 134, at 113–22.
140 Ibid. at 121.
141 See Sobel, *supra* note 136, at 126–33.
142 See Chancellor, *supra* note 2, at 174–7; Sobel, *supra* note 136, at 126–33, 167.
143 See Fraser, *supra* note 134, at 115–17; Chancellor, *supra* note 2, at 180–3. Even his failure to influence Grant did not derail Gould's manipulation of the gold market, which continued as other traders assumed his attempts at improper influence succeeded. See ibid. at 181–3; Sobel, *supra* note 136, at 140–9.
144 Cf. Sobel, *supra* note 136, at 149 (treating with skepticism Gould's denial that he was "in no way instrumental in creating the panic").
145 Sobel, *supra* note 136, at 149. This boom followed a number of other railways schemes that profited due to official corruption. See, e.g., ibid. at 123–4 (describing Daniel Drew's manipulation of the Erie Railroad). Chancellor also discusses how corrupt state and local legislators in New York facilitated the cornering of stocks in two Harlem railroads in 1863 and 1864. Chancellor, *supra* note 2, at 175–6.
146 See generally Chancellor, *supra* note 2, at 169–90 (describing speculation in the mining industry and Gould's manipulation of railroad stock); Sobel, *supra* note 136, at 115–96 (describing the major players in the post-war boom).
147 Fraser, *supra* note 138, at 55–8.
148 In the 1872 Crédit Mobilier scandal, Oakes Ames, a railway promoter and member of Congress, engaged in a complex scheme of graft that involved prominent politicians, including future President James Garfield and former Vice President Schuyler Colfax. Chancellor, *supra* note 2, at 175; Sobel, *supra* note 136, at 165.
149 The Pacific Mail Steamship Company scandal involved lucrative government contracts obtained through bribery of politicians. See Sobel, *supra* note 136, at 165.
150 See ibid. at 171–80 (describing Wall Street's panicked reaction to the collapse of the railroad stocks and government scandals).
151 Ibid. at 175–92.
152 Ibid. at 149.
153 Ibid. at 195, 197; Irwin Unger, The Business Community and the Origins of the 1875 Resumption Act, 35 *Business History Review* 247, 252–3 (1961).
154 Ch. 15, 18 Stat. 296 (1875).
155 See Sobel, *supra* note 136, at 197–9.

156 Ibid. at 193.
157 See Daniel W. Levy, A Legal History of Irrational Exuberance, 48 *Case Western Reserve Law Review* 799, 827–41 (1998) (analyzing the development of Supreme Court opinions handed down in reaction to the financial crises of the post-Civil War period).
158 Ibid. at 834.
159 Ibid. at 835. This passage refers to the Supreme Court's decisions in the "Legal Tender" cases *Juilliard* v. *Greenman*, 110 U.S. 421 (1884) and *Knox* v. *Lee*, 79 U.S. (12 Wall.) 457 (1870). For a fascinating analysis of how the justices in these cases wrestled with reconciling federal power to deal with financial emergencies with the formalism of Court precedent that had limited government powers and elevated individual economic rights, see Levy, *supra* note 157, at 835–41.
160 *Journal of the Missouri Constitutional Convention* Vol. I, 27–33 (1920).
161 Ibid. at 28–31.
162 Ibid. at 32–3.
163 Edwin Lee Lopata, *Local Aid to Railroads in Missouri*, 38 (1981, Arno Press) citing Missouri Constitution, Article IX, Section 6 (1875).
164 Janice C. May, *The Texas State Constitution: A Reference Guide*, 14–16 (1996, Greenwood Press).
165 Ibid. citing Texas Constitution, Art. XVI, Sec. 16 (1876).
166 See Le Grand Powers, Increasing Municipal Indebtedness, 3 *National Municipal Review* 102, 106 (1914) (Panic of 1873 led to state constitutional and statutory restrictions on government indebtedness "in every state"); Joel A. Mintz, Ronald H. Rosenberg, and Larry A. Bakken, *Fundamentals of Municipal Finance*, 47 (2010, American Bar Association) (Panic of 1873 led to state legislatures imposing limitations on state and local indebtedness); Fred Emerson Clark, The Purposes of the Indebtedness of American Cities 1880–1912, PhD Dissertation, University of Illinois (1916, Bureau of Municipal Research) (linking Panic of 1873 to state constitutional restrictions on public indebtedness and noting that, from 1870 to 1877, eighteen states included restrictions on municipal indebtedness in their constitutions).
167 Donald Wayne Hensel, A History of the Colorado Constitution in the Nineteenth Century, PhD Dissertation, University of Colorado (1957), 134–5. Hensel discusses how memories of the Panic of 1873 meshed with the concern of the drafters of Colorado's Constitution over corporate control of the political process. He frames this concern as follows: "would the people discard territorial subjugation only to confront a web of railroad tracks ensnaring them in economic bondage." Ibid. at 135. Hensel then provides an analysis of how this fear shaped state constitutional provisions on regulating railroads and other corporations, restricting government subsidies of corporations (ibid. at 134–55) and limiting public indebtedness (ibid. at 155–65).
168 For a discussion of state constitutions which included anti-subsidy provisions in response to the Panic of 1837, see Susan P. Fino, Cure Worse than the Disease: Taxation and Finance Provisions in State Constitutions, 34 *Rutgers Law Journal* 959, 969–76 (2003). See also Joseph R. Grodin, Calvin R. Massey, and Richard B. Cunningham, *The California State Constitution: A Reference Guide*, 5 (1993, Greenwood Press) (giving later example of California).
169 Paul Erker, *Dampflok, Daimler, Dax: Die Deutsche Wirtschaft im 19. und 20. Jahrhundert*, 84 (2001, Deutsche Verlags-Anstalt).
170 For a discussion of the many causes of the *Gründerboom*, see Friederich-Wilhelm Henning, *Deutsche Wirtschafts- und Sozialgeschichte im 19. Jahrhundert Vol. II*, 792–8 (1996, Verlag Ferdinand Schöningh); Erker, *supra* note 169, at 82.
171 Erker, *supra* note 169, at 81.

172 Henning, *supra* note 170, at 332–40 (liberalism in Germany); A.J.P. Taylor, *The Hapsburg Monarchy: 1809–1918: A History of the Austrian Empire and Austria-Hungary*, 150–1 (1948, Hamish Hamilton, Ltd.) (describing spillover of German liberalism into Austria and end of laissez faire period with Panic of 1873); Herbert Matis, Guidelines of Austrian Economic Policy 1848–1918, in *The Economic Development of Austria since 1870*, 19, 24–6 (Herbert Matis ed. 1994, Edward Elgar) (detailing rise of economic and political liberalism in Austria in 1860s and early 1870s).

173 See Gordon R. Mork, Bismarck and the "Capitulation" of German Liberalism, 43 *Journal of Modern History* 59, 60–9 (1971) (describing formation and rise of party).

174 Jan Thiessen, *"Eine Association von Capitalien": Gründungsrecht und Finanzverfassung von Kapitalgesellschaften im historischen Kontext zwischen 1861 und 1945*, 106–9, 120, Habilitationschrift, Juristischen Fakultät der Humboldt Universität zu Berlin (2008).

175 Jan Lieder, Die 1. Aktienrechtsnovelle vom 11. Juni 1870, in *Aktienrecht im Wandel Vol. I*, 321–4 (Walter Bayer and Mathias Habersack eds., 2007, Mohr Sieback); Henning, *supra* note 170, at 338–9.

176 Art. 173–249a des Allgemeinen Deutschen Handelsgesetzbuchs in der Fassung des Gesetzes vom 11.6.1870 [1870 Joint-stock Company Act] reprinted in *Hundert Jahre modernes Aktienrecht: eine Sammlung von Texten und Quellen zur Aktienrechtsreform 1884 mit zwei Einfuehrungen*, 107–26 (Werner Schubert and Peter Hommelhoff eds., 1985, De Gruyter).

177 Lieder, *supra* note 175, at 324–7.

178 Werner Schubert, Die Abschaffung des Konzessionssystems durch die Aktienrectsnovelie von 1870, 10 *Zeitschrift für Unternehmens- und Gesellschaftsrecht* 285, 289–92 (1981); Lieder, *supra* note 175, at 326–7. See also Thiessen, *supra* note 174, at 107–9.

179 Werner Schubert, Die Enstehung des Aktiengesetzes vom 18. Jun 1884, in *Hundert Jahre modernes Aktienrecht: eine Sammlung von Texten und Quellen zur Aktienrechtsreform 1884 mit zwei Einfuehrungen*, 59–61 (Werner Schubert and Peter Hommelhoff eds., 1985, De Gruyter); Lieder, *supra* note 175, at 329–30.

180 Lieder, *supra* note 175, at 329–30.

181 See Thiessen, *supra* note 174, at 16 (describing French lineage of German commercial statutes). For the origins of the French version of the *Konzessionssystem* in the wake of the Mississippi bubble, see *supra* note 42 and accompanying text. The nineteenth century changes to French law on incorporation influenced drafters of German corporate law in 1870. Schubert, *supra* note 178, at 289–92.

182 Schubert, *supra* note 179, at 59–61; Lieder, *supra* note 175, at 329–30.

183 See Thiessen, *supra* note 174, at 81–3.

184 Ibid. at 70–1.

185 Ibid. at 72–5.

186 See Schubert, *supra* note 178.

187 Henning, *supra* note 170, at 802. The *Aktiengesellschaften* formed during the boom had a total nominal capitalization of 2.9 billion marks compared to a total nominal capital of 2.4 billion for all *Aktiengesellschaften* formed in the previous twenty years. Ibid. In Austria, approximately 1000 *Aktiengesellschaften* were formed between 1867 and 1873 with total nominal capital of 8 billion marks. Ibid. Other scholars come up with totals that are generally in accord with the above figures, but not entirely consistent. For example, one estimate accounts for 843 new *Aktiengesellschaften* founded in Prussia alone from 1871 to 1873 compared to 203 formed in all the previous years together. Sibylle Hofer, Das Aktiengesetz von 1884: ein Lehrstück für prinzipielle Schutzkonzeptionen, in *Aktienrecht im Wandel Vol. I*, 389 (Walter Bayer and Mathias Habersack eds., 2007, Mohr Sieback).

188 See Henning, *supra* note 170, at 820; Erker, *supra* note 169, at 81–2.

189 Deutsche Bank was founded in 1870 before the new corporate law came into effect, but the new law did lead to a boom in bank incorporations, with thirty formed in 1870 alone. Eric Owen Smith, *The German Economy*, 321, 323–4 (1994, Routledge). See also P. Barrett Whale, *Joint Stock Banking in Germany: A Study of the German Creditbanks Before and After the War*, 16–17 (1930, Macmillan).

190 Caroline Fohlin, Does Civil Law Tradition and Universal Banking Crowd Out Securities Markets? Pre-World War I Germany as Counter-Example, 8 *Enterprise and Society* 602, 609–10 (2007) (Germany imposed few laws on banks beyond those applicable to all joint-stock companies). See Henning, *supra* note 170, at 792–6 (discussing expansion of railroad and mining companies), 800–1 (discussing expansion of supply of bank notes and boom); David F. Good, *The Economic Rise of the Hapsburg Empire 1750–1914*, 206–8 (1984, University of California Press) (discussing explosive growth of bank incorporations and stimulus provided by bank credit in Austria and Germany).

191 For a description of the booming Berlin stock market of this era, see Markus Baltzer, *Der Berliner Kapitalmarkt nach der Reichsgründung 1871: Gründerzeit, internationale Finanzmarktintegration und der Einfluss der Makroökonomie* (2007, LIT Verlag).

192 As evidence of the light regulation of exchanges, authorities tolerated a sharp rise in the number of unlicensed brokers on German exchanges. Joost Jonker, Competing in Tandem: Securities Markets and Commercial Banking Patterns in Europe During the Nineteenth Century, in *The Origins of National Financial Systems: Alexander Gerschenkron Reconsidered*, 64, 82 (Douglas James Forsyth and Daniel Verdier eds., 2003, Routledge). Compare Julian R. Franks, Colin Mayer, and Hannes F. Wagner, The Origins of the German Corporation: Finance, Ownership and Control, 10 *Review of Finance* 537, 542 (2006) (before 1896 there was a "virtual complete absence of regulation of transactions on the exchanges"). For a discussion of margin loans (*Lombardkredit*) by banks to stock speculators, see Carsten Burhop, *Die Kreditbanken in der Gründerzeit*, 61–2 (2004, Franz Steiner Verlag).

193 Max Wirth, History of Banking in Austria Hungary: The Austrian National Bank, in *A History of Banking in All the Leading Nations Vol. IV*, 69, 81 (William Graham Sumner ed. 1896, Journal of Commerce).

194 Matis, *supra* note 172, at 28.

195 Max Wirth, History of Banking in Austria Hungary: Austrian Joint-Stock Banks, in *A History of Banking in All the Leading Nations Vol. IV*, 122, 131 (William Graham Sumner ed. 1896, Journal of Commerce). Over this same period, sixty-five provincial banks formed in Austria. Ibid.

196 Matis, *supra* note 172, at 28.

197 Ibid. at 27.

198 Charles P. Kindleberger, *Historical Economics: Art or Science?* 313–14 (1990, University of California Press); See also Alexander Nützenadel, Städtischer Immobilienboom und Finanzkrisen im späten 19. Jahrhundert, 2011/2 *Jahrbuch für Wirtschaftsgeschichte* 97, 98–9.

199 Matis, *supra* note 172, at 28.

200 *Supra* note 169 and accompanying text.

201 Clement Augustus Lounsberry, *Early History of North Dakota*, 506 (1919, Liberty Press).

202 Henning, *supra* note 170, at 801. For a discussion of the severity and economic impact of the crisis, see ibid. at 801–9.

203 David Glasner, Crisis of 1873, in *Business Cycles and Depressions: An Encyclopedia*, 132, 133 (David Glasner ed. 1997, Routledge).

204 Henning, *supra* note 170, at 800 (discussing failure of Franko-Ungarishche Bank in Austria precipitated the July 1 phase of the crisis); Erker, *supra* note 169, at 84 (failure of Quistorpische Vereinsbank in Berlin), Wirth, *supra* note 195, at 131 (of seventy banks formed in Vienna between 1868 and 1873, only eighteen survived

the Panic of 1873 and still operated in 1883; of sixty-five provincial Austrian banks formed in that five year span, only twenty-one survived until 1883), 137 (detailing failures of Austrian cooperative societies following Panic).

205 Henning, *supra* note 170, at 812 (discussing causes of crash).

206 Peter Hommelhof, Eigenkontrolle statt Staatskontrolle: rechtsdogmatischer Überblick zur Aktienrechtsreform 1884, in *Hundert Jahre modernes Aktienrecht: eine Sammlung von Texten und Quellen zur Aktienrechtsreform 1884 mit zwei Einfuehrungen*, 53, 55–6 (Werner Schubert and Peter Hommelhoff eds., 1985, De Gruyter); Hofer, *supra* note 187, at 389. Wolfgang Schoen and Christine Osterloh-Konrad, Rechnungslegung in der Aktiengesellschaft, in *Aktienrecht im Wandel Vol. II*, 891, 904 (Walter Bayer and Mathias Habersack eds., 2007, Mohr Sieback).

207 Henning, *supra* note 170, at 820. Some commentators attributed significant blame for the entire crisis on these *Schwindelgründungen*. Schoen and Osterloh-Konrad, *supra* note 206, at 904.

208 For a discussion of the strategies of deception used in *Schwindelgründungen*, see Hommelhof, *supra* note 206, at 55–6, 64–5.

209 See Thiessen, *supra* note 174, at 145–6; Cornelius Torp, *Die Herausforderung der Globalisierung: Wirtschaft und Politik in Deutschland 1860–1914*, 147–55 (2005, Vandenhoeck & Ruprecht); Henning, *supra* note 170, at 809–18.

210 Henning, *supra* note 170, at 812, 814–18, 823–35.

211 Volker Hentschel, *Wirtschaft und Wirtschaftspolitik im Wilhelminischen Deutschland: Organisierter Kapitalismus und Interventionsstaat?* 99–126 (1978, Klett-Cotta); Erker, *supra* note 169, at 85.

212 Erker, *supra* note 169, at 83.

213 Henning, *supra* note 170, at 809–14; Torp, *supra* note 209, at 147–55. Other nations retaliated and imposed tariffs and protectionist policies of their own. Henning, *supra* note 170, at 813 (discussing United States and Austria-Hungary).

214 Thiessen, *supra* note 174, at 175–6, 184–8.

215 The 1884 statute can be found at Gesetz, betreffend die KGaA und AG vom 18.7.1884 reproduced in *Hundert Jahre modernes Aktienrecht: eine Sammlung von Texten und Quellen zur Aktienrechtsreform 1884 mit zwei Einfuehrungen*, 560–607 (Werner Schubert and Peter Hommelhoff eds., 1985, De Gruyter).

216 For example, the 1884 statute included provisions that increased the power of various institutional bodies within a corporation to check the power of the founders. Hommelhof, *supra* note 206. For example, the 1884 Stock Act gave the *Generalversammlung*, a meeting of a corporation's shareholders, the ability to elect the corporation's *Aufsichtsrat*, akin to one of the corporation's two boards of directors. Ibid. at 87. In turn, the Act strengthened the oversight duties and powers of the *Aufsichtsrat* over corporate management. Ibid. at 87–91. See also Henning, *supra* note 170, at 821–3; Schoen and Osterloh-Konrad, *supra* note 206, at 904–7.

The statute enlarged shareholder rights, including the rights of minority shareholders. Ibid. at 96–102. The statute also implemented new disclosure rules for joint-stock companies, requiring publication of formation documents and prospectuses for investors. Ibid. at 65–8. The German reform thus used many of the same tools – corporate governance and improving securities disclosure – that modern policymakers have deployed in the wake of twentieth century crises.

The 1884 statute is historically important not only for its additions to German law, but also for what the statute did not do. The statute did not reintroduce the old *Konzessionssytem*, which would have required state officials to pre-approve new corporations. Ibid. at 60–1. The drafters of the statute similarly rejected more radical calls to abolish the organization form of the joint-stock company or to restrict this form only to certain enterprises. Ibid. at 57–60 (describing proposals either to abolish this form of entity or to prohibit its use in certain industries). Instead, the law preserved the freedom of entity choice. Ibid. at 61.

217 Fohlin, *supra* note 190, at 612–13.
218 Caroline Fohlin, Regulation, Taxation, and the Development of the German Universal Banking System, 1884–1913, 6 *European Review of Economic History* 221, 227 (2002).
219 For a detailed history of the long political and legislative history of the drafting of the 1884 reform, see Werner Schubert, Die Entstehung des Aktiengesetzes vom 18. Juli 1884, in *Hundert Jahre modernes Aktienrecht: eine Sammlung von Texten und Quellen zur Aktienrechtsreform 1884 mit zwei Einfuehrungen*, 1 (Werner Schubert and Peter Hommelhoff eds., 1985, De Gruyter).
220 Thiessen, *supra* note 174, at 167–84. For a discussion of how Bismarck engaged in ruthless power politics in the economic sphere in the aftermath of the *Gründerkrach*, see Torp, *supra* note 209, at 160.
221 See Taylor, *supra* note 172, at 150–1. Matis, *supra* note 172, at 28–9.
222 Matis, *supra* note 172, at 29. The 1874 joint-stock company act introduced important accounting reforms, restricted the ability of joint-stock companies to pay dividends, and required those companies to hold certain reserve funds. Christian Nowotny and Elisabeth Gruber, The History of Financial Reporting in Austria, in *European Financial Reporting: A History*, 29, 35 (Peter Walton ed. 1995, Academic Press).
223 Matis, *supra* note 172, at 29.
224 Ibid. at 29–30 citing Alois Brusatti, *Wirtschaft- und Sozial Geschichte des industriellen Zeitalters*, 148 (1968, Styria im Styria Pichler) (quoting Lorenz von Stein: "eine für alle Bürger sorgende Verwaltungseinheit").
225 Matis, *supra* note 172, at 30. See also George R. Marek, *The Eagles Die: Franz Joseph, Elisabeth and their Austria*, 182 (1974, Harper & Row) (discussing widespread blame of Jewish population for Panic of 1873 in Austria).
226 John Kenneth Galbraith's economic history of the years leading to the Great Crash blamed the Great Depression on an asset price bubble fueled by stock speculation. John Kenneth Galbraith, *The Great Crash 1929* (1954, Houghton Mifflin).
227 Chancellor, *supra* note 2, at 207–8.
228 Eugene N. White, Lessons from the Great American Real Estate Boom and Bust of the 1920s, National Bureau of Economic Research, *Working Paper No. 15573*, 41 (December 2009) available at www.nber.org/papers/w15573 (last visited July 12, 2013).
229 For extensive accounts of the role of banks in this boom, see William Frazer and John J. Guthrie, Jr., *The Florida Land Boom: Speculation, Money and the Banks* (1995, Praeger); Raymond B. Vickers, *Panic in Paradise: Florida's Banking Crash of 1926* (1994, University of Alabama Press).
230 See Fraser, *supra* note 134, at 375 (characterizing the 1920s as a decade in which "government bent its efforts to serve the narrowest interests of the business classes").
231 Ibid.
232 Ibid. at 376–7.
233 Chancellor, *supra* note 2, at 197, 222–3.
234 Ibid. at 193, 197.
235 Frederick M. Rowe, The Decline of Antitrust and the Delusions of Models: The Faustian Pact of Law and Economics, 72 *Georgetown Law Journal* 1511, 1518–19 (1984).
236 Ibid. at 1519 n.20 citing *U.S.* v. *U.S. Steel Corp.*, 251 U.S. 417 (1920); *U.S.* v. *Int'l Harvester Co.*, 274 U.S. 693 (1927); *FTC* v. *Eastman Kodak Co.*, 274 U.S. 619 (1927).
237 Fraser, *supra* note 134, at 380.
238 Chancellor, *supra* note 2, at 193.
239 By 1932, holding companies dominated the electricity and gas markets in the United States. They owned the majority of electric and gas utilities in the country. Thirteen

holding companies controlled 75 percent of the privately owned electric utilities. Three holding companies generated 45 percent of the nation's electricity. Four holding companies together controlled 56 percent of the natural gas transportation infrastructure. Roberta S. Karmel, Is the Public Utility Holding Company Act a Model for Breaking Up the Banks that Are Too-Big-To-Fail? 62 *Hastings Law Journal* 821, 848 (2011).

240 Fraser, *supra* note 134, at 377–8.
241 William D. Henderson and Richard D. Cudahy, From Insull to Enron: Corporate (Re)Regulation After the Rise and Fall of Two Energy Icons, 25 *Energy Law Journal* 35, 51–9 (2005).
242 Ibid. at 46–50.
243 Ibid. at 54 citing James C. Bonbright and Gardiner C. Means, *The Holding Company: Its Public Significance and Its Regulation*, 7 (1932, McGraw-Hill).
244 273 U.S. 83 (1927). See Henderson and Cudahy, *supra* note 241, at 54, n.109.
245 See Henderson and Cudahy, *supra* note 241, at 54, n.109.
246 Karmel, *supra* note 239, at 849.
247 Henderson and Cudahy, *supra* note 241, at 55.
248 Ibid. at 59–61.
249 Ibid. at 61.
250 Ibid.
251 Karmel, *supra* note 239, at 849.
252 Arthur E. Wilmarth, Jr., Does Financial Liberalization Increase the Likelihood of a Systemic Banking Crisis? Evidence from the Past Three Decades and the Great Depression, in *Too-Big-To-Fail: Policies and Practices in Government Bailouts*, 77, 87–96 (Benton E. Gup ed., 2003, Praeger).
253 Ibid. at 87. Ch. 6, 38 Stat. 251 § 24 (1913).
254 The Act of September 7, 1916, 39 Stat. 753. See Wilmarth, *supra* note 252, at 87.
255 See 69 Pub. L. 639, 44 Stat. 1224. See Wilmarth, *supra* note 252, at 87.
256 Wilmarth, *supra* note 252, at 87.
257 Ibid. at 88.
258 Ibid.
259 Ibid. at 88–9.
260 Ibid. Changes to the liability side of national bank balance sheet also allowed for greater bank investments in illiquid assets. The OCC and the Federal Reserve Act of 1913 allowed national banks to compete more evenly with their state chartered counterparts by accepting time deposits and not just deposits that could be withdrawn upon demand. Ibid. at 88. A 1917 amendment to the Federal Reserve Act made time deposits more attractive by lowering the reserves banks must hold for those deposits compared to the reserves for demand deposits. These changes encouraged banks to invest those deposits in assets that had less liquidity, but offered higher potential returns. These target assets included corporate and foreign securities and loans secured by either real estate or securities. Ibid.
261 White, *supra* note 228, at 41.
262 Ibid. at 41–2.
263 Chapter 4, "The probability of enforcement: causes of action and diluted enforcement." See also Chapter 3, "The problem of diluted enforcement."
264 Vickers, *supra* note 229, at 17.
265 Frazer and Guthrie, *supra* note 229; Vickers, *supra* note 229.
266 White, *supra* note 228, at 44.
267 White, *supra* note 228, at 44–5. For a history of this bank, the Palm Bank and Trust Company, see Vickers, *supra* note 229, at 45–6.
268 White, *supra* note 228, at 45. For a description of the convoluted control of this Palm Beach National Bank, see Vickers, *supra* note 229, at 65–8.
269 White, *supra* note 228, at 45.

270 For an in-depth treatment of banking fraud and corruption in Florida during the 1920s, see Vickers, *supra* note 229.
271 Kenneth A. Snowden, The Anatomy of a Residential Mortgage Crisis: A Look Back to the 1930s, National Bureau of Economic Research, *Working Paper No. 16244*, 8–9 (Building and Loan Associations) (June 2009) available at www.nber.org/papers/w16244 (last visited July 12, 2013).
272 Ibid. at 9–10.
273 Ibid. at 11–12.
274 Kenneth A. Snowden, Mortgage Securitization in the United States: Twentieth Century Developments in Historical Perspective, in, *Anglo-American Financial Systems: Institutions and Markets in the Twentieth Century*, 261, 283–4 (Michael D. Bordo and Richard Sylla eds., 1995, Irwin Professional Publishing). New York authorized the incorporation of mortgage guarantee companies in 1885. Until 1904, however, New York law limited those companies to insuring against defects of title. Ibid. at 283.
275 Ibid. at 284.
276 Ibid. at 285.
277 Ibid.
278 Ibid. at 287.
279 Snowden, *supra* note 271, at 15–18.
280 Ibid. at 13–14, 19.
281 Chancellor, *supra* note 2, at 198–9. Chancellor cites one study that estimates that over sixty of margin loans were provided directly by corporations. Ibid. at 199 citing Barrie A. Wigmore, *The Crash and Its Aftermath: A History of Securities Markets in the United States, 1929–1933*, 94 (1985, Praeger). According to another historian, "call loans" for stock speculation rose from approximately $1 billion in the early years of the decade to $6 billion by 1929. Fraser, *supra* note 134, at 388.
282 Fraser, *supra* note 134, at 387–8, 394.
283 E.g., Paul G. Mahoney, The Stockpools and the Securities Exchange Act, 51 *Journal of Financial Economics* 343 (1999) (questioning whether stock pools were manipulative and arguing that political motivations drove passage of federal securities statute).
284 Chancellor, *supra* note 2, at 201–3. See also Burton G. Malkiel, *A Random Walk Down Wall Street*, 47–9 (1999, W.W. Norton & Company, Inc.) (describing instances of investment pooling and short selling prior to the 1929 crash). For a scholarly account of the Pecora hearings that lays out both abuses uncovered, as well as practices by financial firms that were legal yet nonetheless gave the Roosevelt administration political ammunition for New Deal reforms, see Joel Seligman, *The Transformation of Wall Street*, 21–38 (3rd ed. 2003, Aspen Publishers).
285 Fraser, *supra* note 134, at 388.
286 For a description of financial fraud and scandal in the 1920s, bracketed by the collapse of Charles Ponzi's scheme in 1920 and the trial of Charles Mitchell after the Great Crash, see Fraser, *supra* note 134, at 388–9, 421–2, 427–32.
287 For an overview of economic reform in the New Deal and how it failed to realize "fully the objectives of the Street's harshest critics," see Fraser, *supra* note 134, at 459–71.
288 Ch. 38, 48 Stat. 74 (current version at 15 U.S.C. §§ 77a–77aa (2000)).
289 Ch. 404, 48 Stat. 881 (current version at 15 U.S.C. §§ 78a–78lll (2000)).
290 Ch. 411, 53 Stat. 1149 (current version at 15 U.S.C. § 77aaa et seq.)
291 See 76 Pub. L. 768, 76–768.
292 Ch. 686, title II, Sec. 201, 54 Stat. 847.
293 See, e.g., Seligman, *supra* note 284, at 70–2 (describing compromises in, and criticism of, Securities Act of 1933).
294 See ibid. at 562 (success of disclosure provisions of Securities Act of 1933 and Securities Exchange Act of 1934). See e.g., 15 U.S.C. §§ 77k [Section 11 of the

Securities Act], 78J [Section 10b of the Securities Exchange Act] (examples of civil liability provisions in 1933 and 1934 Acts).

295   Ch. 687, 49 Stat. 838 (current version at 15 U.S.C. §§ 79 to 79z-6 (2000)).

296   Karmel, *supra* note 239, at 850–6.

297   Fraser, *supra* note 134, at 463.

298   Banking Act of 1933, ch. 89, 48 Stat. 162, repealed in part by Gramm-Leach-Bliley Act of 1999, Pub. L. No. 106–102, § 101, 113 Stat. 1338.

299   For a history, see Charles W. Calomiris and Eugene N. White, The Origins of Federal Deposit Insurance, in *The Regulated Economy: A Historical Approach to Political Economy*, 145 (Claudia Dale Goldin and Gary D. Libecap eds. 1994, University of Chicago Press).

300   David C. Wheelock, National Monetary Policy by Regional Design: The Evolving Role of the Federal Reserve Banks in Federal Reserve System Policy, Federal Reserve Bank St. Louis, *Working Paper 1998–010B* (January 1999) available at http://research.stlouisfed.org/wp/1998/1998-010.pdf (last visited July 12, 2013).

301   Act of June 26, 1934, 86 Pub. L. 354, 48 Stat. 1216.

302   See 84 Pub. L. 35, 48 Stat. 847.

303   Federal Home Loan Bank Act of 1932, 72 Pub. L. 304, 47 Stat. 725. See generally Adam Ashcraft, Morten L. Bech, and W. Scott Frame, The Federal Home Loan Bank System: The Lender of Next-to-Last Resort? 42 *Journal of Money, Credit and Banking* 551 (2010). See also Snowden, *supra* note 271, at 20–8 (describing emergence of regulatory structure for federal home loan banks, federal savings and loan associations, Federal Housing Authority, and Federal National Mortgage Association (the predecessor of Fannie Mae)).

304   See 73 Pub. L. 416, 48 Stat. 1064.

305   The existence of a long regulatory cycle between the New Deal and the 1990s does not imply that U.S. financial markets experienced no bubbles, regulatory stimulus, or frauds in the intervening decades. It only means that the patterns that weave through this chapter were not as pronounced. The 1960s boom in U.S. conglomerate stocks serves as but one example of regulatory stimulus, backlash, and fraud during a bubble in this long post-war "quiet" period.

In a harbinger of the SEC's fight against earnings management in the 1990s, the mania for conglomerates in that decade gave rise to, and fed off, a number of deceptive accounting practices that companies used to inflate earnings. For a primer on these accounting techniques, see Malkiel, *supra* note 284, at 62–9; see also Andrew Tobias, *The Funny Money Game* (1971, Playboy Press). These practices became the subject of extensive securities fraud litigation after the stock prices of many conglomerates crashed. Securities fraud litigation involving one of the most prominent conglomerates, National Student Marketing Corporation, led to a seminal decision on the liability of outside counsel for aiding and abetting securities fraud. See *SEC v. Nat'l Student Mktg. Corp.*, 457 F. Supp. 682, 701, 714–15 (D.D.C. 1978).

Although the SEC expressed concern about these practices, it made concerted attempts to regulate them only after the crash in conglomerate stock prices. Malkiel, *supra* note 284, at 67. See also David L. Western, *Booms, Bubbles and Busts in US Stock Markets*, 108–9 (2004, Routledge) (describing political resistance to regulation of financial markets during this time). Fraudulent schemes during this period benefitted from a period of looser enforcement of the securities laws by the SEC dating back to the Eisenhower administration. James Burk, *Values in the Marketplace: The American Stock Exchange Under Federal Securities Law*, 103 (1988, Walter De Gruyter) (arguing that the "fiscal evisceration" of the SEC and the "recession of strict federal oversight" of the capital markets under the Eisenhower administration led to "an efflorescence of fraudulent stock issues and speculative trading abuses"). The Department of Justice and the Federal Trade Commission did not intervene in the mergers of the conglomerate wave because officials narrowly read their statutory authority and concluded that it did not extend to conglomerate mergers. James R. Williamson, *Federal Antitrust Policy during the Kennedy-Johnson Years*, 36 (1995, Greenwood Publishing).

After the crash of conglomerate stocks and the stocks of other "hot" companies, the SEC responded to the pervasive use of deceptive accounting practices that had been used to inflate the post-merger earnings of conglomerates. That agency implemented a host of accounting rules, including requirements that corporations report earnings on a "fully diluted" basis in their securities filings. Malkiel, *supra* note 284, at 65, 67. The SEC also enacted an array of broker–dealer regulations. It launched a broad investigation of the American Exchange in an effort to crack down on market manipulation schemes that had run rampant during the conglomerate boom. Western, *supra*, at 109–10. In 1968, the Federal Trade Commission announced that it would investigate the conglomerate merger wave. Malkiel, *supra* note 284, at 67.

306 For a discussion of the Japanese "style of regulation," see Robert A. Kagan, Introduction: Comparing National Styles of Regulation in Japan and the United States, 22 *Law and Policy* 225 (2000). See also Ulrike Schaede, Change and Continuity in Japanese Regulation, *Berkeley Roundtable on International Economics Working Paper No. 66* (1994).

307 Curtis J. Milhaupt and Geoffrey P. Miller, Cooperation, Conflict, and Convergence in Japanese Finance: Evidence from the "Jusen" Problem, 29 *Law and Policy in International Business* 1 (1997).

308 Ibid. at 6. See also Schaede, *supra* note 306.

309 Milhaupt and Miller, *supra* note 307, at 24–35.

310 Ibid. at 10–24. See also Schaede, *supra* note 306 (describing Japanese financial regulation as "consultative capitalism"); Curtis J. Milhaupt and Geoffrey P. Miller, Regulatory Failure and the Collapse of Japan's Home Mortgage Lending Industry, 22 *Law and Policy* 245, 248–60 (2000).

311 See Chancellor, *supra* note 2, at 289–94, 300–3.

Chapter 6 details how deregulation allowed a number of feedback loops to form. For example, *jusen* borrowed from agricultural cooperatives and loaned money to real estate ventures. Real estate speculation enriched Japanese farmers who sold their land and then invested the proceeds back into cooperatives. Chapter 6, "Japan." Chapter 5 describes how *zaitech*, or financial engineering, allowed other powerful feedback loops to form in stock and real estate speculation. Chapter 5, notes 14–28.

In addition to the dynamics outlined in Chapters 5 and 6, real estate speculation was spurred by yet another regulatory feedback loop. The 1987 Basel I Accord among international bank regulators in G-10 nations fueled bank real estate lending in an indirect, but powerful way. The Accord aimed to raise the standards for bank regulatory capital in each of the participating nations. The drafters of the Basel I Accord made a key concession to Japanese banks that allowed them to count a portion of their equity investments in other companies as regulatory capital. This means that as the Japanese stock market inflated, Japanese banks enjoyed higher levels of regulatory capital, freeing them to invest more funds in real estate or stocks. A feedback loop developed, because the value of company shares in Japan was increasingly driven by the property holdings of firms. When banks increased real estate lending, property values surged. This, in turn, increased both the value of company shares owned by banks and banks' regulatory capital. This feedback loop left Japanese banks with dangerously low regulatory capital when share and real estate prices crashed. Chancellor, *supra* note 2, at 293–4.

312 Chapter 5, note 17 and accompanying text.

313 Chancellor, *supra* note 2, at 305–9.

314 Ibid.

315 Chancellor, *supra* note 2, at 298–9 (describing "Recruit Cosmos" scandal).

316 Chancellor, *supra* note 2, at 305–8.

317 Chancellor, *supra* note 2, at 305.

318 Kazuo Tsuda, Japanese Banks in Deregulation and the Economic Bubble, 22 *Japanese Economic Studies* 122, 152–3 (May/June/August 1994) (extensive government bond issuances in 1970s created pressure for financial deregulation).

319 See, e.g., Assaf Razin and Steven Rosefielde, Currency and Financial Crises of the 1990s and 2000s, National Bureau of Economic Research, *Working Paper No. 16*, 754 (February 2011) available at http://papers.ssrn.com/sol3/papers.cfm?abstract_id=1754907 (last visited July 12, 2013).

320 Milhaupt and Miller, *supra* note 310, 276–7.

321 Ibid. at 277.

322 Ibid. at 278.

323 Ibid. at 278–9.

324 For a history of this period, see Thomas F. Cargill, Michael M. Hutchison, and Takatoshi Ito, *Financial Policy and Central Banking in Japan* (2001, MIT Press).

325 Pub. L. No. 104-104, 110 Stat. 56 (1996).

326 Om Malik, *Broadbandits: Inside the $750 Billion Telecom Heist*, 163–4 (2003, John Wiley & Sons).

327 Charles B. Goldfarb, Telecommunications Act: Competition, Innovation, and Reform, in *Telecommunications Act: Competition, Innovation, and Reform*, 1, 8 (Charles B. Goldfarb ed. 2006, Nova Science Publishers Inc.).

328 Ibid. at 8–9.

329 Malik, *supra* note 326, at 163–80, 185.

330 Ibid. at 171.

331 Ibid. at 169.

332 Ibid. at 173–9.

333 Ibid. at 178.

334 Simon Romero and Riva D. Atlas, WorldCom's Collapse: The Overview; WorldCom Files for Bankruptcy; Largest U.S. Case, *New York Times*, July 22, 2002, at A1.

335 Shawn Young, MCI to State Fraud was $11 Billion: Financial Restatement to Grow by Billions from Reversals in Accounting Practices, *Wall Street Journal*, March 12, 2004, at A3.

336 *U.S.* v. *Ebbers*, 458 F.3d 110 (2nd Cir. 2006) *cert. denied* 549 U.S. 1274 (2007).

337 For example, Global Crossing (the fourth largest in U.S. history at the time) and its executives settled private securities fraud lawsuits for several hundred million dollars. The company's chief executive and its outside law firm contributed approximately $30 million and $19.5 million, respectively, to the settlement. Gretchen Morgenson, Global Crossing Settles Suit on Losses, *New York Times*, March 20, 2004, at C1. The company also admitted to securities disclosure violations in a settlement with the Securities and Exchange Commission, in which three other executives agreed to pay fines. *SEC* v. *Thomas J. Casey et al.*, SEC Litigation Release No. 19, 179 (April 11, 2005).

     Executives of Qwest were convicted and sentenced to jail for insider trading. *U.S.* v. *Nacchio*, 555 F.3d 1234 (10th Cir. 2009) (reinstating conviction of chief executive) *cert. denied* 130 S. Ct. 54 (2009), rehearing denied 130 S. Ct. 784 (2009). The company itself settled a securities fraud suit with the SEC for U.S. $250 million. Carrie Johnson, Qwest to Pay $250 Million in Fraud Probe, *Washington Post*, October 22, 2004, at E1.

     In another high profile telecom case, members of the family controlling Adelphia Communications were convicted of securities fraud in 2004. Brooke A. Masters and Ben White, Adelphia Founder, Son Convicted of Fraud, *Washington Post*, July 9, 2004, at E1.

338 For a summary of federal energy deregulation from the 1970s through the 1990s, see Henderson and Cudahy, *supra* note 241, at 79–83.

339 Pub. L. No. 102–486, 106 Stat. 2776.
340 See Henderson and Cudahy, *supra* note 241, at 81–2.
341 Ibid.
342 Ibid. at 82.
343 Ibid. citing Order 888, Promoting Wholesale Competition Through Open Access Non-Discriminatory Transmission Services by Public Utilities; Recovery of Stranded Costs by Public Utilities and Transmitting Utilities, [Regs. Preambles 1991–1996] F.E.R.C. STATS. & REGS. ¶ 31,036 (1996), 61 *Federal Register* 21,540 (1996) (codified at 18 C.F.R. pts. 35, 385).
344 See Henderson and Cudahy, *supra* note 241, at 82–3.
345 Ibid. at 83.
346 Ibid. at 83–90.
347 Ibid. at 89.
348 Ibid. at 85.
349 Ibid.
350 Ibid. at 86–9.
351 Richard J. Pierce, Jr., How Will the California Debacle Affect Energy Deregulation? 54 *Administrative Law Review* 389, 389–90, 394–5 (2002). See also ibid. at 392 (describing federal deregulation of wholesale markets).
352 See ibid. at 396–401. Professor Pierce calls allegations that the owner of the only natural gas pipeline into the state manipulated prices "plausible." Ibid. at 398.
353 For a detailed historical comparison of Enron with Insull's trusts, See Henderson and Cudahy, *supra* note 241.
354 See Western, *supra* note 305, at 102–3; John C. Coffee, Jr., Understanding Enron: "It's About the Gatekeepers, Stupid," 57 *Business Law* 1403, 1409–10 (2002).
355 Coffee, *supra* note 354, at 1409–10; Stephen Labaton, Now Who, Exactly, Got Us into This? *New York Times*, February 3, 2002, at B1, available at LEXIS, News Library, NYT File.
356 Pub. L. No. 104–67, 109 Stat. 737 (1995) (codified in scattered sections of 15 U.S.C. (2000)).
357 PSLRA sec. 101(b), § 21D(a) (codified as amended at 15 U.S.C. § 78u-4(a) (2000)); see Joel Seligman, Rethinking Private Securities Litigation, 73 *University of Cincinnati Law Review* 95, 105–6 (2004).
358 Sec. 101(b), § 21D(g)(2) (codified as amended at 15 U.S.C. § 78u-4(f)(2) (2000)); see Seligman, *supra* note 357, at 107.
359 Sec. 107 (amending 18 U.S.C. § 1964(c) (2000)).
360 Sec. 102(a), § 27A(c) (codified as amended at 15 U.S.C. § 77z-2(c) (2000)); see Seligman, *supra* note 357, at 106.
361 Pub. L. No. 105–353, sec. 101(a)(1), § 16(b), 112 Stat. 3227, 3228 (codified at 15 U.S.C. § 77p(b) (2000)); Coffee, *supra* note 354, at 1410.
362 Gramm-Leach-Bliley Act, Pub. L. No. 106–102, § 101, 113 Stat. 1338, 1341 (1999) (repealing 20 U.S.C. §§ 78, 377 (1994)).
363 See Floyd Norris, 3 Big Accounting Firms Assail S.E.C.'s Proposed Restrictions, *New York Times*, July 27, 2000, at C9, available at LEXIS, News Library, NYT File. Four accounting firms and the SEC under Levitt ultimately agreed to diluted regulations on auditor independence that imposed much milder restrictions on the non-audit services that accounting firms could provide to the clients whose financial statements they audited than were originally proposed. Floyd Norris, Accounting Firms Accept Rule to Limit Conflicts of Interest, *New York Times*, November 15, 2000, at A1, available at LEXIS, News Library, NYT File.
364 See Coffee, *supra* note 354, at 1411–12. For Levitt's own account of his efforts to reform accounting practices and auditor independence and the stiff resistance he faced due to the political influence of accounting firms, see Arthur Levitt with Paula

Dwyer, *Take on the Street*, 128–39 (2002, Pantheon Books) and Western, *supra* note 305, at 103.

365 See 501 U.S. 350, 359–61 (1991). The ruling bars any federal claims not filed by plaintiffs within one year of when they should have known of the alleged violation and in no event later than three years after the alleged violation. Ibid. at 360. See also Coffee, *supra* note 354, at 1409 and n.29.

366 See 511 U.S. 164, 176–8 (1994). See also Coffee, *supra* note 354, at 1409.

367 See, e.g., In re Donald J. Trump Casino Sec. Litig., 7 F.3d 357, 371 (3d Cir. 1993) ("[C]autionary language [in a prospectus], if sufficient, renders the alleged omissions or misrepresentations immaterial as a matter of law.").

368 E.g., *DiLeo* v. *Ernst & Young*, 901 F.2d 624, 627–28 (7th Cir. 1990) ("[P]laintiffs may not proffer the different financial statements and rest. Investors must point to some facts suggesting that the difference is attributable to fraud.").

369 See Marc I. Steinberg, Curtailing Investor Protection Under the Securities Laws: Good for the Economy? 55 *SMU Law Review* 347, 350–1 (2002); Lynn A. Stout, The Investor Confidence Game, 68 *Brooklyn Law Review* 407, 433 (2002). The Supreme Court created additional limitations in the 1990s on the ability of plaintiffs in private securities litigation to obtain relief. In *Gustafson* v. *Alloyd*, the Supreme Court limited liability under Section 12(a)(2) of the Securities Act to initial sales in connection with a statutory prospectus and thus precluded liability under that section for ordinary or secondary trading. 513 U.S. 561 (1995); Louis Loss and Joel Seligman, *Securities Regulation*, 4206–4220 (3d ed. 2004, Aspen Publishers).

370 Coffee, *supra* note 354, at 1410 and n.33.

371 For a small sample of the legal scholarship analyzing the Sarbanes-Oxley Act of 2002 and other regulatory reactions to the epidemic of fraud epitomized by the Enron scandal, see generally William W. Bratton, Enron, Sarbanes-Oxley and Accounting: Rules Versus Principles Versus Rents, 48 *Villanova Law Review* 1023 (2003) (criticizing the post-Enron focus on principle based accounting standards); Lawrence A. Cunningham, The Sarbanes-Oxley Yawn: Heavy Rhetoric, Light Reform (and It Just Might Work), 35 *Connecticut Law Review* 915 (2003) (arguing that despite being less profound than advertised, the Sarbanes-Oxley Act's sheer complexity may effect some worthwhile reform); Larry E. Ribstein, Market vs. Regulatory Responses to Corporate Fraud: A Critique of the Sarbanes-Oxley Act of 2002, 28 *Journal of Corporation Law* 1 (2003) (questioning whether the Sarbanes-Oxley Act will perform better than market forces in preventing fraud); Roberta Romano, The Sarbanes-Oxley Act and the Making of Quack Corporate Governance, 114 *Yale Law Journal* 1521 (2005); Robert B. Thompson and Hillary A. Sale, Securities Fraud as Corporate Governance: Reflections upon Federalism, 56 *Vanderbilt Law Review* 859 (2003) (listing the Sarbanes-Oxley Act as the latest evidence of the "federalization of corporate governance"); Jeffrey N. Gordon, Governance Failures of the Enron Board and the New Information Order of Sarbanes-Oxley, Columbia Law School Center for Law and Economics Studies, *Working Paper No. 216* (2003) available at http://papers.ssrn.com/abstract=391363 (last visited July 12, 2013) (criticizing provisions of Sarbanes-Oxley Act that require immediate "price-perfecting" disclosure of material corporate developments).

372 Sarbanes-Oxley Act of 2002, Pub. L. No. 107–204, § 302, 116 Stat. 745, 777 (codified at 15 U.S.C.S. § 7241 (LEXIS through Pub. L. No. 109–89)); Management's Reports on Internal Control over Financial Reporting and Certification of Disclosure in Exchange Act Periodic Reports, 68 *Federal Register* 36,636, 36,637 (June 18, 2003) (codified in scattered sections of 17 C.F.R. (2005)).

373 Sarbanes-Oxley Act sec. 301, § 10A(m) (codified at 15 U.S.C.S. § 78j-1(m) (LEXIS through Pub. L. No. 109–89)).

374 Ibid. § 101(a) (codified at 15 U.S.C.S. § 7211(a) (LEXIS through Pub. L. No. 109–89)).

375 Ibid. sec. 201(a), § 10A(g)–(h) (codified at 15 U.S.C.S. § 78j-1(g)–(h)); Strengthening the Commission's Requirements Regarding Auditor Independence, 68 *Federal Register* 6,006, 6,010 (February 5, 2003) (codified in scattered sections of 17 C.F.R. (2005)).

376 Standards of Professional Conduct for Attorneys, 68 *Federal Register* 6296 (codified at 17 C.F.R. pt. 205 (2005)).

377 See 17 C.F.R. § 242.501(a) (2005) (requiring securities analysts to certify that views expressed in research reports reflect personal views of the analyst and to disclose any compensation or payments received for specific recommendations); Order Approving Proposed Rule Changes by the New York Stock Exchange, Inc., 68 *Federal Register* 45,875 (August 4, 2003) (approving NASD and NYSE rule changes regarding security analyst conflicts of interest).

378 New York State Attorney General Eliot Spitzer launched a widely publicized investigation into the practices of stock analysts at major Wall Street firms. Spitzer's investigation found substantial evidence of analysts publicly touting the prospects of companies that they privately believed were not worthwhile investments in order to promote their firm's investment banking services to these companies. See John Cassidy, The Investigation, *New Yorker*, April 7, 2003, at 54, available at LEXIS, News Library, NEWYRK File; Affidavit of Eric R. Dinallo, *In re* Spitzer, No. 02-401522 (New York Supreme Court April 8, 2002), at 3, available at www.ag.ny. gov/sites/default/files/press-releases/archived/MerrillL.pdf (last visited July 12, 2013). This investigation culminated in a settlement where, without admitting guilt, Merrill Lynch and other large investment banks agreed to institute a system of firewalls to insulate their securities analysts from influence by their investment banking businesses and to pay multimillion dollar fines. Cassidy, *supra*.

379 The SEC entered into a settlement agreement with two investment banks that advised Enron on a series of transactions that according to the SEC, "helped Enron mislead its investors by characterizing what were essentially loan proceeds as cash from operating activities." Press Release, SEC, SEC Settles Enforcement Proceedings against J.P. Morgan Chase and Citigroup (July 28, 2003), www.sec.gov/news/press/2003-87.htm (last visited July 12, 2013). These banks agreed to pay $255 million in fines to investors. See ibid. Although neither bank admitted guilt, limiting the precedential value of this settlement, this settlement serves as a warning of the SEC's intention to prosecute advisors of public corporations who help construct transactions designed to mislead investors.

To some extent, judicial "deregulation" also reversed course in the aftermath of the fraud epidemic. For example, a prominent ruling in the Enron litigation has held that secondary actors – including lawyers and accountants – may be held liable as primary participants in securities fraud if plaintiffs can prove these secondary actors had requisite knowledge that misrepresentations authored by these actors would be used to mislead investors. Quoting the SEC's brief, the court stated:

> [W]hen a person, acting alone or with others, creates a misrepresentation [on which the investor-plaintiffs relied], the person can be liable as a primary violator ... if ... he acts with the requisite scienter. Moreover it would not be necessary for a person to be the initiator of a misrepresentation in order to be a primary violator. Provided that a plaintiff can plead and prove scienter, a person can be a primary violator if he or she writes misrepresentations for inclusion in a document to be given to investors, even if the idea for those misrepresentations came from someone else.

> In re Enron Corp. Sec., Derivative & ERISA Litig., 235 F. Supp. 2d 549, 692–3 (S.D. Tex. 2002) (citations omitted) (alterations in original)

This ruling thus sidestepped the Supreme Court's ruling in *Central Bank of Denver* v. *First Interstate Bank of Denver*, 511 U.S. 164, 191 (1991), that precluded "aiding and abetting" liability under Rule 10b-5 actions. See *supra* note 366 and accompanying text. If a wide number of other courts adopt this reasoning, then the scope of *Central Bank of Denver* would be dramatically limited. For reactions from the securities bar and legal scholars on this case, see Kurt Eichenwald, A Higher Standard for Corporate Advice, *New York Times*, December 23, 2002, at A1, available at LEXIS, News Library, NYT File.

Part II

The Regulatory Instability Hypothesis

3 Boom, bust, and the regulatory stimulus cycle in financial markets

Introduction

Chapter 2 reveals a clear historical pattern of deregulation and other regulatory stimulus during the rise of bubbles followed by a sharp regulatory backlash after bubbles implode. This regulatory stimulus cycle represents the first component of the Regulatory Instability Hypothesis.

What explains these recurrent phenomena? Why does the rise of asset price bubble coincide with regulatory stimulus? How does regulatory stimulus contribute to the formation of bubbles? For legal scholars, the more interesting questions may be whether and how bubbles generate regulatory stimulus. Regulatory backlash in the wake of a bubble seems more intuitive. However, can the same theory that explains the causes of regulatory stimulus also explain this aftermath? Can a theory of political economy account for the existence of regulatory cycles in financial markets, such as the cycle of regulatory stimulus, bubble, crash, and backlash that occurred roughly every ten years in nineteenth century Britain? A good theory of political economy should also help explain or predict the different forms that regulatory stimulus and backlash assume.

A number of behavioral finance economists have identified parts of this pattern of regulatory stimulus and backlash. Yet, in the words of one of them, "a full model of economics and politics of bubbles remains to be built."[1] This chapter outlines three models to explain changes in the supply and demand for regulatory stimulus before and after bubbles: a public choice model that analyzes the rational calculus of interest groups and policymakers; a second model (a refinement of the first) based on behavioral biases of market participants and policymakers; and a final model that focuses on deeper shifts in political ideologies and social norms.

In each of these models, financial and political markets generate powerful feedback for one another. Booming markets create strong demand and ideal conditions for the further liberalization of regulatory regimes, as this chapter will explain. At the same time, deregulation or other regulatory stimulus of financial markets fuels speculation and booming prices in financial markets. Market crashes, in turn, create strong demand for a regulatory reaction, which dampen investment further.

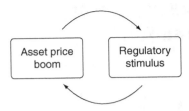

Figure 3.1 The regulatory stimulus cycle.

The potential for feedback between financial and political markets makes untangling cause and effect difficult. In some cases, scholars have found that deregulation of a country's financial services sector or government subsidies of markets created an asset price bubble. Economists have provided both theoretical models and empirical studies of how the liberalization of regulations governing financial institutions and markets can spark credit booms and bubbles.[2] Studies of particular bubble episodes also indicate a causal link between regulation and asset price bubbles. For example, economists have argued that government liberalization of bond markets and banking triggered the rise in Japanese real estate prices in the 1980s.[3] Deeper in the past, the Mississippi bubble likely never would have begun but for John Law receiving extraordinary powers from the French monarchy to securitize the national debt and colonial trade revenues and to print money.[4]

In other cases, it appears that booming markets triggered particular deregulatory events or other forms of regulatory stimulus. The repeal of the Bubble Act came at the tail end of the English railway mania and shortly before the Panic of 1825. The debate in Parliament over repeal focused on how legislators were inundated by requests for private bills to grant corporate charters for new railroad lines. This set the stage for the liberalization of corporate law.[5]

In examining the historical link between deregulation and market bubbles, the old adage, "correlation does not imply causation," bears repeating. In many historical cases, it appears that some underlying cause – industrialization, a new technology, a macroeconomic shift, fundamental political or societal change – propelled both market boom and regulatory stimulus. Rapid industrialization and the development of railroad technologies helps explain England's string of bubbles that formed and crashed roughly every ten years throughout the nineteenth century (1825, 1837, 1847, 1857, 1866...). Industrialization and technological change also explain the surging demand for charters from Parliament for railway corporations during those periods.[6] Industrialization and railroads came later to the United States, Germany, and Austria, where they fueled regulatory stimulus and bubbles, as the previous chapter detailed.[7]

For another example of technological change driving both bubble and regulatory change, consider telecommunications in the United States in the 1990s. The advent of cable television, cell phones, and the internet created enormous investment opportunities in those new technologies. At the same time, this technological shift rendered the decades-old U.S. regulatory architecture for telecommunications obsolete and spurred calls for new legislation. This resultant Telecommunications Act of 1996 served as a regulatory stimulus for an investment boom in telecom companies.[8]

Even if it is difficult to make simple claims that regulatory stimulus caused a boom or bubble or vice versa, a more fundamental insight remains: regulatory stimulus (including deregulation) and market bubbles reinforce one another in powerful ways. Reinforcement in one direction is clear: looser regulation or more government subsidies for financial markets lowers the costs and constraints on financial investment. These legal changes reduce the "regulatory tax" on, or provide subsidies to, investments in, or loans for, a particular asset class. Consider the following small historical sample culled from the previous chapter:

- corporate charters and state-granted monopolies allowed entrepreneurs and shareholders to reap enormous rewards in bubbles in England from the 1690s well into the nineteenth century;[9]
- more permissive rules on incorporation enabled the explosive growth of new joint-stock companies in 1870s Germany;[10]
- outright government loans and donations of land fueled railroad booms in the U.S. Gilded Age;[11]
- new bank charters and regulatory expansion of banking powers fueled real estate and stock speculation in the Roaring Twenties in the United States;[12] and
- legal changes that reduced securities law liability contributed to a boom in stock issuances in the United States at the end of the 1990s.[13]

This sample underscores once again that regulatory stimulus can assume many forms. Yet Chapter 2 argued that no matter the form – whether policymakers repeal a regulatory tax, lower efforts to enforce or collect the tax, or provide a subsidy or legal preference – the effect on investment in an asset market is similar.[14] The form that the regulatory subsidy takes often matters less than the particular kind of investment on which it operates. Indeed, changes in legal rules (or the enforcement of rules) that allow banks to lend more, lend against less collateral, and become more leveraged can have particularly dramatic effects on asset prices and financial markets. Chapter 9 examines these effects in greater detail. Regulatory changes can also have secondary effects. The initial upswing in investment sparked by regulatory stimulus may trigger positive feedback investment. Investors may confuse the effects of one-time changes in the regulatory environment with signals of a lasting change in the fundamentals of particular asset classes.

This chapter focuses on reinforcement in the opposite direction, that is, how market booms or bubbles can promote deregulation and other forms of regulatory stimulus. The chapter also examines how market crashes generate regulatory backlash. To analyze the effect of booming and crashing financial markets on political markets, the chapter constructs three rough models or lenses to explain the factors contributing to regulatory stimulus and backlash.[15]

First, the chapter creates a model of regulation and deregulation that assumes market players and regulators rationally maximize their self-interest. This analysis borrows heavily from public choice scholarship, but also from a broader literature in political science and sociology on the problem of capture.

This chapter then constructs a second behavioral model of regulation during market booms. (This move from rational to behavioral models roughly parallels two economic schools of thought on the formation of bubbles discussed in Chapter 1.) In this model, as markets boom and memories of past financial crises fade, the cognitive limitations of investors and regulators create ideal conditions for financial liberalization and government stimulus of markets. These same limitations and behavioral biases shape the regulatory backlash in the wake of a market crash.

Third, and finally, the chapter looks at how market booms can both trigger and reflect a broader shift in political ideologies and social norms. This third model or lens examines how movements – among market participants, political elites, regulators, and the broader public – that champion the political ideals of economic liberalism and market-oriented social norms can promote greater deregulation. At times, these shifts support "crony capitalism," in which free-market ideals are perverted.

Each model or lens explains some facets and examples of the historical pattern of regulatory stimulus and backlash better than others. The chapter inspects the limitations of each of the three approaches. The end of this chapter looks at the ways in which the three models overlap; the dynamics of interest group politics, cognitive limitations, and ideological changes often resist easy separation and can reinforce one another in powerful ways.

In looking at the pattern of deregulation and government stimulation during booms and regulatory backlash during busts, this chapter looks at both sides of a "market" for regulation: the public that demands legal rules (and changes to those rules) and "policymakers" or "regulators" who supply these rules. This is a fairly coarse distinction; market participants often govern themselves, for example through private ordering, and laws constrain the behavior of public officials, not just private actors. (Furthermore, the use of the term "market" carries with it certain normative overtones.) The overriding point, however, is that both groups – the regulated and the regulators – need to be disaggregated. The regulated public include an array of interest groups, including entrepreneurs in booming markets, their competitors in both new and dying industries, investors (institutional, retail, sophisticated, and naive), and financial institutions of various sizes and regulatory status. Each of these groups has differing (sometimes overlapping) interests, economic and political resources, and degrees of political cohesion. Regulators, likewise, include an assortment of characters: legislators and other elected officials, unelected officials in government ministries and agencies, judges, prosecutors, and even private actors to whom regulatory functions have been delegated (such as credit rating agencies).

The regulated and the regulators interact in institutional contexts that vary greatly according to country and historical moment. The context affects the scope of the respective powers of the regulated and the regulators, the various legal and extralegal constraints on those powers, and their incentives. However, focusing on the institutional (or political or social) context may not explain the recurrent historical pattern of regulatory stimulus during rising bubbles and regulatory backlash after collapse. Indeed, the historical bubble periods surveyed in Chapter 2 were chosen in large part to show how this pattern held in very different legal and political systems, ranging from seventeenth century England to late twentieth century Japan. Some bubbles were chosen to provide points of comparison in the same historical era (the Mississippi versus South Sea bubbles *circa* 1719–1720 and the twin U.S. and German bubbles that imploded in the Panic of 1873).

To explain this recurrent pattern, the three models in this chapter first work to establish overarching theories of the primary influences on the decisions of both regulated and regulators. The analysis then drills down to how these decisions change in different contexts and for different types of actors. One of the more important dimensions of variation is the precise form that regulatory stimulus can take (repeal of written legal rules, exemptions and interpretations of rules, laxer enforcement, failure to adapt legal rules, government subsidies of financial markets, etc.). Here, the legal institutions and political context in which a bubble takes place matter intensely. The forms of regulatory stimulus and backlash depend on the institutions and rules already in place. Predictions on the form that regulatory stimulus and backlash take also vary according to which of the three models is used.

At the same time, the three models yield some common predictions. On a basic level, each predicts a perverse cyclical pattern of regulatory stimulus as markets boom and regulatory backlash only after a crash has occurred. Each model also predicts that political forces may cause regulatory backlash not only to be mistimed, but frequently off-target as well. However, even regulatory reactions that address the causes of a bubble and financial crisis lose political support with the lapse of time. This sets the stage for the cycle to turn and policymakers and interest groups to start a fresh round of regulatory stimulus during the next market boom.

The following provides a roadmap to this chapter. First, the chapter outlines the rational actor/public choice model of deregulation during boom times. On the demand side, this first model looks at how market booms upset the political equilibrium among interest groups, empowering interest groups that would benefit from regulatory stimulus. On the supply side, the first model describes various dynamics that cause rational policymakers and regulators to support regulatory stimulus. The discussion of this first model highlights the problem of diluted enforcement, in which the rising volume of market transactions during a bubble overwhelms even conscientious regulators. The analysis then turns to various games that interest groups and regulators play with respect to regulatory stimulus. The discussion of the first model ends with its predictions for the shape regulatory backlash should assume after a market crash.

The chapter then describes a behavioral model of the same phenomenon: regulatory stimulus during booms and backlash during busts. After outlining how behavioral biases might shape the decisions of regulators and interest groups, the analysis shifts gears to consider an interesting concept by law professor Amitai Aviram. Aviram argues that policy entrepreneurs engage in "bias arbitrage"; policymakers earn political capital by exploiting the difference between public underestimations (or overestimations) of risk and actual risk. This notion of bias arbitrage proves useful not because it helps predict behavior in financial markets in bubble periods. Instead, it is illuminating because of the differences between its assumptions and how the market for financial regulation actually operates during booms and busts. Like financial arbitrage, this bias arbitrage fails to correct asset price bubbles, not least because of deep imperfections in political markets. The discussion of the behavioral model concludes by looking at how these imperfections can distort the regulatory backlash in the aftermath of a burst bubble. These distortions, in turn, sow the seeds for future deregulation and the turning of the regulatory cycle anew.

The chapter then uses a third model (or set of lenses) to examine regulatory stimulus and backlash during bubble times. This third part looks at how ideological shifts – particularly the rise of economic liberalism – have accompanied various bubble periods. This discussion examines how shifts in social norms can facilitate the purchase and sale of regulatory stimuli in political markets. At their worst, changes in social norms can cause government to deform and devolve into crony capitalism. The chapter concludes by evaluating the strengths and weaknesses of the three models, as well as areas in which they overlap.

A rational model

The first model looks to predict the behavior of the regulated and the regulators by assuming that both groups consist of rational actors who maximize their self-interest. Each actor, in deciding whether to push for or against a particular regulatory change, conducts an analysis of her private costs and benefits. What benefits would she expect to enjoy and costs would she foreseeing incurring if she pushed for or opposed regulatory change? What would be her expected benefits and costs should the change actually take place? To simplify the analysis, the model looks first at the "demand" for regulation. How do market booms alter the calculus of the "regulated" in deciding whether to push for (or oppose) regulatory stimulus?

The model then turns to the "supply" of regulation by various types of regulators and policymakers and examines how booms can change their decision-making as well. The model next focuses on the problem of diluted enforcement; a tidal wave of market transactions during a boom can overwhelm even conscientious regulators. The analysis then describes various iterative games that regulated and the regulators play with one another, with "precedent" providing a focal point for negotiation. These games help predict the relative prevalence of different forms of regulatory stimulus. The discussion of the rational model concludes by looking at its predictions for regulatory backlash.

The demand for deregulation and regulatory stimulus: public choice during booms

Prolonged market booms increase the demand for deregulation and other forms of regulatory stimulus by providing discrete interest groups with greater incentives and economic resources to push for regulatory stimulus. Thus, these groups have both the motive and the means to obtain greater deregulation, lower enforcement, and increased government subsidies. These interest groups consist primarily of the promoters of business ventures in booming markets who seek to sell assets and maximize their profits. These groups also include financial institutions that seek to lend, invest, or underwrite investments in those markets. These groups have an interest in lowering the regulatory limitations imposed on their activities and the regulatory "taxes" levied on their profits. They also have an incentive to seek regulatory preferences and government subsidies that afford them advantages over competitors, including new entrants to a market. When asset price booms begin to generate substantial economic gains for the broader investing public, they also create broader political support for continued regulatory stimulus that will keep the party going.

What upsets the political equilibrium? Where is the opposition?

This broad overview of the effects of market booms on demand for deregulation and other regulatory stimulus leaves a number of questions unanswered. First, *what sparks the initial regulatory stimulus?* What overcomes the powerful political inertia that favors the status quo? In a related vein, *why do interest groups that favor regulatory stimulus prevail over interest groups opposed to this regulatory change?*

To answer these two related questions, public choice theory (sometimes called the "economic theory" of regulation) provides a valuable analytical framework.[16] Public choice looks at regulatory change through the lens of the competition of various interest groups in the political marketplace. Interest groups win not necessarily because they have more at stake in a particular regulatory decision. Rather, they succeed because they can overcome collective action challenges and pool group resources to influence the political process. Public choice theory provides a key insight: cohesive and organized groups can extract benefits from the government at the expense of more diffuse groups *even* if the losses to the diffuse groups dwarf the gains to the well organized.[17] According to this theory, net social loss or gain does not determine the course of public policy. Instead, under the right conditions, private interest groups can overcome collective action challenges and commandeer state resources to siphon off social wealth for private rents.[18]

To predict when this occurs, it is therefore important to measure not only the relative economic resources of various interest groups, but their political cohesiveness as well. The few can beat the many in the political marketplace.[19] Note that one can use this particular lens to evaluate the production of regulation without necessarily making more extreme claims that *all* regulations benefit only narrow interest groups and therefore have questionable legitimacy.[20]

Public choice theories can explain not only increased regulation, but also deregulation, as this chapter will demonstrate. The early public choice literature used this logic to answer the question of "why this particular regulation?" Less work has been done to explain "why this particular deregulation?" although a handful of economists have made compelling arguments that the same basic rubric applies.[21]

SHOCKS AND THE INTEREST GROUP EQUILIBRIUM

What upsets the political equilibrium to trigger the kinds of massive regulatory stimuli described in the previous chapter? Many of those historical episodes point to a common answer: an external shock upends the extant political balance among interest groups.[22] This shock to the political marketplace resembles the "displacements" that trigger bubbles according to behavioral finance models.[23] Indeed, the external shock to political and financial markets may be the same event. A political entrepreneur often plays a central role in translating a displacement into the formation of an interest group and that group gaining political influence.[24]

England's eighteenth and nineteenth century bubbles were sparked in part by technological and economic shocks. The initial success of the French Mississippi bubble and the need to finance expanding trade routes sparked England's South Sea bubble in the early eighteenth century.[25] The advent of railways, industrialization, and investment opportunities in the New World set off a cycle of bubbles every ten years in nineteenth century Britain.[26] These shocks did more than fuel a market boom. They also altered the political landscape and empowered new interest groups, namely the promoters of ventures in emerging industries. For example, the emergence of railways in England in the middle of the eighteenth century provided an overwhelming economic threat to canal companies. One of the ways in which railway companies overcame this entrenched group of rivals was by purchasing canals.[27]

Japan in the late 1970s and 1980s provides a more modern and complex example. There, one set of external shocks came in the form of macroeconomic changes: oil shocks, rising public debt, slowing economic growth.[28] These macroeconomic shocks made government caps on bond interest rates and other restrictions on bond markets untenable.[29] Another shock came from external political pressure; the United States urged Japan to liberalize its financial services sector to address trade imbalances and the strong U.S. dollar and to allow foreign competition to enter.[30] Together, these macroeconomic and foreign policy shocks gave Japanese financial firms the incentive and political power to call for liberalizing the regulatory regime governing bond markets.[31] Looser regulations on securities firms then triggered a political cascade. After losing corporate customers to capital markets, Japanese banks pushed for deregulation of their own corner of the financial services industry.[32] Financial liberalization took place in the unique Japanese regulatory environment, in which regulators negotiated with "regulatory cartels" comprising various segments of the Japanese financial services industry.[33]

In these examples, the external shock upset the interests, resources, and alliances of existing groups. It increased the incentives and political cohesion of one interest group to push for regulatory change (for example, railroad promoters in England and securities firms in Japan). Economic shocks have also weakened existing interest groups. Dying industries, like canals, horse coaches, and turnpikes in nineteenth century Britain and the United States, lacked the resources to compete with booming railway industries in the political marketplace.[34]

THE CORPORATE FORM IN THE POLITICAL MARKETPLACE

It is no accident that regulatory stimulus often took the form of granting corporate charters or liberalizing the incorporation process. The use of the corporate form gave promoters not only economic advantages, but political ones as well. The prospects of accessing shareholder capital increased the incentives of promoters to use political influence to obtain corporate charters. Shareholder capital also expanded the resources that promoters could spend in obtaining political support for their ventures. In other words, "other people's money" could be used to purchase regulatory stimulus.[35]

Moreover, the centralization of decision-making authority that comes with the corporate form provides an automatic solution to the problem of organizing collective political action.[36] The boards and managers who run corporations can make decisions to invest in political causes far more easily than diffuse shareholders. The advantage of managers of large corporations in the political marketplace by virtue of their ability to pool shareholder funds assumed center stage in 2010 when the U.S. Supreme Court decided the *Citizens United* case.[37] Historical episodes in which the legal rules changed to facilitate incorporation thus reflect more than the effects of rising bubbles. In fact, liberalized incorporation can create conditions in political economy for certain corporate interest groups to lobby for regulatory stimulus far more effectively.

IF YOU CAN'T BEAT 'EM: FINANCIAL INDUSTRY CONSOLIDATION AND LIBERALIZATION

In some cases, cohesive interest groups have opposed regulatory changes that would threaten their business model or oligopoly position (which is, itself, often created or protected by regulation). However, this opposition can dissipate as relaxed regulations allow for industry consolidation. The steady erosion of the Glass-Steagall Act provides a case study. In the 1970s and 1980s, a series of regulatory interpretations by federal bank regulators allowed banks and bank holding companies to issue and deal in mortgage-backed securities.[38] Section 21 of the Glass-Steagall Act and provisions of the Bank Holding Company Act had previously restricted banks from engaging in this business.[39] The Securities

Industry of America unsuccessfully challenged these new interpretations in federal court in a bid to protect the turf of securities firms (which, at that point, were still statutorily separated from banks by Glass-Steagall).[40]

Even in a losing effort, the securities industry at least provided some opposition to deregulation that favored banks. However, this countervailing force – and any attendant benefits of interest group pluralism – dissipated with the steady erosion of Glass-Steagall's walls among financial industry sectors. After a tipping point was reached – and surely by the time Congress repealed the statute in 1999 – it made more sense for banks, securities firms, and insurance companies to enter each other's markets or merge with one another than to spend political resources to shore up these walls.[41] Among the more pernicious, but less understood effects of the Glass-Steagall repeal was the agglomeration of political power that came with financial consolidation.[42] For all its many costs and weaknesses, legal segmentation of the financial services industry offered one considerable benefit: it created some semblance of political balance among competing industry interest groups.[43]

NO COHESIVE OPPOSITION: CONSUMERS AND RETAIL INVESTORS

This interest group pluralism utterly fails, however, when there is no cohesive interest group opposing financial liberalization or regulatory stimulus. Financial regulations that protect consumers have no cohesive, well-financed interest group champion.[44] The emergence of a few activist groups pushing for financial regulation in the wake of the current global crisis provides an exception that proves this rule.[45]

A similar dynamic characterizes the politics of certain shareholder protection rules. Regulatory changes that remove protections for retail investors, for example, pit cohesive interest groups (like securities issuers, company promoters, and financial institutions) against a diffuse investing public.[46] In recent decades in the United States, plaintiff law firms and institutional investors have provided some political interest group support for securities and corporate law rules that protect minority shareholders.[47] Even so, it is far from clear that these groups counterbalance industry groups pushing for diluting those rules. Moreover, both plaintiffs' attorneys and institutional investors present agency costs of their own, as the interests of the individuals running these groups can diverge from those of retail investors.[48]

THE SPECIAL CASE OF FINANCIAL INSTITUTION REGULATION

One of the most troubling political imbalances lies in the area of prudential banking regulations. When financial institutions seek to loosen prudential regulations – for example to take on more leverage – they may be increasing the systemic risk that they pose for financial markets.[49] When the government responds to a subsequent failure of firms by bailing out their shareholders or creditors, it externalizes the costs onto taxpayers.[50] Even if the government does *not* provide a bailout, financial firm failure might trigger a credit shock to the economy that still externalizes costs onto disparate borrowers, firms, and employees.[51] Thus, the loosening of regulations that mitigate the systemic risk of financial institutions pits the interest of concentrated groups of financial institutions against a very diffuse public.

At first blush, this political imbalance may seem no different from that in other areas, for example, environmental protection, where politically cohesive industries externalize the cost of pollution onto a diffuse public. The regulation of systemic risk by financial institutions, however, raises several problems of political economy not present in environmental law (or other fields). First, the negative externalities associated with financial institutions and systemic risk are more closely coupled with the very services that the public demands. The public wants financial institutions to take risks, extend credit, and provide capital. Too much of these good things, however, can put the government safety net at risk. In environmental law by contrast, there is a traditional tradeoff between the goods that firms provide (products, jobs, and economic growth) and negative externalities (pollution). No one wants dioxin. It is possible that technological advances or Coasean bargains can translate into more jobs without more pollution. But if financial markets are even somewhat efficient, it is hard to have more reward without more risk-taking.[52]

Second, financial markets are subject to cycles, as Chapter 1 described. One recurrent theme of this book and this chapter is the risk that metastasizes when the political cycle becomes too closely coupled with financial cycles. Booming markets and political support for regulatory stimuli mutually reinforce.

Third, environmental law has romance. In environmental issues, there is at least a semblance of interest group pluralism because environmental groups are deeply and ideologically committed to defending wildlife, protecting natural spaces, and fighting pollution.[53] A comparable civil society does not exist in the world of financial regulation, although scholars, like Claire Kelly, have written creatively about the possibility of one developing.[54] Yet, what would motivate citizens to join interest groups battling systemic risk, particularly in the context of hyper-technical financial rules? There is little romance (or psychic or social payoffs) for individuals participating in the process of financial regulation.[55]

THE STRUCTURE OF ADMINISTRATIVE LAW

Even if diffuse public groups could organize, the doctrines and architecture of administrative law may afford them little opportunity to participate in the regulatory process of administrative agencies.[56] In the United States, doctrines such as standing limit the ability of diffuse groups, such as taxpayers or the public at large, to participate in litigation or administrative adjudications.[57] More broadly, U.S. administrative law works to cabin agency power; forcing agencies to take action is not its primary purpose.[58] This creates a structural inclination against aggressive enforcement of financial regulation. It also militates against regulators using existing authority to regulate new financial products or practices.

COST–BENEFIT ANALYSIS, PROPHYLACTIC RULES, AND UNCERTAINTY

Other features of administrative law may frustrate the creation of prophylactic rules designed to protect investors and entire financial markets from emerging risks. U.S. federal law often requires that agencies conduct a cost–benefit analysis to justify new rules.[59] Public choice theory would suggest that concentrated interest groups have a greater ability than diffuse publics to supply agencies with data for this analysis. Moreover, these groups have greater ability to use the cost–benefit requirement to litigate against those rules that agencies ultimately issue.[60]

Against this backdrop, prophylactic rules may fare poorly. Rules designed to regulate new financial products or practices or to mitigate systemic risk may prove particularly vulnerable to challenge. On the one hand, concentrated industry groups can present hard costs associated with rules that constrain their practices and profits. On the other side of the equation, regulators may have difficulty quantifying the benefits to these rules, whether in the form of reduced systemic risk or otherwise. One never sees the crises that don't happen.

Regulators often regulate in the face of radical uncertainty about the risks that new financial products and markets may pose for investors and financial markets. Recent case law demonstrates how administrative law and the cost–benefit requirement have provided industry groups with numerous legal pressure points to challenge new financial rules. For example, the U.S. Securities and Exchange Commission has suffered a string of losses in the D.C. Circuit Court of Appeals over the last decade. That federal court invalidated a bevy of SEC rules that would have prophylactically regulated, among other matters, hedge fund registration, the composition of mutual fund boards, and proxy access by shareholders.[61]

BOOMING MARKETS, RISING TIDES, AND EXPANDING PIES

The observation that the public wants some level of financial institution risk-taking has crucial implications for regulatory stimulus during bubbles. Booming financial markets create economic gains for a broad swath of interest groups, as well as for the public generally. As the rising tide lifts many boats, even initial opponents of regulatory stimulus (for example, a category of financial institutions that is disadvantaged when deregulation makes a financial sector more competitive) may benefit from a reverberating financial boom. Moreover, when the public starts to enjoy investment gains from a bubble, it creates broad political support for policies that sustain the boom. The initial interest groups that support regulatory stimulus may then switch from an "inside" strategy of lobbying regulators to an "outside" strategy of shaping and mobilizing public opinion.[62]

Why do interest groups discount the costs of a bubble?

This last point highlights a deep and lingering question: do supporters of regulatory stimulus not consider the costs they would incur should a bubble collapse?

If they perceive the risk of a bubble, would that not deter them from seeking regulatory stimulus?

Perhaps interest groups supporting regulatory stimulus do not believe a bubble has formed. Alternatively, they may not see their pursuit of regulatory stimulus as contributing to a bubble. Even if they did see a link, they may conclude that their expected personal benefits from obtaining a regulatory stimulus outweigh their expected individual costs. The logic of collective action provides a cogent explanation: if a particular actor does not take advantage of regulatory stimulus (for example, obtaining a corporate charter or exemption from a bank rule), someone else will. That person will then enjoy greater investment returns.

If supporters of regulatory stimulus see the risk of a bubble, they may calculate that they can cash out before it collapses. Promoters of some bubble companies may believe they can protect gains earned during bubble times from regulators or shareholders seeking redress in the wake of a crash. Indeed, a host of factors may remove much of the sting of a bubble's collapse for persons and firms that lobbied for a regulatory stimulus. When benefits to regulatory stimulus come soon but costs are in the far future, the time value of money weighs in favor of taking action. Furthermore, the individuals pushing for regulatory stimulus often are managers of corporate entities. This creates agency costs; managers may not bear the full cost of their actions. Even if shareholders fault these individuals for pushing for regulatory stimulus, a host of rules may still insulate management from legal liability. These include corporate law mechanisms (such as the business judgment rule) that preserve managerial discretion and rules of criminal law (including the prohibition on *ex post facto* laws). More basically, absent graft or corruption, there may be no cause of action against management for pursuing regulatory stimulus.

Financial institution regulation provides another source of moral hazard that may encourage firms to seek regulatory stimulus. The moral hazard created by expected bailouts can make debt cheaper than equity for financial institutions.[63] This gives financial institutions and their creditors additional incentives to push for regulatory changes that externalize the costs of financial institution risk onto taxpayers.[64] This highlights a more fundamental lesson: whenever the costs of a regulatory stimulus can be externalized onto others, demand for regulatory stimulus increases.

The supply of deregulation and regulatory stimulus

In modeling regulatory change, it is important to look not just at the demand side (interest groups supporting or opposing regulatory stimulus), but at the supply side as well. What are the incentives of "regulators" either to enact regulatory change or to favor the status quo? What does the calculus of regulators look like as they decide whether to provide a regulatory stimulus? The answers to these questions reveal the levers that interest groups can use to influence regulators.

A close analysis of the supply side of regulatory stimulus explains how prolonged booms skew the rational calculus of policymakers and regulators towards supporting regulatory stimulus. Booms and well-resourced interest groups create immediate benefits for supporting stimulus and immediate costs to opposition. Meanwhile, several factors mitigate the risk of a regulator being blamed for a crisis. The following discussion initially applies to a generic regulator. Along the way, it considers differences among types of regulators, such as legislators, executives, officials at regulatory agencies, and judges. These various regulators (or policymakers if you prefer that term) operate in different legal and institutional environments, which affects their powers, incentives, risk aversion, responsiveness to different interest groups, and time horizons.

Each regulator, nonetheless, can be thought of as an agent of a larger constituency. Elected officials serve as agents of their electorate. Regulators act as agents of the governmental authority that delegated authority to them (and ultimately as agents of the public). Even an authoritarian leader, like the French sovereign for whom *l'etat c'est moi*, cannot forget to maintain the loyalty of his subjects or he would lose his head. An agency relationship necessarily creates agency costs in the economic sense. The regulator may not act in his constituents' interests and may engage in self-dealing or shirk his responsibility. Recognizing that agency costs permeate the regulatory state is crucial to understanding the conditions under which regulators support regulatory change and regulatory stimulus.

Agency costs arise when regulators enjoy greater private benefits from pursuing a given course of action (like supporting a regulatory stimulus) than the benefits that accrue to their constituents. Alternatively, regulators may not suffer the full social cost of their actions. The discussion below will provide more concrete examples of these abstract formulations. But first, close attention should be paid to two important factors that may exacerbate these agency costs. First, growing asymmetries of information frustrate the ability of constituents to monitor when their regulator is acting in their interest. As we will see, bubbles create several layers of information asymmetries – between regulated and regulator, as well as between regulator and public constituents. Second, regulators may have time horizons that differ markedly from those of their constituents. Agency costs increase when regulators have much shorter time horizons than the public. As we will see, this can lead regulators to take actions (like supporting a regulatory stimulus) in which the short-term benefits accrue to regulators, but the longer-terms costs of a crash afflict the public at large.

Altering the cost–benefit analysis of regulators

According to a rational model, in deciding whether to support a regulatory stimulus, each regulator engages in some form of cost–benefit analysis. Regulators seek to maximize their private benefits.[65] The private benefits to a regulator vary greatly based on the context, but may include the following:

- an increased probability of staying in office;
- money (even judges can care about this, as witnessed by the purchase of judicial support by financial barons during the Gilded Age railroad booms);[66]

- power, or the authority to create deeper and broader rules in the future; and
- personal reputation and legitimacy.

Of course, many regulators also care about fulfilling what they see as their public missions. However, the public interest is subject to competing definitions and claims. The contestability of what constitutes the "public interest" means that ideology matters a great deal. This chapter discusses public interest motivations of regulators in the "norms and ideologies" model later in this chapter.

Balanced against these private benefits to regulators are the costs of support-ing deregulation or other regulatory stimulus. These can include:

- loss of support or hostility from interest groups opposed to the regulatory stimulus; and
- blame should the regulatory stimulus be followed by a market crash, which in turn, might result in a regulator losing employment, power, or reputation.

In seeking to maximize benefits and minimize costs (and for various psychologi-cal reasons), regulators engage in strategies that seek credit for their actions and shift blame. This chapter will discuss some of these credit seeking/blame shift-ing strategies in a moment. The larger point is that prolonged market booms sharply tilt the cost–benefit calculus in favor of supporting regulatory stimulus. This occurs because of several dynamics.

MORE BOOM, MORE INTEREST GROUP PURCHASING POWER

First, financial market booms increase the resources available to interest groups to persuade regulators to support a regulatory stimulus. This chapter has already examined how financial market booms increase the incentives and alter the align-ment of interest groups looking to wield political influence. Booms may also enhance the political levers available to interest groups. Bribes represent the most direct and corrosive means to obtain support for regulatory stimulus. Bubbles increase the amount of money that interest groups can spend on bribes. This pro-vides a partial explanation for the long history of public corruption during bubble periods. Consider the following examples from the previous chapter:

- promoters of English companies seeking royal charters distributed shares to members of Parliament and government ministers in the 1690s, South Sea, and 1825 bubbles;[67]
- in the U.S. Gilded Age, railroad companies bought judges to protect them from legal liability;[68]
- that same era witnessed an epidemic of corruption in the legislative and executive branches as well, as epitomized by the Crédit Mobilier scandal;[69]
- bankers and real estate developers engaged in systematic political bribery during the 1920s Florida land boom;[70] and
- Japan suffered its own wave of public corruption its 1980s bubble.[71]

Other factors made regulators more susceptible to bribes during these bubble periods; this chapter will later examine how changes in social norms and ideologies contributed to public corruption.

Bribes represent only the most extreme form of political influence. Financial market booms also increase the resources available to interest groups to spend on entirely legal forms of political influence, including campaign contributions and lobbyists. Of course, political expenditures by industry groups depend not only on the resources available to groups, but changes in political threats or opportunities, as well.[72] A connection between bubbles and political campaign expenditures appears in the following figures. These figures track campaign contributions over the biennial federal election cycles from 1990 to 2010 by standard industry classification (SIC). The data come from Federal Election Commission filings compiled by the Center for Responsive Politics.[73] Figure 3.2 tracks campaign expenditures by the individuals, companies, and political action committees in the following industries: computer/internet, and telecommunications services and equipment, and telephone utilities.

Figure 3.2 reveals that 2000 represented a watershed campaign year, particularly for contributions from companies in the computer/internet and telecommunications services and equipment sectors. Political expenditures by the computer/internet industry increased almost 400 percent compared to the 1998 election cycle.

Expenditures by these industries increased not only in an absolute sense, but in a relative one as well. This becomes apparent in Figure 3.3, which tracks how the campaign expenditures of each of computer/internet, telecommunications services and equipment, telephone utilities industries rank compared to approximately 80 different industry groups.

Political activity by these industries spiked just as the technology stock bubble inflated in the late 1990s and caused internet and telecom stocks to soar.[74]

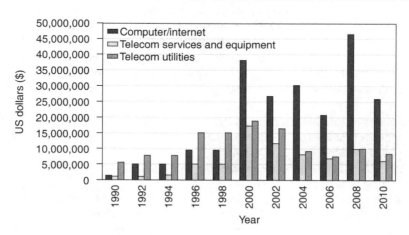

Figure 3.2 Contributions to federal candidates by industry from individuals and political action committees.[75]

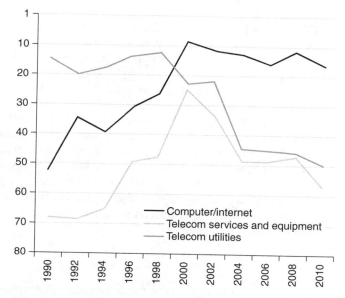

Figure 3.3 Rank of industry contributions to federal candidates among eighty industries.[76]

Data does not suggest, however, that campaign contributions dip after a crash occurs. Indeed, surviving interest group members may even increase expenditures after a crash to shape the regulatory reaction. This may explain the trends in Figure 3.4, which track campaign expenditures by the finance/insurance/estate (FIRE) sector and the "securities and investment" and "real estate" categories within the FIRE sector.

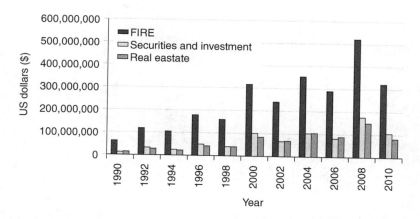

Figure 3.4 Industry contributions to federal candidates from FIRE industry.[77]

The 2008 election cycle (a presidential cycle like 2000) registered a sharp increase in contributions from these sectors. Just as the financial crisis was metastasizing, financial groups poured additional resources into political campaigns. Figure 3.5 disaggregates data on the "securities and investment" category into contributions from venture capital firms, hedge funds, and private equity/investment firms.

Compared with bribes, it is harder to measure the extent to which these legal expenditures influence the decision-making of public officials. Corporations argue that they spend these funds merely to obtain access.[78] Still, it is unlikely that these expenditures have no effect; otherwise rational actors at companies and interest groups would not make them. Indeed, more nuanced theories of regulatory capture look at the subtler ways in which organized interest groups can influence regulators. These include threatening or inflicting reputational damage that can harm the budgets or power of regulatory agencies and the career prospects of individual regulators.[79] Bubbles give interest groups more resources and incentives to deploy these potential weapons.

INFORMATION ASYMMETRIES

Interest groups also make expenditures to shape the information that flows to regulators. Indeed, many scholars claim that this capacity to control information and thus shape the policymaking agenda represents one of the most powerful forms of influence that industry groups can exert over regulators.[80] The interest groups supporting regulatory stimuli may enjoy better information than regulators about the associated economic risks. Some economists theorize that information asymmetries between borrowers and lenders cause bubbles to form.[81] If borrowers have more information than lenders, they may enjoy an even larger information advantage over regulators.

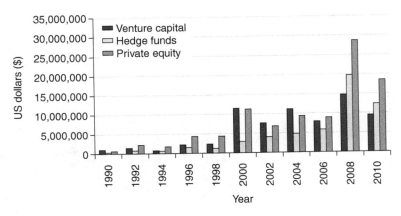

Figure 3.5 Industry contributions to federal candidates from venture capital, hedge funds, and private equity.[82]

Asymmetric information may be exacerbated by the financial innovations that proliferate during bubbles.[83] Consider the extent to which the creators of the following instruments and investment schemes possessed far superior information compared to either government officials or investors: John Law's financial engineering in the Mississippi bubble,[84] joint-stock companies during the South Sea bubble,[85] the complex investment trusts in the 1920s,[86] and credit derivatives in the modern era.[87] A second layer of information asymmetry exists between regulators and their constituents. Even if regulators understand the risks of regulatory stimulus, they enjoy a measure of insulation from punishment by their principals for supporting that stimulus. This chapter will unpack the reason for this insulation.

REVOLVING DOORS AND EXPANDING THE CONCEPT OF CAPTURE

Scholars and policy advocates have long expressed concern that "revolving doors" serve as another form of industry capture of regulators.[88] Commentators worry that regulators and other policymakers favor particular industries or firms in order to obtain lucrative employment after their government service ends.[89] Theoretically, this temptation of regulators would become more acute during bubble periods when salaries and the number of employment opportunities in the private sector increase dramatically.[90] (However, this same dynamic would mitigate the opposite problem of individuals moving from the private sector to government, where they might favor their former industry.)[91]

Some scholars question whether data, in fact, indicate that the revolving door changes regulator behavior in pernicious ways.[92] Nevertheless, scholars have found that the revolving door assumed a significant role in at least one historical bubble period. The revolving door took a peculiarly Japanese shape and played a significant role in regulatory failure during that country's 1980s bubble. Many Japanese financial institutions (particularly the *jusen* real estate finance companies) hired retired senior regulatory officials to serve as executives and board members. The Japanese labeled this *amakudari*, which translates into "descent from heaven." According to scholars, this practice led government officials to refrain from vigorously regulating financial institutions for fear of showing insufficient deference to their former superiors.[93]

This example complicates the framing of the revolving door problem. The *amakudari* problem highlights that social and cultural factors, such as deference to former superiors, may matter just as much in the revolving door as the prospect of economic payoffs.

A number of scholars have expanded the analysis of revolving doors and regulatory capture more generally, to include "softer" forms of capture, including "cognitive" or "ideological" capture. These phenomena describe when regulators identify strongly with the worldview and norms of the industry they oversee.[94] Measuring this form of capture empirically presents challenges. Some scholars have used surveys to measure the correlation between regulator sympathy with industry and regulatory outcomes.[95]

Expanding the concept of capture from economic incentives to "cognitive" or "ideological" capture begins to stretch the rational model of regulatory behavior. This model begins to blur into models of regulation based on either behavioral biases and cognitive limitations or ideologies and norms. Those two other families of models (outlined below in this chapter) may offer richer insights into the ways in which interest groups and regulators process information. These other models may also explain how individuals form beliefs and preferences with respect to how financial markets and regulations work and how they should work. These models might thus fill in cracks in the rational model's assumptions of the preferences of rational actors.

THE COST OF OPPOSING REGULATORY STIMULUS

For now, this chapter will continue to develop the rational model. The costs to a regulator who opposes regulatory stimulus may climb in other ways during a bubble. As noted above, there may be no cohesive interest group that opposes the stimulus and could offer support to a regulator. Moreover, the general public might favor the stimulus for two reasons. First, popular perception might connect the stimulus to a booming market. Regulators would then fear that opposing regulatory stimulus – for example, by strenuously enforcing regulations that would limit financial institution lending – would lead to them being blamed for pricking the bubble and upsetting the economic applecart.[96] Second, and in a related vein, the public might demand to be allowed to invest in a booming asset market. This can translate into political support for liberalizing a broad set of financial regulations that protect retail investors and operate to restrain their access to certain markets. This particular dynamic emerged in the run-up to the U.S. housing bubble. Politicians and some affordable housing advocates joined financial industry groups in support of government policies to stimulate the subprime mortgage market.[97]

RATIONALLY DISCOUNTING THE RISK OF BEING BLAMED FOR A CRISIS

Of course, regulators may suffer public blame for supporting a regulatory stimulus should markets later crash. However, regulators may rationally discount the costs of being blamed for several reasons. First, even if regulators calculate that a crash may occur, it may not happen for an extended period. The present value of any costs to a regulator associated a crash diminish the further out in time that a regulator calculates that the crash will occur.

Second, the timing of crashes far in the future may exacerbate agency costs. An individual regulator may calculate that she will leave her position (perhaps hoping that the revolving door will open to the private sector) before a crisis hits. She may rationally believe it will be difficult to trace decisions back to her as public memory fades. Moreover, it may be difficult to attribute responsibility to her given the multiple decision-makers involved in a regulatory stimulus. If divided government offers checks on policymakers, it also offers opportunities for "blame shifting" (a concept to which this chapter will return in a few moments). In addition, the complexity of crises complicates drawing neat causal lines between particular policy decisions and market crashes. This causal complexity creates yet more avenues for blame shifting.

CAUSAL COMPLEXITY, COLLECTIVE ACTION, AND THE SELFLESS REGULATOR

Causal complexity creates challenges even for more selfless regulators. Even those regulators who want to prevent crises may not see how their individual decisions could contribute to the risk of crises. Moreover, even if regulators intuit a possible connection, they may conclude that opposing a particular regulator stimulus would have negligible effect. Consider a Member of the British Parliament during the South Sea bubble or the 1820s railway mania who was lobbied by a company promoter to sponsor a private bill to charter that company. If the legislator refused, the promoter might simply obtain the backing of another Member. Moreover, if that promoter failed to find political support, promoters of other companies might take his place.

Consider also a Japanese regulator weighing whether to pursue aggressive enforcement against a particular financial institution during the height of the real estate boom in that country. A more stringent approach may have had negligible impact on the lending by other financial institutions or the inflation of the Japanese bubble. At the same time, that course of action could have had very direct consequences for the career prospects of that regulator.

REGULATORY ARBITRAGE AND DEREGULATION

Regulatory arbitrage creates further pressure on regulators to relax legal rules and support regulatory stimulus. A long scholarly literature argues that competition among regulators leads to a race to the bottom. This raises particular concern when financial institutions can externalize risk onto entire financial markets (systemic risk) or onto taxpayers (via government bailouts).[98] In the financial realm, regulators face pressure to relax regulations to discourage investors and financial institutions from shifting capital to less regulated markets.[99] Capital flight can lower regulator budgets, decrease their power by diminishing the firms and capital under their jurisdiction, and anger key constituents. Chapter 5 argues that market booms increase the incentives of firms to engage in regulatory arbitrage.

For this chapter, the point is much simpler: regulatory arbitrage increases the incentives of regulators to deregulate, under-enforce, or support other regulatory stimuli. Note this change in incentives does not depend on capital actually taking flight. In politics, perception matters just as much as empirical facts. If interest groups successfully argue that the risk of capital flight is increasing, regulators may feel significantly threatened to support a regulatory stimulus.

Chapter 6 will describe how this dynamic – regulatory arbitrage spurring deregulation – played out in the Swedish and Japanese bubbles of the 1980s. Here is a short preview. In Sweden, banks began losing lending business to lightly regulated financial companies. Concerns with an expanding, less regulated "grey market" for credit prompted the Swedish government to relax a series of regulatory restrictions on bank lending and investment.[100] Financial liberalization can also spur regulatory arbitrage when capital flows from regulated to freshly deregulated financial institutions and markets. Japan provides an example of this. Japan's deregulation of bond markets and the securities business in the late 1970s and 1980s resulted in Japanese companies obtaining a greater portion of financing from capital markets, including overseas markets. Losing customers, banks pushed for deregulation of their own sector.[101] The Swedish and Japanese examples demonstrate how deregulation and regulatory stimulus can become locked in a dialectical cycle with regulatory arbitrage. Chapter 6 provides a model of this dynamic.

The problem of diluted enforcement

Even "uncaptured" regulators face an uphill battle in seeking faithfully to enforce financial laws during asset price bubbles. Bubble periods dilute enforcement of financial laws, even if regulators remain motivated and vigilant. The increased volume of transactions during a bubble strains the resources – particularly the examination and enforcement resources – of regulators.[102]

Eugene White describes how the banking boom of the 1920s overtaxed the resources of federal bank examiners. While the number of banks and their assets grew during that decade, the resources of the Office of the Comptroller of the Currency – both budget and number of examiners – remained flat. This meant the ratio of bank assets per examiner increased significantly over the 1920s.[103] The dilution of enforcement became particularly severe in Florida, which experienced a massive real estate bubble in that decade. Only one federal examiner was stationed in that state despite the fact that the assets of national banks in the state tripled from 1922 to 1925 alone.[104]

The Securities and Exchange Commission experienced a similar dilution of enforcement during the tech stock boom of the 1990s. Despite increasing dramatically in 2003, the SEC's budget lagged behind both the stock market boom and its crash by several years. This becomes apparent through two simple, novel metrics. Figure 3.6 shows the results of dividing the SEC overall budget by the Dow Jones Wilshire 5000. Figure 3.7 shows the results of dividing that agency's enforcement budget by that same market index.[105]

These graphs show that the SEC overall and enforcement budgets kept pace with the stock market until 1996. The market boom caused a pronounced drop in the SEC's budget relative to market growth from 1997 through 2001. Budget increases in 2002 (combined with market declines) only returned enforcement to the levels it enjoyed at the beginning of the 1990s.

Understandably, during this period, SEC enforcement actions also failed to keep pace with the booming market. Figure 3.8 shows the investigations, administrative proceedings, civil or injunctive actions, and litigation actions initiated or opened in the period from 1990 to 2004.

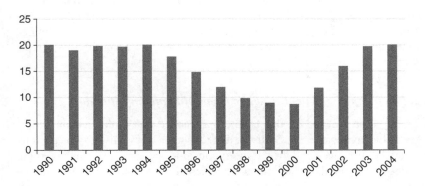

Figure 3.6 Ratio of SEC overall budget to Dow Jones Wilshire Index, 1990–2004.

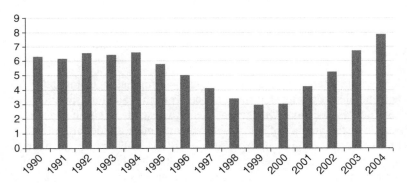

Figure 3.7 Ratio of SEC enforcement budget to Dow Jones Wilshire Index, 1990–2004.

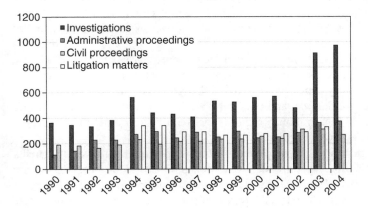

Figure 3.8 SEC proceedings opened, 1990–2004.106

The increased volume of securities transactions during that bubble clearly taxed the resources of the SEC. Market participants – including purveyors of financial fraud – who realize that a regulator's enforcement resources are strained will adjust their calculations of whether to break the law accordingly – a topic discussed in detail in the next chapter.

Deregulation games and predicting the forms of regulatory stimulus

In outlining a rational model, this chapter has looked first at the demand side – changes to the composition, incentives, and resources of interest groups pushing for regulatory stimulus – and then at the supply side – shifting pressures on regulators considering regulatory stimulus. The chapter now looks at various interactions or games within and between these two groups. An analysis of these games generates predictions on the forms that regulatory stimulus will take during bubble periods.

The demand side tradeoff between depth and breadth of regulatory change

Interactions within interest groups may explain the form that regulatory stimulus takes. Discrete interest groups that stand to benefit from regulatory stimulus face a delicate strategic decision. On the one hand, a discrete group has a strong incentive to limit the number of actors with whom it must divide the benefits of change. Limiting the number of beneficiaries allows each group member to enjoy more private benefits of regulatory change. Parties that enjoy the benefits – for example, firms to whom a narrow rule change applies or companies that receive preferential enforcement – may achieve a competitive advantage over those that do not. Moreover, greater private benefits to a smaller number of actors can help a group overcome the challenges of collective action and push for regulatory change. Greater dispersion and spillover of benefits presents more collective action challenges.[107]

On the other hand, drawing a wider circle of beneficiaries can convince more actors to donate political resources – money, votes, influence – to the cause of obtaining a regulatory stimulus. Regulatory change that is "deep" (provides great economic benefits), durable, and politically salient may require the expenditure of greater political capital. It may require more political resources than a narrow, discrete interest group can provide.

However, again, a large group means a greater potential spillover of benefits and an associated increase in collective action problems. This suggests another reason for the rarity of truly deep and durable and legal change. Certain forms of regulatory stimulus (particularly the repeal of statutes) that benefit a wider circle of interest groups should occur less frequently. The repeal of statutes passed in the wake of past financial crises – such as the Bubble Act and the Glass-Steagall Act – that imposed burdens on a broad swath of financial market participants should be rarer still.

Precedent and public choice

This interaction among interest groups seeking regulatory benefits occurs in the context of multi-player games among interest groups and regulators. So far, this chapter has looked at a rational model of the demand and supply of regulatory stimulus. In the real world, the regulated and the regulators do not interact as curves on a chart. Instead, they play various iterative games with one another that shape the development of regulatory change.

In many of these games, precedent assumes particular importance. Precedent matters both in a legal sense and in the context of negotiations that occur in the shadow of the law. A regulated party will attempt to use a prior regulatory decision to obtain the same or more generous treatment from a regulator in the future. For example, a bank or corporation may attempt to extend an existing exemption granted to it by a regulator. Success depends not only on the incentives of the regulator, but on the legal craft of the interest groups involved as well.

Basic rule of law norms mean that a change to a legal rule that benefits one firm or individual should apply equally to other parties. This has important implications for the calculus of regulated firms. A written rule would create spillover benefits for competitors. To retain private benefits, firms and interest groups may favor unwritten forms of regulatory stimulus over written ones. Unwritten regulatory stimulus – such as under-enforcement of laws or the failure of regulators to adapt rules to new contexts – restricts the spillover of private benefits and thus can be particularly attractive to interest groups. The fact that these particular stimuli are harder to identify also lowers the risk of public resistance. However, as noted above, these forms of regulatory stimuli may have shallower and less lasting effects than more visible forms, such as the repeal of a statute.

Regulator games: parceling deregulation

Regulators too must pay close heed to the capacity of precedent, as it restricts their freedom of action. Regulators may attempt to parcel out deregulation for three reasons.

First, deregulation meted out in dribs and drabs allows regulators to gauge the effects on financial markets and financial risk. If regulators care about preventing financial crises (whether for selfish or selfless reasons), an incremental approach allows them to attempt to gauge the effects of deregulation.[108]

On the other hand, even with incrementalism, precedent makes it difficult to reverse course. Moreover, incremental approaches make it hard to see the forest for the trees and detect when a tipping point towards crisis has been reached. Law professor Saule Omarova authored two studies that document how U.S. bank regulators used exemptions to gradually increase the risks that banks could take in the decade leading up the current global financial crisis. In one study, she examines how the Office of the Comptroller of the Currency changed the definition of the "business of banking" incrementally over several years to allow banks to increasingly deal in derivatives.[109] In a later study, Professor Omarova examines how the Federal Reserve granted a series of exemptions to large financial conglomerates that permitted them to use bank affiliates to support and subsidize loans by non-banks.[110] These Federal Reserve exemptions ultimately allowed conglomerates to use government subsidies to banks (deposit insurance, access to government loans, and the government safety net generally) to support subprime mortgage operations by non-bank affiliates.[111] Omarova makes a larger point: by granting incremental exemptions over years, federal regulators failed to see the effects of their decision. They failed to grasp how they had extended the federal bank safety net to riskier activities – subprime mortgage lending, exotic derivatives – that placed banks and entire financial markets at risk.[112]

Second, the parceling of deregulation allows self-interested regulators to conduct another kind of marginal analysis. Self-interested regulators may try to parcel out deregulation to gauge the shape of various interest groups' demand curves for regulatory change. Moreover, self-interested regulators may wish to dole out deregulation in order to preserve leverage (or, viewed in a more negative light, the capacity to extract rents) from interest groups.[113] Incremental change also allows regulators to reverse course if political winds shift and interest groups that favor change in the opposite direction gain power.

These various selfish and selfless motivations provide further reasons that complete deregulation – such as the dismantling of a regulatory regime or agency – occurs only in rare moments. They offer another explanation for the long lives of those statutes passed in the wake of a bubble that give regulators vast powers over industry groups – such as the Bubble Act or the Glass-Steagall Act.

Blame hedging

Yet those statutes were repealed. Massive and salient legal change does occur. Indeed, policymakers sometimes follow a high-political-risk, high-political-reward strategy of sponsoring sweeping regulatory stimulus, such as repeal of prominent statutes. The reward comes in the form of credit for far-reaching deregulation. At the same time, regulators, particularly elected officials, can hedge the risk that they will be blamed should financial crisis ensue. A literature in political economy outlines the motivations and strategies of politicians to engage in "credit-claiming" and "blame avoidance."[114] A number of devices, which I label "blame hedges," allow architects of deregulation to protect themselves. Blame hedges describe strategies that a policymaker can take prospectively to mitigate the future risk of constituents faulting a decision the policymaker made.[115]

For example, legislators can pass sweeping, broad-brush deregulation (or regulation for that matter), but delegate the task of implementing specific regulations to regulatory agencies or ministries. Scholars have noted that delegation allows legislators to reach a political compromise and punt strategic ambiguities for resolution at the agency level.[116] Delegation has a second benefit to legislators; it allows them to claim that later problems are the fault of agencies.[117]

Regulators, in turn, may blame legislators for drafting flawed statutes, placing improper pressure on regulators, or failing to give regulators necessary resources. Regulators also attempt to seek credit and shift blame horizontally – by pinning responsibility for failure on other ministries or agencies. More generally, any division of power in government (among executive, legislative, and judicial branches and among various agencies) offers similar opportunities for blame hedging. Even within the black box of an agency, officials may attempt to share nominal power in order to blame superiors, subordinates, or officials in other units when the crisis hits the fan.

Regulatory backlash

The rational actor model may strain somewhat to explain the regulatory backlash after a bubble collapses. Many variants of public choice theory seem congenitally incapable of admitting that regulation may serve a wider public interest.[118] Public choice analysis can easily slide from a descriptive explanation of how regulations are made to a normative critique that all regulations serve narrow public interests and are therefore suspect.[119] The descriptive side of public choice may, nonetheless, still have insights into regulatory backlash. It may explain, for example, the instances of scapegoating in the wake of bubble collapses, in which social minorities became popular targets. One of the first bubbles, the English stock market boom of the 1690s resulted in restrictions on the number of Jewish stock brokers in London.[120] Jews again received blame for the Panic of 1873 (*Gründerkrach*) in Germany and Austria.[121] Social groups with less political power present attractive regulatory targets as more powerful interest groups attempt to deflect blame.

Beyond this ugly history, lies a larger point: financial industry interest groups may actually support regulation in the aftermath of a crash in order to restrict competition. This phenomenon may take benign forms, as when industry attempts to drive fraudulent competition out of business to preserve public confidence.[122] However, other scholars, such as law professor Jonathan Macey, claim that many banking regulations, including deposit insurance and the Glass-Steagall Act, have their origins in more naked anti-competitive interest group politics.[123] Professor Paul Mahoney makes a similar argument that the disclosure rules of the Securities Act of 1933 hardwired a competitive advantage for large established "wholesale" investment banks over lower status securities dealers.[124] John Morley argues that the investment fund industry pushed for aspects of the New Deal regulation of investment management (including the Investment Company Act of 1940) in order to maintain a "common brand" for a certain type of investment strategy.[125] (The Bubble Act might offer an early example supporting for this public choice theory of regulation. Note, however, that this statute was passed *before* a market crash.)

A rational model is not necessarily inconsistent with financial regulation in the wake of a crisis that serves broader public interests. John Coffee uses the work of Mancur Olson to argue that financial crises prompt latent public groups to overcome collective action problems. These latent groups successfully push through regulations that protect investors and mitigate systemic risk against financial industry opposition. Coffee further argues that, when the crisis recedes into history, the cycle turns. Financial industry groups then regain influence over the political and regulatory process.[126] This account meshes with the theory of the "issue attention cycle" developed by Anthony Downs.[127]

Earlier political science research points out that financial crisis can serve as yet another form of "displacement" that upsets the interest group equilibrium and causes new interest groups to form. For example, David Truman notes how the Panic of 1873 triggered the development of the Grange movement across the United States.[128] Chapter 2 documented how the Grange movement pushed for the wave of state constitutional restrictions on government subsidies to railroads and other corporations in the wake of the Panic.[129]

Regulatory backlash in the wake of bubbles often results in a rough compromise between competing groups. On the one hand, some policy entrepreneurs push for a strenuous regulation of financial markets in the "public interest." On the other hand, financial industry players lobby for measures that lower regulatory taxes while restoring investor confidence and restricting competition. The history of the creation of federal securities laws in the New Deal provides an example of this compromise at work. In the Securities Act of 1933, the Roosevelt administration settled on a regime of mandatory disclosure over the alternative of government "merit regulation" of securities issuances pushed by future Supreme Court Justice William O. Douglas.[130] The final version of the Securities Exchange Act of 1934 reflected the resurgence of financial industry political power in the wake of the landmark Securities Act passed a year earlier.[131]

A behavioral model: disaster myopia and other biases

If a rational model of regulation struggles to explain many forms of regulatory backlash, a behavioral model – or at least a nuanced behavioral overlay on top of a rational model – may provide greater explanatory power. The cognitive biases, limitations, and heuristics described by behavioral economics and social psychology can explain how regulator and interest group behavior changes during booms and busts. In particular, behavioral explanations provide a compelling account of the cyclical and perverse nature of regulatory stimulus during boom times followed by regulatory backlash only after markets have crashed.

In a behavioral model, various cognitive limitations and behavioral biases cause regulators to underestimate the social and personal costs of supporting regulatory stimulus. These limitations and biases cause regulators to underestimate the risks that regulatory stimulus will contribute to a bubble and financial crisis, as well as their personal risk of being blamed for a crisis. Moreover, even if regulators recognize the risk of a bubble, their constituents may suffer from the same cognitive limitations and biases and push regulators to support stimulus.

Behaviorally biased regulators

This model builds off a contention that regulators are not exempt from behavioral biases and cognitive limitations. Law professors Stephen Choi and Adam Pritchard have argued that officials at the U.S. Securities and Exchange Commission may suffer from an array of behavioral biases, including the availability, hindsight, and confirmation biases.[132] Many of these biases (some of which were described briefly in Chapter 1) may contribute to an excessive willingness of regulators to deregulate, under-enforce laws, or provide other regulatory stimuli during market booms. Among the biases that may afflict regulators during market booms and may contribute to excessive support for regulatory stimuli are the following:

Overoptimism. Individuals tend to be overoptimistic about future events.[133] This may translate into policymakers excessively discounting the risks of economic crisis and suffering adverse personal consequences because of a crisis. Excessive discounting may lead them to give excessive support to regulatory stimuli.

Overconfidence. Individuals also tend to be overconfident in their own abilities, particularly their abilities to calculate the probability of future events.[134] Overconfident policymakers may overestimate their ability to predict various negative events: such as the negative consequences of a regulatory stimulus, the probability of a bubble, market crash, or financial crisis, and the probability of being punished because of a crisis.

Hyperbolic discounting. Policymakers may also excessively and subconsciously minimize the expected future costs of a burst bubble because of hyperbolic discounting.[135] This cognitive bias describes how the discount rates of individuals tend to plummet for events in the far future.[136] This translates into a strong desire for immediate reward (and an aversion to immediate pain). Hyperbolic discounting also results in a "dynamic inconsistency" of preferences, in which an individual's desires for the immediate present (such as eating chocolate or stealing) conflict with desires for the future (not getting fat, not going to prison).[137] Hyperbolic discounting means that, in a boom time, policymakers may give excessive weight to the short-term rewards for favoring regulatory stimulus (career opportunities, power, money) and short shrift to long-term risks (economic crisis and its attendant costs for individual regulators).

A number of other cognitive biases may make policymakers susceptible to the arguments of interest groups for a regulatory stimulus. For example, individuals tend to "anchor" or give excessive weight to their initial estimate of a probability.[138] Empirical research also documents a "framing effect" in which individuals reach different conclusions about the same risks and probabilities depending on how problems are described or framed.[139] These behavioral biases may equip interest groups to influence regulators to support regulatory stimulus by changing and framing the information they provide to policymakers. Behavioral biases may prove easier to exploit given the profound information asymmetries enjoyed by industry groups during bubbles periods and with respect to financial innovations. Moreover, behavioral biases of regulators may contribute to their cognitive or ideological capture; boom times may reinforce beliefs that regulatory interventions are unnecessary and that market failures have been identified and mitigated.

The problem with a behavioral explanation for policymaker support of regulatory stimulus is that there are few empirical studies that isolate cognitive limitations or biases as the cause of a regulatory decision. On the other hand, there is an extensive literature documenting behavioral biases in the general population and in financial professionals.[140] There is no reason to think public officials are immune from behavioral biases. Nevertheless, behavioral economics offers a long list of biases and cognitive limitations without specifying which biases lead to particular decisions.[141]

Disaster myopia

Although a laundry list of behavioral biases might afflict policymakers and lead them to discount the risk of a bubble and crisis, two related biases – the availability bias and sample size neglect – assume particular importance. The availability bias, documented by psychological studies, describes how individuals give excessive weight to more recent and salient events when calculating the probabilities of future events. At the same time, they excessively discount the risk of events recurring that happened in the distant past.[142] Sample size neglect encapsulates the frequent error of individuals making risk calculations based on small samples of evidence.[143] Together these biases can cause policymakers to give excessive weight to recent events. Disaster myopia can trigger herd behavior and groupthink inside policymaking circles

These errors can prove disastrous during a bubble or prolonged market boom. Rising prices mask risks to investors, financial institutions, and financial markets as a whole. Jack Guttentag and Richard Herring described how "disaster myopia" – the inability to predict the probability of low frequency, high magnitude financial shocks – afflicts financial institutions in international markets.[144] This same disaster myopia afflicts regulators too.[145]

The crises that don't happen

Two features of bubbles and financial crises play into these behavioral biases. First, bubbles rarely assume the exact same form. A second Tulipomania is unlikely. Chapter 1 noted that bubbles occur in different asset markets and that the similarities between bubbles appear only on an abstract level – for example, rising prices, cheap credit, and an influx of new investors. These factors reinforce the "New Era" or "this time is different" mentality that contributes to the formation of a bubble.[146] These factors also skew the perceptions of policy-makers of the risk of a financial crisis.

Second, as noted above, one never sees the crises that don't happen. This makes prophylactic regulations particularly vulnerable to repeal. Their vulnerability increases as bubbles and crashes recede in the memories of the public and their representatives. The demise of the Glass-Steagall Act in the United States serves as one example. This law, passed in the wake of the Great Depression, imposed a separation between commercial and investment banking. This separation had several rationales; including preventing investment banks from exploiting government insurance of depository banks, stemming contagion from riskier securities firms to banks, and addressing perceived conflicts of interest. As the Great Depression became a distant memory in the United States, policymakers questioned whether this division was still necessary. In the 1980s, regulators allowed exemptions to Glass-Steagall, financial firms ultimately flouted the statute, and Congress repealed Glass-Steagall in 1999.[147] Scholars have questioned whether Glass-Steagall actually lowered risk to the financial system.[148] It is indeed hard to give singular credit to one statute for the lack of major banking crises in the United States for seventy years or to blame its repeal for the current financial crisis. (We will look at how causal complexity impacts policymaker decisions in a moment.) Nevertheless, the political insight remains; prophylactic rules may be the victims of their own success.

Faithful agents but biased principals

Even if a policymaker is unbiased and recognizes the risks of a boom resulting in a crash, she answers to principals or constituents that suffer from cognitive limitations of their own. For example, an agency official may recognize that a given regulatory stimulus – e.g., reduced enforcement of a rule restricting bank leverage – may further inflate a bubble. But she may report to superiors at the agency who believe that a price boom is sustainable or who discount the risk of the regulatory stimulus. Those superiors in turn answer to a President or members of Congress who may also underestimate the risks of looser regulation or the implosion of a bubble. The President and Congress, in turn, face constituents who favor the regulatory stimulus because cognitive biases have led them to believe that a market boom can continue indefinitely.

A faithful and unbiased agent may be punished by biased principals for taking actions in the interest of those principals. In the past, principals have punished agents for betting against a bubble. Consider Markus Brunnermeier and Stefan Nagel's account of how a manager of an investment fund that publicly refused to invest in the technology stock bubble was forced to close the fund as investors fled. The technology bubble popped shortly thereafter.[149] Investors with short horizons sought other funds that earned better returns as the bubble continued to inflate. Government officials can also face adverse consequences for betting against a bubble and opposing a regulatory stimulus.

Interest groups and behavioral biases

Behavioral biases may also shape the demand for deregulation or other regulatory stimulus. These biases may create excessive demand for stimuli. Various groups may press for relaxing a legal rule even when it is against their long-term self-interest should cognitive limitations cause them to underestimate the probability of a financial crisis. This phenomenon may help answer two of the key questions posed above. First, how are interest groups able to overcome inertia in the political marketplace and push through a regulatory stimulus? Second, why might the general public support a regulatory stimulus, even if it provides outsized benefits to a discrete interest group and risks contributing to an asset price bubble?

To answer to these questions consider a more specialized model that grafts behavioral finance onto public choice theory. Discrete interest groups that understand how a regulatory stimulus benefits them and disadvantages the public could be thought of as "political smart money." This smart money can then convince the cognitively biased public to support a regulatory stimulus. The political smart money can take advantage of the regulatory stimulus, inflate their profits, and exploit the investing public. Political smart money can do this by using their superior knowledge of complex financial innovations (like John Law's paper money in the eighteenth century or subprime mortgages and credit derivatives in the modern era).[150] Smart money can also create complex legal structures that exploit the incompleteness of legal rules to the detriment of ordinary investors. Witness how company promoters exploited the loopholes in Germany's new incorporation process in the early 1870s to create *Schwindel-gründungen* (swindle incorporations).[151]

If this behavioral finance terminology is distracting, one could also think of the foregoing as a "Mies Van der Rohe" strategy of interest group behavior. Interest groups that want to push through massive regulatory change (which might harm the broader public) can erect an inspiring edifice and wrap it in a sleek, modern ideology (such as those discussed in the third model below). The public is awed, while the policy entrepreneurs understand the architect's adage that "God is in the details."[152]

Bias arbitrage and its limits

The prevalence of cognitive biases in the marketplace and among the public does not mean that they necessarily will distort public policy. There is an argument that the political marketplace will self-correct. If the public does systematically underestimate the risk of bubble, regulatory stimulus, and crisis, why does some political entrepreneur not warn them? This would correct the "mispricing" of risk in the political marketplace. Indeed, law professor Amitai Aviram posits that politicians and policy entrepreneurs often perform this role. He argues that politicians pass laws or take positions that exploit the difference between public misperceptions of risk and actual risk.[153] Success in correcting misperceptions of risk might offer valuable political rewards to a successful bias arbitrageur, just as a financial arbitrageur earns profits from betting against market mispricings.

However, just as financial arbitrage faces severe limitations in real world financial markets, so too does bias arbitrage face formidable problems in actual political markets. Bias arbitrageurs may face significant opposition from discrete interest groups and an investing public that favors regulatory stimuli. This opposition can persist if a bubble lasts for a prolonged time. In noting the limited capacity of financial arbitrage to correct bubbles, behavioral finance scholars are fond of repeating a quote attributed to John Maynard Keynes: "Markets can remain irrational far longer than you or I can remain solvent."[154] This might be reformulated for policymakers attempting to engage in bias arbitrage against a bubble: "markets can remain irrational far longer than you can hold onto office."

Policymakers betting against a bubble face a more daunting problem in the following paradox: their efforts to stop a bubble from forming likely would not be recognized unless and until a bubble has collapsed. This is another version of the problem described above, that no one sees the crises that don't happen. Many of the Cassandras that warned of the dangers of the Panic of 2007–2008 only received public recognition after the crisis occurred. For Exhibit A, see Brooksley Born, the Chairperson of the U.S. Commodity Futures Trading Commission in the late 1990s. Ms. Born warned of the risk associated with over-the-counter derivatives. Yet she faced bitter opposition from Alan Greenspan, Treasury Secretary Robert Rubin, and Rubin's successor, Lawrence Summers. She was only vindicated a decade later when the global financial crisis erupted.[155]

There is great reason to be skeptical that markets allocate blame and credit fairly or optimally after a financial crisis. This chapter has already described how causal complexity can complicate assigning responsibility to particular policymakers or regulatory stimuli. Blame hedges further frustrate this process. The heavy use of economic vocabulary in this chapter should not obscure that the actual practice of politics is art not science. Policymakers operate in a political environment shaped by narratives, with all their fluidity, irrationality, and messiness. Cultures across time have reacted to collapsed bubbles and financial crises less with a rational economic accounting than with morality plays full of villains, occasional heroes, and religious and quasi-religious lessons.[156] The stories told in the wake of bubbles and crises can have a darker side. As already noted, scapegoating has been not infrequent in the wake of collapsed bubbles.

Predicting regulatory backlash (and the form of regulatory stimulus)

Indeed, behavioral economics would suggest that the regulatory backlash to burst bubbles and financial crises may often be misdirected. If the availability bias might lead policymakers and the public to underestimate the risk of crises in the distant pass recurring, it might also lead to overestimation of risk immediately after a crisis.[157] The salience of the last crisis can lead policymakers to focus on the particular events, instruments, schemes that immediately preceded the crash. The representativeness heuristic and base rate fallacy may reinforce this tendency.[158] The hindsight and overconfidence biases may give regulators unwarranted assurance that they saw the crisis coming, that blame for the crisis lies elsewhere, and that they have full capabilities to prevent future bubbles. Behavioral biases contribute to the considerable risk that policymakers will always prepare to re-fight the last war.[159]

The importance of salience may mean that policymakers give excessive attention to the headline-grabbing stories of fraud and law-breaking. They may discount more systemic causes of crises that are less visible and less easily understood by the general public. Systemic causes do not fit easily into morality plays. It is also bad politics to assign blame for a bubble to the public at large. Psychology plays a role here too. The self-serving bias contributes to individuals taking credit for their success, but blaming others for failure.[160] The tendency of the public and policymakers to blame others may lead to a persistent failure to address the systemic causes of crises.

The availability bias may mean that deeper crashes and more profound financial crises generate more enduring regulatory responses that survive when the political cycle turns. It may take the passage of decades and another large bubble to overcome the salience of the previous crisis and the laws associated with it. The Bubble Act passed during the South Sea bubble in 1720 lasted until 1825, the peak of a railway mania.[161] The fact that the Bubble Act actually represented not a response to the crisis but an anti-competitive measure enacted during the boom to protect the South Sea Company mattered little; the perception of a law's purpose can outweigh its genesis or effects. Similarly, the Glass-Steagall Act and the Public Utility Holding Company Act enacted in the wake of the Great Crash each endured until the late 1990s, when the tech stock bubble inflated.[162] Table 2.a.4 in the Appendix to Chapter 2 sets out the long list of U.S financial regulations birthed during the New Deal that met their demise during this period.

So, behavioral economics may have much to say for the form and timing of regulatory stimulus, as well. If regulatory stimulus can be framed to minimize connections to previous crises, it enjoys a greater chance of being implemented.

Shifting ideologies and norms: market booms and soft capture

Other disciplines besides economics provide alternative explanations for the pattern of regulatory stimulus as markets boom and regulatory backlash after a crash. Economic self-interest may explain only a part of the decisions by policymakers and interest groups to push for or oppose legal change. Political ideologies and social norms shape the preferences and beliefs of interest groups, policymakers, and the public and thus affect legal and regulatory outcomes. Ideologies and norms, however, do not remain fixed. Shifts in the prevailing political ideologies and changes in social norms can animate regulatory stimulus and regulatory backlash.

Liberalism ascendant

Ideological shifts loom particularly large in the history of regulatory stimulus preceding bubbles. Bubbles throughout history started just as markets liberalized and societies became permeated with a market ethos. This ethos elevates the value of private profit-making. It celebrates the entrepreneur, the financier, and the ordinary investor.

Many of the bubble histories outlined in Chapter 2 coincided with periods in which classical liberalism (or neoliberalism) was ascendant in a particular country. This can be seen most clearly in two historical episodes. First, during that railway mania in England preceding the Panic of 1825, avowed liberal Members of Parliament led the charge to the repeal of the Bubble Act. These Members of Parliament belonged to a larger political movement. Emerging political liberalism in early nineteenth century England helped end mercantilism and ushered in a laissez faire approach to regulating capital formation.[163]

Of course, liberalism did not end with the Panic of 1825, but shaped the course of British politics in the nineteenth century.[164] At first blush, ideology may thus seem to offer a weaker explanation for the cycles of regulatory stimulus during bubbles and regulatory backlash after crises. Political ideology in Britain does not appear to have fluctuated to the same extreme extent as financial markets or laws. Yet a closer look at the legal history in the previous chapter is revealing. When the British bubbles in the nineteenth century crashed, the regulatory backlash did not undo previous regulatory stimuli that liberalized corporate law. Instead of reversals, regulatory backlash consisted of modifications and improvements to corporate law. The aftermath of the Panic of 1837 serves as an example. The Gladstone Commission convened in the wake of that crisis made recommendations to move the regulation of corporations away from laissez faire. But the Commission also sought to facilitate the formation of joint-stock companies. These dual impulses resulted in the Joint Stock Companies Act 1844, which expanded access to incorporation by removing the requirement for an Act of Parliament, yet also imposed accounting, audit, and disclosure requirements on new joint-stock companies.[165] The path of eighteenth century British corporate law might be better characterized not in terms of cycles, but as a punctuated evolution. This evolution moved towards easier incorporation, expansion of limited liability for shareholders, and an increased smattering of disclosure, accounting, and corporate governance requirements for companies.

The ascent of political liberalism played a role in a second nineteenth century bubble, namely the 1870s *Gründerboom* in Germany. The National Liberal Party pushed through the corporate law reform of 1870 that liberalized the process for incorporating joint-stock companies. This party espoused *Gewerbefreiheit* (translated as free enterprise or economic freedom). Party members viewed the liberalization of corporate formation not merely as an instrument of economic development. Indeed, the National Liberals saw freer incorporation as serving the ideological purpose of fostering a private economic sphere in Germany separate from the state.[166]

However, this Teutonic example also involves nuances; here too, one cannot draw a simple connection between the rise of a liberal political ideology and regulatory stimulus. German historians tell a more complex story: Chancellor Bismarck aligned himself with the National Liberals in order to push through corporate law reform not because of any personal ideological beliefs. Instead, he viewed the ideological committed liberals as an ideal vehicle for policies that would expand the new nation's economic, political, and military power.[167] After the *Gründerkrach*, Bismarck abandoned his former allies, reversed political course completely, and used the crash as pretext for massive expansion of state control of the economy.[168]

This underscores the need for a richer understanding of how ideology operates in regulatory stimulus and backlash. Ideology may shape the beliefs and preferences of individuals and political groups. At the same time, politicians and interest groups may use ideological movements as instruments in service of more naked self-interest. This raises a series of fascinating questions. To what extent does ideology give birth to economic interest groups and sculpt their preferences? Conversely, do ideological movements gain traction because they mesh with and further the objectives of emerging economic interest groups? These questions – which have occupied historians since at least the nineteenth century – blur the answers to the immediate question of this chapter. It may not be so easy to separate out when regulatory stimulus and backlash result from the dynamics of rational interest group politics from when they reflect deeper, tectonic ideological changes.

Nonetheless, one can see the deep footprints of ideology in regulatory stimulus during other boom periods surveyed in the previous chapter. The 1690s English stock market booms and Mississippi and South Sea bubbles may not have spring directly out of modern political liberalism (Adam Smith was born only in 1723, several years after the South Sea bubble collapsed, and it would be difficult to link directly the thinking of Locke to these episodes). Even these early episodes, however, might be seen as reflecting a kind of proto-liberal belief in the social good that comes with markets.[169]

The respective collapse of the Mississippi and South Sea bubbles damaged this belief in France and England. This can be seen in the ways in which French and English law restricted capital formation well into the next century. The French and English regulatory backlash differed, however, in tone, severity, and impact. Although the Bubble Act imposed constraints on the formation of English joint-stock companies until its demise in 1825, France's regulatory backlash was more draconian.[170] As the previous chapter noted, the Mississippi bubble led to the resurgence in France of religiously inspired usury laws and other legal rules restricting credit. It generated French restrictions on the formation of joint-stock companies. It also set back efforts to reform the nation's public finances over a century.[171] This divergence underscores that, although abstract ideas and ideology matter in history, differences in the soil in which they take root matter too. A nation's political, social, and legal environment give form to the substance of regulatory stimulus and backlash. The divergence between France and England calls into question any notions of mechanical determinism in the legal and political history of bubbles.

A similar divergence in legal, political, and ideological outcomes to bubbles can be seen in the histories of the United States and Germany after the Panic of 1873. Bismarck's Germany embarked on a course of massive state intervention in the economy. The Chancellor promoted the growth of industry and labor cartels to address a perceived threat of over-production and to channel social conflict.[172] During this same time, the United States witnessed the rise of populist, agrarian movements, such as the Grange. The Grange pushed for provisions in state constitutions to limit the powers of states and municipalities to subsidize railroads and other corporations.[173] Meanwhile, other groups pushed for stronger federal monetary powers, leading to a protracted national political struggle over gold and silver standards.[174] This contrast between Germany and the United States suggest that, if there are laws to history, they are not forged of iron.

Political liberalism – even if not labeled as such – marked the political era of the Roaring Twenties in the United States. During this decade, the Progressive movement gave way to the surging success of a pro-business, pro-market Republican Party that held the White House from 1921 through January 1933. The laissez faire political ethos was captured by President Harding's campaign motto: "[L]ess government in business and more business in government" and President Coolidge's equally pithy assertion that "the business of America is business."[175] This political philosophy explains much of the lax enforcement of antitrust and banking laws during the prolonged economic boom.[176]

The 1920s also demonstrates the ways in which the ideals of political liberalism, particularly the belief in free markets, can be perverted during market booms. The Teapot Dome scandal and the political graft that permeated the Florida real estate bubble reveal the ways in which interest groups can hijack free-market ideals in favor of "crony capitalism."

Instead of merely insisting that the government merely stay out of booming markets, interest groups have convinced politicians to grant favors to particular firms or business sectors. The roots of crony capitalism extend back to the corruption surrounding the granting of corporate charters in England from the seventeenth through the nineteenth century. Outright corruption can shade into subtler forms of influence and capture. It is also difficult to draw crisp lines between regulatory stimuli that restrain government intervention in the economy broadly, from stimulus that favors one narrow interest group over another.

There is also an ideological story to be told in late twentieth century bubbles. Consider again the phenomenon of financial liberalization across Western economies that began in the late 1970s and accelerated in the 1980s. The rational model described earlier in this chapter might attribute this liberalization to common economic shocks, such as oil embargoes, inflation, rising public debt, and the end of the Bretton Woods system.[177] However, ideology undoubtedly played a large role as well. Neoliberalism gained ground in a range of Western countries, as the Reagan era began in the United States and Thatcherism took hold in Great Britain. According to some scholars, neoliberalism even accounts for deregulation of the financial services sector in Sweden in the 1980s.[178] Yet it is difficult to answer causal questions of whether neoliberalism triggered financial liberalization or whether liberalization occurred because of underlying economic factors (rising public debt, slowing growth, and resultant changes in the interest group equilibrium). Was neoliberalism symptom or cause?

The neoliberalism explanation for financial deregulation in late twentieth century economies faces more problems when applied to Japan's bubble in the 1980s. The post-war period of one-party rule continued unabated in Japan throughout the 1970s and 1980s.[179] Moreover, scholars attribute much of the impetus for financial liberalization in Japan to interest group pressure: first from securities firms to deregulate in light of economic conditions, then later from banks to compete with securities firms, and still later from external pressures from the United States.[180] A neoliberalism story for Japanese deregulation must therefore take another tack. Perhaps market ideology permeated Japanese political culture in subtler ways. Perhaps Japan reacted to global changes that, in turn, reflected ideological shifts. The latter explanation might focus on how U.S. political pressure on Japan to liberalize its financial services sector was part and parcel of the "Washington Consensus."[181]

In using neoliberalism or liberalism to explain regulatory stimulus during bubbles, there is a not insignificant danger of writing sloppy intellectual history and using ideological explanations as rhetorical makeweight. A more carefully crafted theory of the role of ideology in bubbles would have to account for why the same ideological trends played out in different ways in different nations. For example, why did rising neoliberalism not lead to massive regulatory stimulus in Germany in the 1980s and cause a bubble in that country? Conversely, why did regulatory backlash assume radically different shapes after parallel financial crises (compare France to England in the 1720s or Germany to the United States in the late 1870s)?

Norms and the purchase of regulatory stimulus

If the values of the markets can transform political ideologies during financial booms, they can also change social norms in ways conducive to regulatory stimulus. Some shifts in norms can be utterly toxic. If market values permeate government ("the business of America is business") such that law, regulation, and subsidies seem for sale, then crony capitalism can metastasize. If law and regulation are seen as for sale, then regulators and interest groups will begin the bid and ask. If enough policymakers and interest groups succumb to the temptations of graft and corruption, then the normal societal opprobrium begins to fade. Ideological and norm change can thus spread in nonlinear ways.

If the way society views government and regulation can change policymaker behavior, then the way scholars model the political process can as well. Indeed, it is possible that public choice's influential re-framing of regulation in terms of economic self-interest may become a self-fulfilling prophesy.

The next chapter, which analyzes how compliance with laws deteriorates during bubble periods, will look at how a similar effect may play out in decisions of market participants on whether or not to obey the law. Laws that are bought and sold may lose much of the legitimacy upon which compliance depends.

Conclusion

Evaluating and integrating the models

Each of the three models or lenses described in this chapter has limitations that call for further research. The rational model of regulatory politics struggles to explain regulations in the wake of collapsed bubbles that appear to serve a larger public interest. How does this model account for regulations that mitigate the risk of future crises? The rational model would be improved by better models and further evidence of what happens inside the black box of regulatory agencies. The behavioral model would benefit from empirical or experimental evidence of behavioral biases and cognitive limitations impacting the decision-making of regulators specifically. The ideological and normative model needs greater nuance. It must confront how and why broad ideological currents, such as liberalism or neoliberalism, resulted in dramatically different forms and levels of regulatory stimulus or backlash in different countries during the same eras.

Although this chapter separates out the three models for analytical purposes, in practice they blur together and reinforce one another. As already noted, interest groups may seek to use shifting ideologies as tools to shape regulatory policy. Economic interest may determine which ideology gains traction during particular moments. Witness again Bismarck's use of liberalism to promote his personal political objectives and to further the industrialization and military strength of Germany. Earlier in that century, railroad companies in England took advantage of a climate of political liberalism to repeal the Bubble Act, liberalize the rules on incorporation, and obtain corporate charters and other favorable regulatory treatment. Booming markets may broaden political support for liberal ideas, legal change, and regulatory stimulus

At the same time, ideologies can define the interests of individuals and interest groups. Social norms and ideas form individual and group preferences. Liberals in nineteenth century England and Germany looked to corporate reform not only for instrumental purposes of promoting economic growth, but also for the ideological reasons of increasing economic freedom.

The rational calculus of interest groups and regulators, their behavioral biases, and ideological and normative shifts can reinforce each other. If an economic or technological displacement upsets the interest group equilibrium, it can cause discrete interest groups to lobby for regulatory stimulus. The market boom that results from the original displacement, together with receding memories of past financial crises, also contributes to disaster myopia. During booms, regulators and the public may increasingly support both regulatory stimulus and free-market ideologies. Meanwhile, changing social norms make the purchase and sale of regulatory stimulus more acceptable. When bubbles pop, interest groups pushing for regulatory stimulus lose influence (or they work to shape the inevitable post-crash regulations in order to stifle competitors). The availability bias means regulators and the public overestimate risks in the financial marketplace. Free-market ideologies lose traction (even momentarily), and a regulatory backlash begins.

Whether considered alone or together, the three models in this chapter – rational, behavioral, and ideological – predict that financial regulation will follow a perverse cycle. If regulatory stimulus fuels bubbles, then regulatory backlash occurs only after markets crash and the economic and social damage has been done. The turning of this cycle can be seen in the evolution of British corporate law surveyed in the previous chapter. Roughly every ten years, liberalization during market booms was followed by a crash and new restrictions on the corporate form. The cycle then restarted with a fresh wave of liberalization of corporate law.

A brief look at the quiet period and liberalization's big bang

The cycles, however, are not always constant or rhythmic. For a long period following the Great Depression, the regulatory cycle slowed or stopped. What then explains this long "Quiet Period" of stability in financial regulation in Western Europe, North America, and Japan following World War II? Moreover, what explains the Big Bang of financial liberalization that washed over these same economies in waves starting in the 1970s? Each of the three models yields different but complimentary explanations for the long period of stability and instability. The following presents a brief sketch.

- *The rational model* would explain part of the post-war period of financial stability as resulting from financial regulations that compartmentalized financial institutions. These regulations afforded each segment of institutions a franchise that shielded them from competition and gave them a stake in preserving the regulatory status quo.[182] Macroeconomic and political shocks shattered this regulatory equilibrium and triggered waves of financial liberalization.[183]
- *The behavioral model,* by contrast, would focus on how the severity and salience of the Great Depression gave financial regulations in its wake unprecedented staying power, which would fade only with the passage of decades and long, pronounced market booms.[184]
- *The ideological/norms model* looks how the Great Depression triggered an ideological shift that favored government regulation but that eroded with the rise of neoliberalism in the late 1970s.

Of course, the causes of this period of financial liberalization are much more complex than this capsule analysis indicates. Rising international competition in financial markets, increased regulatory arbitrage and capital flows, and the development of new financial technology (such as derivatives) all destabilized the regulatory architecture. Indeed, Chapter 6 presents a more complex model of the way in which deregulation and regulatory arbitrage reinforce one another. It uses the model to explain the examples of Sweden and Japan in the 1980s.

Radical disequilibrium

For now, the lesson of this chapter is that, under any or all of the three models, there is tremendous political pressure for regulatory stimulus in all its forms – deregulation, under-enforcement, subsidies for booming asset markets – as markets boom. Similarly, there is substantial pressure to impose regulatory taxes on investments after markets crash.

This existence of this regulatory stimulus cycle – the first component of the Regulatory Instability Hypothesis – has far-reaching implications. It suggests that financial regulations may experience periodic bouts of radical disequilibrium. This mirrors the radical disequilibrium of asset price bubbles that can occur in financial markets. Moreover, shocks in financial regulation – the turning of the regulatory stimulus cycle – can exacerbate instability in financial markets. Likewise, bubbles can trigger the turning of the regulatory instability cycle.

The largest danger comes when market booms and regulatory changes begin to move in the same directions and to reinforce one another. Rather than serving as a governor to restrain market excesses or to protect economies from crashes, regulation and other government interventions into financial markets act as stimulants. Instead of controlling a blazing market, regulatory change pours jet fuel onto it.

The pace of regulatory change can mask its destabilizing effects in two very different ways. Incremental reforms – for example the slow drip of changes to regulatory interpretations that allow banks to enter new markets, increase the flow of bank credit, and expand the scope of bank risk – can mean the regulators miss critical tipping points.[185] The government can be blinded to expansions of bank credit and leverage, which turbocharge financial markets and render financial institutions more fragile. At the same time, "Big Bang" style deregulation can lead to sudden booms – witness the booms in Sweden and Japan after massive financial deregulation in those nations in the 1980s (described in Chapter 6). The sudden rise in prices can trigger positive feedback investing in financial markets as investors chase rising prices (whether irrationally – confusing prices driven by government interventions as a change in fundamentals – or rationally). Chapter 9 examines how booms can mask errors in pricing risk on financial markets and interact with a bank "leverage cycle." Disequilibrium in politics and financial regulation can thus spawn cyclones in financial markets with destructive consequences.

Notes

1 Andrei Shleifer, *Inefficient Markets: An Introduction to Behavioral Finance*, 174 (2000, Oxford University Press). Law professor John Coffee has made one of the few attempts to provide such a model. He creates a simple model for what he calls the "sine curve of regulation," i.e., a pattern of financial regulation in the wake of financial crises followed by regulatory roll back in later years. Professor Coffee builds off the work of Mancur Olson and attributes the passage of financial regulation to "latent" citizen groups mobilizing in the wake of financial crises, overcoming daunting collective action challenges thanks to policy entrepreneurs. The passage of time leads a return to normalcy as more cohesive interest groups in the financial industry again dominate the political sphere and push to dilute financial regulation. This very basic model is consistent with the more nuanced articulation of the rational actor/public choice model outlined in this chapter. See John C. Coffee, Jr., The Political Economy of Dodd-Frank: Why Financial Reform Tends to be Frustrated and Systemic Risk Perpetuated, 97 *Cornell Law Review* 1019 (2012).

2 For an overview of some of the economic evidence that financial liberalization contributes to asset price bubbles and financial crises, See Franklin Allen and Douglas Gale, Bubbles, Crises, and Policy, 15 *Oxford Review of Economic Policy* 9 (1999). See also Graciela L. Kaminsky and Carmen M. Reinhart, The Twin Crises: The Causes of Banking and Balance-Of-Payments Problems, 89 *American Economic Review* 473 (1999) (detailing evidence that financial liberalization in various countries starting in 1970s sparked credit booms and led to currency and banking crises). Cf. Asli Demirgüç-Kunt and Enrica Detragiache, Financial Liberalization and Financial Fragility, World Bank Policy Research Center, *Working Paper No. 1917* (June 1, 1998) (study of fifty-three countries from 1980 to 1995 indicates that countries that have liberalized the financial services sector are more likely to experience banking crises, but effects of liberalization on fragility of banking sector weaken in countries with stronger rule of law, lower level of corruption, and good contract enforcement).

   For an alternative model of how bubbles are created by social feedback cycles, see Mitchel Y. Abolafia and Martin Kilduff, Enacting Market Crisis: The Social Construction of a Speculative Bubble, 33 *Administrative Science Quarterly* 177 (1988) (arguing that bubbles are socially constructed by the interaction of competing self-interest social coalitions, including speculators, brokers, bankers, the media, and regulators).

3 Chapter 2, "Japan's real estate bubble," and Chapter 6, "Japan" (describing scholarship arguing that financial liberalization caused Japan's bubble).

4 Chapter 2, "The Mississippi bubble" (describing the origins of John Law's investment scheme).

5 Chapter 2, notes 74–6 and accompanying text (describing Parliamentary debate on repeal of the Bubble Act).

6 The legal history of the Panic of 1825 is provided in "The Panic of 1825: the first emerging markets crisis." For a discussion of regulatory stimulus in the booms that preceded the Panics of 1847 and 1866, see Chapter 2, "1840s railway mania to the crisis of 1847" and "1860s boom in limited liability companies to the Overend, Gurney Crisis of 1866."

7 See Chapter 2, "The Panics of 1869 and 1873 in the United States," "*Gründerboom* and *Gründerkrach*: the Panic of 1873 in Germany and Austria." In the case of Germany, political changes also spurred both boom and regulatory stimulus. Germany's political unification, its victory against France in the Franco-Prussian War, and its subsequent receipt of war reparations generated surplus capital, a new investor class, and demand for railroads and other ventures to develop the nation. At the same time, the overriding political objective of industrial development spurred the

Imperial government to rewrite the law on incorporations. The greater availability of limited liability, in turn, mobilized and channeled private sector investment towards new railroads and other capital intensive enterprises. Chapter 2, "*Gründerboom* and *Gründerkrach*: the Panic of 1873 in Germany and Austria."

8 Chapter 2, "Telecommunications deregulation."

9 Chapter 2, notes 15, 45–6, 53, 71, 92 and accompanying text; Chapter 2, Appendix Table 2.a.3.

10 Chapter 2, notes 175–88 and accompanying text.

11 Chapter 2, notes 134–5 and accompanying text.

12 Chapter 2, "Changes in banking laws facilitate real estate lending and securities activities."

13 Chapter 2, "Securities deregulation."

14 Chapter 2 "Regulatory stimulus and legal backlash: beyond deregulation and re-regulation."

15 By focusing on the link between market booms and regulatory stimulus/deregulation, all three models offer to explain the overall historical pattern of regulatory stimulus/deregulation during boom times, rather than many other studies which focus on explaining particular instances of deregulation in the banking industry or elsewhere. See, e.g., Randall S. Kroszner and Philip E. Strahan, What Drives Deregulation? Economics and Politics of the Relaxation of Bank Branching Restrictions, 114 *Quarterly Journal of Economics* 1437 (1999).

16 The germinal scholarship in public choice or the "economic theory" of regulation includes the following works: George J. Stigler, The Theory of Economic Regulation, 2 *Bell Journal of Economics and Management Science* 3 (Spring 1971); Richard A. Posner, Taxation by Regulation, 2 *Bell Journal of Economics and Management Science* 3 (Spring 1971); Richard A. Posner, Theories of Economic Regulation, 5 *Bell Journal of Economics and Management Science* 335 (Autumn 1974); Sam Peltzman, Toward a More General Theory of Regulation, 19 *Journal of Law and Economics* 211 (1976); Gary Becker, A Theory of Competition among Pressure Groups for Political Influence, 98 *Quarterly Journal of Economics* 371 (1983).

17 The germinal work on the problem of collective action in interest group mobilization is Mancur Olson, *The Logic of Collective Action: Public Goods and the Theory of Groups* (1971, Harvard University Press). For a nuanced discussion of how various factors, including group size and decentralization, impact the formation and structure of interest groups, see Jack L. Walker, *Mobilizing Interest Groups in America: Patrons, Professions, and Social Movements*, 89–94 (1994, University of Michigan Press).

18 For the foundational works on economic rent-seeking, see Gordon Tullock, The Welfare Costs of Tariffs, Monopolies, and Theft, 5 *Western Economic Journal* 224 (1967); Anne O. Krueger, The Political Economy of the Rent-Seeking Society, 64 *American Economic Review* 291(1974).

19 See generally Ernesto Dal Bó, Regulatory Capture: A Review, 22 *Oxford Review of Economic Policy* 203 (2006).

20 Indeed, Mancur Olson's work has been used to argue for various regulations to promote social welfare and solve collective action problems. For a recent example in the context of financial regulation, see Coffee, *supra* note 1.

21 See Randall S. Kroszner and Philip E. Strahan, What Drives Regulation? Economics and Politics of the Relaxation of Bank Branching Restrictions, 114 *Quarterly Journal of Economics* 1437 (1999) (finding that private interest theory provides better explanation than public interest and political institutional explanations for removal of particular banking law restrictions). Cf. Sam Peltzman, The Economic Theory of Regulation after a Decade of Deregulation, *Brookings Papers Economic Activity: Microeconomics*, 1 (1989). Peltzman finds that most cases of deregulation in the 1980s do not challenge the "economic theory" of regulation. Instead, according to Peltzman, the political coalitions behind particular regulations

weakened when the rents created by those regulations declined, which allowed for a regulatory roll back. Peltzman notes two exceptions to this rule – or cases in which deregulation occurred despite the fact that rents to interest groups from those regulations remained high. Ibid. at 39–41.

22 David Truman argued that interest groups owe their formation to a "disturbance" in either economic or social conditions. David B. Truman, *The Governmental Process*, 88 (1951, Alfred A. Knopf); see also Jeffrey M. Berry, *The Interest Group Society*, 65–6 (3rd ed. 1997, Longman); Walker, *supra* note 17, at 42.

23 Chapter 1, "A behavioral-finance model of asset price bubbles." Charles P. Kindleberger, *Manias, Panics and Crashes: A History of Financial Crises*, 14 (4th ed. 2000, Wiley Investment Classics); Andrei Shleifer, *Inefficient Markets: An Introduction to Behavioral Finance*, 169 (2000, Oxford University Press).

24 Berry, *supra* note 22, at 66–7.

25 Chapter 2, note 44 and accompanying text.

26 Chapter 2, "The Panic of 1825: the first emerging markets crisis," "Cycles of corporate law and crises in nineteenth century Britain."

27 Cf. H.G. Moulton, England's Waterway Revival, 19 *Journal of Political Economy* 1, 9–10 (January 1911).

28 Chapter 6, notes 91–4 and accompanying text.

29 Chapter 6, Japan: "Deregulation → Regulatory arbitrage → Deregulation."

30 Chapter 6, note 93 and accompanying text.

31 Chapter 6, Japan: "Deregulation → Regulatory arbitrage → Deregulation."

32 Chapter 6, Japan: "Deregulation → Regulatory arbitrage → Deregulation."

33 Chapter 2, notes 306–10 and accompanying text. See also Chapter 6, Japan: "Deregulation → Regulatory arbitrage → Deregulation."

34 Cf. Rande W. Kostal, *Law and English Railway Capitalism*, 16, 112–13 (1994, Oxford University Press) (describing political opposition of canals and landowners to new railway bills). The development of railways first cheered merchants and manufacturers for breaking the monopoly power of canals and turnpikes, but later raised its own threat of monopoly power. Ibid. at 184. Horse carriage and canal transportation companies could not compete with the speed and efficiency of railways. Ibid. at 188.

35 For a portion of the vast literature exploring the advantages that corporations enjoy in U.S. politics, See, e.g., Lester M. Salamon and John J. Siegfried, Economic Power and Political Influence: The Impact of Industry Structure on Public Policy, in *The Political Economy: Readings in the Politics and Economics of American Public Policy*, 263, 264–5 (Thomas Ferguson and Joel Roger eds. 1984, M.E. Sharpe). For older data on the use of corporate funds in U.S. and U.K. politics, see Charles E. Lindblom, *Politics and Markets: the World's Political Economic Systems*, 194–6 (1977, Basic Books). See also Berry, *supra* note 22, at 218–33.

36 See Stephen M. Bainbridge, *The New Corporate Governance in Theory and Practice*, 156 (2008, Oxford University Press) (outlining advantages of corporate form in centralizing control and overcoming shareholder collective action problems).

37 See 558 U.S. 50, 130 S.Ct. 876 (2010) (overturning laws limiting corporate expenditures on political campaigns made independent of candidates for violating the 1st Amendment). The majority opinion of the Court rejected government rationales for limiting these expenditures, including arguments that corporate expenditures would distort the political marketplace, lead to corruption or the appearance of corruption, and compel shareholders to support a corporation's speech. 130 S.Ct. at 886–917.

In a separate opinion, Justice Stevens dissented from these core holdings, arguing that they represent a "radical departure from what had been settled First Amendment law." 130, S.Ct. 948 (Stevens J. concurring in part, dissenting in part). Stevens offers a history of constitutional treatment of corporate free speech in the United States starting with the Framers. Ibid. at 948–52.

38 Melanie L. Fein, *Securities Activities of Banks*, §§ 13.02[A], 13.02[B] (3rd ed. 2010 Suppl., Aspen Publishers); Eric Smalley, Kristin A. Fisher, Karin R. Jagger, Eliot J. Katz, Kathleen A. Roman, Donald C. Pingleton III, and Tyesha Witcher eds., *Mortgage-Backed Securities: Developments and Trends in the Secondary Mortgage Market 2009–2010*, § 10.8, 748 (2009, West Publishing Group).

39 Section 21 of the later-repealed Glass-Steagall Act prevented depository institutions from engaging "in the business of issuing, underwriting, selling, or distributing" securities for their own account. 12 U.S.C. § 378 (1987). See Smalley *et al.*, *supra* note 38, at 748–9 (§10.8).

Beginning in 1977 and throughout the 1980s and 1990s, the OCC issued a series of interpretations that used an exception to this statutory prohibition to allow national banks to expand incrementally into the issuance, underwriting, and dealing of mortgage-backed securities. Smalley *et al.*, *supra* note 38, at 748–9 (§10.8). The Glass-Steagall Act prohibition included the following proviso:

> nothing in this paragraph shall be construed as affecting in any way such right as any bank, banking association, savings bank, trust company, or other banking institution, may otherwise possess to sell, without recourse or agreement to repurchase, obligations evidencing loans on real estate.
>
> 12 U.S.C. § 378(a)(1) (1987)

For a description of the series of OCC interpretations that allowed banks to issue and sell mortgage-backed securities (and other asset-backed securities), see Fein, *supra* note 39, at § 13.02[A]; Smalley *et al.*, *supra* note 38, at 748–51 (§ 10:8).

The power of national banks to issue and underwrite mortgage-backed securities (and other asset-backed securities) prompted the Federal Reserve Board to issue its own set of regulatory interpretations under the Glass-Steagall Act to permit bank holding companies to conduct the same activities. Fein, *supra* note 38, at § 13.02[B]. The Federal Reserve also issued another series of interpretations permitting these activities under a separate statute, the Bank Holding Company Act. Fein, *supra* note 39, at § 13.02[B].

40 *Securities Industry Association* v. *Clarke*, 885 F.2d 1034 (2d Cir. 1989) *cert. denied*, 110 S. Ct. 1113 (1990). For analysis of the case, see Fein, *supra* note 39, at §§ 4.05[C][6], 13.02[A]. See also *Securities Industry Association* v. *Board of Governors*, 839 F.2d 47 (2d Cir. 1988), *cert. denied*, 486 U.S. 1059 (1988).

41 See Arthur E. Wilmarth, Jr., The Dark Side of Universal Banking: Financial Conglomerates and the Origins of the Subprime Financial Crisis, 41 *Connecticut Law Review* 963 (2009) See ibid. at 972–5 (describing origins of Glass-Steagall Act and its demise), 975–80 (describing merger wave among banks and securities firms in 1980s and 1990s, as deregulation slowly eroded legal barriers between those two lines of business), 980–1002 (outlining convergence of businesses of banks and securities firms during this period in areas such as securitization and derivatives; focusing on activities of large complex financial institutions).

42 Simon Johnson and James Kwak explain how large financial conglomerates flexed their political muscles in the wake of Glass-Steagall's demise to defeat efforts to regulate over-the-counter derivatives. Simon Johnson and James Kwak, *13 Bankers: The Wall Street Takeover and the Next Financial Meltdown*, 133–7 (2010, Random House).

43 Robert Dahl articulated the most coherent and influential vision of interest group pluralism. Robert A. Dahl, *A Preface to Democratic Theory* (1956, University of Chicago Press). For a brief summary of early methodological and normative criticisms of Dahl's theory, including that pluralism favored certain elites, see Berry, *supra* note 22, at 11–13.

44 Cf. Lawrence G. Baxter, "Capture" in Financial Regulation: Can We Channel It Toward the Common Good? 21 *Cornell Journal of Law and Public Policy* 175, 191

(2011) (discussing relative political strength of large financial institutions compared to political weakness of consumers and other diffuse groups in shaping financial regulation).

45 See Kimberly D. Krawiec, Don't "Screw Joe The Plummer": The Sausage-Making of Financial Reform, *Duke Law Faculty Scholarship Paper 2445* (November 11, 2011) available at http://papers.ssrn.com/sol3/papers.cfm?abstract_id=1925431 (last visited July 24, 2013). Professor Krawiec documents that public interest groups have participated in the notice-and-comment process of the Volcker Rule under the Dodd-Frank Act. However, their involvement has been limited primarily to orchestrating a mass submission of short form letter comments. Professor Krawiec notes that the financial industry, by contrast, has had far more intensive and substantive participation in this rule-making process. Cf. Claire Kelly, Financial Crises and Civil Society, 11 *Chicago Journal of International Law* 505 (2011) (arguing that civil society can play a role in international financial regulation in the wake of the global financial crisis).

46 This does not mean, however, that corporations, securities issuers, and financial intermediaries only have incentives to push for legal rules that disadvantage retail investors. Some research indicates that shareholder protection regimes can promote aggregate shareholder investment. Rafael La Porta, Florencio Lopez-de-Silanes, Andrei Shleifer, and Robert Vishny, Investor Protection and Corporate Governance, 58 *Journal of Financial Economics* 3 (2007). Even if this general finding is correct, industry interest groups may not recognize the value of a shareholder protection regime, expend collective resources to defend it, nor equate specific rules with the value of the regime overall. Industry groups still have incentives to push for the removal of particular "taxes" on their profits from minority shareholders. Bubble periods may also alter the calculus by greatly enlarging short-term profit opportunities.

For some of the public choice literature that argues that financial industry groups supported New Deal financial regulation to erect barriers to entry to their markets, see *infra* notes 123–5 and accompanying text.

47 See generally Richard W. Painter, Responding to a False Alarm: Federal Preemption of State Securities Fraud Causes of Action, 84 *Cornell Law Review* 1, 31–9 (1998) (describing battles between issuers, underwriters, and accountants, on the one hand, and plaintiffs' securities bar, on the other, over federal and state legal reform of securities litigation in the 1990s).

See also Robert P. Bartlett III, Do Institutional Investors Really Care About 10b-5? Evidence from Investor Trading Behavior Following *Morrison v. National Australia Bank Ltd.*, Unpublished manuscript (on file with the author) (2012). Professor Bartlett notes that institutional investors publicly opposed the limitation of the extraterritorial application of an important U.S. antifraud securities rule. Yet he finds evidence that the ultimate change in this rule had little apparent effect on the investment behavior of these firms.

48 See Jonathan R. Macey and Geoffrey P. Miller, Plaintiffs' Attorney's Role in Class Action and Derivative Litigation: Economic Analysis and Recommendations for Reform, 58 *University of Chicago Law Review* 1 (1991) (analyzing agency costs associated with plaintiffs' attorneys). Cf. Bernard S. Black, Agents Watching Agents: The Promise of Institutional Investor Voice, 39 *UCLA Law Review* 811 (1992) (concluding that, despite an additional layer of agency costs for retail investors, institutional investors played a positive role in corporate governance).

49 See George G. Kaufman and Kenneth E. Scott, What is Systemic Risk, and Do Bank Regulators Retard or Contribute to It, 7 *Independent Review* 371, 373 (2003) (describing connection between financial institution leverage and systemic risk).

50 See generally Karl S. Okamoto, After the Bailout: Regulating Systemic Moral Hazard, 57 *UCLA Law Review* 183 (2009).

51 See, e.g., Emmanuel Farhi and Jean Tirole, Collective Moral Hazard, Maturity Mismatch, and Systemic Bailouts, National Bureau of Economic Research, *Working Paper No. 15138* (July 2009) available at www.nber.org/papers/w15138 (last visited July 24, 2013) (describing how collective decisions by financial institutions to engage in maturity transformation (creating maturity mismatches) and correlate risk exposures creates systemic risk and pressure for government intervention).

52 Cf. Shleifer, *supra* note 1, at 3 (detailing Efficient Markets Hypothesis and noting "investor rationality implies the impossibility of earning superior risk-adjusted returns").

53 For a description of the rise of citizen interest groups, including environmental groups, in U.S. politics, see Berry, *supra* note 22, at 31–4.

54 Kelly, *supra* note 45.

55 Cf. Krawiec, *supra* note 45 (documenting massive participation in rule-making process of Volcker Rule of financial industry groups compared to much less extensive participation of organized citizen groups despite the public salience of the financial crisis and this regulation in particular).

56 See generally Carolyn Sissoko, Is Financial Regulation Structurally Biased to Favor Deregulation? 86 *Southern California Law Review* 365 (2013).

57 In a germinal case, the U.S. Supreme Court limited standing to sue federal agencies in federal court over environmental laws to only those parties that could show they suffered a particular injury by the agency action. *Lujan* v. *Defenders of Wildlife*, 504 U.S. 555, 560 n.1 (1992). The U.S. Supreme Court and lower federal courts have recently rejected all but a very narrow concept of taxpayer standing. E.g., *Hein* v. *Freedom from Religion Found., Inc.*, 551 U.S. 587, 605–6 (2007) (broadly rejecting taxpayer standing to challenge executive action except in very narrow circumstances); *Bumbgarner* v. *United States*, 2010 U.S. Dist. LEXIS 6851 (rejecting taxpayer standing to challenge federal bailouts in wake of Panic of 2007–2008); *Schultz* v. *U.S. Fed. Reserve Sys.*, 2009 U.S. Dist. LEXIS 13961 (same). See also Anne Abramowitz, Comment: a Remedy for Every Right: What Federal Courts Can Learn from California's Taxpayer Standing, 98 *California Law Review* 1595, 1595–607 (2010) (providing history and academic criticism of taxpayer standing doctrine).

58 Indeed, scholars and policymakers look to administrative law for lessons and tools to constrain the decisions and discretion of a wide range of government actors. E.g., Rachel E. Barkow, Institutional Design and the Policing of Prosecutors: Lessons from Administrative Law, 61 *Stanford Law Review* 869 (2008). See also Michael A. Livermore and Richard L. Revesz, Regulatory Review, Capture, and Agency Inaction, 101 *Georgetown Law Journal* 1337 (2013) (proposing review of agency inactions).

59 Some statutes impose this requirement. E.g., *Chamber of Commerce* v. *SEC*, 412 F.3d 133, 143 (D.C. Cir. 2005) (Securities and Exchange Commission has "statutory obligation to determine as best it can the economic implications" of proposed rules). Various executive orders give the Office of Management and Budget the authority to review rules proposed by federal agencies under a cost–benefit framework. See Robert W. Hahn and Cass R. Sunstein, A New Executive Order for Improving Federal Regulation? Deeper and Wider Cost-Benefit Analysis, 150 *University of Pennsylvania Law Review* 1489 (2001).

60 For arguments that cost–benefit analysis requirements are anti-regulatory, see, e.g., Thomas O. McGarity, Some Thoughts on "Deossifying" the Rule-making Process, 41 *Duke Law Journal* 1385 (1992); David C. Vladeck and Thomas O. McGarity, Paralysis by Analysis: How Conservatives Plan to Kill Popular Regulation, *American Prospect*, Summer 1995.

61 *Chamber of Commerce of the U.S.* v. *SEC*, 412 F.3d 133 (D.C. Cir. 2005) (invalidating for failure to perform requisite cost–benefit analysis an SEC rule governing independent directors on mutual fund boards); *Goldstein* v. *SEC*, 451 F.3d 873

(D.C. Cir. 2006) (striking down hedge fund registration rule as arbitrary); *Business Roundtable* v. *SEC*, 647 F.3d 1144 (D.C. Cir. 2011) (ruling that SEC rule requiring proxy access was arbitrary and capricious because of failure of agency to perform appropriate cost–benefit analysis); *American Equity Inv. Life Ins. Co.* v. *SEC*, 613 F.3d 166 (D.C. Cir. 2010) (vacating annuities regulation).

For a sampling of academic commentary on the SEC's struggles in the D.C. Circuit, see, e.g., Troy A. Paredes, On the Decision to Regulate Hedge Funds: The SEC's Regulatory Philosophy, Style, and Mission, 2006 *University of Illinois Law Review* 975 (2006); Donald C. Langevoort, The SEC as a Lawmaker: Choices about Investor Protection in the Face of Uncertainty, 84 *Washington University Law Review* 1591 (2006) (discussing case in which D.C. Circuit struck down SEC rule on mutual funds for failure to perform cost–benefit analysis); Edward Sherwin, The Cost-Benefit Analysis of Financial Regulation: Lessons from the SEC's Stalled Mutual Fund Reform Effort, 12 *Stanford Journal of Law, Business and Finance* 1 (2006) (arguing financial regulators need to justify regulation according to federal rules requiring cost–benefit analysis).

62 For an analysis of when interest groups deploy inside strategies versus outside ones, see Walker, *supra* note 17, at 103–21.

63 Viral V. Acharya, Thomas F. Cooley, Matthew Richardson, and Ingo Walter, Capital, Contingent Capital, and Liquidity Requirements, in *Regulating Wall Street: The Dodd-Frank Act and the New Architecture of Global Finance*, 145, 157 (Viral V. Acharya, Thomas F. Cooley, Matthew P. Richardson, and Ingo Walter eds., 2011, John Wiley & Sons); Viral V. Acharya, Matthew Richardson, Stijn van Nieuwerburgh, and Lawrence J. White, *Guaranteed to Fail: Fannie Mae, Freddie Mac, and the Debacle of Mortgage Finance*, 27–8 (2011, Princeton University Press) (analyzing too-big-to-fail guarantees and leverage of government-sponsored entities).

64 Cf. Rebel A. Cole, Joseph A. McKenzie, and Lawrence J. White, Deregulation Gone Awry: Moral Hazard in the Savings and Loan Industry, in *The Causes and Costs of Depository Institution Failures*, 29 (Allin F. Cottrell, Michael S. Lawlor, and John H. Wood eds. 1995, Springer) (detailing how deregulation and a government safety net created moral hazard for federal thrifts during the U.S. Savings and Loan crisis). Chapter 5 will explore how the expectation of government bailouts and the presence of government guarantees create incentives for regulatory capital arbitrage by financial institutions.

65 The public choice view of self-interested regulators has been heavily criticized. See, e.g., Mark Kelman, On Democracy-Bashing: A Skeptical Look at the Theoretical and "Empirical" Practice of the Public Choice Movement, 74 *Virginia Law Review* 199, 202 (1988).

66 See Chapter 2, notes 137–8, 145 and accompanying text.

67 Chapter 2, notes 17, 46, 49–51, 72 and accompanying text. Historian Stuart Banner describes how critics of "stock-jobbing" during the South Sea bubble were concerned about an incestuous relationship between the financial community and politicians had led to a ballooning government.

> As the government grew larger, and as it came to have more and more funds at its disposal, opportunities for patronage grew. This new bureaucratic state, as the critics saw it, was self-perpetuating: as more and more people depended on the bureaucracy's existence for their livelihood, they developed a vested interest in keeping the bureaucracy alive, by issuing more and more debt to finance ever more extensive military projects. And a similarly vicious circle was driving the stock jobbers: as they invested more deeply in government securities, they developed a greater interest in keeping that profitable relationship going, by encouraging the government to incur expenditures of increasing magnitude (often through an aggressive military policy), which would require more borrowing in

the future. The result was public policy made with a view, not to the overall good, but to the benefit of a faction – the people involved in this new fiscal-military state. Stuart Banner, *Anglo-American Securities Regulation: Cultural and Political Roots, 1690–1860*, 64 (1998, Cambridge University Press).

68   Chapter 2, notes 137–8, 145 and accompanying text.
69   Chapter 2, notes 136–45, 148–50 and accompanying text.
70   Chapter 2, "Regulating banks in the Sunshine State."
71   Chapter 2, notes 314–15 and accompanying text.
72   The importance of political threats becomes apparent in a series of case studies by David Hart of the political activity of five computer firms (AOL, Cisco Systems, IBM, Intel, Microsoft) from their foundation through 2000. Hart found that three of these companies (IBM, Intel, and Microsoft) began serious political lobbying efforts only after they faced outside threats which the government could allay (government antitrust litigation in the case of IBM and Microsoft and foreign competition in the case of Intel). David M. Hart, Political Representation Among Dominant Firms: Revisiting the "Olsonian Hypothesis," Harvard Kennedy School of Government Faculty Research, *Working Paper RWP02-045* (October 2002) available at http://papers.ssrn.com/sol3/papers.cfm?abstract_id=357540 (last visited July 24, 2013).
73   This data can be accessed at www.opensecrets.org/industries/index.php (last visited July 24, 2013).
74   News stories from that era provide accounts of politicians courting support from Silicon Valley donors for the first time. E.g., Karen Breslau, Valley of the Dollars, *Newsweek*, November 8, 1999, at 36.
75   Ibid. OpenSecrets.org and the Center for Responsive Politics collects this data from Federal Election Commission filings. The data are based on contributions of $200 or more from PACs and individuals to federal candidates and from PACs, soft money (including directly from corporate and union treasuries), and individual donors to political parties and outside spending groups, all as reported to the Federal Election Commission. Although election cycles are shown in charts as 1996, 1998, 2000 etc., they actually represent two-year periods. For example, the 2002 election cycle runs from January 1, 2001 to December 31, 2002. Ibid.
76   Ibid. (explaining methodology and source of data).
77   See *supra* note 75 for an explanation of data and methodology.
78   Berry, *supra* note 22, at 154–8 (surveying debate on what campaign contributions and lobbying buys).
79   See Dal Bó, *supra* note 19, at 212–13 (surveying literature on how interest groups can affect regulatory incentives in different ways, including by inflicting reputational damage).
      Even independent agencies are subject to various forms of capture. This occurs despite the fact that one of the core rationales for agency independence is to prevent this capture and limit political influence over certain government processes. Recent administrative law scholarship has focused on the less visible mechanisms by which interest groups and politicians can shape decision-making in independent agencies. For a careful analysis of the various and subtle ways in which agencies can be captured, see Rachel E. Barkow, Insulating Agencies: Avoiding Capture Through Institutional Design, 89 *Texas Law Review* 15 (2010). Cf. Lisa Schultz Bressman and Robert B. Thompson, The Future of Agency Independence, 63 *Vanderbilt Law Review* 599 (2010) (discussing pathways by which U.S. President can influence independent agencies).
80   See Dal Bó, *supra* note 19, at 211–12 (surveying literature on interest group provision of information as means of influencing regulators rather than changing regulator incentives).
81   For economic theories that claim information asymmetries contribute to bubbles, see Franklin Allen and Douglas Gale, Bubbles and Crises, 110 *Economic Journal* 236

(2000); Franklin Allen, Stephen Morris, and Andrew Postlewaite, Finite Bubbles with Short Sale Constraints and Asymmetric Information, 61 *Journal of Economic Theory* 206 (1993).

82 Ibid.

83 For a small sample of the economic literature on financial innovations during bubble periods, see James C. Van Horne, Of Financial Innovations and Excesses, 40 *Journal of Finance* 620 (1984); Carlota Perez, *Technological Revolutions and Financial Capital: The Dynamics of Bubbles and Golden Ages*, 138–145 (2003 Edward Elgar); John C. Persons and Vincent A. Warther, Boom and Bust Patterns in the Adoption of Financial Innovations, 10 *Review of Financial Studies* 939 (1997).

84 Chapter 2, "The Mississippi bubble."

85 Chapter 2, "The South Seas bubble."

86 Chapter 2, note 285.

87 For an introduction to credit derivatives and the risks they pose, see Frank Partnoy and David A. Skeel, Jr., The Promise and Perils of Credit Derivatives, 75 *University of Cincinnati Law Review* 1019 (2007). Professors Partnoy and Skeel declare themselves "agnostic" on the question of whether these economic risks justify additional disclosure regulations. Ibid. at 1046. For other perspectives on information asymmetries in credit derivatives, particularly those which leave regulators under-informed of the risks and macroeconomic effects of these instruments, see Margaret M. Blair and Erik F. Gerding, Sometimes Too Great a Notional: Measuring the "Systemic Significance" of OTC Credit Derivatives, 1 *Lombard Street* 10 (August 31, 2009); Erik F. Gerding, Credit Derivatives, Leverage, and Financial Regulation's Missing Macroeconomic Dimension, 8 *Berkeley Business Law Journal* 29 (2011).

88 See Dal Bó, *supra* note 19, at 214–19 (surveying literature).

89 Kay Lehman Schlozman and John T. Tierney, *Organized Interests and American Democracy*, 342 (1986, Harper & Row).

90 Erik F. Gerding, The Next Epidemic: Bubbles and the Growth and Decay of Securities Regulation, 38 *Connecticut Law Review* 393, 422 (2006).

91 Cf. Toni Makkai and John Braithwaite, In and Out of the Revolving Door: Making Sense of Regulatory Capture, 12 *Journal of Public Policy* 61, 61 (1992) (describing capture involving both leaving government service for industry and vice versa).

92 See, e.g., ibid. In evaluating revolving door patterns in the Australian nursing home sectors, Professors Makkai and Braithwaite found little evidence that regulators either exiting the public sector for industry or vice versa leads to lower enforcement outcomes. Instead, they argue for seeing the problem of regulatory capture as a situational, rather than as a unitary, phenomenon that is determined by interest group structure.

93 For an in-depth analysis of the *amakudari* phenomenon, see Chikako Usui and Richard A. Colignon, Government Elites and Amakudari in Japan, 1963–1992, 35 *Asian Survey* 682 (July 1995). See also Curtis J. Milhaupt and Geoffrey P. Miller, Cooperation, Conflict, and Convergence in Japanese Finance: Evidence from the "Jusen" Problem, 29 *Law and Policy in International Business* 1, 14–15, 27 (1997); Akiyoshi Horiuchi and Katsutoshi Shimizu, Did *Amakudari* Undermine the Effectiveness of Regulator Monitoring in Japan? 25 *Journal of Banking and Finance* 573 (2001) (finding that banks that engaged in *amakudari* by hiring former Ministry of Finance officials had lower capital adequacy levels and increased levels of non-performing loans).

94 E.g., Johnson and Kwak, *supra* note 42, at 93. See also Simon Johnson, The Quiet Coup, *The Atlantic*, May 2009, at 47. Economist Raghuram Rajan attaches a similar label of "cognitive capture" to the belief of financial regulators that the interest of the industry they regulate constitutes the public interest. Raghuram G. Rajan, *Fault Lines: How Hidden Fractures Still Threaten the World Economy*, 181 (2010, Princeton University Press).

95 E.g., Makkai and Braithwaite, *supra* note 91.
96 Central banks also face this disincentive to prick an asset price bubble. See generally Geoffrey P. Miller, The Role of a Central Bank in a Bubble Economy, 18 *Cardozo Law Review* 1053, 1055 (1996) (discussing the Bank of Japan's pivotal role in the creation and ultimate bursting of the Japanese economic bubble).
97 For a brief overview of the various political groups that pressured Freddie Mac and Fannie Mae to invest in subprime mortgages, see Erik F. Gerding, Deregulation Pas de Deux: Dual Regulatory Classes of Financial Institutions and the Path to Financial Crisis in Sweden and the United States, 15 *NeXuS* 135, 152–4 (2010).
98 Chapter 5 discusses regulatory arbitrage in detail. For recent empirical work on regulatory arbitrage in international banking, see, e.g., Joel F. Houston, Chen Lin and Yue Ma, Regulatory Arbitrage and International Bank Flows, Unpublished manuscript (December 18, 2009) available at http://papers.ssrn.com/sol3/papers.cfm?abstract_id=1525895 (last visited July 24, 2013) (analyzing capital flows from banks in jurisdictions with heavier regulations to more lightly regulated jurisdictions).
99 Cf. Eric Helleiner, *States and the Reemergence of Global Finance: From Bretton Woods to the 1990s*, 167 (1996, Cornell University Press).
100 Chapter 6, note 52 and accompanying text.
101 Chapter 6, "Deregulation → Regulatory arbitrage → Deregulation." See also Chapter 2, note 311 and accompanying text.
102 Makkai and Braithwaite argue that the particular problem of volume of enforcement work represents a potentially more worrisome pressure on regulators to under-enforce laws than "revolving doors" or capture. They speculate that regulators may make a conscious choice not to enforce laws intensively, because that would tie up too many resources on one individual violation. Makkai and Braithwaite, *supra* note 92, at 75.
103 Eugene N. White, Lessons from the Great American Real Estate Boom and Bust of the 1920s, National Bureau of Economic Research, *Working Paper No. 15573*, 41 (December 2009) available at www.nber.org/papers/w15573 (last visited July 24, 2013). White offers the following assessment of the OCC's performance during the decade's real estate boom:

> Overall, the OCC, which most contemporary observers conceded was the best bank regulatory agency, did not noticeably respond to the real estate boom. It garnered no additional resources nor did it redirect its existing funds or manpower to increase supervision of rapidly expanding banking systems in hot regional markets. It may even have mildly encouraged the boom by easing entry into banking.
>
> Ibid. at 46

104 Ibid. at 45–6.
105 For the sake of simplicity, calculations were made by dividing the overall and enforcement budget amounts for the SEC by the average of the Dow Jones Wilshire 5000 on the last day of each of the twelve months of the given year.
    Data on the SEC's overall budget is taken from SEC, SEC Budget History vs. Actual Expenses, available at www.sec.gov/foia/docs/budgetact.htm (last modified March 3, 2005). Data on the SEC's enforcement budget is taken from the "Prevention and Suppression of Fraud" line in the federal budget compendia for the fifteen federal fiscal years from 1990 to 2004. Office of Management and Budget, Budget of the United States Government, Fiscal Year 1992, at 1177 (1991); Office of Management and Budget, Budget of the United States Government, Fiscal Year 1993, at 1031 (1992); Office of Management and Budget, Budget of the United States Government, Fiscal Year 1994, at 1140 (1993); Office of Management and Budget, Budget of the United States Government Appendix, Fiscal Year 1995, at 961 (1994); Office of Management and Budget Appendix: Budget of the United States Government, Fiscal Year 1996, at

1054 (1995); Office of Management and Budget, Appendix: Budget of the United States Government, Fiscal Year 1997, at 1051 (1996); Office of Management and Budget, Appendix: Budget of the United States Government, Fiscal Year 1998, at 1112 (1997); Office of Management and Budget, Appendix: Budget of the United States Government, Fiscal Year 1999, at 1134 (1998); Office of Management and Budget, Appendix: Budget of the United States Government, Fiscal Year 2000, at 1198 (1999); Office of Management and Budget, Appendix: Budget of the United States Government, Fiscal Year 2001, at 1203 (2000); Office of Management and Budget, Appendix: Budget of the United States Government, Fiscal Year 2002, at 1215 (2001); Office of Management and Budget, Appendix: Budget of the United States Government, Fiscal Year 2003, at 1178 (2002); Office of Management and Budget, Appendix: Budget of the United States Government, Fiscal Year 2004, at 1102 (2003); Office of Management and Budget, Appendix: Budget of the United States Government, Fiscal Year 2005, at 1182 (2004); Office of Management and Budget, Appendix: Budget of the United States Government, Fiscal Year 2006, at 1220–1 (2005).

Dow Jones Wilshire 5000 Composite Index, available at Bloomberg (search terms: "DJ Wilshire 5000 TR"; range: "1/31/90" to "12/31/04"; period: monthly; market: "mid/trd") (on file with author).

106 Office of Management and Budget, Budget of the United States Government, Fiscal Year 1992, at 1177 (1991); Office of Management and Budget, Budget of the United States Government, Fiscal Year 1993, at 1032 (1992); Office of Management and Budget, Budget of the United States Government, Fiscal Year 1994, at 1141 (1993); Office of Management and Budget, Budget of the United States Government Appendix, Fiscal Year 1995, at 962 (1994); Office of Management and Budget, Appendix: Budget of the United States Government, Fiscal Year 1996, at 1055 (1995); Office of Management and Budget, Appendix: Budget of the United States Government, Fiscal Year 1997, at 1052 (1996); Office of Management and Budget, Appendix: Budget of the United States Government, Fiscal Year 1998, at 1112–13 (1997); Office of Management and Budget, Appendix: Budget of the United States Government, Fiscal Year 1999, at 1135 (1998); Office of Management and Budget, Appendix: Budget of the United States Government, Fiscal Year 2000, at 1199–200 (1999); Office of Management and Budget, Appendix: Budget of the United States Government, Fiscal Year 2001, at 1204–5 (2000); Office of Management and Budget, Appendix: Budget of the United States Government, Fiscal Year 2002, at 1216–17 (2001); Office of Management and Budget, Appendix: Budget of the United States Government, Fiscal Year 2003, at 1179–80 (2002); Office of Management and Budget, Appendix: Budget of the United States Government, Fiscal Year 2004, at 1103–4 (2003); Office of Management and Budget, Appendix: Budget of the United States Government, Fiscal Year 2005, at 1182–3 (2004); Office of Management and Budget, Appendix: Budget of the United States Government, Fiscal Year 2006, at 1221–2 (2005).

107 Dal Bó, *supra* note 19, at 205.

108 A host of commentators have argued for incremental responses to the financial crisis for policy reasons. E.g., Lawrence A. Cunningham and David Zaring, The Three or Four Approaches to Financial Regulation: A Cautionary Analysis Against Exuberance in Crisis Response, 78 *George Washington Law Review* 39 (2009); Charles K. Whitehead, The Goldilocks Paradigm: Financial Risk and Staged Regulation, 97 *Cornell Law Review* 1267 (2012).

109 Saule T. Omarova, The Quiet Metamorphosis: How Derivatives Changed the "Business of Banking," 63 *Miami Law Review* 1041 (2009).

In addition, the OCC issued a series of interpretations allowing national banks to enter into certain credit default swaps. Fein, *supra* note 39, at § 14.05[G] citing OCC Interpretative Letter No. 1051 (February 15, 2006). This same interpretation allowed national banks to hold below-investment grade debt to hedge risks from derivatives activities. Ibid.

110 Saule T. Omarova, From Gramm-Leach-Bliley to Dodd-Frank: The Unfulfilled Promise of Section 23A of the Federal Reserve Act, 89 *North Carolina Law Review* 1683 (2011) (discussing Section 23A of the Federal Reserve Act).

Omarova argues that the demise of Glass-Steagall division between commercial and investment banking placed much of the work for counteracting subsidy leakage from depository banks on an obscure Depression era statutory provision, namely Section 23A of the Federal Reserve Act. Ibid. at 1695–7. Section 23A imposes quantitative limitations on certain extensions of credit and other transactions between a bank and its affiliates that expose a bank to an affiliate's credit or investment risk. Section 23A also prohibits banks from purchasing low-quality assets from their non-bank affiliates. Finally, it imposes strict collateral requirements with respect to extensions of credit to affiliates. Ibid. at 1692–5.

Omarova details how banks sought exemptions from these strictures "to leverage their subsidiary banks' high credit ratings and access to cheap sources of funding to increase profitability of their nonbank subsidiaries." Ibid. at 1707.

The Federal Reserve granted numerous exemptions from 1996 until 2010 to allow financial conglomerates to use their bank affiliates to support loans by non-banks, including to support shadow banking operations. Ibid. at 1706–28 (describing exemptions to allow bank affiliates to purchase assets such as mortgage and hedge fund loans). For example, between 2000 and 2006, the Federal Reserve gave Citigroup multiple exemptions to allow its banking subsidiary to purchase subprime mortgage assets from a series of mortgage lenders that Citigroup had acquired. Ibid. at 1708–17. Omarova argues that this allowed Citigroup to expand its non-banking mortgage lending operations and reap more profits from securitization. Ibid.

She also details a separate set of Federal Reserve exemptions that allowed conglomerates to use bank affiliates to support securities lending by broker-dealer affiliates. Ibid. at 1717–27. This eased the ability of financial conglomerates to engage in derivatives and repo transactions, among other shadow banking operations. Ibid. at 1726–7. See also R. Kent Weaver, The Politics of Blame Avoidance, in *Princeton Readings in American Politics* (Richard M. Valelly ed., 2009, Princeton University Press); Christopher Hood, *The Blame Game: Spin, Bureaucracy, and Self-Preservation in Government* (2011, Princeton University Press).

111 Ibid. at 1689–90.

112 Ibid. at 1727–9.

113 Fred McChesney has articulated one of the darker versions of public choice theory, in which regulators attempt to use regulation to extract rents and extort interest groups. Fred S. McChesney, *Money for Nothing: Politicians, Rent Extraction, and Political Extortion* (1997, Harvard University Press).

114 See Charlotte Twight, From Claiming Credit to Avoiding Blame: The Evolution of Congressional Strategy for Asbestos Management, 11 *Journal of Public Policy* 153, 155–6 (1991) (surveying this literature).

115 Blame hedges are a variation on blame avoidance devices. See ibid. (detailing blame avoidance devices used by Congress). See also R. Kent Weaver, The Politics of Blame Avoidance, 6 *Journal of Public Policy* 371 (1986) (developing concept of blame avoidance strategies).

116 For a broad overview of the various reasons legislatures draft incomplete statutes, see Scott Baker and Kimberly D. Krawiec, The Penalty Default Canon, 72 *George Washington Law Review* 663, 671–2 (2004).

117 Ibid. at 672–3 (2004) (labeling delegation for this reason "responsibility-shifting delegations"). Baker and Krawiec cite a literature arguing that congressional delegation often reflects attempts by members of Congress to claim credit but avoid blame. Ibid. at 671–81 citing David Epstein and Sharyn O'Halloran, *Delegating Powers* (1999, Cambridge University Press) and Peter H. Aranson, Ernest Gellhorn, and Glen O. Robinson, A Theory of Legislative Delegation, 68 *Cornell Law Review* 1

(1982). For a critique of this theory of congressional delegation, see Baker and Krawiec, *supra* this note, at 677–9, citing Daniel A. Farber and Philip A. Frickey, *Law and Public Choice: A Critical Introduction* 81 (1991, University of Chicago Press); Jerry L. Mashaw, *Greed, Chaos, and Governance: Using Public Choice to Improve Public Law*, 146–7 (1997, Yale University Press).

118 For critiques of public choice theory on both empirical and normative fronts, see, e.g., Mark Kelman, On Democracy-Bashing: A Skeptical Look at the Theoretical and "Empirical" Practice of the Public Choice Movement, 74 *Virginia Law Review* 199 (1988). For other critiques of public choice, see, e.g., Edward L. Rubin, Public Choice, Phenomenology, and the Meaning of the Modern State: Keep the Bathwater, but Throw Out That Baby, 87 *Cornell Law Review* 309 (2002) (disputing the microeconomic foundations of public choice theory that political actors are rational maximizers of self-interest); Abner J. Mikva, Foreword to Symposium on the Theory of Public Choice, 74 *Virginia Law Review* 167, 169 (1988).

119 For a particularly caustic version of this critique of public choice theory, see Kelman, *supra* note 118, at 236–73.

120 Chapter 2, note 26 and accompanying text.

121 Chapter 2, notes 214, 225 and accompanying text.

122 Tamar Frankel, Regulation and Investors' Trust in the Securities Markets, 68 *Brooklyn Law Review* 439, 441–2 (2002). Professor Frankel argues that securities firms supported passage of the federal securities laws during the New Deal for this reason, but simultaneously attempted to water down the provisions of those laws. Their objective, she claims, was to create a public perception that the SEC was regulating securities markets, while reducing their regulatory costs. Ibid. See also Ronald J. Gilson and Reinier H. Kraakman, The Mechanisms of Market Efficiency, 70 *Virginia Law Review* 549, 605–6 (1984). Professors Gilson and Kraakman explain why some firms support regulation

> well-defined and energetically enforced legislation of this type turns the lemon problem on its head and drives low-quality producers from the market. This process may explain in part why trade associations that are dominated by high-quality firms often lobby for more stringent legislative standards and greater enforcement of those standards. Ibid. at 605.

> Gilson and Kraakman cite Section 11 liability under the U.S. Securities Act of 1933 as an example. Ibid. at 605–6.

123 Jonathan R. Macey, The Political Science of Regulating Bank Risk, 49 *Ohio State Law Journal* 1277 (1989) (making public choice argument bank regulations, such as deposit insurance, serve objectives of bank interest groups more than addressing public interest of mitigating bank crises); Jonathan R. Macey, Special Interest Groups Legislation and the Judicial Function: The Dilemma of Glass-Steagall, 33 *Emory Law Journal* 1 (1984) (arguing that Glass-Steagall statute represented victory of investment bank interest groups over commercial banks). Compare William F. Shugart II, A Public Choice Perspective of the Banking Act of 1933, in *The Financial Services Revolution*, 87 (Catherine England and Thomas Huertas eds. 1988, Springer) (positing public choice explanation that Glass-Steagall Act benefitted both commercial and investment banks).

124 Paul G. Mahoney, The Political Economy of the Securities Act of 1933, 30 *Journal of Legal Studies* 1 (2001).

125 John Morley, Collective Branding and the Origins of Investment Fund Regulation, 6 *Virginia Law and Business Review* 341 (2012). Morley argues that changes to tax rules governing investment funds may have stemmed from efforts by open-end funds to remove assets from closed-end funds. Ibid. at 392–4.

126 Coffee, *supra* note 1.

127 Anthony Downs, Up and Down with Ecology: The Issue Attention Cycle, 28 *Public Interest* 38 (1972).
128 Truman, *supra* note 22, at 88.
129 Chapter 2, note 165 and accompanying text.
130 For a history of the enactment of the Securities Act of 1933, see Joel Seligman, *The Transformation of Wall Street*, 39–72 (3rd ed. 2003, Aspen Publishers).
131 See ibid. at 73–100 (describing history of the Securities Exchange Act of 1934, its political compromises, and the resurgent political power of business and Wall Street firms behind those compromises).
132 Stephen J. Choi and Adam C. Pritchard, Behavioral Economics and the SEC, 56 *Stanford Law Review* 1 (2003). Unfortunately, Choi and Pritchard offer scant evidence to support their claims, but use behavioral economics more as a rhetorical device to counter arguments that behavioral biases among market participants support a need for regulatory intervention.
133 See Neil D. Weinstein, Unrealistic Optimism about Future Life Events, 39 *Journal of Personality and Social Psychology* 806 (1980).
134 Richard P. Larrick, Katherine A. Burson, and Jack B. Soll, Social Comparison and Confidence: When Thinking You're Better than Average Predicts Overconfidence (and When It Does Not), 102 *Organizational Behavior and Human Decision Processes* 76, 76–8 (2007) (surveying literature on overconfidence and "better than average" effects). This study reconciles evidence that individuals tend to be overconfident in their ability when performing difficult tasks, but underconfident when performing easy tasks. See also Nicholas Barberis and Richard Thaler, A Survey of Behavioral Finance, in *1B Handbook of the Economics of Finance*, 1054, 1065–6 (George M. Constantinides, Milton Harris, and René M. Stulz, eds., 2003, Elsevier North Holland) (discussing overconfidence in context of behavioral finance).
135 David Laibson conducted early, influential research that provided evidence of hyperbolic discounting. David Laibson, Golden Eggs and Hyperbolic Discounting, 112 *Quarterly Journal of Economics* 443, 445–6 (1997).
136 Ibid. See also Christine Jolls, Cass R. Sunstein, and Richard Thaler, A Behavioral Approach to Law and Economics, 50 *Stanford Law Review* 1471, 1539 (1998) (surveying literature on hyperbolic discounting and discussing applications to law).
137 See Laibson, *supra* note 135 (discussing this inconsistency).
138 Amos Tversky and Daniel Kahneman, Judgment under Uncertainty: Heuristics and Biases, 185 *Science* 1124, 1128 (1974).
139 See generally Richard S. Thaler, Mental Accounting Matters, in *Choices, Values and Frames*, 241 (Daniel Kahneman and Amos Tversky eds., 2000, Cambridge University Press).
140 Chapter 1 provided evidence of behavioral biases of noise traders. Chapter 1, "Behavioral finance models of bubbles." Chapter 8 provides evidence that even financial professionals bid asset prices higher than fundamental value in experimental asset market settings. Chapter 8, "Evaluating the evidence."
141 Chapter 1 set forth some of the criticisms of behavioral finance. Chapter 1, "Criticism of behavioral finance: open questions."
142 See Tversky and Kahneman, *supra* note 138, at 1127–8.
143 Barberis and Thaler, *supra* note 134, at 1067.
144 Jack M. Guttentag and Richard J. Herring, Disaster Myopia in International Banking, Princeton University, *Essays in International Finance No. 164* (September 1986).
145 Richard J. Herring and Susan Wachter, Real Estate Booms and Banking Busts: An International Perspective, Wharton Financial Institutions Center, *Working Paper 99-27*, 15 (1999) available at http://fic.wharton.upenn.edu/fic/papers/99/9927.pdf (last visited July 24, 2013).
146 Chapter 1, note16 and accompanying text.

147 Arthur Wilmarth chronicled the demise of Glass-Steagall in a series of articles. Arthur E. Wilmarth, The Transformation of the U.S. Financial Services Industry, 1975–2000: Competition, Consolidation, and Increased Risks, 2002 *University of Illinois Law Review* 215 (2002); Arthur E. Wilmarth, Jr., The Dark Side of Universal Banking: Financial Conglomerates and the Origins of the Subprime Financial Crisis, 41 *Connecticut Law Review* 963, 972–1002 (2009).

148 E.g., Jonathan R. Macey, Special Interest Groups Legislation and the Judicial Function, *supra* note 124.

149 Markus K. Brunnermeier and Stefan Nagel, Hedge Funds and the Technology Bubble, 59 *Journal of Finance* 2013, 2030–2 (2004) (providing an example of a hedge fund that was forced to liquidate after refusing to invest in technology stocks during the 1990s technology stock bubble).

150 Chapter 2, "The Mississippi bubble," Chapter 11, "Regulatory stimulus and the legal origins of the shadow banking system."

151 Chapter 2, notes 207–8.

152 Franz Schulze, *Mies Van Der Rohe: A Critical Biography*, 281 (1995 University of Chicago Press) (noting that this phrase has been attributed to Van Der Rohe, but questioning its actual provenance).

153 Amitai Aviram, Bias Arbitrage, 64 *Washington and Lee Law Review* 789 (2007). Professor Aviriam argues that laws can have a "placebo effect," or a counter-bias that balances out the public misperception of risk.

154 Paul Krugman, How Did Economists Get It So Wrong? *New York Times* Magazine, Section MM 36 (September 6, 2009) (linking this phrase to the behavioral finance literature on the limits of arbitrage); Justin Fox, *The Myth of the Rational Market*, 260 (2011, Harper Business) (arguing quote is likely misattributed to Keynes).

155 PBS Frontline, The Warning (October 2009) available at www.pbs.org/wgbh/pages/frontline/warning/ (last visited July 24, 2013).

156 For a cultural and political history of securities regulation that details the moral cultural reaction to financial crises, see Banner, *supra* note 67.

157 The late legal scholar Larry Ribstein argued that the collapse of bubbles routinely led to regulatory overreaction. Larry E. Ribstein, Bubble Laws, 40 *Houston Law Review* 77 (2003).

158 Cf. Maya Bar-Hillel, The Base-rate Fallacy in Probability Judgments, 44 *Acta Psychologica* 211 (1980) (describing and documenting evidence of base-rate fallacy).

159 See generally, A.C. Pritchard, The SEC at 70: Time for Retirement, 80 *Notre Dame Law Review* 1073, 1093–6 (2005) (arguing that behavioral biases and other "pathologies" mean that the Securities and Exchange Commission will be constantly fighting the last way and using wrong tools to address securities market failures). Professor Pritchard's support for this attack on the SEC is somewhat slim. Other legal scholars have lamented the tendency of regulators to "fight the last war." Adam J. Levitin, In Defense of Bailouts, 99 *Georgetown Law Journal* 435, 462 (2011).

160 Paul Brest and Linda Hamilton Krieger, *Problem Solving, Decision Making, and Professional Judgment: A Guide for Lawyers and Policy Makers*, 244–9 (2010, Oxford University Press) (describing self-serving bias). Cf. Tom Pyszczynski, Jeff Greenberg, and Kathleen Holt, Maintaining Consistency between Self-Serving Beliefs and Available Data: A Bias in Information Evaluation, 11 *Personality and Social Psychology Bulletin* 179, 186–8 (1985) (analyzing whether self-serving interpretations arise from cognitive effects or personal motivation). For literature questioning the existence of this bias, see Dale T. Miller and Michael Ross, Self-serving Biases in the Attribution of Causality: Fact or Fiction? 82 *Psychological Bulletin* 213 (1975).

161 Chapter 2, note 74 and accompanying text.

162 Chapter 2, note 347 and accompanying text; Chapter 2, Appendix Table 2.a.4; Chapter 11, "The demise of Glass-Steagall and subsidy leakage."

163 See Chapter 2, notes 77–8 and accompanying text.
164 For a classic work that places British political liberalism in the nineteenth century in context, moves beyond economic liberalism, and explores the movement's cultural underpinnings and ties to American and Canadian political movements, see Robert Lloyd Kelley, *The Transatlantic Persuasion: The Liberal-Democratic Mind in the Age of Gladstone* (1990, Transaction Publishers).
165 Chapter 2, notes 94–9 and accompanying text.
166 Chapter 2, notes 172–5 and accompanying text.
167 Chapter 2, note 174 and accompanying text.
168 Chapter 2, note 220 and accompanying text. See also Chapter 2, notes 209–13.
169 Edward Chancellor, *Devil Take the Hindmost: A History of Financial Speculation*, 60 (1999, Plume Books) (describing political origins of South Sea bubble in "ideology of self-interest").
170 Chapter 2, note 62 and accompanying text (effects of Bubble Act).
171 Chapter 2, notes 40–2 and accompanying text.
172 Chapter 2, notes 209–13, 220 and accompanying text.
173 Chapter 2, note 165 and accompanying text. See also notes 156, 160–4, 166 and accompanying text.
174 Chapter 2, notes 154–9 and accompanying text.
175 Frank Freidel, *Presidents of the United States of America*, 62 (1994, Diane Publishing) (Harding quote); Arthur F. Fleser, *A Rhetorical Study of the Speaking of Calvin Coolidge*, 73 (1990, Edwin Mellen Press) (Coolidge quote).
176 Chapter 2, "Regulatory stimulus during a decade of laissez faire politics."
177 For a description of how these factors helped birth modern international financial regulation, see Pierre-Hugues Verdier, The Political Economy of International Financial Regulation, 88 *Indiana Law Journal* (forthcoming 2013).
178 See Timothy A. Canova, The Swedish Model Betrayed, 37 *Challenge* 36 (May–June 1994) (describing politics of deregulation); Brian Burkitt and Phil Whyman, The Origins of the Recent Swedish Crisis: A Lesson for the European Left, 93 *European Business Review* 33 (1993); Bengt Larsson, Neo-liberalism and Polycontextuality: Banking Crisis and Re-regulation in Sweden, 32 *Economy and Society* 428 (2003).
179 For an account of long-term rule by the Liberal Democratic Party in Japan for most of the post-war period until 1993, see Masaru Kohno, *Japan's Postwar Party Politics*, 66–7 (1997, Princeton University Press).
180 Chapter 6, "Japan."
181 See generally Laura D'Andrea Tyson, From the Anglo-American Model to Market Pluralism, 16 *New Perspectives Quarterly* 4 (Winter 1999) (situating Plaza Accord between Japan and the United States and widespread relaxation of capital controls across countries in the 1980s within the "Washington Consensus").
182 See generally Gary B. Gorton, *Slapped by the Invisible Hand: The Panic of 2007*, 54–5 (2010, Oxford University Press) (providing explanation for the Quiet Period); Gary B. Gorton, *Misunderstanding Financial Crises: Why We Don't See Them Coming* (2012, Oxford University Press). Ibid. at 10–28 (defining historical characteristics of a "Quiet Period" in banking systems), 125–33 (analyzing conditions leading to post-war "Quiet Period").
183 Chapter 6, "Japan." See also Verdier, *supra* note 177.
184 The disaster myopia literature provides one of the clearest examples of this explanation. See *supra* notes 144–5 and accompanying text.
185 Law professor Saule Omarova has carefully documented a series of incremental interpretative changes by different U.S. bank regulators in the last several decades. See *supra* notes 109–12 and accompanying text.

4   Epidemics of fraud and compliance rot

Chapter 2 documented two historical patterns. The last chapter looked at the first pattern: the regulatory subsidy cycle, in which governments enact regulatory stimulus during market booms and respond with a regulatory backlash after bubbles collapse. This chapter examines the second pattern. It explores the causes and contributing factors to the epidemics of fraud that have historically accompanied asset price bubbles. This exploration, in turn, sheds light on how compliance with financial laws and regulation radically deteriorates during bubble periods. The fecund market of a bubble promotes widespread disobedience of financial rules, or what this book labels "compliance rot."

Charles Kindleberger, the economic historian of bubbles, devotes a significant section of his book *Manias, Panics, and Crashes* to the "emergence of swindles."[1] Yet he provides a fairly simplistic explanation for this historical trend. He argues that this fraud is "demand determined" and results from the prevalence of foolhardy investors.[2] This chapter provides a deeper and more nuanced explanation for epidemics of fraud by analyzing not only the "demand" side of fraud, but the supply side as well. Market booms distort the incentives of market participants to engage in fraud in four broad ways. These four dynamics roughly parallel the models used in the last chapter to explain regulatory changes through bubbles and busts:

First, booms or bubbles distort the rational economic calculus of whether to commit fraud by enhancing the immediate benefits to committing fraud, while pushing the legal liability and other costs further into the future. Legal rules thus under-deter fraud.

Second, a market boom can exacerbate behavioral biases that cause market participants to underestimate potential liability and other costs of committing fraud.

Third, bubbles undermine norms that constrain fraud. Moreover, social norms shift during boom times, as both the financial industry and investor communities undergo rapid change and welcome an influx of new businesspeople and first time investors.

Fourth, the crony capitalism and selling of regulatory stimuli that can accompany bubbles (described in the previous chapter) undermines the legitimacy of financial laws. Legitimacy, psychologist Tom Tyler argues, provides a key determinant of why people obey the law. By comparison, an instrumental framework, in which individuals conduct a rational cost/benefit analysis in deciding whether to comply with the law, offers an incomplete picture, according to Tyler.[3]

These four dynamics explain more than just how compliance rot afflicts antifraud rules. They also predict lower obedience by financial market participants with a host of other financial laws during bubble times. In particular, this quartet of bubble dynamics generates compliance rot in those financial regulations that curb financial institution leverage, risk-taking, and profit. Systematic non-compliance with prudential regulations that aim to ensure the safety and soundness of banks and other financial institutions poses a deep challenge for the functioning of financial markets and laws.

This chapter is organized as follows. It begins with a brief analysis of data that suggest deregulation alone may not explain the rise of antifraud rules, particularly during the 1990s technology stock boom. It then outlines a "demand" side explanation for financial fraud that is more nuanced than Kindleberger's theory that foolish (or behaviorally biased) investors present attractive targets. The chapter then focuses on the "supply" side of fraud. In modeling the supply side, the chapter proceeds through each of the four dynamics described above. These models explain how bubble conditions can trigger compliance rot with respect to antifraud rules by undermining rational deterrence, exacerbating behavioral biases, altering social norms, and eroding the legitimacy of laws. The chapter concludes by telescoping out to discuss how these four dynamics predict the deterioration of compliance with financial regulations that restrict risk-taking and leverage during bubble times. This final section contrasts how compliance rot during bubble periods may differ with respect to antifraud and prudential regulations.

Deregulation alone may not explain epidemics of fraud

In examining what exacerbates fraud, it is helpful to isolate potential contributing factors. The last chapter examined in detail the dynamics of deregulation and other forms of regulatory stimulus. Nevertheless, deregulation (defined for immediate purposes as the roll back of antifraud rules) does not appear to provide a complete explanation for outbreak of epidemics of fraud during a bubble. In many historical bubble episodes, it does not appear that legislatures, regulators, or courts repealed or changed antifraud rules.[4]

In the years preceding the 1990 technology stock boom, Congress and federal courts *did* alter many antifraud provisions of U.S. securities laws. Chapter 2 outlined many of these changes, including a statute that imposed tougher pleading requirements on plaintiff lawsuits and various federal court rulings that limited the scope of liability under certain securities laws.[5] Can deregulation alone explain the epidemic of fraud in the Enron era? Or was something else at work?

Law professor John Coffee blames deregulation. He contends that this wave of deregulation in the 1990s undermined the deterrent effect of securities laws with respect to key actors in securities markets called "gatekeepers."[6] Gatekeepers are outside accountants, lawyers, bankers, and other intermediaries who lend their reputation to securities issuers and verify their securities disclosure. Gatekeepers thus allow issuers to access capital markets.[7] This lower deterrence effect, combined with increasing conflicts of interest for gatekeepers, Coffee argues, caused the Enron scandal and the epidemic of fraud during the tech stock bubble.[8]

This chapter will create a model for the deterrence theory of antifraud in a moment. At this point, however, it is important to see why deregulation and conflicts of interest theories offer only an incomplete explanation for the epidemic of fraud in the tech stock bubble. Consider that the deregulation of antifraud rules (described in Chapter 2) and the proliferation of gatekeeper conflicts of interest progressed steadily and incrementally throughout the 1990s.[9] For example, Congress passed the two principal statutes that changed antifraud liability, the Private Securities Litigation Reform Act and the Securities Litigation Uniform Standards Act, in 1995 and 1998 respectively.[10] Significant judicial opinions that cabined private rights of action in securities fraud also came down throughout the decade. For example, the Supreme Court issued its decision in *Lampf, Pleva* (strengthening an important statute of limitations) in 1991 and *Central Bank of Denver* (removing a private cause of action against "aiders and abettors") in 1994.[11]

A reasonable prediction, based on Coffee's theory, would be that gatekeeper acquiescence and the incidence of corporate fraud would have also risen steadily and incrementally. Yet this does not appear to be the case. Instead, corporate fraud appears to have reached epidemic proportions only in the last years of the decade.[12] Financial restatements by corporations serve as a bellwether for the presence of fraud. Restatements send a dire message to Wall Street about the integrity of a company's financial disclosure, and stock prices react swiftly and harshly. As Coffee notes, a number of studies of restatements during the 1990s show a sharp spike occurring at the end of the decade.[13] Figure 4.1 shows the incidence of companies restating their earnings and companies restating their

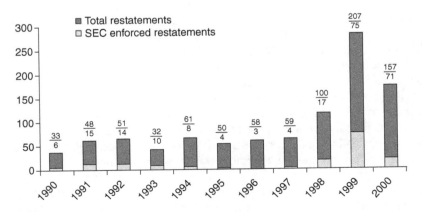

Figure 4.1 Number of restatements, 1990–2000.[14]

financial statements as a whole from 1990 to 2000. Restatements are counted in the financial period being restated.

The end of the decade witnessed not only a sharp rise in the number of earnings and financial restatements, but in the magnitude of these restatements as well. This magnitude can be measured by stock price losses that occurred immediately after the announcement of a restatement. These losses for earnings and financial restatements are depicted in Figure 4.2.

This sharp spike in restatements at the end of the decade strongly suggests that another factor came into play in the late 1990s to drive the epidemic of fraud. The most likely candidate is the dynamics of the booming stock market in the late 1990s. Economist Robert Shiller cites the historically unprecedented spike in the price to earnings ratio of the U.S. stock market from 1997 to 2000 as one sign that a stock market bubble had formed.[15] Figure 4.3 displays the price/earnings ratio from 1990 to 2000 calculated, using Shiller's data, by dividing the S&P Composite Index (corrected for inflation) by the ten-year moving average real earnings on that index.

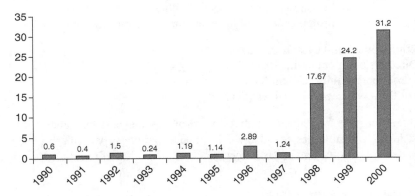

Figure 4.2 Market value of losses due to restatements, 1990–2000 (in billions of dollars).[16]

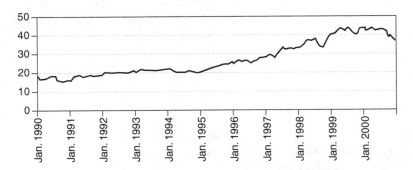

Figure 4.3 Price to earnings ratio, S&P Composite Index, 1990–2000.[17]

This price earnings trend strongly correlates with the trends in earnings restatements over this same decade described above. Comparing this price/earnings data to the total number of restatements from 1990 to 2000 yields a correlation coefficient of 0.898527.[18] The old maxim that correlation does not imply causation again applies. Nevertheless, the data lends strong support to a conclusion that a skyrocketing stock market was a key driver of securities fraud.[19]

The question then is: how do stock market booms and bubbles contribute to epidemics of financial fraud?

The "demand" for fraud

Kindleberger's view that fraud during bubbles is "demand determined" represents the conventional wisdom. This under-theorized theory holds that the swelling ranks of inexperienced, foolish investors present easier prey for the purveyors of financial fraud.[20] Demand theories are deeply engrained in popular thought. They mesh with the "greater fool" metaphor for investing during a bubble. They also resonate in many of the historical cultural accounts of financial fraud. Witness the following 1720 poem "Bubble" by satirist Jonathan Swift that mocks both the promoters of, and investors in, the South Sea Company:

> While some build Castles in the Air,
> Directors build'em in the Seas;
> Subscribers plainly see 'um there,
> For fools will see as Wise men please.[21]

This view that the foolishness of investors provides the best explanation for losses during a bubble has found favor in judicial opinions, particularly when judges have not allowed plaintiffs to recover.[22]

Behavioral explanations of fraud

This demand side theory also accords with behavioral economic explanations of investor behavior. One can easily imagine how the behavioral biases described in detail in Chapters 1 and 3 might contribute to investors underestimating the risk of fraud. Consider the following potential causal links between biases and estimations of fraud risk:

- *overoptimism*: fraud won't affect this company;[23]
- *overconfidence*: fraud may occur, but I can detect it;[24] and
- *the availability bias*: stock prices are skyrocketing and I have not heard about a major financial fraud case recently.[25]

Behavioral biases may cause investors to be less guarded against financial fraud during market bubbles and thus to present fraudsters with attractive targets. Behavioral economics and social psychology mesh with, and provide a modern scholarly gloss on, Kindleberger's demand side theory. When severe behavioral biases cause investors to ignore warning signs of fraud, they render the vast disclosure system of federal securities laws less effective.[26] Behavioral biases may explain evidence from the Panic of 2007–2008 that even sophisticated investors did not use the disclosure available to them to assess the risk of their investments. Law professor Bobby Bartlett documents how investors in monoline bond insurers apparently failed to use publicly available information about the bonds these companies insured to gauge the firms' worsening financial condition.[27]

Trust in excess

Behavioral biases may lead to a superabundance of investor trust in the integrity of financial markets in boom times. "Trust" was the subject of a wave of legal scholarship at the turn of this last century.[28] It has been defined as a learned, internalized behavior where one person comes to rely on, have confidence in, and believe in the integrity of, another.[29] Trust reflects a willingness to be vulnerable to possible exploitation by the recipient of that trust because of internalized beliefs, and not merely because of a series of individual rational economic calculations.[30] In the 1990s, political theorists, psychologists, economists, and legal scholars all analyzed trust as a form of "social capital" and explored how a lack of widespread trust in society – trust in government, social institutions, and civil society – can hamper economic and political development.[31] Indeed, some measure of trust between investors, firms, and financial intermediaries is essential to the functioning of any market.

Law professor Lynn Stout applies this learning on trust to the securities markets, and argues that investor confidence in the fairness of the market and in the trustworthiness of market intermediaries has been dangerously eroded by an epidemic of corporate scandals.[32] If investors fear being defrauded by issuers, broker dealers, exchanges, or other market intermediaries, or that the investment odds are otherwise rigged, they will no longer invest in the stock market.[33]

Investors can also overly trust the market and place too much confidence in securities issuers and market intermediaries. Because they would have little reason to question a market that provides consistent high returns to them, investors can fail to notice evidence that calls into question the integrity of the market. Investors – because they suffer from behavioral biases and engage in irrational herding,[34] or because they rationally base their investment decisions on the decisions of other investors (a phenomenon known as an information cascade)[35] – observe others placing their trust in the market and in market participants, and decide to do the same.

Since trust is a behavioral phenomenon, the behavioral biases that contribute to investor euphoria and the development of a bubble can lead to an excess of trust in the integrity of market participants, just as they can lead to excesses in market prices. Excessive trust in the integrity of the market explains why the history of bubbles is to a large extent the history of massive financial fraud. Just as bubbles may generate feedback with political cycles, they may also both gather steam from, and exacerbate cycles of investor trust in, markets.[36]

Fraud and rational risk-taking

Behavioral biases may not be necessary for a demand side explanation of why investors are susceptible to fraud. It may also be perfectly rational for investors to take less precaution in a bubble. During a bubble, many investors have significantly shorter time horizons for their investments because they are looking to "flip" stocks or real estate. They therefore may care less about whether fraud is later discovered and results in a drop in asset value beyond that horizon. Indeed, Chapter 1 described rational-bubble models in which rational investors continue to bid prices above fundamental value.[37] It may be completely rational for investors to discount future price crashes, whether they stem from a collapsed bubble, the uncovering of fraud, or both.

Moreover, if investors insist on additional precautions, they may be shut out of a hot investment market in which sellers insist on quick transactions. This pressure affects investors on both ends of the sophistication spectrum. During the boom of the last decade, prospective homebuyers routinely waived various inspection rights as a condition to closing in order to succeed in purchasing a home.[38] Meanwhile, sophisticated financial institutions agreed to extend "covenant-lite" loans to finance leveraged buyouts and other sophisticated corporate transactions. Under these stripped-down loan documents, borrowers did not have to make various customary contractual agreements that lenders normally demand for their protection.[39]

Rational investors also face more pronounced information asymmetries during asset price bubbles.[40] Investors may face higher information costs in evaluating new technologies (such as railroad, radio, or the internet) or investments in far flung, inaccessible locations (for example, English investors investing in South American mines in 1825, or investors in New York or Berlin evaluating railroad companies in the American Wild West of the early 1870s). Moreover, the innovative financial instruments associated with bubbles may heighten these information asymmetries. The most recent crisis provides the example of asset-backed securities, including collateralized debt obligations. In these transactions, investors in capital markets purchased securities created from securities that, in turn, were created by cash streams from mortgages and other loans. The structure of these instruments meant investors were several transactions removed from the ultimate assets that generated their risk and rewards.[41] Investors may remedy information asymmetries during a bubble by spending additional resources and time. Doing so, however, in a seller's market may mean other investors snap up investment opportunities.

The "supply" of fraud: the deterioration of deterrence

Demand-determined theories, however, provide an incomplete account of the rise of financial fraud during bubbles. While investors may be less wary of fraud, few investors buy into an obviously fraudulent scheme and consent to being defrauded. It takes two to tango in fraud, and the incentives of market participants to supply fraud must also be considered. Ultimately, to borrow from the eco-nomic analysis of tort law, the question is which party – the supplier of fraud or the investors – can most efficiently take precautions against fraud.[42] Economic research demonstrates that the behavioral biases of investors are particularly robust. An array of policies designed to dampen bubbles and correct the propen-sity of individuals to trade on "noise" have proven largely ineffective.[43] This argues for focusing greater attention on the suppliers of fraud, who might be more susceptible to changed incentive structures.

Demand-determined theories ignore how prolonged market bubbles can increase dramatically the incentives of market participants to commit financial fraud. One way to understand how bubbles skew these incentives is through a rational model of the decision potential fraudsters make. To construct this model, assume that a market participant (say the promoter of a company selling shares, a broker or other middleman, or one of the "gatekeepers" described above) con-ducts a rough cost–benefit analysis. He or she will weigh the monetary benefits of participating in the fraud (profits from the sale of the assets or side payments from another fraudster) against various costs.

These costs include legal liability from various common law or statutory anti-fraud rules, as well as reputation costs. In this model, the principal purpose of antifraud liability is to exert a deterrent effect (as opposed to retribution or victim compensation).[44] As we will see, however, the structure of many antifraud rules, including those under U.S. securities laws, limits their deterrent effect.

A model of deterrence

In modeling the deterrence that undergirds any antifraud liability rules (whether under U.S. federal securities laws or otherwise), the calculation by a seller or a market intermediary (such as a gatekeeper) on whether to commit fraud would look something like the following:

$$B <> P_d * ((P_e * L_1) + L_r)$$

In this model:

B represents the benefits an actor realizes from participating in a fraud.

P_d represents the probability of the fraud being detected. Any expected liability for someone committing fraud, whether legal or reputational, is contingent on the probability of fraud being detected and attributed to the actor.

P_e represents the probability of the antifraud laws being successfully enforced. This variable reflects the probability that governmental bodies or private plain-tiffs will bring a case in the first place, as well as the likelihood that the case will succeed. Likelihood of success depends in large part on the procedural hurdles that prosecutors and plaintiffs must clear and the substantive elements they must prove under a given antifraud rule.

L_l represents the legal liability under antifraud rules. Settlement may lower this liability, but increase the plaintiff or prosecutor's probability of success.[45]

L_r represents market, reputational, and other non-legal losses that the participant in a fraud will suffer if the fraud is detected. Reputational loss is particularly important for gatekeepers and market intermediaries, but also for sellers who prize their credibility in the marketplace.[46] For example, securities issuers may value highly their ongoing reputation with stock analysts and investors.

In plain English, under this model, a rational actor will commit or participate in fraud when her individual benefits outweigh her costs. She incurs liability and other costs (like reputational damage) only when fraud is detected. The detection of fraud does not automatically lead to legal liability. A separate variable captures the probability of successful enforcement or prosecution of antifraud rules.[47]

How a bubble affects the calculus

The prospect of a sustained boom in prices in a particular asset class significantly alters this equation. It increases the immediate benefits of fraud, as participants can sell assets at higher prices. Booming prices may also benefit market intermediaries and gatekeepers who are not selling the assets themselves. The intermediaries and gatekeepers may own a stake in the assets being sold (such as when law firms take an equity stake in a client selling shares).[48] They may receive greater direct or indirect payments during a boom from the principal architects of the fraud. For example, as noted above, critics charged that accounting firms in the years leading up to the Enron scandal suffered from severe conflicts of interest. They received a significant source of their overall revenue from consulting fees from the same clients whose books they were auditing.[49]

At the same time, market booms postpone the moment in which market participants realize any legal liability and reputational costs associated with participating in fraud. The reasons for this delay will be examined in a moment. For now, note that increased immediate benefits, more remote costs, and the time value of money would tip the scales further in favor of committing fraud. Compliance rot can thus begin to decay the effectiveness of antifraud rules.

The probability of detection: swimming naked while the tide rolls in

Prolonged asset price booms delay the incurrence of legal and reputational costs, first, because the probability that fraud will be detected may drop precipitously unless and until prices go down. Warren Buffet's adage that "you only find out who is swimming naked when the tide goes out" applies to cases of financial fraud.[50] While investors continue to bid up prices, fraudulent schemes remain submerged. Even Ponzi schemes, like the Bernie Madoff fraud, that begin well before a bubble period can be sustained by a bull market encouraging new investors to enter a market. (Conversely, a market drop can cause investors to withdraw money, triggering the collapse of Ponzi schemes, as was the case in the Madoff episode.)[51]

The probability of enforcement: causes of action **and** *diluted enforcement*

Market booms also reduce the probability of enforcement of antifraud rules for several reasons. Without a drop in prices, there may be no legal cause of action. Consider Rule 10b-5 under the Securities Exchange Act of 1934, one of the core antifraud rules in U.S. securities law.[52] Many of the requisite elements of a plaintiff's cause of action under this rule can typically be shown only with a drop in a security's price. Notably, plaintiffs must prove damages to recover under this rule.[53] A plaintiff that purchased a security and alleges fraud will find it impossible to prove damages if the stock price continued to rise after the purchase.[54] Plaintiffs can prove other elements of a 10b-5 case, such as materiality and loss causation through the movement of security prices.[55] Consistently rising prices during a bubble can frustrate their ability to prove these elements.

A rational potential participant in a fraud will also realize that public enforcement of antifraud rules will be overtaxed by the sheer transaction volume of a market boom. The previous chapter explained how a rising market can spread thin enforcement resources.[56] In other words, the same number of cops walk the beat, but the neighborhood they must patrol has become a lot larger. Potential participants in fraud are likely fully aware of these legal and practical constraints on both prosecutors and private plaintiffs. Rational participants might adjust their calculations on whether to comply with antifraud laws accordingly.

Reputational costs and lemons

If a significant number of any given category of market participants engage in disreputable conduct, the deterrence effect of a reputational loss drops. This dynamic particularly affects gatekeeper behavior; gatekeepers care about their reputation not only in an absolute sense, but also in a relative sense compared to the reputations of their competitors. In a game increasingly full of cheaters, the marginal reputational loss from deciding to cheat plummets.[57]

This chapter discusses the role of norms in legal compliance in a moment. For now, it is worth outlining an economic analysis of how prolonged market booms and bubbles could transform both asset markets *and* the market for gatekeeper services into "lemons" markets. Economist George Akerlof explained how producers of poor quality goods (like used car "lemons") can drive out producers of high-quality goods if consumers cannot easily determine product quality.[58] Producers of high-quality goods – for example, nonfraudulent companies issuing shares or honest gatekeepers – have a possible solution. They can preserve their market share and prevent the market from unraveling by sending a credible signal to consumers that distinguishes their higher quality assets and services.[59]

Market booms and bubbles, however, disrupt these signals. An influx of noise traders creates sufficient informational noise that can overpower even credible signals about quality. Asset prices become relatively more influenced by trend-chasing and positive feedback strategies by investors. They become relatively less affected by information on fundamental values, including information on fraud risk.[60] Continually rising prices can frustrate investors in attempting to distinguish between legitimate and fraudulent investments and between honest and dishonest gatekeepers. Even investors interested in distinguishing quality face the problem that market prices are set by the highest bidder, not the average or most rational one. Again, someone considering committing or participating in fraud would realize that bubbles conceal lemons and then adjust his behavior accordingly.

Rising information and agency costs

Even those issuers and market intermediaries that seek to comply with the law may be frustrated by two types of costs that rise with the inflation of a bubble. First, the increased transaction flow during a market boom translates into increased information processing costs.[61] These costs affect both the internal compliance function of securities issuers and, particularly, external gatekeepers.[62] Overworked gatekeepers can miss signs of misconduct.[63] The rapid growth of an issuer means that resolving accounting issues and establishing internal quality controls at that company becomes exponentially more difficult. Increased work and the accompanying pressure to close deals and satisfy clients can lead to an industry-wide decline in the professional norms critical to gatekeeping (a topic that will be explored in more detail below).[64] This rise in the costs of information represents a private sector version of the problem of diluted government enforcement described in the last chapter.

Moreover, a bubble exacerbates agency costs. Institutional controls and memory suffer as a booming economy creates alternative job opportunities and increases staff turnover. With shorter careers at firms, individuals become less invested in the long-term future of the firm. They discount their personal legal liability if the firm is not expected to realize that liability for several years.[65] Individuals may choose to commit malfeasance or shirk monitoring duties because, by the time the costs of such actions are realized, the individual will likely be employed elsewhere.[66] High staff turnover makes it difficult to trace responsibility for misconduct back to specific individuals. When potential misconduct is identified, the individuals that stay with firms tend to blame those employees that conveniently left the firm.[67] (This is akin to the "blame hedging" that occurs in the public sector, a phenomenon described in the previous chapter.) With a tighter labor market and competition for "stars," firms become more reluctant to discipline employees.[68]

Final period problems: when fraud pays

The dynamics of a boom create final period problems on several layers. First, for sellers, their immediate benefits to defrauding a buyer may outweigh any future benefits they would enjoy from maintaining a continued relationship with buyers. (Matters become worse if a fraudster can disappear, as Gregor MacGregor, the *cacique* of Poyais, did in 1825. MacGregor absconded with the proceeds of that fictional republic's sovereign debt issuance.)[69] Firms, however, may have a longer time horizon. Yet they suffer from a cocktail of the final period problem and agency costs; their employees and agents may conclude that the benefits to fraud outweigh a continued relationship with their employer.

Even if being caught in the future is a near certainty, fraud or misconduct may still pay. Those individuals or firms that were caught and penalized for their conduct during the late 1990s might still rationally conclude that it was worth it. The multimillion-dollar penalties paid by stock analysts Henry Blodgett and Jack Grubman to the SEC pale when compared to the compensation they received both during the boom period and in golden parachutes.[70] Moreover, these penalties are incurred long after the benefits to malfeasance were realized. The time value of money weakens the deterrence effect of liability.

Punitive damages may counteract the problems of weakened deterrence – whether from delayed or lower probabilities of detection and enforcement. However, many areas of Anglo-American law disfavor or disallow punitive damages. For example, punitive damages are foreign to the law of contract.[71] Antifraud liability in securities law is also generally limited to rescission or actual damages.[72] In other areas of the law, U.S. courts have sharply cut back on the availability of punitive damages. For example, the Supreme Court limited punitive damages in the Exxon Valdez oil spill to a 1:1 ratio to compensatory damages.[73] It sidestepped the question of the impact of this cap on deterrence, particularly in cases in which a plaintiff's probability of recovery is reduced.[74]

A behavioral overlay

Even if misconduct would be irrational, securities issuers and market intermediaries might still choose to engage in malfeasance because of behavioral biases exacerbated by a stock market bubble. These behavioral biases come into play on two levels. First, they can affect directly the judgment of sellers of assets and market intermediaries contemplating financial fraud. Second, these sellers and market intermediaries must judge the decision-making of investors, who may themselves suffer from behavioral biases. If cognitive limitations frustrate and delay the detection of fraud by investors or prosecutors, savvy sellers and market intermediaries would lower the estimates of their expected liability for fraud.

Behavioral biased sellers and market intermediaries

Even financially sophisticated market players suffer from the behavioral biases that drive investor confidence and stock market bubbles.[75] For example, accountants, who would be expected to be both adept and conservative in estimating their own potential liability in securities litigation, suffer from the full range of behavioral biases, including overconfidence and overoptimism.[76] The same behavioral analysis of how the cognitive limitations of investors can create a bubble also explains how issuers and market intermediaries misjudge the liability and other costs associated with committing fraud during a bubble.

The availability bias may cause gatekeepers to believe the booming stock market will continue. This would make falling stock prices and shareholder suits appear remote. Overconfidence and overoptimism lead market participants to heavily discount the chances either that fraud can be detected or that they will be caught in misconduct. Other biases reinforce this thinking. The self-attribution bias describes how individuals attribute successes to their own personal skill yet attribute failure to bad luck or sabotage.[77] This may lead those who commit fraud to discount the possibility of punishment.

Similarly, the "hot-hand" phenomenon[78] may cause bad actors to think that their string of success will continue. Hyperbolic discounting exacerbates under-deterrence; fraudsters recognize immediate benefits but incur liability only after a bubble bursts.[79] Lastly, belief perseverance and anchoring mean that market participants are unlikely to judge correctly when the market tide has turned and the risk of being punished for fraud has increased.[80]

Sellers and market intermediaries considering behaviorally biased investors: the problem of materiality

In deciding whether to commit financial fraud, sellers of assets and market intermediaries also consider the decision-making of investors, who themselves suffer from behavioral biases. Potential purveyors of fraud may look to exploit the cognitive limitations of investors. However, the behavioral biases of investors may color the calculations of potential suppliers of fraud in subtler ways.

Behavioral biases have an outsized effect on securities law compliance because of the amorphous legal standard of materiality that lies at the heart of U.S. securities law. The U.S. Supreme Court defines materiality by reference to a reasonable investor. A fact in securities disclosure is material if there is a substantial likelihood that it "would have been viewed by the reasonable investor as having significantly altered the 'total mix' of information made available."[81]

But this standard becomes problematic when a stock market bubble makes reasonable investors a scarce commodity. Although it is unlikely that a court would revise this objective standard during temporary periods of market irrationality,[82] these periods could distort the *perception* by market participants of what constitutes a reasonable investor. Their estimation of whether an ideal, objective reasonable investor would judge any given fact pattern to be material can become colored by the prevalence of irrationally exuberant and euphoric investors in the market.

This misperception would be reinforced because market prices serve as a gauge of materiality in fraud litigation.[83] This use of stock prices in securities litigation owes much to the U.S. Supreme Court's acceptance of the basic tenets of the Efficient Market Hypothesis.[84] This finance theory has led many courts to use stock price movements following the public release of information as a strong indication that that information was material.[85] Yet when corporations and gatekeepers observe stock prices soaring due to market euphoria, they could mis-judge the materiality of information. They may erroneously believe that euphoric investors would not care – and stock prices would not plummet – even if certain harmful information was disclosed.

In making materiality judgments during the drafting of disclosure or the per-formance of due diligence in a securities offering, corporations and their gate-keepers do not have the luxury of viewing market prices in hindsight after hypothetical disclosure. They are forced to use rules of thumb or heuristics. The first stage of due diligence typically involves discussions between issuers and underwriter's counsel on what heuristic should be used as a proxy for material-ity.[86] Dollar thresholds may be debated, despite that fact that the law does not set a numerical threshold on materiality.[87] But setting these thresholds based on a company's stock prices would be a grave legal and logical error. This is particu-larly true if the stock price is already inflated, either by frenzied speculation or fraud.[88] Materiality thresholds based on a company's earnings or asset values can be similarly skewed by fraud or price increases during a bubble.

This can lead to an end result of behaviorally biased market participants basing their decisions on legal compliance on their perceptions of behaviorally biased investors.

Shifting norms

Social norms may have a greater influence than rational cost–benefit calculus on decisions by market participants to comply with the law or commit fraud. Legal scholars have used the term "norm" in various ways.[89] By norm, or social norm, this chapter means a "decentralized behavioral standard that individuals feel obligated to follow."[90] This obligation may stem from a desire to win esteem in a community or because individuals have internalized the standard.[91] On the other hand, failure to abide by a norm may result in an individual facing sanctions from other members of a group – whether in the form of stigma and other repu-tational penalties or otherwise.[92] Norms are social phenomena created within a community. More closely knit communities can foster stronger social norms that can govern individual behavior within that group even in the absence of laws enacted and enforced by the state.[93]

Defined in this way, social norms may not be quantified as easily as economic costs and benefits. However, this should not lead to a casual dismissal of these powerful determinants of community behavior. Indeed, the rise of a bubble may trigger several seismic shifts in social norms that may encourage financial fraud. The last chapter described how bubbles often herald or trigger a broader shift in political ideologies and social norms.[94] The values of the marketplace supplant those supplied by religion and other traditional sources of authority. The same ideological and normative shifts that drive regulatory stimulus during bubble times also promote compliance rot. The values of the market include a strong strain of *caveat emptor*. During many bubble periods, the norm of *caveat emptor* has devolved into predatory capitalism. Buyer beware became an invitation for financiers to deceive investors and to celebrate and be celebrated in doing so.

It is difficult to discern and measure the rise of these norms in historical bubbles with precision. To map societal shifts affecting financial markets some historians have looked to court cases of the time, as well as to newspapers, pamphlets, and even fiction.[95] Accordingly, many of the sources cited below look to a range of cultural texts to ascertain shifts in norms within financial markets during bubble periods.

During the rise of the English stock market in the 1690s, commentators decried how the flourishing culture of speculation in London's "Exchange Alley" also promoted a culture of fraud and political corruption.[96] The verbs "to bubble" and "to stockjob" were coined to connote committing a fraud on investors.[97] Stuart Banner describes how commentators during the South Sea bubble feared that the norms of the new stock market were permeating society. He writes:

> The unique incentives faced by securities traders, it was argued, created a subculture where lying was the norm.... It was bad enough that this localized ethos existed: What made it so dangerous was the possibility that it might spread beyond the market into the wider culture.[98]

Commentators in the U.S. Gilded Age similarly blamed epidemics of political corruption and financial fraud on the changing social mores of the age.[99] Fast forward to the 1920s and, again, booming financial markets upended societal values. Edward Chancellor writes, "In the stock market of the Roaring Twenties, Americans found a secular religion whose ludic qualities, cynicism, and materialism reflected the zeitgeist of the Jazz Age."[100] He then describes how this cultural shift coincided with an epidemic of manipulation of stock markets, in which pools of speculators earned fortunes.[101] These historical vignettes detail how booming markets have transformed norms within financial markets to sanctify a Darwinian exploitation of investors.

Buy side changes: new investors, norms of reciprocity, and norm asymmetries

The problem, however, is that, during these transformative periods, the ascendance of *caveat emptor* norms may not be recognized and internalized by all market participants. Bubbles bring together different groups of asset sellers, buyers, and market intermediaries who have not transacted with one another previously. These groups may have radically different expectations of appropriate behavior in the marketplace. The new investors that flood into markets during bubbles and extended market booms can encourage fraud in ways other than by presenting easy, unsophisticated prey. This influx of newcomers enlarges the social group with whom regular sellers and market intermediaries interact. This larger group means that many sellers and buyers are interacting for the first, and possibly the last, time. This presents not only a final period problem, of the type described above, but, moreover, a profound challenge to the critical norm of reciprocity. This norm serves as a bulwark against fraud by discouraging members of a group from taking advantage of one another.[102]

Bubbles do more than enlarge social groups and introduce new investors. They also have fundamentally changed the demographics of investors. Bubble periods present opportunities for new groups – women, immigrants, racial, ethnic, and religious minorities, and members of groups with lower socio-economic status – to invest in financial markets for the first time.[103] Stuart Banner documents this mingling of different races and religions during the South Sea by citing popular texts from the age. The following quote comes from a set of South Sea bubble playing cards from 1721:

> Here Stars and Garters, Jews and Gentiles, Crowd,
> The Saint, the Rake, the Humble and the Proud.[104]

Banner also documents the expanding number of women investors during this age.[105] Women comprised almost 12 percent of the original investors in the Bank of England and purchased almost 6 percent of the Bank's initial issuance.[106] The emergence of women in financial markets prompted both opprobrium and bitter satire from some quarters.[107]

Over a century later, England's stock market boomed once more. Again, new social groups entered the market unaware of its dangers. Rande Kostal describes the situation during the railway mania of the 1830s:

> England's rapidly expanding ranks of railway securities investors was almost wholly unschooled in the ways (and potential hazards) of the stock markets. Many new investors were country gentlemen who, a contemporary study asserted, had "no means of obtaining that correct information which might engender or justify suspicion."[108]

A decade later, an even more feverish railway mania reached even deeper into England's social strata to lure first time investors. Kostal cites a newspaper of the time that describes the extent of the boom of the early 1840s thus:

> The whole population of the empire was infected by the railway mania. No class, from the highest to the lowest, was exempt. Like a fever, it spread through every rank. The statesmen, the noblemen, the manufacturer, the man of independent property, the literary, the commercial man, peer, printer, clergymen, naval men, M.P.'s, special pleaders, professors, cotton spinners, gentlemen's cooks and attorneys, with their clerks ... bankers, beersellers, and butlers, domestic servants, footmen – all have joined in the excitement.[109]

Decades later, the Gilded Age bubbles in the United States also democratized investment. Edward Chancellor evokes how investors came from "all classes and

backgrounds": "On the sidewalks of the financial district, young dandy speculators from Broadway jostled with farmers, store owners, lawyers, doctors, clergy-
men, mechanics, and penniless 'gutter-snipes.'"[110] As in previous ages, women
too joined these American manias in large numbers.[111] The stock market became
central to American culture during the Roaring Twenties, and the ranks of investors swelled with women and religious and ethnic minorities. By some estimate,
women conducted 35 percent of stock market trades during the period.[112]

This kind of demographic change can erode the norm of reciprocity. Norms
restrain opportunistic behavior within particular social groups.[113] Community
norms serve as a strong regulator of fraud.[114] The disciplining effect of norms
works far more effectively within a close-knit community that can impose reputational penalties (including blaming and shaming) and other costs on cheaters.[115] The discipline of norms may be largely absent when a large number of
individuals from different social groups transact for the first time.

Moreover, interactions, particularly first time interactions, between social
groups may demonstrate norm asymmetries that disadvantage one group. Sometimes this can also be seen in the aftermath of bubbles too. For example, in the
wake of the Panic of 2007–2008, large numbers of homeowners continued to
make mortgage payments even though they were "underwater" and faced dim
prospects of regaining equity in their homes in the near future.[116] In this case, the
rational response would have been to default on the mortgages,[117] particularly in
those U.S. states in which lenders would have no further legal recourse against
the borrowers other than foreclosing on the mortgaged property.[118]

Why then did homeowners fail to take the rational, self-interested action of
walking away from underwater mortgages? Law professor Brent White argues
that community norms ("a deal is a deal") reinforced emotional responses
(such as shame and fear) and prevented mass efficient breach by homeowners.[119]
He characterizes this state of affairs, in which individual borrowers face
normative constraints against breach but corporate lenders do not, as "norm
asymmetry."[120]

Norm asymmetry may characterize even higher echelons of financial markets.
Even sophisticated buyers of assets may have markedly different expectations
and norms from sophisticated sellers. Consider the following front page example
from the recent financial crisis. In 2010, after financial markets collapsed, the
U.S. Securities and Exchange Commission brought a headline-grabbing suit
against the investment bank Goldman Sachs. The SEC alleged that Goldman
failed to disclose key facts to European financial institution clients about
complex securities (called synthetic collateralized debt obligations) that
Goldman sold to them. According to the SEC, Goldman failed to tell these European firms that another client of the investment bank, a prominent hedge fund,
was involved in designing those securities *and* had bet that the securities the
Europeans had purchased would lose money. The SEC alleged that, unknown to
the investors (but known to Goldman), the hedge fund entered into derivative
contracts betting that the securities sold to investors would lose money. Essentially, two sets of Goldman clients were on opposite sides of a transaction, but,

only one side allegedly knew that the other was adverse. The SEC claimed Goldman failed to disclose material facts of this conflict of interest.[121]

Less interesting than the legal outcome of the case (it settled) was the public debate over whether Goldman had done anything illegal or unethical. Many commentators took the side of Goldman Sachs and argued that Goldman did not have to disclose the particular role the hedge fund played. Under this view, investors should have anticipated that Goldman allowed a party with interests adverse to their own to structure the securities. The European firms placed excessive trust in Goldman Sachs.[122] Other commentators argued that the European financial firms were entitled to operate under a radically different set of assumptions, namely that Goldman at least owed them a duty to disclose the role of the hedge fund, if not to act in their "best interests" more broadly defined.[123] According to some accounts, the dispute stemmed from the naiveté of the European traders, but also from their radically different cultural assumptions about the prevailing norms in the U.S. derivatives marketplace.[124]

This debate highlights that norms may differ not only between retail investors and sophisticated financial institutions, but also among financial firms and across national borders. One group's sharp deal is another group's financial fraud. Because bubbles throw together different groups of investors, sellers, and financial intermediaries, norm asymmetries proliferate and open the path for opportunism.

Sell side norms: new financial industry participants

If bubbles change the norms that govern the interactions between investors on the one hand and sellers and market intermediaries on the other, they can also alter the norms solely within the "sell side" of the financial community and inside individual firms. Just as bubbles open up opportunities for new groups of investors, they also create new employment opportunities within the financial community. An influx of new financial professionals can trigger or reinforce dramatic shifts in norms within that community.

Two dynamics warrant particular mention. The first is that market booms can usher in youth movements in the financial sector. The young and ambitious have played prominent roles in questionable conduct in a long historical line of bubbles. For example, in the South Seas bubble, a teenaged Benjamin Disraeli, future British Prime Minister, received employ as a drafter of pamphlets that extolled the fanciful prospects of new speculative companies.[125] Fresh faced youths would follow in his path in bubbles to come. In the recent "subprime" crisis, the U.S. mortgage industry paid recent college graduates six figure salaries to hawk exotic "subprime" mortgages. The culture at these mortgage lenders promoted fraud; staff at several large mortgage lenders routinely forged loan documents to get loans approved and to make risky loans appear safe.[126]

Youth bring more than love of risk and braggadocio to financial markets. They also often come less burdened with more conservative social norms. The younger generation that goes to work for brokers and other financial intermediaries during boom times has not been socialized with the prevailing norms of the established financial community. During boom times, popular culture alternately glorifies and satirizes the rise of young financial traders and their cavalier attitude towards risk, law, and traditional values. In the 1980s, the decade of Oliver Stone's film *Wall Street* and Tom Wolfe's novel *The Bonfire of the Vanities*, young bond traders exulted in "ripping the faces off" their clients.[127]

Second, bubbles unsettle those existing norms via other demographic changes. Bubbles create massive disruptions in financial markets and social orders. This allows new social groups, including social, religious, and ethnic minorities, to enter business and financial communities. This influx can unsettle the norms by which these communities govern themselves. There is no evidence that the new entrants into the markets are any more likely to commit fraud. Instead, new members weaken the bonds by which the "club" governs itself.

Throughout history, the rise of minorities in the financial community during bubble times has disturbed members of the establishment. Daniel Defoe decried the growing numbers of lower class and Jewish stock brokers after England's 1690s bubble and during the South Sea bubble.[128] In the Gilded Age bubbles in the United States, many of the most prominent tycoons and stock operators came not from wealth or the Establishment, but sprung onto financial markets from the humblest of origins.[129] Two of the most powerful railroad financiers of the era, "Jubilee Jim" Fisk and Daniel Drew worked in traveling circuses as young men and learned the basics of con games there.[130]

The organizers of some of the largest speculative pools in the Roaring Twenties were Irish and other minorities outside Wall Street's mainstream. Chancellor writes of Irish financiers, such as Joseph Kennedy (father of the future U.S. President): "Born mostly into poverty and excluded by their religion from the East Coast financial elite, which was dominated by Wasps and German Jews, these men were prepared to take great risks to establish themselves."[131] Immigrant outsiders, such as Charles Ponzi and Swedish "Match King" Ivar Kreuger, made and lost fortunes in this time and caused the ruin of many of their investors.[132]

One must again take great care in making claims about financial fraud here. The entrance of these outsiders during bubble times has led to ugly episodes of scapegoating in the wake of financial crises.[133] The point is not that outsiders are more or less likely to commit fraud. There is *no* evidence to suggest that minorities have been more culpable during bubble periods or otherwise. Indeed, ensconced members of the financial community may see in the influx of outsiders a competitive threat or an excuse to dishonor long-held rules of the club. During the Roaring Twenties, paragons of Wall Street's WASP Establishment also engaged in misconduct. When New York Stock Exchange President Richard Whitney, scion of an old, wealthy family and educated at Groton and Harvard, was sent to prison for fraud and embezzlement, President Franklin Roosevelt, his former prep school classmate, lamented, "Not Dick Whitney."[134] Furthermore, many investment pools in the 1920s were run by a different kind of "outsider," namely executives from the automobile industry. This "Detroit Crowd" may not have differed from Wall Street leaders in religion or ethnicity, but one scholar notes that, "[t]hey did not come into the market hampered by the heavy armour of tradition."[135]

Demographic change remains important, not to pin blame on minority groups, but rather because it exerts powerful, potential subsurface tension that places stress on the foundational norms that govern communities, financial and otherwise. When communities are in flux, crucial norms become unstable.

Deteriorating legal legitimacy

Perhaps the most important but least understood determinant of compliance with law is the perceived legitimacy of those laws. Psychologist Tom Tyler authored a path-breaking study that documented evidence of what determines compliance with laws.[136] According to Tyler, in deciding whether to follow legal rules, people consider the legitimacy of those rules. They do not merely perform an economic cost–benefit analysis of the rewards and penalties for following or breaking the law.[137] Tyler argues that an analysis of norms and legitimacy must supplement the incomplete "instrumental perspective" of why people obey the law.[138]

Tyler argues that individuals consider legitimacy not only in terms of substantive outcomes (including distributive justice), but moreover in terms of procedural fairness.[139] Personal experience shapes individual perceptions of this fairness.[140] Crucial to perception of procedural fairness are beliefs that government decision-makers should be neutral and unbiased.[141] Perceptions about the motivations of legal and political authorities therefore matter intensely.[142] Although Tyler did not study compliance in financial market contexts, his work offers insights for compliance with financial laws and regulations. His work meshes with how some legal scholars are starting to view compliance inside complex financial institutions.[143]

Still, the application of Tyler's findings to behavior inside corporate entities raises vexing questions. How does working within an institutional context affect the importance of legitimacy as a determinant of whether individuals obey the law? How does the for-profit nature of corporations shape compliance?[144] How do actors within these entities reconcile social norms and legal legitimacy with norms of shareholder wealth maximization? Do institutional dynamics, the profit motive, or shareholder wealth maximization assume more importance than legitimacy and social norms? Further study of the impact of legitimacy and norms on legal compliance within corporate entities and financial institutions is sorely needed.

It is important, however, to underscore that the norm of shareholder wealth maximization for corporate is not immutable. In the legal academy, this norm is, in fact, highly contested.[145] Descriptive accounts of how managers of corporations actually behave often shade into normative claims of how they should act. It is difficult to separately cleanly claims of "is" from claims of "ought." The tricky thing about norms is that, if individuals believe in them, they exist. If individuals doubt their existence, norms disintegrate.

Crony capitalism and legitimacy

If the legitimacy of laws assumes any importance in compliance with financial laws, then the political consequences of asset price bubbles pose a serious challenge to that compliance. Chapter 2 detailed the long history of political corruption that accompanies asset price bubbles. Chapter 3 then set out several models to explain how bubbles can increase the incentives and resources of financial industry to obtain regulatory stimulus. At the same time, the previous chapter argued that the dynamics of a bubble can increase the incentives of policymakers to grant legal favors to particular interest groups.

When bubbles usher in crony capitalism or cause market participants to perceive that the law is increasingly for sale, then the legitimacy of legal regimes deteriorates drastically. Three centuries ago, Daniel Defoe lamented, "when statesmen turn jobbers, the state may be jobbed."[146] Both commentators during bubble times and historians alike have found deep links between fraud in financial markets and political corruption. They often characterized this connection in epidemiological terms. Writing about the wake of the South Sea bubble, Edward Chancellor writes that the corruption trials of prominent government officials "revealed how contagious the mores of the moneyed men had become."[147] During the 1820s railway mania, *The Times* of London criticized Members of Parliament who were serving as directors of new ventures (which were seeking or had obtained charters from Parliament) as suffering "the leprous infection of avarice."[148]

Historian Steve Fraser details how the crony capitalism of the Gilded Age bubbles undermined legitimacy at all levels of government. He focuses on how four titans of industry, Daniel Drew, Jim Fisk, Jay Gould, and Cornelius Vanderbilt, amassed wealth with the help of corrupted legislators, judges, and executives in a political era that came to be called the "Great Barbecue." These men vied to expand and protect their railroads and other ventures by bribing state legislators, judges, and members of President Grant's cabinet.[149] Fraser describes the effects of these political machinations thus:

> Without the active collaboration of state legislators, sitting judges, mayors and city machine bosses, congressmen and cabinet members, the vast wealth amassed by our four horsemen is inconceivable.... However, this intimacy with government, some of it skirting or crossing the borders of legality, did mean that the state was in danger of being converted into a client-state whose legitimacy could naturally be called into question. So the elevation of the financial pathfinder was, in a bizarre fashion, given its special lift by the debauching of republican government.[150]

Commentators of the time lamented the government's loss of legitimacy. Charles Francis Adams, and Henry Adams described how legislatures were devolving into: "a mart in which the prices of votes was haggled over and laws, made to order, were bought and sold."[151] The rampant political corruption produced both public outcry, but little effective political resistance as the boom times rolled on.[152] "Crony capitalism" took root outside Great Britain and the United States. It eroded the legitimacy of Japan's government and financial laws during the 1980s bubble. The corrupted Japanese political class "utilised speculation to serve its fathomless financial demands."[153]

Even if the public at large still believes in the justness of financial laws, if a significant subset of financial professionals do not, their obedience to antifraud or other laws may wane. These financial sophisticates break into two groups: those that successfully wield significant political power and those that do not. The former group may worry less about the legitimacy of the law or their compliance with it. They bought it, and they can break it. In extreme examples, like those cited by Fraser, financial mandarins "comply with the law" by simply buying legislatures, regulators, and judges. Of course, one of the insights of the broader literature on capture is that there are many degrees of purchasing political influence below outright corruption.[154] The concern of this group with legal legitimacy, if any, is more that widespread public outcry over corruption does not rise to a level that threatens their political or economic interests.

The latter group, largely shut out of significant political power, may question the procedural fairness of the legal system. According to Tyler's research, disbelief that a legal regime is procedurally fair has corrosive effects on individual and social group decisions to obey the law.

Booms and norms in the legal profession

Lawyers play a crucial role in the development of social norms – both within the profession and in the broader public – that affect legal compliance. Moreover, the legal profession can affect, for better or worse, the public's perception of the legitimacy of laws. Viewed through this lens, the story of lawyers during boom times is checkered. Rande Kostal's magisterial study of the role that lawyers played in the development of English railways in the nineteenth century illustrates the ways in which lawyers have undermined legal legitimacy. During various railway bubbles, lawyers served as architects and facilitators of fraudulent schemes. In the Panic of 1825, Rande Kostal contends that, "[t]he legal profession was merely the most prolific breeding-ground of sham railway organizers."[155]

English lawyers also undermined the legitimacy of laws when they opposed railway companies. Kostal describes how rival rail lines, landowners, and other interest groups entangled railway companies in a thicket of litigation.[156] The legal profession's abuses of England's archaic legal system during this era inspired Dickens's savage satire of the legal profession in *Bleak House*.[157] Again, the public perception of lawyers matters perhaps more than the substantive accuracy. If the public perceives that law and lawyers represent mere rent-seekers, then the perceived legitimacy of financial laws could deteriorate significantly. Tyler's research would then lead to a prediction that levels of compliance with these laws would drop and compliance rot will set in.

Law professor Ronald Gilson offers a modern response to criticisms that lawyers merely engage in rent-seeking behavior. Gilson argued that corporate lawyers provide value to clients by serving as "transaction cost engineers" that reduce the transaction costs to contracting.[158] Yet this view, if taken to extreme, also creates problems for legal legitimacy. Financial laws and regulations, of course, could be thought of as transaction costs to be reduced. Indeed, Chapter 2 described regulatory stimulus to include legal changes that reduced the "regulatory tax" on investments.[159] Viewing legal compliance or non-compliance as a cost of doing business fundamentally alters the way in which the law is seen. Conceiving of law as transaction cost and lawyers as transaction cost engineers operates not only on a descriptive level but a normative one too. Law may be drained of its normative force, as well as of its effective influence on human behavior, when modeled as a mere drag coefficient on economic activity. This echoes earlier parts of this book that underscored the potential normative undertones to descriptive scholarship on public choice theory and shareholder wealth maximization. The lens through which the law is observed, analyzed, taught, and perceived by lawyers and their clients matters immensely for legal compliance.

The next chapter discusses the critical role of lawyers in assisting clients in "regulatory arbitrage," which can shade into evasion of laws. That chapter also sketches how changes in the norms and economics of the U.S. legal profession over the last three decades contributed to a loosening of normative constraints on regulatory arbitrage.[160] For now, it is important to highlight that a number of the information and agency cost dynamics described above can also operate to undermine social norms within law firms, the legal profession, and in other professional gatekeeper communities. Higher transaction volume, higher staff turnover, and the greater power of "stars" do more than increase information and agency costs within firms. They can undermine the concern of employees for the reputation of their firms and for preserving the reputation and norms of their profession.

Deteriorating compliance with prudential regulations

Many of the dynamics that reduce the effectiveness of antifraud rules during bubbles apply equally to cause compliance with a host of other financial laws and regulations to rot. Financial booms can undermine the incentives of market participants – particularly financial institutions and other market intermediaries – to comply with legal rules that would otherwise curb their profits. Compliance with prudential regulations on financial firms can deteriorate significantly, because these legal rules stand in the way of firms and individuals earning additional profits from booming asset markets. Regulations that restrict investments in booming asset classes or constrain lending and leverage may suffer from the same general dynamics that reduce compliance with antifraud rules. Rather than repeat the lengthy analysis above for compliance with antifraud laws, the remainder of this chapter highlights the similar and different effects of bubbles on compliance with prudential regulations compared to rules on fraud.

Rational calculus

First, financial booms can alter the *rational* calculus of financial institutions, market intermediaries, and individuals at those firms in determining whether to comply with prudential rules. The same cost–benefit calculus rubric set forth above for antifraud rules explains how bubbles can lead to compliance rot afflicting a host of banking laws.

Skewing benefits and reputational "costs." Market booms offer immediate benefits to making investments in booming asset markets that regulations would otherwise restrict. *Not* making these investments may leave market participants at a competitive disadvantage as others profit from the frenzy. Moreover, if financial institutions can sidestep leverage restrictions during a boom, they can supercharge returns to shareholders. Shareholders did not seek to be defrauded, but they might be more welcoming of less-than-legal means to increase their profits.

Those individuals who manage other people's money may face pressure to increase profits or see their investors flee. This phenomenon serves as a one leitmotif of this book. Recall that "smart money" arbitrageurs faced the same risk in attempting to sell short during a bubble; investors punish fund managers who forego the opportunity of investing in a bubble.[161] Indeed, reputational considerations may cut *against* compliance with prudential regulations that limit risk-taking during bubble periods.

Delayed detection. At the same time, the liability for breaking those rules can be pushed off into the far future. Rising prices can hide violations of prudential regulations from both regulators and from financial markets. Indeed, market discipline breaks down when markets go haywire in bubble times. Fewer investors or creditors care about risk-taking or leverage while bubbly investment returns pour in. A rising tide of asset prices tends to hide excessive risk-taking from market scrutiny, just as it conceals fraud.[162] Regulatory interventions, such as deposit insurance, if poorly designed, may work to insulate financial institutions from market discipline rather than reinforce it.[163] Moreover, as Chapter 9 explains, when financial institutions increase their leverage en masse, the effective money supply increases and adds fuel to an asset price boom. Rising asset prices, in turn, cover up the risks of loans defaulting. It also masks the risk of excessive leverage to individual financial institutions that have become more fragile and more susceptible to collapse in a downturn.

Diluted enforcement. If market discipline erodes during bubble periods, so too does government enforcement.[164] Diluted enforcement can plague prudential regulations just as much as it affects antifraud rules. Chapter 3 describes how the Office of the Comptroller of the Currency became overwhelmed by the banking boom of the Roaring Twenties.[165] The ballooning size of banks and the volume of transactions they conduct during bubbles can swamp bank examiners when their personnel resources remain fixed.

Moreover, the last chapter outlined the various ways that booms dull the incentives of policymakers to enforce prudential regulations actively, including being reluctant to take action that would upset the economic applecart during a bubble.[166] These dynamics add to the particular incentives that bank regulators have to forbear from taking action against banks facing potential insolvency.[167] Bankers and other market participants recognize the limitations – in resources, incentives, and cognitive abilities – that regulatory enforcers face. They may then adjust their levels of compliance with financial laws downwards accordingly.

Information and agency costs. As with detecting fraud, rising transaction volume frustrates the efforts of departments within a financial institution to police compliance with prudential regulations. As with fraud, agency costs may also rise. Booming markets increase the employment opportunities for bank employees. Departures reduce institutional memory and stunt the development of loyalty to the firm and the inculcation of firm norms. Firms may be reluctant to discipline "star" traders who bring profits.[168]

Agency costs and short-termism among the employees at financial institutions may lead to inappropriate pricing of long-term risk. In other words, if the compensation of employees at financial firms creates incentives for short-term profit, then the employees may be unlikely to take more conservative, long-term assessments of risk and ride a boom for all its worth.[169]

These varieties of agency costs and a breakdown in internal monitoring within financial institutions may explain the return during boom times of that hardy perennial: rogue traders. However, rogue traders may not be so roguish. Law professor Kim Krawiec argues that popular notions of rogue traders who lost hundreds of millions or more at large financial institutions may be wrong. Management may stand to gain from the risk-taking of these traders. Accordingly they create incentive structures, permissive corporate governance systems, and cavalier institutional cultures that encourage risky trading. When some trades fail spectacularly, management may disavow the traders and feed public misconceptions of "rogues" to protect their own interests.[170]

Moving yardsticks. A more charitable theory for why compliance with financial regulation deteriorates during bubbles focuses on the changing regulatory standards during these periods. Chapter 2 described the prevalence of regulatory stimulus during bubbles in history. Regulatory stimulus includes policymakers rolling back, granting exemptions to, and engaging in more permissive interpretation and enforcement of, financial regulations. One knock-on effect of these legal changes is that firms will have difficulty predicting their legal liability. Constantly moving the legal yardsticks downfield may encourage lower compliance by financial firms, particularly if individuals at those firms are overly aggressive, confident, or optimistic. These individuals might well gamble that the law may soon change (a prominent example of this during the demise of Glass-Steagall will follow shortly).

A behavioral overlay

Overconfidence and overoptimism lead to a behavioral theory of compliance rot. Compliance with prudential regulations can also deteriorate because of the behavioral biases afflicting individuals both within financial firms and regulatory agencies. These biases – among them overconfidence, overoptimism, the availability bias – can lead bankers to discount the probability of getting caught and the costs of noncompliance with the law. They can similarly lead the internal compliance cops of financial firms to underestimate the probability of legal violations escaping their notice. As noted above, cognitive limitations may also impair the performance of regulators. Overoptimism may cause regulators to discount the risk of a market crash. Overconfidence would cause them to overestimate their ability to spot misconduct or excessive risk in the firms or markets which they oversee.

Economists Jack Guttentag, Richard Herring, and Susan Wachter have described how a cluster of behavioral biases, which they call "disaster myopia," combine to cause both bankers and bank regulators to severely underestimate the risk of banking crises. The passage of time since a previous market crash, bank run, or other systemic crisis leads to excessive risk-taking by bankers and excessive complacency by regulators.[171] This phenomenon leads to several perversities. First, as more time elapses since a catastrophe, the dangers of disaster myopia grow larger. Second, as noted in the previous chapter, this has consequences for the durability of regulation; again, one never sees the crises that don't happen.

Norms: Citigroup and the last days of Glass-Steagall

The same shifts in social norms that drive deregulation and fraud also stimulate compliance rot in prudential regulations. Indeed research links norms to compliance with a host of legal rules, such as tax laws.[172] In fact, the erosion may be much more severe with respect to prudential rules than for antifraud rules for several reasons. First, fraud involves identifiable human victims, including the proverbial widows and orphans. Violating prudential regulations may seem, in comparison, like a victimless crime. Although bank failures harm employees, shareholders, creditors, communities, and taxpayers, these victims may appear more diffuse and anonymous than in many financial frauds.

Moreover, the failure of a firm may seem remote during a bubble. Thus the value of a prudential regulation may appear negligible. "Disaster myopia" and the free-market ideologies that accompany many bubble periods can mix into a potent cocktail that makes many prudential regulations seem quaint, obsolete, and even illegitimate in the eyes of both bankers and regulators. Booming markets may appear more capable of governing themselves.

This perceived obsolescence explains the dismantling of one of the cornerstones of the post-war architecture of U.S. financial regulation. What may be forgotten in the story of Glass-Steagall's twilight, was that just before the U.S. Congress repealed the statute in 1999, one Wall Street firm brazenly challenged it. When Citicorp announced its prospective merger with Traveler's Insurance in 1998, its executives and lawyers knew that the transaction would violate a clear command of Glass-Steagall that banking and insurance businesses could not coexist under the same corporate umbrella. Facing the prospect of having to divest assets that would have negated much of the value of the deal, the firms sought regulatory relief from the Federal Reserve.[173] The Chairman of the Federal Reserve, in turn, pushed Congress to repeal Glass-Steagall, calling its walls between banking and commerce obsolete and inefficient. Congress promptly complied and passed the Gramm-Leach-Bliley Act that repealed the Depression-era statute.[174] The Citigroup–Traveler's merger looks in retrospect like a game of "chicken": even a form of strategic, public noncompliance with the law. The sheer size of the deal increased the pressure on regulators and legislators to remove the offending law or challenge the legal offender.

The story of Glass-Steagall's end has a rough parallel in the demise of the Bubble Act, another foundational statute that endured for decades. As the English stock market boomed, many joint-stock companies flouted the legal prohibitions in the Act. During the parliamentary debates leading to the Bubble Act's repeal in 1825, many Members of Parliament noted diminished compliance with the statute and criticized the law for both under- and over-deterring firms.[175] When firms openly flout a law and lawmakers question the law's wisdom, its normative force has all but evaporated.

Conclusion

It is difficult to distill which of changing costs and benefits, behavioral biases, or shifting social norms has the greatest effect on compliance rot with respect to antifraud and prudential rules in bubble periods. These three different dynamics reinforce one another in promoting compliance rot in myriad ways. For example, diluted enforcement, disaster myopia, and market based norms may combine to cause individuals at financial firms to discount the downsides to committing fraud or bending the law to take additional risks.

This difficulty in the descriptive analysis will cascade down to thorny problems in crafting policy prescriptions. Indeed, some scholars claim that increasing legal penalties to ensure compliance may have the perverse effect of undermining social norms of compliance.[176] This assertion, however, raises problems. First, it may not accurately describe the relationship between all laws and norms. Indeed, many laws may express and reinforce social norms. Yet, assuming there is a tension between law and norms, financial regulation faces a Faustian dilemma in responding to bubble periods; financial booms and manias undermine the architectures of *both* legal liability and social norms. If shoring up one weakens the other, which should policymakers chose to address: legal costs and benefits or norms?

The concluding chapter of this book takes up this question and other tensions between instrumental and norm-based views of market and regulator behavior.

Notes

1 Charles P. Kindleberger, *Manias, Panics and Crashes: A History of Financial Crises*, 73–90 (4th ed. 2000, Wiley Investment Classics).
2 Ibid. at 76.
3 Tom R. Tyler, *Why People Obey the Law* (2006, Princeton University Press). For a theoretical analysis that complements Tyler's work, see Janice Nadler, Flouting the Law, 83 *Texas Law Review* 1399 (2005).
4 Even if antifraud rules were not repealed or altered, it *is* possible that they were under-enforced. The previous chapter discussed how market booms can dilute enforcement: Chapter 3, "The problem of diluted enforcement." Later, this Chapter 4 explores the consequences of diluted enforcement on the potential suppliers of fraud and on market participants considering whether to comply with financial laws.
5 See Chapter 2, "Securities deregulation." The Private Securities Litigation Reform Act of 1995 (PSLRA) imposed strict new pleading requirements. Pub. L. No. 104–67, 109 Stat. 737 (1995) (codified in scattered sections of 15 U.S.C. (2000)). Among the most significant judicial opinions of the 1990s that cabined federal securities law liability was the Supreme Court's 1994 ruling in *Central Bank of Denver* v. *First Interstate Bank of Denver*. This case abolished "aiding and abetting" theories of liability for certain securities laws. 511 U.S. 164, 191 (1994).
6 John C. Coffee, Jr., Understanding Enron: "It's About the Gatekeepers, Stupid," 57 *Business Lawyer* 1403, 1403–5, 1409–10 (2002) [hereinafter Coffee, Understanding Enron].
7 For seminal works on the role of gatekeepers in policing the securities markets, see generally Stephen Choi, Market Lessons for Gatekeepers, 92 *Northwestern University Law Review* 916 (1998); Ronald J. Gilson and Reinier H. Kraakman, The Mechanisms of Market Efficiency, 70 *Virginia Law Review* 549 (1984); Victor P. Goldberg, Accountable Accountants: Is Third-Party Liability Necessary? 17 *Journal of Legal Studies* 295 (1988); Reinier H. Kraakman, Corporate Liability Strategies and the Costs of Legal Controls, 93 *Yale Law Journal* 857 (1984) [hereinafter Kraakman, Corporate]; Reinier H. Kraakman, Gatekeepers: The Anatomy of a Third-Party Enforcement Strategy, 2 *Journal of Law, Economics and Organization* 53 (1986) [hereinafter Kraakman, Gatekeepers].

Over two decades of research, scholars have employed two definitions of gate-keepers. The first definition focuses on the *certification* role of gatekeepers. This definition views gatekeepers as "reputational intermediaries who provide verification and certification services to investors." Coffee, Understanding Enron, *supra* note 6, at 1405. For other scholarship that employs this definition, see, for example, Choi, *supra*, at 918. Under the second definition, gatekeepers *restrict access* to the market by securities issuers who do not conform to legal (and market) standards. The gate-keeper stakes its reputation on those firms who are granted access. See Kraakman, Gatekeepers, *supra*, at 53 (defining gatekeepers as "private parties who are able to disrupt misconduct by withholding their cooperation from wrongdoers").

Coffee is not alone in examining the failure of gatekeepers to police securities fraud during the tech stock era. For other works in the aftermath of Enron, see, for example, Stephen J. Choi and Jill E. Fisch, How to Fix Wall Street: A Voucher Financing Proposal for Securities Intermediaries, 113 *Yale Law Journal* 269 (2003); Jill E. Fisch and Kenneth M. Rosen, Is There a Role for Lawyers in Preventing Future Enrons? 48 *Villanova Law Review* 1097 (2003); Jill E. Fisch and Hillary A. Sale, The Securities Analyst as Agent: Rethinking the Regulation of Analysts, 88 *Iowa Law Review* 1035 (2003); Assaf Hamdani, Assessing Gatekeeper Liability, 77 *Southern California Law Review* 53 (2003); Frank Partnoy, Barbarians at the Gate-keepers? A Proposal for a Modified Strict Liability Regime, 79 *Washington University Law Quarterly* 491 (2001).

8 Coffee, Understanding Enron, *supra* note 6, at 1403–5, 1409–10. John C. Coffee, Jr., What Caused Enron? A Capsule Social and Economic History of the 1990s, 89 *Cornell Law Review* 269 (2003–2004) [hereinafter, Coffee, What Caused Enron?].

9 One measure of growing conflicts of interest during the decade was the increasing percentage of auditor revenue derived from non-audit services. See Coffee, What Caused Enron? *supra* note 8, at 291. Two studies that together tracked this percentage for major accounting firms in the years 1990, 1994–1996, and 1999 show a steady increase in the percentage of auditor revenue derived from non-audit services over the decade. The Panel on Audit Effectiveness, Report and Recommendations (2000), 112 available at www.pobauditpanel.org/download.html (last visited July 24, 2013) (breaking down the percentage of revenue for the Big 5 accounting firms among "accounting and auditing," "tax," and "consulting" services for the years 1990 and 1999); Andrew Crockett, Frederic S. Mishkin, and Eugene N. White, *Conflicts of Interest in the Financial Services Industry*, 33 (2003, Centre for Economic Policy Research) (breaking down the percentage of revenue for the Big 6 accounting firms among "auditing and accounting," "management advisory," and "tax" services for each of years 1994, 1995, and 1996). The author is not aware of any study showing that the conflicts of interest for other gatekeepers spiked at any point during the decade.

10 Chapter 2, notes 354–61 and accompanying text.

11 Chapter 2, notes 365–9 and accompanying text.

12 See Coffee, What Caused Enron? *supra* note 8, at 282–3 (showing that the number of earnings restatements by publicly held corporations skyrocketed between 1998 and 2000).

13 Ibid.

14 George B. Moriarty and Philip B. Livingston, Quantitative Measures of the Quality of Financial Reporting, 17 *Financial Executive* 54–5 (2001). This data was also used by Coffee, What Caused Enron? *supra* note 8, at 282, 285, n.60.

15 Robert J. Shiller, *Irrational Exuberance*, 7–8 (2001, Broadway Books).

16 Moriarty and Livingston, *supra* note 14, at 55.

17 Ibid. at 6. For an explanation of Shiller's sources and methodology in making the calculations for price/earnings ratios, see ibid. at 257 n.2. Shiller's data on price/earnings ratio and other stock market metrics from 1990 to 2000 are available at www.irrationalexuberance.com/ie_data.xls (last visited October 26, 2005).

18 The correlation coefficient that comparing this price/earnings data to the total market value of losses due to restatements is even higher at 0.909787. But one would expect a higher correlation in this number because rising stock prices would be reflected in both price/earnings data and the market value of losses due to restatements. Both of these coefficients reflect the correlation of (i) the average of Shiller's twelve monthly price to earnings ratio data points for each year, and (ii) the annual numbers on restatements.

19 Others have offered alternative theories of causation for the rise in restatements in 1998. For example, Moriarty and Livingston attribute the spike in restatements in 1998 to changing SEC enforcement priorities due to then SEC Chairman Levitt's campaign against earnings management abuses. Moriarty and Livingston, *supra* note 14, at 56. But the timing of the SEC's earnings management crusade does not fully support this theory. The SEC first began its efforts to combat earnings management in 1998, the year that Levitt gave his influential speech on the topic. Ibid.; see Arthur Levitt, Chairman, SEC, The Numbers Game, Remarks at the NYU Center for Law and Business (September 28, 1998) (transcript available at www.sec.gov/news/speech/speecharchive/1998/spch220.txt) (last visited July 25, 2013). Since restatements are, by nature, retrospective, one would expect that, if the SEC efforts were the primary driver of restatements (and, by extension, triggered the revelation of fraud) then the years affected by restatements would have dramatically increased *before* 1998.

20 Kindleberger, *supra* note 1, at 76.

21 Cited in Edward Chancellor, *Devil Take the Hindmost: A History of Financial Speculation*, 47 (1999, Plume Books).

22 For example, in the 2003 case of *In re Merrill Lynch & Co.*, a federal judge ruled that the technology stock market bubble was an intervening cause that precluded relief in a securities class-action suit. 273 F. Supp. 2d 351, 364–5, 382 (S.D.N.Y. 2003). That same judge also used the existence of a bubble as a bar to plaintiff recovery when he invoked the separate "bespeaks caution" doctrine that holds that disclosure had adequately cautioned investors of the risk of the investment. Ibid. at 376. For an analysis of this decision and its implications for the loss-causation element of securities-fraud litigation, see Jay W. Eisenhofer, Geoffrey C. Jarvis, and James R. Banko, Securities Fraud, Stock Price Valuation, and Loss Causation: Toward a Corporate Finance-Based Theory of Loss Causation, 59 *Business Lawyer* 1419, 1438 (2004).

23 For some of the literature on the overoptimism bias, see Chapter 1, note 45 and accompanying text.

24 For some of the literature on the overconfidence bias, see Chapter 1, note 46 and accompanying text.

25 For some of the literature on the availability bias, see Chapter 1, notes 47–8 and accompanying text.

26 See generally Coffee, Understanding Enron, *supra* note 6, at 1412–13; Coffee, What Caused Enron? *supra* note 8, at 293 (euphoric investors may ignore auditors and other gatekeepers).

27 Robert P. Bartlett, III, Inefficiencies in the Information Thicket: A Case Study of Derivative Disclosures During the Financial Crisis, 36 *Journal of Corporation Law* 1 (2010).

28 See, e.g., Margaret M. Blair and Lynn A. Stout, Trust, Trustworthiness, and the Behavioral Foundations of Corporate Law, 149 *University of Pennsylvania Law Review* 1735 (2000) (exploring how the learned, socially determined nature of trust is reflected in the structure of corporate law); Lawrence A. Mitchell, Fairness and Trust in Corporate Law, 43 *Duke Law Journal* 425 (1993) (arguing that courts and legislatures have jeopardized the integrity of corporate fiduciary law by ignoring the essential role of trust); Eric A. Posner, Altruism, Status, and Trust in the Law of Gifts and Gratuitous Promises, 1997 *Wisconsin Law Review* 567, 577–8 (discussing the role of trust in gifts and relational contracts); Carol M. Rose, Trust in the Mirror of Betrayal, 75 *Boston University Law Review* 531 (1995) (examining the resilience of trust in light of the notion that pure rationality counsels against trusting others).

29 See generally Blair and Stout, *supra* note 28, at 1745–6.

30 See ibid. at 1745, 1750–3.

31 See, e.g., Francis Fukuyama, *Trust: The Social Virtues and the Creation of Prosperity*, 10–11 (1995, Free Press) (arguing that trust, being necessary for people to work together for common purposes, is essential to American civil society); Karen Cook, Trust in Society, in *Trust in Society*, xi, xi (Karen S. Cook ed., 2001, Russell Sage Foundation) (discussing a national decline in trust of everything from prominent professionals to the very idea of a team or family); cf. Peter Brann and Margaret Foddy, Trust and the Consumption of a Deteriorating Common Resource, 31 *Journal of Conflict Resolution* 615 (1987) (describing a study that examined the relationship between trust and resource consumption).

32 See Lynn A. Stout, The Investor Confidence Game, 68 *Brooklyn Law Review* 407, 415–20 (2002) (comparing the reactions of a solely rational investor and a "trusting investor" in light of recent corporate scandals).

33 See Tamar Frankel, Regulation and Investors' Trust in the Securities Markets, 68 *Brooklyn Law Review* 439, 443 n.17, 448 (2002) ("[Investors] care about a fair, not necessarily a level, playing field.... They are willing to lose fair and square but not to be taken by fraud.").

34 Chapter 2, "Bounded rationality and noise traders," "Herding and positive-feedback investment loops."
35 An information cascade occurs when individuals make decisions in sequence, and, after observing the behavior decisions of those who acted before, it is optimal for an individual to follow that behavior regardless of his or her own information. For two influential articles in the economic literature on information cascades, see Abhijit V. Banerjee, A Simple Model of Herd Behavior, 107 *Quarterly Journal of Economics* 797 (1992) and Sushil Bikchandani, David Hirshleifer, and Ivo Welch, A Theory of Fads, Fashion, Custom, and Cultural Change as Informational Cascades, 100 *Journal of Political Economy* 992 (1992).
36 Erik F. Gerding, The Next Epidemic: Bubbles and the Growth and Decay of Securities Regulation, 38 *Connecticut Law Review* 393, 418–21 (2006). For an empirical study that shows a connection between investor beliefs about the prospects of companies engaged in an initial public offering and fraud, see Tracy Yue Wang, Andrew Winton, and Xiaoyun Yu, Corporate Fraud and Business Conditions: Evidence from IPOs, 65 *Journal of Finance* 2255 (2010). This study also finds that monitoring of fraud by underwriters is less effective during financial booms. The authors conclude that these dynamics mean that regulators and auditors "should be especially vigilant" for fraud during booms. Ibid. at 2287.
37 Chapter 1, "Rational bubbles."
38 Deborah K. Dietsch, 10 Things You Need to Know About Buying or Selling a Home, *Washington Post*, October 31, 2011 available at www.washingtonpost.com/realestate/ten-things-you-need-to-know-about-buying-or-selling-a-home/2011/10/20/gIQApgYzIM_story.html (last visited July 25, 2013) ("Waiving the inspection was one way to beat the competition during the go-go market of 2005–07.").
39 Ana Lai and Steven M. Bavaria. The Leveraging of America: Covenant-Lite Loan Structures Diminish Recovery Prospects, Standard & Poor's Ratings Direct, July 18, 2007.
40 Cf. Pascal Blanqué, Crisis and Fraud, 11 *Journal of Financial Regulation and Compliance* 60, 63 (2003) (discussing information asymmetries, financial fraud and bubbles).
41 Erik F. Gerding, Code, Crash, and Open Source: The Outsourcing of Financial Regulation to Risk Models and the Global Financial Crisis, 84 *Washington Law Review* 127, 175 (2009).
42 Cf. Guido Calabresi, *The Cost of Accidents: A Legal and Economic Analysis* (1970, Yale University Press) (developing the idea of a "least-cost avoider" in tort law).
43 Andrei Shleifer, *Inefficient Markets: An Introduction to Behavioral Finance*, 11–12 (2000, Oxford University Press). The robustness of bubbles themselves is discussed in more detail in Chapter 8.
44 Economic scholarship on deterrence theory grows out of the seminal analysis of Nobel laureate Gary Becker. See generally Gary S. Becker, Crime and Punishment: An Economic Approach, in *Essays in the Economics of Crime and Punishment*, 1 (Gary S. Becker and William M. Landes eds., 1974, National Bureau of Economic Research/Columbia University Press). For an analysis of deterrence theory and the Sarbanes-Oxley Act, see Michael A. Perino, Enron's Legislative Aftermath: Some Reflections on the Deterrence Aspects of the Sarbanes-Oxley Act of 2002, 76 *St. John's Law Review* 671 (2002).
45 There is an extensive legal literature on the economic calculations involved in litigation and settlement. For a relatively recent contribution that also summarizes past scholarship, see Robert J. Rhee, A Price Theory of Legal Bargaining: An Inquiry into the Selection of Settlement and Litigation Under Uncertainty, 56 *Emory Law Journal* 619 (2006).
46 See generally *supra* note 7 (literature on gatekeepers and reputational intermediaries);

Frank H. Easterbrook and Daniel A. Fischel, Mandatory Disclosure and the Protection of Investors, 70 *Virginia Law Review* 669, 675 (1984) (discussing how issuer concern with maintaining reputation mitigates fraud).

47 Coffee's theories of misaligned incentives and under-deterrence due to deregulation focuses on the benefits received from fraud, *B*, and the legal liability under the securities laws, *Ll*. His misaligned incentives theory posits that gatekeepers had more to gain from participating or acquiescing in fraud. He also argues that deregulation lowered the expected value of legal liability. See Coffee, Understanding Enron, *supra* note 6, at 1414–15.

48 Donald C. Langevoort, When Lawyers and Law Firms Invest in their Corporate Clients' Stock, 80 *Washington University Law Quarterly* 569 (2002) (evaluating this practice of lawyers during the tech stock period). See also John S. Dzienkowski and Robert J. Peroni, The Decline in Lawyer Independence: Lawyer Equity Investments in Clients, 81 *Texas Law Review* 405 (2002).

49 Coffee, Understanding Enron, *supra* note 6, at 1415. This arguably compromised the role of auditors as gatekeepers that policed the accuracy of financial disclosure. Ibid. at 1414. Conflicts of interest in the 1990s could be found among gatekeepers in other areas of the financial sector. For example, stock analysts in investment banking firms came under internal pressure to deliver positive ratings for the stock of corporate clients of their firms. These clients could provide other revenue (such as merger and acquisition advisory fees or securities underwriting fees) to the investment bank. Ibid. at 1407.

In each case, gatekeepers saw their interests become aligned more with pleasing corporate clients and seeing stock prices rise, and less in serving their traditional role as independent watchdogs; any potential reputational losses from acquiescing to client misdeeds were dwarfed by the potential gains to gatekeepers from other revenue streams.

This logic of misaligned incentives also explains the failure of corporate governance in the 1990s. Because executives and directors received increasing amounts of compensation through stock and stock options, they became obsessed with increasing short-term share prices to the detriment of their fiduciary roles. Coffee, Understanding Enron, *supra* note 6, at 1413–14. Thus the incentives of the "internal gatekeepers" of companies became just as corrupted as the external gatekeepers. Ibid. at 1414.

50 This quote comes from the following source: Letter from Warren E. Buffett, Chairman of the Board to the Shareholders of Berkshire Hathaway Inc. (February 28, 2002) available at www.berkshirehathaway.com/2001ar/2001letter.html (last visited July 25, 2013).

51 Liaquat Ahmed, How Bernard Madoff Did It, *New York Times*, May 13, 2011, Book Review at 30 (noting how Madoff scheme almost collapsed during 1987 stock market crash, recession of early 1990s, and bursting of tech stock bubble, only to be revived by new sources of funds).

52 See 17 C.F.R. § 240.10b-5 (2011). For a brief discussion, of the elements of a private plaintiff's cause of action under this rule, see *Dura Pharmaceuticals, Inc.* v. *Broudo*, 544 U.S. 336, 341–2 (2005).

53 *Dura*, 544 U.S. at 341. 15 U.S.C. § 78u-4(b)(4) (2011).

54 In *Dura*, the Supreme Court ruled that merely alleging that the purchase price was inflated by a misrepresentation is insufficient to prove the misrepresentation caused the plaintiff's loss, which is a required element under a Rule 10b-5 case. *Dura*, 544 U.S. at 342–6.

55 The Supreme Court analyzed the element of loss causation in *Dura*, 544 U.S. 336. For a discussion of the use of stock prices to determine materiality in securities litigation, See *infra* note 76, and accompanying text. The Supreme Court's decision in *Basic Inc.* v. *Levinson*, 485 U.S. 224, 244–5 (1998 in *re Merck & Co. Securities*

Litigation, 432 F.3d 261 (3d Cir. 2005)), established how plaintiffs can obtain a presumption of reliance (through the "fraud-on-the-market" theory) by proving that the market for a particular stock was efficient.

56   Chapter 3, "The problem of diluted enforcement."

57   Evaluating the merits of this argument requires consideration of the "race to the bottom" versus "race to the top" debate that recurs throughout corporate, securities, and financial regulation scholarship. In other words, would the cheating of a few gatekeepers cause other gatekeepers to cheat and the market for gatekeepers to unwind? Or would other gatekeepers be able to compete and win market share by distinguishing themselves from cheaters and touting their trustworthiness? For divergent views on this question in the context of gatekeepers, see Choi, *supra* note 7, at 919 (proposing a self-tailored liability scheme, because a gatekeeper's choice of liability level would send a signal to market on the gatekeeper's reliability); Hamdani, *supra* note 7, at 89–90 (suggesting that market stability depends on gatekeepers' capacity to foil unlawful conduct); Partnoy, *supra* note 7, at 492, 494–6 (arguing for strict liability for gatekeepers because regulatory licenses enjoyed by gatekeepers reduce potential reputational loss).

58   George A. Akerlof, The Market for Lemons: Quality Uncertainty and the Market Mechanism, 84 *Quarterly Journal of Economics* 488 (1970). For one article that analyzes the conditions for when the market for gatekeepers services will and will not devolve into a lemon's market, see Choi, *supra* note 7.

59   See, e.g., Gilson and Kraakman, *supra* note 7, at 585, 602–5.

60   Law professor Claire Hill argues that noise trading and consequent market inefficiencies during the subprime bubble explain why investors did not demand a sufficient "lemons" premium for investing in securities backed by subprime mortgage related mortgages. Claire A. Hill, Why Didn't Subprime Investors Demand a (Much Larger) Lemons Premium, 74 *Law and Contemporary Problems* 47 (2011).

61   Cf. Troy A. Paredes, Blinded by the Light: Information Overload and Its Consequences for Securities Regulation, 81 *Washington University Law Quarterly* 417, 419 (2003).

62   See ibid. at 446 n.133.

63   See ibid. at 440–1 (explaining that "people can only process a finite amount of information during any particular period of time.... [T]he decision maker's decision quality decreases if she is given additional information.").

64   John Coates provides one example of professional standards declining during a boom. He documents the widespread failure of law firms to draft standard antitakeover defenses into the organizational documents of many of the new companies they advised during the late 1990s. See John C. Coates IV, Explaining Variation in Takeover Defenses: Blame the Lawyers, 89 *California Law Review* 1301, 1303, 1309 (2001).

65   See James A. Fanto, Subtle Hazards Revisited: The Corruption of a Financial Holding Company by a Corporate Client's Inner Circle, 70 *Brooklyn Law Review* 7, 28 (2004) ("[I]nvestment bankers are today little more than hired guns with weak commitments to their current employer investment bank and more loyalty to their corporate clients, whom they often bring along to any new employer").

66   Ibid.

67   For an analysis of excuses and the assignment of blame in organizations from the perspective of social psychology and organizational behavior, see Raymond L. Higgins and C.R. Snyder, The Business of Excuses, in *Impression Management in the Organization*, 73, 78 (Robert A. Giacolone and Paul Rosenfeld eds., 1989, Psychology Press) (noting that the most successful blaming strategy is to direct blame outside the organization); Nancy Bell and Phillip Tetlock, The Intuitive Politician and the Assignment of Blame in Organizations, in *Impression Management in the Organization*, 105, 110 (Robert A. Giacolone and Paul Rosenfeld eds., 1989, Psychology Press).

68 See Coffee, Understanding Enron, *supra* note 6, at 1412–13 (discussing the celebrity status of high-profile securities analysts during the 1990s boom).
69 For MacGregor's story, see Chapter 2, note 83 and accompanying text.
70 Compare *SEC* v. *Grubman, Litigation Release No. 18,111* (April 28, 2003) available at www.sec.gov/litigation/litreleases/lr18111.htm (last visited July 25, 2013) (announcing a $15 million settlement) and *SEC* v. *Blodgett, Litigation Release No. 18,115* (April 28, 2003) available at www.sec.gov/litigation/litreleases/lr18115.htm (last visited July 25, 2013) (announcing a $4 million settlement), with John Cassidy, The Investigation, *New Yorker*, April 7, 2003, at 54 (reporting salary and fringe benefits enjoyed by Blodgett and Grubman during the boom period).

Of course, Blodgett and Grubman may have liability under investor litigation. Even so, corporation-provided insurance and indemnification can blunt the deterrence effect of this litigation. James. D. Cox, Private Litigation and the Deterrence of Corporate Misconduct, 60 *Law and Contemporary Problems* 1, 21–38 (1997) (analyzing the extent to which third-party insurance undermines deterrence versus whether insurance market reestablishes deterrence effect).
71 E. Allan Farnsworth, *Contracts*, § 12.8 (4th ed. 2004, Aspen Law and Business).
72 For example, Section 12(a) of the Securities Act of 1933 provides that rescission is the only remedy for violations of that provision. For other causes of action, Congress has limited the amounts plaintiffs can recover to actual damages. E.g., 15 U.S.C. § 78u-4(e).
73 *Exxon Shipping Co.* v. *Baker*, 554 U.S. 471 (2008). In this case, the U.S. Supreme Court gave a tour of punitive damages in Anglo-American jurisprudence.
74 Many scholars have supported this choice to view punitive damages through the lens of retribution and punishment rather than deterrence. E.g., Leo M. Romero, Punitive Damages, Criminal Punishment, and Proportionality: The Importance of Legislative Limits, 41 *Connecticut Law Review* 109 (2008). As an aside, it is somewhat odd to think of moral retribution against a corporate entity that in the words of Baron Thurlow, has "no soul to be damned, no body to be kicked." See John C. Coffee, Jr., "No Soul to Damn, No Body to Kick": An Unscandalized Inquiry into the Problem of Corporate Punishment, 79 *Michigan Law Review* 386 (1981).
75 Chapter 8, "Restricting access of unsophisticated investors and 'tiering'." See also Chapter 1, "Behavioral finance models of bubbles."
76 Robert A. Prentice, The Case of the Irrational Auditor: A Behavioral Insight into Securities Fraud Litigation, 95 *Northwestern University Law Review* 133, 154–5 (2000).
77 Kent Daniel, David Hirshleifer, and Avanidhar Subrahmanyam, Investor Psychology and Security Market Under- and Overreactions, 53 *Journal of Finance* 1839 (1998) (analyzing the extent to which self-attribution bias and other biases affect the under-reaction and over-reaction by investors to new information).
78 Thomas Gilovich, Robert Vallone, and Amos Tversky, The Hot Hand in Basketball: On the Misperception of Random Sequences, 17 *Cognitive Psychology* 295, 296 (1985) (defining the "hot-hand" phenomenon as the belief that a basketball player has a better "chance of hitting a basket after one or more successful shots than after one or more misses").
79 See Chapter 3, "Behaviorally biased regulators."
80 See Chapter 3, "Behaviorally biased regulators" (discussing effects of behavioral biases on regulators); Chapter 1, "Bounded rationality and noise traders" (discussing behavioral economics literature on behavioral biases).
81 *TSC Indus., Inc.* v. *Northway, Inc.*, 426 U.S. 438, 449 (1976) (defining materiality in context of a fact omitted from a proxy statement); see also *Basic Inc.* v. *Levinson*, 485 U.S. 224, 249 (1988) (applying the *TSC Industries* standard to other securities fraud cases). In *TSC Industries*, the Court articulated the standard in a second way. To prove that a statement that was omitted from disclosure was material requires,

according to the Court, "a showing of substantial likelihood that, under all the circumstances, the omitted fact would have assumed actual significance in the deliberation of the reasonable shareholder." *TSC Industries*, 426 U.S. at 449.

82 Indeed, an empirical study of securities fraud litigation by David Hoffman demonstrates that courts do not factor the considerable evidence that investors exhibit behavioral biases in making investment decisions into judicial determinations of what constitutes materiality under the reasonable investor standard. David A. Hoffman, The "Duty" to be a Rational Shareholder, 90 *Minnesota Law Review* 536, 593 (2006). Hoffman criticizes this judicial pattern as effectively imposing a duty on shareholders to act rationally. See ibid. at 593–603.

83 See Securities and Exchange Commission, Staff Accounting Bulletin No. 99, Release No. SAB 99, 64 *Federal Register* 45, 150, 45, 152 (August 19, 1999) available at www.sec.gov/interps/account/sab99.htm (last visited July 25, 2013). A failure of a price movement after a disclosure, however, does not mean that the disclosed fact was immaterial. The SEC has rejected applying strict quantitative thresholds for materiality determinations. Ibid. See also *ECA & Local 134 IBEW Joint Pension Trust of Chi.* v. *JP Morgan Chase Co.*, 553 F.3d 187, 204 (2d Cir. N.Y. 2009) (precipitous price drop is factor in proving materiality); In re Merck & Co. Sec. Litig., 432 F. 3d 261, 274 (3d Cir. 2005) ("in efficient markets materiality is defined as 'information that alters the price of the firm's stock'").

84 See *Basic*, 485 U.S. at 245–7.

85 For a seminal case, see *Elkind* v. *Liggett & Myers, Inc.*, 635 F.2d 156, 166 (2d Cir. 1980), holding that information was not material when it was insufficient by itself to trigger a downturn in price. For an early analysis of the impact of the Efficient Market Hypothesis on determinations of materiality, see Roger J. Dennis, Materiality and the Efficient Capital Market Model: A Recipe for the Total Mix, 25 *William and Mary Law Review* 373 (1984).

86 For a practical, general overview of the due diligence process written for those lawyers most likely to be conducting diligence, see generally Mark Schonberger and Vasiliki B. Tsaganos, Top Twelve Most Frequently Asked Questions by Junior Associates Conducting Due Diligence, in *Conducting Due Diligence*, 9–70 (2004, Practising Law Institute). For practical surveys of due diligence in securities offerings written from the perspective of underwriters' counsel, see Craig E. Chapman, Underwriters' Due Diligence Revisited, in *Conducting Due Diligence*, 71–92 (2004, Practising Law Institute); Valerie Ford Jacob, The Due Diligence Process from the Underwriter's Perspective, in *Conducting Due Diligence*, 93–128 (2004, Practising Law Institute).

87 SEC, Staff Accounting Bulletin No. 99, *supra* note 83.

88 For a discussion of the problematic gap between the qualitative legal standard for materiality and the quantitative standards of materiality employed by the accounting profession, see Manning Gilbert Warren III, Revenue Recognition and Corporate Counsel, 56 *SMU Law Review* 885, 898–906 (2003).

89 Marcel Kahan, The Limited Significance of Norms for Corporate Governance, 149 *University of Pennsylvania Law Review* 1869, 1870–1 (2001) (surveying definitions of term by law and economics scholars and questioning its usefulness).

90 Richard H. McAdams, The Origin, Development, and Regulation of Norms, 96 *Michigan Law Review* 338, 381 (1997).

91 Ibid.

92 See Thomas Voss, Game-Theoretical Perspectives on the Emergence of Social Norms, in *Social Norms*, 105, 109 (Michael Hechter and Karl-Dieter Opp eds., 2001, Russell Sage Foundation).

93 For the classical study of social norms in closely knit communities, see Robert Ellickson, *Order without Law: How Neighbors Settle Disputes* (1991, Harvard University Press).

94 Chapter 3, "Shifting ideologies and norms: market booms and soft capture."
95 Stuart Banner, *Anglo-American Securities Regulation*, 10–12 (1998, Cambridge University Press) (describing advantages and limitations of these sources).
96 Chancellor, *supra* note 21, at 48–9, 54–5.
97 Ibid. at 48.
98 Banner, *supra* note 95, at 49.
99 Chancellor, *supra* note 21, at 187–8.
100 Ibid. at 203.
101 Ibid. at 201–3.
102 Legal scholarship has just scratched the surface of the importance of norms in miti-gating the risk of fraud, cheating, and "corruption" (often, defined in the economic terms of agency costs, i.e., when an agent cheats a principal). See, e.g., Dan M. Kahan, The Logic of Reciprocity: Trust, Collective Action, and Law, 102 *Michigan Law Review* 71, 99 (2003); Peter H. Huang and Ho-Mou Wu, More Order Without Law: A Theory of Social Norms and Organizational Cultures, 10 *Journal of Law, Economics, and Organization* 390 (1994) (providing game theoretical model of role of norms in mitigating "corruption" in agent–principal relationships). See generally Eric A. Posner, Law and Social Norms: The Case of Tax Compliance, 86 *Virginia Law Review* 1781, 1781–2 n.2 (2000) (listing growing legal scholarship on role of norms in law); Jon Elster, *The Cement of Society: A Study of Social Order*, 268–70 (1989, Cambridge University Press). See also Robert D. Putnam, *Bowling Alone: The Collapse and Revival of American Community*, 21 (2001, Touchstone Books/ Simon & Schuster) (discussing social science research of social networks and norms of reciprocity).
103 E.g., Banner, *supra* note 95, at 38 (describing how by the South Sea bubble "invest-ing in securities was a practice that had trickled well down the social scale, to include all elements of propertied English society"), 44–5, 65–72.
104 Ibid. at 65 citing South Sea Bubble playing cards (Carrington Bowles, 1721). Among the other texts that Banner quotes is the following passage from the 1720 play *South-Sea*:

> PLOW: A Stock-jobber! Pray, Sir, what Religion may he be of?
> SCRAPE: Religion! Why, they don't mind Religion in *Change-Alley*. But Turks, Jews, Atheists, and Infidels, mingle there as if they were a-kin to one another.

Banner, *supra* note 95, at 65 citing W.R. Chetwood, *South-Sea; or, the Biters Bit* 16 (1720).
105 Banner, *supra* note 95, at 69–72; see also Chancellor, *supra* note 21, at 78–80.
106 Banner, *supra* note 95, at 69–70.
107 Ibid. at 69–72.
108 Rande W. Kostal, *Law and English Railway Capitalism 1825–1875*, 23 (1994, Oxford University Press).
109 Ibid. citing Railway Director (January 9, 1846).
110 Chancellor, *supra* note 21, at 166.
111 Ibid. at 166–7.
112 Ibid. at 203–5.
113 For the germinal work in the legal literature on how social or community norms regulate behavior, see Ellickson, *supra* note 93.
114 The community of Jewish diamond merchants in New York City provides an example of the ability of community norms to police fraud. Barack D. Richman, How Community Institutions Create Economic Advantage: Jewish Diamond Mer-chants in New York, 31 *Law and Social Inquiry* 383 (2006). See also Robert C. Ellickson, A Hypothesis of Wealth-Maximizing Norms: Evidence from the Whaling Industry, 5 *Journal of Law, Economics, and Organization* 83 (1989) (discussing

norms in close-knit eighteenth and nineteenth century New England whaling industry).

115 See, e.g., Pamela H. Bucy, Game Theory and the Civil False Claims Act: Iterated Games and Close-knit Groups, 35 *Loyola University Chicago Law Journal* 1021, 1035–8 (2004). Professor Bucy summarizes Ellickson's research on how the force of norms among cattle ranchers in a remote rural county depended on the close-knit nature of a social group. Ellickson, *supra* note 93, at 9–10, 48–64 (describing community of ranchers), 57–64 (describing penalties imposed within community for violating norms).

116 Brent T. White, Underwater and Not Walking Away: Shame, Fear and the Social Management of the Housing Crisis, 45 *Wake Forest Law Review* 971, 973–9 (2010).

117 Ibid. Indeed, U.S. contract law generally permits parties to breach a contract and then pay damages. Contract damages are not intended to deter breach, but merely to compensate the non-breaching party as if the contract had been performed. Arthur Linton Corbin, John E. Murray, and Timothy Murray, *Corbin on Contracts*, § 55.3, 11–55 (2012, Matthew Bender).

This has led some legal economists to champion a doctrine or theory of "efficient breach." See, e.g., Charles J. Goetz and Robert E. Scott, Liquidated Damages, Penalties and the Just Compensation Principle: Some Notes on an Enforcement Model and a Theory of Efficient Breach, 77 *Columbia Law Review* 554 (1977); Richard A. Posner, *Economic Analysis of Law*, § 4.9, at 89–90 (2nd ed. 1977, Little, Brown). For one of many critiques of economic theories of "efficient breach," see Ian R. Macneil, Efficient Breach of Contract: Circles in the Sky, 68 *Virginia Law Review* 947, 969 (1982). Aside from this debate, the point remains that U.S. courts will compel a party to perform a contract (specific performance) only if fairly demanding standards are met, including that a court finds that damages would be inadequate to compensate the non-breaching party. See Corbin et al., *supra*, at § 1136, 12–63.

118 White, *supra* note 116, at 979–86.

119 Ibid. at 972–3, 989–96 (arguing that emotions played a role in homeowner choice not to default).

120 Ibid. at 972–3.

121 *Securities and Exchange Commission* v. *Goldman, Sachs & Co. and Fabrice Tourre*, 10 Civ. 3229 (BJ) S.D.N.Y. filed April 16, 2010, Litigation Release No. 21,489 (April 16, 2010) available at www.sec.gov/litigation/litreleases/2010/lr21489.htm (last visited July 25, 2013).

122 E.g., Bianna Goldodryga, Maureen White, and Lee Ferran, Warren Buffett: Nothing Improper in Goldman Transaction, ABC News (May 3, 2010) available at http://abcnews.go.com/GMA/buffett-improper-goldman-transaction/story?id=10535378#. T8vfktXpMTY (last visited July 25, 2013) (quoting Warren Buffett that investors should expect to trade with Goldman Sachs not receive "investment advisory" services); Nicole Gelinas, A Third Party Problem, *New York Times* Room for Debate Blog (April 16, 2010) available at http://roomfordebate.blogs.nytimes.com/2010/04/16/what-goldmans-conduct-reveals/ (last visited July 25, 2013) ("It's simple: the German bank that bought the mortgage securities shouldn't have relied on a consultant.")

123 Yves Smith, Immoral, Destructive Behavior, *New York Times* Room for Debate Blog (April 16, 2010) available at http://roomfordebate.blogs.nytimes.com/2010/04/16/what-goldmans-conduct-reveals/ (last visited July 25, 2013) ("No matter what happens to this particular lawsuit, it's critical not to lose sight of the fact that immoral, destructive behavior has become deeply entrenched on Wall Street, and it will take concerted action to root it out."); Megan McArdle, Undermining Trust in Markets, *New York Times* Room for Debate Blog (April 16, 2010) ("If the S.E.C. is correct, this isn't merely evidence of a crime, but of a distressingly cavalier attitude toward basic rules of market conduct.").

124 For a (surprisingly scatological) journalistic account arguing that Wall Street banks exploited the lack of sophistication, market naiveté, trust, and cultural assumptions of German financial institutions, see Michael Lewis, It's the Economy, Dummkopf! 53 *Vanity Fair* 304 (September 2011). For a more in-depth narrative of how Wall Street investment banks sold CDOs and other derivatives to European banks to allow the European firms to arbitrage capital regulations, see Nicholas Dunbar, *The Devil's Derivatives* (2011, Harvard Business Review Press).

 The discordant views of the duties that Goldman Sachs owed to its institutional clients were on display in a heated U.S. Senate Committee hearing on the lawsuit. See Wall Street and the Financial Crisis: The Role of Investment Banks: Hearing Before the Permanent Subcommittee on Investigations of the Sub Committee on Homeland Security and Governmental Affairs, 111th Congress (2010). See also Robert B. Thompson, Market Makers and *Vampire Squid*: Regulating Securities Markets After the Financial Meltdown, 89 *Washington University Law Review* 323, 323–7 (2012) (providing background of Senate hearing and surveying differing views of Goldman Sachs' duties as market intermediary in this type of transaction).

125 Chancellor, *supra* note 21, at 101–4.

126 Bethany McLean and Joe Nocera, *All the Devils Are Here: The Hidden History of the Financial Crisis*, 125–37 (2011, Portfolio/Penguin).

127 Chancellor, *supra* note 21, at 254.

128 Banner, *supra* note 95, at 36 citing Daniel Defoe, *The Villainy of Stock-Jobbers Detected*, 26 (1701, Anne Baldwin), Daniel Defoe, *The Anatomy of Exchange-Alley: Or a System of Stock-Jobbing*, 41 (1719, E. Smith).

129 Chancellor, *supra* note 21, at 160–4 (describing origins of Daniel Drew and Cornelius Vanderbilt, among others).

130 Steve Fraser, *Wall Street: America's Dream Palace*, 74–5 (2008, Yale University Press).

131 Chancellor, *supra* note 21, at 202.

132 Fraser, *supra* note 130, at 78–80. For an excellent account of Kreuger, see Frank Partnoy, *The Match King: Ivar Kreuger, the Financial Genius Behind a Century of Wall Street Scandals* (2009, PublicAffairs).

133 Chapter 3, "Regulatory backlash"; Chapter 2, notes 26, 214, 225 and accompanying text (historical examples of scapegoating after collapsed bubbles). Many of the commentators who decried the moral lapses during financial manias veered into prejudice, as seen, for example, in the anti-Semitism of Charles Francis and Henry Adams. Fraser, *supra* note 130, at 158.

134 Fraser, *supra* note 130, at 82–4.

135 Chancellor, *supra* note 21, at 201 quoting Charles Amos Dice cited in John Kenneth Galbraith, *The Great Crash*, 42 (1994, Penguin).

136 Tyler, *supra* note 3.

137 Ibid. at 165.

138 Ibid.

139 Ibid. at 161–5.

140 Ibid. at 162.

141 Ibid. at 164.

142 Ibid.

143 Annelise Riles, *Collateral Knowledge: Legal Reasoning in the Global Financial Markets*, 233–9 (2011, University of Chicago Press). Professor Riles advocates reordering the way we think about improving compliance with law within financial institutions.

> The greater ambition, rather, should be to fundamentally change the culture of financial practice, to create a world in which actors of their own free will, indeed before even being admonished, incentivized, pushed, or prodded by regulators, make socially optimal choices, the very choices regulators would enshrine in regulation. Ibid. at 236.

144 For some skepticism of whether norms is a useful construct in understanding corporate law, see Kahan, *supra* note 89 (reviewing literature).

145 For a small (somewhat more recent) sample of the long debate on this norm, compare Stephen M. Bainbridge, In Defense of the Shareholder Wealth Maximization Norm: A Reply to Professor Green, 50 *Washington and Lee Law Review* 1423 (1993) with Lynn A. Stout, Bad and Not-so-Bad Arguments for Shareholder Primacy, 75 *Southern California Law Review* 1189 (2002). See also Mark J. Roe, Shareholder Wealth Maximization Norm and Industrial Organization, 149 *University of Pennsylvania Law Review* 2063 (2000) (comparing strong shareholder primacy in United States where product markets are competitive to Europe where markets are less competitive and shareholder primacy less pronounced).

146 Chancellor, *supra* note 21, at 49–50, citing Defoe, *Anatomy, supra* note 128.

147 Chancellor, *supra* note 21, at 49.

148 Ibid. at 107.

149 Steve Fraser, *Every Man a Speculator: A History of Wall Street in American Life*, 113–35 (2005, Harper).

150 Ibid. at 113.

151 Charles Francis Adams and Henry Adams, *Chapters of Erie* (1886) cited in Fraser, *supra* note 130, at 33.

152 Fraser, *Every Man a Speculator, supra* note 149 at 120–35.

153 Chancellor, *supra* note 21, at 299.

154 Chapter 2, notes 137–40 and accompanying text (bribes and corruption during U.S. Gilded Age bubbles); Chapter 3, "More boom, more interest group purchasing power" (analysing different modes of influencing financial regulatory policy).

155 Rande W. Kostal, *Law and English Railway Capitalism 1825–1875*, 12 (1994, Oxford University Press).

156 Ibid. at 53–109 (describing litigation in wake of stock market crash in 1845); 322–57 (describing enormous profits of lawyers from representing railway companies). Kostal devotes much of his book to litigation involving railroads, including suits on personal injury and litigation over land that railways sought to expand.

157 Charles Dickens, *Bleak House* (1853, Bradbury & Evans).

158 Ronald J. Gilson, Value Creation by Business Lawyers: Legal Skills and Asset Pricing, 94 *Yale Law Journal* 239, 255 (1984).

159 Chapter 2, "Regulatory stimulus and legal backlash: beyond deregulation and re-regulation."

160 Chapter 5 "Professional norms." See also Victor Fleischer, Regulatory Arbitrage, 89 *Texas Law Review* 227, 265–9 (2010).

161 Chapter 1, notes 66–9. Chapter 3, "Bias arbitrage and its limits" (describing risks facing policymakers attempting to "bet" against a bubble).

162 Cf. Claudio Borio and Haibin Zhu, Capital Regulation, Risk-taking and Monetary Policy: A Missing Link in the Transmission Mechanism, Bank for International Settlements, *Working Paper No. 268* (2008). Borio and Zhu posit that changes in monetary policy may affect financial institution lending and investments through a "risk taking" channel. They argue that changes in monetary policy may alter the perceptions of risk by financial institutions or their tolerance for risk. Ibid. at 9.

163 Richard Herring and Susan Wachter, Bubbles in Real Estate Markets, in *Asset-Price Bubbles: The Implications for Monetary, Regulatory, and International Policies*, 217 (William C. Hunter, George G. Kaufman, and Michael Pomerleano, eds., 2003, MIT Press).

164 Unlike fraud, however, prudential regulators may have a legal cause for an enforcement action even absent a drop in asset prices. See, e.g., 12 U.S.C. § 1818 (enforcement statute for institutions insured by U.S. Federal Deposit Insurance Corporation).
      However, some penalties may still depend in large part on a bank suffering actual losses. For example, the highest category of civil monetary penalties that U.S.

federal banking agencies can apply requires not only knowing and reckless conduct, but also either a substantial loss to the bank or substantial benefit to the person being fined. 12 U.S.C. § 1818(i)(2)(C).

A booming market may mean that a legal violation – for example, a prohibited investment – does not cause losses for an extended period of time.

165 Chapter 3, "The problem of diluted enforcement."
166 Chapter 3, "Altering the cost benefit analysis of regulators," "The cost of opposing regulatory stimulus."
167 E.g., George J. Benston and George G. Kaufman, FDICIA After Five Years, 11 *Journal of Economic Perspectives* 139 (1997) (discussing how deposit insurance and other government interventions create perverse incentives for regulators to forbear taking action against failing banks and arguing that Federal Deposit Insurance Corporation Improvement Act of 1991 did not address this problem adequately).
168 Gerding, *supra* note 36, at 441.
169 Cf. Patrick Bolton, José Scheinkman, and Wei Xiong, Executive Compensation and Short-Termist Behaviour in Speculative Markets, 73 *Review of Economic Studies* 577 (2006) (presenting a model of compensation leading to excessive short-term behavior by managers).
170 Kimberly D. Krawiec, Accounting for Greed: Unraveling the Rogue Trader Mystery, 79 *Oregon Law Review* 301 (2000); see also Kimberly D. Krawiec, The Return of the Rogue, 51 *Arizona Law Review* 879 (2009) (arguing that, under self-enforcement regime, financial firms with highest operational risk are least likely to recognize risk and set aside sufficient reserves).
171 See Jack M. Guttentag and Richard J. Herring, Disaster Myopia in International Banking, *Princeton University Essays in Internationl Finance No. 164* (September 1986); Richard J. Herring and Susan Wachter, Real Estate Booms and Banking Busts: An International Perspective, Wharton Financial Institutions Center, *Working Paper 99-27*, 15 (1999) available at http://fic.wharton.upenn.edu/fic/papers/99/9927.pdf (last visited July 25, 2013).
172 Kahan, *supra* note 102, at 80–5. See also Posner, *supra* note 102 (analyzing norms as signals rather than through lens of reciprocity).
173 Mitchell Martin, Citicorp and Travelers Plan to Merge in Record $70 Billion Deal: A New No. 1: Financial Giants Unite, *New York Times*, April 7, 1998, at A1.
174 See, e.g., Leslie Wayne, Shaping a Colossus: The Politics; Deal Jump-Starts a Stalled Banking Bill, *New York Times*, April 9, 1998, at D4; Leslie Wayne, House Acts to Ease 30's Banking Curbs By One-Vote Margin, *New York Times*, May 14, 1998, at A1 (describing political coalition behind legislation). See also Arthur E. Wilmarth, Jr., The Dark Side of Universal Banking: Financial Conglomerates and the Origins of the Subprime Financial Crisis, 41 *Connecticut Law Review* 963, 972–5 (2009); Arthur E. Wilmarth, The Transformation of the U.S. Financial Services Industry, 1975–2000: Competition, Consolidation, and Increased Risks, 2002 *University of Illinois Law Review* 215, 219–22, 306–7 (2002).
175 Bishop Carleton Hunt, *The Development of the Business Corporation in England 1800–1867*, 37–41 (1936, Harvard University Press).
176 Kahan, *supra* note 102; Elster, *supra* note 102.

5   Regulatory arbitrage frenzies and the hydraulics of investor demand

If asset price bubbles and prolonged market booms skew the calculus of market participants against compliance with financial laws, they also increase incentives to skirt legal rules in lawful ways. When legal rules hamper market participants from enjoying the immense profits available in booming asset markets, those parties will seek loopholes in those rules. The prospect of law or regulation shutting these parties out of lucrative investment opportunities sharpens their legal creativity and whets their appetite for legal risk. The greater the potential profits in booming asset classes that are foreclosed by regulation, the greater the incentives to game legal rules (if not break them altogether).

Market participants – sellers of assets, buyers, middlemen, and lenders – can almost always find loopholes because of the inherent "incompleteness" of all legal rules. Legal rules are incomplete because their language cannot unambiguously provide for every future contingency.[1] New laws provide fresh opportunities to find loopholes, and bubbles often provide a bumper crop of new laws and legal change. (Chapters 2 and 3 described how bubbles foster regulatory stimulus, as interest groups and policymakers look to jumpstart investment in financial markets.) Consider the following example from Chapter 2: entrepreneurs in Germany in the early 1870s exploited the incompleteness in that country's newly liberalized legal regime governing the incorporation of joint-stock companies in order to create fraudulent companies and abscond with investor money.[2]

Yet market participants can use far more sophisticated techniques than finding simple loopholes to evade the law. Indeed, they employ sophisticated legal planning techniques to exploit the differences between the formal treatment of investments and their economic substance. These legal planning techniques, known as regulatory arbitrage, allow market participants to avoid regulatory "taxes" on investments.[3] Regulatory arbitrage techniques allow participants to make the same investments or invest in close economic substitutes but with lower regulatory costs.[4] This chapter argues that regulatory arbitrage can take one of two forms. In pursuit of higher investment returns and lower regulatory taxes, market participants will engage in one or both of the following:

- *Investment switching.* In the face of regulatory restrictions that might lower or foreclose investment returns, investors and financial institutions divert to alternative channels for making investments or obtaining credit that are subject to lower regulatory taxes. Investment switching often involves moving capital to parallel financial markets or other legal jurisdictions that offer close economic substitutes for a loan or investment but impose lower regulatory taxes.

• *Investment structuring.* Financial institutions or sophisticated investors also engage lawyers and other advisors (accountants, bankers, etc.) to develop legal structures to exploit the incompleteness of financial regulation. Legal innovation provides these parties with regulatory "work-arounds." These legal structures creatively interpret legal definitions and exemptions to avoid the application of regulatory restrictions to a particular investment or source of credit. Work-arounds allow market participants to enjoy the same economic benefits of a loan or investment at a lower regulatory "tax rate." Developing regulatory "work-arounds" for clients represents an essential role of transactional and regulatory attorneys, whom Professor Ronald Gilson famously called "transaction cost engineers." By lowering transaction costs, Gilson argues that lawyers facilitate the efficient pricing of assets.[5]

These two techniques are by no means mutually exclusive. Indeed, investment structuring – creating novel forms of transactions – often facilitates investment switching. For example, American Depository Receipts (or "ADRs") are instruments that represent an interest in the securities of a non-U.S. company. These ADRs trade on U.S. financial markets and enable U.S. investors to invest in foreign companies without having to purchase shares directly on a foreign exchange.[6]

Regulatory arbitrage resembles financial arbitrage (described in Chapter 1) in several key respects. Like financial arbitrage, market participants who engage in regulatory arbitrage seek to exploit the price differences between economic substitutes. In regulatory arbitrage, these price differences stem from different legal rules (or regulatory "tax rates"). In regulatory arbitrage, market players might not hedge in the same way that financial arbitrageurs do (who sell an overpriced security short and hedge by purchasing a close economic substitute).[7] Even so, regulatory arbitrage, like financial arbitrage, places pressure on prices of economic substitutes to converge. Sellers of assets that are priced higher because of regulatory taxation may be forced to slash prices (and profit margins) if they lose significant sales due to investment switching or structuring. Alternatively, these sellers may push policymakers to lower regulatory taxation (i.e., deregulate) to equalize prices (a political dynamic this chapter will explore later).

Note that the term "regulatory arbitrage" provides a new bottle for some very old wine. Law professor Michael Knoll traces back regulatory arbitrage to sophisticated legal structures and financial instruments used over 2000 years ago to evade usury laws.[8] Financial innovation plays a crucial role in regulatory arbitrage and vice versa; Nobel laureate Merton Miller argues that regulatory arbitrage is one of the most significant drivers of financial innovation.[9]

Asset price bubbles provide particularly fertile grounds for regulatory arbitrage. They increase the incentives of individuals and firms to engage in investment switching and structuring. As we will see, regulatory arbitrage becomes contagious: the increased profits enjoyed by those that partake in gaming financial rules encourages others to join in a frenzy of regulatory arbitrage.

One can find examples of both investment switching and investment structuring throughout the legal history of asset price bubbles. Look first at investment switching: Chapter 6 offers a stark example of this phenomenon in the Swedish banking sector in the 1970s and 1980s. As described in Chapter 6, Sweden subjected its banks to a number of stringent regulations, including requirements that a certain percentage of their assets consist of public sector and housing bonds. These constraints on banking allowed less regulated finance companies to flourish and grab a growing share of loan markets. The government fretted over the hollowing out of the regulated financial sector and the development of a "grey market."[10] Japanese financial regulators also liberalized their banking sector because of a similar fear of *kudoka* ("hollowing out"); earlier deregulation that allowed Japanese corporations to obtain financing from foreign capital markets jeopardized the competitive position of Japanese banks and frightened policymakers.[11]

This same concern with hemorrhaging of capital from more regulated jurisdictions to less regulated jurisdictions animates various international efforts to harmonize financial regulations, such as the Basel Accords and bank capital requirements (a topic discussed below).[12] Whenever financial institutions offer functionally equivalent financial services yet are subject to different legal regimes and different levels of regulatory taxation, regulatory arbitrage can flourish. Greater legal restrictions on institutions in one regime may merely push borrowers or investors to those institutions operating in another regime. Even the prospect of hemorrhaging capital because of different levels of regulation leaves enough traces of blood in the water for a regulatory arbitrage frenzy to start.

Examples of investment structuring during asset price bubbles also abound. Take a straightforward case: in England's 1825 bubble, Latin American sovereign bonds being offered to English investors would have violated England's usury laws. To avoid these restrictions, the sovereigns executed the indentures for the bonds in France.[13]

Regulatory arbitrage can take far more complex forms. The Japanese real estate bubble of the 1980s both spawned, and was fueled by, forms of regulatory arbitrage called *zaitech* (translated as financial engineering). In the mid-1980s, Japanese brokerage firms (with the consent of the Ministry of Finance) began offering corporate customers special accounts, called *tokkin* accounts, that allowed the corporations to trade in securities without paying capital gains taxes.[14] Changes in Japanese accounting rules allowed corporations owning these accounts to record them at the higher of book or market value.[15] This allowed firms to disclose investment profits, but not losses.[16]

As the Ministry of Finance looked the other way, brokerage houses introduced a further (illegal) version of this account called *eigyo tokkin*. This second type of account allowed corporate customers to speculate in securities and guaranteed them a minimum return above market interest rates.[17] Annual corporate profits from *tokkin* accounts increased from U.S.$2 billion in 1985 to U.S.$7 billion in 1987, even as operating profits declined over that period. *Zaitech* created a feedback loop; it increased paper profits for firms, which fueled a rocketing stock market. Increased market gains encouraged more speculation.[18] When losses started to occur, the managers of the *tokkin* accounts hid them by transferring them back and forth between different companies through a technique called *tobashi* (or "shuttlecocking").[19]

Japanese companies financed the speculation they conducted through *tokkin* and *eigyo tokkin* accounts by issuing special "warrant bonds" in the London Eurobond market.[20] These warrant bonds (first permitted by the Ministry of Finance in 1981 as part of Japan's financial liberalization) combined traditional bonds with an option for the bondholder to purchase the issuer's shares in five years at a fixed price.[21] Rising share prices of Japanese companies raised the value of this warrant feature and lowered the interest rates on the bond component of the instrument.[22] Of particular importance, the bonds were denominated and payable in U.S. dollars.[23] The rising exchange rate of the yen to the dollar (which many in financial markets expected to continue) lowered the expected liability in real terms for the Japanese companies issuing the bonds.[24] Edward Chancellor explains that the financial engineering of *zaitech* exploited these market conditions such that companies issuing the bonds enjoyed a negative interest rate.[25] Japanese companies would funnel the proceeds of the warrant bonds into their *tokkin* and *eigyo tokkin* accounts (with their guaranteed returns).[26] This resulted in an extraordinary phenomenon described by Chancellor: "Japanese companies were actually paid to borrow the money to finance their speculations.... *Zaitech* was a game with no losers."[27] *Zaitech* thus encouraged Japanese corporations to engage in tax-free and apparently risk-free speculation. This speculation sidestepped the traditionally tightly regulated Japanese bank credit markets and fueled the growth of enormous stock and real estate bubbles.[28]

It is no accident that regulatory arbitrage flourishes during an asset price bubble. As the opening of this chapter noted, booms in particular asset markets push investors and intermediaries to seek ways to avoid regulations that thwart or tax access to those markets. This chapter examines both the incentives for parties to engage in regulatory arbitrage and how bubbles increase those incentives. In modeling the factors that drive and constrain regulatory arbitrage, this chapter argues that surging investor demand can exert a hydraulic effect in financial markets. These hydraulics can overwhelm the levies and floodgates of financial regulation built to channel and control investment and risk-taking. These hydraulic effects can have cascading and contagious effects; the success of one firm in using regulatory arbitrage to access a bubble market drives others to follow. This dynamic in turn places pressure on regulators to lower the floodgates.

The chapter later turns from looking at why regulatory arbitrage increases and frenzies ensue during booms and bubbles, to the effects of this increase. The hydraulics of rising levels of regulatory arbitrage can subvert critical financial regulations. Regulatory arbitrage can also exert a political hydraulic effect. This chapter explains how market participants who lose profits from regulatory arbitrage (perhaps because they cannot engage in regulatory arbitrage cheaply) can form an alliance with policymakers concerned about markets under their jurisdiction being "hollowed out." This alliance exerts political influence to loosen regulations, using the threat of regulatory arbitrage and the perceived loss of "competitiveness" as rhetorical ammunition.

The chapter next develops a case study of one form of regulatory arbitrage that assumed great importance in international and domestic financial markets over the last three decades; it traces the development of "regulatory capital arbitrage" and its co-evolution with bank regulatory capital requirements.[29] Regulatory capital arbitrage arguably reached an apogee in the years immediately before the Panic of 2007–2008, with severe consequences for that crisis.

The chapter concludes by arguing that "complex adaptive systems" provides a lens for analyzing both the dialectical co-evolution of bank capital regulations and regulatory capital arbitrage, and regulatory arbitrage more generally.

The calculus of regulatory arbitrage: the hydraulics of investor demand

The calculus of whether to engage in regulatory arbitrage is not all that different from the calculus of legal compliance explored in the preceding chapter. Indeed, aggressive regulatory arbitrage transactions may skirt the edge of legality. On the benefit side of the equation, regulatory arbitrage may allow market participants to enjoy increased profits by avoiding regulatory restrictions and taxes. Conversely, investors that refrain from regulatory arbitrage while their competitors partake may be disadvantaged.

Regulatory arbitrage also entails costs and risks similar to non-compliance with the law. As with non-compliance, regulatory arbitrage – particularly investment structuring – involves legal risk. For example, Victor Fleischer notes that statutes and regulations often include a number of anti-evasion provisions that allow regulators to "look through" the form of transactions and regulate them according to their economic substance.[30] Regulators may be able to penalize parties that engage in aggressive regulatory arbitrage.[31]

Just as they skew the calculus of compliance with financial laws, bubbles radically tilt the incentives in favor of regulatory arbitrage. Booming prices in particular asset markets increase the benefits of engaging in investment switching or structuring. Meanwhile, booms increase the opportunity cost and penalties in a competitive market for abstaining from those practices; competitors that arbitrage quickly gobble up profits. Money managers that engage in regulatory arbitrage and increase investment returns bleed away investors and capital from those that abstain.[32] This mirrors the dynamics described in previous chapters of even sophisticated money managers being punished for betting against a bubble. Bubbles increase the possibility of regulatory arbitrage contagion.

Costs – including legal risk associated with regulatory arbitrage – can also plummet during a market boom. To understand how these costs can drop and how asset price bubbles increase levels of regulatory arbitrage, it is helpful to model and analyze the calculus of investment switching separate from the calculus of engaging in investment structuring.

The calculus of investment switching

In deciding whether to switch capital from one market or jurisdiction to another, a market participant would look at the marginal benefits of moving one dollar versus the marginal costs. The marginal benefits have already been outlined above: switching investments might lead to an increase on the margin in an investor's rate of return. A particular booming asset market would offer higher rates of return (because of lower regulatory taxation rates) and thus increase the marginal benefits of investment switching.

Of course, a rational investor should adjust rates of return for risk, including market risk (greater volatility in prices in the new market),[33] credit risk (the risk to lenders of loans in a new market defaulting),[34] liquidity risk (the risk of being unable to find a deep pool of buyers or sellers for an asset at any given moment),[35] and political risk (for example, the risk that the government will expropriate investments or not allow investors to repatriate capital).[36] Fraud risk may also increase if antifraud rules are weaker or more weakly enforced. Switching capital to a new (and possibly overheating) market may increase these risks. The regulatory taxes that investors seek to avoid in a market may, in many cases, have the benefit of making that pricier market less risky. For example, if a jurisdiction subjects financial institutions to higher capital requirements, those institutions enjoy a greater cushion against market shocks and may be less likely to default should a shock hit.[37] Similarly, higher tighter margin rules that cap loans to stock investors (or tighter margin rules on derivative transactions) may reduce the risk of default by counterparties.[38]

Yet investors may discount the benefits of these regulatory taxes and the increased risk of a heating market for the usual reasons people discount risks during a bubble. Rising prices may mask risk if investors only look to the immediate past to measure risk.[39] Behavioral biases, again, may cause investors to underestimate the risks of new markets.[40] Money managers may recognize increased risks of switching to an overheating market, but they may have an excessively short-term focus because of either poorly designed incentive contracts or because their investors may abandon their fund because of their own short-term horizons.[41] In short, a booming market can radically increase the perceived benefits of investment switching.

Moreover, investment switching to avoid certain financial regulations – such as bank regulations that mitigate systemic risk may be particularly attractive; firms that switch can externalize much of the costs (such as the systemic risk from bank failures) onto third parties. This chapter will return to the heightened incentives to arbitrage systemic risk regulations in a few moments.

The surging benefits of moving capital to a less regulated market may swamp the transaction costs of investment switching. These costs include the following:

1   *taxes and third-party fees*: switching from one market to another may cause an investor to incur additional taxes or brokerage fees for executing the transactions;[42]
2   *loss of regulatory preferences*: investments in an investor's home jurisdiction may offer various regulatory benefits, such as reduced capital charges when financial institutions make domestic investments;[43]
3   *asymmetric information and agency costs*: investing in new markets, particularly overseas, may complicate an investor's ability to track her investments.[44]

Many of these costs, however, may be reduced (or appear to be reduced) by other developments during a market boom. Technology and regulatory changes may deepen interlinkages between capital markets and facilitate movement of capital.[45] New technology, from telegraphs to telephony to the internet to Bloomberg terminals, can reduce the information costs of tracking and comparing investments across markets.[46] At the same time, new media sources – printed pamphlets, newspapers, radio, and the internet – both accompany and spur many asset price bubbles.[47] This new media also can convince investors that information asymmetries associated with switching investments have fallen. (Although, throughout the history of bubbles, the information provided by many new media sources – from the pamphlets penned by a young Benjamin Disraeli for bubble ventures in 1825 to the stock analysts during the 1990s tech stock bubble – has been of dubious quality.)[48]

Governments may also facilitate investment switching by changing regulations to attract investment. Consider how England attempted to mimic the success of the Mississippi bubble by creating the South Sea Company.[49] Germany's creation of the Neuer Markt during the 1990s U.S. technology stock bubble provides a more complex example. To mimic the success of the United States in promoting high-tech start-ups, the Deutsche Börse created a new segment of the stock market with looser listing requirements. Yet the German exchange also increased certain disclosure requirements based on economic theory that greater investor protection facilitated stock market growth.[50] Bubbles increase the incentives of regulators to change legal rules to attract investment and lower regulatory taxes. Bubbles thus generate a kind of contagion of regulatory stimulus (as Chapter 3 detailed).

Finally, financial innovations and new transaction structures (investment structuring in other words) may reduce the transaction costs of investment switching. Lawyers, accounting, and consulting firms, and market intermediaries (particularly investment banks) offer new financial products to assist in investment switching. Consider the following example for recent history. German banks created particularly elaborate transaction structures to invest in risky U.S. asset-backed securities in the years leading to the Panic of 2007–2008. For example, IKB Deutsche Industriebank incorporated a conduit entity under Delaware law and listed the company on the Dublin Stock Exchange in order to invest in collateralized debt obligations (CDOs) based on U.S. subprime mortgages. IKB ultimately foundered during the Panic due to investments in these securities, which were sold to it by Wall Street investment banks. IKB's investment in these securities took center stage in the U.S. Securities and Exchange Commission's 2010 lawsuit against Goldman Sachs for selling CDOs.[51]

The calculus of investment structuring

If investment structuring can facilitate investment switching, it becomes critical to understand what drives this dynamic too. Bubbles also alter the calculus in favor of market participants engaging in investment structuring. Investors will engage in investment structuring to the extent the marginal benefits of structuring outweigh the marginal costs.[52] As with investment switching, the benefits to investment structuring come in the form of a marginal increase in risk-adjusted returns. This increase stems from a reduction in regulatory tax rates. At the same time, several factors impose costs and constraints on investment structuring. Yet these too may be reduced during bubble times. Consider the following constraints:

Legal risk. As noted above, regulators may have powers to void and even penalize aggressive regulatory arbitrage transactions.[53] The Dodd-Frank Act contains over two dozen separate anti-evasion provisions that give regulators authority to pass rules to prevent circumvention of statutory requirements.[54]

However, regulators may not exercise the powers they have. Chapter 3 described various dynamics that lower the incentives and capacities of regulators to enforce the law aggressively during boom times. These dynamics include the following:

- enforcement resources being spread thinly;
- regulator disincentives to opposing powerful market players or stopping an economic boom; and
- cognitive biases that make financial risks appear smaller.

All of the limitations that cause regulators to under-enforce the law during booms would also cause them to under-exercise their powers to void investment structuring and counter regulatory arbitrage.

Regulatory arbitrage presents particular problems for regulators that law-breaking does not. The opacity of sophisticated financial transactions may be hard to understand for even well-resourced regulators.[55] Regulators may struggle to adapt legal rules to financial innovation, particularly as the pace of that innovation increases during boom times.[56] The sheer volume of transactions during bubble periods alone taxes the resources of regulators.[57]

The outcome of an arms race between an innovating financial industry and regulators depends in large part on the legal ground rules. Regulators enjoy more of an advantage in regimes in which financial products must be pre-approved by them as opposed to when regulators must challenge already implemented transactions.[58]

In challenges to regulatory arbitrage transactions, the allocation of legal burdens between the regulators and the regulated is crucial. Chapter 3 noted that procedural features of administrative law, such as standing, and substantive rules, such as requirements that regulators conduct cost–benefit analyses, provide industry groups with additional leverage to challenge agency actions.[59] That chapter also described how public choice theory suggests that concentrated industry groups will participate in agency determinations to a much greater degree than diffuse publics that may be impacted, such as retail investors or tax-payers that fund bailouts.[60]

Regulators may also have a hard time discerning the true economic purpose of particular transactions, and the purpose of those transactions may shift over time. Regulators lauded asset-backed securities and credit derivatives for their capacity to allocate and spread financial risks efficiently.[61] Yet, as we will see later in this chapter, financial institutions increasingly used these instruments to game bank capital rules.

Bubbles may whet the appetite of investors for legal risk. The last chapter described various factors that cause market participants to discount the risk of being penalized for fraud. These include rational factors (such as the time value of money lowering expected liability for legal penalties imposed in the far future), agency costs (which occur when a firm cannot or does not pass on a legal penalty to responsible employees), and behavioral biases (when cognitive limitations cause an actor to underestimate legal liability). The previous chapter also described how a bubble may exacerbate these factors and further undermine the deterrence effect of various financial laws. For example, increasing regula-tory arbitrage may create a jailbreak effect, as market participants wager that regulators cannot punish everyone. These same factors that drive compliance rot militate in favor of more aggressive investment structuring during bubbles despite the legal risk of regulators voiding these transactions and imposing sanctions.

Third-party and internal structuring costs. As with any new technology, designing regulatory arbitrage transactions requires investment. Investors must often incur out-of-pocket expenses to third parties, such as fees to bankers, accountants, lawyers, and credit rating agencies.[62] Firms also incur internal costs, such as when a firm must dedicate employees and invest in new assets (such as computer or management information systems) to support a novel transaction.[63]

However, there may be economies of scale to these investments.[64] After the initial investment in the design phase, a firm can reuse a particular transaction structure again and again. Moreover, the benefits of a particular regulatory arbi-trage benefit may spill over, as firms copy the transaction structures of early adopters.[65] Again, law firms, accounting and consulting firms, and investment banks often act as merchants of regulatory arbitrage devices and contribute to their diffusion.

Intellectual property rights may provide some check on copycatting and dampen the use of financial innovations for regulatory arbitrage.[66] Curiously, through the late 1990s, financial firms seldom sought to create intellectual property protections (trademarks, copyrights, and patents) for novel financial instruments that they created.[67] Yet since that time period, one study documents that patents with respect to financial products and services have been litigated at twenty-seven to thirty-nine times the rate of litigation of patents as a whole.[68] Financial services firms are disproportionately the defendants in these lawsuits.[69] Further study is needed to see the extent to which intellectual property litigation dampens financial innovation and regulatory arbitrage.[70]

Successful arbitrage devices may generate regulatory spillover effects as well. When a regulator approves a transaction by an early adopter it sets legal precedent that inures to the benefit of industry laggards. (Chapter 3 outlined how firms calculate whether to seek a legal exemption or other regulatory preference. The ability of competitors to piggyback off regulator decisions because of legal precedent is a crucial variable in this calculus.)[71] Precedent may also convince legislators and regulators to approve or enable similar transaction structures. The state of Wyoming's creation of the limited liability company serves as a case in point. Once the U.S. Internal Revenue Service ruled that this entity could receive partnership tax treatment (despite owners enjoying the same limited liability of corporate shareholders), use of the limited liability company (LLC) form exploded. Other U.S. states quickly passed their own LLC statutes to compete with Wyoming.[72]

Information asymmetries and agency costs. Professor Fleischer notes that the complexity of regulatory arbitrage transactions can exacerbate information asymmetries within a firm. Management and shareholders must grapple with the increased complexity of a firm's capital structure.[73] This increased complexity can allow managers to take advantage of shareholders. The complex financial innovations of investment trusts in the 1920s provide stark examples of this. Electric utilities devised complex holding company structures with affiliates in multiple states to take on high amounts of leverage.[74] In this same decade, Swedish "Match King" Ivar Krueger pioneered many financial and corporate law structures that would become widely used in later decades, including corporations with dual share structures (with one class of shares holding more control rights),[75] the forerunner of American Depository Receipts,[76] off-balance sheet financings,[77] and certain foreign exchange options, convertible debt instruments, and other derivatives.[78]

Even if information asymmetries and agency costs mushroom, there are the separate questions of whether investors recognize the risk or even care. The previous chapter argued that, for rational and behavioral reasons, investors take less care to protect themselves from fraud during bubble periods.[79] That same logic applies to regulatory arbitrage. This gives managers greater freedom to engage in complex investment structuring.

Financing costs. The higher information asymmetries and agency costs in normal times may translate into a higher cost of capital for firms that use complex regulatory arbitrage techniques.[80] However, as we have seen before in this book, bubbles can mean the discipline of capital markets erodes as lenders relax their standards to compete in a frenzy of cheap credit.[81]

Professional norms

Professor Fleischer argues that professional norms of attorneys function as an additional check on aggressive regulatory arbitrage transactions that entail significant legal risk.[82] Attorneys and law firms have a strong incentive to preserve reputational capital and not endorse arbitrage transactions of questionable legality that regulators might later void or penalize.[83] His logic applies equally to other professional "gatekeepers" that play necessary roles in creating arbitrage transactions, such as accountants and bankers.[84]

Fleischer argues that deep changes in the U.S. legal profession may have weakened these professional norms. These changes include the following:

1   *Opinion shopping.* Clients increasingly ask multiple outside law firms to provide legal opinions. Competition increases pressure on law firms to endorse regulatory arbitrage transactions.[85] This pressure mirrors the pressure felt by rating agencies when issuers shop for ratings.[86]
2   *Decline of general partnerships and lockstep compensation:* Few law firms remain general partners in which partners are jointly and severally liable for each other's malpractice. Moreover, firms have moved away from compensating partners in lockstep according to seniority. This increases the incentives of individual partners to build a personal book of business. The decline both of general partnerships and lockstep compensation reduces incentives of partners to protect the firm's reputational capital in the face of clients asking for support for aggressive regulatory arbitrage.[87]
3   *Increasing lateral mobility.* The growing employment prospects for partners moving from one firm to another and the growing tendency of firms to fire "underperforming" partners further weakens incentives of lawyers to guard a firm's reputational capital.[88]

Other scholars concur with many of Fleischer's assessments. Larry Ribstein has written extensively about weakening reputational "bonds" among partners in big law firms and between firms and their clients.[89] Fleischer's views accord with the discussion in the previous chapter of how bubbles exacerbate the agency and information processing costs of gatekeepers. Increased staff turnover and higher transaction volume promote sloppiness and decrease incentives to maintain a firm's reputation.[90]

Bubbles may further accelerate changes in professional norms in other ways. The previous chapter argued that various trends that tend to recur during bubble periods delegitimize law and legal norms. These include the following: a waxing liberal ideology that elevates the value of markets, the tendency to see laws and lawyers as impediments to economic growth, the boom in the purchase and sale of laws to stimulate markets (i.e., regulatory stimulus), and crony capitalism.[91]

The last chapter pushed this analysis even deeper. It argued that the very way the profession and the academy think about law and the role of lawyers can have a profound effect on these norms. Viewing law as simply a transaction cost and lawyers as "transaction cost engineers" encourage corporate lawyers to see their primary function as serving clients, including by facilitating regulatory arbitrage.[92] Fleischer notes that some practitioners believe that changes in legal education have fostered a more relativistic approach to interpreting statutes and regulations in order to please clients.[93] Other roles of lawyers – such as upholding the law as officers of the court or defending the "franchise" of law – recede further into the background.[94]

It is hard to measure whether recent changes to norms and ideologies within the legal profession are contributing to greater regulatory arbitrage and legal nihilism. Concerns about a declining moral force to "the law" do have a certain ahistorical feel to them. After all, a more "realistic" (and relativistic) view of "law" as merely being forecasts of the judgments and penalties that courts would impose on a lawbreaker dates back at least to Oliver Wendell Holmes, Jr. and "The Path of the Law."[95] Again, regulatory arbitrage is nothing new under the sun and dates back thousands of years.[96]

Even so the dynamics of a bubble create conditions for regulatory arbitrage to metastasize.

Effects of regulatory arbitrage: political and legal hydraulics

Political hydraulics

Regulatory arbitrage – whether investment switching or structuring – can cause those firms that cannot engage in regulatory arbitrage themselves (or cannot do so cheaply) to lose business to competitors. Investment switching means capital will flow to asset sellers, lenders, and market intermediaries in less regulated markets. Market participants may be able to deploy investment structuring to different extents. Those with greater capacity for investment structuring can lower their cost of capital.[97]

When regulatory arbitrage places firms or investors at a competitive disadvantage, they push policymakers to lower regulatory taxes to level the playing field. Policymakers themselves may be concerned that regulatory arbitrage causes markets under their jurisdiction to become "hollowed out." They may conclude that it is better to reduce regulations than to regulate a shrinking market or see regulations subverted.[98] In other words, regulatory arbitrage – or the fear of regulatory arbitrage – can drive deregulation. It can also undermine incentives of regulators to enforce financial laws or to apply them to new technologies, financial products, or transactions.[99]

The hydraulics of capital flowing around regulations via investment switching and structuring undermines the political support for financial regulations. The next chapter examines and models the interaction between regulatory arbitrage and deregulation in greater detail. It looks at the example of Sweden in the

1980s, where regulators relaxed various regulations on banks after those institutions lost lending business to less regulated finance companies. The next chapter also returns to Japan in the 1980s. As already noted in Chapter 2, financial liberalization allowed Japanese corporations to move to international capital markets for their financing needs. This triggered a cascade of political and market events. After losing much of their core lending business to capital markets, heavily regulated Japanese banks pushed for deregulation of their own corner of the financial services industry. They also moved into the residential mortgage business. This caused the *jusen* firms that dominated that residential sector to move into even riskier segments of the real estate lending market.[100]

Legal hydraulics

The social costs of regulatory arbitrage can be significant. However, before outlining these costs, it is critical to note the regulatory arbitrage may also have benefits. Whether arbitrage has net positive or negative social benefits depends on the type of legal rules being arbitraged.

For some legal rules, a strong argument can be made that regulatory arbitrage has beneficial effects. It can facilitate movement to a legal regime that will optimize the contractual benefits for all parties to a transaction. A choice of legal regimes arguably allows parties to select a set of legal rules that will best structure their economic (or social) relationship.[101] For example, both shareholders and management may benefit from the freedom to choose the jurisdiction in which to incorporate a business. This allows them to choose a set of laws to govern their legal relationships with one another that best fit their preferences. This is the core insight of the vast literature on corporate federalism in the United States.[102] This same argument has been made in the context of allowing same-sex couples in the United State to marry in any state that will recognize their union.[103]

These examples, however, do not involve significant externalities on third parties. By contrast, the arbitraging of regulation that mitigates externalities poses much higher social costs. Chapter 3 argued that financial regulations that mitigated systemic risk posed unique problems of political economy.[104] Consider bank prudential regulations, such as capital requirements, leverage caps, liquidity requirements, and assorted other restrictions on bank investments and risk-taking. Prudential regulations aim to prevent the widespread failure of banks (whether from insolvency or a bank run).[105] Bank failure, whether of numerous banks or one large bank, could result in a credit crunch and crisis in financial markets. The effects would be felt by more than just the shareholders and creditors of the failed banks.[106] The victims of a financial market crisis can do little to protect themselves, either by negotiating with particular banks or diversifying their investments. This inability of individual market participants to protect themselves through investment diversification is the hallmark of systemic risk.[107]

For regulations that mitigate externalities on third parties, regulatory arbitrage will be a robust and persistent phenomenon. If regulatory arbitrage exploits the difference between legal form and economic substance, theory suggests that the way to reduce the incidence of regulatory arbitrage is to align legal rules with economic substance.[108] However, regulated actors have a persistent incentive to avoid legal rules designed to force them to internalize social costs that they could otherwise impose on third parties. This incentive sharpens when a regulated actor can externalize costs on a set of diffuse parties who could not easily bargain or otherwise mitigate the risk of the regulated actor's behavior. These regulated actors have persistent opportunities for regulatory arbitrage because of the unavoidable incompleteness of legal rules and a multiplicity of different legal jurisdictions to which they can move capital.[109]

Regulatory arbitrage can have at least four pernicious effects on regulation. First, regulatory arbitrage can undermine the effectiveness of regulations. This occurs in investment structuring, in which parties create financial structures specifically to lower regulatory "taxes." The case study of regulatory capital arbitrage that follows explains how particular transactions allowed banks and other financial institutions to lower the effective capital that they were required to hold as a cushion against losses in their investment portfolio. This leaves banks more exposed to economic shocks, increases their risk of failure, and elevates systemic risk.[110]

Investment switching lowers the effectiveness of regulations even if policymakers do *not* lower regulatory standards in a "race to the bottom."[111] Scholars and policymakers have still been concerned that investment switching means that more capital will shift from regimes with high regulatory taxes to those with low tax rates.[112] In the case of regulatory capital arbitrage, investment switching means that shareholders and creditors will move money from banks with high amounts of effective capital to those with lower capital.[113] The banks with lower effective capital will grow and pose more of a systemic danger, while the more heavily "taxed" banks atrophy. In the aggregate, regimes with lower regulatory taxes can attract capital, while higher tax regimes face the risk of becoming hollowed out. Even if no regime lowers its regulatory standards as a result, capital will shift to lightly regulated jurisdictions and overall global systemic risk will increase.

The potential for financial regulation to drive capital to less regulated jurisdictions appears in a recent economic study, provocatively entitled "Bubble Thy Neighbor." In this study, economists found that tighter capital controls in one country reduced capital inflows and pushed investment to other countries. The authors expressed concern that these controls may lower the risk of an asset price bubble in the implementing country, but increase the risk of market distortions in other countries.[114]

Regulatory arbitrage poses particular dangers when it undermines the effectiveness of certain financial regulations. Chapter 9 discusses how the subversion of regulations that curb the leverage of financial institutions and the overall supply of credit in financial markets may create a triple whammy. Increases in leverage and the supply of credit can cause asset prices to skyrocket, fueling the inflation of a bubble. Rising prices can attract more investors, and feedback effects begin to develop. A bubble can promote greater arbitrage of regulations, which can further inflate the bubble. At the same time, highly leveraged financial institutions face a greater danger of insolvency should a market crash cause investment losses.[115]

Regulatory arbitrage may have particularly powerful effects on regulations that seek to steer investors away from higher risk investments. Chapter 8 discusses how certain securities and financial laws create "tiers" of investors and aim to offer more sophisticated investors greater access to investments perceived to involve higher risk.[116] However, when prices in "riskier" asset classes skyrocket, incentives for regulatory arbitrage increase; buyers in less sophisticated tiers and sellers (like financial intermediaries) have incentives to work around restrictions on investor access.

Regulatory arbitrage has a second pernicious effect or social cost beyond undermining the effectiveness of regulation. Regulatory arbitrage can also mask risks. This chapter has already described how regulatory arbitrage, particularly investment structuring, can increase information asymmetries for management and shareholders of firms. For example, regulatory arbitrage can render the capital structure of a firm and the risks it faces more complex and opaque. This opacity problem extends to creditors and other market participants with exposure to the firm, as well as to regulators. Complex arbitrage transactions and investment switching can prevent regulators from understanding the risk exposures of individual firms and of financial markets.[117] Regulatory arbitrage that occurs during, or contributes to, an asset price bubble proves particularly worrisome, as rising asset prices mask the mispricing of risk. Chapter 9 looks at this effect as well. The problem of opacity also becomes particularly significant in the context of regulatory capital arbitrage, as described in the case study below.

Third, regulatory arbitrage can distort competition in markets to the extent that participants – particularly financial institutions – cannot engage in the regulatory arbitrage to the same degree.[118] This can radically distort competition in the financial services sector. The following chapter explores how this distortion can create political pressure for deregulation and push some financial firms into riskier asset segments.

Fourth, regulatory arbitrage can waste public resources and increase the complexity of laws. Victor Fleischer notes that regulatory arbitrage can encourage wasteful legal planning and structuring by firms and individuals.[119]

Regulatory arbitrage also wastes public resources as policymakers and regulators must continuously respond to investment switching and structuring and adapt legal rules. This arms race often results in thicker and more complicated legal codes. This growing complexity makes it harder to comply with and enforce legal rules. It can shroud the true purposes of legal rules and erode their political support and legitimacy. Increasingly complex legal rules, in turn, open up new avenues for regulatory arbitrage.[120]

A case study: regulatory capital arbitrage

To illustrate more vividly regulatory arbitrage in practice and how it can under-mine vital prudential regulations and exacerbate asset price bubbles, the follow-ing case study examines a particularly complex and important species of regulatory arbitrage: regulatory capital arbitrage. Regulatory capital arbitrage occurs when financial institutions or their investors engage in either investment switching or investment structuring to avoid regulatory capital requirements. Regulatory capital arbitrage played a crucial role in the Panic of 2007 and 2008. Chapter 10 will delve into aspects of the current financial crisis more deeply. The immediate goal of this case study is to describe the following:

- the incentives for financial institutions to engage in regulatory capital arbi-trage to lower the cost of capital regulations;
- how the presence of government guarantees and systemic risk externalities make regulatory arbitrage prevalent and persistent and render capital requirements inherently unstable;
- how regulatory capital requirements and regulatory capital arbitrage evolved together over time in a dialectical manner;
- the techniques financial institutions have used to engage in regulatory capital arbitrage with an emphasis on strategies that involve complex finan-cial instruments, such as asset-backed securities;
- how, in the years just before the Panic of 2007–2008, financial institutions increasingly used asset-backed securities and similar instruments for regula-tory capital arbitrage and less for their (purported) original economic purpose of transferring credit risk; and
- the severe consequences of this massive regulatory capital arbitrage.

Regulatory capital arbitrage appears to have increased as massive real estate bubbles inflated in the United States and in Europe. At the same time, regulatory capital arbitrage fueled the production of asset-backed securities that fed the boom. Regulatory capital arbitrage also masked dangerous increases in the leverage of financial institutions.

Capital requirements as regulatory tax

To understand why and how banks engaged in this form of regulatory arbitrage, it is critical first to highlight the functions of capital regulations. Regulatory capital requirements require that a financial institution retain a certain amount of equity based on the amount of assets it owns.[121] The regulatory capital cushion has two interrelated functions. First, it protects the bank (particularly its cred-itors) from unexpected losses on its investments.[122] Lowering the risk of bank insolvency mitigates the negative externalities of bank failures on financial markets and taxpayers who provide deposit insurance.[123] Second, bank capital requirements reduce a firm's leverage.[124] Increased leverage of financial institu-tions not only leaves those firms more exposed to economic shocks and insolvency, it also can increase the effective supply of money in the economy and fuel asset price booms and bubbles. Chapter 9 will explore these macro-economic effects in greater detail.

When regulations require banks to hold more capital than they would due solely to market discipline (i.e., the level of capital that their creditors and investors demand), banks view these requirements as a form of regulatory taxation.[125] As they do with respect to other forms of taxation, banks incur structuring costs to reduce the regulatory burden imposed by capital requirements.[126] The goal of this arbitrage – called regulatory capital arbitrage – is to enable firms to reduce their capital ratios for regulatory purposes but without a corresponding reduction in economic risk (or to maintain regulatory capital ratios while *increasing* economic risk).[127] Regulatory arbitrage may reduce a firm's cost of capital.[128]

Cheap debt: government guarantees, systemic risk, and the instability of regulatory capital requirements

Financial institutions have tremendous incentives to game capital requirements and increase their leverage because of the relative inexpensiveness of debt to equity financing for them.[129] Yet the cheapness of debt for financial institutions violates the Miller–Modigliani theorem from corporate finance. This theory holds that, under certain assumptions, a firm should have the same cost of financing whether it finances itself entirely through equity, entirely through debt, or with any mix of the two.[130] Several factors may explain why debt is cheaper for financial institutions than equity.[131] The tax-deductibility of interest payments on debt provides one distortion.[132]

Government guarantees of financial institutions – whether explicit or implicit – provide another powerful force that makes debt cheaper than equity. By offering to bail out financial institution creditors, these guarantees make debt relatively cheap. Like black holes, guarantees exert a powerful gravitational pull towards leverage that warps regulatory space. Financial institutions have powerful incentives to exploit these guarantees and arbitrage capital requirements.[133]

Attempting to remove these guarantees may not provide a realistic remedy. Governments provide these guarantees to mitigate systemic risk and to lower the cost of bank failures externalized on financial markets.[134] Policymakers cannot easily foreswear government guarantees and bailouts altogether because of these potential systemic externalities of bank failures.[135] These externalities and the prospect of government bailouts make financial regulation inherently unstable because of moral hazard (which, because of the financial crisis and government bailouts, is a concept many taxpayers understand all too well).[136] Indeed, governments impose capital requirements to mitigate the moral hazard of financial institutions taking excessive risk at the ultimate expense of taxpayers.[137] However, the prospect of government guarantees rescuing creditors of financial institutions makes debt relatively cheap and creates powerful incentives for financial institutions to game these capital requirements and increase leverage.

Financial institution leverage (as Chapter 9 explains) has effects beyond moral hazard. This leverage feeds asset price bubbles by increasing the effective money supply. Rising prices can cover up market mispricing of risk. Leverage also leaves individual financial institutions and entire financial markets more susceptible to economic downturns.

Chapter 7 will examine how implicit government guarantees can become self-fulfilling prophesies. The widespread belief in the marketplace that the government will bail the creditors of a financial institution out will lead creditors to over-lend to that institution. If the level of lending becomes large enough, the risk of the institution failing may threaten the stability of financial markets generally. This creates strong pressure on the government to provide an actual bailout. This same logic applies to lending to entire classes of financial institutions. If creditors think the government will guarantee an entire class of institution, lending to that entire class will increase. The government may have no economically, politically, or legally principled way to bail out some institutions in the class but not others. Again, Chapter 7 will look at how government guarantees promote investor herding and how investor herding induces government guarantees. Chapter 6 will explore the ways in which market players play games with the government and each other to conjure up and exploit implicit guarantees.

The Basel Accords: the dialectics of capital requirements and regulatory capital arbitrage

This primal impulse of financial institutions to escape capital requirements shaped the development of international and national banking regulation. A brief history of the Basel Accords, a set of international agreements among bank regulators, reveals that capital regulations and regulatory capital arbitrage co-evolved in a dialectical manner.[138] The evolution of capital requirements provides a prime example of a "regulatory dialectic" described by Edward Kane in 1986. Kane argued that financial innovation responds to regulator actions and regulators, in turn, adjust regulations in light of financial innovation.[139]

In the 1980s, bank regulators in several nations (members of the Basel Committee on Banking Supervision) became concerned about the prospect of an international race to the bottom in regulatory capital requirements for banks. The regulators feared that banks in countries with lower capital regulations would gain a competitive advantage and would attract cross-border capital flows. In other words, regulators worried about the effects of massive investment switching on bank regulation, bank stability, and the risk of cross-border financial crises. These concerns animated the creation of the Basel I Accord.[140]

In 1988, bank regulators in various countries agreed to set recommended minimum capital requirements for banks in their jurisdictions that were ultimately adopted by the G-10 countries.[141] Basel I established regulatory capital requirements for the credit risk exposure of banks.[142] The Basel I rules required that certain large banks maintain capital equal to 8 percent of the value of their risk-weighted assets.[143] The drafters recognized that not all assets posed equal credit risk and created different categories for assets based on their perceived credit risk. Assets that posed minimal credit risk required zero capital. On the other end of the spectrum, higher credit risk assets required 100 percent capital.[144]

This crude approach of placing assets into risk buckets created problems. The regulatory risk weights did not match the true economic risk that assets posed for banks. In many cases, the actual credit risk was lower than the regulatory weight, which created strong incentives for banks to engage in regulatory capital arbitrage (including through the techniques described below).[145]

To remedy the failings of Basel I, the Basel Committee on Banking Supervision drafted the Basel II Accord.[146] This second agreement supplemented the Basel I Accord (the risk-bucket approach was tweaked, but remains in place for many banks) and allowed certain large banks to set their capital requirements according to a bank's own proprietary risk models. The accord's drafters created this policy innovation on the theory that these models would better reflect the true economic risk faced by large banks. Theoretically, the freedom to set risk capital according to their own models would not only enable banks to deploy capital more efficiently, it would also curb their incentives to engage in regulatory capital arbitrage.[147]

However, as we will see, banks and other financial institutions found ways to game these rules and used the internal-model approach to increase dramatically their leverage.[148] In December 2010, the Basel Committee responded to the flaws in Basel II, which were exposed by the Panic of 2007–2008 with a third accord (Basel III).[149] Time will tell how banks will arbitrage this third Basel incarnation.

An overview of how regulatory capital arbitrage works

Banks and other financial institutions game the types of capital requirements envisioned by Basel I and II in a number of different ways. The most important forms of regulatory capital arbitrage have involved various types of investment structuring facilitated by securitization (as well as other financial instruments described in Chapter 10 on shadow banking).[150]

Regulatory capital arbitrage generally entails banks gaming traditional bank capital ratios by playing with the numerator and denominator of those ratios.[151] Simple regulatory capital requirements mandate that financial institutions maintain a capital ratio comprising equity in the numerator and assets in the denominator.[152] The Basel I and Basel II accords contained complex rules for what types of equity instruments could count towards the numerator.[153] As noted above, the Accords also required different ratios of capital for different categories of assets in the denominator, depending on the believed riskiness of the assets.[154]

Banks could game these traditional capital rules by cosmetically increasing the numerator in the ratio, for example through gains trading or under-provisioning for loan loss reserves.[155] Banks also gamed the numerator by developing hybrid securities, such as trust preferred securities. These securities are treated like debt for tax purposes (with interest payments being subject to deductions), but as capital for bank regulatory purposes.[156] Trust preferred securities had debt-like features, including required "interest" payments to holders (with some ability of the bank to defer payments for limited time periods).[157] Commentators have faulted the performance of these instruments during the financial crisis. The responsibility of banks to make "debt payments" combined with a freeze in the market for issuances of trust preferred securities during the crisis underscored that these securities did not provide the same cushion against losses as plain vanilla equity.[158]

The games that banks have played with the numerator of regulatory capital ratios pale in comparison to the prevalence and complexity of their strategies to manipulate the denominator.[159] Securitization has played a vital role in these efforts.[160] Chapter 10 will explain securitization more thoroughly, but for now the following description suffices. In a securitization transaction, an investment vehicle purchases and pools together various loans or other assets that have predictable future cash streams. Those cash streams collateralize and fund securities that the vehicle issues to investors in capital markets. The investment vehicle typically issues different classes (or tranches) of securities, with senior classes having prior contractual claims on the cash streams. The tranches thus offer investors different mixes of risk and reward.[161]

Securitization has evolved into numerous specialized variants, including asset-backed commercial paper (ABCP). Companies seeking financing create asset-backed commercial paper by first selling cash-producing assets into an investment vehicle. The investment vehicle then issues short-term securities with maturities of between 90 and 180 days.[162] Aside from issuing securities with shorter maturities, asset-backed commercial paper differs from traditional securitization in several other respects. First, the investment vehicle in asset-backed commercial paper (called a "conduit") may purchase a revolving set of assets that may change over time.[163] Second, as commercial paper matures, the conduit will issue new paper to investors (the proceeds of which will be used to purchase fresh assets and pay the fees of the various service providers to the transaction).[164] These first two features mean that conduits may suffer an asset-liability mismatch, as they have short-term obligations to investors yet hold longer-term assets. This mismatch potential leads to a third feature of ABCP that differs from traditional securitizations: in exchange for a fee, a third party often agrees to provide liquidity support to the vehicle in the form of infusions of cash or liquid assets as needed.[165] Like securitizations, asset-backed commercial paper issuances often include credit support (in the form of bond insurance, credit derivatives, or other financial guarantees) from another financial institution.[166]

Securitization, in whatever form, offers the lenders who sell assets to an investment vehicle for cash a way to solve a mismatch between long-term assets and short-term liabilities. It affords investors the ability to participate in lending markets with securities that can be more liquid than loans themselves and that are tailored to particular investment needs. More generally, securitization provides a mechanism to transfer and spread credit risk from lenders to investors.[167]

Yet securitization has also been a valuable tool in gaming regulations. This latter role, as we will see later in this chapter, may have eclipsed its other economic benefits. The use of securitization in regulatory capital arbitrage can be understood through two insights. First, securitization can game the fact that traditional capital regulations place assets in certain risk buckets. By unbundling and reassembling the cash streams and risk from underlying assets, securitization allows firms to create instruments that fit into a particular regulatory bucket yet have much more risk "stuffed" into the instrument than the regulatory capital required for that bucket assumes.[168]

Second, securitization plays with the regulatory treatment of guarantees. David Jones explains using the following example. Assume a bank has a balance sheet with assets of $100 in loans, liabilities of $95 in deposits and $5 in equity. This firm's implied leverage ratio is thus 5 percent. If a firm were to sell $50 in loans to a third party and provide an off-balance sheet guarantee for those loans (for example, through a standby letter of credit or other form of credit enhancement), it would have the same economic risk. Yet its capital ratio per its balance sheet would dramatically improve, jumping to 10 percent ($5 in equity divided by $50 in on-balance sheet loans).[169] The first two Basel Accords prohibit this simple form of regulatory capital arbitrage by imposing regulatory capital requirements on financial guarantees. The Accords require that when the bank issues a guarantee on assets that it has sold itself, the guarantee is deemed to be "recourse." This generally means that the bank must hold capital equal to the bank's maximum potential credit loss under the guarantee. Nevertheless, banks use securitization and other shadow banking instruments to create effective guarantees that do not require that the financial institution hold regulatory capital for the full amount of economic risk it retains.[170]

Six strategies for regulatory capital arbitrage

These two insights help explain six common strategies for regulatory capital arbitrage:

1   *Concentrate credit risk and cherry pick.* Under this first strategy, banks structure asset-backed securities so that subordinated tranches of asset-backed securities bear high concentrations of economic risk (that is, they are more at risk of losses should the loans that back the securitization default) yet are subject to low regulatory capital requirements. Thus, the capital that a bank must hold against these securities according to regulation is lower than the economic risk of those securities. The senior tranches in the securitization contain a correspondingly low degree of economic risk, but would require relatively higher capital; they would bear the brunt of the regulatory capital requirements. The issuing bank then retains the subordinated securities and sells the senior securities to outside investors.[171]

Scholars have also claimed that banks used the flip side of the same strategy: banks would securitize assets and then purchase the resultant AAA-rated senior securities. These securities would contain more economic risk than regulatory capital requirements.[172] These AAA-rated securities were treated as having minimal credit risk and no liquidity or funding risk.[173] Banks could thus have their cake (enjoy fat premiums on their asset-backed security investments, which were particularly high for securitizations backed by subprime mortgages) and eat it too (lower their regulatory capital below economic risk).[174]

2   *Remote origination.* The second strategy is to ensure "remote origination," namely that the issuer of the asset-backed securities is not affiliated with the original lender that made the underlying loans. Securitizations involve remote originators for many reasons (primarily bankruptcy law).[175] However, bank regulations provide another reason; capital regulations require only an 8 percent capital ratio if the bank is issuing a guarantee of loans owned by someone else. This provides an explanation for one structural feature of some asset-backed commercial paper programs: the credit enhancements provided by the sponsoring bank require lower capital when some other entity (other than the sponsoring bank) originates the assets that will back the commercial paper sold to investors.[176]

3   *Indirect credit enhancements and creative guarantees.* The third strategy exploits the regulatory treatment of other forms of economic guarantees provided by banks for securitization vehicles. In essence, these guarantors bear more economic risk than suggested by the regulatory capital required.[177]

For example, banks carefully structured the liquidity enhancements that they provided to asset-backed commercial paper vehicles to obtain lower risk weights for these guarantees under capital regulations.[178] Careful design allowed banks that provided liquidity enhancements to hold only 0.8 percent capital against the value of assets in the asset-backed commercial paper vehicle (compared to the 8 percent capital that would be required had these assets been on the bank's balance sheet).[179] U.S. bank regulators effectively exempted these liquidity enhancements from capital requirements for the sponsoring banks.[180] The asset-backed commercial paper market responded with explosive growth. It doubled from $600 billion to $1.2 trillion outstanding from 2004 to the second quarter of 2007.[181]

The crisis triggered these liquidity guarantees and revealed the mistake of this light regulatory capital treatment.[182] Asset-backed commercial paper transactions were structured so that, when the crisis struck, investors bore only 4.3 percent of the loss of the $1.25 trillion outstanding in asset-backed commercial paper. Guarantors bore the remainder.[183] Empirical studies show when asset-backed commercial paper investment vehicles suffered losses during the crisis, sponsoring banks – and not investors – generally bore the losses.[184] Risk materialized on the balance sheets of sponsoring banks despite the light capital treatment.[185] This led several scholars to brand asset-backed commercial paper as "securitization without risk transfer" and to conclude that a primary driver of these securitization structures was regulatory capital arbitrage.[186]

In addition to liquidity enhancements, banks designed other creative, indirect guarantees. For example, banks designed complex credit enhancements for asset-backed securities that resembled revolving credit facilities (such as collateralized loan agreements (a form of CDO) and securitizations of credit card facilities).[187] Careful structuring meant that these credit enhancements required no or minimal regulatory capital for the banks that provided them.[188]

Still other guarantees from banks and financial institutions were implicit. Although many sponsors of securitizations had no contractual obligation to support a failing investment vehicle, the marketplace expected that the firm would step in should the vehicle experience extreme losses.[189] A financial institution that failed to honor these expectations might suffer a severe reputation loss and be unable to find financing in the future.[190] Scholars have found that, to avoid this fate, sponsors would go to great lengths to support investment vehicles.[191] If sponsors of securitization could provide "moral recourse" for these vehicles without agreeing explicitly and contractually to provide a guarantee, they could avoid capital requirements and other legal costs.[192]

4   *Third-party guarantees*. Banks also engaged in regulatory capital arbitrage when they purchased asset-backed securities that enjoyed third-party guarantees via credit derivatives or bond insurance. Those guarantees allowed the banks that invested in senior asset-backed securities to hold as little as zero capital against those investments. Regulations allowed banks to hold no capital even though capital markets priced the credit risk on those assets (when adjusted for the guarantees) at more than zero. Banks widely exploited this loophole. For example, AIG's 2007 Annual Report disclosed that $379 billion of its $527 billion credit derivative exposure (created by its infamous Financial Products Group) represented derivatives sold to financial institutions seeking to engage in this form of regulatory capital arbitrage.[193]

5   *Moving assets from banking book to trading book*. The 1997 Market Risk Amendment to the Basel Accords facilitated additional forms of regulatory capital arbitrage. These amendments allowed certain banks to set regulatory capital for certain risks in their trading books. This encouraged banks to move asset-backed securities and other shadow banking instruments from their banking book to their trading books to dramatically lower their regulatory capital.[194]

6   *Exploiting Basel II's do-it-yourself capital requirements*. As noted above, the Basel II Accord allowed certain large financial institutions to set their own regulatory capital levels according to their proprietary risk models. When the SEC extended this approach to certain large investment banking conglomerates, many of those firms dramatically increased their leverage

ratios to over 30:1 within a three year span.[195] In other words, financial institutions used these models to lower their capital requirements.[196] Financial institutions used these same models to measure firm risk management policies and price asset-backed securities, credit derivatives, and other shadow banking instruments.[197]

Regulatory capital arbitrage as compound arbitrage

Many of the six evasion strategies described above depended on asset-backed securities or other shadow banking instruments and counterparties receiving investment grade ratings from credit rating agencies.[198] Financial institutions played a different set of games to achieve higher ratings. For example, scholars have examined how the financial institutions that designed and marketed asset-backed securities shopped among rating agency firms for higher ratings. The firms that put together securitizations determined which ratings firm would get hired for a particular transaction. Competition among ratings firms, combined with negligible liability for giving unwarranted investment grade ratings, created perverse incentives for the agencies to please the firms holding the purse strings.[199]

The gaming of rating agencies may have taken even more sophisticated forms. In the wake of the SEC's 2010 lawsuit against Goldman Sachs, newspapers reported that the investment bank had exploited the disclosure by rating agencies of their methodologies in rating asset-backed securities. Goldman Sachs and other banks were able to reverse engineer rating agency models to obtain higher ratings for riskier asset-backed securities.[200] In short, even regulation outsourced to private entities can suffer from regulatory arbitrage.[201] These various games that financial institutions played with rating agencies assumed fresh importance in the context of regulatory capital arbitrage; these games further undermined capital regulations.

Similarly, interpretations of bank regulators that allowed lenders to lower their regulatory capital requirements by securitizing assets depended on the securitization qualifying as a true sale for bankruptcy and accounting purposes.[202] Thus the gaming of bankruptcy and accounting rules also contributed to regulatory capital arbitrage.[203]

The crisis and the effects of regulatory capital arbitrage

Taking a step back from individual arbitrage strategies, a troubling picture of the effect of regulatory capital arbitrage emerges. Although, the various shadow banking instruments were designed to spread risk, most of the credit risk stayed within the financial system. A 2008 study reports that banks, thrifts, government-sponsored entities, and broker-dealers held $789 billion – or roughly 50 percent – of the AAA-rated CDO tranches outstanding.[204] At the same point, banks, broker dealers, and monoline bond insurers held $320 billion of the $476 billion of subordinated CDO tranches.[205] A 2008 IMF report documented how balance sheets of a sample of ten very large financial institutions doubled from 2004 to 2007, yet the implied risk of their balance sheets under the Basel Accord registered only a modest uptick.[206]

This suggests that the most troubling problem with securitization (and shadow banking generally) is not that financial institutions unloaded high credit risk assets onto non-financial institution investors. On the contrary, too much of the toxic risk stayed on the balance sheets of financial institutions or was passed from one institution to another.[207] The system did not diffuse risk, but hid, recycled, and concentrated it in complex daisy chains. Securitization only pantomimed its stated role of transferring risk in the service of letting banks escape capital rules. Professors Acharya and Richardson explain that this evasion of capital regulations was the driving force behind securitization in the years leading up to the crisis. They write:

> especially from 2003 to 2007, the main purpose of securitization was not to share risk with investors, but to make an end run around capital adequacy regulations. The net result was to keep the risk concentrated in the financial institutions – and, indeed, to keep the risk at a greatly magnified level, because of the over-leveraging it allowed.[208]

These statistics support the earlier predictions of scholars on the pernicious effects of regulatory capital arbitrage. Well before the crisis, some scholars worried that regulatory capital arbitrage would result in an effective deterioration of risk based capital standards.[209] They worried that regulatory capital arbitrage could mask growing financial problems at banks and frustrate both market discipline and regulatory actions to address failing banks.[210] Some scholars attribute to regulatory arbitrage the fact that many large complex financial institutions that failed during the crisis – Bear Stearns, Washington Mutual, Lehman Brothers, Wachovia, and Merrill Lynch – actually had higher capital than required by regulation. This arbitrage masked the true economic risk of these firms.[211] Moreover, regulatory capital arbitrage can discourage a true hedging of economic risks.[212] As already noted, higher leverage can effectively externalize more of a firm's risk on the marketplace and on the government.[213]

Conclusion and complex adaptive systems

Regulatory arbitrage in general and regulatory capital arbitrage in particular will remain features of the landscape of the financial markets and financial regulation well into the future. Financial institutions and other market participants have a strong incentive to game financial rules that restrict their risk-taking and profits. Financial institutions have particularly sharp incentives to engage in regulatory capital arbitrage. The presence of government guarantees – explicit and implicit – and externalities from financial institution failure continue to make debt relatively cheaper for financial institutions than equity. The presence of government guarantees – explicit and implicit – continue to make debt a relatively cheaper source of financing for financial institutions than issuing equity.

This explains the dialectical co-evolution of capital regulations and regulatory capital arbitrage described above. Regulators must impose capital requirements to reduce the systemic effects of excessive financial institution leverage and the moral hazard from government guarantees. However, each and every historical attempt to set capital requirements has resulted in new forms of regulatory capital arbitrage. The United States and Britain worried that their early regulatory capital requirements would drive capital overseas to less regulated jurisdictions. This resulted in the first Basel Accord. Yet financial institutions found ways to game that agreement's crude risk-bucket approach. So bank regulators responded with the Basel II Accord and allowed large banks to set capital according to their proprietary risk models. Not surprisingly, financial conglomerates used this approach to lower effective capital and raise leverage. Now regulators have rolled out Basel III. And so it goes...

The incentives to engage in regulatory arbitrage and regulatory capital arbitrage increase during prolonged market bubbles. The prospect of being shut out of increased profits from a booming asset market sharpens the legal creativity and appetite for legal risk of investors and financial institutions. Chapter 9 argues that increased arbitrage and the decreased effectiveness of some legal rules – particularly those that restrain leverage and credit – in turn feed bubbles.

In reviewing this chapter's findings, it may be helpful to take a step back from the details of regulatory arbitrage and regulatory capital arbitrage and look at overall patterns with a different scholarly lens. Research into complex adaptive systems may help explain the regulatory arbitrage described above.[214] Complex adaptive systems are the centerpiece of complexity science, a somewhat amorphous interdisciplinary field that engages economists, computer scientists, and natural scientists. These scholars study how simple interactions between adaptive agents (which could mean anything from investors in a market to organisms in an ecosystem to cells within an organism) can evolve into increasingly complex adaptive systems.[215] The ability of agents to adapt to the changes in the system, including those caused by the interaction of the agents, leads the overall system – the market, ecosystem, or organism – to develop in nonlinear ways.[216]

Economists have looked at how a financial market represents a complex adaptive system[217] and may therefore exhibit nonlinear behavior[218] and suffer bouts of disequilibrium and unpredictable swings.[219] Accordingly, models of market risk may suffer spectacular failures.[220]

If a financial market is a complex adaptive system, then so too is a regulated financial market. The agents in the system are financial market traders and the regulators are looking to govern the risk-taking of those traders. As regulators set rules for the market, the traders (with the help of their lawyers) find ways to adapt around these rules or to move capital to a less regulated part of the system. The co-evolution of financial regulation and regulatory arbitrage provides an example of what scholars of complex adaptive systems call "emergence." Legal scholar J.B. Ruhl defines emergence as:

the appearance of unforeseen qualities from the self-organizing interaction of large numbers of objects, which cannot be understood through study of any one of the objects. The key to emergence is understanding that the emergent behaviors of dynamical systems are high-level patterns arising from the indescribably complex interaction of lower-level subsystems. Hence, removing or otherwise changing any interacting component of the system potentially changes the entire system since the interactions leading to the global emergent behaviors may no longer be possible.[221]

Emergence and the complex interactions of agents on the microlevel frustrate the prediction of changes to the overall system.[222]

One could analogize the complex adaptive system of a regulated financial market to a Petri dish in which traders and regulators adapt to one another. This interaction may make predictions about the stability of financial markets and regulation hard enough in normal times. Yet asset price bubbles place that Petri dish under a heat lamp. The heat creates the conditions for frenzies of regulatory arbitrage that destabilize the architecture of financial regulation.

Notes

1 Katharina Pistor and Chenggang Xu, Incomplete Law, 35 *New York University Journal of International Law and Politics* 931 (2003). Pistor and Xu argue that incompleteness may take many forms. Legal rules may be incomplete because they attempt to regulate comprehensively a set of activities but omit some substantively equivalent actions. Other legal rules are incomplete because of vague or ambiguous language which leaves the boundaries of legal rules unclear. Pistor and Xu describe how incompleteness can result not only from bad drafting, but also because of technological or social changes or because legal drafters deliberately made legal rules ambiguous (whether for political reasons or to allow courts and agencies to fill in gaps). Ibid. at 932–3.

This account of incomplete legal rules has a mirror image in legal and economic scholarship on "incomplete" contracts. See, e.g., Oliver Hart and John Moore, Foundations of Incomplete Contracts, 66 *Review of Economic Studies* 115 (1999) (providing theoretical economic framework for analysis of incomplete contracts); Ian Ayres and Robert Gertner, Filling Gaps in Incomplete Contracts: An Economic Theory of Default Rules, 99 *Yale Law Journal* 87 (1989).

2 Chapter 2, notes 207–8 and accompanying text.

3 Victor Fleischer provides a framework for understanding regulatory arbitrage and the conditions under which it flourishes. He describes regulatory arbitrage as a legal planning technique that exploits the gap between the economic substance of a transaction and its legal or regulatory treatment, taking advantage of the legal system's intrinsically limited ability to attach formal labels that track the economics of transactions with sufficient precision. Victor Fleischer, Regulatory Arbitrage, 89 *Texas Law Review* 227, 229 (2010).

Fleischer later describes the practice as: "the manipulation of the structure of a deal to take advantage of a gap between the economic substance of a transaction and its regulatory treatment." Ibid. at 230.

For another, less expansive definition, see Frank Partnoy, Financial Derivatives and the Costs of Regulatory Arbitrage, 22 *Journal of Corporation Law* 211, 227 (1997) ("Regulatory arbitrage consists of those financial transactions designed specifically to reduce costs or capture profit opportunities created by differential regulations or laws.").

4 Fleischer argues that three different conditions can generate opportunities and incentives to engage in regulatory arbitrage:

> *Regulatory regime inconsistency:* This occurs when a particular transaction can receive different regulatory treatment (and thus incur different regulatory costs) under different regimes. These different regimes might be different legal jurisdictions. For example, a transaction might be structured to be governed by the law of different nations or states. Alternatively, a transaction might be governed by alternative regulators with overlapping jurisdictions (such as two banking regulators in the same nation).

> *Economic substance inconsistency:* This occurs when two transactions that have the same economic functions (for example, they provide the same future cash flows) receive different regulatory treatment (and incur different regulatory costs) under the same regulatory regime.

> *Time inconsistency:* This occurs when the same transaction receives different regulatory treatment (and incurs different associated costs) at different points in time.

> Fleischer, *supra* note 3, at 244–50

5 See Ronald J. Gilson, Value Creation by Business Lawyers: Legal Skills and Asset Pricing, 94 *Yale Law Journal* 239, 243 (1984).

6 Brian P. Murray and Maurice Pesso, The Accident of Efficiency: Foreign Exchanges, American Depository Receipts, and Space Arbitrage, 51 *Buffalo Law Review* 383, 389 (2003) (describing ADRs). Some economists have found that ADRs may enable financial arbitrage of foreign company securities, as arbitrageurs exploit price differences between a company's ADRs and equivalent amounts of its stock traded on foreign exchanges. Mahmoud Wahab, Malek Lashgari, and Richard J. Cohn, Arbitrage Opportunities in the American Depository Receipts Market Revisited, 2 *Journal of International Financial Markets, Institutions and Money* 97 (1993).

7 Chapter 1, notes 35, 60 and accompanying text.

8 Michael S. Knoll, The Ancient Roots of Modern Financial Innovation: The Early History of Regulatory Arbitrage, 87 *Oregon Law Review* 93 (2008).

9 Merton H. Miller, *Financial Innovations and Market Volatility*, 5–9 (1991, Wiley); Merton Miller, Financial Innovation: The Last Twenty and the Next, 21 *Journal of Financial and Quantitative Analysis* 459 (1986). See also Peter Tufano, Financial Innovation, in *1A The Handbook of the Economics of Finance*, 307, 318–20 (George M. Constantinides, Milton Harris, and René M. Stulz, eds., 2003, Elsevier North Holland).

10 Chapter 6, notes 49, 52 and accompanying text.

11 Ulrike Schaede, Change and Continuity in Japanese Regulation, Berkeley Roundtable on the International Economy, *Working Paper No. 66* (1994).

12 Heidi Mandanis Schooner and Michael W. Taylor, *Global Bank Regulation: Principles and Policies*, xvii–xxii (2010, Academic Press).

13 Chapter 2, note 66 and accompanying text.

14 Edward Chancellor, *Devil Take the Hindmost: A History of Financial Speculation*, 290 (1999, Plume Books). See also Kazuo Tsuda, Japanese Banks in Deregulation and the Economic Bubble, 22 *Japanese Economic Studies* 122, 140–1 (May/June/August 1994).

15 Chancellor, *supra* note 14, at 290; Tsuda, *supra* note 14, at 141–3.

16 Chancellor, *supra* note 14, at 290.

17 Ibid.

18 Chancellor, *supra* note 14, at 290–1. See also Tsuda, *supra* note 14, at 140–4. Tsuda

discusses how investment decisions with respect to *tokkin* accounts were largely left to the discretion of the brokerage/securities companies and how securities companies issued implicit non-contractual guarantees against losses in these accounts. Ibid. at 143–7.

Tsuda also examines how banks set up "investment consulting firms" to enter the *tokkin* market and work around legal restrictions that prevented them from entering the asset management segment of the securities business. Ibid. at 144–6.

19 Tsuda, *supra* note 14, at 147.
20 Ibid.
21 Ibid.
22 Ibid. at 290–1.
23 Ibid. at 291.
24 Ibid.
25 Ibid.
26 Ibid.
27 Ibid.
28 Chapter 2, note 312 and accompanying text.
29 David Jones, Emerging Problems with the Basel Capital Accord: Regulatory Capital Arbitrage and Related Issues, 24 *Journal of Banking and Finance* 35 (2000).
30 Fleischer, *supra* note 3, at 253–7.
31 Ibid.
32 See generally Arnoud W.A. Boot, Silva Deželan, and Todd T. Milbourn, Regulatory Distortions in a Competitive Financial Services Industry, 17 *Journal of Financial Services Research* 249 (2000) (analyzing effects of regulatory arbitrage given competition among financial institutions).
33 Market risk describes risks that the value of a firm's investments or other assets will decline (or that its liabilities will increase) due to changes in market prices. Hennie van Greuning and Sonja Brajovic Bratanovic, *Analyzing and Managing Banking Risk: Framework for Assessing Corporate Governance and Financial Risk*, 111 (2003, World Bank Publications). Because a firm's investment portfolio may be subject to price fluctuations in different types of markets, market risk covers several different subcategories of risk, including: *interest rate risk*, or the risk exposure from changes in interest rates (Joël Bessis, *Risk Management in Banking*, 17 (2nd ed. 2002, Wiley)); and *equity risk*, or risk arising from fluctuations in stock returns (Aswath Damodaran, *Investment Valuation*, 60 (2002, Wiley) (discussing measurement of equity risk through equity-risk premiums)).
34 Bessis, *supra* note 33, at 13. Bessis notes that credit risk also covers the decline in the credit standing of an obligor, or bonds or stock held by the institution even short of default, as this decline "triggers an upward move of the required market yield to compensate [for] the higher risk and triggers a value decline" of the security. Ibid. Credit risk includes counterparty risk in derivative transactions, i.e., the risk that a counterparty which has contractual obligations to make payment to an institution (upon an event specified in the derivative contract) will not perform those obligations. Ibid. at 499–504 (discussing credit risk in the context of derivatives). For an economic analysis of the effects of counterparty risk on the pricing of derivatives and other complex financial instruments, see generally Robert A. Jarrow and Fan Yu, Counterparty Risk and the Pricing of Defaultable Securities, 56 *Journal of Finance* 1765 (2002).
35 Liquidity risk takes two related forms. *Trading-liquidity risk* (also called market liquidity risk) is the risk that a firm cannot find a counterparty in the market willing to buy or sell the asset at fair market value. This raises the question of what constitutes "fair market value." There are other variations on the definition of "trading-liquidity risk" or "market-liquidity risk" that have their own ambiguities. According to the Bank for International Settlements, market-liquidity risk occurs when "a firm

cannot easily offset or eliminate a position at the market price because of inadequate market depth or market disruption." Bank for International Settlements, Principles for Sound Liquidity Risk Management and Supervision 1 n.2 (June 2008). *Funding-liquidity risk* means "the risk that [a] firm will not be able to meet efficiently both expected and unexpected current and future cash flow and collateral needs without affecting either daily operations or the financial condition of the firm." Ibid.

36 Charlotte H. Brink, *Measuring Political Risk: Risks to Foreign Investment* (2004, Ashgate Publishing).
37 Jeff Madura, *Financial Markets and Institutions*, 492 (9th ed. 2010, Cengage Learning).
38 Erik F. Gerding, Credit Derivatives, Leverage, and Financial Regulation's Missing Macroeconomic Dimension, 8 *Berkeley Business Law Journal* 42, 64, 67–8 (2011).
39 Erik F. Gerding, Code, Crash, and Open Source, 84 *Washington Law Review* 127, 170–1 (2009) (describing errors in risk models stemming from failure to go far back enough in time to gather data on historical risk).
40 See Chapter 1, "Bounded rationality and noise traders" (introducing behavioral biases); Chapter 3, "A behavioral model: disaster myopia and other biases" (applying behavioral economic research to decisions of policymakers during bubble periods).
41 See generally Chapter 1, "Limited arbitrage." See also Li Jin, How Does Investor Short-termism Affect Mutual Fund Manager Short-termism, European Finance Association Moscow Mtgs Paper (February 27, 2005) available at http://papers.ssrn.com/sol3/papers.cfm?abstract_id=675262 (last visited July 25, 2013).
42 Amir N. Licht, Regulatory Arbitrage for Real: International Securities Regulation in a World of Interacting Securities Markets, 38 *Virginia Journal of International Law* 563, 570 (1998). But See Linda L. Tesar and Ingrid M. Werner, Home Bias and High Turnover, 14 *Journal of International Money and Finance* 467 (1995) (providing evidence that tax effects and transaction costs cannot explain why firms have bias for investing in domestic securities).
43 Japan provides an odd example of this. Japanese regulators negotiated an exception to the Basel Accord that allowed Japanese banks to count shareholdings in other Japanese corporations as regulatory capital. Chancellor, supra note 14, at 294.
44 Chapter 4, "Fraud and rational risk-taking."
45 Cf. Licht, *supra* note 42 (analyzing effects of regulatory arbitrage conducted by trading among increasingly connected international securities markets).
   In his classic history of bubbles, Charles Kindleberger gave an example of how investors could arbitrage around margin regulations on the New York Stock Exchange by purchasing futures in Chicago. Charles P. Kindleberger, *Manias, Panics, and Crashes: A History of Financial Crises*, 63 (1996, Wiley).
46 For a sociological look at how traders use technology to evaluate investments across markets, see Daniel Beunza and David Stark, Tools of the Trade: The Sociotechnology of Arbitrage in a Wall Street Trading Room, 13 *Industrial and Corporate Change* 369 (2004).
47 Robert J. Shiller, *Irrational Exuberance*, 71–95 (2001, Broadway Books).
48 See Chapter 2, note 85 and accompanying text.
49 For a description of how England and France competed for investor funds (particularly for Dutch investors) during these parallel bubbles, see Eric S. Schubert, Innovations, Debts, and Bubbles: International Integration of Financial Markets in Western Europe, 1688–1720, 48 *Journal of Economic History* 299 (1988).
50 Sigurt Vitols and Lutz Engelhardt, National Institutions and High Tech Industries: A Varieties of Capitalism Perspective on the Failure of Germany's "Neuer Markt," Wissenschaftszentrum Berlin für Sozialforschung, *Discussion Paper SP II 2005-03*, 3–6 (February 2005) available at http://papers.ssrn.com/sol3/papers.cfm?abstract_id=670764 (last visited July 25, 2013).

51 For one dry and one colorful account of IKB's doomed investment structuring to access the U.S. CDO market, see James Wilson and Patrick Jenkins, IKB's Experience is Thin End of the Wedge, *Financial Times*, April 19, 2010, at 23; and Michael Lewis, It's the Economy, Dummkopf! 53 *Vanity Fair* 304 (September 2011). For a more in-depth narrative of how Wall Street investment banks sold CDOs and other derivatives to European banks to allow the European firms to arbitrage capital regulations, see Nicholas Dunbar, *The Devil's Derivatives* (2011, Harvard Business Review Press).

52 The rational actor calculus for investors in choosing whether to attempt to fit into a loophole can be simplified and modeled as follows:

$$B <> C + Pc(Lc + Pl*Cl)$$

Where:

B represents the additional rate of return (adjusted for risk) the investor would get from the otherwise unavailable investment when compared to the legally available alternative investment with the best return.

C represents the transaction costs of taking advantage of the exemption, including the costs of obtaining legal and other professional advice.

Pc represents the probability that a regulator would challenge the exemption or investment structure (which would also include the probability that a regulator would detect the use of the exemption)

Lc represents the costs of challenging the regulator, including legal costs and reputational loss.

Pl represents the probability of the investor losing the challenge with the regulator.

Cl represents the costs of losing the challenge including legal fines, loss of licenses, criminal liability, and any additional reputational loss.

Under this model, investors will choose to adopt a legal structure, if the marginal profit that could be gained from the otherwise prohibited investment outweighs the expected costs (including the expected legal liability if the structure is challenged by a regulator or court).

53 Fleischer, *supra* note 3, at 253–7.

54 Dodd-Frank Wall Street Reform and Consumer Protection Act, Pub. L. 111–203, 124 Stat. 1399, 1400, 1561, 1618, 1619, 1627, 1669, 1670, 1673, 1675, 1678, 1732, 1759, 1764, 1802 (two provisions), 1820, 1960, 1980, 1995, 2068, 2071, 2084, 2090, 2108, 2133, 2141, 2148, 2161 (2010).

55 Chapter 3, "Altering the cost–benefit analysis of regulators," "Information asymmetries."

56 Richard Zeckhauser, Causes of the Financial Crisis: Many Responsible Parties, Harvard Kennedy School Faculty Research, *Working Paper Series No. 10-016*, 2–3 (June 2010) available at http://dash.harvard.edu/handle/1/4448877 (last visited July 25, 2013) (financial industry and its innovation will win arms race with regulators); see also Dan Awrey, Complexity, Innovation and the Regulation of Modern Financial Markets, 2 *Harvard Business Law Review* 235 (2012) available at http://papers.ssrn.com/sol3/papers.cfm?abstract_id=1916649 (last visited July 25, 2013) (discussing challenges of regulators in understanding and regulating innovation in financial markets).

57 Chapter 3, "The problem of diluted enforcement."

58 Several academics made influential proposals in the wake of the Panic of 2007–2008 to create consumer financial regulators with the powers to pre-approve financial products. The U.S. Food and Drug Administration and Consumer Product Safety Commission served as templates for these proposals. E.g., Oren Bar-Gill and Elizabeth Warren, Making Credit Safer, 157 *University of Pennsylvania Law Review* 1 (2008). See also Daniel Carpenter, Justin Grimmer, and Eric Lomazoff, Approval Regulation and Endogenous Consumer Confidence: Theory and Analogies to Licensing, Safety, and Financial Regulation, 4 *Regulation and Governance* 383

(2010) (arguing that government pre-approval could increase consumer usage of financial products and discussing implications for newly created Canadian Financial Consumer Agency and U.S. Consumer Financial Protection Bureau).

59 Chapter 3, "The structure of administrative law."

60 Chapter 3, "What upsets the political equilibrium? Where is the opposition?," "No cohesive opposition: consumers and retail investors," "The special case of financial institution regulation."

61 For a description of how certain asset-backed securities and credit derivatives can spread risk efficiently in capital markets, see Ronald J. Gilson and Charles K. Whitehead, Deconstructing Equity: Public Ownership, Agency Costs, and Complete Capital Markets, 108 *Columbia Law Review* 231 (2008) (describing how advances in quantitative finance have led to the development of sophisticated derivatives and other financial products that promise both to lead to "complete" capital markets and drain liquidity from equity markets).

  Then-Federal Reserve Chairman Alan Greenspan expressed concern about how over-regulation of OTC derivatives might impair market efficiency and threaten U.S. competitiveness. Working Group Report on OTC [Over-the-Counter] Derivatives: Hearing Before the Senate Committee on Agriculture, Nutrition and Forestry, 106th Congress (February 10, 2000) (statement of Alan Greenspan, Chairman, Board of Governors of the Federal Reserve System) available at www.federalreserve.gov/boarddocs/testimony/2000/20000210.htm (last visited July 25, 2013). Chairman Greenspan also touted the ability of loan securitization to increase market efficiency and to open "doors to national credit markets for both consumers and businesses." Alan Greenspan, Remarks at the JumpStart Coalition's Annual Meeting (April 3, 2003) available at www.federalreserve.gov/boarddocs/speeches/2003/20030403/default.htm (last visited July 25, 2013).

62 Jones, *supra* note 29, at 39.

63 Ibid.

64 Ibid.

65 Legal innovations, like other technologies, can spread quickly as the diffusion of innovations literature suggests. See Michael J. Powell, Professional Innovation: Corporate Lawyers and Private Lawmaking, 18 *Law and Social Inquiry* 423 (1993) (looking at spread of "poison pill"). That does not mean, however, that legal innovation necessarily leads to uniform practices or some equilibrium point. See Anna Gelpern and Mitu Gulati, Innovation After the Revolution: Foreign Sovereign Bond Contracts Since 2003, 4 *Capital Markets Law Journal* 85 (2009). Cf. W. Scott Frame and Lawrence J. White, Technological Change, Financial Innovation, and Diffusion in Banking, Federal Reserve Bank Atlanta, *Working Paper 2009-10* (March 2009).

66 See generally Heidi Mandanis Schooner, Financial Innovation, Business Methods Patents, and the Regulation of Systemic Risk (November 2, 2011) (unpublished manuscript, on file with the author).

67 Tamar Frankel, Cross-Border Securitizations: Without Law, But Not Lawless, 8 *Duke Journal of Comparative and International Law* 255 (1998).

68 Josh Lerner, The Litigation of Financial Innovations, 53 *Journal of Law and Economics* 807 (2010).

69 Ibid.

70 For an outline of the connections between intellectual property rights and financial institution regulation, see Schooner, *supra* note 66.

71 Chapter 3, "Deregulation games and predicting the forms of regulatory stimulus."

72 David J. Cartano, *Federal and State Taxation of Limited Liability Companies*, ¶ 101, 1–2 (2009, CCH Inc.) (covering this history).

73 Fleischer, *supra* note 3, at 259–61.

74 See Chancellor, *supra* note 14, 207–10.

75 Frank Partnoy, *The Match King: Ivar Kreuger, The Financial Genius Behind a Century of Wall Street Scandals*, 76–7 (2009, PublicAffairs).
76 Ibid. at 43. American Depository Receipts are described above. *Supra* note 6 and accompanying text.
77 Partnoy, *supra* note 75, at 52.
78 Ibid. at 42–3 (describing gold debentures), 81 (describing use of foreign exchange options), 108–9 (describing convertible debt debentures).
79 Chapter 4, "Fraud and rational risk-taking," "Sellers and market intermediaries considering behaviorally biased investors: the problem of materiality."
80 Cf. Jones, *supra* note 29, at 29, David Jones cites higher net interest costs associated with off-balance sheet financings (such as securitizations) as a constraint on using those transactions for regulatory capital arbitrage. He notes: "banks having high investment-grade credit ratings, securitizations often imply weighted average yields on the ABSs (inclusive of fees to third party credit enchanters [sic]) that exceed yields on the bank's directly-issued debt." Ibid. at n. 2.
81 E.g., Ch. 4, note 39 and accompanying text (providing example of covenant lite loans).
82 Fleischer, *supra* note 3, at 264–72 (discussing professional and ethical constraints on lawyers assisting clients in regulatory arbitrage).
83 Ibid. at 265–6.
84 For the literature on gatekeepers, see Chapter 4, notes 6, 7 and accompanying text.
85 Fleischer, *supra* note 3, at 266–7.
86 Chapter 4, note 49; Chapter 11, "Rating agency games."
87 Fleischer, *supra* note 3, at 267–8.
88 Ibid. at 269.
89 E.g., Larry E. Ribstein, The Death of Big Law, 2010 *Wisconsin Law Review* 749 (2010). But see Jordan Barry, On Regulatory Arbitrage, 89 *Texas Law Review* 69 (2011) (arguing that professional norms provide more of a check on regulatory arbitrage than Fleischer contends).
90 Chapter 4, "Rising information and agency costs."
91 Chapter 4, "Shifting norms," "Deteriorating legal legitimacy."
92 Chapter 4, "Booms and norms in the legal profession."
93 Fleischer, *supra* note 3, at 269–70.
94 For one example of a continuing bumper crop of books and scholarship lamenting the decline of professional norms in legal practice, see Anthony T. Kronman, *The Lost Lawyer: Failing Ideals of the Legal Profession* (1995, Belknap/Harvard University Press) (describing vanishing ideal of "lawyer-statesman").
95 Oliver Wendell Holmes, Jr., The Path of the Law, 10 *Harvard Law Review* 457 (1897).
96 *Supra* note 8.
97 See generally Jones, *supra* note 29, at 36–8.
98 Chapter 6, notes 52 (fear of Swedish financial regulators during 1980s boom), 111 (fear of Japanese regulators during 1980s boom) and accompanying text.
99 For a discussion of the impact of the elimination of currency exchange and capital market controls on investor protection and prudential regulation in European Union member countries in the 1980s, see Manning Gilbert Warren III, Global Harmonization of Securities Laws: The Achievements of the European Communities, 31 *Harvard International Law Journal* 185, 187–90 (1990).
100 Chapter 6, "Sweden" and "Japan." See also Chapter 2, "Japan's real estate bubble."
101 For a comprehensive analysis of the market for laws and jurisdictional competition, see Erin A. O'Hara and Larry E. Ribstein, *The Law Market* (2009, Oxford University Press).
102 See, e.g., Roberta Romano, *The Genius of American Corporate Law*, 1–51 (1993, American Enterprise Institute).

103 For an analysis, see O'Hara and Ribstein, *supra* note 101, at 162–71.
104 Chapter 3, "The special case of financial institution regulation."
105 See Adam Feibelman, Commercial Lending and the Separation of Banking and Commerce, 75 *University of Cincinnati Law Review* 943, 967 (2007) (equating concerns in banking law with the "safety and soundness" of banks with efforts to mitigate systemic risk). See also Erik F. Gerding, The Subprime Crisis and the Link between Consumer Financial Protection and Systemic Risk, 5 *Florida International University Law Review* 93, 100–1 (2009) (providing examples of bank safety and soundness regulations designed to mitigate system risk).
106 See Viral V. Acharya, Thomas F. Cooley, Matthew Richardson, and Ingo Walter, Capital, Contingent Capital, and Liquidity Requirements, in *Regulating Wall Street: The Dodd-Frank Act and the New Architecture of Global Finance*, 143, 145 (Viral V. Acharya, Thomas F. Cooley, Matthew P. Richardson, and Ingo Walter eds., 2011, John Wiley & Sons) (describing solvency and liquidity risks in financial markets).
107 Systemic risk arises from a broader market failure; this form of risk denotes potential losses that affect the entire market. It has been defined as "the risk of a breakdown in an entire system, as opposed to breakdowns in individual parts or components." George G. Kaufman and Kenneth E. Scott, What is Systemic Risk, and Do Bank Regulators Retard or Contribute to It? 7 *Independent Review* 371, 371 (2003); see also Steven L. Schwarcz, Systemic Risk, 97 *Georgetown Law Journal* 193 (2008).

Systemic risk thus cannot be mitigated through diversification. See Larry E. Ribstein, Fraud on a Noisy Market, 10 *Lewis and Clark Law Review* 137, 142 (2006) (discussing how arbitrageurs cannot diversify away systemic risk).

Systemic losses may begin with an external shock that disrupts entire financial markets, or with a chain reaction in which one financial institution fails, causing its creditors to fail as well. Kaufman and Scott, *supra* at 372–3. Systemic risk represents a prime concern of financial regulators, due to its enormous repercussions and the inability of any individual financial institution to mitigate this form of risk through diversification. See Schwarcz, *supra*, at 200–2. Professor Schwarcz argues that not only do financial institutions lack the capacity to deal with systemic risk individually (because of an inability to diversify away the risk), but that they also lack incentives due to collective action failure; no one firm can capture all of the benefit of an action it takes to reduce systemic risk. Ibid.
108 *Cf.* Fleischer, *supra* note 3, at 247–8.
109 Pistor and Xu, *supra* note 1.
110 See generally Acharya *et al.*, *supra* note 106, at 143–6.
111 For an analysis of when competition among bang regulators may result in a race to the bottom, see John A. Weinberg, Competition Among Bank Regulators, 88 *Federal Reserve Bank Richmond Economic Quarterly* 19 (Fall 2002).
112 *Supra* note 11 and accompanying text.
113 Ibid.
114 Kristin Forbes, Marcel Fratzscher, Thomas Kostka, and Roland Straub, Bubble Thy Neighbor: Direct and Spillover Effects of Capital Controls, IMF 12th Jacques Polak Annual Research Conference Paper (November 6, 2011) available at www.imf.org/external/np/res/seminars/2011/arc/pdf/forbes.pdf (last visited July 25, 2013).
115 Chapter 9, "Dangerous feedback: when the Regulatory Instability Hypothesis matters most."
116 Chapter 8, notes 22–30 and accompanying text.
117 Jones, *supra* note 29, at 49.
118 Ibid. at 36.
119 Fleischer, *supra* note 3, at 276.
120 For a nuanced and critical analysis of the interplay among financial innovation, regulation, and complexity, see Awrey, *supra* note 56.

121 Madura, *supra* note 37, at 492.
122 Ibid.
123 See Richard Herring and Til Schuermann, Capital Regulation for Position Risk in Banks, Securities Firms, and Insurance Companies, in *Capital Adequacy Beyond Basel: Banking, Securities, and Insurance*, 15, 19 (Hal S. Scott ed., 2005, Oxford University Press) (describing rationale for capital adequacy rules of reducing systemic risk); Stéphanie M. Stulz, *Bank Capital and Risk-taking: The Impact of Capital Regulation, Charter Value, and the Business Cycle*, 11 (2007, Springer) (describing literature on capital requirements mediating moral hazard of deposit insurance).
124 Acharya *et al.*, *supra* note 106, 146–7.
125 Jones, *supra* note 29.
126 Ibid. at 38–9.
127 See ibid. at 36, 38–9.
128 Jones, *supra* note 29, at 38–40.
129 Acharya *et al.*, *supra* note 106, at 157.
130 Franco Modigliani and Merton H. Miller, The Cost of Capital, Corporation Finance and the Theory of Investment, 48 *American Economic Review* 261 (1958).
131 For reasons that debt is a relatively cheaper source of financing, see Chapter 9. For a comprehensive analysis of when the assumptions of the Miller–Modigliani theorem do not hold, see Peter H. Huang and Michael S. Knoll, Corporate Finance, Corporate Law and Finance Theory, 74 *Southern California Law Review*. 175, 178 (2000) (presenting the "reverse" Miller–Modigliani theorem).
132 Tax Reform and the Tax Treatment of Debt and Equity, Joint Hearing Before the Senate Committee on Finance and House Committee on Ways and Means, 112th Congress (July 13, 2011) (statement of Victor Fleischer, Associate Professor, University of Colorado Law School) available at http://finance.senate.gov/imo/media/doc/Fleischer%20Testimony.pdf (last visited July 25, 2013). Professor Fleischer cites the use of hybrid instruments, such as trust preferred, as evidence that the asymmetrical tax treatment of debt and equity induces leverage. Ibid. These hybrid instruments are discussed below. See *infra* notes 150–2 and accompanying text.
133 See Acharya *et al.*, *supra* note 106, at 157; Allen N. Berger, Richard J. Herring, and Giorgio P. Szegö, The Role of Capital in Financial Institutions, 19 *Journal of Banking and Finance* 393 (1995). See also Robert C. Merton and Zvi Bodie, On the Management of Financial Guarantees, 21 *Financial Management* 87, 95–6 (1992) (discussing limitations of capital requirements as means that guarantor can govern the debtor).
134 See ibid. See also Viral Acharya and Matthew Richardson, Causes of the Financial Crisis, 21 *Critical Review* 195, 197–8 (2009).
135 Acharya *et al.*, *supra* note 106, at 157.
136 See Matthew Richardson, Large Banks and the Volcker Rule, in *Regulating Wall Street: The Dodd-Frank Act and the New Architecture of Global Finance*, 181, 184 (Viral V. Acharya, Thomas F. Cooley, Matthew P. Richardson, and Ingo Walter eds., 2011, John Wiley & Sons).
137 See Richard Herring and Til Schuermann, *supra* note 123, at 15, 19 (describing rationale for capital adequacy rules of reducing systemic risk); Stulz, *supra* note 123, at 11 (describing literature on capital requirements mediating moral hazard of deposit insurance).
138 Basel I and II are accords among bank regulators and central bankers from countries that belong to the Basel Committee on Banking Supervision (members come from the so-called "Group of Ten" countries: Belgium, Canada, France, Germany, Italy, Japan, Netherlands, Sweden, Switzerland, United Kingdom, and United States). Each accord consists of a series of recommended bank regulations and principles that national regulators should implement in their home countries. Each accord thus

attempts to set minimum international banking standards to mitigate both regulatory arbitrage by international banks and financial risks caused by bank failure that could spread from one economy to another. For capsule summaries of the Basel accords, see Robert Hugi, Jason H.P. Kravitt, and Carol A. Hitselberger, U.S. Adoption of Basel II and the Basel II Securitization Framework, 12 *North Carolina Banking Institute Journal* 45 (2008); Eric Y. Wu, Basel II: A Revised Framework, 24 *Annual Review of Banking and Financial Law* 150 (2005).

Although non-binding, national regulators exert pressure on one another to comply with the accord, giving it the quality of "soft law." See Michael S. Barr and Geoffrey P. Miller, Global Administrative Law: The View from Basel, 17 *European Journal of International Law* 15, 17 (2006) (reciting critiques of law-making by networks of bank regulators and international bureaucrats in the Basel Accord including that the process lacks accountability and legitimacy, but arguing that Basel II is subject to a subtle structure of international administrative law); Dieter Kerwer, Rules that Many Use: Standards and Global Regulation, 18 *Governance* 611 (2005).

139 Edward J. Kane, Technology and the Regulation of Financial Markets, in *Technology and the Regulation of Financial Markets: Securities, Futures and Banking*, 187 (Anthony Saunders and Lawrence J. White eds. 1986, Lexington Books).

140 For historical background on adoption of the original Basel Accord, see Joseph Jude Norton, Capital Adequacy Standards: A Legitimate Regulatory Concern for Prudential Supervision of Banking Activities? 49 *Ohio State Law Journal* 1299, 1336–42 (1989). See also Richard Scott Carnell, Jonathan R. Macey, and Geoffrey P. Miller, *Banking Law and Regulation*, 281–82 (3d ed. 2001, Aspen Publishers/Wolters Kluwer) (discussing history of U.S. risk based capital standards leading to Basel I).

141 Charles Goodhart, *The Basel Committee on Banking Supervision: A History of the Early Years 1974–1997*, 170, 180–1, 190–1 (2011, Cambridge University Press) (detailing history of adoption of Basel I).

142 Basel Committee on Banking Supervision, International Convergence of Capital Measurement and Capital Standards (July 1988, updated to April 1998) [hereinafter "Basel I"] available at www.bis.org/publ/bcbsc111.pdf?noframes=1 (last visited July 25, 2013).

143 Ibid. at Part III.

144 Ibid. at Part II (establishing risk weight system).

145 Raj Bhala, Applying Equilibrium Theory and the FICAS Model: A Case Study of Capital Adequacy and Currency Trading, 41 *St. Louis University Law Journal* 125, 159–62, 178, 183–7 (1997) (detailing arguments for superiority of banks' internal models to measure risk and set capital requirements compared to regulatory methods).

146 Basel Committee on Banking Supervision, International Convergence of Capital Measurement and Capital Standards: A Revised Framework (June 2006) [hereinafter "Basel II"] available at www.bis.org/publ/bcbs128.pdf (last visited July 25, 2013). Basel II allowed certain large banks to use proprietary risk models to set their capital requirements for not only credit risk (ibid. at 59–60), but market risk (ibid. at 191–203) and operational risk (ibid. at 147) as well.

147 See Joseph J. Norton, A Perceived Trend in Modern International Financial Regulation: Increasing Reliance on a Public-Private Partnership, 37 *International Law* 43, 53–8 (2003) (discussing mechanics and rationale for Basel II). See also Bhala, *supra* note 145 (providing arguments for use of internal models approach).

148 See Gerding, *supra* note 39, at 159, 180–2.

149 Basel Committee on Banking Supervision, Basel III: A Global Regulatory Framework for More Resilient Banks and Banking Systems (December 2010) available at www.bis.org/publ/bcbs189_dec2010.pdf (last visited July 25, 2013).

150 Some senior regulators recognized this potential and expressed concern as early as 1998. E.g., Financial Globalization and Efficient Banking Regulation, Remarks by

Federal Reserve Governor Laurence Meyer before the Annual Washington Conference of the Institute of International Bankers, Washington, D.C. (March 2, 1009) available at www.federalreserve.gov/boarddocs/speeches/1998/19980302.htm (last visited July 25, 2013).
151 Jones, *supra* note 29, at 36.
152 Madura, *supra* note 37, at 429.
153 Benton E. Gup, Capital Games, in *Capital Markets, Globalization, and Economic Development*, 17 (Benton E. Gup ed., 2005, Springer).
154 Ibid.
155 Ibid.
156 See Acharya *et al.*, *supra* note 106, at 161, 175.
157 Ibid. at 161. Trust preferred securities were in turn securitized to develop more liquid markets for these securities. Ibid.
158 Ibid. at 161, 176–7. The Dodd-Frank Act restricts their use for meeting regulatory capital purposes. Ibid. at 176–7.
159 Jones, *supra* note 29, at 36.
160 Ibid.
161 For a description of the mechanics and economic benefits of securitization, see Gerding, *supra* note 39, at 147–9; Anand K. Bhattacharya and Frank J. Fabozzi, Expanding Frontiers of Asset Securitization, in *Asset-backed Securities*, 1 (Anand K. Bhattacharya and Frank J. Fabozzi eds., 1996, Wiley); Leon T. Kendall, Securitization: A New Era in American Finance, in *A Primer on Securitization*, 1 (Leon T. Kendall and Michael J. Fishman eds., 1997, MIT Press); Steven P. Baum, The Securitization of Commercial Property Debt, in *A Primer on Securitization*, 45 (Leon T. Kendall and Michael J. Fishman eds., 1997, MIT Press); Joshua Coval, Jakub Jurek, and Erik Stafford, The Economics of Structured Finance, 23 *Journal of Economic Perspectives* 3 (2009).
162 Acharya and Richardson, *supra* note 134, at 201.
163 Fitch Ratings, Structured Finance: Asset-backed Criteria Report: Asset-backed Commercial Paper Explained (November 8, 2001) available at http://pages.stern.nyu.edu/~igiddy/ABS/fitchabcp.pdf (last visited October 1, 2010).
164 Ibid.
165 Viral V. Acharya, Philipp Schnabl, and Gustavo Suarez, Securitization Without Risk Transfer, National Bureau of Economic Research, *Working Paper No. 15730*, 2 (February 2010).
166 In addition, some conduits purchase a mix of different assets to diversify the portfolio. Fitch Ratings, *supra* note 163.
167 Gerding, *supra* note 39, at 148–9.
168 Jones, *supra* note 29, at 41–4.
169 Ibid. at 40–1.
170 Ibid.
171 Ibid. at 42–4.
172 See Acharya *et al.*, *supra* note 106, at 149.
173 Ibid. at 148.
174 Acharya and Richardson, *supra* note 134, at 204–5.
175 If the originator is deemed to have made a "true sale" of the assets to the SIV (special investment vehicle), the assets are no longer considered part of the estate of the originator in bankruptcy. The SIV is then the outright owner of the consumer mortgages, and the originator no longer has any impact on the risk being transferred from borrowers to the SIV and investors. For a discussion of "true sales" in securitizations, see Steven L. Schwarcz, Securitization Post-Enron, 25 *Cardozo Law Review* 1539, 1543–8 (2004).
176 Jones, *supra* note 29, at 44–5.
177 Ibid. at 45–6.

178 Ibid. See also Acharya *et al.*, *supra* note, at 165; Acharya *et al.*, *supra* note 106, at 148.

179 Viral V. Acharya and Phillip Schnabl, Do Global Banks Spread Global Imbalances? Asset-Backed Commercial Paper during the Financial Crisis of 2007–09, 58 *IMF Economic Review* 37, 89 (2010).

180 Acharya et al., *supra* note 165, at 12–13.

181 See Acharya *et al.*, *supra* note 106, at 148–9.

182 Acharya *et al.*, *supra* note 165.

183 See Acharya *et al.*, *supra* note 106, at 149.

184 Acharya and Schnabl, note 179, at 90–2.

185 Ibid.

186 Acharya *et al.*, *supra* note 165, at 31–4.

187 Jones, *supra* note 29, at 46. The assets backing these securitizations may be paid off ("drawdowns") by borrowers quickly, yet investors purchasing the asset-backed securities may prefer a much longer maturity on their securities. Banks sponsoring these securitizations covered any potential resulting mismatches between an investment vehicle's fluctuating assets and its issued securities by creating "master trusts." Under these trusts, the bank "designates" lines of credit for the investment vehicle. Ibid. at 46–7.

188 The sponsoring bank's credit exposure under these lines of credit was considered minimal. Thus, a bank's credit enhancement was considered to constitute not credit risk (which would require regulatory capital under Basel) but operational risk (which would not require regulatory capital). Ibid.

189 Gary B. Gorton and Nicholas S. Souleles, Special Purpose Vehicles and Securitization, in *The Risks of Financial Institutions*, 549, 551–2 (Mark Carey and René M. Stulz eds. 2007, National Bureau of Economic Research/University of Chicago Press). Gorton and Souleles provide a model for implicit recourse. Ibid. at 575–8. The model explains how "[t]he sponsoring bank and the investors in the SPV collude in adopting a contractual mechanism that cannot be written down because of accounting and regulatory rules." Ibid. at 576.

190 Ibid. As financial institutions judged that the probability of this non-contractual liability was low, they decided that they did not need to treat these moral recourse obligations as a balance sheet liability. Stephen G. Ryan, Accounting in and for the Subprime Crisis, 83 *Accounting Review* 1605, 1632 (2008).

191 Gorton and Souleles, *supra* note 189, at 565 (surveying others studies finding moral recourse), 580–7 (testing for and finding evidence of marketplace assumption of moral recourse by securitization sponsors).

192 See generally Gorton and Souleles, *supra* note 189 (discussing how regulators recognized the problem of moral recourse, but providing tests that show sponsors of securitizations nonetheless appear to have provided non-contractual guarantees).

193 Ibid. at 149–50.

194 Jones, *supra* note 29, at 48. See also Robert P. Bartlett, III, Making Banks Transparent, 65 *Vanderbilt Law Review* 293 (2012).

195 See Gerding, *supra* note 39, at 159 citing Stephen Labaton, Agency's '04 Rule Let Banks Pile Up New Debt, and Risk, *New York Times*, October 3, 2008, at A1.

196 See Gerding, *supra* note 39, at 154–9.

197 Ibid. at 139–43, 147–64.

198 Acharya and Schnabl, *supra* note 179, at 85.

199 Edward I. Altman, T. Sabri Öncü, Matthew Richardson, Anjolein Schmeits, and Lawrence J. White, Regulation of Rating Agencies, in *Regulating Wall Street: The Dodd-Frank Act and the New Architecture of Global Finance*, 443, 448–53 (Viral V. Acharya, Thomas F. Cooley, Matthew P. Richardson, and Ingo Walter eds., 2011, John Wiley & Sons) (describing conflict of interest when issuer of securities pays rating agencies for rating).

Law Professor Frank Partnoy has been a longtime critic of rating agency regulations. Professor Partnoy has long argued that regulation is part of the problem. See, e.g., Frank Partnoy, The Siskel and Ebert of Financial Markets? Two Thumbs Down for the Credit Rating Agencies, 77 *Washington University Law Quarterly* 619, 681 (1999). Instead of creating incentives for better monitoring, regulators have undermined those incentives by granting rating agencies a kind of oligopoly power. See ibid. at 698.

This power stems from the fact that the securitization market, including the market for mortgage-backed securities, focuses largely on institutional investors. Kendall, *supra* note 161, at 15.

Many of these institutional investors are restricted by regulation to purchasing only securities with an investment-grade credit rating. E.g., James Hedges, Hedge Fund Transparency, in *Hedge Funds: Strategies, Risk Assessment, and Returns*, 320, 321 (Greg N. Gregoriou, Vassilios N. Karavas, Fabrice Rouah eds., 2003, Beard Books) (discussing regulations that discourage mutual funds from investing in debt below investment grade). For example, regulations restrict much of the securities investments of many pension funds, and regulated financial institutions, including banks and insurance companies, to investment-grade debt. See, e.g., General Accounting Office, Community and Economic Development Loans: Securitization Faces Significant Barriers, Report to Congressional Requestors 04-21 (October 2003) available at http://www.gao.gov/products/GAO-04-21 (last visited July 25, 2013) (discussing requirements on pension funds); 12 U.S.C. § 1831e(d)(4)(A) (2009) (provision of Federal Deposit Insurance Act permitting insured savings banks to invest in investment-grade debt, i.e., debt securities "rated in one of the 4 highest rating categories by at least one nationally recognized statistical rating organization"); Partnoy, *supra* at 700–1 (outlining use by state regulators of rating agencies' ratings in insurance regulations).

These "investment-grade" restrictions are designed to ensure the safety of an entity's assets, and, in the case of a bank or other regulated financial institution, to mitigate systemic risk. Cf. Viral V. Acharya, A Theory of Systemic Risk and Design of Prudential Bank Regulation, Unpublished manuscript (January 9, 2001) (analyzing whether prudential bank regulations, including limitations on investments, mitigates systemic risk) available at http://papers.ssrn.com/sol3/papers.cfm?abstract_id= 236401 (last visited July 25, 2013).

These investment-grade regulations, in turn, provide that only rating agencies that have a special license from the SEC as "Nationally Recognized Statistical Rating Organizations" (NRSROs) can give an investment-grade rating. Partnoy, *supra* at 623.

The handful of NRSROs, and the models they use to rate securities, thus possess great responsibility for regulating the riskiness of investments made by a large number of financial institutions. Professor Partnoy contends that rating agencies rent out the regulatory license they enjoy by virtue of this web of regulations. Partnoy, *supra*.

200 Gretchen Morgenson and Louise Story, Rating Agency Data Aided Wall Street in Deals, *New York Times*, April 23, 2010, at A1.
201 See generally, Gerding, *supra* note 39.
202 Melanie L. Fein, *Securities Activities of Banks*, § 13.04 (3rd ed. 2010 Suppl., Aspen Publishers).
203 See Chapter 11, "Regulatory capital arbitrage revisited."
204 See Acharya *et al.*, *supra* note 106, at 149.
205 Ibid.
206 Ibid. at 150 citing International Monetary Fund, *Global Financial Stability Report: Containing Systemic Risks and Restoring Financial Soundness*, 31 (April 2008) available at www.imf.org/external/pubs/ft/gfsr/2008/01/pdf/text.pdf (last visited July 25, 2013).

207 See Hyun Song Shin, Securitisation and Financial Stability, 119 *Economic Journal* 309 (2009).
208 Acharya and Richardson, *supra* note 134, at 196–7 (2009).
209 Jones, *supra* note 29, at 49.
210 Ibid.
211 See Acharya *et al.*, *supra* note 106, at 147.
212 Jones, *supra* note 29, at 37.
213 See Acharya *et al.*, *supra* note 106, at 157. See also Acharya and Richardson, *supra* note 134, at 197–8.
214 For a provocative application of complex adaptive systems to financial institution regulation, see Lawrence G. Baxter, Internationalization of Law: The "Complex" Case of Bank Regulation, in *The Internationalisation of Law: Legislating, Decision-making, Practice and Education*, 3 (Mary E. Hiscock and William Van Caenegem eds. 2010, Edward Elgar).
215 Complex adaptive systems are systems in which multiple independent agents interact with one another. The capacity of the agents to adapt to changes in the system causes the system to evolve into progressively more complex forms and to change in a non-linear manner. Simon A. Levin, Complex Adaptive Systems: Exploring the Known, Unknown and the Unknowable, 40 *Bulletin of the American Mathematical Society* 3, 4 (2002) (defining complex adaptive systems).
216 Ibid.
217 See, e.g., Cars H. Hommes, Financial Markets as Nonlinear Adaptive Evolutionary Systems, 1 *Quantitative Finance* 149 (2001).
218 Risk models or regulations that rely on linear causality falter when applied to complex adaptive systems. Professor J.B. Ruhl has written extensively on the failures of law to manage nonlinear causality. See J.B. Ruhl, Thinking of Environmental Law as a Complex Adaptive System: How to Clean Up the Environment by Making a Mess of Environmental Law, 34 *Houston Law Review* 933, 979 (1997) (criticizing environmental statutes for this flaw).
219 John Foster, From Simplistic to Complex Systems in Economics, 29 *Cambridge Journal of Economics* 873 (2005). Many complex adaptive systems may tend towards disequilibrium because of the concept of emergence (described *supra* note 215). Ruhl, *supra* note 218, at 990–1.
220 See generally Alejandro Reveiz Herault and Sebastian Rojas, The Case for Active Management from the Perspective of Complexity Theory, 495 *Borradores de Economía* 11 (2008) available at www.banrep.gov.co/docum/ftp/borra495.pdf (last visited July 25, 2013). Cf. Carlo C. Jaeger, Ortwin Renn, Eugene A. Rosa, and Thomas Webler, *Risk, Uncertainty and Rational Action* (2001, Earthscan Publications). Legal scholars have analyzed how individuals severely underestimate risk when confronted with complex adaptive systems. E.g., Lawrence A. Cunningham, Too Big to Fail: Moral Hazard in Auditing and the Need to Restructure the Industry Before it Unravels, 106 *Columbia Law Review* 1698, 1724–6 (2006) (discussing accounting firms' underestimation of their legal exposure); see also Lawrence A. Cunningham, From Random Walks to Chaotic Crashes, 62 *George Washington Law Review* 546 (1994).
221 J.B. Ruhl, Complexity Theory as a Paradigm for the Dynamical Law-And-Society System: A Wake-Up Call for Legal Reductionism and the Modern Administrative State, 45 *Duke Law Journal* 849, 877–8 (1996) (internal quotations omitted).
222 See ibid.

6 Deregulation and regulatory arbitrage spirals

A dance for two

Thus far, this book has looked at the first three elements of the Financial Instability Hypothesis – the regulatory stimulus cycle (in Chapter 3), deteriorating legal compliance (or "compliance rot" in Chapter 4), and regulatory arbitrage frenzies (in Chapter 5) – in isolation. Of course, in real financial markets and real financial history, these phenomena do not operate independently of one another. On the contrary, regulatory stimulus – particularly deregulation – and regulatory arbitrage occur simultaneously or in sequence. Moreover, deregulation and regulatory arbitrage can reinforce and generate powerful feedback for one another. This feedback gains strength during bubble times.

This chapter explores the spirals that form between deregulation and regulatory arbitrage that exacerbate asset price bubbles. Since feedback mechanisms make untangling cause and effect difficult, this chapter studies one particular context or phenomenon. It isolates cases in which two (or more) different categories of financial institutions operate in the same jurisdiction. Deregulation allows firms in one category to compete in the same market as another category and to provide economically equivalent financial services to customers. In these cases, the chapter examines how regulatory arbitrage can trigger deregulation and vice versa.

On the one hand, regulatory arbitrage may spark deregulation. For example, financial institutions in a more heavily regulated category may push legislatures or regulatory agencies to deregulate them if less regulated competitors begin to "steal" lending or investment business or appear to raise capital more cheaply. Less regulated competitors may be able to earn additional profits from a heating asset market, while regulation prevents a more regulated class of institution from investing in that same market. Alternatively, regulation may impose restrictions on the ability of one class of institutions to offer favorable market terms to depositors or other investors. Another class may not face similar regulatory restrictions and can attract additional capital if market conditions shift. Even the perceived loss of competitive position gives regulated firms rhetorical ammunition to use in a political fight over deregulation.[1]

On the other hand, deregulation may fuel regulatory arbitrage. Deregulation may allow one class of institution to enter a new market and compete with another class to provide the same financial services or make the same investments.

However, deregulation may not remove all the regulatory differences between the two classes. For example, the deregulated class may enjoy fewer legal restrictions on its ability to raise capital. Or deregulation may not remove government subsidies (including explicit or implicit guarantees) of the deregulated class. Fewer regulatory restrictions (i.e., a lower regulatory tax) or a regulatory subsidy can have the same effect; they may give institutions in the deregulated class a lower cost of capital than, or other competitive advantage over, their counterparts. This allows the deregulated firms to steal business and ultimately capital from their competitors. The shift of capital to exploit regulatory differences represents "investment switching" – one of the two forms of regulatory arbitrage described in the preceding chapter.

This chapter unpacks the interactions of deregulation and regulatory arbitrage by creating a model of how two classes of regulated financial institutions interact in the financial services and political marketplaces. These two classes become locked in an elaborate "dance-for-two" (or *pas de deux*, if you are a Francophile) as they compete for business and look to influence policymakers.

The chapter then evaluates how this "dance-for-two" model explains the histories of the Swedish and Japanese real estate bubbles in the 1980s. In both episodes, two or more classes of regulated lending institutions within the given country – banks and finance companies in Sweden and securities firms, banks, and *jusen* companies in Japan – co-existed with one another until an external shock upset the market and political equilibrium. The dynamics in these two nations may have differed in whether the shock triggered deregulation or regulatory arbitrage first. In both cases, however, deregulation and regulatory arbitrage started to fuel one another in a spiral of competition and financial liberalization. In Sweden, the pattern looked more like:

Shock → regulatory arbitrage → deregulation → regulatory arbitrage …

In Japan, the spiral appears to have been:

Shock → deregulation → regulatory arbitrage → deregulation …

As previous chapters have noted, the regulatory history in Japan is complex. External shocks in the 1970s and 1980s triggered cascading competitive and regulatory effects in a highly segmented financial services sector.[2]

In the model – and in the case of Sweden and Japan – the spiral of deregulation and regulatory arbitrage contributed to a lending and investment boom. This, in turn, fueled an asset price bubble. The chapter and the dance-for-two model unpack several dynamics that destabilize the regulatory architecture in a country:

1   *Destabilizing deregulation.* When financial institutions in a more highly regulated category successfully push for deregulation to compete in a new market with a second category, they often retain explicit or implicit

government subsidies. These residual subsidies, if not counteracted by prudential regulation, create regulatory and market distortions beyond simple
moral hazard, including the following:

a   *subsidy transfer and leakage*: financial conglomerates seek to transfer
    and exploit the subsidies afforded to certain affiliates to underwrite
    additional risk-taking by less regulated affiliates;
b   *market distortion and displacement*: when a more heavily regulated cat-
    egory of financial institutions is deregulated but not de-subsidized, the
    continuing subsidies may afford it a lower cost of capital. Alternatively,
    the deregulated class may face fewer restrictions on its ability to raise
    capital. In either case, regulation affords the deregulated class with a
    significant advantage over competitors. In ordinary times, this distor-
    tion might drive competitors out of the market. During bubble times,
    however, it can displace competitors into riskier market segments.
    These riskier market pockets survive as long as the bubble and the mis-
    pricing of risk continues. Indeed, the displacement can contribute to the
    severity of mispricing in a bubble.

2   *Destabilizing regulatory arbitrage.* Less regulated financial institutions may
    start out in the margins of the financial services sectors. As the boom con-
    tinues, the total lending by these marginal institutions may mushroom. The
    displacement effects described above may cause these institutions to move
    into riskier lending segments. However, these institutions still fit into the
    crevices of financial regulatory architecture; regulators may not perceive the
    additional risk that this category poses for financial markets.

This risk materializes when the bubble bursts. The failure of the less regulated
category of financial institutions can drag down subsidized financial institutions
(particularly those enjoying explicit or implicit government guarantees). The risk
of contagion stems from the less visible ways that the subsidized firms have
invested in their marginal counterparts (both through loans or equity investments). Often, subsidized firms have structured these investments to work
around regulatory restrictions that would have prevented them from investing in
riskier market segments directly.

After describing the dance-for-two model and the Swedish and Japanese
examples, the chapter briefly considers whether the model might explain deregulation and regulatory arbitrage in other historical bubbles. It looks at the relationship in the United States during the subprime mortgage bubble between Freddie
Mac and Fannie Mae, on the one hand, and "private label" securitizations, on the
other. The chapter concludes by discussing broader implications of the dance-
for-two model, including spirals of *cross-border* regulatory arbitrage and
deregulation.

The model

Many countries regulate financial institutions by placing them into distinct regulatory categories or segments. However, when a shock causes financial institutions that face different regulatory treatment or different levels of government subsidies to compete in the same market, a spiral of destabilizing deregulation and regulatory arbitrage can begin. The following model explains how. It provides a template for understanding:

- the ways in which two regulatory classes of institutions interact to generate regulatory arbitrage and deregulation;
- how regulatory arbitrage and deregulation can reinforce one another;
- how regulatory arbitrage and deregulation can destabilize the architecture of financial regulation; and
- how these two dynamics can also increase lending and risk-taking by financial institutions, and fuel the growth of an asset price bubble.

The model has six elements:

1   *Financial regulation creates two (or more) categories of institutions* that initially provide similar, but not functionally equivalent financial services. Regulation treats these two institutions differently:

    a   One class of institution faces greater restrictions on its lending or investment activities. These restrictions may limit their ability to enter the market of the second class. However, this class often enjoys an explicit or implicit guarantee from the government or other regulatory subsidies that the second class does not.

    b   A second class is more loosely regulated and can take on more risk by making certain kinds of loans or investments. Again, regulations prevent the more regulated from making these same risky investments (at least directly).

These two categories co-exist until the competitive equilibria in the financial services and political marketplaces are upset by...

2   *An exogenous shock* disturbs the competitive and political equilibria. The shock may be an external political or economic event.

3   *The shock starts a spiral of regulatory arbitrage and deregulation.* The shock might first cause financial institutions in one regulatory category to push policymakers to deregulate them. When deregulation occurs, it allows the firms in the deregulated category to compete directly with the second class. However, the playing field is not even. The deregulated class retains certain government subsidies that the second class does not. Alternatively, the second class continues to endure certain additional regulatory restrictions (for example, restrictions on potential sources of capital) not imposed on the deregulated class. This regulatory imbalance allows the deregulated firms to win profits and market share from the other class of financial

institutions. Deregulation thus begets regulatory arbitrage. Institutions in the category on the losing end may then push policymakers to deregulate them as well.

Alternatively, the shock might steer borrowers or investors to a less regulated category of financial institutions. The more regulated financial institutions then lobby policymakers for deregulation. This, in turn, gives these firms a competitive advantage if they enjoy regulatory preferences (whether by retaining government subsidies or avoiding the regulatory taxes imposed on the second class). In this case, regulatory arbitrage begets deregulation, which begets regulatory arbitrage.

4   *Both deregulation and regulatory arbitrage destabilize the architecture of financial regulation.* As summarized above, this instability results from several different dynamics. These include *destabilizing deregulation* which results from a deregulated class of institution retaining a government subsidy, which prudential regulation fails to negate or counteract. This results not only in moral hazard, but the potential for both *subsidy transfer and leakage* and *market distortion and displacement* as well. These dynamics are described in detail below.

Destabilizing regulatory arbitrage also subverts financial regulation. Regulators fail to understand the growing systemic risk posed by the less regulated class moving into riskier lending and investment sectors. This risk can spread to the more regulated, government-guaranteed financial institutions because those firms have invested in the less regulated class. The firms make these *investment linkages* to work around regulatory restrictions on their direct participations in riskier loan and investment markets.

5   *Deregulation and regulatory arbitrage spurs additional lending, which fuels an asset market boom.* The additional lending also increases overall leverage in the financial system. This makes individual financial institutions and entire financial markets more vulnerable to economic downturns and increased losses. The risks of this financial fragility materialize when…

6   *Asset prices collapse and contagion spreads.* Contagion from the insolvency of the less regulated financial institutions spreads to government-guaranteed institutions via the investment linkages.

Each of the six elements of the dance-for-two model is described in further detail below.

Two categories of financial institutions

The model assumes a regulatory regime that has (at least) two categories of financial institutions that initially provide similar but distinct economic services to investors and borrowers.

The first category of institution is more tightly regulated. These institutions face restrictions on their business activities, including on the types of loans or other investments they can make. These restrictions might take various forms,

including: regulations that limit financial institutions to particular lines of business to shield them from excessive losses;[3] restrictions on the types of investments that financial institutions may make (e.g., restrictions on investments in
real estate[4] and riskier classes of securities, such as equity);[5] prudential restrictions on the number of loans to certain types of borrowers;[6] and caps on interest
rates that banks may charge their borrowers[7] or offer to their depositors.[8] These
regulations can serve to segment the financial services marketplace and prevent
this category of institution from competing with other regulatory classes.

In return for being subject to these regulatory restrictions, this first class of
institution often enjoys certain regulatory subsidies. This subsidy may take the
form of a government guarantee that may be explicit (for example, deposit insurance)[9] or implicit (for example, a widely held perception in the marketplace that
a government would back the debts of this type of institution should it become
insolvent). One variant on this implicit guarantee is the "too-big-to-fail" (or
"too-interconnected-to-fail") financial institution. This particular guarantee stems
from the fact that many investors believe that the government would have to
assume the obligations of large, "systemically significant" financial institutions –
even absent an explicit guarantee – because the insolvency of those institutions
would threaten to unleash severe and cascading losses in financial markets.[10]
Regulatory subsidies may take still other forms, including tax breaks or exemptions from other financial laws, such as certain securities regulations.

Institutions in the second regulatory category do not enjoy these subsidies (or
at least not to the same extent as the first category), but are also not subject to the
same restrictions on lending, investment, or business operations. This regulatory
distinction allows firms in this second category to operate in a second, adjacent,
market space to the first class.

The tradeoff in this dual regulatory scheme has a certain economic logic. If
the government grants a regulatory subsidy – particularly a guarantee – to a class
of institution, it wants to limit the institution's risk-taking to mitigate moral
hazard.[11] This division may also offer creditors of (including depositors), and
investors in, financial institutions a choice between lower risk (the first class)
and higher reward (the second class). The restrictions on the first class of institution not only limit excessive risk-taking, but also prevent that class of institution
from using its regulatory subsidy to gain a competitive advantage over the
second class (a topic discussed in more detail below). This crafted regulatory
balance allows financial institutions in different segments to co-exist.[12]

An exogenous shock

The competitive equilibrium between the two categories of financial institutions
endures until an exogenous shock shatters it. This shock (as with the shocks
described in Chapter 3 that trigger regulatory stimulus) may take the form of significant changes in the macroeconomic environment, such as inflation or interest
rate spikes. In other cases, political changes or a mix of political and economic
changes (such as rising government debt) may upset the existing equilibrium.

Spirals of deregulation and regulatory arbitrage

This exogenous shock may spark either deregulation or regulatory arbitrage. In either case, deregulation creates conditions ideal for regulatory arbitrage. Or regulatory arbitrage sparks deregulation. These feedback mechanisms between these two phenomena are described below.

Deregulation → regulatory arbitrage → deregulation

This shock might first cause financial institutions in one regulatory category to push policymakers to deregulate them to let them compete with other classes of financial institutions.

Chapter 3 outlined how an exogenous shock can give interest groups the incentives and resources to overcome collective action problems and political opposition to push for regulatory stimulus. In this Chapter 6 model, the exogenous shock serves the same function and yields the same result. The shock alters the incentives (or resources) of firms in this regulatory class such that they have a greater ability to overcome collective action problems and influence policymakers than firms in other regulatory categories. An economic shock might exert stress on the existing business model of a regulated class of institution. For example, those banks that are subject to caps on the interest rates they can offer depositors may lose business in an environment of rapidly rising inflation or market interest rates.[13] Alternatively, a displacement may cause prices and profits in a particular asset market to skyrocket. One category of institution might enjoy these profits if only policymakers would lift restrictions on them investing in that asset class.

Policymakers may also find that deregulation serves a larger policy goal beyond placating or preserving the status of a particular interest group of financial institutions. Policymakers may seek to expand investment in particular asset markets or increase the access of particular borrowers to credit. They may be lobbied by groups pursuing broader social objectives, such as increasing the availability of credit to consumers and businesses. Policymakers might also seek to make subsidized entities less dependent on government subsidies. Alternatively, they may face external pressure from other countries to liberalize their financial sector and open it to foreign competitors. In other words, the exogenous shock may take the form of a political or ideological change and not just economic factors. (Chapter 3 examines rational/public choice, behavioral, and ideological/norm based explanations for deregulation and other regulatory stimulus during bubble periods).

When it occurs, deregulation removes many restrictions on ability of a regulated class of institution to either raise or invest capital. Deregulation may enable institutions in a particular regulatory class to compete directly with firms in another category for the first time. In this case, deregulation enables one category of financial institutions to offer functionally equivalent financial services (such as intermediating for corporate customers seeking financing) to those of firms in a second category.

However, deregulation leaves the playing field un-level. As explained below, the newly deregulated class may enjoy explicit or implicit government subsidies that the second class does not. Or the second class may face regulatory restrictions that the first class does not. For example, regulations may prohibit firms in the second class from financing themselves through offering customers deposit accounts. This distortion (described in more detail in the next element of the dance-for-two model) allows the newly deregulated class of firms to win profits and market share from other classes of financial institutions that provide functionally equivalent services. The newly unshackled firms may offer more competitive terms when bidding to make loans or investments. Investment success may help these firms on the other side of the balance sheet, as well, by attracting additional capital. The removal of regulations may also liberalize the ability of these firms to attract debt and equity financing (for example, by removing caps on interest rates on deposit accounts). The flow of business and capital to institutions in this deregulated category because of regulatory change represents a classic case of "investment switching," as defined in the previous chapter. Deregulation thus begets regulatory arbitrage.

Regulatory arbitrage may in turn beget further deregulation. Institutions that have lost business or capital to the deregulated category may then push policymakers to deregulate them as well. They may argue for the need to compete on a level playing field with the deregulated class. Another political strategy is for institutions in a regulatory category that "lost" in the initial round of liberalization to seek deregulation to compete "down market." That is, they may seek regulatory changes to allow them to enter into a market space occupied by a third category of financial institutions. This third category may comprise more diffuse firms who wield even less political or market power. The down-market strategy allows the second class to avoid political conflict with the already deregulated class of institutions, which demonstrated enough clout to push through the initial round of deregulation.

Regulatory arbitrage → deregulation → regulatory arbitrage

Alternatively, the shock may trigger regulatory arbitrage and not deregulation first. In this case, regulatory arbitrage starts the spiral wheel spinning. The shock might alter economic conditions and push parties seeking to invest capital (such as depositors) or raise capital (such as borrowers) to a less regulated category of financial institution. For example, inflation or a spike in market interest rates may allow one class of institution to offer investment opportunities with better rates of return than another class. To repeat an earlier example: regulations may cap the rates that banks can offer depositors. The shock may drive investors to alternative financial institutions not subject to these caps.

Alternatively, regulation may restrict a certain class of institution from investing in, or lending to, a particular asset market. The shock may increase the demand for financing and the returns to investing in this market. This allows the financial institutions that can lend or invest in this asset market without regulatory encumbrance to enjoy higher profits.

The more regulated financial institutions may then lobby policymakers for deregulation. Deregulation, in turn (as described above), may give these firms a competitive advantage. Policymakers may be motivated to liberalize the financial sector to minimize regulatory arbitrage caused by dual classes of entities and stanch the subversion of financial laws. In this case, regulatory arbitrage begets deregulation, which begets regulatory arbitrage.

Regulatory architecture destabilized: subsidy games

Both deregulation and regulatory arbitrage subvert the architecture of financial regulation. Under the old regime of segmented financial institutions, regulators understand the business models of, and systemic risks posed by, different classes of institutions. Institutions in certain classes might receive regulatory subsidies, particularly government guarantees, to mitigate these systemic risks. Deposit insurance to mitigate the risk of bank runs serves as one canonical example of such a subsidy.[14] Regulators, under the old regime, then work to counteract or negate this subsidy to address moral hazard and any competitive distortions. For example, governments charge deposit insurance premia and impose prudential regulations on insured entities.[15] Meanwhile, other categories of financial institutions might not need subsidies or regulation because the type or volume of their business do not raise systemic concerns.

Deregulation upsets this ecosystem when it occurs without de-subsidization. In other words, policymakers relax prudential regulations without removing the government subsidy or taking other steps to counter it. This can occur because it is difficult to quantify the benefits of a government guarantee or other subsidy. It may also prove difficult to measure the extent to which regulation counteracts the subsidy.[16] Implicit government guarantees magnify this measurement problem.[17]

Of course, the management and owners of institutions pushing for deregulation have every incentive to keep and expand a government subsidy. A government guarantee allows that firm to lower its cost of capital and externalize part of its risk-taking onto taxpayers. Thus, as deregulation proceeds, the deregulated class has an incentive to minimize the appearance of a net subsidy. The difficulty of quantifying a net subsidy creates "plausible deniability" for both deregulated financial firms and policymakers. This explains part of how deregulation succeeds politically. "Government guarantee? What government guarantee?"[18]

After deregulation, policymakers often place the responsibility for counteracting subsidies on untested or more obscure rules. In the case of financial conglomerates, these rules may include complex firewalls that limit transactions between government-insured and non-insured affiliates. The deregulated entities have strong incentives to push for a gradual relaxation of these rules.[19]

Subsidy transfers and leakage. When deregulation results in a class of financial institutions enjoying a higher net subsidy – particularly a guarantee – they have incentives to exploit it. This goes beyond simple moral hazard. These firms also look to engage in *subsidy transfers* and *subsidy leakage.* These terms describe how financial conglomerates seek to transfer the subsidy from a regulated affiliate to less regulated ones. The government subsidy of a deregulated firm's core activities – such as bank lending financed by government-insured deposits – begins to leak to the new investment activities of the institution.[20] This leakage or transfer may be *intra-firm* – if a conglomerate uses funds from a subsidized affiliate to fund investment operations of a less regulated affiliate.[21] The transfer may also be *inter-firm*; this occurs when the institution uses subsidized funds to invest in an apparently unaffiliated entity (such as by investing in financial institution in the second, less regulated class). In either case, the transfer shifts the risk of newly permitted investments onto taxpayers. It extends the umbrella of government guarantees and other subsidies to cover new business operations.[22]

Market distortions and displacement. Financial institutions can use residual government subsidies to compete aggressively with unsubsidized firms.[23] Again, deregulation may remove restrictions on a more regulated category of institutions competing in the same markets (whether when raising capital or investing it) as unsubsidized categories. The residual government subsidy affords the first class a lower cost of capital.[24] For example, deposit insurance or an implicit government guarantee allows the first class of institution to raise capital more cheaply. If deregulation allows the first class to form a new business unit to compete with the second class in a new market, this lower cost of capital may enable institutions in the first class to cross-subsidize that business unit.[25] This competitive advantage enjoyed by the first class of institution enables those institutions to gain market share.

The flip side of one category enjoying a government subsidy is the other category of institution continuing to face a unique regulatory restriction or "tax." For example, deregulation may allow one class to compete with a second class for the first time. However, regulation may leave the playing field uneven, by restricting the ways that second class may raise money. As demonstrated in the examples below, a second class faces difficulty competing if they cannot offer deposit accounts, but their new competitors can.

Whether regulation distorts the playing field by residual subsidies or hidden taxes, the distortionary effect on financial institution competition may be the same. Competition from subsidized/less-taxed firms may push unsubsidized class of institution into riskier market segments to seek profits and maintain business. For example, the second class of institution newly forced to compete in a loan market with the first class may lower underwriting standards and extend loans to less creditworthy borrowers. In ordinary market times, this increased risk might drive those unsubsidized/taxed firms out of business. However, during asset price bubbles, when markets misprice risk, these firms may survive or even thrive in riskier market segments.

When unsubsidized, less regulated firms succeed in riskier, but booming markets, they may attract capital from investors. In particular, they may attract investments from their subsidized competitors from another regulatory class. Those subsidized competitors may seek to participate in riskier market segments that regulation restricts them from investing in directly. By investing in a less regulated class of financial institution, these regulated firms form "investment linkages." These dynamics represent regulatory arbitrage in both of the forms described in previous chapters. Investors engage in *investment switching*, as they move capital to less regulated firms. Regulated financial institutions employ *investment structuring*; their equity and debt investments in less regulated competitors allow them to make investments in markets that regulation would otherwise preclude.

This regulatory arbitrage can destabilize regulatory architecture in a number of ways. First, these less regulated firms may have existed on the periphery of financial regulation. They pose little systemic danger so long as their share of loan or investment markets remains small. However, when the volume of their lending or investment mushrooms, regulation may not keep pace. Regulators may fail to track, and adjust to, the consequent increase in the systemic risk that this class of institutions poses. Second, these investments by subsidized entities may exploit government subsidies and represent risk-taking on the taxpayer dime. Third, investment linkages (those investments by subsidized entities in less regulated counterparties) provide transmission lines for contagion. Should the less regulated entities suffer losses in a financial downturn, they may drag their regulated investors down with them.

Increased lending fuels market boom

Deregulation or regulatory arbitrage may increase the total volume of financial institution lending by lowering the regulatory constraints (or the effective regulatory "tax rate") on lending. Residual government subsidies – including a moral hazard-creating government guarantee – also translate into increased lending. Deregulation or regulatory arbitrage may also allow financial institutions to increase their leverage. The previous chapter noted how government guarantees create incentives for financial institutions to increase leverage.[26] As Chapter 9 explains, increases in the volume of credit or financial institution leverage can increase asset prices and contribute to an asset price bubble.

Higher asset prices may in turn generate various feedback loops. For example, higher prices may encourage further risky lending, mask inadequate underwriting standards, and lull regulators, creditors, and investors into a false sense of security.[27] Chapter 9 discusses the ways in which looser credit – and looser credit regulations – can fuel a bubble and generate feedback loops.

Asset prices collapse and financial crisis

In the final stage of the model, asset prices collapse. This threatens the solvency of financial institutions starting with the institutions with higher exposure to the particular collapsing asset markets. Those unsubsidized, less regulated classes of financial institutions that entered riskier market segments (for example, by lending to less credit-worthy borrowers) may be the first to fail. Their failure may, in turn, threaten the more regulated financial institutions that loaned to or invested in them. Investment linkages between regulated categories spread the contagion of financial crises. A deep enough crash may trigger the government guarantees of these more regulated institutions.

Sweden

The preceding model provides a good template for understanding how regulatory arbitrage and deregulation of financial institutions in Sweden in the 1980s led to the severe 1990 real estate crisis in that country.[28] The Swedish real estate bubble was exacerbated by interaction of two regulatory classes of financial institutions: banks and finance companies. The changing regulatory treatment of these two types of institutions created feedback loops between the financial and political marketplaces; deregulation, riskier lending practices, and booming asset prices reinforced one another.

Two categories of financial institutions. In the 1970s, Sweden had a highly regulated banking sector that was subject to a series of legal restrictions designed to maintain stable and low interest rates and to direct credit towards favored economic sectors such as housing and public finance.[29] These regulations included various measures that restricted the volume of a bank's lending, including high reserve requirements, placement requirements, and liquidity ratios.[30] Working in concert, placement requirements and liquidity ratios required that a certain percentage of bank's lending portfolio consist of government and housing bonds.[31] The Swedish central bank also controlled the volume of bank credit by using regulation, moral suasion, and access to central bank loans to impose quantitative restrictions on lending by each bank.[32] Swedish banks were also subject to ceilings on the average interest rates they could charge on their loans.[33] Although Sweden removed legal caps on the interest rates that banks could offer depositors in the 1970s, a few large banks continued to dominate the industry, and the absence of competition[34] kept deposit rates low.[35] Together, Swedish bank regulations ensured that Swedish banks enjoyed steady, but low profits[36] and minimal risk.[37] Sweden had no explicit deposit insurance scheme before or immediately after deregulation. Nevertheless, scholars argue that financial markets believe in the existence of implicit deposit insurance – i.e., that the government would not allow banks to fail in a financial crisis.[38]

Finance companies did not face these same restrictions and thus were able to gain a competitive advantage over banks.[39] Finance companies were founded decades earlier in Sweden.[40] These lenders started by lending to consumers and small businesses.[41] By the 1980s, they had moved into numerous other lending markets, including factoring and leasing.[42] At the same time, finance companies faced limitations on funding sources not applicable to banks. Swedish regulations prohibited finance companies from accepting deposits from the public or issuing certificates of deposit or bonds.[43] Finance companies relied heavily either on short-maturity loans from banks and other lenders or on issuing investment certificates, also with short maturities.[44] Banks thus provided a significant source of financing for finance companies. This increased bank exposure when finance companies later faltered in Sweden's financial crisis.[45]

Shock and regulatory arbitrage. These less regulated finance companies began to gain market share over banks in loans to both businesses and households.[46] Scholars attribute this to the shock of ballooning public sector debt. As public debt increased, the requirements that banks hold government bonds in their portfolio required them to compensate by curbing loans to the private sector.[47] Finance companies filled the void in credit markets. Their ranks swelled from 67 finance companies in Sweden in 1970 to 292 in 1988.[48] Scholars have categorized the rise of finance companies in Sweden as part of the growth of a "grey credit market."[49]

Swedish banks responded to competition from the grey market by establishing their own finance company subsidiaries.[50] This represented one *investment linkage* between the two categories of financial institution per this chapter's model.

Deregulation. From 1983 to 1985, among other liberalization reforms, Sweden repealed liquidity ratios, removed ceilings on bank loan rates, lifted volume restrictions on loans, and abolished placement ratios.[51] The Swedish government grew concerned that its bank regulatory regime was increasingly being circumvented by the growth of finance companies and other sources of credit.[52] Scholars have also claimed that regulators were motivated by a desire to increase bank profits.[53] Other scholars have characterized deregulation of the financial sector as part of a larger "neoliberal" political movement that aimed to shrink the public sector and welfare state.[54]

The consequences of deregulation. In the wake of deregulation, pent up consumer and business demand for credit exploded.[55] Deregulated banks dramatically expanded lending in part to meet surging demand and recapture market share in an increasingly competitive market.[56] Competitive pressures and the pursuit of increased profits drove banks to increase lending dramatically. In particular, banks expanded real estate lending, but they also increasingly lent to other cyclical economic sectors.[57] Deregulation resulted in a shift in bank portfolios that dramatically increased bank exposures to credit risk.[58]

Deregulation of banks resulted in displacement; it pushed finance companies to riskier market segments. For example, the ensuing competition in real estate loans pressed finance companies to enter more marginal lending markets and take on higher credit risk.[59] Finance companies began extending loans to applicants previously rejected by banks, making real estate loans with only junior security interests, investing in highly leveraged commercial real estate projects, and financing customer speculation in equity securities.[60]

Analyzing whether subsidy leakage occurred is more complex. The government guarantee of bank obligations was at best implicit.[61] Nevertheless, banks continued to enjoy lower funding costs via regulatory restrictions on the funding sources of finance companies.[62] This regulatory advantage of banks may also have played a role in the displacement of finance companies.[63] Moreover, banks provided significant levels of credit to finance companies (yet another investment linkage between the two classes of institutions).[64]

Increased lending and asset market boom. Increased lending and lower underwriting standards fueled a dramatic lending boom; the ratio of bank loans to total GDP skyrocketed just as financial sector deregulation ended in 1986.[65] Increases in bank real estate lending resulted in a feedback loop; a surge in lending stimulated further increases in real estate prices and demand for real estate.[66] This boom reinforced risky loan underwriting practices.[67] Lenders dramatically increased their loan-to-value ratios for mortgages for owner-occupied residences.[68] The boom also lowered the guard of regulators; scholars have faulted Swedish bank regulators for failing to strengthen and adapt prudential safety-and-soundness bank regulation to a more competitive, deregulated lending environment.[69]

Some economists contend that bank deregulation precipitated the boom in lending and asset prices.[70] Others find that, although this deregulation was not the catalyst for the initial lending boom and economic expansion, it did magnify those trends.[71] Deregulation stimulated competition among financial institutions, in which lenders focused on expansion rather than prudent lending practices.[72]

Crisis. The lending boom and rise in asset prices ended in dramatic fashion in 1989, as depreciation of the Swedish currency triggered massive defaults on the growing number of domestic loans denominated in foreign currencies.[73] A rise in nonperforming loans and declining collateral values triggered a banking crisis, with finance companies facing financial difficulties first.[74] Financial losses spilled over to banks via their investments in finance companies.[75] In the early stages of the Swedish financial crisis, losses on real estate loans mushroomed, and losses eventually spread to other types of loans.[76] Losses in real estate loans were mirrored by steep declines in real estate prices, which in turn paralleled declines in bank share prices.[77] The worsening crisis led the Swedish government to take extraordinary measures to guarantee bank loans and bail out financial institutions. The government ultimately nationalized two large banks.[78]

Japan

Like Sweden, Japan experienced a real estate bubble in the 1980s. Chapter 2 began to tell the legal history of this bubble. This chapter will revisit that history in greater detail to see how it fits into the dance-for-two model of this chapter.

Two (or more) categories of financial institutions. Entering the 1980s, Japan's financial sector had some clear parallels to that of Sweden. In the post-war period, the financial sector was populated by numerous categories of lenders and financial intermediaires, each subject to a different regulatory regime.[79] Japanese financial regulation compartmentalized financial services into narrow and distinct sectors – including securities firms, commercial banking, trust banking, long-term credit banking, and regional banking – with each sector serving a distinct market.[80] Another category of financial institution, called *jusen*, originally provided residential home loans. *Jusen* originally existed at the margins of Japanese financial markets and financial regulation. Yet they came to play a pivotal role in Japan's bubble and crisis.[81] This chapter will focus on the interaction of securities firms, banks, and *jusen*.[82]

In the post-war period through the 1970s, Japan tightly regulated securities firms and bond markets. Japanese monetary authorities imposed caps on the interest rates of virtually every type of bond.[83] Regulations also required that most types of domestically issued bonds be backed by collateral. This left corporations with few alternatives for financing other than banks.[84]

Meanwhile, banks, regulated by the Japanese Ministry of Finance, faced an array of prudential banking regulations that restricted their sources of financing.[85] The government capped the interest rates that banks could offer on deposit accounts.[86] *Jusen*, on the other hand, represented a class of non-depository finance companies in Japan created in the early 1970s for the principal purpose of providing residential housing mortgages.[87] *Jusen* enjoyed light regulation, as the Ministry of Finance considered them to exist on the periphery of the Japanese financial system.[88] *Jusen* were, however, often connected to more central players in the country's finance; banks often owned *jusen* and steered higher credit risk or more "unsavory" customers (including gangsters) to these less regulated affiliates.[89] Bank ownership or investments in *jusen* serve as textbook examples of the *investment linkages* described by the model in this chapter.

Japan also restricted foreign competition and access by Japanese corporations and financial firms to foreign markets through a series of measures including the following: exchange controls, limiting the number of licenses issued to domestic financial firms permitted to engage in foreign exchange transactions, and restrictions on the foreign activities of Japan's financial institutions. These measures effectively segregated and quarantined Japanese finance from overseas capital markets.[90]

Shocks. The well-ordered financial ecosystem of Japan absorbed multiple outside shocks in the 1970s and 1980s that led the government to deregulate the financial sector in waves. In the late 1970s Japan faced dramatic macroeconomic shifts, including ballooning government debt, oil shocks and inflation, and slowing economic growth.[91] The end of the Bretton-Woods system of fixed international exchange rates coincided with the globalization of financial services.[92] In the 1980s, the United States placed increasing pressure on Japan to remedy growing trade imbalances and to open up its financial services markets to foreign institutions.[93] At the same time, the Japanese government and firms sought ways to invest vast piles of cash generated by Japan's large trade surpluses and a household savings glut.[94]

Deregulation → Regulatory arbitrage → Deregulation. Japan deregulated its financial markets in several waves. The economic and political shocks described above initially led policymakers to deregulate bond markets and securities firms. This resulted in Japanese banks losing corporate customers, who increasingly raised financing and invested their cash via capital markets. The banks then pushed for the Japanese Ministry of Finance to deregulate them as well. The following paragraphs summarize this cascade of deregulation, regulatory arbitrage, and deregulation.

Japan began deregulating securities firms and its bond markets in the late 1970s. In 1977 and 1978, the Bank of Japan and the Ministry of Finance liberalized the process for government bond issues. Previously, the Ministry of Finance pressured Japan's banks to purchase and hold low-yielding government bonds. The government made a tacit promise that it would later repurchase (and "monetize") these bonds. Macroeconomic pressures in the 1970s – the growing government deficit, the oil shocks, inflation, and slowing economic growth – made this policy riskier for banks. They doubted the continuing ability of the government to repurchase bonds. Under pressure from banks, the Ministry of Finance began selling government bonds by auction. It then permitted banks to resell these bonds into a secondary market.[95]

This initial deregulation had a knock-on effect. The trading of government bonds threatened to crowd out corporate bonds, which Japan historically subjected to interest rate restrictions. Accordingly, after the liberalization of government bond markets, the government relaxed interest rate caps on corporate bond issues as well.[96] (Interestingly, interest rates on convertible bonds were not regulated.)[97]

Subsequently the government lowered restrictions on the ability of Japanese corporations to issue bonds in overseas markets. The Foreign Exchange Law Reform of 1980 removed the requirement that firms obtain prior government consent for foreign bond issuances and replaced it with a mere notice requirement.[98] At the same time, Japan relaxed foreign exchange controls that previously permitted only a small number of licensed firms to engage in foreign exchange transactions.[99] The Ministry of Finance reported that by 1983 Japanese firms received almost 50 percent of their financing from foreign capital markets.[100] The opening of foreign markets enabled Japanese corporations and financial firms to engage in creative forms of regulatory arbitrage around interest rate restrictions on bonds; with the help of financial firms, Japanese corporations routed financing transactions through overseas markets.[101]

The Japanese government approved the issuance of warrant bonds in June 1981.[102] These warrant bonds represented a bond coupled with a warrant that gave the investor the right to purchase the issuer's shares at a set price in the future.[103] According to the Ministry of Finance, by 1986, over 20 percent of new corporate financing came from warrant bonds.[104] Japanese corporations preferred issuing bonds and warrant bonds in overseas markets to escape legal requirements that bonds issued domestically be backed by collateral.[105]

Later, the government expanded the number of firms that could legally issue unsecured bonds domestically. Only two Japanese companies could issue unsecured bonds prior to 1983 (Toyota Motors and Matsushita Electric). By 1987, 180 firms could issue unsecured bonds, and 330 firms could issue unsecured domestic convertible bonds.[106]

Deregulation acted as catalyst for a transformation of the financial services sector in Japan. Large Japanese firms increasingly raised money through capital markets as opposed to bank loans.[107] The percentage of external financing of

Japanese manufacturing firms provides one measure of the extent of this shift. The percentage of external funds raised by these firms from capital markets increased from 11.6 percent in the period 1971–1975 to 38.2 percent in 1981–1985. The portion of capital raised by Japanese corporations via bond issuances climbed from 4.6 to 22.7 percent in these same two periods. Comparing these same time periods, the percentage of external funds raised by borrowing from financial institutions dropped from 84 to 56.6 percent.[108]

This deregulation of securities firms and bond markets had the cumulative effect of causing banks to suffer on both sides of their balance sheets. On the financing side, banks lost deposit business when investors moved to bonds issued in capital markets as well as novel investment products created by securities firms. These capital markets investments were not subject to the regulatory caps on the interest rates banks could offer on deposit accounts.[109] This squeeze prompted banks to push policymakers to remove restrictions on the financing sources for banks. In a move to market based financing, regulators allowed banks to issue certificates of deposit and access international capital markets. Moreover, starting in 1983, the government encouraged banks to raise capital through publicly traded equity offerings.[110]

On the other side of the bank balance sheet, Japanese bank regulators became concerned that banks were losing loan business. Regulators feared that domestic bank regulations would continue to drive corporate customers to issue bonds on capital markets instead of borrowing from banks. More troubling, leakage to foreign capital markets could lead to a "hollowing out" (*kudoka*) of the Japanese financial system. This nightmare prompted regulators to adapt a reactive and accommodating stance towards the risk-taking of banks and financial institutions. When Japanese securities firms started mimicking Wall Street firms in their use of advanced financial instruments, such as exotic swaps, Japan's regulators had little experience to guide them or formal rules to deploy. Regulators feared losing capital to foreign markets, disadvantaging their home country financial firms, and losing power over their own financial system.[111] Accordingly, they adopted an approach of consulting with industry over these financial practices (which meshed with an established regulatory paradigm in Japan).[112] This resulted in councils, comprising public officials and financial industry representatives, issuing reports that may have largely mouthed industry views in lieu of vigorous oversight and regulation of financial institution investments.[113]

Consequences of deregulation: a competitive cascade. Deregulation thus triggered a competitive cascade that affected each tier of the segmented Japanese financial services sectors. Securities firms flourished as corporations increasingly met their financing needs through the capital markets (particularly foreign capital markets), while legal rules prevented banks from entering the securities business.[114] The loss of corporate lending business to capital markets led banks to seek alternative sources of revenue. For example, city banks reacted to a loss of corporate lending business by increasing loans to smaller businesses, which had previously received financing from regional banks, credit cooperatives, and large corporations in the form of trade credit.[115]

Further down the food chain, banks entered the residential home loan market, the traditional domain of the *jusen*.[116] The *jusen*, in turn, made up for the loss of their core business, by financing riskier commercial real estate projects.[117] *Jusen* faced a competitive disadvantage in that they did not finance themselves through deposits. Accepting deposits would have placed them under the jurisdiction of the Ministry of Finance.[118]

Increased lending and asset market boom. Lending fueled speculation in capital markets and fueled a securities bubble. Credit also fed a parallel real estate bubble. For example, the *jusen* dramatically increased lending to corporate borrowers. Many of these borrowers, in turn, used the loans for real estate development.[119] Increased real estate lending by *jusen* and banks has been cited as a contributing factor to the massive real estate boom in Japan.[120]

One feedback loop bears mentioning here. *Jusen* could not raise money through deposits, but they could borrow from agricultural cooperatives comprising Japanese farmers. A 1980 rule change by the ministry that oversaw the cooperatives (the Ministry of Agriculture, Forestry, and Fisheries) allowed them to lend unlimited amounts to *jusen*, provided that the loans were used to finance the purchase of residential real estate. *Jusen* loans fueled real estate speculation that enriched Japanese farmers who sold farmland. The farmers invested the proceeds in agricultural cooperatives who loaned more to *jusen*.[121]

Crisis. When Japan's real estate prices collapsed, *jusen* institutions faced insolvency due to billions of dollars of losses on their real estate loans.[122] The nonperforming loans of the *jusen* were part of a larger economic crisis in which the nation's financial institutions were crippled by bad loans on their books; scholars estimate that the size of Japanese bad loans from the collapse of the real estate and stock market bubble during the 1980s was twice as large as the loan losses from the U.S. savings and loan crisis of the 1980s, as measured as a percentage of gross domestic product.[123] The Japanese government engaged in protracted negotiations to persuade Japanese banks to absorb the massive losses from their *jusen* affiliates.[124]

Extending the model and further research

The "dance-for-two" model in this chapter might explain how deregulation and feedback reinforced one another in other bubbles, both recent and historical. The following presents a preliminary analysis of whether the model explains one particular spiral of deregulation and regulatory arbitrage during the subprime mortgage crisis. The chapter then moves to outline a research agenda for applying the model to other historical episodes.

Securitization and the U.S. subprime crisis

This chapter's "dance-for-two" model offers a useful lens for looking at deregulation and regulatory arbitrage in the U.S. subprime mortgage securitization market in the years leading up to the Panic of 2007–2008. In particular, the model provides a template for studying the interactions of government-sponsored entities (i.e., Freddie Mac and Fannie Mae), on the one hand, and investment banks that sponsored so-called "private label securitizations," on the other. A brief look at the interactions of these two categories of financial institutions over the last decade indicates that many of the spiral dynamics of the dance-for-two model were indeed at play in the United States.

Two categories of financial institutions. Up until the Panic of 2007–2008, the U.S. residential-mortgage securitization market was bifurcated. Two very different categories of financial institutions were involved in sponsoring these securitizations. Government-sponsored entities (GSEs) (chiefly Freddie Mac and Fannie Mae) pioneered and dominated this market for decades. Yet they faced growing competition from investment banks and other parties that put together "private label" securitizations. These private label transactions did not face the same regulatory restrictions that limited the GSEs to purchasing mortgages of a certain size and credit quality.

A little history helps understand these two classes of institutions and their differences. Congress chartered Freddie Mac and Fannie Mae as privately owned companies to create a liquid national market for residential mortgages to promote increased homeownership.[125] To fulfill their missions, Freddie and Fannie engaged in two lines of business. First, they (together with the Government National Mortgage Association) pioneered the creation of mortgage-backed securities. The GSEs would purchase pools of residential mortgages of certain loan sizes that met certain credit standards and other criteria ("conforming mortgages"). The future cash streams from these mortgages would be used to make payments on securities issued and sold to investors. Freddie and Fannie would also guarantee payments on these securities. Second, the GSEs purchased for their own investment portfolios both mortgages and mortgaged-backed securities issued by others.[126]

Before the financial crisis, scholars debated whether or not these two GSEs enjoyed an implicit guarantee from the federal government of their obligations in the event of their insolvency.[127] (As discussed below, the financial crisis settled the argument. The government took over the GSEs, placing them in conservatorship and bailing out their creditors. The government's guarantee is no longer quite so implicit.)[128]

Beyond an implicit guarantee, Freddie and Fannie enjoyed a raft of other regulatory subsidies, including tax exemptions, exemptions from various securities laws, and laws granting special status to GSE securities making them equivalent to government securities. This last preference enabled federal agencies, fiduciaries, and federally regulated lenders to invest in GSE securities whereas they could not purchase other private sector securities (at least to the same extent).[129] Moreover, Freddie and Fannie were subject to weaker capital requirements than other federally regulated financial institutions. This enabled these two GSEs to take on more leverage and hence more risk.[130]

The success of the GSEs in the first line of business – issuing and guaranteeing residential mortgage-backed securities – spawned copycatting. Other financial institutions entered the residential mortgage-backed securities market in several waves from the 1970s to the early 2000s. These financial institutions sponsored new issuances of residential mortgage-backed securities in what are called "private label" securitizations. Freddie and Fannie retained a dominant position in "conforming mortgages," while the private label securitizations focused on segments of the mortgage market foreclosed to Freddie and Fannie by regulation, including "jumbo" mortgages (mortgages above a certain dollar threshold) and riskier "subprime" mortgages (mortgages to less creditworthy borrowers). The sponsors of those private label issuances did not benefit from the implicit guarantee and other regulatory subsidies enjoyed by Freddie and Fannie.[131]

Deregulation. In the case of Freddie and Fannie, deregulation took the form of government pressure for the two companies to loosen their standards for their respective retained investment portfolios. Many policymakers wanted to enable and push the GSEs to purchase higher risk "subprime" mortgages in which low-income individuals were the borrowers.[132] Although Freddie and Fannie retained dominance in the conforming mortgage market, regulations had prevented them from participating in the surging profits of the subprime mortgage market.[133] Press accounts describe the pressure that the chief executive of Fannie Mae was under in 2004 to allow his company to purchase riskier mortgages from mortgage lenders:

> [H]is company was under siege. Competitors were snatching away lucrative parts of its business. Congress was demanding that Mr. Mudd help steer more loans to low-income borrowers. Lenders were threatening to sell directly to Wall Street unless Fannie bought a bigger chunk of their riskiest loans.[134]

One scholar dates the decision of the GSEs to lower their purchasing standards to the 1990s, and attributes the decision in part to political pressure from Congress, the Executive Branch, and the U.S. Department of Housing and Urban Development.[135] Other accounts fault the George W. Bush administration; animated by a belief in free markets and the importance of encouraging home ownership, that administration pursued a broad set of regulatory initiatives to stimulate mortgage lending.[136] The President pushed Freddie Mac and Fannie Mae to increase support of lending to low-income borrowers.[137] On the same day that the head of the federal agency that regulated Freddie and Fannie issued a report outlining the risk that those firms could default on their obligations and spark a market crisis, the White House attempted to fire him.[138] Only later did the administration join with certain members of Congress in a failed legislative attempt to impose stricter regulations on Freddie and Fannie.[139]

At the same time that Congress and the White House were pressuring Freddie and Fannie, those firms were also using extensive lobbying efforts to thwart attempts to regulate them.[140] This tangled web of political lobbying by the GSEs and pressure from the Executive and Legislative Branches makes it difficult to determine cause and effect. To what extent did Freddie and Fannie push to lower investment standards so they could participate in the lucrative subprime mortgage market? To what extent were these changed investment standards pushed on these firms by their overseers?[141] The lingering question is whether the GSEs were pushed, did they jump, or was it some combination of both?

Consequences of deregulation. Whether because of competitive or political pressure, Freddie and Fannie dramatically increased their direct purchases of riskier "subprime" and "alt-A" mortgages. They also increased their investments in private label asset-backed securities, including securities backed by those same two riskier mortgage classes.[142] These two kinds of investments by the GSEs meant that they were acting simultaneously as competitor of, and investor in, private label securitizations. Like Swedish banks with finance companies and Japanese banks with *jusen*, the GSEs had a twin strategy of competing with, and investing in, their less regulated counterparties.

The GSEs competed with private label securitizations to acquire subprime mortgages. This opens up the possibility that the deregulation of Freddie and Fannie described above resulted in displacement. Displacement would occur if GSEs, competing to purchase risky mortgages, pushed private label securitizations to purchase even riskier mortgages. More study is needed on this point.

At the same time, as noted above, Freddie and Fannie increased their purchases of private label securities. This represents another example of the *investment linkages* described in this chapter. This investment in private label securities has a rough parallel to Swedish banks owning their own finance companies and Japanese banks owning *jusen*.

Increased lending and *asset market boom.* The subprime investments by the GSEs contributed to a spike in subprime mortgage lending. The contribution of the GSEs to this lending boom remains to be quantified and requires further study. Unfortunately, public data on the magnitude of Freddie and Fannie's investment in subprime mortgages and private label securitizations is not readily available.

However, a very cursory examination of data that is available on both subprime mortgages and assets reveals a marked increase in the number of subprime mortgages being underwritten by mortgage lenders in 2004. Figure 6.1[143] reveals a 2004 spike both in the volume of subprime mortgages and in their percentage share of all mortgage originations in the United States. This came at roughly the same time that the GSEs changed their investment policies and began investing in subprime mortgage assets.

Assuming the supply of subprime mortgages was elastic, the new purchases of these mortgages by Freddie and Fannie should have increased the number of these mortgages. However, detailed econometric studies are needed to determine a more precise causal link between new GSE purchases of subprime mortgages and private label mortgage-backed securities, on the one hand, and this surge in subprime originations on the other.

Crisis. Freddie and Fannie's investments in subprime mortgages and asset-backed securities based on those mortgages proved catastrophic. When the

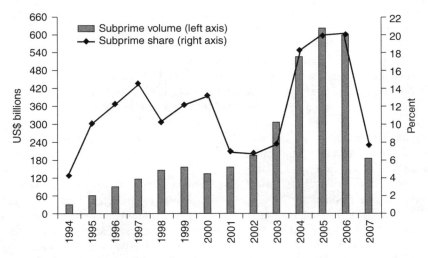

Figure 6.1 Volume of subprime mortgages originated in the United States and share of subprime mortgages of overall U.S. mortgage market 1994–2007.

subprime crisis accelerated, defaults on subprime mortgages and resultant losses on private label asset-backed securities increased and damaged the financial health of the GSEs. Freddie and Fannie's thin capitalization meant losses on their retained portfolios devastated these two firms.[144] The financial collapse of these two firms prompted a government takeover of both firms.[145] The government takeover appears to vindicate those who argued that Freddie and Fannie enjoyed and exploited implicit government guarantees.

Other historical examples?

The model outlined in this chapter might also be used to examine other bubble periods to see if the dual classes of financial institutions drove regulatory arbitrage and deregulation. One candidate for study is the Panic of 1825, which involved speculation in shares funded in part by lending from the Bank of England, on the one hand, and smaller, lightly regulated "country banks," on the other.[146]

This model might also serve as a template for examining other aspects of the current global financial crisis. For example, the model argues for further study of the repeal of the Glass-Steagall wall between commercial and investment banks. Did the repeal of Glass-Steagall result in subsidy leakage inside financial conglomerates? Did insured banks cross-subsidize investments by their un-insured and less regulated affiliates?

The model also argues for study of whether displacement occurred in the run-up to the Panic of 2007–2008. Did the entry of banks into the securities business push investment banks into riskier markets? Did subsidies enjoyed by conglomerates with significant bank affiliates allow them to undercut those conglomerates that lacked a substantial depository bank business? Two intriguing clues stand out:

- the prominent failure of conglomerates with small (or no) depository banking business, such as Lehman Brothers and Bear Stearns); and
- the larger U.S. financial conglomerates that survived the crisis were either bank holding companies or converted into bank holding companies.[147]

Both of these facts suggest that the "dance-for-two" model and the dynamics of displacement – and their application to the interaction between commercial and investment banks – are ripe for study.

The dance-for-two model might also explain competitive dynamics in the bond insurance business. In 2000, Congress shielded credit derivatives and other OTC derivatives from regulation by the Commodity Futures Trading Commission (CFTC), the SEC, and state regulators by passing the Commodity Futures Modernization Act.[148] This statute exempted credit derivatives not only from disclosure regulations, but also from regulations under the Commodity Exchange Act and other statutes that could have applied capital requirements to counterparties to these contracts.[149] OTC credit derivatives thus enjoyed a lower level of regulation than state-regulated monoline bond insurers. Did this uneven regulatory playing field and competition from OTC credit derivatives push monoline bond insurers to insure riskier bonds?[150]

Lessons

The dance-for-two model highlights the ways in which financial institution deregulation and regulatory arbitrage may create powerful feedback effects for one another. An exogenous shock may trigger powerful competitive and political spirals in which financial liberalization and efforts by financial firms to sidestep regulation reinforce one another. These spirals radically destabilize the foundations of a country's financial architecture. The dance-for-two model – between regulatory arbitrage and deregulation and between two classes of regulated institutions – also calls for further and closer examination of the following dynamics:

Regulatory distortion and displacement. The model in this chapter casts a harsh light on the dangers inherent in subsidy transfers between linked financial institutions – those that enjoy government guarantees or other subsidies but are subject to greater regulation, on one side, and their less subsidized and less regulated counterparts, on the other. Subsidy transfers exploit and extend the government safety net and increase moral hazard.

Displacement also has severe consequences for financial regulation. When liberalization allows a subsidized category of financial firms to enter the same market space as an unsubsidized category of firms, it distorts the regulatory landscape. The less subsidized category may have to make riskier loans and investments to survive. In normal times, these firms might fail. However, in bubble times, increased risks may not immediately materialize. Instead, riskier investments may feed the bubble and delay a reckoning. These potential regulatory distortions of subsidy transfers and displacement may pose risks that are subtler, but no less important than the now infamous "too-big-to-fail" problem.

The problems of subsidy transfer and displacement both have their origins in botched financial deregulation. Financial deregulation inevitably creates market distortions when it subjects two classes of institutions to different regulatory treatment: whether it allows one firm to retain residual subsidies (including, but not limited to, a government guarantee) or subjects institutions in the second class to continuing regulatory taxes (such as limitations on their ability to finance themselves by taking deposits). Either creates an un-level playing field in the marketplace. This may push the second class to take extreme measures to compete. They might push policymakers to deregulate them or otherwise move "down market" and make riskier investments.

Subsidy games. Policymakers often botch deregulation because a deregulated class has every incentive to keep, hide, and exploit residual government subsidies. Part of the problem for scholars and policymakers and part of the opportunity for financial firms is that it remains difficult to detect an implicit guarantee *ex ante*. For scholars, there is some danger of hindsight bias in analyzing implicit subsidies after the fact; the ultimate government takeover of those firms does not mean the market and those firms acted beforehand as if a government guarantee existed. At the same time, the takeover cannot but strengthen the "I told you so" argument of scholars and policymakers who argued that an implicit guarantee existed.

Implicit guarantees remain tricky to measure *ex ante*. This presents problems for determining when the dynamics of this "dance-for-two" model apply. One indication of the existence of an implicit guarantee comes when the market prices the debt issued by an entity with an alleged guarantee significantly more cheaply than the debt of comparable financial institutions that lack a guarantee. The rub lies in finding "comparable" institutions. It may be that comparable institutions also enjoy a guarantee. For example, when institutions are large enough (or interconnected enough), they may all enjoy a "too-big-to-fail" guarantee.

Moreover, implicit guarantees have fuzzy edges. This stems, in part, from the fact that implicit guarantees can be self-fulfilling prophesies. If enough creditors of a firm believe or act as if the government will bail them out should a firm fail, the government may have no choice but to bail them out.[151] Implicit guarantees also have fuzzy edges due to strategic behavior. Firms (and their creditors) have every reason to disclaim the existence of a guarantee. "What government guarantee?" (This same incentive exists with respect to financial conglomerates and subsidy transfers: "No subsidy transfer here.")

Even competitors who do not enjoy this guarantee may lack the incentive to complain. These competitors may rely on the guaranteed firms for capital or business and wish to avoid agitating them. This suggests that guaranteed firms benefit by investing in less regulated counterparties not only through regulatory arbitrage, but also by coopting political rivals. The competitors may also wish to avoid calling attention to their own government guarantees (explicit or implicit) or to their efforts to obtain an implicit guarantee of their own.

Investment linkages. The financial connections between heavily and lightly regulated firms pose other challenges to the stability of financial region. Firms with residual guarantees may also seek to engage in regulatory arbitrage around regulations that restrict them from making certain risky loans or investments. They can accomplish this through equity investments or loans to less regulated competitors. Meanwhile, these investment linkages provide a vehicle for subsidy leakage. Extending the government safety net to less regulated institutions (without extending regulation) causes those institutions to make excessive loans or investments, which can fuel a boom. When the bust occurs, the same investment linkages provide a transmission line for financial crisis from less regulated to more regulated and guaranteed institutions.

Credit booms. The historical evidence in this chapter also meshes with the conclusions of Chapter 9. In the cases of Sweden and the United States, scholars have faulted loose monetary policy for contributing to the asset price bubble.[152] This macroeconomic explanation is not inconsistent with, but rather complements, the regulatory analysis of this chapter. Chapter 9 argues that loose monetary policy may combine with deregulation of prudential standards to create a lethal one-two-three punch. Lighter prudential regulations can translate into increased financial institution leverage and lending. This in turn leads to a further *effective* increase in the money supply. Loose monetary policy can also cover up shortcomings in prudential regulation, as low interest rates can mask the high credit risk of a swath of loans. Higher leverage increases the financial fragility both of individual financial institutions and of entire financial markets when the tide turns, a bubble bursts, and risk materializes.

Thus the evidence of this chapter supports one of the policy conclusions in Chapter 9; monetary policy and prudential regulation need to be tightly coordinated. This becomes even more urgent during periods of severe regulatory change – whether from regulatory arbitrage, deregulation, or some cocktail of both.

Deregulation-done-wrong. Deregulation may or may not be justified on its own policy merits. However, this chapter underscores how careless deregulation can increase the risk of a crisis. Firms have every incentive to encourage deregulation but to retain their government subsidies. Furthermore, deregulation can fuel booms that can spark noise trading and camouflage financial risks.

Many genies, many bottles. It is also unlikely that the problems inherent in the interaction of regulatory arbitrage and deregulation will soon vanish. Regulatory arbitrage is likely to remain a feature of modern financial markets given multiple categories of financial institutions within countries and differing regulatory regimes across jurisdictions. Moreover, financial firms have enduring incentives to game regulations, particularly those that seek to cabin systemic risk and prevent firms from externalizing the costs of their risk-taking on taxpayers and financial markets.

It is thus unlikely that even if reforms succeed in creating "narrow banks," that regulatory arbitrage will end. Constraining the business of banks does not address the fact that other financial institutions and financial products may only move into the emptied market segments. Regulatory arbitrage is to a large extent a byproduct of the emergence of more "complete" capital markets. Financial markets have evolved and offer firms and investors an ever-expanding array of new financial institutions and products, such as derivatives, to extend credit and transfer risk.[153] This proliferation of new products also facilitates regulatory arbitrage, as Chapter 5 explained. This genie will not go gently back into that bottle.

Even if firms could be segmented and regulatory subsidies contained and countered, an economic shock that causes an asset market to boom will cause one category of financial institution to enjoy profits. When regulations preclude other firms from investing in these markets to the same extent, those firms will push for deregulation to the extent they cannot engage in regulatory arbitrage cheaply.

These regulatory and political dynamics are compounded by the globalization of international finance. The model and examples described above focus on deregulation and liberalization within one country's borders. The dance-for-two dynamics outlined in this chapter apply in spades with respect to international financial regulation. Cross-border regulatory arbitrage and domestic deregulation can become locked in particularly strong spirals. Even successful cabining of subsidies within one nation may be undermined if investors can invest or borrow from foreign capital markets. The specter of cross-border capital flight would set the wheels of deregulation in motion in a country that fears a "hollowing out." Then again, liberalization in one country may trigger regulatory arbitrage across national borders. Deregulation and regulatory arbitrage spirals can thus spin across borders and destabilize the architecture of financial regulation within and among nations. Tornadoes respect neither political boundaries nor careful carpentry.

Notes

1 Wall Street firms made arguments for deregulation based on the perceived loss of business to overseas markets. They claimed these losses stemmed from "excessive" U.S. financial regulations in the Sarbanes Oxley era. U.S. companies, stock market officials, and politicians argued that the increased regulatory burdens and liability were driving companies to deregister and delist securities in the United States and to move their capital raising efforts to either private placements or overseas markets. E.g., Greg Ip, Kara Scannell, and Deborah Solomon, Panel Urges Relaxing Rules For Oversight, *Wall Street Journal*, November 30, 2006, at C1 (describing recommendations of blue-ribbon government Committee on Capital Markets Regulation); Cf. Greg Ip, Maybe U.S. Markets are still Supreme, *Wall Street Journal*, April 27, 2007, at C1 (describing academic study questioning claims that Sarbanes Oxley Act caused U.S. exchanges to lose listings to overseas competitors).

   If it did occur, this movement of capital to lower regulatory costs represents "investment switching," one of the two variants of regulatory arbitrage described in the previous chapter.

For one scholarly argument that the increased regulatory burdens of the statute would promote regulatory arbitrage and capital flight, See Larry E. Ribstein, International Implications of Sarbanes Oxley: Raising the Rent on U.S. Law, 3 *Journal of Corporate Law Studies* 299 (2003). The extent to which this flight actually occurred and was driven by that statute has been the subject of intense empirical study and controversy. For a small sampling of the studies related to this controversy, see Kate Litvak, Sarbanes-Oxley and the Cross-Listing Premium, 105 *Michigan Law Review* 1857 (2007) (finding evidence that investors expected that cross-listed firms would, on net, incur costs because of Sarbanes Oxley); William J. Carney, The Costs of Being Public after Sarbanes-Oxley: The Irony of Going Private, 55 *Emory Law Journal* 141 (2006); Robert P. Bartlett III, Going Private but Staying Public: Reexamining the Effect of Sarbanes-Oxley on Firms' Going-private Decisions, 76 *University of Chicago Law Review* 7 (2009) (concluding from subordinated debt financings that non-Sarbanes Oxley related factors may better explain many going-private transactions).

2 Chapter 2, "Japan's real estate bubble," Chapter 3, "Shocks and the interest group equilibrium." See *infra*, Chapter 6, "Deregulation→Regulatory arbitrage→ Deregulation."

3 For example, U.S. federal banking law circumscribes the non-banking commercial business in which banks may engage or own. See e.g., 12 U.S.C. § 24 (2008) (enumerating powers of national banks).

4 E.g., 12 U.S.C. § 29 (2008) (restricting ability of national banks to invest in real estate).

5 E.g., 12 U.S.C. § 24(Seventh); 12 C.F.R. § 1; Office of the Comptroller of the Currency, Comptroller's Handbook (Section 203): Investment Securities: Narrative and Procedures (March 1990) available at www.occ.gov/publications/publications-by-type/comptrollers-handbook/investsecurities1.pdf (last visited July 26, 2013) (each defining investment securities that national banks may purchase).

6 For example, U.S. federal banking laws limit the loans that banks may have outstanding to one borrower. 12 U.S.C. §§ 84, 1464(u) (2008); 12 C.F.R. § 32.1(b) (2008). Another set of laws restrict a bank's loans to other depositary institutions to prevent the collapse of one institution from threatening others. 12 U.S.C. § 371b-2 (2008); 12 C.F.R. § 206 (2008).

7 For a description of how federal law in the United States has cut back on state usury laws, See Michael S. Barr, Banking the Poor, 21 *Yale Journal on Regulation* 121, 148 (2004); Christopher L. Peterson, Federalism and Predatory Lending: Unmasking the Deregulatory Agenda, 78 *Temple Law Review* 1, 35–7 (2005); Elizabeth R. Schlitz, The Amazing, Elastic, Ever-Expanding Exportation Doctrine and its Effect on Predatory Lending Regulation, 88 *Minnesota Law Review* 518 (2004).

8 For example, the Federal Reserve Board's now defunct Regulation Q imposed caps on the interest rates depository institutions could offer to depositors. 12 C.F.R. Pt. 217 (1979). The Depositary Institutions Deregulation and Monetary Control Act of 1980 required the phased elimination of Regulation Q. Pub. L. No. 96–221, 94 Stat. 132 (codified as amended in scattered sections of 12 U.S.C.) See R. Alton Gilbert, Requiem for Regulation Q: What It Did and Why It Passed Away, *Federal Reserve Bank St. Louis Review* 22 (February 1986).

9 Steven L. Schwarcz, Systemic Risk, 97 *Georgetown Law Journal* 193, 210 (2008) (describing deposit insurance as a tool to mitigate systemic risk).

10 For an earlier article analyzing "too-big-to-fail" financial institutions, See Arthur E. Wilmarth, Jr., Too Big to Fail, Too Few to Serve? The Potential Risks of Nationwide Banks, 77 *Iowa Law Review* 957 (1992). See also John R. Walter, Can a Safety Net Subsidy Be Contained? 84 *Federal Reserve of Bank Richmond* 1, 7–8 (1998). A more recent variant of the "too-big-to-fail" concern is the "too-interconnected-to-fail" financial institution. Under this theory, a government may not allow some

financial institutions to fail for fear of the repercussions to their financial institution counterparties. See Onnig H. Dombalagian, Requiem for the Bulge Bracket? Revisiting Investment Bank Regulation, 85 *Indiana Law Journal* 777, 797–801 (2010).

11 Moral hazard refers to the perverse incentives for insured parties to take on excessive risk. For an analysis of how deposit insurance may contribute to moral hazard, See Patricia A. McCoy, The Moral Hazard Implications of Deposit Insurance: Theory and Evidence, in *International Monetary Fund, Current Developments in Monetary and Financial Law, Vol. 5*, 417 (2008, International Monetary Fund) available at www.imf.org/External/NP/seminars/eng/2006/mfl/pam.pdf (last visited January 30, 2010).

12 Gary Gorton explains the long "Quiet Period" in U.S. banking from 1934 to 1990. During this period, the U.S. enjoyed an absence of severe financial crises. Part of the reason, Gorton argues, is that regulation restricted competition for banks, increasing their "franchise value." This explains why banks did not seek to engage in the moral hazards provided by deposit insurance. Gorton argues that competition for banks emerged in the early 1990s and deregulation lowered the franchise value for banks. Gary Gorton, Slapped in the Face by the Invisible Hand: Banking and the Panic of 2007, National Bureau of Economic Research, *Working Paper* (May 9, 2009) available at http://papers.ssrn.com/sol3/papers.cfm?abstract_id=1401882 (last visited July 26, 2013).

13 This is indeed what happened to U.S. banks during the late 1970s and what prompted the removal of these interest rate caps in 1980. *Supra* note 8. In this case, however, bank deregulation was preceded by regulatory arbitrage, as banks lost business to money market mutual funds that could offer investors higher interest rates. See William A. Birdthistle, Breaking Bucks in Money Market Mutual Funds, 2010 *Wisconsin Law Review* 1155, 1156–81 (2010) (describing evolution of money market mutual funds).

14 Charles M. Kahn and João A.C. Santos, Allocating Bank Regulatory Powers: Lender of Last Resort, Deposit Insurance and Supervision, 49 *European Economic Review* 2107 (2005).

15 See McCoy, *supra* note 11.

16 Cf. Lie Yu, On the Wealth and Risk Effects of the Glass-Steagall Overhaul: Evidence from the Stock Market, NYU Stern School of Business Salomon Center, *Working Paper No. S-01-6* (January 2001) (attempting to measure whether repeal of Glass-Steagall Act resulted in subsidy transfers from banks with deposit insurance to other affiliates).

17 Consider the academic debate pre-crisis over whether Freddie Mac and Fannie Mae enjoyed an implicit guarantee from the United States government. *Infra* notes 127–8 and accompanying text.

18 Cf. Arthur E. Wilmarth, How Should We Respond to the Growing Risks of Financial Conglomerates?, in *Financial Modernization after Gramm-Leach-Bliley*, 65 (Patricia A. McCoy ed. 2002, Matthew Bender/LexisNexis) (arguing that policymakers were discounting risks of subsidy transfers and too-big-to-fail guarantees in wake of Glass-Steagall repeal).

19 E.g., Saule T. Omarova, From Gramm-Leach-Bliley to Dodd-Frank: The Unfulfilled Promise of Section 23A of the Federal Reserve Act, 89 *North Carolina Law Review* 101, 109–11 (2011). Professor Omarova analyzes how, in the wake of Glass-Steagall's demise, financial conglomerates sought exemptions from Section 23A of the Federal Reserve Act. These exemptions allowed conglomerates to cause their bank subsidiaries to extend credit to, and purchase assets from, non-banking affiliates. These exemptions allowed conglomerates to transfer the government subsidies banks enjoyed to support subprime mortgage lending and other investments. Ibid.

20 Walter, *supra* note 10, at 11. Arthur Wilmarth argued in 2002 that banks that were "too-big-to-fail" could transfer this implicit subsidy to ("cross-subsidize") non-bank

affiliates. Arthur E. Wilmarth, Jr., The Transformation of the U.S. Financial Services Industry, 1975–2000: Competition, Consolidation, and Increased Risk, 2002 *University of Illinois Law Review* 215, 446–9 (2002).

21 Intra-firm subsidies may take the form of intra-company loans, or asset purchases, dividends, or equity investments in direct subsidiaries. Walter, *supra* note 10, at 11–13.

22 Ibid. at 11.

23 Ibid.

24 Ibid. at 10.

25 See Walter, *supra* note 10.

26 Chapter 5, "Cheap debt: government guarantees, systemic risk, and the instability of regulatory capital requirements."

27 This is what some scholars argue happened in Sweden after deregulation of banks in the 1980s. See *infra* notes 65–9 and accompanying text.
    Rising asset prices may enable some riskier forms of loans. For example, in the recent subprime mortgage bubbles, less credit-worthy borrowers were able to take out exotic mortgages, including adjustable-rate-mortgages (ARMs) that they could not hope to repay. Rising prices allowed these borrowers to exit by refinancing or "flipping" the real estate. Both of these exit strategies depended on housing prices appreciating. See Stephen G. Ryan, Accounting in and for the Subprime Crisis, 83 *Accounting Review* 1605, 1615 (2008) (analyzing the "binary" nature of ARMs as only functioning when housing prices rise).

28 The Norwegian and Finnish banking sectors experienced similar deregulation in the 1980s and a crisis at roughly the same time as Sweden. For economic literature comparing deregulation in Sweden with that of other Scandinavian countries in the same period, See Lars Jonung, Lessons from Financial Liberalisation in Scandinavia, 50 *Comparative Economic Studies* 564 (2008); Burkhard Drees and Ceyla Pazarbaşioğlu, The Nordic Banking Crises: Pitfalls in Financial Liberalization, International Monetary Fund, *Occasional Paper No. 161* (April 1998); Peter Englund and Vesa Vihriälä, Financial Crises in Developed Economies: The Cases of Sweden and Finland, Pellervo Economic Research Institute, *Working Paper No. 63* (March 2003) available at www. ptt.fi/dokumentit/tp63_1809080802.pdf (last visited September 10, 2009).

29 Drees and Pazarbaşioğlu, *supra* note 28, at 3. See also Bengt Larsson, Neoliberalism and Polycontextuality: Banking Crisis and Re-regulation in Sweden, 32 *Economy and Society* 428 (2003).

30 Drees and Pazarbaşioğlu, *supra* note 28, at 4.

31 Ibid. at 5; Peter Englund, The Swedish Banking Crisis: Roots and Consequences, 15 *Oxford Review of Economic Policy* 80, 83 (1999).

32 Drees and Pazarbaşioğlu, *supra* note 28, at 5. Englund, *supra* note 31, at 83. The Swedish Central Bank applied moral suasion through weekly meetings among the heads of that institution and senior executives of private sector banks. Ibid.

33 Drees and Pazarbaşioğlu, *supra* note 28, at 3.

34 This absence of competition resulted from legal prohibitions on entry. From 1945 to 1983, Sweden granted no new banking licenses. E. Phillip Davis, *Debt, Financial Fragility and Systemic Risk*, 256 (1995) Oxford University Press.

35 Drees and Pazarbaşioğlu, *supra* note 28, at 3.

36 Ibid. at 7.

37 Jonung, *supra* note 28, at 567 ("Banking was rendered an almost risk-free enterprise in this system"). Sweden also restricted access by foreign banks to the Swedish market. See Drees and Pazarbaşioğlu, *supra* note 28, at 6.

38 Drees and Pazarbaşioğlu, *supra* note 28, at 15.

39 L. Peter Jennergren, The Swedish Finance Company Crisis: Could It Have Been Anticipated? 50 *Scandinavian Economic History Review* 7 (2002); see also Davis, *supra* note 34, at 256; Dwight M. Jaffee, The Swedish Real Estate Crisis, 82,

Unpublished manuscript (October 1994) available at http://faculty.haas.berkeley.edu/jaffee/Papers/Sweden.pdf (last visited September 10, 2009).

40 There is some disagreement over when finance companies first began. Compare Davis, *supra* note 34, at 256 (asserting finance companies were an innovation of the 1920s and 1930s) with Jennergren, *supra* note 39 ("Finance companies started in the 1960s.").

41 Davis, *supra* note 34, at 256.

42 Ibid.; Englund, *supra* note 31, at 85; see generally Jennergren, *supra* note 39 (describing forms of credit provided by finance companies).

43 Jennergren, *supra* note 39.

44 Ibid.; Englund, *supra* note 31, at 85.

45 Englund, *supra* note 31, at 85.

46 Jennergren, *supra* note 39; Drees and Pazarbaşioğlu, *supra* note 28, at 9. See also Englund, *supra* note 31, at 85.

47 Drees and Pazarbaşioğlu, *supra* note 28, at 9.

48 Davis, *supra* note 34, at 256. In 1988, finance companies collectively held assets of 171 billion Swedish kroner. Ibid.

49 Drees and Pazarbaşioğlu, *supra* note 28, at 9.

50 Ibid. at 9–10.

51 Ibid. at 10; Davis, *supra* note 34, at 256; Peter Englund, Financial Deregulation in Sweden, 34 *European Economic Review* 385, 385–6 (1990); Englund, *supra* note 31, at 83.

52 Ibid.; Englund, *supra* note 31, at 84.

53 Jaffee, *supra* note 39, at 89–90.

54 See Timothy A. Canova, The Swedish Model Betrayed, 37 *Challenge* 36 (May–June 1994) (describing politics of deregulation); Brian Burkitt and Phil Whyman, The Origins of the Recent Swedish Crisis: A Lesson for the European Left, 93 *European Business Review* 33 (1993); Larsson, *supra* note 29.

55 Drees and Pazarbaşioğlu, *supra* note 28, at 12–14.

56 Ibid. at 84. See also Englund, *supra* note 31, at 84.

57 Drees and Pazarbaşioğlu, *supra* note 28, at 15; Jaffee, *supra* note 39, at 86–9 (noting, however, that Swedish bank statistics do not track real estate loans as a separate category).

58 Jaffee, *supra* note 39, at 84–7.

59 Jennergren, *supra* note 39; Englund, *supra* note 31, at 85.

60 Jennergren, *supra* note 39; Davis, *supra* note 34, at 256.

61 See *supra* note 38, and accompanying text.

62 See *supra* notes 43–4, and accompanying text.

63 See Jennergren, *supra* note 39; Englund, *supra* note 31, at 89–90.

64 See *supra* note 45, and accompanying text.

65 Drees and Pazarbaşioğlu, *supra* note 28, at 13. For other data on the extent of the lending boom, see Englund, *supra* note 31, at 84–6.

66 Jaffee, *supra* note 39, at 88.

67 Drees and Pazarbaşioğlu, *supra* note 28, at 15. In terms of lowered loan underwriting standards, the following account of Drees and Pazarbaşioğlu has eerie parallels to accounts of the U.S. subprime crisis: the shift to more price competition weakened traditionally close banking relationships and impaired banks' ability to assess credit risks and monitor borrowers. Ibid.

68 Englund, *supra* note 31, at 85.

69 Drees and Pazarbaşioğlu, *supra* note 28, at 21; Davis, *supra* note 34, at 581–2, 587–8; Urban Bäckström, What Lessons Can be Learned from Recent Financial Crises? The Swedish Experience, 1997 *Federal Reserve Bank of Kansas City Proceedings* 129, 138 (1997); Martin Andersson and Staffan Viotti, Managing and Preventing Financial Crises: Lessons from the Swedish Experience, 1 *Sveriges Riksbank Quarterly Review* 71, 77 (1999).

Some commentators fault regulators for failing to recognize the dangers of high concentrations of real estate loans and the foreign exchange risk created by a large number of loans being denominated in foreign currencies but in which the assets were denominated in the local currency. See Stefan Ingves and Goran Lind, Stockholm Solutions, International Monetary Fund *Finance and Development*, 21, 22 (December 2008) available at https://www.imf.org/external/Pubs/FT/fandd/2008/12/pdf/ingves.pdf (last visited January 5, 2010).

Another scholar questions whether real estate lending was directly regulated at all and faults bankers and supervisors for failing to consider excessive concentrations of loans in specific sectors, the need for conservative initial underwriting in new loan markets, and the importance of careful valuations of the collateral and cash flows available to service each loan. Jaffee, *supra* note 39, at 90.

For a devastating critique of the lack of understanding of regulators of the need to adjust prudential regulation in a deregulated financial sectors, see Director Stefan Ingves, Monetary and Exchange Affairs Department, Banking, Insurance and Securities Commission of Norway, The Nordic Banking Crisis from an International Perspective, Remarks at the International Monetary Fund (September 11, 2002) available at www.imf.org/external/np/speeches/2002/091102.htm (last visited January 20, 2010).

Mr. Ingves said:

> Another contributing cause to banking crisis is premature financial liberalization, together with inadequate preparation among bankers and supervisors. The former may not have the needed skills to manage and price risk, and the latter may not be given adequate resources and competencies to monitor the more complex new risks. This can easily create a situation with pure ignorance about the risks involved among relevant parties. Not having a clue about what is going on is sometimes a much more important cause of serious difficulties than the [*sic*] in academia so often discussed moral hazard.

70 See Davis, *supra* note 34, at 256. See Lars Jonung, Jaakko Kiander, and Pentti Vartia, The Great Financial Crisis in Finland and Sweden: The Dynamics of Boom, Bust and Recovery 1985–2000, in *The Great Financial Crisis in Finland and Sweden: The Nordic Experience of Financial Liberalization*, 19, 35 (Lars Jonung, Jaakko Kiander, and Pentti Vartia eds. 2009, Edward Elgar). Cf. Bäckström, *supra* note 69, at 130 ("Credit market deregulation in 1985 ... meant that monetary conditions became more expansionary.")

71 Englund, *supra* note 31, at 88–9, 95–6. Cf. Jonung, *supra* note 28, at 577 (describing general trend of financial deregulation in Scandinavian countries triggering asset price booms). Other economists have found no causal link between Swedish deregulation of financial institutions and a more general boom in consumption. Jonas Agell and Lennart Berg, Does Financial Deregulation Cause a Consumption Boom? 98 *Scandinavian Journal of Economics* 579 (1996). Agell and Berg do note that their study does not consider whether deregulation might have affected "investment patterns, asset choice and borrowing for commercial purposes." Ibid. at 597. For one dissenting view of the contribution of financial liberalization to the Swedish crisis, see Massimiliano Rimarchi, Financial Liberalization, Credit Boom and Recession: A Business Cycle Accounting Perspective for Sweden, Unpublished manuscript (paper for University of Cambridge Faculty of Economics Conference on "Macroeconomic and Financial Linkages: Theory and Practice") (December 8, 2008) available at www.econ.cam.ac.uk/events/mafc/Rimarchi.pdf (last visited September 10, 2009). Rimarchi concludes that bank deregulation did not loosen bank credit, did not spur growth in asset markets, and did not contribute to the vulnerability of the Swedish economy to financial crisis. Ibid. at 23.

72 Englund, *supra* note 31, at 95–6; Andersson and Viotti, *supra* note 69, at 72.

73 Drees and Pazarbaşioğlu, *supra* note 28, at 22–3. See generally Englund, *supra* note 31, at 89–92.

74 Drees and Pazarbaşioğlu, *supra* note 28, at 23; Englund, *supra* note 31, at 89–90.
75 Drees and Pazarbaşioğlu, *supra* note 28, at 23; Englund, *supra* note 31, at 90.
76 Drees and Pazarbaşioğlu, *supra* note 28, at 23.
77 See ibid. at 23.
78 Ibid. at 29–30.
79 For a brief introduction to some of these categories of financial institutions, See Christopher Wood, *The Bubble Economy*, 44–47 (1992, Grove/Atlantic).
80 Curtis J. Milhaupt and Geoffrey P. Miller, Cooperation, Conflict, and Convergence in Japanese Finance: Evidence from the "Jusen" Problem, 29 *Law and Policy in International Business* 1, 6 (1997). See also Ulrike Schaede, Change and Continuity in Japanese Regulation, Berkeley Roundtable on International Economics, *Working Paper No. 66* (1994).
81 Milhaupt and Miller, *supra* note 80, at 24–35.
82 For a description of the general bank regulatory environment in Japan during the 1980s, see Curtis J. Milhaupt and Geoffrey P. Miller, Regulatory Failure and the Collapse of Japan's Home Mortgage Lending Industry: A Legal and Economic Analysis, 22 *Law and Policy* 245 (2000).
83 See Allen B. Frankel and Paul B. Morgan, Deregulation and Competition in Japanese Banking, 78 *Federal Reserve Bulletin* 579, 579, 581 (August 1992) (describing regulation and deregulation of Japanese banks in late 1970s and 1980s).
84 Ibid.
85 Ibid. at 581–91.
86 Ibid. at 581.
87 Milhaupt and Miller, *supra* note 82, at 260.
88 Ibid. at 260–1.
89 Ibid. at 261. Banks also used *jusen* subsidiaries to take non-performing assets off their books and to evade lending restrictions. Ibid.
90 Frankel and Morgan, *supra* note 83, at 579.
91 Frankel and Morgan, *supra* note 83, at 579–80; Kazuo Tsuda, Japanese Banks in Deregulation and the Economic Bubble, 22 *Japanese Economic Studies* 122, 123 (May/June/August 1994) (increase in government bond issuances in 1970s created pressure for financial deregulation).
92 See generally Philip G. Cerny, The Dynamics of Financial Globalization: Technology, Market Structure, and Policy Response, 27 *Policy Sciences* 319 (1994).
93 Edward Chancellor, *Devil Take the Hindmost: A History of Financial Speculation*, 295–6 (1999, Plume Books); see also Tsuda, *supra* note 91, at 123–5. Tsuda argues that a 1984 study co-authored by the U.S. and Japanese government that addressed the causes of the strong dollar provided the blueprint for deregulation. He writes: "the impetus for serious deregulation, internationalization, and securitization occurred when the 'U.S.-Japan Dollar-Yen Committee Report' was published in 1984." Ibid. at 123.
94 Chancellor, *supra* note 93, at 287, 295.
95 Takeo Hoshi, Anil Kashyap, and David Scharfstein, Bank Monitoring and Investment: Evidence from the Changing Structure of Japanese Corporate Banking Relationships, in *Asymmetric Information, Corporate Finance, and Investment*, 105, 109 (R. Glenn Hubbard ed. 1990, National Bureau of Economic Research/University of Chicago Press).

Before reform, Japanese banks purchased government bonds with the understanding that the Bank of Japan would later buy the bonds and ensure some profit. However, as public debt and government bond issuances mushroomed, banks feared that the Bank of Japan could not continue this practice and still follow prudent monetary policy. Frankel and Morgan, *supra* note 83, at 580.
96 Hoshi *et al.*, *supra* note 95, at 109. See also Frankel and Morgan, *supra* note 83, at 580, 583. Some official interest rate restrictions on the interest rates banks could charge remained in place. Ibid.

97   Hoshi *et al.*, *supra* note 95, at 109.
98   Hoshi *et al.*, *supra* note 95, at 109; Frankel and Morgan, *supra* note 83, at 582.
99   See Frankel and Morgan, *supra* note 83, at 579, 582.
100 Hoshi *et al.*, *supra* note 95, at 109. The Ministry of Finance gradually eased "suggested" standards for the amount of money that firms could raise through bond issuances. Tsuda, *supra* note 91, at 135.
101 Frankel and Morgan, *supra* note 83, at 582.
102 Hoshi *et al.*, *supra* note 95, at 109. Tsuda, *supra* note 91, at 135.
103 Chancellor, *supra* note 93, at 290. Initially, warrant bond holders were legally prohibited from detaching or transferring the option separate from the bond, but in December 1985, the government approved the detachability of options. Hoshi *et al.*, *supra* note 95, at 109.
104 Hoshi *et al.*, *supra* note 95, at 109. Warrant bonds represented only the most prominent of a range of innovative debt and equity products that Japanese securities firms developed to help corporate customers raise funds without being subject to interest rate caps. Other products included floating rate notes, "note issuance facilities," and "revolving underwriting facilities." Tsuda, *supra* note 91, at 137–8.
105 See Tsuda, *supra* note 91, at 135–6.
106 Hoshi *et al.*, *supra* note 95, at 109. Bonds issued in overseas markets had enjoyed an advantage in that they were not required to be secured. See Tsuda, *supra* note 91, at 135.
107 Frankel and Morgan, *supra* note 83, at 582–3. Schaede, *supra* note 80.
108 Hoshi *et al.*, *supra* note 95, at 110.
109 Financial institutions developed a particular kind of repurchase agreement to engage in regulatory arbitrage around these caps. Frankel and Morgan, *supra* note 83, at 580–1 (describing *gensaki* market in which corporations borrowed from non-bank institutions via short-term repurchase agreements). The higher interest rates offered on these repurchase agreements attracted a wave of investors. See ibid.; Tsuda, *supra* note 91, at 123, 126.
     The *gensaki* market allowed Japanese corporations to engage in a form of financial and regulatory arbitrage: they could borrow from banks at government-set rates and invest in government bonds at higher market based rates. During the same period, Japanese firms used the *gensaki* market as a source of financing for their inventory of government bonds. Frankel and Morgan, *supra* note 83, at 580–1.
     Japanese securities firms developed other products to arbitrage around regulations and compete with banks in their core business. For example, they sold a kind of mutual fund in government bonds (the "medium-term government bond fund") to investors. This competition alarmed banks, who pushed even harder for deregulation. Ibid. at 126–7.
110 Frankel and Morgan, *supra* note 83, at 581–2. In 1985, regulators allowed mutual banks to offer money market certificates as an alternative investment product to deposit accounts. Regulators then gradually liberalized restrictions on the terms of this product and which types of banks could offer it. Ibid. at 583; Tsuda, *supra* note 91, at 123, 127. Also, in 1985, regulators allowed banks to offer long-term deposit accounts and then gradually eased interest rate caps and other restrictions on the product, as well. Ibid. This formed part of a larger movement by regulators and banks to ease interest rates on long-term borrowings by banks. Ibid. at 129–34.
     Deregulation of interest rates that banks could offer took more technical forms. In the late 1980s, regulators approved changes in the ways that banks calculated interest rates. Ibid. at 129–34.
111 Schaede, *supra* note 80.
112 Ibid. For a description of the ecosystem of Japanese financial regulation before and during the bubble, see Chapter 2, notes 306–10 and accompanying text.
113 See Schaede, *supra* note 80.
114 Tsuda, *supra* note 91, at 134–5.

115 Frankel and Morgan, *supra* note 83, at 586.
116 Milhaupt and Miller, *supra* note 80, at 29.
117 Ibid. at 29–40.
118 Cf. Milhaupt and Miller, *supra* note 80, at 26.
119 Milhaupt and Miller, *supra* note 82, at 262. In 1980, *jusen* had loaned ¥15 billion (the equivalent of U.S.$150 million) to corporations compared to ¥317 billion (U.S.$3.17 billion) to individuals. By the end of the decade, *jusen* lending shifted significantly towards corporate borrowers; in 1990, loans by *jusen* to corporations increased to ¥973 billion (U.S.$9.73 billion), while loans to individuals decreased to ¥265 billion (U.S.$2.65 billion). Ibid. For a description of the bubble and how the credit boom fueled it, see Chapter 2, "Japan's real estate bubble."
120 Milhaupt and Miller, *supra* note 82, at 264; see also Geoffrey P. Miller, The Role of a Central Bank in a Bubble Economy, 18 *Cardozo Law Review* 1053, 1062 (1996) (noting "bank" lending to real estate developers as one of five contributing factors to Japanese real estate boom). Chapter 2, "Japan's real estate bubble."
121 Milhaupt and Miller, *supra* note 80, at 34–40.
122 Milhaupt and Miller, *supra* note 82, at 264–5.
123 Ibid. at 246.
124 Milhaupt and Miller, *supra* note 82, at 265–78; Milhaupt and Miller, *supra* note 80, at 42–68.
125 David Reiss, The Federal Government's Implied Guarantee of Fannie Mae and Freddie Mac's Obligations: Uncle Sam Will Pick Up the Tab, 42 *Georgia Law Review* 1019, 1028 (2008).
126 Ibid. at 1027–33.
127 Compare Reiss, *supra* note 125 (arguing an implicit guarantee existed) with Richard Scott Carnell, Handling the Failure of a Government-Sponsored Enterprise, 80 *Washington Law Review* 565 (2005). Professor Carnell documented government disavowals of a guarantee and argued that the guarantee was more a matter of investor perception. Ibid. at 584.
128 For an analysis of the regulatory privileges enjoyed by the GSEs after Freddie and Fannie were placed into conservatorship and taken over by the Federal government, See David J. Reiss, Fannie Mae and Freddie Mac and the Future of Federal Housing Finance Policy: A Study of Regulatory Privilege, 61 *Alabama Law Review* 907 (2010).
129 Reiss, *supra* note 125, at 1055–5.
130 Ibid. at 1065.
131 Ibid. at 1030–3 (describing private label securitizations), 1052–68 (describing unique regulatory privileges enjoyed by GSEs).
132 Binyamin Appelbaum, How Washington Failed to Rein in Fannie, Freddie, *Washington Post*, September 14, 2008, at A1.
133 See ibid. See *supra* note 93 and accompanying text. Christopher L. Peterson, Fannie Mae, Freddie Mac, and the Home Mortgage Foreclosure Crisis, 10 *Loyola University (New Orleans) Journal of Public Interest Law* 149, 161–5 (2009). Professor Chris Peterson describes the competition from private label securitizations giving rise to abusive mortgage lending practices:

> By the 1990s, the private label securitization market specializing in subprime mortgages, jumbo mortgages, and an expanding array of alternative mortgage products with non-amortizing features were rapidly capturing market share from more traditional GSEs. With the new access to large pools of capital, unscrupulous and thinly capitalized mortgage brokers and lenders began to aggressively market a new crop of questionable subprime and manufactured home mortgage loans. Legal aid attorneys, consumer advocates, and the press began to see an increase in the volume of what America would come to call predatory mortgages.
> Ibid. at 160

134 Charles Duhigg, Pressured to Take More Risk, Fannie Reached a Tipping Point, *New York Times*, October 5, 2008, at A1.

135 Richard E. Mendales, The Fall and Rise of Fannie and Freddie: Securitization After the Meltdown, 42 *Uniform Commercial Code Law Journal* 33, 36 (2009) citing Carol D. Leonnig, How HUD Mortgage Policy Fed the Crisis, *Washington Post*, June 10, 2008, at A1; Steven A. Holmes, Fannie Mae Eases Credit to Aid Mortgage Lending, *New York Times*, September 30, 1999, at C2; Stephen Labaton, New Agency Proposed to OverSee Freddie Mac and Fannie Mae, *New York Times*, September 11, 2003, at C1; Charles W. Calomiris and Peter J. Wallison, Blame Fannie Mae and Congress for the Credit Mess, *Wall Street Journal*, September 23, 2008, at A29.

136 Jo Becker, Sheryl Gay Stolberg, and Stephen Labaton, White House Philosophy Stoked Mortgage Bonfire, *New York Times*, December 21, 2008, at A1.

137 Ibid.

138 Ibid.

139 Ibid.

140 Duhigg, *supra* note 134, at A1; Appelbaum, *supra* note 132, at A1.

141 Some accounts of the decision at Fannie to expand purchases of subprime mortgages focus on management making the decision because of competitive pressures rather than responding to political pressure. E.g., Damon Silvers and Heather Slavkin, The Legacy of Deregulation and the Financial Crisis: Linkages between Deregulation in Labor Markets, Housing Finance Markets, and the Broader Financial Markets, 4 *Journal of Business and Technology Law* 301, 326–7 (2009).

142 Peterson, *supra* note 133, at 163.

143 George Selgin, Guilty as Charged, The Independent Institute (November 7, 2008) available at www.independent.org/publications/article.asp?id=2368 (last visited February 1, 2010).

144 See Peterson, *supra* note 133, at 164–7.

145 Ibid.

146 See Chapter 2, notes 79–81 and accompanying text.

147 Jon Hilsenrath, Goldman, Morgan Scrap Wall Street Model, Become Banks in Bid to Ride Out Crisis: End of Traditional Investment Banking, as Storied Firms Face Closer Supervision and Stringent New Capital Requirements, *Wall Street Journal*, September 22, 2008, at A1.

148 Pub. L. No. 106–554, 114 Stat. 2763.

149 Michael Greenberger, Out of the Black Hole: Regulatory Reform of the Over-The-Counter Derivatives Market, in *Make Markets Be Markets* (Robert Johnson and Erica Payne eds., 2009, Roosevelt Institute).

150 For a suggestion that these factors did induce monoline bond insurers to take additional risks, see Thomas Nelthorpe, The Sure Thing, American Securitization Forum 35 (Winter/Spring 2007).

151 Chapter 5, "Cheap debt: government guarantees, systemic risk, and the instability of regulatory capital requirements," Chapter 7, "Expected government bailouts and too-correlated-to-fail."

152 E.g., sources *supra* note 70 (expansionary monetary policy in Sweden), John B. Taylor, *Getting Off Track: How Government Actions and Interventions Caused, Prolonged, and Worsened the Financial Crisis*, 1–13 (2009, Hoover Institution Press) (arguing that loose monetary policy caused current financial crisis).

153 See Ronald J. Gilson and Charles K. Whitehead, Deconstructing Equity: Public Ownership, Agency Costs, and Complete Capital Markets, 108 *Columbia Law Review* 231 (2008).

7 Procyclical regulation and herd-promoting regulation

This book has thus far unpacked three elements of the Regulatory Instability Hypothesis. Chapter 3 examined the regulatory cycle and explored how feedback effects can develop between asset price bubbles, on the one hand, and deregulation and other regulatory stimuli, on the other. Chapter 4 explored how bubbles promote fraud and undermine compliance by market participants with financial law and regulation. Chapter 5 analyzed how bubbles and regulatory arbitrage reinforce each other in spirals that feed bubbles. The last chapter looked at how deregulation and regulatory arbitrage create feedback for one another and can fuel asset price bubbles.

Bubbles and financial regulation destabilize one another in yet two additional ways. This chapter outlines the last two elements of the Regulatory Instability Hypothesis: procyclical regulations, on the one hand, and the dangers of investment herding and homogeneity, on the other. Procyclical regulations represent legal rules that, by their operation in the ordinary course, exacerbate boom and bust cycles. These regulations promote more investment and more lending as markets boom and then constrict investment as markets contract. These procyclical effects occur in the regular operation of these legal rules. They do not require changes in the substance of legal rules or in the behavior of policymakers or regulators (as is the case with deregulation, reduced enforcement, regulatory preferences, and the other forms of regulatory stimulus described in Chapter 3). Nor do these procyclical effects stem from changes in legal compliance (the topic of Chapter 4) or increasing gamesmanship of financial rules (per Chapter 5). Instead these effects arise, more or less automatically, as firms fully comply with existing financial rules. It is the interaction of these rules with market cycles that push market booms higher and market crashes lower. This general description may seem a bit abstract. Accordingly, a few concrete examples of procyclical regulations will follow in a moment.

After exploring procyclical regulation, the chapter explores a second (and the final) element of the Regulatory Instability Hypothesis, namely the problem of investment herding and homogeneity. Chapter 1 described in detail economic theories of how herd behavior by investors, both irrational and rational, drives asset price bubbles.[1] This chapter examines the danger of this herding from two fresh angles. First, herding by financial institutions into particular investments and asset classes leaves those institutions with dangerous correlations in their risk exposure, which increases systemic risk. Second, the herd behavior that drives asset price bubbles and crashes has an analogue in the herding that drives bank runs. Economists have provided powerful models of bank runs.[2] The economic literature, however, has delved to a far lesser extent into herding *into* liquid asset classes, a type of bank run-in-reverse. Herding that generates liquidity can set the stage for bank runs, as investors stampede out of liquidity.

Both of these dynamics – investment herding that generates dangerous risk correlations and liquidity herding that propels bank runs – have legal and regulatory dimensions, which this chapter will unpack. First, financial regulations may encourage herding, including by granting legal preferences to certain asset classes. Moreover, the prospect of receiving a government bailout increases the collective incentives of financial institutions to make investments with correlated risks. Second, traditional financial regulation does too little to address herding and homogeneity.

These regulations that promote investment herding share several features with procyclical regulations. Both types of regulations intensify market booms and deepen market crashes. These effects occur because of the manner in which both herd-promoting and procyclical regulations shape the collective behavior of market participants, particularly financial institutions. However, procyclical regulations differ from regulations that promote investment herding in several respects. Procyclical regulations interact directly with market cycles. The requirements that they impose on market participants change as the cycle turns. For example, as explained below, boom times may trigger certain loan loss regulations to require lower reserves from banks, while market downturns cause these regulations to impose higher reserves. The substantive obligations imposed by regulations that promote investment herding, by contrast, do not necessarily change as economic cycles turn. Nonetheless, the herding of market participants, as reinforced by regulations, can shift overnight; as boom turns to bust, the herd moves in a different direction. Per one example (detailed further below), the combination of capital requirements and government guarantees can induce financial institutions to herd into investment classes with low regulatory capital weights. These weights stay the same even when a crash occurs and the value of investments in a particular asset class plummets.[3]

Both of the subjects of this chapter – procyclical regulation and herding/ homogeneity – have become centerpieces of a burgeoning literature on "macroprudential" regulation.[4] Macroprudential scholars argue that the traditional emphasis of financial regulation on the safety and soundness of individual financial institutions (on a one-by-one basis) ignores *and can even enhance* risks faced by financial institutions and markets in the aggregate.[5] This chapter will return at several junctures to macroprudential scholarship.

For now, note that the division in the chapter between procyclical regulation and the problem of herding and homogeneity roughly parallels a distinction made by some macroprudential scholars, such as Claudio Borio. Borio argues that the macroprudential regulatory approach is concerned with systemic risk along two dimensions. First, the macroprudential approach focuses on changes in systemic risk over *time*. In particular, systemic risk may increase over time as regulation exacerbates economic cycles. As an example of the macroprudential approach's concern with the time dimension, Borio cites the same procyclical regulations discussed below.[6] Second, Borio argues that macroprudential scholarship is concerned with the distribution of risk along another dimension, which he labels *cross-sectional*. The regulatory concern in this second dimension is that financial institutions make investment decisions that subject them to correlated risk.[7] This chapter does not use Borio's exact rubric (which might be cheekily be renamed "time" and "space"), because the second dimension – common exposures to risks – can also change over time and even cyclically. Indeed, as we will see, this is what makes financial institution herding so difficult to detect and so dangerous.

Procyclical regulation

For over a decade policymakers and economists have worried about the problem of procyclical regulations.[8] Perhaps the first and canonical example of this type of regulation comes in the area of loan loss reserves. Regulations typically base the amount of reserves that a bank must hold against potential losses in its loan portfolio on the level of recent defaults on that bank's loans. However, many of these regulations base those reserves on default data that does not go back far enough in time. This causes regulations to interact with economic cycles to generate a procyclical effect.

Consider the following example: when the economy cycles and turns to a boom phase, asset prices rise. Fewer borrowers default as they have more income and rising asset prices give them two exit options for loans: cheap refinancing or reselling (or "flipping") the asset. Fewer loan defaults cause bank loan losses to dip. This dynamic would also lower loan loss reserve requirements (at least under poorly designed regulations). These regulations might look back to data on bank losses only from the most recent quarter or year to set required reserves. However, this takes a snapshot only of a boom period and misses earlier quarters or years in which the economy was much worse and bank loan losses much higher.[9]

Lower required reserves, in turn, free banks to make additional loans. Additional lending adds more fuel to a market boom.[10] Meanwhile, other feedback mechanisms during a bubble may stoke markets. Rising prices allow borrowers to borrow more, by making assets (such as stock or real estate) more valuable as collateral.[11] Rising prices also permit borrowers to sell assets and then repay loans in full. For example, rising residential real estate prices allow mortgage borrowers either to refinance or to sell a home, prepay the mortgage, and pocket a tidy profit.)[12] A stronger boom lowers the rate of loan defaults, which further reduces loan loss requirements further. A feedback loop has formed.[13]

This feedback mechanism lurches sharply into reverse when the economic cycle turns, financial markets sputter, and asset prices flatten or drop. An economic downturn and lower asset prices translate into higher loan default rates, which then trigger higher reserve requirements. This, in turn, throttles back lending.[14] Lower lending, in turn, further depresses economic growth and asset prices. Speculators in asset markets find two of their potential exit strategies closed. Falling asset prices preclude either reselling the assets (whether stocks or real estate) or obtaining cheap refinancing.[15]

Loan loss reserve regulations can thus amplify the boom and bust cycle.[16] Beyond this direct macroeconomic impact, they have a second, but no less important effect. Procyclical loan loss reserve requirements also render financial institutions more vulnerable to market downturns. Financial institutions that reduce their reserves during boom times can be dangerously exposed to insolvency – caught with their proverbial pants down – when markets crash and loan defaults spike. This increased vulnerability has microeconomic implications: it reduces the effectiveness of financial regulations designed to safeguard the solvency of individual financial institutions. It also has indirect macroeconomic effects, because increasing the fragility of financial institutions ratchets up systemic risk.[17] Failing financial institutions choke off credit, which makes economic downturns more severe and lasting.[18] The failure of one financial institution raises the specter of other financial institutions – particularly its creditors – falling like dominoes. Cascading failures of financial institutions causes a classic form of systemic risk to materialize and metastasize.[19]

The feedback loop created by traditional loan loss reserve regulations has led economists to call for dynamic loan loss provisioning regulations to exert a countercyclical effect. Countercylical regulations – how they operate and the necessary conditions for them to function effectively – are described in more detail in the concluding chapter of this book. For now, the following brief description suffices: dynamic loan loss provisioning uses financial models and data to increase loan loss reserves as a market cycle turns to a boom. This theoretically should throttle back bank lending and leave banks with an extra reserve cushion when a downturn arrives. When it does, dynamic loan loss provisioning requires lower loan loss reserves to encourage greater lending. The final chapter discusses Spain's recent experience with this type of countercyclical regulation.[20]

Capital requirements

Economists have argued that other forms of prudential bank regulation can have procyclical effects. For example, Samuel Hanson, Anil Kashyap, and Jeremy Stein contend that the traditional approach of regulators to bank capital can exacerbate boom and bust cycles. When a bank suffers losses and its regulatory capital ratios deteriorate, its equity cushion against financial failure begins to thin. Regulators would then push banks to take action either by selling new equity or reducing the asset side of their balance sheet. A bank may then choose to sell assets and curtail new lending.[21]

This regulatory approach may make sense from the standpoint of ensuring the safety and soundness of individual banks. However, when many banks suffer losses at the same time, economic havoc ensues. When numerous banks curb their lending simultaneously, the economy contracts. This can trigger a fresh wave of losses for the banks. Moreover, a concurrent attempt by banks to shrink their balance sheets and unload assets creates fire sale conditions in financial markets. As prices plummet, banks encounter great difficulty finding willing buyers. These credit crunch and fire sale dynamics reinforce one another.[22] Banks, arguably, must reduce assets, because of the difficulty in selling new equity. The "debt overhang" – that is the prior claims of creditors on the assets of a troubled institution – make equity unattractive to potential investors.[23] More-over, when many troubled firms seek to access the capital markets simultan-eously, the glut of new share issuances drives down prices and the proceeds that any firm can expect to receive.[24]

Claudio Borio argues that other (more modern) approaches to capital regula-tions can also have procyclical effects. He examines the Basel II Accord, which allows certain large banks to set their own regulatory capital levels according to their proprietary risk models. Borio argues that many of these risk models are inherently flawed because they do not measure changes in risk over long enough time periods.[25] This causes models to alternately underestimate and then overes-timate risk to financial institutions, which "rises in booms, as imbalances build up, and materializes in recessions, as they unwind."[26] Underestimation of risk allows banks to lower capital requirements at precisely the wrong moment: when markets boom and the probability of crisis spikes.[27]

The theory of capital regulations having procyclical effects, however, has out-paced empirical evidence, particularly with respect to procylicality during market busts. In the Panic of 2007–2008, financial institutions did suffer pro-found losses on various mortgages, mortgage-related asset-backed securities, and credit derivatives. A credit crunch then hit. However, producing solid evidence that capital regulations forced banks to conduct fire sales remains a work in progress.[28]

Bankruptcy fire sales

Some evidence of fire sale-like dynamics during the Panic comes from the work of the late legal scholar Sarah Woo. She argued that in the late 2000s concerns of bank regulators with the concentration risk of banks with respect to real estate loans drove individual banks to take individually rational but collectively coun-terproductive measures. Woo contended that this regulatory preoccupation prompted banks to force borrowers into foreclosure or bankruptcy even when banks could have recovered more from individual borrowers through less drastic measures, such as renegotiating loans. These actions by banks depressed the value of real estate loans and real estate generally, triggering further write-downs by banks and reductions in capital. This in turn sparked subsequent waves of foreclosures and created a downward price spiral in the real estate market. Con-cerns with the concentration risk of individual banks thus contributed to real estate market declines that afflicted the banking industry collectively.[29]

Woo's work, however, only infers that banks took these actions because of capital regulations. She demonstrates that banks were more likely to push borrowers into bankruptcy when the banks had high concentration ratios, that is, highly concentrated exposures to particular real estate markets. Although bank regulators track these ratios carefully and factor them into regulatory decisions, Woo's data do not show a direct causal link: she does not demonstrate that regulators forced fire sale behavior by banks. Banks may have individually taken harsh actions with respect to borrowers in order to withdraw money quickly from a collapsing market, before other lenders. This would mirror the rational logic that animates bank runs (described below).[30] Banks might also have acted quickly to retain the confidence of creditors and investors. In other words, banks may have been driven by the perverse logic of a collective action failure instead of by regulation.

Woo's research leaves open whether other examples of bank regulatory policy triggered market-wide fire sales. Moreover, her research did not focus on what caused the high degree of concentration risk among banks in the first place. To understand how these concentrations came about, it is important to turn in a moment to the fifth piece of the Regulatory Instability Hypothesis: investment herding.

Mark-to-market accounting rules?

Banks, policymakers, and a number of scholars blamed another alleged regulatory suspect for exacerbating the Panic of 2007–2008. They claim that the interaction of mark-to-market accounting rules and bank capital requirements (as well as the interaction of mark-to-market with debt covenants or rating agency determinations) caused banks to engage in fire sales when losses on investments mounted.[31] Mark-to-market accounting rules require banks to adjust the value of certain categories of financial investments for fluctuations in the market prices of those assets. This contrasts with historical cost accounting, in which firms record the value of assets on a balance sheet at the price paid for those assets (as adjusted by amortization).[32] Several scholars theorize that, by causing banks to write-up the value of assets during a boom, mark-to-market accounting increases bank leverage. This additional leverage would add further fuel to a boom. Under historical cost accounting, on the other hand, banks could not raise the value of assets. The hidden increase in asset values would create a buffer should banks suffer a downturn.[33]

Other economic studies provide models to explain how mark-to-market accounting might deepen liquidity crises. Losses on financial assets can have contagious effects, as losses on assets force banks to mark down the value of assets. Some mix of capital regulations, bond covenants, and rating agency standards then, the theory goes, forces banks to sell assets to maintain capital ratios and reduce leverage. Simultaneous write downs and asset sales by multiple banks further depresses asset prices, causing a fresh wave of write-downs and fire sales.[34]

This theory, however, runs into problems when confronted with empirical evidence. Studies have found little evidence that mark-to-market accounting led to a decline in the regulatory capital of banks during the financial crisis or that banks conducted significant fire sales of assets because of mark-to-market accounting or fire sales in general.[35] Several factors may have blunted the procyclicality of mark-to-market in practice. First, only a portion of the assets on financial institution balance sheets were subject to mark-to-market requirements.[36] Second, mark-to-market accounting rules are not mechanical; when market prices are not readily available for a certain asset (e.g., because of a market freeze), firms can value those assets according to models. In other words, firms retain a large measure of discretion in measuring assets that trade in markets subject to bouts of illiquidity.[37] One study indicates that banks actually overvalued distressed assets on their balance sheets in crisis years.[38]

Moreover, even the alleged procyclicality of mark-to-market accounting does not necessarily argue for switching to the alternative of historical cost accounting. Historical cost accounting can also be gamed. For example, a firm can cherry pick those assets that have gained in value during a boom and sell them. Yet the firm can retain assets that have not increased, continuing to value them at historic cost.[39] This practice (called "gains trading") inflates the apparent value of the firm, masks its risks, and allows it to game bank capital requirements.[40] During a financial crisis, historical cost accounting can mask the extent of bank losses. The resultant opacity of banks' financial conditions can discourage investment in banks, as investors could not distinguish sick from healthy institutions.[41] Many scholars labeled the criticism of mark-to-market accounting during the Panic of 2007–2008 as a calculated distraction from the real culprit: bank losses that stemmed from bad investments. These scholars likened the criticism of mark-to-market to "shooting the messenger."[42]

Scholars also argue that any procyclical effects of mark-to-market accounting during liquidity crises could be addressed in more productive ways than switching to historical cost accounting and obscuring losses.[43] One mechanism would give banks greater (temporary) flexibility to value assets in a frozen market according to models and not market prices. Alternatively, bank capital regulations and debt covenants could be decoupled from strict mark-to-market accounting metrics during liquidity crises.[44] Finally, some scholars advocated using technology to provide investors and regulators with simultaneous asset valuations under mark-to-market and historical cost methods.[45]

Capital buffers during booms

The doubts as to whether regulations forced fire sales by banks during the Panic of 2007–2008 should not obscure the fact that financial institutions became critically undercapitalized during the crisis. Moreover, financial institutions dramatically increased their leverage and the riskiness of their asset portfolio in the years before the crisis.[46] Chapter 5 described research on how banks heavily engaged in regulatory capital arbitrage during this period to mask leverage and risk-taking and reduce the effectiveness of capital rules.[47] Capital regulations did not bite during the boom times and allowed banks to increase their leverage and fragility.

Therefore, policymakers and scholars have looked to increase capital buffers countercyclically – that is to require banks to hold more equity as a cushion against losses as financial markets enter the boom phase of a cycle.[48] Other scholars recommend a slightly different approach: instead of timing regulations to market cycles, capital requirements could automatically increase or decrease over time according to simpler measures of leverage or asset-liability mismatches in the marketplace.[49] The concluding chapter to his book discusses the advantages of making financial regulations more automatic and countercyclical, including mitigating the political and psychological factors that militate against vigorous regulation during boom times. Yet that chapter also analyzes the limitations of putting regulation on autopilot.

Herd-promoting regulation and homogeneity

The dangers

Investment herding is central to economic theories of how bubbles form. Chapter 1 outlined theories for why investors may swarm into a particular asset class for either rational or irrational reasons. The risks of herding, however, go beyond merely inflating an asset price bubble that will pop and cause investor losses. Two particular dynamics can transform asset price bubbles into far more catastrophic economic events. First, herd behavior by financial institutions leaves those firms with dangerously correlated risk exposures. Second, when financial firms and their investors herd into certain asset classes, they make those assets highly liquid. Although liquidity offers great economic benefits, the herd can reverse course and stampede out of those asset classes. What would be a crash in ordinary stock or real estate markets becomes a bank run for financial institutions. These two dynamics are unpacked below before the analysis turns to the ways that regulation has sown the seeds for systemic risk and liquidity crises.

Financial institution herding and homogeneity

Herd behavior can have a very specific and particularly pernicious effect on the safety and soundness of financial institutions. Consider a group of banks that lend money en masse to railroad companies or that purchase triple A-rated bonds backed by residential real estate mortgages. These banks now face a common risk exposure – either to the railroad industry or to residential real estate and bond markets. When these common loans or investments make up a significant portion of the balance sheets of a significant number of banks, systemic risk elevates. These banks now have a dangerous common exposure to an economic shock. An event that causes severe losses to railroad industry or that causes a broad decline in home prices can place a wide swath of banks in financial peril.[50]

The simultaneous failures of multiple financial institutions can result in a credit crunch. Credit crunches, in turn, trigger cascading problems throughout the economy. Tighter credit causes more businesses to lay off employees, default on loans, and enter insolvency. Again, a feedback loop rears its head; nonlinear herd behavior leads to nonlinear economic fallout.[51]

Herd behavior by financial institutions has another insidious feature; this collective behavior tends to mask the very risks it creates. When financial institutions simultaneously invest in the same assets or lend to the same class of borrowers, the resultant boom diminishes the appearance of risk in those markets. Booming prices can make silly railroad ventures seem more promising and high-credit-risk home buyers appear more solid by reducing their default rates. Rising prices, lower loan defaults, and increased liquidity in asset classes all cloak the dangers of correlated risk exposures for financial institutions.

The Japanese real estate and stock market bubbles of the 1980s provide a stark example of the dynamics and dangers of bank herding in bubbles. Several econometric studies have documented how Japanese banks, across an array of different regulatory categories, herded into specific loan markets. After Japan deregulated its financial services sector (as described in Chapters 2 and 6), banks faced increased competition from securities firms and bond markets in providing capital to large corporations. In response, Japanese banks moved en masse to extend loans to "emerging industries," particularly real estate and financial services.[52] Several studies indicate that herding was particularly strong within each regulatory category of financial institution. Moreover, this bank herding followed a cyclical pattern, with extreme herd behavior in the late 1980s.[53]

It was at this time that Japan's real estate and stock market peaked. Indeed, this bank herding intensified during, and contributed to, a bubble in those sectors.[54] When the Japanese bubble burst, the exposures of these lenders to the same asset classes translated into a contagion of losses, an avalanche of bank failures, and a credit crunch.[55] The herding of banks conjured up systemic risk, and systemic risk then attacked the herd.

Liquidity herding: bank runs and reverse bank runs

Investment herding can take more refined and potentially more dangerous forms. The herd behavior that drives both asset price bubbles and subsequent crashes has a direct analogue in the herding that drives bank runs. Economists model these runs as "self-fulfilling prophesies." One model, created by Douglas Diamond and Philip Dybvig, revolutionized the way economists think about bank runs. Instead of seeing these events as panics driven by irrational behavior, Diamond and Dybvig explain why *rational* depositors would withdraw funds from banks and trigger a bank run. Bank customers may demand the return of their deposits if they expect that other depositors might do so first and strip the cupboard bare. This creates yet another feedback loop: an initial wave of depositor withdrawals prompts more withdrawals, eventually leaving a bank with no money to return to its customers.[56] Franklin Allen and Douglas Gale subsequently developed another model to explain which events might trigger the initial set of withdrawals. According to Allen and Gale, depositors may begin the rush to withdraw funds if they anticipate a downturn in a business cycle that might cause other depositors to need cash and withdraw bank funds.[57]

Economists have extended this same logic behind bank runs to explain how liquidity in capital markets can vanish.[58] To see how bank runs can occur in financial markets and not just in traditional banks, it is important first to define "liquidity." This chapter will explore several different (but related) uses of that term. The first definition of liquidity involves "asset liquidity," or the ability to convert an asset readily into cash.[59] For assets that trade on markets, this first form of liquidity roughly translates into a second form. "Trading liquidity" (also called "market liquidity") describes the ability to find buyers and sellers at any given moment in an asset market. A greater depth of buyers and sellers in a given market means that a sale of a given quantity of an asset will cause less of a movement in the market price.[60] Measuring the impact of the sale of a certain quantity of assets on market prices provides a standard gauge for trading liquidity.[61] In markets with a greater number or "depth" of buyers or sellers, individual trades should cause less of a price change. Investors in financial markets face trading liquidity risk (also called market liquidity risk), which represents the potential losses should a firm not be able to find a counterparty in the market willing to buy the asset at fair market value.[62]

If holders of otherwise liquid market-traded assets become concerned that other investors will begin to sell those assets en masse (for example, because of an economic downturn, or because fears that an asset class has become overvalued in a bubble and will suffer a substantial price decline), they will begin to sell themselves. As with runs on depository banks, these sell-offs can become a self-fulfilling prophecy. Investors may fear selling too late after prices have plummeted and willing buyers in the marketplace have vanished. Accordingly, investors begin to:

- sell asset-backed securities;
- curtail new lending (whether via purchases of new bonds, repurchase agreements, or selling credit protection in credit derivatives); and
- hike requirements for collateral or interest rates on repurchase agreements and other loans.[63]

Liquidity in credit markets dries up as liquidity spirals and a credit crunch reinforce one another.[64] These spirals may take at least two forms. First, "loss spirals" occur when financial institutions experiences losses on their investments because of declines of asset prices. This weakens the institutions' balance sheets and induces them to reduce leverage and shrink balance sheets. When institutions take these steps en masse, asset prices decline further.[65] A second form of spiral, a margin/haircut spiral, initial losses create funding problems for financial institutions, which then reduce their investments and their leverage. This causes asset prices to drop, which causes lenders to these institutions to demand higher margins or more collateral for loans. This pinches financial institutions who engage in a fresh wave of deleveraging.[66] At the same time, when financial institutions simultaneously sell the same assets, they create a "fire sale externality": it may be rational for each firm to unload assets, but this collective behavior triggers a free fall in asset prices that imposes significant market-wide losses.[67]

Chapter 11 surveys economic research on how various capital markets (including markets for asset-backed securities and "repo" lending) suffered "shadow bank runs" during the Panic of 2007–2008. For investors, a run can lead to severe losses or the inability to sell or value their assets. The consequences can be even more devastating for borrowers. Many companies finance themselves through issuing "liquid" instruments to investors; just as banks offer demand deposits to customers, other firms issue short-term securities in capital markets. For these firms, a run turns off the spigot of credit necessary for their survival. This presents a problem of "liquidity" in yet another sense of the word, namely the ability of a firm to pay off short-term debts as they come due.[68] Firms that have a mismatch of long-term assets but short-term liabilities are susceptible to runs – whether of the traditional bank variety or of the post-modern flavor of a financial market freeze.

If the economic literature on bank runs and the evaporation of liquidity is particularly rich, the literature on herding *into* liquid asset classes – a kind of bank run-in-reverse – has been less prominent. The logic behind bank runs can be inserted to explain the emergence of liquidity in certain asset classes. Consider the example of a depository bank. If a bank can convince sufficient investors that other investors will keep deposits in the bank, it can offer investors the ability to withdraw funds upon demand. Sufficient investment herding into the deposits of a bank creates the necessary liquidity, even if there is a risk of a bank run.[69] The same logic applies to market investments. If investors believe that enough other investors will continue to buy, sell, and invest in a particular asset, then they will place a higher value on that asset because of its expected liquidity. When investors herd into a particular asset class, they create trading liquidity.[70]

Investment and liquidity herding together

Herding by financial institutions into certain investments can generate bubbles, correlated credit risk, and market liquidity all at the same time. The economic literature on asset price bubbles tends to be separate from research on bank runs.[71] Yet the two phenomena can be intertwined. The herd behavior that creates bubbles in particular asset markets can also make those assets highly liquid. Indeed, as Chapter 11 will explain further, massive investments in mortgage-related securities fueled a bubble in those instruments and in residential real estate in the United States more generally. This investment herding also made many of those instruments appear highly liquid. Those mortgage-related securities could be traded on financial markets where (at least in theory) a deep pool of buyers and sellers existed.

Scholars often attempt to make distinction between solvency crises (in which financial institutions and other institutions fail because investment losses cause the value of their assets to fall below liabilities) from bank runs and other liquidity crises (in which otherwise solvent firms cannot pay their immediate obligations because short-term financing has evaporated). The distinction turns on whether the crisis can be ended merely by temporary government loans or liquidity injections.[72] Yet the real world can make a mess of such neat divisions.[73] One form of crisis can trigger or morph into the other. A bank run can destroy solvent financial institutions that cannot raise sufficient cash quickly. On the other hand, fears of severe investment losses and potential insolvency can catalyze a run on a bank or financial market. Chapter 11 untangles how solvency and liquidity crises became entangled in the Panic of 2007–2008: losses on mortgage-related securities led to liquidity evaporating in asset-backed securities and "repo" markets. The drying up of short-term credit, in turn, bankrupted many financial institutions large and small.

Note that the herd behavior that precipitates asset price bubbles, bank runs and reverse-bank runs is mirrored by another species of herd behavior in credit markets. Chapter 9 describes how financial institutions have been trapped in a leverage cycle, in which they dramatically increase their leverage during boom times and dramatically contract their leverage in an economic downturn. This leveraging and deleveraging can further reinforce investment herding.

How financial regulation contributes to investment herding

A thorny question remains: how do investors first coordinate their actions to form a herd? In particular, what allows them to create sufficient market depth and liquidity? A combination of contractual and institutional mechanisms – including bank intermediaries offering deposit accounts and financial exchanges complete with market-makers and specialists on those exchanges – provide vessels for liquidity. Central banks and government regulators often seek to enhance these vessels – for example by mandating disclosure for securities[74] or requiring market-makers on exchanges to provide liquidity when it dries up in particular securities.[75] More importantly, regulatory preferences granted to particular institutions – such as when central banks offer payment clearing services[76] access to emergency loans,[77] and (as we will see) deposit insurance to select financial institutions – create a chrysalis for a liquid market to coalesce. These regulatory preferences provide a prime example of how regulators and regulations can promote investment and liquidity herding.

Capital requirements and investment herding

Some regulations encourage, at the margin, herding into particular investment classes. Chapter 5 explained how capital requirements categorize bank assets according to their perceived riskiness and then assign risk weights to each category. Assets with lower risk weights require banks to hold less equity against them.[78] That chapter also explained how various government interventions, including deposit insurance and other explicit and implicit government guarantees of financial institutions and tax preferences for debt, create powerful incentives for financial institutions to game capital requirements and invest in debt securities with higher returns (and levels of economic risk) but lower capital charges. This creates a strong urge for financial institutions to herd into particular asset classes.

Law professor Roberta Romano explains how the details of capital regulations promoted this herding. She contends that capital regulations created under the Basel Accords promote dangerous homogeneity in the investments of banks by providing strong incentives to invest in particular asset categories.[79] She contends that the structure of capital requirements led banks to invest in the same types of assets – for example, investment grade mortgage-backed securities or Greek sovereign debt.[80] Herding into these supposedly safe assets left banks exposed to the same economic risks. When the value of the financial instruments crashed, their liquidity also vanished.

One can accept that capital requirements can contribute herding without necessarily accepting Professor Romano's broader argument against harmonizing capital requirements.[81] Placing too much blame on regulations discounts the tendency for investors and financial institutions to engage in investment herding of their own accord. Indeed, early asset price bubbles developed and crashed in the absence of capital requirements or other modern financial regulations.

Legal preferences for financial instruments and trading liquidity

Regulation also promotes herding into liquidity by granting certain investments legal preferences. Deposit insurance provides a basic example. Designed as a remedy for bank runs, government-provided insurance encourages investors to invest funds in demand deposits. The government safety net also provides a coordinating mechanism that encourages liquidity formation in bank deposits. By solving the collective action problem described above, deposit insurance catalyzes the initial investor herding that creates a liquid asset class.

Deposit insurance regulations foster trading liquidity in a secondary way, as well. To counter the moral hazard that comes with insurance, governments charge premia and impose various liquidity regulations on banks. In many countries, these liquidity regulations include requirements that banks hold a certain quantity of specified categories of assets deemed to be highly liquid. Often these assets are limited to government bonds.[82] By steering banks towards a narrow band of instruments, these regulations create a deeper and more liquid trading market in those instruments.

Regulations can promote liquidity herding via subtler means. Chapter 11 describes how, in 1983, the financial industry successfully lobbied the U.S. Congress to grant certain exemptions from normal bankruptcy rules for repurchase agreements ("repos"). In 2005, the financial industry convinced Congress to grant similar exemptions for certain derivatives ("swaps").[83] Thus, a party to one of these derivative contracts is no longer subject to the automatic stay and voidable preferences provisions of the bankruptcy code that would restrict their remedies as a creditor should their counterparty enter bankruptcy. This means that should the counterparty file for bankruptcy, the creditor party in a derivative contract does not face the normal legal restrictions on terminating the derivative contract, accelerating the debtor's obligations, foreclosing on collateral, and exercising set-off rights. Nor is the creditor subject to potential claw-back of pre-bankruptcy payments from the debtor.[84] The market volume of repos and swaps skyrocketed after Congress granted each of these exemptions.[85]

These legal exemptions or preferences did more than just stimulate the markets for these two types of financial contract. They also made them liquid. Economists Gary Gorton and Andrew Metrick argue that these exemptions made repos more attractive as an investment substitute for the demand deposits offered by banks. According to Gorton and Metrick, repos offer firms a short-term investment backed by collateral that has many of the same features of demand deposits, namely low risk and the ability to withdraw funds quickly.[86] Gorton and Metrick explain that bankruptcy exemptions allowed repos to become "informationally insensitive debt," just like bank deposits.[87] Informationally insensitive debt describes obligations that are "immune to adverse selection by privately informed traders."[88] In other words, investors do not have to worry that more informed traders can reap a profit at their expense by using private information.[89] Information insensitivity also translates into very low search costs for investors seeking to value the debt instrument. Under normal circumstances (and thanks in part to government insurance), customers do not need to expend considerable resources in assessing the risk of losing money in a bank deposit account. Similarly, the bankruptcy exemptions mean that parties to repo and swap contracts must spend less time assessing the risk that their counterparties will become insolvent.

By becoming more like bank deposits, repos and other financial instruments assumed many of the economic features of "money," as explained further in Chapter 9. That chapter also analyzes how regulatory preferences thus work to increase the effective supply of money in the economy. Chapter 11 looks at this monetary dynamic in the context of the Panic of 2007–2008; it argues that legal preferences (together with regulatory arbitrage) midwifed the birth of a "shadow banking system." This shadow system enlarged the effective money supply and fueled prices in real estate and capital markets in the years leading up to the Panic.

Expected government bailouts and too-correlated-to-fail

According to a number of economists, the prospect of receiving a government bailout increases the incentives of financial institutions to engage in investment herding and to take correlated risks.[90] The government may be unwilling to let a large group of financial institutions fail at the same time for fear of widespread damage to the economy.[91] The government accordingly bails out financial institutions, which provides a windfall for their creditors (and possibly their shareholders too).[92] The prospect of receiving a bailout encourages financial institutions to take correlated risks.[93] Firms that stay outside the herd can be more safely allowed to fail by the government. Meanwhile, there may be no economically, politically, or legally principled way for the government to bail out some firms in the herd but not others.

A market-wide expectation of government bailouts can thus become a self-fulfilling prophesy. The resultant herd behavior can leave the government with no choice but to intervene. Moreover, as noted above, when firms herd into particular asset classes, they increase systemic risk.

Economists Emmanuel Farhi and Jean Tirole contend that bailouts (or merely the prospect of bailouts) promote not only herding into particular asset classes, but other forms of herd behavior by financial institutions as well. They argue that bailouts encourage financial institutions to engage in maturity transformation en masse. Maturity transformation occurs when a financial firm invests in long-term assets and finances itself with short-term debt. Maturity transformation leaves institutions susceptible to bank runs and other liquidity crises. To prevent destructive liquidity crises from savaging the wider economy, government must provide bailouts to firms that engage in maturity transformation.[94] The upshot of this vicious circle is that the mere expectation of government action promotes a stampede by financial institutions.

Farhi and Tirole also contend that market expectations of bailouts encourage financial institutions collectively to increase leverage.[95] When numerous financial institutions become over-leveraged simultaneously, they become, individually and collectively, more vulnerable to an economic downturn. Moreover, market-wide expectations of a bailout for creditors make debt a relatively cheaper source of financing for financial institutions than equity. (As Chapter 5 explained, this not only encourages financial institutions to increase their leverage, it also increases incentives to engage in regulatory capital arbitrage.)[96] The government cannot afford to let a large number of leveraged financial institutions fail and must provide a bailout.

Increased leverage has knock-on macroeconomic effects. It not only leaves financial institutions vulnerable to increased losses, it also has the macroeconomic effects described in detail in Chapter 9, which include enlarging the effective money supply *and* fueling the growth of a bubble. Perversely, bailouts, a tool used to dampen systemic risk, can operate to increase that risk.

In all of these scenarios, financial institutions essentially play a game of "chicken" with the government. Like the sheriff played by Cleavon Little in the classic Mel Brooks film *Blazing Saddles*, financial institutions hold a collective gun to their head – whether via correlated investments, maturity transformation, or excessive leverage. They tell the town folk to give them what they want or "we'll shoot."

The problem of investment herding creates a different version of a much-discussed problem: in addition to "too-big-to-fail," policymakers must also worry about "too-correlated-to-fail." The preoccupation with the size of financial institutions (or their interconnectedness) may distract from the risks posed by many smaller financial institutions increasing systemic risk through herding and correlated risk exposures. It also obscures the even more nuanced problems of collective maturity transformation and excessive leveraging en masse. The moral hazard created by government guarantees and bailouts may be far easier to understand and to explain to the public than how the expectation of government intervention stimulates herd behavior.

Unfortunately, there are no easy solutions to the problems created by government bailouts. The government could search for a way to send a credible signal to the marketplace that it will not bail out financial institutions. This, however, is much easier said than done. After firms already form a herd and face collective extinction, a government may feel it has no choice but to provide bailouts. Hardwiring bailout prohibitions into law, as the Dodd-Frank Act allegedly attempts,[97] may provide false comfort. Who would enforce the prohibition? What would prevent the law from being amended? As the concluding chapter to this book explains, legal principles prevent present legislatures and sovereigns from binding their future counterparts.[98]

Moreover, would society want to restrict government bailouts even if it meant economic devastation? Economists call this "time-inconsistency." Before a crisis, the government should forswear providing bailouts. Yet, during a crisis, the public may want the government to avert Armageddon.[99] This time inconsistency interferes with the government transmitting a credible signal that it will not provide bailouts. It allows market participants to continue to play chicken with the state.

Regulators failing to detect herding

If forswearing bailouts is less than credible, the alternative is to regulate to mitigate herd behavior by financial institutions. Yet, scholars lament the systematic failure of financial regulators to recognize and mitigate herd behavior in financial markets. This represents one of the core criticisms of financial regulation by macroprudential scholars. They argue that regulation focuses too much on individual financial institutions in isolation and misses the dangerous correlations in the risk exposures among different financial institutions.[100]

Economists working under the macroprudential umbrella have put forth a number of policy solutions to address this homogeneity. First, regulators need to be able to detect and measure correlations in risk among financial institutions. Moreover, they need to track these correlations as they change over time. To achieve this scholars have proposed novel tools and metrics. For example, economists Tobias Adrian and Markus Brunnermeier propose a new measure of systemic risk called "CoVar" which measures the value-at-risk of financial institutions stemming from the potential financial distress of other financial institutions.[101] Of course, CoVar and other refined tools still require regulators with the capacities and incentives to use them properly. Scholars have advocated using new regulatory agencies, such as the Office of Financial Research created by the Dodd-Frank Act, to track changes in risk correlations in the financial system.[102]

The problem of correlated risk demands much of regulators. It requires mechanisms (both technical and legal) to gather and process massive amounts of information from individual financial institutions to spot emerging correlations. It would also depend upon a fundamental reorientation of regulators; they must look not only at the health of individual firms, one-by-one, but at the collective behavior and collective risks of many institutions.

Indeed, a bevy of macroprudential scholarship, new risk management tools, and changes to the organizational chart of financial regulators alone should not give the public false hope that the problems of herd behavior or procyclical regulations can be easily cured. Macroprudential scholars realize that countercyclical regulations and other macroprudential tools may prove difficult to calibrate. As a cushion against mistakes by the market and regulators, they also recommend increasing the buffers that financial institutions must hold against various forms of financial risk materializing.[103]

However, firms have strong incentives to game these requirements too. Chapter 5 explained how the presence of government guarantees and the market's expectation of government guarantees make debt cheap *and* create strong incentives for regulatory capital arbitrage.

Moreover, expectations placed on any regulatory fix must be tempered by over three centuries of history that underscore how the regulatory pathologies created by asset price bubbles persist in, pervade, and permeate financial markets. Efforts to impose tougher capital regulations, create countercyclical loan loss regulations for banks, or address risk correlations in the portfolios of investment funds all crash head on into the dynamics of the Regulatory Instability Hypothesis. Bubbles reduce demand for any and all of these regulations. They atrophy the incentives and capacities of policymakers to maintain and enforce laws. At the same moment, bubbles rot away the incentives of market participants to comply with legal rules, while supercharging regulatory arbitrage. Countercyclical regulations that bite harder during booms or rules that discourage investments in sizzling asset classes may only exert a hydraulic effect as capital seeks to surge and flow around legal dams and levees. If one class of financial institution faces higher regulatory "taxes," investors will move money to less regulated competitors. Or they will devise new transaction structures to sidestep regulation. If investors and financial institutions cannot find a legal avenue to access booming markets, they may look to illicit back alleys or lobby policymakers to loosen the screws.

In other words, a bubble's rise jolts the regulatory stimulus cycle into motion, starts compliance rot, and promotes regulatory arbitrage. The various pieces of the Regulatory Instability Hypothesis – the regulatory cycle, compliance rot, increasing regulatory arbitrage, procyclical regulations, and laws that fail to retard and even promote investment herding – interlock and reinforce one another.

The questions then become: what, if anything, can financial laws do about asset price bubbles? What can they do about the pernicious feedback loops that form between booming markets and deteriorating financial regulation? The next chapter begins to address the first question – by asking what regulations can do to retard bubble formation.

Notes

1 See David Hirshleifer and Siew Hong Teoh, Herd Behaviour and Cascading in Capital Markets: A Review and Synthesis, 9 *European Financial Management* 25 (2003) (reviewing economic theories and empirical evidence behind herding (convergence in investor behavior) and cascading (when investors ignore private information signals and base decisions on behavior of others) in capital markets); Sushil Bikchandani and Sunil Sharma, Herd Behavior in Financial Markets, 47 International Monetary Fund, *Staff Papers No. 279* (2001).
2 See *infra* notes 56–7 and accompanying text.
3 See *infra* notes 78–81 and accompanying text.
4 For a survey of this scholarship, see Gabriele Galati and Ricchild Moessner, Macroprudential Policy: A Literature Review, Bank for International Settlements, *Working Paper No. 337* (2011) available at www.bis.org/publ/work337.pdf (last visited July 27, 2013).
5 See generally Samuel G. Hanson, Anil K. Kashyap, and Jeremy C. Stein, A Macroprudential Approach to Financial Regulation, 25 *Journal of Economic Perspectives* 3 (2011).
6 Claudio Borio, Towards a Macroprudential Framework for Financial Supervision and Regulation? Bank for International Settlements, *Working Paper No. 128*, 11–17 (February 2003) available at http://papers.ssrn.com/sol3/papers.cfm?abstract_id=841306## (last visited July 27, 2013).
7 Ibid. at 10.
8 E.g., Claudio Borio, Craig Furfine, and Philip Lowe, Procyclicality of the Financial System and Financial Stability: Issues and Policy Options, in Marrying the Macro and Microprudential Dimensions of Financial Stability, Bank for International Settlements, Monetary and Economics Department, *Working Paper No. 1* (March 2001); Charles A.E. Goodhart, The Historical Pattern of Economic Cycles and Their Interaction with Asset Prices and Financial Regulation, in *Asset-Price Bubbles: The Implications for Monetary, Regulatory, and International Policies*, 467 (William C. Hunter, George G. Kaufman, and Michael Pomerleano, eds., 2003, MIT Press). Cf. Jeffrey Carmichael and Neil Esho, Asset Price Bubbles and Prudential Regulation, in *Asset-Price Bubbles: The Implications for Monetary, Regulatory, and International Policies*, 481, 491–8 (William C. Hunter, George G. Kaufman, and Michael Pomerleano, eds., 2003, MIT Press) (analyzing ability of various regulations to counter procyclicality in bank lending and stem growth of asset price bubbles).
9 Jaime Caruana, Banking Provisions and Asset Price Bubbles, in *Asset-Price Bubbles: The Implications for Monetary, Regulatory, and International Policies*, 537, 540–2 (William C. Hunter, George G. Kaufman, and Michael Pomerleano, eds., 2003, MIT Press).
10 Ibid. at 538–9, 541–2; Carmichael and Esho, *supra* note 8, at 481 (detailing how increased bank lending and market booms reinforced one another in various episodes of Australia's financial history, creating risk of crises).
11 Ibid. at 538; Goodhart, *supra* note 8, at 67, 474.
12 Cf. Stephen G. Ryan, Accounting in and for the Subprime Crisis, 83 *Accounting Review* 1605, 1607, 1615 (2008) (describing how subprime mortgage market

flourished when housing prices rose, but had "binary" quality; when prices declined, borrowers could no longer sell or refinance and markets collapsed).

Chapter 9 describes recent economic research on the leverage cycle. Chapter 9, "Leverage cycles."

13 Caruana, *supra* note 9, at 538–9, 541–2.

14 Caruana, *supra* note 9, at 538–9, 541.

15 Caruana, *supra* note 9, at 538–9; Ryan, *supra* note 12, at 1615.

16 Caruana, *supra* note 9, at 538–42.

17 George G. Kaufman and Kenneth E. Scott, What is Systemic Risk, and Do Bank Regulators Retard or Contribute to It? 7 *Independent Review* 371, 371 (2003) (defining systemic risk as "the risk of a breakdown in an entire system, as opposed to breakdowns in individual parts or components"). See also Steven L. Schwarcz, Systemic Risk, 97 *Georgetown Law Journal* 193 (2008). Systemic risk thus cannot be mitigated through diversification. See Larry E. Ribstein, Fraud on a Noisy Market, 10 *Lewis and Clark Law Review* 137, 142 (2006) (discussing how arbitrageurs cannot diversify away systemic risk). Systemic losses may begin with an external shock that disrupts entire financial markets, or with a chain reaction in which one financial institution fails, causing its creditors to fail as well. Kaufman and Scott, *supra*, at 372–3.

Systemic risk represents a prime concern of financial regulators, due to its enormous repercussions and the inability of any individual financial institution to mitigate this form of risk through diversification. See Schwarcz, *supra*, at 200–2. Professor Schwarcz argues that not only do financial institutions lack the capacity to deal with systemic risk individually (because of an inability to diversify away the risk), but that they also lack incentives due to collective action failure; no one firm can capture all the of the benefit of an action it takes to reduce systemic risk. Ibid.

18 Goodhart, *supra* note 8, at 471.

19 See Kaufman and Scott, *supra* note 17, at 372–3 (describing chain reaction form of systemic risk).

20 See Caruana, *supra* note 9.

21 Hanson *et al.*, *supra* note 5, at 4–5.

22 Ibid. at 5–6.

23 Ibid. at 6.

24 At the same time, any one firm might be reluctant to attempt to raise equity on its own during a crisis for fear of sending a signal to the marketplace of its financial weakness. See Markus K. Brunnermeier, Deciphering the Liquidity and Credit Crunch 2007–2008, 23 *Journal of Economic Perspectives* 77, 89 (2009) (discussing failure of Lehman Brothers to raise equity during crisis as its financial condition deteriorated).

25 Borio, *supra* note 6, at 11–16.

26 Ibid. at 8, 11–15.

27 Goodhart, *supra* note 8, at 474–5. For an early critique of Basel II of having procyclical effects, see Jón Danielssón, Paul Embrechts, Charles Goodhart, Con Keating, Felix Muennich, Olivier Renault, and Hyun Song Shin, An Academic Response to Basel II, London School of Economics and Financial Markets Group, *Special Paper No. 130* (May 2001). For a more recent model of the procyclical effects of Basel II, see Rafael Repullo and Javier Suarez, The Procyclical Effects of Bank Capital Regulation, 26 *Review of Financial Studies* 452 (2013).

28 The empirical evidence that *bank* capital requirements had procyclical effects and contributed to fire sales during the Panic of 2007–2008 is mixed at best. See *infra* notes 35–6 and accompanying text. However, evidence that various regulatory constraints may have forced *insurance companies* into fire sales during the crisis is somewhat stronger. E.g., Andrew Ellul, Chotibhak Jotikasthira, and Christian Lundblad, Regulatory Pressure and Fire Sales in the Corporate Bond Market, 101 *Journal*

of Financial Economics 596 (2011); Craig B. Merrill, Taylor D. Nadauld, René M. Stulz, and Shane Sherlund, Did Capital Requirements and Fair Value Accounting Spark Fire Sales in Distressed Mortgage-Backed Securities? National Bureau of Economic Research, *Working Paper No. 18270* (August 2012) available at www. nber.org/papers/w18270 (last visited July 27, 2013).

29 Sarah Pei Woo, Regulatory Bankruptcy: How Bank Regulation Causes Fire Sales, 99 *Georgetown Law Journal* 1615 (2011).

30 See *infra* notes 56–7 and accompanying text.

31 E.g., Peter J. Wallison, Fixing Fair Value Accounting, 6 *Journal of Law, Economics and Policy* 137 (2010).

32 For a concise summary of mark-to-market accounting rules in effect in the United States at the time of the Panic of 2007–2008 (including Statements of Financial Accounting Standards Nos. 107, 157, and 159), see John C. Heaton, Deborah Lucas, and Robert L. McDonald, Is Mark-to-market Accounting Destabilizing? Analysis and Implications for Policy, 57 *Journal of Monetary Economics* 64, 66–8 (2010).

33 Guillaume Plantin, Haresh Sapra, Hyun Song Shin, Fair Value Accounting and Financial Stability, Banque de France, *Financial Stability Review No. 12*, 85, 89–92 (October 2008); Avinash D. Persaud, Regulation, Valuation and Systemic Liquidity, Banque de France, *Financial Stability Review No. 12*, 75 (October 2008). See also Christian Laux and Christian Leuz, The Crisis of Fair-Value Accounting: Making Sense of the Recent Debate, 34 *Accounting, Organizations and Society* 826, 829 (2009) (reviewing theory of procyclical effects); Haresh Sapra, The Economic Trade-Offs in the Fair Value Debate, 6 *Journal of Law, Economics and Policy* 193 (2010).

34 Franklin Allen and Elena Carletti, Mark-to-market Accounting Liquidity Pricing, 45 *Journal of Accounting and Economics* 358 (2008); Guillaume Plantin, Haresh Sapra, and Hyun Song Shin, Mark-to-market: Panacea or Pandora's Box? 46 *Journal of Accounting Research* 435 (2008) (constructing a model that shows inefficiencies of mark-to-market accounting can be particularly severe for assets that are of long duration, illiquid, and senior); Heaton *et al.*, *supra* note 32, at 69–71. See also Laux and Leuz, *supra* note 33, at 829.

35 E.g., Brad A. Badertscher, Jeffrey J. Burks, and Peter D. Easton, A Convenient Scapegoat: Fair Value Accounting by Commercial Banks during the Financial Crisis, 87 *Accounting Review* 59 (2012); Sanders Shaffer, Fair Value Accounting: Villain or Innocent Victim: Exploring the Links between Fair Value Accounting, Bank Regulatory Capital and the Recent Financial Crisis, Federal Reserve Bank of Boston, *Working Paper No. QAU10-01* (January 31, 2010) available at http://papers. ssrn.com/sol3/papers.cfm?abstract_id=1543210 (last visited July 27, 2013) (sample of large banks during crisis shows no clear link between mark-to-market losses and declines in regulatory capital, but suggests other factors – particularly loan losses – reduced that capital). See also Amir Amel-Zadeh and Geoff Meeks, Bank Failure, Mark-to-Market and the Financial Crisis, Unpublished manuscript (November 1, 2011) available at http://papers.ssrn.com/sol3/papers.cfm?abstract_id=1494452 (last visited July 27, 2013) ("preliminary results … do not provide consistent evidence of investors perceiving increased risk of externalities and feedback loops in bank balance sheet valuations due to mark-to-market accounting."); Office of the Chief Accountant, Division of Corporation Finance, U.S. Securities & Exchange Commission, Report and Recommendations Pursuant to Section 133 of the Emergency Economic Stabilization Act of 2008: Study on Mark-to-Market Accounting (2008).

Some studies conducted well prior to the crisis have indicated that fair market value accounting creates more volatility, is more subject to manipulation, and puts more stress on bank regulatory capital levels than historical cost accounting. Mary E. Barth, Wayne R. Landsman, and James M. Wahlen, Fair Value Accounting: Effects on Banks' Earnings Volatility, Regulatory Capital, and Value of Contractual Cash Flows, 19 *Journal of Banking and Finance* 577 (1995).

Two studies purported to show that fair market value accounting contributed to contagion. Urooj Khan, Does Fair Value Accounting Contribute to Systemic Risk in the Banking Industry? *Columbia Business School Research Paper* (November 15, 2010) available at http://ssrn.com/abstract=1911895; Robert M. Bowen, Urooj Khan, and Shivaram Rajgopal, The Economic Consequences of Relaxing Fair Value Accounting and Impairment Rules on Banks during the Financial Crisis of 2008–2009, Unpublished manuscript (January 10, 2010) available at http://papers.ssrn.com/sol3/papers.cfm?abstract_id=1498912 (event study of effect of relaxation of mark-to-market rules on stock prices). However, these studies relied on stock returns or prices, which measure the perceived effect of mark-to-market accounting rather than actual bank behavior, in contrast with the Badertscher *et al.* and Shaffer studies above. See Badertscher *et al.*, at 12–13.

36 However, even large banks, which held a greater proportion of assets subject to mark-to-market rules, do not appear to have conducted fire sales due to deteriorating regulatory capital. Shaffer, *supra* note 35.
37 See Nicole Gelinas, Mark to Market: A False Culprit, 6 *Journal of Law, Economics and Policy* 145, 149–50 (2010).
38 Harry Huizinga and Luc Laeven, Accounting Discretion of Banks During a Financial Crisis, European Banking Center, *Discussion Paper No. 2009-17* (July 2009).
39 Laux and Leuz, *supra* note 33, at 829.
40 David Jones, Emerging Problems with the Basel Capital Accord: Regulatory Capital Arbitrage and Related Issues, 24 *Journal of Banking and Finance* 35, 36–7, 49–50 (2000) (including gains trading as form of regulatory capital arbitrage and discussing policy consequences of regulatory capital arbitrage).
41 See Laux and Leuz, *supra* note 33, at 828.
42 Raymond C. Niles, Eighty Years in the Making: How Housing Subsidies Caused the Financial Meltdown, 6 *Journal of Law, Economics and Policy* 165 (2010); See also Gelinas, *supra* note 37, at 151–2.
43 Laux and Leuz, *supra* note 33, at 832.
44 Heaton *et al.*, *supra* note 32, at 74–5.
45 James J. Angel, In Praise of Mark to Management: The Need for Three-Dimensional Accounting, 6 *Journal of Law, Economics and Policy* 153 (2010).
46 Tobias Adrian and Hyun Song Shin, Liquidity and Leverage, 19 *Journal of Financial Intermediation* 418 (2010).
47 Chapter 5, "A case study: regulatory capital arbitrage."
48 Mathias Drehmann, Claudio Borio, Leonardo Gambacorta, Gabriel Jiménez, and Carlos Trucharte, Countercyclical Capital Buffers: Exploring Options, Bank for International Settlements, *Working Paper No. 317* (July 2010) available at http://papers.ssrn.com/sol3/papers.cfm?abstract_id=1648946 (last visited July 27, 2013); Hanson *et al.*, *supra* note 5, at 7–9.
   Countercyclical capital requirements became key elements of both the U.S. Dodd-Frank Act and the Basel III Capital Accord. Michal Kowalik, Countercyclical Capital Regulation: Should Bank Regulators Use Rules or Discretion? *Federal Reserve Bank of Kansas City Economic Review* 63 (2nd Q. 2011).
49 Markus K. Brunnermeier, Andrew Crockett, Charles A. Goodhart, Avinash Persaud, and Hyun Song Shin, *The Fundamental Principles of Financial Regulation*, 31–6 (2009, Centre for Economic Policy Research).
50 Kaufman and Scott, *supra*, note 17, at 372–3 (naming three causes of systemic risk, including when many financial institutions have common exposures to particular economic shocks).
51 Goodhart, *supra* note 8, at 471; Carmichael and Esho, *supra* note 8 (discussing Australia's historical experience). See also Brunnermeier, *supra* note 24 (discussing dynamics of credit and liquidity crunches in Panic of 2007–2008).
52 Ryuichi Nakagawa and Hirofumi Uchida, Herd Behaviour by Japanese Banks after

Financial Deregulation, 78 *Economica* 618 (2011); Hirofumi Uchida and Ryuichi Nakagawa, Herd Behavior in the Japanese Loan Market: Evidence from Bank Panel Data, 16 *Journal of Financial Intermediation* 555 (2007); Ryuichi Nakagawa, Hidekazu Oiwa, and Fumiko Takeda, The Economic Impact of Herd Behavior in the Japanese Loan Market, 20 *Pacific-Basin Finance Journal* 600 (2012).

53 Uchida and Nakagawa, *supra* note 52. In addition, studies indicate that a significant portion of this herding stemmed from "irrational" decision-making. Ibid.

54 Nakagawa *et al.*, *supra* note 52; Uchida and Nakagawa, *supra* note 52. For a description of the Japanese real estate and stock market bubbles, see Chapter 2, "Japan's real estate bubble," Chapter 6, "Japan."

55 Chapter 2, "Japan's real estate bubble," Chapter 6, Japan: "Increased lending and asset market boom," and Japan: "Crisis."

56 Douglas W. Diamond and Philip H. Dybvig, Bank Runs, Deposit Insurance, and Liquidity, 91 *Journal of Political Economy* 401 (1983).

57 Franklin Allen and Douglas Gale, Optimal Financial Crises, 53 *Journal of Finance* 1245 (1998).

58 E.g., Gary Gorton and Andrew Metrick, Securitized Banking and the Run on Repo, 104 *Journal of Financial Economics* 425 (2011).

59 E.g., Jaroslaw Morawski, *Investment Decisions on Illiquid Assets: A Search Theoretical Approach to Real Estate Liquidity*, 13 (2009, Springer Gabler); Roger A. Lyon, *Investment Portfolio Management in the Commercial Bank*, 29 (1960, Rutgers University Press); Loren A. Nikolai, John D. Bazley, and Jefferson P. Jones, *Intermediate Accounting*, 601 (11th ed. 2010, South-western Cengage Learning) (providing text book accounting definition of liquidity).

60 See Sanford J. Grossman and Merton H. Miller, Liquidity and Market Structure, 43 *Journal of Finance* 617 (1988) (presenting model for how market liquidity is created). Similarly, "liquid" assets are assets that can be bought or sold readily without major price changes. Economists often measure "market liquidity" along three dimensions: *range*, or the spread between bid and ask prices in a market; and *depth*, which means the volume of trades that can occur without moving the market price, and *resiliency*, which describes how quickly market prices revert to previous levels after a price shock. Charles Adams, Donald J. Mathieson, Garry Schinasi, and International Monetary Fund Research Staff, *International Capital Markets: Development, Prospects, and Key Policy Issues*, 70 (1999, International Monetary Fund).

61 See Peter L. Bernstein, Liquidity, Stock Markets, and Market Makers, 16 *Financial Management* 54, 54 (1987).

62 This raises the question of what constitutes "fair market value." There are other variations on the definition of "trading-liquidity risk" or "market-liquidity risk" that have their own ambiguities. According to the Bank for International Settlements, market-liquidity risk occurs when "a firm cannot easily offset or eliminate a position at the market price because of inadequate market depth or market disruption." Bank for International Settlements, *Principles for Sound Liquidity Risk Management and Supervision*, 1 n.2 (June 2008, Bank for International Settlements).

63 For some of the literature on bank runs in the shadow banking sector, see Gary Gorton, Slapped in the Face by the Invisible Hand: Banking and the Panic of 2007, National Bureau of Economic Research, *Working Paper* (May 9, 2009) available at http://papers.ssrn.com/sol3/papers.cfm?abstract_id=1401882 (last visited July 27, 2013); Gary Gorton and Andrew Metrick, Securitized Banking and the Run on Repo, 104 *Journal of Financial Economics* 425 (2012); Gary B. Gorton, *Slapped by the Invisible Hand: The Panic of 2007* (2010, Oxford University Press).

64 Brunnermeier, *supra* note 24 (describing these dynamics in theory and in the Panic of 2007–2008).

65 Brunnermeier *et al.*, *supra* note 49, at 16–18.

66 Ibid. at 18–23.

67 Ibid. at 23–4. For a model of the "flight to quality" during a market crisis, see Ricardo J. Caballero and Arvind Krishnamurthy, Collective Risk Management in a Flight to Quality, 63 *Journal of Finance* 2195 (2008).

68 This is often labeled "funding liquidity risk," which has been defined as "the risk that [a] firm will not be able to meet efficiently both expected and unexpected current and future cash flow and collateral needs without affecting either daily operations or the financial condition of the firm." Bank for International Settlements, *supra* note 61, at 1.

69 Diamond and Dybvig provide a model to explain this in the first (less heralded) section of their classic article on bank runs, Diamond and Dybvig, *supra* note 56, at 405–10.

70 See, e.g. Andrea Devenow and Ivo Welch, Rational Herding in Financial Economics, 40 *European Economic Review* 603, 606–7 (1996) (summarizing literature on "payoff externalities" creating liquidity in financial markets); Anat R. Admati and Paul Pfleiderer, A Theory of Intraday Patterns: Volume and Price Variability, 1 *Review of Financial Studies* 3 (1988) (developing theory explaining intraday trading patterns on exchanges based on strategic interactions of "liquidity" and "informed" traders, who seek to benefit from concentrating trading in the same windows). Cf. Bhagwan Chowdry and Vikram Nanda, Multimarket Trading and Market Liquidity, 4 *Review of Financial Studies* 483 (1991) (actions by market makers in liquid markets defeat informed traders acting on "inside information").

71 Cf. Devenow and Welch, *supra* note 70, at 605–6 (surveying literatures on rational herding in stock markets and bank runs); David Hirshleifer and Siew Hong Teoh, Herd Behaviour and Cascading in Capital Markets: A Review and Synthesis, 9 *European Financial Management* 25, 50–3 (2003).

72 See Andrew Dewit, Masaru Kaneko, and Yukiko Yamazaki, The Politics of Fixing Financial Crises: Liquidity versus Solvency, in *Keynes and Modern Economics*, 243, 244–5 (Ryuzo Kuroki ed. 2012, Routledge).

73 Ibid. See also Michael D. Bordo, An Historical Perspective on the Crisis of 2007–2008, National Bureau of Economic Research, *Working Paper No. 14569* (December 2008) available at www.nber.org/papers/w14569 (last visited July 27, 2013) (comparing interaction of solvency and liquidity problems for financial institutions in Panic of 2007–2008 with earlier historical financial crises).

74 Marcel Kahan, Securities Laws and the Social Costs of "Inaccurate" Stock Prices, 41 *Duke Law Journal* 977, 992–4, 1017–25 (1992) (discussing how inaccurate securities prices reduce liquidity and how securities laws theoretically address these inaccuracies). See also John C. Coffee, Jr., Market Failure and the Economic Case for a Mandatory Disclosure System, 70 *Virginia Law Review* 717 (1984) (providing economic justification for mandatory securities disclosure).

75 These regulatory obligations on market-makers have fallen out of favor in the United States. See Onnig H. Dombalagian, The Expressive Synergies of the Volcker Rule, 54 *Boston College Law Review* 469, 480–3 (2013).

76 C.A.E. Goodhart, Why Do Banks Need a Central Bank? 39 *Oxford Economic Papers* 75 (1987) (arguing private sector could provide same clearing and transaction services).

77 Xavier Freixas, Bruno M. Parigi, and Jean-Charles Rochet, Systemic Risk, Interbank Relations, and Liquidity Provision by the Central Bank, 32 *Journal of Money, Credit and Banking* 611 (2000).

78 Chapter 5, "The Basel Accords: the dialectics of capital requirements and regulatory capital arbitrage."

79 Roberta Romano, For Diversity in the International Regulation of Financial Institutions: Redesigning the Basel Architecture, *Yale Law and Economics Research Paper No. 452*, 40–6 (August 10, 2012) available at http://papers.ssrn.com/sol3/papers.cfm?abstract_id=2127749 (last visited January 10, 2013). See also Roberta Romano,

Against Financial Regulation Harmonization: A Comment, *Yale Law and Economics Research Paper No. 414* (November 20, 2010) available at http://papers.ssrn.com/sol3/papers.cfm?abstract_id=1697348 (last visited July 27, 2013).

80 Roberta Romano, For Diversity in the International Regulation of Financial Institutions, *supra* note 79 at 40–6.

81 Sources *supra* note 79. Romano makes a number of interesting and nuanced proposals for allowing countries to deviate from the strictures of the Basel regime to make capital requirements more adaptive and diverse. Roberta Romano, For Diversity in the International Regulation of Financial Institutions, *supra* note 79.

82 E.g., U.K. Financial Services Authority, Strengthening Liquidity Standards, *Policy Statement 09–16* (October 2009), 45–49 available at www.fsa.gov.uk/pubs/policy/ps09_16.pdf (last visited July 27, 2013).

83 Chapter 11, "Regulatory preferences and money creation: bankruptcy exemptions for repos and swaps."

84 See Mark J. Roe, The Derivatives Players' Payment Priorities as Financial Crisis Accelerator, 63 *Stanford Law Review* 539 (2011) (explaining bankruptcy "preferences" for swaps).

85 Chapter 11, notes 16 and 20.

86 Gary Gorton and Andrew Metrick, Regulating the Shadow Banking System, *Brookings Papers Economic Activity*, 261, 266, 277 (Fall 2010).

87 Gorton and Metrick, *supra* note 86; Gorton, [Oxford University Press], *supra* note 63, at 27.

88 Gorton and Metrick, *supra* note 63.

89 Ibid. at 3–4.

90 E.g., Emmanuel Farhi and Jean Tirole, Collective Moral Hazard, Maturity Mismatch, and Systemic Bailouts, 102 *American Economic Review* 60 (2011); Viral V. Acharya and Tanju Yorulmazer, Cash-in-the-Market Pricing and Optimal Resolution of Bank Failures, 21 *Review of Financial Studies* 2705, 2706–8, 2725 (2008).

91 Viral Acharya and Tanju Yorulmazer provide a further gloss on the theory that when the number of failing financial institutions reaches a tipping point, the government is pushed to provide bailouts. They explain that when the number of bank failures is small, failed banks and their assets can be acquired readily by surviving banks. However, when the number of bank failures is large, the regulator finds it *ex-post* optimal to bail out some or all failed banks. Bailouts give banks incentives to herd and increase the risk that many banks may fail together. Viral V. Acharya and Tanju Yorulmazer, Too Many to Fail: An Analysis of Time Inconsistency in Bank Closure Policies, 16 *Journal of Financial Intermediation* 1, 1–31 (2007).

92 Ibid.

93 Farhi and Tirole, *supra* note 90, at 22; Acharya and Yorulmazer, *supra* note 91, at 2725.

94 Farhi and Tirole, *supra* note 90.

95 Ibid.

96 Chapter 5, "Cheap debt: government guarantees, systemic risk, and the instability of regulatory capital requirements."

97 Cf. Lissa Lamkin Broome, The Dodd-Frank Act: TARP Bailout Backlash and Too Big to Fail, 15 *North Carolina Banking Institute Journal* 70, 78–9 (2011) (questioning effectiveness and scope of restrictions on bailouts and emergency Federal Reserve loans created by provisions of Dodd-Frank).

98 Conclusion, notes 135–6 and accompanying text.

99 E.g., V.V. Chari and Patrick J. Kehoe, Bailouts, Time Inconsistency and Optimal Regulation, Federal Reserve Bank of Minneapolis Research Department Staff Report (November 2009).

100 Borio, *supra* note 6, at 2–3, 10. Compare Brunnermeier *et al.*, *supra* note 49, at 27–9 (describing how institutions may not pose systemic risks on an individual basis, but may be "systemic as a part of herd").
101 Tobias Adrian and Markus K. Brunnermeier, CoVar, Federal Reserve Bank of New York, *Staff Report No. 348* (August 27, 2009) available at http://papers.ssrn.com/sol3/papers.cfm?abstract_id=1269446 (last visited July 27, 2013).
102 Brett McDonnell and Daniel Schwarcz, Regulatory Contrarians, 88 *North Carolina Law Review* 1629, 1670–1 (2011).
103 Cf. Brunnermeier *et al.*, *supra* note 49, at 32–5 (proposing modifying capital requirements to focus on leverage and asset-liability mismatches).

Part III

Fighting bubbles, feeding bubbles

8   Anti-bubble laws

The most direct approach to dealing with the pernicious effects of asset price bubbles is to prevent bubbles from occurring or mitigate the severity of asset mispricings if they do occur. Indeed, policymakers and scholars have long implemented or proposed various regulations designed to dampen bubbles or otherwise combat "excessive speculation." In recent years, examples of actual or proposed anti-bubble laws included the following:

- In May 2007, the Chinese government imposed a tax on securities transactions to curb speculation in stocks as fears rose that the Chinese stock market was in a bubble.[1] This action followed in the wake of a long line of economic scholarship advocating for transaction taxes to remedy excessive speculation.[2]
- Economic and legal scholars have long seen arbitrage[3] as a cure for speculative mispricings and as a means to short circuit asset price bubbles (as Chapter 1 described in detail).[4] Scholars advocated enabling arbitrage to perform these roles better by removing a Depression-era federal securities regulation that restricted short sales.[5] In June 2007, the Securities and Exchange Commission (SEC) repealed this restriction.[6] However, after the Panic of 2007–2008, the SEC reversed course and re-imposed restrictions on short sales for securities that fall below a certain price range on a given day.[7]
- Scholars have also characterized circuit breakers, which halt exchange trading after dramatic price declines, as a means of preventing excessive speculation and bubbles.[8] Other scholars have advocated reverse circuit breakers, which would halt trading after precipitous price gains, to quell excessive speculation.[9]

The question is whether any of these laws are effective in preventing or mitigating the severity of asset price bubbles. Answering that question, however, proves extremely problematic. Chapter 1 detailed how difficult and contentious it is to identify bubbles in real financial markets. Even if bubble can be identified, it is hard to assess the impact of specific financial laws or regulations on a bubble given the multiple causal factors – macroeconomic and microeconomic – at work in financial markets. Moreover, one never sees the bubbles that do not occur.

Therefore, to assess the effectiveness of anti-bubble laws, this chapter looks primarily at evidence from experimental asset markets. This chapter will detail how economists have developed sophisticated experiments in which individuals trade financial assets on computer based virtual markets. In this experimental setting, researchers specify the fundamental value of an asset and allow traders to calculate that value. When traders bid prices in the experimental market far above that fundamental value, researchers know that a bubble has formed. Researchers can then introduce a series of controls into the experiments that mimic various regulations, market rules, or conditions to see if they have any effect on the growth of a bubble.

This chapter begins by creating a template to categorize various anti-bubble laws. This template roughly tracks behavioral finance theories of how bubbles form (as described in Chapter 1). The chapter then looks at the general design and conduct of this experimental economic research into bubbles to assess its validity for making conclusions about real financial markets. Then, the chapter looks at the results of various experiments to assess the potential effectiveness of various anti-bubble laws. In the case of several of these laws, it compares results from experimental asset markets to empirical evidence, however imperfect that evidence may be. Another class of anti-bubble laws – regulations that restrict credit to investors in asset markets – is discussed in the next chapter.

A genealogy of anti-bubble laws

Financial laws and regulations that aim to prevent asset price bubbles or mitigate the mispricing that occur during bubbles can be broken into three general categories.

1   *Disclosure.* Those legal rules that require enhanced disclosure or investor education may have two potential effects on bubbles. First, they might focus investor attention on information regarding fundamental value rather than noise. Alternatively, these rules might remedy information asymmetries that lead to asset mispricing. A more aggressive variant of these laws would attempt to "debias" investors and correct the cognitive mistakes that may spark bubbles.
2   *Short circuiting positive-feedback loops.* Other laws and regulations attempt to break or dampen the positive feedback created when investors chase rising asset prices. This category of anti-bubble laws includes transaction taxes and circuit breakers. It also includes laws that attempt to either restrict investor access to certain markets or channel less sophisticated investors to less risky assets.
3   *Enabling arbitrage.* This third category would roll back restrictions on short selling to enable arbitrageurs to correct mispricings.

This three-part template roughly mirrors behavioral finance theories of how bubbles form. As Chapter 1 details, behavioral finance scholars counter neoclassical finance theory by preventing evidence that:

- Investors do not exhibit economic rationality, but instead chase price trends and focus on "noise" (information not related to fundamental value) due to behavioral biases and cognitive limitations.[10]
- The resultant "irrational" decisions made by different investors do not cancel each other out. Instead, these decisions are highly correlated. Noise trading can create feedback and reinforce itself.[11]
- Arbitrageurs face substantial risk and constraints in real world markets that limit their ability and incentives to correct asset mispricings.[12]

The deeper theory behind and examples of each category of anti-bubble law is examined immediately below.

Improving information to investors and information processing of investors

Some scholars have argued that the development of asset price bubbles or excessive speculation can be hindered by providing investors with higher quality information on fundamental values or improving investor ability to process that information.[13] Some behavioral finance scholars contend that with clearer information on fundamentals, investors will focus less on noise, such as price trends.[14] Scholars who follow rational-bubble models have also advocated enhanced securities disclosure to remedy information asymmetries that can cause bubbles. For example, Randall Krozner, then a member of the Council of Economic Advisors, framed the George W. Bush administration's 2002 ten-point securities-disclosure initiative as a means of reducing the likelihood of asset mispricing and bubbles.[15]

Beyond disclosure recommendations, scholars recommend investor-education programs – including government-sponsored or government-mandated programs – to mitigate the risk of speculative excess.[16] Other economists focus on more innovative, market based solutions to provide investors with better information on fundamental value. For example, some economists advocate creating new futures markets to provide clearer signals to investors when short-time price increases appear to be unsustainable.[17]

Yet, with the exception of creating futures markets, these proposals for enhanced securities-law-disclosure regulations and investor education are somewhat inchoate. It is unclear what disclosure proposals would concretely add to existing U.S. federal securities laws. It is equally unclear what investor education programs would involve and how they would be evaluated. Formulating more concrete disclosure proposals (or investor-education programs) faces a problem identified in Chapter 1: if it is hard to determine fundamental value, it is hard to specify which information is most important to calculating fundamental value. Indeed, a great deal of information might shed light on an asset's future income potential.

Short circuiting positive-feedback investment loops

Chapter 1 summarized empirical evidence that a large group of investors persist in trading on noise.[18] In response, some economists and legal scholars advocate policies to break down the positive-feedback loops caused by these investors. These policies can take several forms. First, several scholars have argued that, if noise traders create a severe risk of widespread mispricing of assets, then the government should restrict their access to markets or channel their investments to less risky assets.[19] These proposals turn the traditional logic of investor protection on its head: rather than protecting individual investors from the ravages of markets, these policies look to protect markets from the ravages of individual investors.

A second approach to counter positive-feedback investing would be to use tax policy to increase the costs to investors who rapidly flip assets. A number of prominent economists and legal scholars have advocated various forms of taxes – from increasing short-term–capital-gains tax rates to instituting a transaction tax – to curb excessive speculation and improve market efficiency.[20]

Circuit breakers and reverse circuit breakers represent a third alternative to combating asset price bubbles and excessive speculation. These mechanisms would temporarily halt market trading when an asset's price falls beyond a set range in a given day (or when prices rise below a specified range, in the case of a reverse circuit breaker). One rationale for circuit breakers is to provide investors with a cooling-off period. This might allow investors to reconsider their participation in the herd behavior that may be driving a meteoric price crash or rise.[21]

Many of these ideas to break feedback loops can be found in existing law and regulation. The first approach, restricting the access of unsophisticated investors to certain markets or channeling these investors into less risky investments, is implicit in the structure of U.S. securities law. Various securities law exemptions create tiers of investors. Certain exemptions from the registration requirements of federal securities law allow institutional investors,[22] investors with high net worth,[23] or investors that meet certain sophistication standards[24] to invest in securities that are accompanied by less disclosure. Furthermore, the Investment Company Act contains exemptions for issuers whose stock is owned by certain institutions or high-net-worth individuals.[25] These exemptions allow many hedge funds to act outside the purview of that statute.[26] Commodities laws and regulations contain similar exemptions for institutions and high-net-worth individuals.[27]

This tiering of investors tailors the disclosure requirements of the federal securities laws to the needs of certain classes of investors based on the perceived need of those classes for protection.[28] Yet tiering does much more. It effectively channels lower-net-worth and less sophisticated individual investors towards (what are perceived to be) less risky investments.[29] Admittedly, this channeling of investors towards lower risk operates in a very rough manner. Questions remain on whether the legal categories for tiering are appropriate proxies for the relative need for investor protection. Moreover, it is debatable whether those assets open to a broader spectrum of the investing public in fact pose lower risks.[30]

Using tax policy to curb speculation – the second approach to cutting positive-feedback investment loops – is an element of existing tax and securities rules in the United States. The difference between short-term and long-term capital gains taxes[31] and securities rules that require certain inside investors to disgorge short-swing profits[32] combine to impose costs on flipping and discourage speculation. Other countries have also experimented with more direct transaction taxes to cool speculation and correct mispricings from potential bubbles. Most recently, in May 2007, China imposed higher taxes on stock trades to curb what many saw as a rising stock-market bubble.[33]

Circuit breakers, the third approach noted above, are already in place at several U.S. financial exchanges. For example, the New York Stock Exchange has imposed circuit breakers for over two decades.[34]

Removing barriers to arbitrage

The final category of anti-bubble laws consists of proposals to remove short sale restrictions and other barriers to arbitrage to allow the market to correct mispricings. A number of prominent scholars (with differing views on the rationality of markets) argued that restrictions on short sales, such as the uptick test, should be removed to promote market efficiency.[35] In June 2007, the SEC repealed the tick test in part to promote efficient pricing in stock markets.[36]

However, after securities markets suffered massive price declines and hemorrhaged liquidity during the Panic of 2007–2008, the SEC abruptly reversed course. The agency re-imposed restrictions on selling a given security short if the price of that security fell below a specified range in a given day (in a combination of a circuit-breaker and a short sale prohibition).[37] In addition, the SEC banned certain "naked" short sales, in which a seller sells a security that it neither owned nor borrowed.[38]

Using experimental asset markets to evaluate effectiveness

Evaluating the effectiveness of the laws described above with empirical evidence alone is difficult for at least three reasons. First, it is extremely hard to identify which price booms in history constituted asset price bubbles, for all the reasons outlined in Chapter 1.[39] Unless bubbles can be identified, it is impossible to determine which regulations or other factors prevent them. Unless the magnitude of asset mispricing in a bubble can be identified, it is impossible to determine which regulations or factors mitigate the severity of bubbles. Second, it is hard to determine if certain regulations prevent bubbles in financial markets because no one sees the bubbles that do not form. Third, in actual financial markets, a given regulation is only one of a host of causal factors that can affect asset mispricings.

Experimental asset markets offer novel solutions to all of these problems. Economists can create simulated markets in which they can specify the fundamental value of the securities being traded.[40] In these experimental markets, subjects trade a fixed-income security with each other on a computer trading system over a set number of trading periods.[41] The individuals trading know that the security would mature at the end of the last trading period. They are informed of the probabilities that a fixed dividend will be paid at the end of every trading period. This means that there is a true fundamental value to the security and that traders can calculate this value as of each trading period.[42] In more technical economic language, the traders in the experiments face *risk* (which means losses and gains are based on known probabilities) and not Knightian *uncertainty* (in which probabilities of future losses or gains are unknown).[43] Yet in experiment after experiment, traders engage in bidding wars that drive the prices of securities higher than fundamental values. Prices return to fundamental value, often via crash, only in the last trading period.[44] Any experiment in which prices diverge significantly from fundamental value means that an asset price bubble formed.[45]

Experimental asset markets also allow researchers to measure the effects of particular regulations. Economists can mimic anti-bubble laws in these markets by introducing experimental controls. The careful design of these controls allows experimental economists to isolate causal links with greater precision than many empirical tests.[46] Bubbles in these experimental markets have proven remarkably robust under various conditions.[47]

Validity of experimental economics in general

Generating conclusions from the laboratory that would apply to the real world requires that the experiments have a requisite degree of realism or "validity." Experimental economists have identified three assumptions that must hold true for experiments to generate implications for real-world markets.[48] First, experiment subjects must prefer receiving more money to less.[49] This assumption is critical as researchers use monetary payoffs to motivate research subjects to behave as if they were trading in real financial assets. In technical economic language this assumption can be restated as follows: monetary payoffs made to subjects according to their performance in the experiment must induce preferences in the subjects.[50] But does receiving monetary payoffs cause experiment subjects to behave like investors in real financial markets? Over the last two decades, experimental economists have provided extensive support for this first assumption. Studies have shown that even small payoffs cause experimental subjects to behave in predictable ways.[51] Experimental economists have responded to a persistent critique that the small stakes involved undermine the internal validity of experiments,[52] with extensive support that even small payoffs cause participants to take their performance in the experiments seriously.[53] Economists further argue that monetary payoffs in experimental asset markets, such as those discussed below, improve validity over experiments with nonmonetary payoffs,[54] such as experiments in which coffee mugs are traded.[55]

This concern over the realism of incentives in experiments points to the second assumption underlying experimental economics – that the basic rules governing individual behavior in the real economy also govern subjects in the experiment.[56] Experimental economics rests on a third and final assumption – sometimes labeled "parallelism" – that all relevant features of actual markets have been incorporated into simulated markets.[57]

A closer look at the design of experimental asset markets

In evaluating whether the experimental asset markets that test for bubbles meet the second and third criteria, it is crucial to carefully evaluate their design.[58] When constructing these markets, Professor Vernon Smith established an experiment protocol to allow other researchers to replicate the research.[59] According to the protocol (and in addition to the basic design of experimental asset markets described above)[60] a fixed number of traders bought and sold a uniform security in a double-continuous auction conducted through a computer network. Traders were given an initial endowment of shares and cash. At the end of the experiment, they received the sum of any cash remaining, all dividends paid on shares when held, and any net capital gains from trading. In any trading period, a trader could either buy or sell by pressing a simple series of keys on her or his computer terminal. A trader could buy the security if he or she had sufficient cash holdings to pay the purchase price. A trader could sell as long as he or she had the shares to complete the sale.[61]

Experiments lasted for a preannounced number of trading periods.[62] Each trading period ended either with unanimous consent of all participants or at the end of a preannounced period of time.[63] The markets combined a bid-ask–spread-reduction rule with a rank-queue limit-order file. This means that bids to buy below the highest standing bid and offers to sell above the lowest standing offer were not rejected but queued in a limit-order file. Once a bid and offer were matched and a contract occurred, the highest queued bid and the lowest queued offer became the new bid-ask spread. Traders were aware of the position of their bids and offers in the limit-order file and could withdraw them at any time.[64]

This basic protocol has been followed in numerous experiments over the last two decades. In each experiment, economists were able to compare period by period the prices set by the traders with the fundamental, or "intrinsic price," of the security being traded. (Fundamental value equaled the expected dividend value multiplied by the number of trading periods remaining in the experiment). In a wide range of experiments, trade prices shot far above intrinsic value and crashed back down to that value only in the final trading period.[65]

Experimental controls and their effects on bubbles

These bubble results prompted early reviewers to note how these experimental markets may not have reflected material attributes of real markets that might prevent such mispricings.[66] In response to these critiques, Smith and other researchers introduced new variables in the experiments to test whether alternative conditions found in real-world securities markets might prevent, prick, or dampen bubbles. These new control variables included:

- informing traders of the results of previous experiments;[67]
- repeating experiments to give traders "experience";[68]
- allowing traders to enter into futures contracts;[69]
- varying the financial sophistication of traders;[70]
- changing the relative initial endowments of cash and shares held by traders;[71]
- charging a fee for trades;[72]
- implementing capital-gains taxes;[73]
- instituting circuit breakers;[74]
- restricting the resale of purchased securities;[75]
- allowing traders to make short sales;[76] and
- allowing traders to buy securities on margin.[77]

The introduction of these controls gave experimental asset markets many features of real securities markets and replicated many anti-bubble laws. As described below, bubbles in asset markets proved robust to the introduction of most of these controls.

External validity and limitations of basic design

It is crucial, however, to highlight some of the limitations of these experiments before attempting to draw legal and policy conclusions from them. This section highlights certain limitations to the general design of the experimental asset markets described above. Results from specific experiments that mimic anti-bubble laws are discussed later in this chapter.

By necessity, experiments need to simplify the complex mechanisms present in real-world markets. However, these simplifications lead to at least five criticisms of the general design of experimental asset markets. First, traders were given the rewards of their performance,[78] but, in many experiments, they did not have to pay losses from their own pockets.[79] This may have skewed experimental results somewhat. Several behavioral economic studies suggest that individuals make much different decisions when they stand to lose money compared to when they may enjoy gains. For example, studies indicate that gamblers playing with house money tend to make riskier bets.[80] Yet this first concern is not fatal to the validity of results from experimental asset markets. A subset of experimental asset market studies in which subjects traded their own money also produced bubbles.[81] The results reached in this subset of experiments roughly paralleled results in experiments in which traders did not pay out-of-pocket. This suggests that the Smith protocol (in which traders do not lose their own money) can produce valid results.[82]

The second potential criticism of the design of these experiments is that real securities markets do not end after a predetermined number of trading periods.

This leads to a possible objection that crashes would chasten traders.[83] Experimenters considered this, and many studies repeated the experiments several times with the same traders.[84] Indeed, experience did significantly dampen the propensity of traders to pay prices above fundamental value.[85] Thus, experience dampens bubbles in the experiments, but "experience" means participating in experimental asset markets and experiencing a bubble and crash, not real-world financial experience. Experiments featuring individuals with real-world financial experience as traders – small-business owners, stock brokers, and executives – produced bubbles.[86]

According to a third critique, it is possible that a looming final horizon in each experiment made traders try to achieve unrealistically high short-term gains. This objection is harder to assess. Limiting the number of trading periods is necessary to be able to set a definite fundamental value for the securities.[87]

The elegance of the experimental controls creates a fourth potential limitation. Several experiments introduced various policies and environmental features in combination. Nevertheless, the experiments may have missed potential combinations of controls that might together have reduced the incidence or severity of mispricings. It is possible that the aggregate effect of multiple anti-bubble laws on reducing mispricings may be greater than a sum of their individual effects. Without resorting to a "kitchen sink" approach, future experiments might productively test additional combinations of controls, such as allowing short sales and futures contracting, simultaneously.

The fifth criticism of the experiments concerns their applicability to real estate markets. Chapter 1 explained that real estate assets have different economic properties from securities, including durability, heterogeneity, and consumption value.[88] These differences might limit the ability to draw conclusions for real estate markets based on experiments in which liquid, fungible securities were traded.[89] Therefore, an evaluation of the effectiveness of anti-bubble laws with respect to real estate markets must give much greater weight to empirical evidence than to experimental studies.

Legal scholars might raise a final concern about the use of experimental asset markets to justify laws or regulations, namely that motivated individuals will find loopholes in real-world laws. Note that there is a certain asymmetry to this objection. It may lead us to doubt the effectiveness of anti-bubble laws. Yet it does not support the reverse conclusion, namely that anti-bubble laws that appeared ineffective in experiments may have greater effect in actual markets.

Evaluating the evidence

Bearing in mind these limitations of experimental asset markets, experimental evidence can be used, together with empirical evidence, to evaluate the effectiveness of each of the three categories of anti-bubble laws.

Improving fundamental information to investors and information processing of investors

Evidence from experimental asset markets draws into question the effect that enhanced disclosure requirements and mandated investor-education programs would have in preventing, pricking, or mitigating the severity of asset price bubbles.

Disclosure

Bubbles formed in experimental asset markets even when investors were given all the information necessary to compute fundamental value.[90] Calculating expected future dividends required investors to perform simple multiplication.[91] The experimenters could have performed the math for the investors. However, in real-world markets, disclosure is unlikely to ever provide as clear an indication of an asset's fundamental value as the information given to the subjects in these experiments.[92] The fact that bubbles formed when dividend uncertainty was removed (or, more accurately, when this uncertainty was converted into risk) suggests that even very high-quality disclosure to investors with respect to fundamental value will not eliminate bubbles.

Nevertheless, these results do not lead to a conclusion that mandatory-disclosure regimes have *no* prophylactic effect on mispricings. Even if supplying investors with near-perfect information on fundamentals does not eliminate bubbles, disclosing imperfect information on fundamental value might still reduce the incidence or magnitude of bubbles. Bubbles may have been more severe had the information on fundamental value been more opaque, noisy, or even absent.

It is important to underscore again that these experimental asset markets allowed researchers to create known fundamental value and thus test investors under conditions of risk but not uncertainty. In real markets, investors face uncertainty about true fundamental value. It is possible, although not convincing, that under conditions of uncertainty, investors would be more responsive to disclosure (or to other anti-bubble laws for that matter) than when facing conditions of risk. It is possible that investors were less risk averse and exhibited more overconfidence in experiments because they thought they could calculate risk probabilities and that they would have been more conservative if they knew they were operating with uncertainty.[93]

These concerns with using experimental research to judge the effects of disclosure laws on bubbles lead to a greater need to consider empirical studies. Empirical data comparing the incidence of bubbles in countries with varying levels of securities disclosure requirements has indicated that countries with weaker requirements tend to suffer more asset price bubbles. Moreover, their asset price bubbles tend to last longer and have a greater magnitude of mispricing.[94] In Asia, in particular, economists have noted an inverse correlation between the incidence of asset price bubbles and the strength and enforcement of a country's securities laws and financial disclosure rules.[95]

Although there is evidence that disclosure requirements may decrease the incidence and magnitude of bubbles, enhancing disclosure may have a decreasing marginal effect. It would be a mistake to conclude that more disclosure is inevitably better. Investors can face "information overload" and may be unable to cognitively process more information.[96] In the case of more complex financial products, information asymmetries may be impossible to overcome with disclosure and education.[97]

Unfortunately, the empirical research outlined above was not intended to design optimal disclosure. As noted above, proposals to use disclosure to mitigate bubbles provide little specifics as to what enhanced disclosure might look like. Any additional disclosure will have to contend with several further challenges. First, the information marketplace becomes particularly crowded during booms. New legal rules would have to select carefully which information will cut through the noise. As Chapter 1 noted, even cogent evidence that asset prices exceed fundamental values will face competing claims. Bubble periods are often marked by "New Era" economic logic, in which various parties contend that fundamental changes in the economy have rendered conventional means of asset valuation obsolete.[98] This cacophony of opinions may explain the repeated failure throughout history of attempts by central bankers and other governmental officials to talk down or "jawbone" suspected asset price bubbles.[99]

Second, the cognitive limitations of investors may hinder their ability to process additional disclosure and improve their investment decisions. Chapter 1 detailed economic research on how behavioral biases may cause or contribute to bubbles. These same biases may limit the effectiveness of providing more information to investors. One recent vein of legal scholarship has advocated re-engineering consumer disclosures to counteract these behavioral biases. Some of these "debiasing" proposals focus on ways to use behavioral biases to correct biases. For example, research into the availability bias might make consumer disclosure more salient.[100] Other research focuses on the capacity of emerging technologies to deliver disclosure more effectively.[101] However, this research on debiasing is still in its infancy. It has yet to lead to concrete proposals for a redesign of securities disclosure that can reliably overcome deeply ingrained cognitive biases.

Third, you can lead a horse to water, but you cannot make it drink. Chapter 4 provided both theory and evidence of how it may be completely rational for investors to ignore disclosure (or waive rights to information) during bubble periods.[102] For example, throughout much of the last decade, bidders who hoped to buy a house in "hot" real estate markets, such as Washington, D.C., decided that they needed to waive inspection and appraisal rights in their offers.[103] Insisting on information rights, taking the time to pour through disclosure, and carefully calculating risk can mean that investors miss opportunities during boom times.

Information from futures markets

Futures markets appear to provide information to investors that is much more effective in reducing the magnitude of asset price bubbles. Certain experiments permitted experienced traders to enter into futures contracts and allowed other traders to see the prices of these contracts.[104] Based on the results, experimenters concluded that "futures markets dampen, but do not eliminate, bubbles by speeding up the process by which traders form common expectations."[105] Traders who can better calculate fundamental values can set futures prices and send a clear signal to others in the market of long-term expectations for these values.

Experimental evidence would support arguments by economists that developing futures markets for real estate and other asset classes will not only allow investors to mitigate risk, but also will provide them with clearer information on potential mispricings.[106] Nevertheless, real-world futures are complex financial instruments, and it is questionable whether many "noise traders" would be able to understand the price signals created by these new markets.

Investor education

Perhaps investor education programs could remedy the inability of investors to understand futures or investor mistakes more generally. However, as with disclosure, the evidence supporting investor education is mixed. Even in experimental asset markets with more financially sophisticated traders – small-business persons,[107] securities brokers,[108] and corporate executives[109] – bubbles formed. On the other hand, in experiments with subjects who were advanced graduate students in economics and familiar with game theory, prices closely tracked fundamental value.[110]

In one experiment, researchers even attempted one form of investor education by giving graduate-student subjects copies of earlier studies that analyzed how bubbles formed in similar experimental asset markets. Merely providing this information did not prevent a bubble from occurring; only a combination of having subjects read these studies *and* repeat the experiment *and* be allowed to engage in short selling led to prices tracking fundamental value and, even then, only roughly so.[111]

Any inference that investor-education policies might work to counter bubbles based on the success of graduate students literate in game theory must be severely tempered. Economics graduate students familiar with experimental literature are likely to intuit the researchers' objectives. Awareness of the experimental conceit undermines the second fundamental assumption of experimental economics – that human behavior in the experiments mirrors behavior in real markets.[112]

It is difficult to extrapolate from experimental asset markets lessons on how education programs should be designed. Investor education and financial literacy programs have come under sustained attack. Legal scholars have questioned whether data supports the effectiveness of investor and consumer education.

Some scholars have argued that the poor track record of financial literacy programs stems from the stubborn persistence of behavioral biases and the resultant inability of individuals to process complex financial information.[113]

Experiencing a bubble and a crash

The ultimate form of investor education, and the one most effective in preventing bubbles, appears to be the harsh experience of participating in the rise and crash of a bubble. One of the strongest findings in experimental economics has been the positive effects of experience. After investors experience an asset price bubble and a subsequent crash in one experiment, they are much less likely to bid prices higher than fundamental value in subsequent iterations of the experiment.[114] In experiments that introduce multiple factors to try to dampen bubbles, the results indicate that it is trader experience with prior bubbles, much more than any other factor, that reduces the magnitude of mispricings.[115] Experiencing bubbles in prior experiments also reduces the volatility and turnover of trading.[116]

Experimental evidence of the chastening effects of experiencing a bubble and crash accords with the findings of economic historians that asset price bubbles tend to form in the same market only after a lapse of a significant period of time.[117] However, the historical evidence is not uniform in this regard. Witness the recurrence of asset price bubbles in U.S. railroad stock in 1869 and 1873.[118]

Indeed, one should not take great comfort in the ability of a bubble to inoculate investors from future speculative fevers. Several factors can cause recurrent or serial bubbles. First, some economists have speculated that the crash of a bubble in one asset market can drive liquidity to another asset market and ignite speculation there. This is a particular risk if a central bank lowers interest rates after the collapse of the first bubble. Many economists link the credit boom that resulted in the Panic of 2007–2008 to the Federal Reserve keeping interest rates low in the wake of the bursting of the technology stock bubble in 2000.[119] Economists have posited that international links between economies allow investors to shift returns earned from an asset bubble in one country to fund speculation in other countries.[120] The following chapter will discuss this "whack-a-bubble" problem and the pattern of easy credit/bubble/crash/easy credit in more detail.

Second, when investors experience a bubble and crash in a particular asset class or financial market, they may not be able to extrapolate lessons for other assets and markets. Bubbles appear similar only when viewed at a certain level of abstraction. The different causes of economic booms reinforce the "New Era" or "This Time is Different" logic.[121]

Third, even if one group of investors learns from a particular crash, markets can attract capital from new investors. Foreign investors may not have learned the hard lessons from the crash. For example, soon after U.S. railroad stocks crashed in 1869, German investors, flush with cash, began investing in new U.S. railroad companies. This fueled the Panic of 1873.[122] Moreover, new generations of investors may inflate future bubbles. Indeed, many economic models incorporate multiple groups of investors entering a market in stages.[123]

Even with these potential limitations, the experimental evidence that experiencing a crash can mitigate bubbles raises profound questions for policymakers and scholars. If a particular bubble can be prevented or pricked, does that deprive investors of an invaluable education? Might a mild bubble forming and crashing prevent more damaging bubbles from forming later? Might effective anti-bubble laws lead to less frequent but more severe bubbles? More concretely, policies that may not prevent bubbles but that remove their sting for investors create a very real risk of moral hazard. If investors feel less pain from losing money during a bubble crash, the positive effects on investor learning would be compromised.

Short circuiting positive-feedback investment loops

Restricting access of unsophisticated investors and "tiering"

Much of the same evidence against the effectiveness of disclosure and investor education also draws into question whether policies that restrict access of certain investors to markets will mitigate mispricings. More precisely, this evidence calls into question assumptions about who should be restricted from riskier markets. In experimental asset markets, small-business people, corporate executives, and securities dealers created bubbles.[124] This suggests that existing categories for tiering investors may have faulty assumptions. Securities law exemptions that rely on high-net-worth and "financial-sophistication" standards may not use adequate proxies for rational financial decision-making.

Yet it remains unclear what would constitute an appropriate category to define sophisticated investors who require less legal protection. There is a significant tension in the behavioral-finance literature: on the one hand, behavioral finance differentiates between irrational noise traders and "smart money," or arbitrageurs.[125] On the other hand, many behavioral-finance studies document behavioral biases in securities professionals and arbitrageurs. Even individuals who would likely fall in the smart-money camp can suffer from cognitive limitations and make "irrational" investment decisions.[126]

"Noise traders" and "smart money" are useful as theoretical constructs for models. However, formulating sound policy based on this distinction requires much more evidence of which types of investors fall into which category. Much work remains in constructing a more nuanced demographic profile of noise traders. Experimental economics could prove a valuable tool in this regard. Some experimental-asset-market studies have already attempted to screen traders based on personality and risk preference and then measure which traders drive bubble prices.[127] Being able to categorize investors by their propensity for certain decision-making errors might allow scholars to determine whether certain anti-bubble laws are more effective with certain classes of investors.

Transaction and capital-gains taxes

An array of evidence suggests that transaction and capital-gains taxes will have mixed results in preventing bubbles. In one experimental asset market, a moderate transaction tax[128] did not eliminate bubbles or reduce their duration, but it did reduce the amplitude of a bubble.[129] Oddly, this transaction tax increased the turnover of shares for traders with no previous experience with experimental asset markets.[130] In another experiment, a 50 percent capital-gains tax likewise did not reduce the tendency of bubbles to occur.[131]

This experimental evidence accords with the observation by one economist that real estate markets, which have higher transaction costs than stock markets, still experience bubbles.[132] Moreover, countries that impose higher transaction costs on trades do not seem to enjoy less stock-market volatility.[133] Of course, at a high-enough rate, transaction taxes will deter speculation. Yet this would come at the cost of choking-off liquidity in the market.

Proponents of these taxes argue that they will affect short-term speculators more than long-term investors given that short-term speculators base their decision on prices during more recent and narrower time windows.[134] However, arbitrageurs are by nature also short-term speculators. Transaction taxes would also impose additional costs on arbitrageurs and might deter them from correcting mispricings. Determining the relative effects of transaction taxes on noise traders compared to arbitrageurs would require a comparison of each group's elasticity of demand for a particular asset. Given the long-running debate about the slope of demand curves for stocks in general,[135] it is unlikely a consensus will emerge on this question any time soon. Nonetheless, the surprising evidence from experimental asset markets – that transaction taxes actually increase stock turnover among inexperienced traders but decrease turnover for experienced traders[136] – does not suggest that transaction taxes can target noise traders and avoid arbitrageurs.

Circuit breakers

In both experiments and empirical studies, circuit breakers and reverse circuit breakers appear to do little to prevent or mitigate bubbles and often appear to exacerbate mispricings. Experimental asset markets have introduced limited price-change rules similar to those imposed by stock and futures markets. Trading is halted in the experiment when prices decline or rise beyond a set band around the price in a previous trading period.[137] Researchers have found that these rules exacerbate the magnitude of mispricings above fundamental value when compared to baseline experiments.[138]

Empirical evidence also does not support the effectiveness of circuit breakers in staving-off or mitigating price bubbles. Circuit breakers that shut markets down for short periods of time are designed to provide a cooling-off period for massive, short-term price swings. They are not designed and remain unproven as a device for preventing long-term mispricing, such as prolonged stock-market bubbles.[139]

Other resale restrictions

Evidence that holding periods that restrict resale of assets prevent or mitigate the severity of bubbles is also very weak. On the experimental side, one experimental asset market completely forbade resale. Yet a bubble still formed with results mirroring those in other experiments.[140] This result calls into question the effectiveness of holding periods and other resale restrictions. The result is also in tension with the theory that bubbles are driven by expectations of capital gains (i.e., that investors drive up prices because they are following a "greater-fool" strategy).[141]

Enabling arbitrage

Experimental and empirical evidence suggests that short sales can prevent or dampen bubbles only if a number of conditions are met. In an experimental asset market that allowed a minority of "more sophisticated" traders to engage in short sales,[142] bubbles still formed. In some experiments the magnitude and duration of mispricing during a bubble increased.[143] Reviewing the short sale experiments, researchers noted that the "bubble forces are so strong that the insiders[144] are swamped by the buying wave."[145] Results from other experimental-asset-market studies also document the limited effectiveness of short sales in preventing or dampening bubbles.[146] The conclusions from the short sale experiments must remain tentative since it is possible that these experiments may have overly constrained short selling.[147] In particular, with only one security being traded on the market, traders selling short could not hedge by purchasing substitute securities.[148]

However, behavioral finance provides evidence that short selling and arbitrage faces constraints in real-world markets.[149] The empirical evidence of the "limits of arbitrage," together with experimental evidence, suggests that arbitrage is no panacea for bubbles and that removing legal barriers to short selling may not have a significant impact on preventing, pricking, or dampening bubbles.

The collective results from experimental asset markets and empirical studies accords with historical evidence that bubbles are robust phenomena. None of the three categories of anti-bubble laws described in this chapter have experienced great success in preventing bubbles from occurring. The following chapter will describe a fourth category that enjoys a much better record of success against asset price bubbles. However, it comes with its own costs and constraints. For now, the mixed record of anti-bubble laws, together with the long history of asset price bubbles in different countries and economies, suggests that policymakers should not hope to prevent bubbles. A more productive course might seek to mitigate their effects when they do occur.

Notes

1 David Barboza and Keith Bradsher, Tax Increase Batters Chinese Stocks, but There's Little Wider Damage, *New York Times*, May 31, 2007, at C4.

2 See, e.g., Lawrence H. Summers and Victoria P. Summers, When Financial Markets Work Too Well: A Cautious Case for a Securities Transactions Tax, 3 *Journal of Financial Services Research* 261 (1989) (positing that a transaction tax may curb excessive speculation that results from excess liquidity); Theresa A. Gabaldon, John Law, with a Tulip, in the South Seas: Gambling and the Regulation of Euphoric Market Transactions, 26 *Journal of Corporation Law* 225, 281 (2001); Joseph E. Stigliz, Using Tax Policy to Curb Speculative Short-Term Trading, 3 *Journal of Financial Services Research* 101 (1989).

3 Arbitrage means investment trades that exploit a perceived short-term mispricing of an asset. For example, if an arbitrageur believes a certain stock is overvalued, he or she sells that stock short (i.e., borrows shares of that stock and then sells them). The arbitrageur profits if the stock price declines from the amount owed the lender of the stock (but loses if the price rises). Arbitrageurs hedge their risks when entering into short sales by simultaneously buying a close substitute of the stock. Andrei Shleifer and Robert W. Vishny, The Limits of Arbitrage, 52 *Journal of Finance* 35 (1997) (analyzing how risks cannot be completely removed from arbitrage). For an in-depth discussion of the roles arbitrage plays (and does not play) in dampening bubbles, see Chapter 1, "Behavioral finance models of bubbles," and "Limited arbitrage."

4 For a survey of the economic literature on the role of arbitrage (specifically short sales) in preventing asset price bubbles and promoting the efficient pricing of stocks and an analysis of the legal restrictions on short sales, see Michael R. Powers, David M. Schizer, and Martin Shubik, Market Bubbles and Wasteful Avoidance: Tax and Regulatory Constraints on Short Sales, 57 *Tax Law Review* 233 (2004).

5 E.g., ibid. at 264, 270 (advocating repeal of the "uptick rule," which permitted short sales on a security only if the previous trade increased the price of that security). For a comprehensive analysis of the uptick rule, see Jonathan R. Macey, Mark Mitchell, and Jeffry Netter, Restrictions on Short Sales: An Analysis of the Uptick Rule and Its Role in View of the October 1987 Stock Market Crash, 74 *Cornell Law Review* 799 (1989) (concluding that the uptick rule impairs market efficiency). The uptick rule was previously codified at 17 C.F.R. § 240.10a-1 (2007).

6 Regulation SHO and Rule 10a-1, 72 *Federal Register* 36,348 (July 3, 2007) (codified at 17 C.F.R. pts. 240, 242 (2008)). In enacting this rule change, the SEC stated that the benefits of removing this restriction would include improving the "price efficiency" of stock markets but did not explicitly reference the role of short sales in preventing asset price bubbles. Ibid. at 36,355. Some scholars have noted that one of the historical purposes for the now-repealed uptick rule was to prevent bubbles. See Robert J. Shiller, *Irrational Exuberance*, 226 (2001, Broadway Books).

7 Amendments to Regulation SHO, Exchange Act Release No. 34-61595 (February 26, 2010) available at www.sec.gov/rules/final/2010/34-61595.pdf (last visited July 27, 2013).

8 See Shiller, *supra* note 6, at 225–6. The New York Stock Exchange initiated a circuit breaker after the 1987 stock-market crash. See NYSE, Inc., Rules and Constitution, Rule 80B (1998) ("Trading Halts Due to Extraordinary Market Volatility"). For background on the introduction of this circuit breaker and a proposal to modify the regulation to take into account how investors experience market time periods in "nonlinear" ways, see Lawrence A. Cunningham, From Random Walks to Chaotic Crashes: The Linear Genealogy of the Efficient Capital Market Hypothesis, 62 *George Washington Law Review* 546, 598–602 (1994).

9 Gabaldon, *supra* note 2, at 283.

10 Chapter 1, "Bounded rationality and noise traders." Andrei Shleifer, *Inefficient Markets: An Introduction to Behavioral Finance*, 10–11 (2000, Oxford University Press).

11 Chapter 1, "Herding and positive-feedback investment loops." Shleifer, *supra* note 10, at 12–13.

12 Chapter 1, "Limited arbitrage." Shleifer, *supra* note 10, at 13–16.

13 Some scholars who have advocated disclosure as an antidote for bubbles subscribe to the theory that bubbles stem from the heterogeneous expectations of investors; disclosure could mitigate the incidence and severity of bubbles by encouraging investors to form common expectations of future asset prices. Gabaldon, *supra* note 2, at 283–4; Lynn A. Stout, Are Stock Markets Costly Casinos? Disagreement, Market Failure, and Securities Regulation, 81 *Virginia Law Review* 611, 695–7 (1995). By contrast, a few scholars have recommended tailoring securities-disclosure requirements to take into account behavioral and emotional responses to information by investors. See, e.g., Peter H. Huang, Regulating Irrational Exuberance and Anxiety in Securities Markets, in *The Law and Economics of Irrational Behavior*, 501, 518–22 (Francesco Parisi and Vernon L. Smith eds., 2005, Stanford University Press).

14 Nicholas L. Georgakopoulos, Why Should Disclosure Rules Subsidize Informed Traders, 16 *International Review of Law and Economics* 417, 424 (1996) (arguing that disclosure may cause noise traders to reconsider beliefs). Some scholars take an alternative approach and argue that disclosure reduces the effect of noise traders by increasing the number and influence of "informational traders." Ibid.; Zohar Goshen and Gideon Parchomovsky, The Essential Role of Securities Regulation, 55 *Duke Law Journal* 711, 739 (2006). Other scholars have used the findings of behavioral finance to argue that mandatory disclosure promotes noise trading. E.g., Paul G. Mahoney, Is There a Cure for "Excessive" Trading? 81 *Virginia Law Review* 713, 743 (1995).

15 Randall S. Kroszner, Asset-Price Bubbles, Information, and Public Policy, in *Asset-Price Bubbles: The Implications for Monetary, Regulatory, and International Policies*, 3, 8–12 (William C. Hunter, George G. Kaufman, and Michael Pomerleano eds., 2003, MIT Press). In this same article, Kroszner also argues that Bush administration proposals to alter the Employee Retirement Income Security Act would serve these same goals by giving employers greater flexibility to sponsor investment advice for employees and clarifying the employer's legal liability in doing so. Ibid. at 8–10.

16 Werner De Bondt, Bubble Psychology, in *Asset-Price Bubbles: The Implications for Monetary, Regulatory, and International Policies*, 205, 212 (William C. Hunter, George G. Kaufman, and Michael Pomerleano eds., 2003, MIT Press); Gabaldon, *supra* note 2, at 280–3; cf. Lawrence A. Cunningham, Behavioral Finance and Investor Governance, 59 *Washington and Lee Law Review* 767, 788–96 (2002) (proposing investor-education programs to remedy investor behavioral biases).

17 Robert J. Shiller, *Macro Markets: Creating Institutions for Managing Society's Largest Economic Risks*, 204–5 (1993, Oxford University Press).

18 Chapter 1, notes 62, 64–6.

19 Stephen Choi has argued for an investor-licensing regime that would classify investors according to their informational resources and provide more securities law protection to those investors with less information. Stephen Choi, Regulating Investors Not Issuers: A Market-Based Proposal, 88 *California Law Review* 279 (2000). Choi summarizes the scheme: "much like a pilot's license, investors would need an investment license to deal with particular types of capital market participants." Ibid. at 283. Choi compares his proposal to the existing securities law regime of exemptions to issuer registration that attempts to tailor information requirements according to the sophistication of investors. Ibid. at 305–7; see also Gabaldon, *supra* note 2, at

279, 282–3 (considering restricting access of investors to markets or investor licensing schemes to combat investor speculation).

20 See, e.g., Summers and Summers, *supra* note 2 (positing that a transaction tax may curb excessive speculation that results from excess liquidity); Gabaldon, *supra* note 2, at 281 (advocating increasing short-term-capital-gains tax rates to curb investor gambling); Stigliz, *supra* note 2.

21 See Gabaldon, *supra* note 2, at 283 (advocating reverse circuit breakers for this reason); Shiller, *supra* note 6, at 225–6 (describing this rationale but questioning the effectiveness of circuit breakers).

22 Rule 144A of the Securities Act of 1933 allows private resale of securities to "qualified institutional buyers." 17 C.F.R. § 230.144A (2007).

23 Rules 505 and 506 of Regulation D of the Securities Act of 1933 do not require disclosure to "accredited investors" and do not count these investors towards the limit on the number of purchasers in their respective exemptions. Ibid. §§ 230.505–6. Regulation D defines "accredited investors" as certain institutions and individuals whose net worth exceeds certain thresholds. Ibid. § 230.501(a).

24 Under an exemption in Rule 506, issuers may still sell securities to investors that are not accredited, note 162 provided that these nonaccredited investors meet certain sophistication standards. 17 C.F.R. § 230.506(b)(2)(ii).

25 See 15 U.S.C. § 80a-3(c)(7) (2000).

26 William W. Bratton, Hedge Funds and Governance Targets, 95 *Georgetown Law Journal* 1375, 1382 n.33 (2007).

27 Arthur E. Wilmarth, Jr., The Transformation of the U.S. Financial Services Industry, 1975–2000: Competition, Consolidation, and Increased Risks, 2002 *University of Illinois Law Review* 215, 333 n.488 (2002).

28 This logic of tailoring disclosure to meet the needs of investors for protection was adopted by the Supreme Court in *SEC* v. *Ralston Purina Co.*, 346 U.S. 119, 124–5 (1953) (determining whether a securities offering was a "public offering," and thus not entitled to the private-offering exemption from registration requirements, by looking to the sophistication of investors).

29 Interpreting exemptions with an eye towards matching investors with risk accords with the way many in the federal-securities bar interpret *Ralston Purina*. Note 167, Federal Regulation of Securities Committee, American Bar Association, Section 4(2) and Statutory Law, 31 *Business Lawyer* 485, 491–5 (1975) (arguing that one factor in interpreting *Ralston Purina* and applying the private-placement exemption from federal securities laws should be the purchaser's risk-bearing ability). However, the mere fact that securities are registered with the SEC and are sold with increased disclosure does not guarantee that they are less risky than securities sold pursuant to an exemption.

This tiering effect is reinforced by other securities laws that require securities intermediaries to take into account the specific circumstances of individual clients in providing advice and facilitating investments. The suitability requirements imposed on broker-dealers by the Financial Industry Regulatory Association ("FINRA," the successor to the National Association of Securities Dealers) represents the most prominent example of this type of rule. See Daniel G. Schmedlen, Jr., Broker-Dealer Sales Practice in Derivatives Transactions: A Survey and Evaluation of Suitability Requirements, 52 *Washington and Lee Law Review* 1441, 1456 (1995) (analyzing National Association of Securities Dealers suitability requirements in the context of derivative sales); FINRA Rule 2111 (Suitability) available at http://finra.complinet. com/en/display/display_main.html?rbid=2403&element_id=9859 (last visited July 27, 2013).

30 For older critiques of U.S. securities law exemptions for sophisticated investors, see C. Edward Fletcher, III, Sophisticated Investors under the Federal Securities Laws, 1988 *Duke Law Journal* 1081; Howard M. Friedman, On Being Rich, Accredited

and Undiversified: The Lacunae In Contemporary Securities Regulation, 47 *Oklahoma Law Review* 291 (1994).

31 C. Thomas Paschall, U.S. Capital Gains Taxes: Arbitrary Holding Periods, Debatable Tax Rates, 73 *Southern California Law Review* 843, 861–4 (2000) (arguing that legislators in the United States and Europe intended that holding periods for capital-gains taxes would discourage speculation).

32 Comment, Short-Swing Profits and the Ten Percent Rule, 9 *Stanford Law Review* 582, 586 (1957) (noting that Congress intended section 16(b) of the Securities Exchange Act to discourage insider speculation).

33 See, e.g., Barboza and Bradsher, *supra* note 1, at C4 (reporting that the Chinese stock market plummeted in response to a new transaction tax designed to curb stock-market speculation "as a growing number of economists and analysts warn about the danger of a market bubble.").

34 See Shiller, *supra* note 6, at 225–6. The New York Stock Exchange initiated a circuit breaker after the 1987 stock-market crash. See NYSE, Inc., Rules and Constitution, Rule 80B (1998) ("Trading Halts Due to Extraordinary Market Volatility"). For background on the introduction of this circuit breaker and a proposal to modify the regulation to take into account how investors experience market time periods in "nonlinear" ways, see Cunningham, *supra* note 8, at 598–602.

35 E.g., Powers *et al.*, *supra* note 4, at 264–70 (arguing for removal of the uptick rule and other legal restrictions on short sales); Lynn A. Stout, Why the Law Hates Speculators: Regulation and Private Ordering in the Market for OTC Derivatives, 48 *Duke Law Journal* 701, 761–2 (1999) (noting that easing restrictions on short sales may be a remedy for bubbles but may also increase market volatility).

36 Regulation SHO and Rule 10a-1, 72 *Federal Register* 36,348 (July 3, 2007) (to be codified at 17 C.F.R. pts. 240, 242). In enacting this rule change, the SEC stated that the benefits of removing this restriction would include improving the "price efficiency" of stock markets but did not explicitly reference the role of short sales in preventing asset price bubbles. Ibid. at 36,355. Some scholars have noted that one of the historical purposes for the later-repealed (and then reinstated) uptick rule was to prevent bubbles. See Shiller, *supra* note 6, at 226. When it repealed the uptick rule, the SEC did place additional restrictions on "naked" short selling, that is, when the investor does not own and has not borrowed the securities it is selling short.

37 *Supra* note 7.

38 Amendments to Regulation SHO, Exchange Act Release No. 34-60388 (July 27, 2009) available at www.sec.gov/rules/final/2009/34-60388.pdf (last visited July 27, 2013).

39 See Chapter 1, "Definitional problems: bubbles and fundamental value."

40 See David P. Porter and Vernon L. Smith, Stock Market Bubbles in the Laboratory, 1 *Applied Mathematical Finance* 111, 111 (1994).

41 Gunduz Caginalp, David Porter, and Vernon L. Smith, Overreactions, Momentum, Liquidity, and Price Bubbles in Laboratory and Field Asset Markets, 1 *Journal of Psychology and Financial Markets* 24, 24 (2000); Ronald R. King, Vernon L. Smith, Arlington W. Williams, and Mark Van Boening, The Robustness of Bubbles and Crashes in Experimental Stock Markets, in *Nonlinear Dynamics and Evolutionary Economics*, 183, 183 (Richard H. Day and Ping Chen eds., 1993, Oxford University Press); Porter & Smith, *supra* note 40, at 111.

42 See Caginalp *et al.*, *supra* note 41, at 24–5; David P. Porter and Vernon L. Smith, Futures Contracting and Dividend Uncertainty in Experimental Asset Markets, 68 *Journal of Business* 509, 509–10 (1995).

43 The economic distinctions between risk and (Knightian) uncertainty are discussed in Chapter 1, "Conflation of risk and uncertainty."

44 Caginalp *et al.*, *supra* note 41, at 26; King *et al.*, *supra* note 41, at 199–200; Porter and Smith, *supra* note 40, at 121–2.

45 Vernon L. Smith, Gerry L. Suchanek, and Arlington W. Williams, Bubbles, Crashes, and Endogenous Expectations in Experimental Spot Asset Markets, 56 *Econometrica* 1119, 1125–8 (1988).

46 Vernon L. Smith, Microeconomic Systems as an Experimental Science, 72 *American Economic Review* 923, 923–35 (1982).

47 See Caginalp *et al.*, *supra* note 41, at 26–32 (surveying experiments where bubbles occurred despite various changes in experimental market conditions). For samples of experiments testing for the occurrence of bubbles under various economic conditions and policies, see King *et al.*, *supra* note 41, at 185–200; Vivian Lei, Charles N. Noussair, and Charles R. Plott, Nonspeculative Bubbles in Experimental Asset Markets: Lack of Common Knowledge of Rationality vs. Actual Irrationality, 69 *Econometrica* 831 (2001); Smith *et al.*, *supra* note 45.

48 Elizabeth Hoffman and Matthew L. Spitzer, Experimental Law and Economics: An Introduction, 85 *Columbia Law Review* 991, 991 (1985).

49 Ibid.

50 Vernon L. Smith, Experimental Economics: Induced Value Theory, *American Economic Review* 274, 274–7 (May 1976).

51 See, e.g., Colin F. Camerer and Robin M. Hogarth, The Effects of Financial Incentives in Experiments: A Review and Capital-Labor-Production Framework, 19 *Journal of Risk and Uncertainty* 7 (1999) (analyzing seventy-four experimental studies to determine whether incentive levels or monetary versus nonmonetary payoffs improved subject performance).

52 Even early reactions among legal scholars reflected this concern. See, e.g., Stewart E. Sterk, Neighbors in American Land Law, 87 *Columbia Law Review* 55, 73 n.69 (1987) (critiquing whether experiments used to support Coase Theorem are valid given the small stakes involved).

53 E.g., Camerer and Hogarth, *supra* note 51.

54 Ralph Hertwig and Andreas Ortmann, Experimental Practices in Economics: A Methodological Challenge for Psychologists? 24 *Behavioral and Brain Sciences* 383, 401 (2001).

55 As one example, proponents of behavioral law and economics have referenced various experiments in which subjects traded coffee mugs as evidence of the "endowment effect" (the propensity for individuals to place a higher value on objects they already own than on objects they do not). See, e.g., Christine Jolls, Cass R. Sunstein, and Richard Thaler, A Behavioral Approach to Law and Economics, 50 *Stanford Law Review* 1471, 1483 (1998) citing Daniel Kahneman, Jack L. Knetsch, and Richard H. Thaler, Experimental Tests of the Endowment Effect and the Coase Theorem, 98 *Journal of Political Economy* 1325, 1329–42 (1990). This reliance of behavioral economics on fairly basic experiments, many with nonmonetary payoffs, may explain persistent criticism of behavioral law and economics. See, e.g., Richard A. Posner, Rational Choice, Behavioral Economics, and the Law, 50 *Stanford Law Review* 1551, 1565–7 (1998) (critiquing conclusions drawn by the authors above from coffee-mug experiments).

56 Hoffman and Spitzer, *supra* note 48, at 992–3.

57 Ibid.

58 Ibid. at 993.

59 For the basic formulation of this protocol, see Smith *et al.*, *supra* note 45, at 1122–5. This section describes the general parameters of the experiments conducted by Smith and colleagues. When other experimental asset markets that had different parameters are considered this chapter, differences from this general design are noted.

60 See, e.g., Caginalp *et al.*, *supra* note 41, at 24; King *et al.*, *supra* note 41, at 183.

61 Smith *et al.*, *supra* note 45, at 1122–5.

62 In most of the experiments of Smith and his collaborators there were fifteen trading periods. See, e.g., King *et al.*, *supra* note 41, at 183.

63 Generally, the trading period lasted a maximum of four minutes. Smith *et al.*, *supra* note 45, at 1124.

64 King *et al.*, *supra* note 41, at 184; Smith *et al.*, *supra* note 45, at 1122–5.

65 Caginalp *et al.*, *supra* note 41; King *et al.*, *supra* note 41; Porter and Smith, *supra* note 40; Smith *et al.*, *supra* note 45.

66 See Caginalp *et al.*, *supra* note 41, at 26–32 (describing changes to the experimental environment to make experiments match attributes of real markets).

67 Traders were given copies of previous studies of experimental asset markets that showed prices exceeded fundamental value. E.g., King *et al.*, *supra* note 41, at 190–4.

68 Multiple experiments were rerun with at least some traders having participated in earlier experiment iterations. See, e.g., King *et al.*, *supra* note 41, at 186–200; Smith *et al.*, *supra* note 45, at 1133–6.

69 Porter and Smith, *supra* note 40, at 120.

70 Criticisms of the validity of early experiments that used undergraduate economics students as traders were addressed by later experiments that used small-business people, corporate executives, and stock-market dealers as subjects. Caginalp *et al.*, *supra* note 41, at 28.
      Compare Smith *et al.*, *supra* note 45, at 1124 (using unequal endowments of cash and assets), with King *et al.*, *supra* note 41, at 189 ("buyers [tend] to be those subjects with endowments large in cash and small in shares; the reverse holds for sellers.").

71 Compare Smith *et al.*, *supra* note 45, at 1124 (using unequal endowments of cash and assets), with King *et al.*, *supra* note 41, at 189 ("buyers [tend] to be those subjects with endowments large in cash and small in shares; the reverse holds for sellers.").

72 King *et al.*, *supra* note 41, at 190.

73 Vivian Lei, Charles Noussair, and Charles R. Plott, Asset Bubbles and Rationality: Additional Evidence from Capital Gains Tax Experiments, California Institute of Technology, *Working Paper No. 1137*, 1–2 (June 2002) available at www.hss.caltech.edu/SSPapers/wp1137.pdf (last visited July 27, 2013).

74 King *et al.*, *supra* note 41, at 194–5.

75 Lei *et al.*, *supra* note 47, at 834.

76 King *et al.*, *supra* note 41, at 186–8.

77 Ibid. at 188–9.

78 Caginalp *et al.*, *supra* note 41, at 26.

79 Camerer and Hogarth, *supra* note 51, at 36 ("Because it is generally difficult to impose losses or punishments on subjects for bureaucratic reasons – university committees that approve protocols involving human subjects strongly object to it – we do not know how earning money and losing money differ.").

80 Behavioral-economics literature often recites the "loss-aversion" bias (i.e., that individuals are willing to take on less risk that would lead to losses than risk that would lead to the same amount of gains). See, e.g., Daniel Kahneman, Jack L. Knetsch, and Richard H. Thaler, Anomalies: The Endowment Effect, Loss Aversion, and Status Quo Bias, 5 *Journal of Economic Perspectives* 193 (Winter 1991); Robert A. Prentice and Jonathan J. Koehler, A Normality Bias in Legal Decision Making, 88 *Cornell Law Review* 583, 601–2 (2003).

81 James S. Ang and Thomas Schwarz, Risk Aversion and Information Structure: An Experimental Study of Price Variability in the Securities Markets, 40 *Journal of Finance* 825, 830–1 (1985).

82 Nevertheless, the Ang and Schwarz experiments in which traders invested with their own money did not feature the full set of controls – including all of the controls that mimic the various anti-bubble laws – that the experiments following the Smith protocol did. See *supra* note 81. The potential for skewed results in the Smith

protocol experiments – because subjects were "playing with house money" – argues for re-running the Ang and Schwarz experiments with controls that mimic more anti-bubble laws.

83 Smith *et al.*, *supra* note 45, at 1133 (noting this potential flaw).

84 See *supra* note 68.

85 Caginalp *et al.*, *supra* note 41, at 26.

86 King *et al.*, *supra* note 41, at 196–7.

87 Other experiment based asset-market research supports the hypothesis that short horizons promote bubble formation. See Shinichi Hirota and Shyam Sunder, Price Bubbles Sans Dividend Anchors: Evidence from Laboratory Stock Markets, 31 *Journal of Economic Dynamics and Control* 1875 (2007).

   Some scholars have raised a related criticism, namely that Smith's design predetermined a crash by setting fundamental values to decline to zero. These scholars found that when fundamental value was held constant prices of securities traded close to fundamental value. Dean Johnson and Patrick Joyce, Bubbles and Crashes Revisited, Unpublished manuscript (October 2006) available at www.bapress.ca/ref/ref-2012-3/Bubbles%20and%20Crashes%20Revisited.pdf (last visited July 27, 2013). But this research does not appear to have been replicated. Other studies of experimental asset markets with a flat fundamental value showed recurring bubbles. E.g., Charles Noussair, Stephane Robin, and Bernard Ruffieux, Price Bubbles in Laboratory Asset Markets with Constant Fundamental Values, 4 *Experimental Economics* 87 (2001); A.J. Bostian, Jacob Goeree, and Charles A. Holt, Price Bubbles in Asset Market Experiments with a Flat Fundamental Value, Unpublished manuscript (August 30, 2005) available at www.atl-res.com/finance/conference_pdf/HoltFinal.pdf (last visited July 27, 2013).

88 Chapter 1, "Real estate bubbles."

89 For example, traders in these virtual markets could not have enjoyed any consumption value from the securities being traded, but real estate investors often do place such a value on their properties. Real estate represents not only an investment good that can be leased or sold for a return, but also a consumption good used for work or living space; and investors often purchase a real estate asset for both investment and consumption functions. Michael Ball, Colin Lizieri, and Bryan D. MacGregor, *The Economics of Commercial Property Markets*, 14 (1998, Routledge).

90 Porter and Smith phrase the conclusion: "Public information in intrinsic dividend (or net asset) value is not sufficient to induce common expectations and trading at fundamental value." Porter and Smith, *supra* note 40, at 114.

91 Fundamental value equaled (1) the probability of a dividend multiplied by (2) the amount of a possible dividend multiplied by (3) the number of trading periods remaining in the experiment. See King *et al.*, *supra* note 41, at 183.

92 Porter and Smith, *supra* note 40, at 121–2; Caginalp *et al.*, *supra* note 41, at 24–5; Porter and Smith, *supra* note 42, at 509–10; Smith *et al.*, *supra* note 45, at 1124.

93 Because the value of experimental asset markets lies in large part on having known fundamental values and thus being able to identify bubbles with certainty, it would be logically problematic to test whether experiment subjects operating in an environment of true uncertainty would be more or less likely to create bubbles. Again, using risk as a proxy for uncertainty may be unavoidable in this area of economics, but it also limits the validity of research.

94 William R. White, What Have We Learned from Recent Financial Crises and Policy Responses? in *Global Financial Crises: Lessons from Recent Events*, 177 (Joseph R. Bisignano, William C. Hunter, and George G. Kaufman eds., 2000, Springer). These findings mesh with broader studies that have found a connection between investor-protection laws and the depth of a nation's securities markets. Shleifer, *supra* note 10, at 191–2 (surveying studies showing a correlation between nations' investor-protection regimes and success in developing well-functioning and deep securities markets).

95 See, e.g., Stephan Haggard, *The Political Economy of the Asian Financial Crisis*, 19 (2000, Institute for International Economics); Robert Chote, Financial Crises: The Lessons of Asia, in Financial Crises and Asia, Centre for Economic Policy Research, *Conference Report No. 6*, 1, 10 (1998).

96 Troy A. Paredes, Blinded by the Light: Information Overload and its Consequences for Securities Regulation, 81 *Washington University Law Quarterly* 417, 441 (2003).

97 Jeffrey Carmichael and Neil Esho, Asset-Price Bubbles and Prudential Regulation, in *Asset-Price Bubbles: The Implications for Monetary, Regulatory, and International Policies*, 481, 491 (William C. Hunter, George G. Kaufman, and Michael Pomerleano eds., 2003, MIT Press).

98 See Shiller, *supra* note 6, at 96–132 (describing how popular perceptions during stock market expansions that "the future is brighter or less uncertain than it was in the past" can lead to asset price bubbles).

99 The warning by Federal Reserve Chairman Greenspan in 1996 that the stock market was "irrationally exuberant" represents a recent example of such a failed attempt. Charles P. Kindleberger, *Manias, Panics and Crashes: A History of Financial Crises*, 7 (4th ed. 2000, Wiley Investment Classics). For historical surveys of the futility of official warnings that a bubble may be occurring (in part, because of contrary statements by other officials), see ibid. at 91–4; Edward Chancellor, *Devil Take the Hindmost: A History of Financial Speculation*, 151, 230–1 (1999, Plume Books).

100 Christine Jolls and Cass R. Sunstein, Debiasing through Law, 35 *Journal of Legal Studies* 199 (2006).

101 E.g., Scott Peppet, Freedom of Contract in an Augmented Reality: The Case of Consumer Contracts, 59 *UCLA Law Review* 676 (2012); M. Ryan Calo, Against Notice Skepticism in Privacy (and Elsewhere), 87 *Notre Dame Law Review* 1027 (2012).

102 Chapter 4, "Fraud and rational risk-taking."

103 Daniela Deane, Higher Prices, Tougher Choices, *Washington Post*, March 23, 2005, at H1.

104 Porter and Smith, *supra* note 40, at 120. Experimenters first conducted a series of two-period training sequences in which traders could enter into futures contracts in period one and the contracts would mature in period two. This taught traders "that a futures contract is equivalent to a cash contract in the period in which it expires, and should trade at the same price." Caginalp *et al.*, *supra* note 41, at 30. In the actual experimental markets with fifteen trading periods, traders could enter into spot and futures contracts for the first eight periods, with futures contracts expiring in period eight. After the eighth period, traders could only enter into spot contracts. Ibid.

105 Porter and Smith, *supra* note 40, at 120; see also Charles Noussair and Steven Tucker, Futures Markets and Bubble Formation in Experimental Asset Markets, 11 *Pacific Economic Review* 167 (2006).

106 See Karl E. Case and Robert J. Shiller, The Behavior of Home Buyers in Boom and Post-Boom Markets, *New England Economic Review* 29, 44–45 (November–December 1988); Shiller, *supra* note 17, at 204–5.

    This finding meshes with the heterogeneous-expecations model of bubbles. See Chapter 1, note 75.

107 Smith *et al.*, *supra* note 45, at 1130–1.

108 King *et al.*, *supra* note 41, at 196–7.

109 Ibid.

110 Caginalp *et al.*, *supra* note 41, at 28–9. Undergraduate economics students produced dramatic bubbles in trading. Ibid.

111 King *et al.*, *supra* note 41, at 190–3. But, if the percentage of traders who lacked experience in the experimental asset markets and were not informed of the studies is too high, bubbles formed as "experienced" and "informed" traders did not have sufficient resources to undercut bubble prices through short selling. Ibid. at 193–4.

112 Cf. Hoffman and Spitzer, *supra* note 48, at 992–3

113 Lauren E. Willis, Against Financial Literacy Education, 84 *Iowa Law Review* 197 (2008).

114 Caginalp *et al.*, *supra* note 41, at 26; Smith *et al.*, *supra* note 45, at 1133–6.

115 See King *et al.*, *supra* note 41, at 188–200.

116 Ibid.

117 Kindleberger, *supra* note 99, at 13 ("[S]ome time must elapse after one speculative mania that ends in crisis before investors have recovered sufficiently from their losses and disillusionment to be willing to take a flyer again."); see also Shiller, *supra* note 6, at 96–117 (surveying episodes of "new era economic thinking" in the United States in the twentieth century, which occurs "in pulses.").

118 Chapter 2, "The Panics of 1869 and 1873 in the United States."

119 For an accessible account of this theory, see Greg Ip and Jon E. Hilsenrath, Debt Bomb, *Wall Street Journal*, August 7, 2007, at A1.

120 Some economists believe that currency crises in China are having this effect on markets in other countries. Ibid. Economists have also studied the reverse problem of crashes in one market having cross-border effects through stock-market and other economic interlinkages. See, e.g., Michael D. Bordo and Antu Panini Murshid, Globalization and Changing Patterns in Crisis Transmission, in *Asset-Price Bubbles: The Implications for Monetary, Regulatory, and International Policies*, 309, 309–22 (William C. Hunter, George G. Kaufman, and Michael Pomerleano eds., 2003, MIT Press).

121 Chapter 1, note 16 and accompanying text.

122 Chapter 2, note 169 and accompanying text.

123 Economists have created "overlapping-generations" models to study the potential effects of new investors entering markets. See, e.g., Jean Tirole, Asset-Price Bubbles and Overlapping Generations, 53 *Econometrica* 1071 (1985) (concluding that new generations of investors overlapping with older generations allow bubbles to form). If new generations enter asset markets more quickly, the chastening effect of asset bubble crashes may have a shorter duration. See also Chapter 1, note 70 and accompanying text.

124 *Supra* note 86 and accompanying text.

125 See, e.g., Shleifer, *supra* note 10, at 172.

126 E.g., Gregory La Blanc and Jeffrey J. Rachlinski, In Praise of Investor Irrationality, in *The Law and Economics of Irrational Behavior*, 570–4 (Francesco Parisi and Vernon L. Smith eds., 2005, Stanford University Press).

127 Shyam Sunder, Experiment Asset Markets: A Survey, in *The Handbook of Experimental Economics*, 445, 489 (John H. Kagel and Alvin E. Roth Sunder eds., 1995, Princeton University Press) (summarizing one set of studies).

128 King *et al.*, *supra* note 41, at 190. One experiment charged an exchange fee of $0.20 on each transaction, split equally between buyer and seller. To give a sense of the reasonableness of this tax, the intrinsic value of one share started at $3.50 at the beginning of the experiment and declined linearly to zero at the end of fifteen trading periods. Assuming turnover of six-times total shares, $0.20 represents an average cost of $1.20 per share. See ibid.

129 Ibid.

130 Ibid. The tax did have the expected effect of reducing turnover by experienced traders. Ibid.

131 Lei *et al.*, *supra* note 73, at 2, 4.

132 Shiller, *supra* note 6, at 227; see also James R. Repetti, The Use of Tax Law to Stabilize the Stock Market: The Efficacy of Holding Period Requirements, 8 *Virginia Tax Review* 591, 627–30 (1989) (arguing that holding-period requirements of long-term-capital-gains tax preferences and short sale restrictions are not justified as ways to deter speculation and may reinforce irrational investing and mispricing). Other tax rules might help address mispricing during a bubble, but further study is needed.

133 Richard Roll, Price Volatility, International Market Links, and Their Implications for Regulatory Policies, 3 *Journal of Financial Services Research* 211, 238 (1989).
134 Shiller, *supra* note 6, at 227.
135 For one early salvo in this debate, see Andrei Shleifer, Do Demand Curves for Stocks Slope Down? 41 *Journal of Finance* 579 (1986).
136 See *supra* note 128 and accompanying text.
137 King *et al.*, *supra* note 41, at 194–5. The price band used in the experiment was plus or minus thirty-two cents (which equaled twice the expected dividend for any period). Ibid. at 195.
138 Ibid. at 195. The experimenters posited that the circuit breaker "accentuates the severity of bubbles because traders perceive that their downside risk is limited by the 32 or 48 cent bounds on price declines in each period." Ibid. Only when the experiment was rerun with traders "experienced" with previous experimental iterations, did prices track fundamental value. But, this was the same result as in baseline experiments comparing inexperienced and experienced traders without a circuit breaker, which suggests that it is the experience of past bubbles and crashes, not circuit breakers, that prevents mispricings. Ibid.; see also Lucy F. Ackert, Bryan K. Church, and Narayanan Jayaraman, An Experimental Study of Circuit Breakers: The Effects of Mandated Market Closures and Temporary Halts on Market Behavior, 4 *Journal of Financial Markets* 185 (2001) ("[The] presence of a circuit breaker rule does not affect the magnitude of the absolute deviation in price from fundamental value.").
139 Shiller, *supra* note 6, at 226.
140 Lei *et al.*, *supra* note 47, at 841–5.
141 Ibid.
142 One experiment placed three graduate students who had read earlier experimental asset studies (labeled "insiders") in a market with six to nine undergraduates who had not read the studies ("outsiders"). Insiders and outsiders had the same share endowments, but insiders could sell two shares borrowed from experimenters. Each of these shares had to be repurchased and repaid to the experimenters or a penalty of one-half the initial dividend value would be imposed on each share not repaid. It is unclear what the initial share endowment was. Caginalp *et al.*, *supra* note 41, at 27.
143 King *et al.*, *supra* note 41, at 186–8. When short sale experiments were rerun to give traders experience, bubble magnitude decreased. However, as with the circuit-breaker experiments, it appears as if experience, not short sales, was the primary factor mitigating mispricings. See ibid. at 188–9, 199.
144 The insiders were the graduate students who were informed of past experimental-asset-market research and had the capability of selling short.
145 Caginalp *et al.*, *supra* note 41, at 27–8.
146 See Sunder, *supra* note 127, at 448 (surveying other experimental asset markets that tested for effects of short selling).
147 Conclusions on the limited effectiveness of short selling in reducing bubbles could be made more robust by rerunning these experiments and changing the parameters to further decrease the costs of short selling. For example, the experiment could be rerun with the following parameters varied: (1) increasing the number of shares the short sellers could borrow (it is difficult to interpret the results of the initial survey because, while the number of shares that could be borrowed (two) is known, the share endowments of each trader is not disclosed); (2) decreasing the penalty for not repaying shares borrowed; (3) increasing the proportion of traders that could sell short compared to the total number of traders; and (4) increasing the time horizon of the short sellers.
148 The ability to purchase substitute securities allows arbitrageurs to mitigate risk and is therefore critical to fully effective arbitrage. Shleifer, *supra* note 10, at 3–4.
149 See Chapter 1, "Limited arbitrage".

9 Credit and leverage

The monetary dimension of financial regulation

Introduction

The last chapter described the mixed success of various laws and regulations in preventing, pricking, or mitigating the severity of asset price bubbles. This chapter explores one of the few effective means of controlling bubbles, restricting credit. It explores how various financial regulations that govern credit and leverage may control the size and severity of asset price bubbles. Conversely, changes in these regulations, including deteriorating regulations, may exacerbate bubbles.

Consider first the evidence: in experimental asset markets, restrictions on credit to investors have been shown to mitigate the severity of bubbles. More precisely, when inexperienced traders in these experimental markets could borrow funds to purchase shares, the magnitude of a bubble increased significantly. The ability to invest on credit drove asset prices much higher than fundamental values.[1] These experiments demonstrate the effectiveness of credit restrictions in mitigating the severity of bubbles in a laboratory environment. These results led the economists conducting the experiments to rank regulations that restrict credit to investors as one of the most promising policy tools for addressing asset price bubbles.[2]

These experimental results accord with a significant body of macroeconomic research that focuses on the role of credit in driving mispricings. Macroeconomists studying the effects of monetary policy describe a pattern of higher interest rates pricking inflation in asset markets.[3] Although there may be a lingering debate over whether any particular bout of inflation in an asset market constituted a bubble, a broad consensus exists among macroeconomists that tighter monetary policy could prick bubbles should they form.[4]

There is less consensus on the mechanisms by which credit contributes to a bubble. Chapter 1 summarized microeconomic models of how investing with borrowed money created agency costs and incentives for investors to bid prices above fundamental value. According to these models, investors speculating with other people's money will take more risks if they are shielded from liability to their creditors.[5] These agency cost theories, however, do not provide a good explanation for the results in experimental asset markets: investors in those experiments who borrowed funds were not shielded from liability but were required to repay the loans.[6]

Macroeconomists theorize about multiple "channels" by which monetary policy can impact household and business wealth, shape the expectations of individuals and firms, and thus affect their investment decisions.[7] This chapter focuses on a simple mechanism by which changes in the supply of money impact asset prices. When investors supplement their own funds with borrowed money the *liquidity* – which this chapter uses in the sense of the effective supply of money[8] – in a given financial market increases.[9] An increased effective supply of money drives up the prices of assets. More dollars chase the same amount of assets.

Monetary expansion through increased financial institution leverage

The effective supply of money in an entire economy can grow in at least two ways, as this chapter will explain. First, the money supply expands when financial institutions either hold lower reserves or increase their effective *leverage* – that is borrow more and commit less of their own capital to fund their investments. The capacity of financial institution leverage to increase the effective money supply has been the subject of cutting edge economic research surveyed below. Financial institution leverage has a monetary impact. When this leverage increases, it can fuel asset price inflation and bubbles.[10]

Unfortunately, these monetary effects of financial institution leverage have been obscured by the more readily understood capacity of leverage to magnify losses to a firm's equity holders. A great deal of scholarship and press after the Panic of 2007–2008 has focused on the dangers of excessive financial institution leverage.[11] This trove of literature centers on how leverage renders financial institutions more fragile and susceptible to economic shocks and how the failures of these institutions deepen economic crises.[12] Systematic failures of financial institutions indeed have a macroeconomic effect. However, the focus on leverage causing financial institution fragility has overshadowed the monetary dimension of financial institution leverage and, in turn, regulations that govern that leverage.[13] This chapter spotlights the monetary dimension of financial regulation.

Monetary expansion through the creation of money-like instruments

Regulation also plays a crucial role in the second way in which the effective supply of money grows, namely by endowing new financial instruments with the economic features of "money." Instruments become more like money, when they serve as a:

- *a medium of exchange*;
- *a unit of account*; and
- *a store of value*.[14]

Cash, of course, has all the functions of money, but other financial instruments may possess many of them as well. The fact that financial instruments may serve these three functions to a greater or lesser degree explains why economists and central banks have developed different measures (from narrow to broad) of the money supply.[15]

Policymakers can help financial instruments take one or more of these three features by granting them certain regulatory preferences. The bankruptcy exemptions for repos and swaps (previewed in Chapter 7 and analyzed more fully in Chapter 11) serve as one example of these preferences.[16] This chapter analyzes those exemptions anew and explains how they not only spurred investment in those instruments, but also increased the money supply.

Why do monetary changes trigger bubbles? Information problems or irrationality

Pause for a moment to consider the link between increases in the effective money supply and asset price bubbles. According to neoclassical economics, increases in the money supply or lower interest rates may cause the price of assets to rise, but not necessarily to rise above fundamental value. Indeed, a rational investor should recognize that price changes stem from fluctuations in the amount of money or the supply of credit. Rational investors would distinguish increases in "nominal" values from higher "real" prices.[17]

How then can monetary changes lead to asset price bubbles? There are two explanations. First, investors may not see even dramatic changes in the monetary environment. The next two chapters argue that the evolution of a massive channel of lending, the so-called "shadow banking system," grew incrementally alongside the traditional depository banking sector.[18] This shadow banking sector turbocharged the growth of the money supply and the provision of economic credit.[19] Yet, just as this shadow system exerted more of an effect on the economy, the U.S. Federal Reserve chose to abandon tracking more inclusive metrics of the money supply. In other words, instead of looking at broader gauges of the supply of money, the Federal Reserve looked at narrower measures.[20] (This chapter and particularly the following two will discuss the implications of the Federal Reserve's failure to track changes in the money supply in greater detail.) If central banks have trouble measuring monetary changes, so too can private sector investors.

Second, investors do not always make rational distinctions between the real and nominal values of assets. Individuals often mistake changes in nominal values (e.g., those driven by increases in the amount of money) for changes in real values. Economists call this bias or distorted perception "money illusion."[21] Moreover, spikes in asset prices can trigger positive feedback investing; as Chapter 1 notes, once an asset market booms, noise traders may chase the price trend and a bubble begins.[22]

If macroeconomists widely agree that monetary policy *could* prick or prevent an asset price bubble, they have no consensus on whether it *should* be used for this purpose. In fact, macroeconomists have engaged in a long debate on whether monetary policy should be used to prevent bubbles from forming or pricking bubbles that have already developed. This debate has largely assumed that a central bank will use traditional monetary policy tools – namely "open market operations" and changing the interest rate of central bank loans to private sector banks – to change the money supply and market interest rates.

This chapter begins (in "The traditional tools of monetary policy") by explaining how those traditional monetary policy tools work. The second section, "The macroeconomist debate: should monetary policy address bubbles?" then outlines the debate among macroeconomists on whether monetary policy should be used to address asset price bubbles. One of the principal objections to using monetary policy for this purpose is that a tighter monetary policy will have spillover effects beyond the particular asset market that is overheating. The third section of the chapter, "Financial regulations as substitutes for monetary policy," looks at how financial regulations can have more a targeted (if not surgical) monetary impact with less spillover effects. The chapter explains how reserve requirements and leverage regulations can change the effective supply of money. Policymakers once saw this macroeconomic or monetary potential of financial regulation, but it long ago faded into obscurity.

In the fourth section, "Advantages and drawbacks to using regulation as monetary tools," the chapter looks at the significant drawbacks to using these different types of regulation to address bubbles. Then, "Regulatory preferences and the creation of money" switches gears and examines how regulatory preferences can have a monetary impact by endowing certain financial instruments with the economic characteristics of money.

Finally, "The implications" argues that, even if financial regulation is not used as a substitute for monetary policy, both central banks and financial regulators need to understand the monetary impacts of changes in regulation, including via regulatory stimulus, deteriorating compliance, and regulatory arbitrage. This final section also details the deep challenges to an accurate understanding of the monetary effects of financial regulation.

The traditional tools of monetary policy

Before delving into the link between monetary policy and bubbles, it is crucial to understand the basic monetary tools in a central banker's tool box. Understanding the everyday levers by which monetary policy works sets the stage for a later discussion of how financial regulation can *and must* be added to the quiver of macroeconomic policymakers. Currently, central bankers most commonly use the following two monetary policy tools:

- *Open market operations.* A central bank can reduce the overall supply of money in the economy by selling other assets it owns, such as government bonds, into the open market. The cash the government receives is thus withdrawn from circulation in the marketplace. A central bank can reverse course and expand the supply of money in the economy by purchasing assets in financial markets with cash (which the central bank might produce, among other ways, by simply printing more money).[23]

• *Lending to banks.* As lender-of-last-resort, a central bank regularly extends loans to private sector banks to help them cover their short-term obligations.[24] Increasing the interest rate on these loans causes market rates to increase because government loans act as a substitute for private sector credit. Moreover, higher interest rates on central bank loans raise the cost of capital for the private sector private banks that borrow from the government. It forces them to raise interest rates for their own borrowers. In this way, private sector banks that borrow from the central bank act as a "transmission belt" for monetary policy.[25]

Central banks have other, more seldom-used tools for implementing monetary policy, including some of the financial regulations discussed below in this chapter. One of these tools deserves a preview because it illustrates nicely how financial regulation more generally can have a monetary impact. Central banks and other bank regulators can adjust the monetary transmission belt by changing the amount of money that banks are required to hold in reserve.[26] Regulators have required banks to hold cash and certain other highly liquid assets in reserve. These reserves are intended to cover potential demands by the banks' depositors for the return of funds in their accounts, other short-term obligations of the bank, and losses on bank loans.[27] By increasing the amount that banks must hold in reserve, regulators effectively reduce the supply of money available for investment. In the last decades, however, many central banks have reduced traditional reserve requirements significantly and have largely abandoned using them as a tool for monetary policy.[28]

These reserve requirements factor into a central bank's calculations of how bank lending in general increases the money supply. For example, after the Federal Reserve lends money to a private sector bank, the supply of money increases by a multiplier. This occurs because the borrowing bank, after keeping money in reserve, may lend money to a second bank, that in turn may lend to a third bank, which lends to its customers. This process of lending more money than the lender has in assets is the essence of "fractional-reserve banking."[29]

The following example illustrates how fractional-reserve banking results in a multiplier effect.[30] Assume that banks face a requirement that they hold 10 percent of their funds in reserve. If the Federal Reserve lends $1000 to Bank A, Bank A then lends the maximum amount allowed (taking into account the reserve requirement) to Bank B, Bank B lends the maximum amount to Bank C, and Bank C finally lends the maximum amount to Company D, then the initial $1000 loan from the central bank increased the effective money supply to $3439.[31] Ultimately, that initial $1000 loan should create $10,000 assuming a 10 percent reserve requirement.[32] Figure 9.1 depicts the amount of money created along this chain.

Now, if the capital requirement is lowered to 5 percent, the supply of money would increase (by more than 5 percent) over these same four loans to

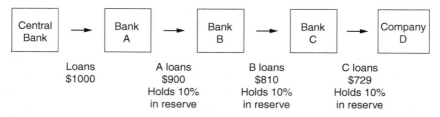

Figure 9.1 Money-creation via a central bank loan.

$3709.88.[33] The money multiplier effect would mean that the $1000 loan ultimately creates $20,000 of money given a 5 percent reserve requirement.

Note that the money multiplier effect continues to operate even if money is not loaned from one bank to another, as in the above examples. The multiplier effect continues so long as the money stays in the banking system. For example, if money is loaned to a company that uses it to purchase equipment and the seller of that equipment deposits the proceeds of the sale into a bank account, the multiplier effect is still at work. It ends only if it proceeds of a loan are not re-deposited with a bank, but "stuffed under a mattress."[34]

The macroeconomist debate: should monetary policy address bubbles?

Having provided an overview of the tools available to central banks, the central question becomes: should these tools of monetary policy be used to prevent, dampen, or prick asset price bubbles? This very question has been the subject of a fierce and long-running debate among macroeconomists.

The Bernanke camp

One camp in this debate, led by former Princeton economics professor and current Federal Reserve Chairman Ben Bernanke, has argued against using monetary policy to prick bubbles.[35] The Bernanke view contends that central banks (assuming they are pursuing an inflation-targeting policy)[36] should focus only on aggregate inflation in the economy and not on inflation in specific asset markets. Under this view (which once prevailed among leaders of the U.S. Federal Reserve and other central banks),[37] deploying monetary policy to address bubbles entails too much risk for several reasons. First, prices in a particular asset market may not send clear signals about overall inflation in the economy.[38] Second, economists in this camp believe it is too difficult to determine whether and when a booming asset market represents a bubble. Even skyrocketing prices may reflect the fundamental value of assets rather than the market mispricings of a bubble.[39] This concern stems from the deep questions and controversies sketched out in Chapter 1 on whether various market booms in history constituted bubble episodes or could be explained by other economic factors. If it is difficult to determine with any certainty that a bubble occurred after the fact, these economists argue, how can central bankers have any confidence that they can predict bubbles beforehand or identify them as they inflate?[40]

Central bankers, of course, regularly make decisions under uncertainty, but using the lever of monetary policy to address asset prices still has considerable costs. This leads to a third concern: it is difficult for central bankers to calibrate changes in interest rates or the money supply to achieve precise results in an asset market. The Bernanke camp fears that crude changes in monetary policy could push asset markets from boom to crash.[41]

Finally, monetary policy can have uncertain but potentially huge spillover effects on many different aspects of the economy beyond the particular financial market that is booming. Monetary policy might affect, among other things, inflation, unemployment, and foreign exchange rates. For example, raising interest rates dampens inflation across the entire economy. Higher interest rates might thus cool one overheating market yet also depress other asset markets that are not "irrationally" priced. Addressing a potential bubble in a stock market, for example, may lead to stagnating housing prices that had not suffered from any excessive inflation. Monetary policy can have other drastic spillover effects; higher interest rates may increase unemployment or raise the value of a country's currency, making exports less competitive. These spillover effects of monetary policy led Bernanke and other macroeconomists to liken using monetary policy to address bubbles to conducting "brain surgery with a sledgehammer."[42]

"Leaning into the wind" and the Greenspan Put

Several prominent macroeconomists do not subscribe to the Bernanke view.[43] They argue that, in certain circumstances, monetary policy should address potential asset price bubbles as they develop. This policy approach has been called "leaning into the wind."[44] This view, shared by the heads of central banks in Europe[45] and Canada,[46] breaks into several parts. First, booming prices in a particular asset class may send a warning signal about the risk of inflation in the entire economy.[47] Second, the risk that a collapsed bubble poses to a country's financial stability justifies taking action even in the face of spillover costs and potential uncertainty as to whether booming prices represent a bubble.[48] Third, central bankers can exercise judgment as to whether prices in a particular market constitute a bubble or are otherwise justified by economic fundamentals.[49] Finally, economists in this camp underscore that central banks should not target asset prices, per se, but take prices in certain potentially overheating markets into consideration in formulating monetary policy and promoting macroeconomic stability.[50]

The global financial crisis may have tipped the scales in the debate in favor of leaning into the wind. Economists at the IMF and a number of important central banks worldwide recently endorsed using monetary policy to mitigate potential asset price bubbles.[51] This change comes as the neoclassical approach and the entire field of macroeconomics faces sustained and withering criticism after the Panic of 2007–2008.[52]

Critics of the Bernanke camp have underscored the serious problems created by the so-called "Greenspan Put." This colorful term describes the Federal Reserve's decades-old reluctance to wield monetary policy to stop bubbles, while championing the use of monetary policy to address the aftermath of a collapsed bubble. During his tenure as chairman of the Federal Reserve, Alan Greenspan opposed using interest rate hikes to deflate potential asset price bubbles. Yet he advocated lowering interest rates after a crash in asset prices in order to stimulate growth and prevent financial markets from freezing in a liquidity crisis.[53] In the first half of the 2000s, Greenspan followed this policy to the letter. In the wake of the collapse of technology stocks, the Enron wave of scandals, and the September 11 attacks, the Federal Reserve slashed key interest rates and kept them at historic low levels for several quarters.[54]

Detractors labeled his policy the "Greenspan Put" because it allowed investors in an asset market to enjoy a prolonged price boom, but also placed a monetary safety net under them in case prices fell too far too fast. The Greenspan Put may have created a form of systemic moral hazard, as speculating investors felt insulated from the risk of a market collapse.[55] A long roster of scholars and policymakers faulted Alan Greenspan for keeping interest rates too low too long in the wake of the collapsed technology stock market in 2000–2001. These critics argue that low interest rates led to an influx of foreign capital and cheap credit, which spurred a housing market bubble.[56] When this bubble popped, it generated the worst global financial crisis since the Great Depression. In using monetary policy to respond to the collapse of one bubble, Greenspan may have sown the seeds for a larger bubble.[57] In a series of columns, Paul Krugman criticized the Federal Reserve for blowing serial bubbles.[58] To mix metaphors, by wielding the monetary sledgehammer only upon the collapse of a bubble, the Federal Reserve may have sparked a game of "whack-a-bubble."

Lingering concerns: the unavoidable costs of broad-brush monetary policy tools

Even if the view that monetary policy should be used to address bubbles is ascendant, employing the broad-brush monetary tools of open market operations and central bank loans still entails serious risks. Using these tools pits a central banker's judgment against the judgment of the financial markets. Government officials will face strong political pressure not to tighten monetary policy and upset the economic applecart.[59] The same political dynamics described in Chapter 3 that reinforce regulatory stimuli also militate for monetary stimulus. Using judgment without articulating clear policy standards to the public may interfere with the central bank sending a clear signal of its future monetary policy. This frustrates the formation of market expectations that are integral to a successful monetary policy. A central bank signal on monetary policy must also be credible, that is, the market must believe that the central bank is committed to taking a monetary course of action against inflation in an asset class. If participants in the market do not believe in the resoluteness of the central bank, they may trade against the central bank's actions (including by bidding asset prices higher) and undermine efforts to deflate a boom.[60]

A central bank might overcome these concerns (it might exercise good judgment and make a credible commitment to address asset price bubbles), but this still leaves the final concern expressed by the Bernanke camp. Bubble-fighting monetary policy would still have spillover effects. Tighter monetary policy could, among other things, chill other markets that are not irrationally priced, increase unemployment, alter exchange rates, and trigger capital movement across borders.

Financial regulations as substitutes for monetary policy

These spillover effects provide powerful motivation to search for more narrowly tailored means of targeting the credit, liquidity, and leverage that fuel asset price bubbles. The fierce debate among macroeconomists has overshadowed the availability of tools beyond open-market operations and central bank loans, both of which act to change monetary conditions across the entire economy. Policy makers have more than just these two controls to fly the macroeconomic plane.

Central bankers and financial regulators can use a variety of regulatory levers to adjust the effective supply of money in the economy. These levers operate by restricting the credit that financial institutions provide and the leverage they take on. These tools described below have the potential advantage of being more surgical. They may allow central bankers and regulators to target the flow of credit to specific overheating asset markets. Tailoring regulations to particular markets thus avoids the spillover effects associated with broad-brush monetary tools.

The discussion below starts with a traditional tool, namely reserve requirements, that has fallen into disuse at central banks. It then discusses adapting the logic of reserve requirements to adjust the credit supplied by, and the leverage embedded within, certain financial instruments, such as repos and credit derivatives. The analysis then moves to the federal margin regulations in the United States, which restrict the amount of credit which banks, broker dealers, and others may provide to stock-market investors. This chapter then looks at whether capital requirements could be used to throttle back financial institution lending in particular asset markets. This last point touches on a current heated public policy debate on raising capital requirements.

As explained below, many of these potential regulatory tools could potentially be narrowly tailored to apply to particular assets and asset markets. Reserve requirements, for example, could require that banks set aside higher amounts of reserves for particular asset classes – such as real estate or securities. This potential narrow tailoring, however, comes at the cost of losing effectiveness, a topic addressed in "Advantages and drawbacks to using regulation as monetary tools," below.

Reserve requirements and leverage regulations

As noted above, bank reserve requirements used to form part of a central bank's monetary toolkit. A few countries, such as China, continue to use this regulatory lever to address inflation.[61] If China's efforts succeed, perhaps reserve requirements will experience a renaissance and reenter the arsenal of other central banks.

Reserve requirements are still used heavily for bank regulatory purposes if not as monetary instruments. For example, loan loss regulations require that financial institutions set aside funds to cover the risk of default on their loan portfolios.[62] Chapter 7 discussed how poorly designed loan loss reserve regulations can exert procyclical effects. That discussion of procyclicality provided clues to how loan loss regulations and various other kinds of reserve regulations can have an indirect (and often unintended) monetary impact.

Consider if regulators required banks to increase loan loss reserves across the board for real estate lending. This would create a bigger cushion for banks in the event of a real estate downturn. Yet this regulatory change would also decrease the amount of credit and the effective supply of money (or liquidity) in real estate markets. Restricted credit and less liquidity could put downward pressure on real estate prices. Successfully using reserve requirements to achieve monetary results, however, is subject to significant caveats (discussed in "Advantages and drawbacks to using regulation as monetary tools," below.)

Margin, embedded leverage, and financial instruments

The economic logic of reserve requirements also explains how certain contractual provisions in modern financial instruments can also exert a monetary effect. In particular, those contractual provisions in repurchase agreements (or "repos") and credit derivatives that govern collateral control the amount of leverage embedded within those instruments. These provisions also affect the amount of credit that one financial institution can provide via these instruments. Accordingly financial regulations that mimic these contractual provisions and require more (or less) collateral can also have a monetary impact. To explain how this works, the following discussion provides an overview of these instruments. It also introduces some cutting edge macroeconomic research on the link between leverage and overall market liquidity (i.e., the effective supply of money).

Repos

That line of economic research began with repo agreements. Tobias Adrian and Hyun Song Shin examined the repo market, which has become a critical source of short-term credit for financial institutions.[63] In a repo transaction, a borrower sells a security at a price below the current market value and agrees to repurchase it at a higher agreed price in the future.[64] This sale and repurchase has the same economic effect as a secured loan, with the security serving as collateral.[65]

The difference between the current market price of the security and the price at which the borrower sells it represents the repo's "haircut."[66] Larger haircuts (when the security is sold to the repo lender for far below market price) mean more collateral for the lender and lower leverage for the borrower.[67] Smaller haircuts translate into less collateral and more leverage.[68] The following two chapters revisit the economic function and legal history of repos.

Smaller haircuts have the same economic effects – increasing leverage and freeing up capital – as lowering a reserve requirement for bank lending does.[69] The lending of financial institutions one to one another in sequence via repos also generates the same money multiplier effect. This multiplier effect is amplified when lenders decrease the haircut and dampened when they increase it.[70] A regulation governing the size of a repo haircut would thus affect the supply of money being created in the repo market.

Credit derivatives

This same logic also applies to credit derivatives and their collateral provisions. Credit derivatives are financial instruments whose values depend on the credit risk of a firm or other financial contract. Although credit derivatives come in forms as varied and complex as financial wizards can conjure, the basic economics can be understood through a common variant, the credit default swap (CDS). In a simple CDS, one party (the "credit protection buyer" or Party A in Figure 9.2) pays a premium to another party (the "credit protection seller" or Party B in Figure 9.2). In exchange, the credit protection seller agrees to make specified payments to the credit protection buyer should a specified "credit event" occur.[71] For example, the credit protection seller might agree to make payments to the buyer should a payment default occur on specific bonds or other financial instruments. A CDS thus functions as kind of financial guarantee or "insurance" on those bonds.[72]

The following two chapters explain and explore credit derivatives in greater detail. For now, note that the credit protection seller in a CDS can turn around and hedge the credit risk it is assuming by itself purchasing credit protection (i.e., becoming a credit protection buyer) in a second CDS. The credit protection seller under that contract (Party C) can, in turn, hedge its risk with a third CDS (with yet a another party, Party D, serving as credit protection seller). Rinse, lather, repeat.[73] Figure 9.2 depicts this chain of credit derivatives.

The credit protection seller can be leveraged in several ways. Most basically, it can borrow money from third parties. But leverage is also embedded within the derivative contract itself.[74] The credit protection seller is leveraged to the extent that it does not post collateral to cover its expected obligations to make any future payment under the derivative contract. The credit protection buyer may become worried about its counterparty risk from the seller (i.e., the risk that a credit event will occur and the credit protection seller will default on its obligations to make payment to the buyer). To mitigate this risk, the buyer may demand that the credit protection seller post collateral. The amount of

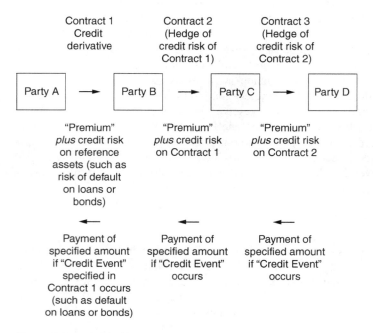

Figure 9.2 A chain of credit derivatives.

collateral required fluctuates according to contract and the creditworthiness of the seller.[75]

When counterparties lower collateral requirements along a chain of credit derivatives, then credit protection sellers must commit fewer funds to cover their obligations under the contracts. Lowering (or raising) the collateral or margin requirements increases (or decreases) geometrically the amount of credit risk that can be transferred by a chain of credit derivatives.[76]

By enlarging the carrying capacity of existing credit derivatives and increasing the capital available for credit protection sellers to underwrite new derivatives, lower collateral requirements turbocharge credit markets.[77] This occurs because financial institutions often use CDSs and other credit derivatives to hedge the risk of loans they have made or bonds that they have purchased. A number of empirical studies document that lenders purchase credit derivatives to offload credit risk, and then make fresh loans (or purchase more bonds).[78] The more credit risk that financial institutions hedge with derivatives, the more new loans they can provide and fresh credit risk they can assume.

This also means that errors in the pricing or collateralization of credit derivatives that allow credit protection sellers to become excessively leveraged lead to excessive increases in liquidity. When credit protection sellers sell too many derivatives too cheaply, financial institutions can offload too much risk, and extend too much new credit.[79] Furthermore, if credit protection sellers must post too little collateral to cover their obligations, they take on too much credit risk from financial institutions and allow too much new lending.

As with repos, regulations that require credit protection sellers to post higher collateral reduces the embedded leverage with the associated derivatives. By dampening the carrying capacity of those financial instruments to transfer credit risk, this type of regulation would also lower their capacity to increase the provision of credit and the creation of money.

The exchanges upon which futures and some standardized derivatives are traded typically impose restrictions, called margin rules, which govern the collateral that parties trading on the exchange must post to cover their obligations.[80] Traders that buy and sell futures and derivatives on an exchange typically do not settle the trades directly with one another. Instead, they settle with a third party, namely a "clearing company" affiliated with the exchange.[81] This clearing company intermediates between all exchange trades to facilitate trading. Accordingly, two traders looking to trade with one another no longer have to worry about the credit risk of each other; the clearing company assumes the counterparty risk of both. To mitigate its counterparty risk, the clearing company requires all members of the exchange to post a certain amount of collateral, which may consist of cash or securities.[82] This collateral covers a member's future obligations to deliver the futures or derivatives that it sold or to pay for futures or derivatives it bought. The clearing company constantly adjusts the collateral requirements for each member based on the open positions and perceived creditworthiness of the member.[83] These margin rules are functionally equivalent to the collateral provisions described above in private, off-exchange (so-called "over-the-counter") derivatives.[84]

The purpose of these exchange margin rules is usually thought of as solely to mitigate this counterparty risk (and, possibly, to prevent a chain reaction of financial firm failures). However, by adjusting collateral and embedded leverage, margin rules for credit derivatives also affect the creation of money.

Indeed, there is some precedent for using exchange margin rules to address asset price bubbles. Some 2011 accounts credit the Chicago Mercantile Exchange's decision to raise margin requirements on silver futures with popping a global commodities bubble.[85] This essentially replicated the result in experimental asset markets, in which changes to margin rules have pricked bubbles.

Asset-backed securities

The same dynamics of leverage and money creation with respect to credit derivatives can also apply to asset-backed securities (instruments described in detail in the following two chapters). Asset-backed securities are financial instruments created when multiple loans, mortgages, or other assets that produce a predictable future cash stream are pooled together and sold to an investment vehicle that issues securities to investors.[86] The investment vehicle uses the cash from the sale to investors to purchase the pool of loans, mortgages, or other underlying assets from lenders. The vehicle later applies the cash received from the borrowers of those underlying loans, mortgages, or assets, to make scheduled payments on the asset-backed securities to investors.[87]

By purchasing these asset-backed securities, investors provide cash to the lenders that extend credit in the underlying mortgages or loans (who are known as "originating lenders" or "originators"). Originating lenders can use this cash to make new loans. Figure 9.3 depicts the creation of a basic asset-backed securities transaction.[88]

If asset-backed securities serve as pipelines for credit, they also spread credit risk in the opposite direction. Securitization transfers credit risk from the original borrowers to the originating lenders and onto the investment vehicle and ultimately to investors in capital markets. As with CDSs, when an originating lender can offload more credit risk via asset-backed securities, it can make more new loans to borrowers.

Moreover, regulations that require originating lenders to retain more credit risk clamp down on the new credit than can be provided. This means that credit risk retention regulations for securitization must be seen in a new light. A brief detour explains how these rules operate. After the Panic of 2007–2008, policymakers became concerned that the increasing tendency of originating lenders to sell these assets to an investment vehicle (the first stage in Figure 9.3) dulled their incentive to check the creditworthiness of borrowers.[89] This concern generated numerous proposals, including a provision ultimately found in the Dodd-Frank Act that requires regulators to consider new rules mandating that originating lenders retain a portion of loans sold in a securitization (i.e., retain some "skin" in the game).[90] But, as with credit derivatives and counterparty risk, credit retention comprises only the microeconomic half of the story. Requiring that lenders hold onto part of their loans restricts the capital they can deploy for new loans. This throttles back the amount of additional credit that can flow back to consumers and businesses.

Chapter 11 also argues for rethinking the purposes of leverage regulations. Generally, regulators address the leverage of financial institutions to mitigate the

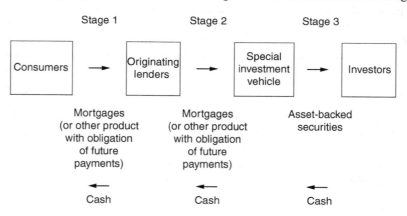

Figure 9.3 A simplified securitization transaction.

risk of their failure and the system impact it would cause. Similarly, margin for repos or the collateral for derivatives is seen as reducing counterparty risk. Policymakers have considered regulating this margin in order to reduce the possibility of important firms falling like dominoes. Yet leverage also has a systemic effect by changing the monetary environment. Increased leverage can spark unsustainable financial market booms.

U.S. federal margin regulations

This use of prudential regulation for monetary policy has precedent. Federal margin regulations in the United States provide one example. These rules, introduced in the New Deal, restrict the ability of banks and broker dealers to lend money to investors to purchase stock.[91] These regulations stemmed from concerns in the wake of the 1929 Crash that credit had fueled excessive speculation.[92] In response, the U.S. Securities Exchange Act of 1934 gave the Federal Reserve the responsibility to establish margin regulations and the SEC the responsibility to enforce them.[93] The Federal Reserve passed separate regulations restricting the extension of credit by broker-dealers,[94] banks, and all other types of lenders.[95] The fact that Congress gave the Federal Reserve responsibility for setting the level of margin regulations suggests that policymakers realized that a broader policy kit was necessary for addressing overheating markets and that monetary policymaking might encompass other tools.[96]

Capital requirements?

It is possible that other banking regulations that govern financial institution leverage can restrict the provision of bank credit and change the effective supply of money. Capital requirements provide an interesting test case. However, the extent to which higher capital requirements reduce the provision of bank credit remains controversial.

Indeed, in the wake of the financial crisis, policymakers have considered dramatically raising capital requirements on banks to increase their cushion against economic turmoil. This would reduce the risk of bank failure and its spillover costs on the economy and on the taxpayers who fund bank bailouts. Capital requirements are intended to ensure that a financial institution has sufficient "patient capital" to weather significant losses and economic downturns.[97]

Chapter 5 discussed how capital regulations work. To review: these regulations require that banks maintain a ratio of equity to assets. Only certain kinds of capital (which shareholders cannot easily redeem) count towards the numerator. Capital regulations place assets into different buckets, with more capital required for asset categories considered to involve higher risk.[98]

Banks have sharply criticized these proposals claiming that they would cause banks to cut back on lending. The banks argue that if they were forced to hold more capital against their assets, they would have to cut back on the size of their assets. Since their principal assets are loans, this arguably translates into less lending.[99] This current debate is also largely about politics, as banks attempt to use continued anemic economic growth in the United States and Europe as a reason to dilute tougher bank capital rules.

Economists, such as Anat Admati and Martin Hellwig have attacked the bankers' logic on several fronts. First, they note that capital requirements are not the same as reserves. Reserves are considered "contra" assets and are recorded on the left side of a bank's balance sheet. Reserves necessarily restrict lending. Capital, by contrast, sits on the right side of the balance sheet. Moreover, imposing higher ratios of capital to assets does not necessarily mean that assets will be reduced. Banks could meet higher capital requirements in ways other than by curbing lending, including by issuing more stock, reducing their debt level, and changing the makeup of their assets to include more lower risk assets. Finally, the economists point to the Miller–Modigliani theorem (discussed in Chapter 5) to note that, under certain assumptions, the value of a firm does not depend on whether it finances itself with more debt or more equity. This implies that, when a financial institution must finance itself to a greater extent with equity, the size of its overall balance sheet should not change, nor should it necessarily have to reduce its lending.[100]

Despite this counterattack by economists, there are a number of circumstances in which capital *might* indeed restrict bank lending, and this might be a *good* thing if policymakers sought to use capital requirements in the future to cool overheating markets. Raising capital by issuing new shares is not costless for banks, which means higher capital requirements might force banks to reduce the asset side of their balance sheet. Moreover, the assumptions behind the Miller–Modigliani theorem do not always hold. Notably, markets are not always efficient. Indeed, the economic theory and evidence of bubbles, laid out in Chapter 1, describes when capital markets are most *in*efficient. To the extent that it is costly for firms to raise capital (even leaving aside tax rules and government guarantees that make debt relatively cheaper, as Chapter 5 explains), higher required levels of capital *might* constrain lending. To the extent this occurs, higher capital requirements would also constrain money creation in the macroeconomy.

Beyond capital requirements, a host of other prudential regulations that govern financial institution leverage might be used as tools of monetary policy. Candidates include direct caps on the leverage of a financial institution,[101] loan-to-value requirements,[102] taxes levied on banks based on the size of their balance sheets,[103] and premia charged for government deposit insurance.[104]

Advantages and drawbacks to using regulation as monetary tools

Using margin or collateral requirements and prudential regulations as monetary tools offers several benefits. If the Bernanke camp worries that raising interest rates across the entire economy is attempting brain surgery with a sledgehammer, collateral and margin regulations could provide macroeconomic policymakers with a set of scalpels. Regulators could narrowly tailor (or "Taylor") rules such as collateral requirements for credit derivatives for specific classes of assets. For example, regulators could require higher collateral requirements for a credit derivative that hedges credit risk from mortgages. Regulations could require higher collateral for loans to specific economic sectors. Regulators could then recalibrate these asset-class-specific regulations when particular asset markets appear to overheat or collapse. To continue the airplane metaphor introduced above, these tools would provide pilots with finer controls of trim.

The narrowness of these tools, however, could often be their undoing. Collateral regulations only apply to specific financial instruments. When regulators increase collateral requirements on a given instrument, they only encourage traders to find (or devise) unregulated economic substitutes. In other words, the narrowness of these tools invites regulatory arbitrage. Chapter 5 explained in detail how booms foment regulatory arbitrage, including by raising the benefits to evading regulation. If prudential regulations are to be used to combat asset price bubbles, the very dynamics of bubbles may weaken prudential regulations. By contrast, the sledgehammer nature of broad-brush monetary policy tools gives them their power. When interest rates rise market-wide, there are fewer avenues for regulatory arbitrage.

Regulatory preferences and the creation of money

Financial regulation can change the money supply in a second way beyond changing the reserves or leverage of financial institutions. Chapter 7 described how statutes and regulations can give legal preferences to certain financial instruments that endow those contracts with many of the economic characteristics of "money." Again, the three canonical economic functions of money are serving as a medium of exchange, a unit of account, and store of value. Cash, of course, performs all of these functions (except in the most extreme cases in which public confidence in a government currency fails).

Private sector obligations can also take on these three functions. To do so, these obligations or instruments must enjoy a low degree of credit risk. In other words, the holders of the instrument must be assured that the risk that the obligor will not pay is low. Instruments are more like money if they can be readily converted into cash, for example, when they are traded on a deep market. (Chapter 7 explains different concepts of liquidity – including liquidity in the sense of the overall supply of money in a market, the ability to convert assets into cash, and "trading liquidity.")

As noted in Chapter 7, economist Gary Gorton frames the ability of financial instruments to achieve the economic characteristics of money in a slightly different manner. He writes that instruments become money to the degree they become "informationally insensitive debt."[105] Debt becomes informationally insensitive when it is "immune to adverse selection by privately informed traders."[106] In layperson's terms, this means that holders of this debt need not worry that there is inside information about the value of the instrument.[107] Nor do they have to incur extensive search costs to ascertain that value.

Financial instruments may enjoy lower credit risk and higher liquidity – and thus take on features of money – by virtue of contractual features. For example, bank deposit accounts may give holders the right to withdraw funds on demand. However, Chapter 7 also outlined how various government preferences can help various financial instruments achieve lower credit risk and higher liquidity. For example, government deposit insurance helps convince investors to deposit money in banks. As Chapter 7 explained other regulatory preferences can induce investors to "herd into liquidity." That discussion provided a preview of Chapter 11, which describes how various preferences helped foster liquidity in "shadow banking" instruments. For example, the Congress provided repos and various derivatives ("swaps") exemptions from the Bankruptcy Code that reduced the need for creditors under those contracts to assess the bankruptcy risk of their counterparties. These regulatory preferences helped create a deep, liquid market for these instruments

Together, these regulatory preferences – whether provided *ex ante* or *ex post* – also had a significant monetary dimension. By endowing more financial instruments with money-like features, policymakers increased the supply of money in the economy. If regulations can make financial instruments more like money, several scholars, such as Morgan Ricks, also argue that they can and should also be used to restrict the creation of money.[108]

The implications

Knowing is half the battle

Central bankers may balk at using prudential regulations to implement monetary policy. As noted above, prudential regulations may be too narrow to be effective instruments of monetary policy. There may also be times in which macro-economic objectives – e.g., promoting job growth – conflict with the primary purposes of prudential regulations – ensuring the safety and soundness of banks.

However, even if these regulations are not used to implement monetary policy, central bankers still need to worry about them because these regulations can still have monetary effects. By increasing financial institution leverage or endowing financial instruments with the characteristics of money, these regulations change the effective supply of money. This can occur *even if this was not the principal intent of policymakers*.

Changes to these regulations can have unseen monetary consequences. Deregulation or the under-enforcement of prudential regulations can allow financial institutions to increase their leverage. Reduced legal compliance or increased regulatory arbitrage can yield the same result. Increased financial institution leverage or more money-like instruments, in turn, increase the money supply and can fuel an asset price bubble.

Dangerous feedback: when the Regulatory Instability Hypothesis matters most

The potential for destructive feedback loops is extreme. Previous chapters explained at length how asset price bubbles promote deregulation, lower enforcement, compliance rot, and regulatory arbitrage. The deterioration of financial regulation can feed a bubble which causes regulation to deteriorate further. This means that the implications of the Regulatory Instability Hypothesis become most dire when they apply to legal rules that govern financial institution leverage and the creation of money-like instruments. When the regulatory stimulus cycle, compliance rot, or regulatory arbitrage frenzies impact these types of legal rules, they threaten to generate or exacerbate bubbles.

Moreover, the deteriorating effectiveness of regulations of financial institution leverage during bubbles can provide a devastating one-two-three punch. Financial institutions can fuel a bubble, and then, when the bubble implodes, highly leveraged financial institutions can collapse. Furthermore, as Chapter 7 explained, when asset prices nosedive, investors can herd out of markets, causing liquidity to evaporate in bank run-like dynamics.

Bubbles then beget banking crises. A wave of bank failures can trigger a contraction of credit, which further depresses asset prices, atrophies economic activity, and poses further threats to bank solvency and liquidity. These feedback dynamics are not merely theoretical, but in fact explain some of the worse financial crises of the modern era. In their masterly book, *This Time is Different*, Carmen Reinhart and Kenneth Rogoff document the links between asset price bubbles and banking crises.[109] In this book, Chapter 11 outlines how the Panic of 2007–2008 represented the confluence of the solvency and liquidity crises described immediately above.

Leverage cycles

This empirical data meshes with cutting edge macroeconomic theories of how leverage cycles can form. Economist John Geanakoplos has presented an influential new theory of a macroeconomic leverage cycle.[110] Geanakoplos observed that equilibrium in credit markets depends not only on interest rates, but also on the margin or collateral that lenders demand for loans.[111] The level of margin or collateral for a loan dictates the leverage of the borrower. Geanakoplos theorized that leverage in the economy experiences cycles.[112] During boom times, lenders demand less collateral and leverage increases.[113] Increased lending fuels the economy and drives margins lower and leverage even higher. When the economy sours, lenders demand more collateral. Reduced leverage and lending throttles back the economy.[114]

Chapter 11 discusses how Geanakoplos's theoretical work has received empirical support in the wake of the crisis. Economists Tobias Adrian and Hyun Song Shin present evidence that major financial institutions dramatically increased their leverage in the boom years in the United States, and then dramatically decreased leverage after crises struck in 1987, 1998, and 2007.[115] They also show that the repo market, which these financial institutions rely on for short-term financing, grew significantly in the boom years leading to the Panic of 2007–2008, peaked in March 2008, and then crashed.[116]

Geanakoplos's model of a leverage cycle follows other macroeconomic models of how credit more generally can generate economic cycles. For example, the influential Kiyotaki–Moore model illustrates a mechanism in which collateralized lending can amplify exogenous shocks to the economy. Similar to Geanakoplos's analysis, above, if these shocks cause the value of collateral to drop, lenders can dramatically curtail lending, choking economic growth.[117]

Masking risk

These multiple feedback dynamics complicate efforts to understand the interactions among regulatory changes, financial institution leverage, liquidity in the markets for credit instruments, and asset prices. The fog thickens more, because rising asset prices in bubble periods mask the mispricing of the risks faced by individual financial firms and financial markets as a whole. Masking the mispricing of risk is, after all, the essence of asset price bubbles.

Collective action and information problems in the marketplace

Moreover, individual market participants may not see the collective changes to financial institution leverage that come from their individual decisions to reduce margin or collateral requirements or to invest in particular credit instruments. If the markets for credit instruments are opaque, investors may not perceive the herd behavior that generates systemic increases in leverage or stampedes into liquidity. The participants in these markets have less ability to factor macroeconomic consequences into their decisions to price contracts and set collateral requirements than they do with respect to counterparty risk.[118]

They may also have little incentive to address these macroeconomic risks. Indeed, in a recurrent leitmotif of this book, market participants may be punished by their principals for attempting to sit out a bubble. The logic of short time horizons and herd behavior reinforce another. Individual market participants can do little to counteract the macroeconomic effects of investing in these credit markets. When the music keeps playing, you keep dancing.[119]

The gathering storm

Central banks and monetary policymakers have better incentives to consider the systemic impacts of changes to macroeconomic conditions. Yet they may have neither the tools nor the inclination to pay attention to profound, subsurface effects of regulatory change. Changes to leverage or money creating regulations – whether from regulatory stimulus, compliance rot, or regulatory arbitrage – represent a large blindspot for macroeconomists and central banks. Legal rules and changes to legal rules tend to get washed out in models that focus on macro-economic aggregates. Central bankers and macroeconomists are trained to watch interest rates and unemployment levels not changes in regulation, legal compliance, or regulatory arbitrage.

The danger looms that, when they affect credit regulations, deregulation, deteriorating legal compliance, and regulatory arbitrage can generate a bubble without central bankers, regulators, or the marketplace even being aware. This is in fact, what Chapter 11 argues happened in the run-up to the Panic of 2007–2008. Deregulation and regulatory arbitrage incubated a shadow financial system that served the same functions as the traditional banking system – *including serving as a transmission belt for monetary policy* – while the Federal Reserve and bank regulators slept. In essence, thanks to an agglomeration of legal changes, financial markets grew a turbocharged engine under the pilots' noses. As we will see, the pilots even decided to turn off some of their instruments as the plane raced into a gathering storm.

Notes

1 Ronald R. King, Vernon L. Smith, Arlington W. Williams, and Mark Van Boening, The Robustness of Bubbles and Crashes in Experimental Stock Markets, in *Non-linear Dynamics and Evolutionary Economics*, 183, 188–9 (Richard H. Day and Ping Chen eds., 1993, Oxford University Press).

   The results were more mixed in experiments in which traders could both buy on margin and sell shares short. Ibid. In situations in which traders were allowed to repeat previous experiments and gain experience in investing with margin loans, prices more closely tracked fundamentals. However this result did not significantly differ from the baseline. This bolsters the inference that having experienced a bubble and crash was the key factor that reduced the incidence and severity of bubbles. Ibid. The previous chapter discusses the effect on the incidence and severity of bubbles in experimental asset markets when traders could gain experience with bubbles in previous iterations of the experiment. Chapter 8, "Experiencing a bubble and a crash."

2 King *et al.*, *supra* note 1. One group of researchers concluded: "[t]his suggests that the common social policy of imposing margin requirements may be effective in moderating stock market bubbles." Ibid. at 199.

3 Robert J. Shiller, *Irrational Exuberance*, 222–4 (2001, Broadway Books).

4 This consensus includes economists who think monetary policy should be used to address asset price bubbles, as well as those who argue that it should not. Compare Stephen G. Cecchetti, Hans Genberg, and Sushil Wadhwani, Asset Prices in a Flexible Inflation Targeting Framework, in *Asset-Price Bubbles: The Implications for Monetary, Regulatory, and International Policies*, 427 (William C. Hunter, George G. Kaufman, and Michael Pomerleano eds., 2003, MIT Press) (arguing that monetary policy should take into account asset price "misalignments") with Ben Bernanke and Mark Gertler, Monetary Policy and Asset Price Volatility, *Federal Reserve Bank of Kansas City Economic Review* 17 (4th Quarter, 1999) (arguing against using monetary policy to combat asset price bubbles). Cf. Jean-Claude Trichet, Asset Price Bubbles and Their Implications for Monetary Policy and Financial Stability, in *Asset-Price Bubbles: The Implications for Monetary, Regulatory, and International Policies*, 14, 16–17 (William C. Hunter, George G. Kaufman, and Michael Pomerleano, eds., 2003, MIT Press).

5 Chapter 1, "Agency costs and the role of credit." See, e.g., Franklin Allen and Gary Gorton, Churning Bubbles, 60 *Review of Economic Studies* 813 (1993); Franklin Allen and Douglas Gale, Bubbles and Crises, 110 *Economic Journal* 236, 236 (2000); Franklin Allen and Douglas Gale, Asset-Price Bubbles and Stock Market Interlinkages, in *Asset-Price Bubbles: The Implications for Monetary, Regulatory, and International Policies*, 323, 325–9 (William C. Hunter, George G. Kaufman, and Michael Pomerleano eds., 2003, MIT Press).

6 Cf. King *et al.*, *supra* note 1.

7 See generally Frederic S. Mishkin, The Channels of Monetary Transmission: Lessons for Monetary Policy, National Bureau of Economic Research, *Working Paper No. w5464* (May 1996) available at http://papers.ssrn.com/sol3/papers. cfm?abstract_id=265157 (last visited July 27, 2013) (summarizing macroeconomic research on interest rate and "credit" channels).

8 This chapter uses "liquidity" in the sense of the total money supply, that is, those financial instruments that have the characteristics of "money." These features are described *infra* Chapter 9, note 14 and accompanying text.

   Chapter 7 noted other related meanings of liquidity, including "market liquidity" or "trading liquidity," which refers to the volume (or depth) of buyers and sellers in a market. Greater market liquidity means that larger volumes of assets can be bought or sold without each trade significantly affecting the asset's market price. Chapter 7, notes 59–62 and accompanying text.

9 In the legal literature, Margaret Blair was one of the first to examine how increases in leverage can enlarge the effective money supply. Margaret M. Blair, Financial Innovation, Leverage, Bubbles, and the Distribution of Income, 30 *Review of Banking and Financial Law* 225, 229–32 (2010).

   Tobias Adrian and Hyun Song Shin have authored much of the recent and germinal macroeconomic literature on the connection between leverage and liquidity in the "shadow banking" sector. See Tobias Adrian and Hyun Song Shin, Money, Liquidity, and Monetary Policy, 99 *American Economic Review* 600 (2009); Tobias Adrian and Hyun Song Shin, Liquidity and Leverage, 19 *Journal of Financial Intermediation* 418 (2010); Tobias Adrian and Hyun Song Shin, The Shadow Banking System: Implications for Financial Regulation, Federal Reserve Bank of New York, *Staff Report No. 382* (2009) available at www.newyorkfed.org/research/staff_reports/sr382.pdf (last visited July 27, 2013); Tobias Adrian and Hyun Song Shin, The Changing Nature of Financial Intermediation and the Financial Crisis of 2007–2009, 2 *Annual Review of Economics* 603 (2010); Tobias Adrian and Hyun Song Shin, Liquidity, Monetary Policy, and Financial Cycles, Federal Reserve Bank of New York, 14 *Current Issues in Economics and Finance* 1 (2008) available at www.newyorkfed.org/research/current_issues/ci14-1/ci14-1.html (last visited July 27, 2013).

10 The monetary impact of financial institution leverage has been largely overlooked in legal scholarship with a few notable exceptions. See Blair, *supra* note 9.

11 See e.g., Steven L. Schwarcz, Systemic Risk, 97 *Georgetown Law Journal* 193, 223–4 (2008).

12 Ibid.

13 E.g., Erik F. Gerding, Credit Derivatives, Leverage, and Financial Regulation's Missing Macroeconomic Dimension, 8 *Berkeley Business Law Journal* 29 (2011).

14 N. Gregory Mankiw, *Macroeconomics*, 75–7 (5th ed. 2003, Worth/Palgrave Macmillan).

15 See ibid. at 80–1.

16 Chapter 7, "Legal preferences for financial instruments and trading liquidity," Chapter 11, "Regulatory preferences and money creation: bankruptcy exemptions for repos and swaps."

17 Economists have questioned the ability of investors to make distinctions between

real and nominal prices in practice. For an early example of scholarship in this vein, see Franco Modigliani and Richard Cohn, Inflation, Rational Valuation, and the Market, 35 *Financial Analysts Journal* 3 (March–April 1979).

18 The shadow banking system is in detail in Chapter 10. For a sample of influential economic research on the shadow banking system, see Zoltan Poszar, Tobias Adrian, Adam Ashcraft, and Hayley Boesky, Shadow Banking, Federal Reserve Bank of New York, *Staff Report No. 458* (July 2010), 8 available at www.newyorkfed.org/research/staff_reports/sr458.html (last visited July 27, 2013); Gary Gorton, Slapped in the Face by the Invisible Hand: Banking and the Panic of 2007, National Bureau of Economic Research, *Working Paper* (May 9, 2009) available at http://papers.ssrn.com/sol3/papers.cfm?abstract_id=1401882 (last visited July 27, 2013); Gary Gorton and Andrew Metrick, Securitized Banking and the Run on Repo, 104 *Journal of Financial Economics* 425 (2012); Morgan Ricks, Shadow Banking and Financial Regulation, *Columbia Law and Economics Working Paper No. 370* (August 30, 2010) available at http://papers.ssrn.com/sol3/papers.cfm?abstract_id=1571290 (last visited July 27, 2013).

19 Chapter 10, "Provision of credit," "Meteoric growth: shadow banking eclipses depository banking," Chapter 11, "Money: the emergence of a shadow monetary transmission belt, financial regulation, and herding." See generally Adrian and Shin, Money, Liquidity, and Monetary Policy, *supra* note 9.

20 See Blair, *supra* note 9, at 270–3.

21 Markus K. Brunnermeier and Christian Julliard, Money Illusion and Housing Frenzies, 21 *Review of Financial Studies* 135 (2008); Eldar Shafir, Peter Diamond, and Amos Tversky, Money Illusion, 112 *Quarterly Journal of Economics* 341 (1997).

22 Chapter 1, "A behavioral-finance model of asset price bubbles."

23 For a description of how the Federal Reserve has conducted open market operations, see Cheryl L. Edwards, Open Market Operations in the 1990s, 83 *Federal Reserve Bulletin* 859 (1997).

24 In the United States, the Federal Reserve lends to financial institutions through its discount window. By law, only private sector depositary institutions are eligible to borrow from the discount window *unless* the Federal Reserve Board finds that an emergency requires that other firms also be allowed to borrow. 12 U.S.C. § 343 (2009). The Federal Reserve used emergency powers to extend this borrowing privilege to securities dealers during the current financial crisis. Ben S. Bernanke, The Crisis and the Policy Response, Remarks at the Stamp Lecture at the London School of Economics, (January 13, 2009) available at www.federalreserve.gov/newsevents/speech/bernanke20090113a.htm#fn3 (last visited July 27, 2013). This was the first time since the Great Depression that non-banks were allowed to borrow from the discount window. Thomas O. Porter, The Federal Reserve's Catch-22: A Legal Analysis of the Federal Reserve's Emergency Powers, 13 *North Carolina Banking Institute Journal* 483, 502 (2009).

25 The "transmission belt" metaphor was popularized by Gerald Corrigan in a 1982 speech. E. Gerald Corrigan, Are Banks Special? Annual Report Essay, Federal Reserve Bank of Minneapolis (1982) available at www.minneapolisfed.org/pubs/ar/ar1982a.cfm (last visited July 27, 2013).

26 Gordon H. Sellon, Jr. and Stuart E. Weiner, Monetary Policy Without Reserve Requirements: Analytical Issues, *Federal Reserve Bank of Kansas City Economics Review* 5 (1996).

27 The principal Federal Reserve regulations imposing reserve requirements on banks can be found at Reserve Requirements of Depository Institutions (Regulation D), 12 C.F.R. § 204 (2009).

28 Sellon and Weiner, *supra* note 26, at 5.

29 For a discussion of bank regulations governing liquidity in the context of fractional reserve banking, see George J. Benston and George G. Kaufman, The Appropriate Role of Bank Regulation, 106 *Economic Journal* 688, 694 (1996).

30 This example is based on N. Gregory Mankiw, *Principles of Macroeconomics*, 348–9 (2008, Cengage Learning). Economist and law professor Margaret Blair uses a similar example to show how financial institution leverage increases the effective money supply. See Blair, *supra* note 9, at 229–31.

31 Here is the simple arithmetic:

> $1000 (original amount loaned from Fed to A)
> +$900 (amount that A loans to B while holding 10% in reserve)
> +$810 (amount that B loans to C while holding 10% in reserve)
> +$729 (amount that C loans to D while holding 10% in reserve)
> $3439

For a slightly more elaborate example, see Mankiw, *supra* note 30, at 348–9.

32 Per introductory macroeconomics, the money multiplier is the inverse of the reserve ratio, as expressed by the following equation: Money multiplier = 1/reserve ratio. Ibid.

33 Here is the calculation:

> $1000.00 (original amount loaned from Fed to A)
> +$950.00 (amount that A loans to B while holding 5% in reserve)
> +$902.50 (amount that B loans to C while holding 5% in reserve)
> +$857.38 (amount that C loans to D while holding 5% in reserve)
> $3709.88

34 See Blair, *supra* note 9, at 253–4.

35 Bernanke and Gertler, *supra* note 4, at 18 (1999). ("[The inflation targeting approach] implies that policy should *not* respond to changes in asset prices, except insofar as they signal changes in expected inflation." (emphasis in original)).

36 Federal Reserve Governor Ben S. Bernanke, Remarks at the Annual Washington Policy Conference of the National Association of Business Economists, Washington, D.C. ("A Perspective on Inflation Targeting") (March 25, 2003) available at www. federalreserve.gov/Boarddocs/Speeches/2003/20030325/default.htm (last visited July 27, 2013) (describing history of inflation targeting by various central banks).

37 At least until the current global financial crisis, many macroeconomists believed that monetary policy should not address potential bubbles. Cf. Benjamin M. Friedman, Comments on Implications of Bubbles for Monetary Policy, in *Asset-Price Bubbles: The Implications for Monetary, Regulatory, and International Policies*, 459, 460 (William C. Hunter, George G. Kaufman, and Michael Pomerleano eds., 2003, MIT Press).

38 Ibid.; Marvin Goodfriend, Interest Rate Policy should Not React Directly to Asset Prices, in *Asset-Price Bubbles: The Implications for Monetary, Regulatory, and International Policies*, 445 (William C. Hunter, George G. Kaufman, and Michael Pomerleano eds., 2003, MIT Press).

    Note that this particular objection to using monetary policy to target asset prices does not rely on an argument that asset price bubbles are difficult to identify, only that increases in the prices of one asset class send a signal about overall inflation.

39 Bernanke and Gertler, *supra* note 4, at 18–19.

40 Ibid. at 19.

41 Ibid. at 18, 42.

42 Governor Ben S. Bernanke, Asset Price "Bubbles" and Monetary Policy, Remarks at the New York Chapter of the National Association for Business Economics, New York (October 15, 2002) available at www.federalreserve.gov/BoardDocs/ Speeches/2002/20021015/default.htm (last visited July 27, 2013).

43 E.g., Steven G. Cecchetti, Hans Genberg, John Lipsky, and Sushil Wadhwani, *Asset Prices and Central Bank Policy* (2001, International Center for Monetary and Banking Studies/Centre for Economic Policy Research).

44 Frank H. Westerhoff and Cristian Wieland, Spillover Dynamics of Central Bank Interventions, 54 *German Economic Review* 435 (2004).

45 Andrew Mountford, Leaning into the Wind: A Structural VAR Investigation of UK Monetary Policy, 67 *Oxford Bulletin of Economics and Statistics* 597 (2005).

46 Mark Carney, Governor of the Bank of Canada, Some Considerations on Using Monetary Policy to Stabilize Economic Activity, Remarks for Federal Reserve Bank of Kansas City Symposium, Jackson Hole, Wyoming (August 22, 2009) available at www.kansascityfed.org/publicat/sympos/2009/papers/carney.08.22.09.pdf (last visited July 27, 2013).

47 Cf. Cechetti *et al.*, *supra* note 4, at 430.

48 Claudio E.V. Borio and Phillip W. Lowe, Asset Prices, Financial and Monetary Stability: Exploring the Nexus, *BIS Working Paper No. 114* (July 2002) available at http://papers.ssrn.com/sol3/papers.cfm?abstract_id=846305 (last visited July 27, 2013).

49 William C. Dudley, President, Federal Reserve Bank of New York, Remarks at the Eighth Annual BIS Conference, Basel, Switzerland (July 3, 2009) available at www. newyorkfed.org/newsevents/speeches/2009/dud090702.html (last visited July 27, 2013).

50 Cechetti *et al.*, *supra* note 4, at 429.

51 International Monetary Fund, *World Economic Outlook: Sustaining the Recovery*, 93–117 (October 2009, IMF) (surveying economic theory and data and concluding that although monetary policy does not appear to be primary cause of asset bubbles, monetary policymakers may be acting "too narrowly" in responding to potential bubbles; these policymakers can use monetary policy to address asset bubbles to promote macro-stability).

52 See generally Paul Krugman, How Did Economists Get It So Wrong? *New York Times*, September 2, 2009, §MM (Magazine), at 36. Questions on neoclassical macroeconomics have also come from more "conservative" intellectual quarters. See John Cassidy, After the Blowup, *New Yorker* (January 11, 2010), at 28 (describing criticism made by Judge Richard Posner).

53 Federal Reserve Chairman Alan Greenspan, Remarks, New Challenges for Monetary Policy: Proceedings of the Federal Reserve Bank of Kansas City, 143 (1999).

54 Edmund L. Andrews, Greenspan Concedes Error on Regulation, *New York Times*, October 23, 2008, at B1.

55 E.g., Marcus Miller, Paul Weller, and Lei Zhang, Moral Hazard and the U.S. Stock Market: Analyzing the "Greenspan Put"? 112 *Economic Journal* 171 (2002).

56 E.g., John B. Taylor, *Getting Off Track: How Government Actions and Interventions Caused, Prolonged, and Worsened the Financial Crisis* (2009, Hoover Institution Press).

57 Peter S. Goodman, Taking Hard New Look at a Greenspan Legacy, *New York Times*, August 2, 2002, at A1; see also Richard A. Posner, *A Failure of Capitalism*, 30, 38–40, 46, 105–6 (2009, Harvard University Press) (attributing housing bubble to low interest rates and foreign investment in early 2000s).

In a caustic 2002 column, Paul Krugman argued that the only policy the Federal Reserve could pursue to resuscitate the U.S. economy in the wake of the collapse of the technology stock bubble was to create a housing bubble.

> To fight this recession the Fed needs more than a snapback; it needs soaring household spending to offset moribund business investment. And to do that, as Paul McCulley of Pimco put it, Alan Greenspan needs to create a housing bubble to replace the NASDAQ bubble. Paul Krugman, Dubya's Double Dip? *New York Times*, August 2, 2002, at A21.

Chairman Greenspan himself admitted that the slashing of the fed funds rate in 2002 and 2003 may have contributed to rising housing prices, but he rejects the assertion that this contributed to the growing use of adjustable rate mortgages. Alan

Greenspan, The Roots of the Mortgage Crisis, *Wall Street Journal*, December 12, 2007, at A19.

58 E.g., Paul Krugman, Running Out of Bubbles, *New York Times*, May 27, 2005, at A23.

59 Geoffrey P. Miller, The Role of a Central Bank in a Bubble Economy, 18 *Cardozo Law Review* 1053 (1996) (describing this political disincentives that prevented the Japanese central bank from acting against the real estate bubble in that country in the 1980s).

60 See generally, Christopher Allsopp, Macroeconomic Policy Rules in Theory and in Practice, Bank of England External MPC Unit, *Discussion Paper No. 10* (September 2002) available at www.bankofengland.co.uk/publications/Documents/externalmpc-papers/extmpcpaper0010.pdf (last visited July 27, 2013) (concluding that using monetary tools to address bubbles would weaken credibility of monetary policy.)

61 China Moves to Cool Its Inflation, *BBC News* (November 11, 2007) available at http://news.bbc.co.uk/2/hi/business/7089307.stm (last visited July 27, 2013).

62 Jeffrey Carmichael and Neil Esho, Asset Price Bubbles and Prudential Regulation, in *Asset-Price Bubbles: The Implications for Monetary, Regulatory, and International Policies*, 481, 495 (William C. Hunter, George G. Kaufman, and Michael Pomerleano eds., 2003, MIT Press).

63 Adrian and Shin, Money, Liquidity, and Monetary Policy, *supra* note 9, at 602 (2009). For a description of the repo market, its importance as a source of short-term financing for financial institutions, and how the market seized up in the financial crisis, see Gorton and Metrick, *supra* note 18.

64 Adrian and Shin, Money, Liquidity, and Monetary Policy, *supra* note 9, at 602.

65 Gorton and Metrick, *supra* note 18.

66 Adrian and Shin, Money, Liquidity, and Monetary Policy, *supra* note 9, at 602.

67 Ibid.

68 Ibid.

69 Ibid.

70 Ibid.

71 Michael Durbin, *All About Derivatives*, 61–62, 65 (2007, McGraw-Hill).

72 However, the CDS contract is not regulated as insurance due to the craft and lobbying of the lawyers who devised this type of instrument. See Robert F. Schwartz, Risk Distribution in the Capital Markets: Credit Default Swaps, Insurance and a Theory of Demarcation, 12 *Fordham Journal of Corporate and Financial Law* 167, 181–8 (2007) (describing history of lawyers and insurance regulators grappling with whether CDSs should be regulated as insurance products). For an argument that credit derivatives do not constitute, and should not be regulated as, insurance, see M. Todd Henderson, Credit Derivatives are not "Insurance," 16 *Connecticut Insurance Law Journal* 1 (2009).

73 Gerding, *supra* note 13, at 50–4.

74 There is a fascinating debate in finance literature on whether CDSs should be analogized to options or swaps. CDSs typically have an asymmetric payoff structure, which makes them resemble options. However, the price performance of CDSs is more like a swap than an option. See Mark J.P. Anson, Frank J. Fabozzi, Moorad Choudhry, and Ren-Raw Chen, *Credit Derivatives: Instruments, Assets, and Pricing*, 56–7 (2004, John Wiley & Sons).

75 Sharon Brown-Hruska, The Derivatives Marketplace: Exchanges and the Over-the-Counter Market, in *Financial Derivatives: Pricing and Risk Management*, 21, 29–30 (Robert W. Kolb and James A. Overdahl eds., 2010, John Wiley & Sons) (comparing collateral mechanisms in over-the-counter and centrally cleared derivatives).

76 Returning to Figure 9.1 and modifying it to add a few additional credit transfers illustrates this geometric effect. First, consider if all credit protection buyers demand that credit protection sellers post 10 percent of the maximum credit exposure as collateral. Assume all credit protection sellers have $100 in total capital to invest in credit derivatives or otherwise. If Party A "insures" $100 in bonds with Party B (the

second column in Table 9.1), Party B must post $10 in collateral (the third column Table 9.1), but still has $90 in capital to deploy elsewhere (the right hand column), whether in selling more credit protection or in making other investments. If Party B insures the residual credit risk ($90 or $100 minus the collateral amount) with Party C, Party C must post $9 in collateral, but still has $91 in capital it can invest elsewhere. Party C could then insure its residual credit risk with Party D who insures with Party E. The chain of seven credit derivatives continues to Party H. Table 9.1 shows that the total credit risk transferred by these seven derivatives is $521.70 (and the total capital remaining available to the credit protection sellers is $647.83).

Table 9.1 Credit transfer with 10 percent collateral requirement on credit derivatives

Credit derivative (protection seller on right)	Credit risk transferred	Collateral posted by credit protection seller	Residual credit risk (not covered by collateral)	Remaining capital available to seller
Party A → Party B	$100	$10	$90	$90
Party B → Party C	$90	$9	$81	$91
Party C → Party D	$81	$8.10	$72.90	$91.90
Party D → Party E	$72.90	$7.29	$65.61	$92.71
Party E → Party F	$65.61	$6.56	$59.05	$93.44
Party F → Party G	$59.05	$5.91	$53.14	$94.09
Party G → Party H	$53.14	$5.31	$47.83	$94.69
Total	$521.70	$52.17		$647.83

Now assume that all credit protection buyers drop their collateral requirements to 5 percent of the maximum credit exposure. When Party A insures $100 in bonds, Party B must post only $5 in collateral and has $95 in capital remaining. Table 9.2 shows how this lower collateral requirement means that the same seven derivatives now transfer $603.37 in credit risk (and the seven credit protection sellers now have approximately $669.83 in capital to invest elsewhere).

Table 9.2 Credit transfer with 5 percent collateral requirement on credit derivatives

Credit derivative (protection seller on right)	Credit risk transferred	Collateral posted by seller	Residual credit risk	Remaining capital available to seller
Party A → Party B	$100	$5	$95	$95
Party B → Party C	$95	$4.75	$90.25	$95.25
Party C → Party D	$90.25	$4.51	$85.74	$95.49
Party D → Party E	$85.75	$4.29	$81.46	$95.71
Party E → Party F	$81.46	$4.07	$77.39	$95.93
Party F → Party G	$77.39	$3.87	$73.52	$96.13
Party G → Party H	$73.52	$3.68	$69.84	$96.32
Total	$603.37	$30.17		$669.83

A drop in collateral requirements from 10 percent to 5 percent results in an increase in credit risk transferred of over 15 percent. The effects of lower collateral would increase geometrically with longer chains of credit derivatives.

Finally, consider if collateral requirements are changed to 50 percent. Table 9.3 shows that the same chain of credit derivatives now transfers only $198.43 in credit risk.

Table 9.3 Credit transfer with 50 percent collateral requirement on credit derivatives

Credit derivative (protection seller on right)	Credit risk transferred	Collateral posted by seller	Residual credit risk	Remaining capital available to seller
Party A → Party B	$100	$50	$50	$50
Party B → Party C	$50	$25	$25	$75
Party C → Party D	$25	$12.50	$12.50	$87.5
Party D → Party E	$12.5	$6.25	$6.25	$93.75
Party E → Party F	$6.25	$3.13	$3.12	$96.87
Party F → Party G	$3.12	$1.56	$1.56	$98.44
Party G → Party H	$1.56	$0.78	$0.78	$99.22
Total	$198.43	$99.22		$600.78

77 In describing the monetary effects of financial institution leverage in general (but not leverage via credit derivatives), Margaret Blair coins the term "credit multiplier." Blair, *supra* note 9, at 266.

78 A number of studies document expanded lending by banks that use credit derivatives. E.g., Beverly Hirtle, Credit Derivatives and Bank Credit Supply, 18 *Journal of Financial Intermediation* 125, 126 (2009). Oddly, this study also finds that increased use of credit derivatives by a bank correlates with a decrease in the bank's lending under existing commitments (such as extensions of existing loans). Ibid.; see also Benedikt Goderis, Ian W. Marsh, Judit Vall Castello, and Wolf Wagner, Bank Behaviour with Access to Credit Markets, Bank of Finland, *Research Discussion Paper No. 4* (2007) available at http://papers.ssrn.com/sol3/papers.cfm?id=1010101 (last visited July 27, 2013). This study finds that banks that transfer risk via credit derivatives increased their lending levels by 50 percent. The authors compared banks that had issued at least one collateralized loan obligation to a control group that had not. Ibid.; see also Günter Franke and Jan Pieter Krahnen, Default Risk Sharing between Banks and Markets: the Contribution of Collateralized Debt Obligations, in *The Risks of Financial Institutions*, 603, 628 (Mark Carey and René M. Stulz eds., 2007, National Bureau of Economic Research/University of Chicago Press) (finding evidence that some banks use the risk reduction achieved through securitization to take new risks). These findings are consistent with other empirical studies that show that banks use sales of loans to take on new credit risk rather than reduce overall risk. See, e.g., A. Sinan Cebenoyan and Philip E. Strahan, Risk Management, Capital Structure and Lending at Banks, 28 *Journal of Banking and Finance* 19 (2004).

    Note that repo lenders and credit protection buyers have different mechanisms to control the leverage of their respective counterparties. Repo lenders set the haircut once, when the repurchase agreement is entered into. Nevertheless, the short term of many repurchase agreements allows lenders to reset the haircut quickly in subsequent transactions to compensate for changing credit risk or market conditions. The longer term of many CDSs explains why collateral requirements can change during the term of the contract. Cf. Dimitris N. Chorafas, *Introduction to Derivative Financial Instruments: Options, Futures, Forwards, Swaps, and Hedging*, 275–6 (2008, McGraw-Hill) (describing dynamic nature of margin requirements on futures and options markets).

79 Gerding, *supra* note 13, at 53–4.

80 E.g., New York Stock Exchange, Rule 431 (Margin Requirements) available at www.nyse.com/nysenotices/nyse/rule-interpretations/pdf?number=191 (last visited July 27, 2013).

81 Bank for International Settlements, Clearing Arrangements for Exchange-Traded Derivatives, 50, n.8 (March 1997) available at www.bis.org/publ/cpss23a.pdf (last

visited July 27, 2013). See Ben S. Bernanke, Clearing and Settlement During the Crash, 3 *Review of Financial Studies* 133 (1990) (analyzing clearing arrangements during 1987 stock market crash).

82 If the value of collateral declines, a trader may suffer a margin call, which would require *that* he or she post additional collateral. If the trader cannot meet the margin call, his or her broker may seize and sell the collateral. Margin calls may accelerate stock market declines; declines in the value of collateral may lead to *market-wide* margin calls and widespread sell-offs by brokers. This is one way in which deleveraging during the downside of the leverage cycle operates. See "Chapter 11, "Financial institutions and the leverage cycle."

83 See ibid.; Franklin R. Edwards, The Clearing Association in Futures Markets: Guarantor and Regulator, 3 *Journal of Futures Markets* 369 (1983).

84 Brown-Hruska, *supra* note 75.

85 William Neuman and Graham Bowley, Response to Volatility in Silver Takes Hold, *New York Times*, May 8, 2011, at B1. However, officials of that exchange deny using margin requirements as a tool to affect prices on the exchange. Ibid.

86 Ibid. at 147–9 (describing process and purposes of securitization).

87 Ibid.

88 This securitization process can be repeated again as asset-backed securities themselves can be pooled together, sold to a second investment vehicle, and used to use another class of asset-backed securities (called collateralized debt obligations or "CDOs"). CDO securities can in turn be securitized. Just as with hedging credit derivatives with other credit derivatives, after rinsing, lathering, and repeating, long chains are created. Ibid. at 162–3. Professors Partnoy and Skeel categorize CDOs as another form of credit derivative. Frank Partnoy and David A. Skeel, Jr., The Promise and Perils of Credit Derivatives, 75 *University of Cincinnati Law Review* 1019, 1022 (2007).

89 Dwight M. Jaffee, Bank Regulation and Mortgage Market Reform, 8 *Berkeley Business Law Journal* 8 (2011).

90 See 15 U.S.C. § 78o-11 (2011).

91 Margin regulations have their statutory basis in Section 7 of the Securities Exchange Act of 1934. 15 U.S.C. § 78g (2009).

92 Gikas Hardouvelis and Steve Peristiani, Do Margin Requirements Matter? Evidence from U.S. and Japanese Stock Markets, 14 *Federal Reserve Bank of New York Quarterly Review* 16 (1989–1990).

93 See 15 U.S.C. § 78g (2012).

94 Credit by Brokers and Dealers (Regulation T), 12 C.F.R. § 207 (2009).

95 Credit by Banks and Persons other than Brokers or Dealers for the Purpose of Purchasing or Carrying Margin Stock (Regulation U), 12 C.F.R. § 221 (2009); see also Borrowers of Securities Credit (Regulation X), 12 C.F.R. § 224 (2009).

96 For historical background on the federal margin regulations, see Roberta S. Karmel, The Investment Banker and the Credit Regulations, 45 *New York University Law Review* 59 (1970).

97 Ibid. at 493–4.

98 Chapter 5, "The Basel Accords: the dialectics of capital requirements and regulatory capital arbitrage."

99 See Jack Ewing, Banks Win an Easing of Rules on Assets, *New York Times*, January 7, 2013, at B1 (describing successful effort by banks to ease Basel bank capital regulations).

100 For a comprehensive argument, see Anat Admati and Martin Hellwig, *The Bankers' New Clothes: What's Wrong with Banking and What to Do about It* (2013, Princeton University Press).

101 See Rosa María Lastra, Systemic Risk, SIFIs and Financial Stability, 6 *Capital Markets Law Journal* 197, 200 (2011) (discussing this regulation as a potential "macroprudential" tool).

102 Ibid.
103 Ibid.
104 Anna J. Schwartz, Asset Price Inflation and Monetary Policy, National Bureau Economic Research, *Working Paper No. W9321* (November 2002) available at http://papers.ssrn.com/sol3/papers.cfm?abstract_id=352020 (last visited July 27, 2013).
105 Gary B. Gorton, *Slapped by the Invisible Hand: The Panic of 2007*, 27 (2010, Oxford University Press).
106 Gorton, *supra* note 18.
107 Ibid. at 3–4.
108 Morgan Ricks, Regulating Money Creation After the Crisis, 1 *Harvard Business Law Review* 75 (2011).
109 Carmen M. Reinhart and Kenneth S. Rogoff, *This Time is Different: Eight Centuries of Financial Folly*, 158–62 (2009, Princeton University Press).
110 See John Geanakoplos, The Leverage Cycle, Cowles Foundation, *Discussion Paper No. 1715* (2009) available at http://papers.ssrn.com/sol3/papers.cfm?abstract_id=144 1943 (last visited July 12, 2013). See also Ana Fostel and John Geanakoplos, Leverage Cycles and the Anxious Economy, 98 *American Economic Review* 1211 (2008).
111 Geanakoplos, *supra* note 110.
112 Ibid.
113 Ibid. Note that the value of non-cash assets held as collateral may also increase during boom times. If the dollar value of collateral stays the same, and assets posted as collateral rise in value, the lender may withdraw assets from collateral and deploy them for other purposes.
114 Ibid.
115 Adrian and Shin, Money, Liquidity, and Monetary Policy, *supra* note 9, at 602–3.
116 Adrian and Shin, The Changing Nature of Financial Intermediation and the Financial Crisis of 2007–2009, *supra* note 9, at 606–7.
117 Nobuhiro Kiyotaki and John Moore, Credit Cycles, 105 *Journal of Political Economy* 211 (1997).
118 Indeed, a party to a shadow banking instrument such as a credit derivative has (however imperfect) incentives and mechanisms to mitigate its exposure to a counterparty's default. By contrast, the contribution of one credit derivative to aggregate monetary effects is much harder to see. Counterparties may miss how macroeconomic effects mask mispricing of credit risk.
    Moreover, even if counterparties are aware of the macroeconomic effects of shadow banking instruments, derivatives, the logic of collective action dulls incentives to counter these affects in individual contracts. Financial institutions and managers that swim against the tide and curb investment in credit derivatives or insist on tighter collateral during boom times may be punished for doing so by angry investors. Cf. Markus K. Brunnermeier and Stefan Nagel, Hedge Funds and the Technology Bubble, 59 *Journal of Finance* 2013, 2030–2 (2004) (providing an example of a hedge fund that was forced to liquidate after refusing to invest in technology stocks during the 1990s tech stock bubble).
119 See Erik F. Gerding, Laws Against Bubbles: An Experimental-Asset-Market Approach to Analyzing Financial Regulation, 2007 *Wisconsin Law Review* 977, 996–9 (describing economics of herd behavior during bubbles and behavioral finance accounts of bubble formation). The music metaphor is a paraphrase of a famous quote from Citigroup CEO Charles Prince during the height of the recent bubble, in which he explained his firm's continued bullish investments with the following statement: "When the music stops, in terms of liquidity, things will be complicated. But as long as the music is playing, you've got to get up and dance. We're still dancing." See Markus K. Brunnermeier, Deciphering the Liquidity and Credit Crunch 2007–2008, 23 *Journal of Economic Perspectives* 77, 82 (2009) (providing quote).

Part IV

The panic of 2007–2008 as master class in regulatory instability

The shadow banking bubble

10 The shadow banking system
A thumbnail sketch

If credit and leverage matter in bubbles, they played major roles in the most recent bubble which popped in the Panic of 2007–2008. Financial institution credit and leverage fueled the real estate and securities bubbles in the United States and Europe. These factors also made the crashes in both continents more severe and the ensuing financial crises more destructive, economically and socially. Following historical pattern, these latest debt bubbles proved far more dangerous than equity bubbles, not least because they became intertwined with a banking boom, bust, and crisis.

This book has thus far largely skirted the current financial crisis. However, just as they played crucial roles in three centuries of bubbles, the dynamics outlined earlier in this book that destabilized financial regulation reappeared in spades as the current crisis brewed. Moreover, these dynamics – the regulatory stimulus cycle, compliance rot, regulatory arbitrage frenzies, and herd-promoting and procyclical regulations – worked to supercharge the lending and leverage of U.S. and European financial institutions. Regulatory stimulus and regulatory arbitrage came together to incubate massive real estate and capital markets bubbles in the United States and Europe. As the bubbles inflated, they, in turn, promoted more regulatory stimulus and arbitrage, as market participants sought both changes in legal rules and to use novel financial instruments to skirt those rules that endured. At the same time, regulation promoted herding by financial institutions into real estate and certain related capital markets and classes of financial instruments. The metastasizing growth of these markets and instruments fueled real estate and security prices. As the real estate and capital market bubbles inflated further, they promoted more herd behavior, as well as outbreaks of fraud and law-breaking. The story of how regulatory change sowed the seeds for these bubbles thus presents a master class in the Regulatory Instability Hypothesis.

Indeed, the Regulatory Instability Hypothesis provides a unique lens through which to view the origins of the Panic of 2007–2008. This lens focuses attention on regulatory stimulus, compliance rot, regulatory arbitrage, and herding, not as abstract or disconnected phenomena. Rather, these dynamics had their most far-reaching effects by midwifing the birth and suckling the growth of an alternative channel of credit in the economy called the shadow banking system. This system formed from the fusion of disparate markets for financial instruments, each of which emerged in the last decades. These instruments include asset-backed securities, asset-backed commercial paper, money market mutual funds, credit derivatives, and repos. These separate markets later ultimately fused together to form an intricate system that connected borrowers to investors in capital markets. This system funneled credit to consumers and businesses and transferred and spread credit risk to investors.

This system did not grow, however, in a vacuum, merely to meet the economic needs of borrowers and investors. Rather, it formed as a bypass around depository banking; it developed in the shadow of that heavily regulated traditional financial sector. Banking law and other financial regulation functioned as the dark matter that exerted a hidden gravitational pull on shadow banking markets. Regulation and the impulse to evade regulations gave the shadow banking system its contours. Moreover, the urge to use regulatory subsidies and lower regulatory taxes formed part of the system's molecular structure, its DNA, and, to a large extent, its very reason for existence. The individual constituent parts of the shadow banking system developed and flourished because of deregulation, the creation of regulatory preferences, and regulatory arbitrage.

When these individual markets fused together, they created an alternative system for credit and investment that, by the eve of the Panic, rivaled the size of the depository banking sector. The creation of an alternative credit system is critical because, as the last chapter explained, credit pours jet fuel onto the fire of an asset price bubble. Indeed, shadow banking instruments, together, funneled massive amounts of credit into inflating real estate markets. Moreover, as the twin bubbles in real estate and shadow banking markets expanded, they promoted further regulatory arbitrage and herding, as well as regulatory stimulus and law-breaking. Indeed, scholars argue that, in the later stages of the bubble, investments in the shadow banking sector boomed because financial institutions sought to use its component instruments to engage in a saturnalia of regulatory capital arbitrage.

The formation of vicious feedback loops provide a time lapse film of the dynamics described in this book. Regulatory stimulus, increasing regulatory arbitrage, deteriorating legal compliance, and regulation-fueled herding created a credit system that turbocharged financial markets and sparked a bubble. This system enabled meteoric increases in financial institution leverage, which enlarged the effective money supply in financial markets. At the same time, this leverage rendered financial institutions extremely vulnerable to a crash. The risk of a crash worsened because of the herd behavior of financial institutions, who – driven in large part by regulatory preferences and subsidies – stampeded into shadow banking markets. The herd created dangerous correlations of risk, yet masked that risk with the illusion of safety and liquidity. Unfortunately, the Federal Reserve and bank regulators paid too little heed to the creation of this shadow banking system and to its consequences – in terms of both monetary impacts and systemic risk.

The next chapter tells the story of the rise and fall of the shadow banking system through the lens of the Regulatory Instability Hypothesis. But before this story can be told, this chapter defines and examines the anatomy of the shadow banking system.

The shadow banking system defined

Policymakers and scholars often define the shadow banking system by reference to specific financial instruments.[1] However, the alternative approach of defining shadow banking through its economic functions and features is far preferable. This functional approach helps pinpoint when and how certain financial instruments (and financial institutions) fit under the rubric of shadow banking. Moreover, the functional approach clarifies the economic roles played by those instruments, as well as the economic risks they create. It also provides criteria for when yet-to-be-invented instruments could perform the same functions and pose the same dangers.

On a high level, the shadow banking system and its component financial instruments serve many of the functions of traditional depository banking, yet operate by connecting borrowers to investors in capital markets. The shadow banking system represents a hybrid: it plays the role of bank, yet harnesses capital markets like bonds. Investors in capital markets purchase instruments that funnel credit to households and firms. This system provides also a means for borrowers (and financial institutions that originate loans to them) to spread credit risk widely. While shadow banking transfers and spreads credit risks, it also subjects its participants to a different set of risks, including market risk, or the risk of losses from changing market prices.[2]

Bonds also funnel credit to individuals and firms and spread credit risk. Yet the instruments in shadow banking markets – asset-backed securities, asset-backed commercial paper, credit derivatives, money market mutual funds, and repos – differ in marked respects from traditional corporate bonds. Beyond providing credit and transferring credit risk, each of these categories of shadow banking instruments has many, if not all, of the following seven additional features that distinguish them from bonds:

1 *Credit intermediation.* Unlike with bonds, these instruments interpose an intermediary between borrowers and investors.[3]
2 *Pooling.* Intermediation, in turn, allows the cash streams and financial risks of different loans or financial assets to be pooled together.[4]
3 *Structuring.* Complex contractual features of these instruments permit "structuring." Structuring describes how the cash streams and risks of underlying loans or assets can be unbundled, rearranged, and rewoven into new instruments sold to investors. These instruments can thus offer specific combinations of risk and reward tailored to meet the needs of investors.[5]
4 *Maturity or liquidity transformation.* Pooling, intermediation, and structuring enable shadow banking markets to perform another function, namely

"maturity transformation." This feature captures how some shadow instruments effectively convert assets with longer maturities (such as thirty year mortgages) into instruments with shorter terms that are sold to investors.[6] Other shadow banking markets converted cash streams from instruments into assets with similar maturities (such as thirty year mortgages into thirty year bonds). However, these newly created instruments enjoyed theoretically higher liquidity; the ability of investors to sell these shadow instruments into a liquid market gave them an option to exit (and to limit their credit risk) similar to that associated with short-term loans. This "liquidity transformation," nonetheless, creates economic problems similar to those of maturity transformation. As the next chapter describes, when many investors seek to exercise this option to liquidate market instruments simultaneously, the herd creates bank run dynamics.[7]

5   *Credit transformation.* Pooling, intermediation, and structuring also enable shadow banking markets to convert low credit quality assets into higher quality/lower credit risk instruments.[8] These safer instruments appeal to a wider range of investors.

6   *"Money" creation.* All five functions described above together allow certain shadow banking instruments to offer theoretical low risk and high liquidity to investors.[9] These instruments thus exhibit, to a degree, one or more of the three canonical economic characteristics of "money" mentioned in the previous chapter: namely serving as a medium of exchange, a unit of account, and store of value.[10]

7   *Opacity.* Finally, the existence of one or more intermediaries between borrowers and investors creates a degree of opacity that complicates the ability of investors to assess how financial risk, including credit risk, courses from underlying assets to the instruments they have purchased.[11]

These seven features plus credit risk/credit transfer do not manifest themselves in the same manner or to the same degree in the various instruments of the shadow banking system. Indeed, the various instruments described in detail below, from asset-backed securities to repos, have different transactional structures. They serve a mix of different economic functions to differing degrees. They thus pose different kinds and gradients of risk. It is therefore important to analyze these instruments individually. "Anatomy: the instruments of shadow banking," below, will describe each of the instruments listed above one-by one. It will then compare these various instruments side-by-side to gauge the extent to which they exhibit the eight features (including credit risk and transfer) listed above.

Shadow banking compared to depository banking: revisiting the "specialness" of banks

These shadow banking instruments – whether considered individually or as a system – came to provide at least three of the core economic functions of banks as described in an influential 1982 speech by Gerald Corrigan (then a senior Federal Reserve official).[12] In that speech, Corrigan claimed banks had three "special" attributes that made them deserving of different regulatory treatment from other financial institutions.[13] The emergence of the shadow system belied this specialness of banking.

First, Corrigan argues that banks are special because they provide "backup" liquidity to households, businesses, and financial markets.[14] Corrigan claimed that this function becomes crucial when financial markets undergo profound stress.[15] However, most of these "shadow" instruments also provided credit or liquidity to consumers and businesses via cash raised from instruments sold to investors in capital markets.[16]

Second, Corrigan claimed that banks alone provide "transaction accounts" (namely, checking and savings deposits) that allow the account holders both to withdraw funds – at par and on demand – and then to transfer them to other parties easily.[17] Providing customers with assurance that they will have liquid, transferable funds also becomes particularly critical during times of financial crisis, according to Corrigan.[18] Many shadow banking instruments were designed to offer investors much of the same liquidity and relative security of bank deposits.[19] By creating instruments with many of the economic features of "money," the shadow banking system replicates the transaction account feature that Corrigan claimed made banks distinct.

These first two ways in which shadow banking mimics the "special" features of banking are easy to grasp compared to the third. Corrigan argued that banks also serve as a "transmission belt" for monetary policy.[20] Yet, shadow banking too can dramatically expand (or contract) the effective supply of money in the economy in one or two ways. One: the system allows financial institutions to borrow and lend to one another in long chains. When institutions along this chain collectively increase their effective leverage, the liquidity in financial markets (or the effective money supply) increases – almost magically – just as when depository banks lower reserve requirements.[21] Two: by creating money-like instruments, the system increases broad measures of the money supply.[22] The next chapter looks at the monetary dimension of the shadow banking system in detail.

This is not to say that central banks monitor (let alone manipulate) the shadow banking system in the same way they look to the traditional banking sector to implement monetary policy. They have not. Indeed, central banks and monetary policymakers not only did not use these tools, they also failed to track the growth of the shadow banking system and its monetary impacts.[23] The shadow banking system and the regulations that helped foster it provide a case study for the lessons of the previous chapter. Unfortunately, too few scholars and policymakers recognized this monetary dimension of shadow banking instruments and the regulations that govern them.[24] The next chapter analyzes this intellectual too.

Some at the time did, however, cast doubt on Corrigan's premise that banks were unique. Soon after his 1982 speech, a number of scholars who argued for deregulating banks pointed to counterexamples of the specialness of these financial institutions. For example, in 1983, Richard Aspinwall challenged Corrigan's thesis by pointing to a range of financial instruments and institutions (all of which came to form parts of what this chapter calls the shadow banking system).[25] Aspinwall argued that the best response to the increasing ability of non-banks to provide the same economic functions as banks is to reduce the regulatory impediments to banks to allow them to compete.[26] Other scholars have echoed Aspinwall's deregulatory argument through the decades, up through and even past the onset of the current global financial crisis (which this book labels the "Panic of 2007–2008").[27]

Banking risks

This deregulatory argument was, however, premised on assumptions that the non-banks that provided the economic functions of banks did not create or pose the same economic risks as banks. In other words, the champions of deregulation discounted the possibility that shadow banks imposed the same economic externalities as banks. If non-banks did in fact pose the same risks and inflict the same negative externalities as banks, regulating these entities as opposed to merely deregulating banks might have been the more sensible policy solution.[28]

To foreshadow the next chapter, the Panic of 2007–2008 belied these assumptions that non-banks did not face the same economic risks and pose the same negative externalities as banks.[29] At the time, however, the assumption may not have been entirely unreasonable. Indeed, elements of shadow banking, like securitization, offered novel structures to address two of the formidable and intertwined risks inherent in traditional banking: liquidity risk and solvency risk.

Liquidity risk arises because, when banks borrow from depositors and lend to households and businesses, they suffer from an asset–liability mismatch.[30] On the one side of their balance sheet, they have long-term assets (like thirty year mortgages).[31] While, on the other side, they have short-term liabilities, as depositors can typically withdraw funds from their accounts on short notice.[32] This asset–liability mismatch leaves banks susceptible to runs, when depositors rush to withdraw funds.[33] Although bank runs may seem like irrational panics, economists have shown that they may result from completely rational behavior. To reinforce Chapter 7, investors may seek to withdraw funds knowing that if a mass of other investors withdraw first, they would strip the cupboard bare. Bank runs thus can become self-fulfilling prophesies.[34] A run at one bank threatens to trigger runs on others if depositors and other creditors cannot distinguish a safe bank from an unsafe one.[35] A rash of runs can cause credit to evaporate in financial markets and the economy generally.[36] It is this prospect of bank runs and liquidity drying up quickly that animates the three core governmental interventions in banking markets: a central bank acting as lender-of-last-resort, government-provided deposit insurance, and requirements that banks maintain a certain level of highly liquid assets in their portfolio.[37]

Banks also suffer solvency crises, which may strike for several reasons.[38] When banks hold onto the loans they make, they face credit risk, i.e., the risk of loans defaulting.[39] Credit risk may be compounded if banks have long-term exposure to particular borrowers, types of borrowers or sectors of the economy;

this creates concentration risk.[40] Moreover, banks become more financially fragile when they become more highly leveraged.[41] As with liquidity risk, the insolvency of one bank can have dire spillover effects on other banks. A bank's failure can cause severe losses for banks that have loaned money to it. This raises the specter of a chain reaction of failing banks.[42] This specter becomes more frightening if banks have exposures to common risks (such as similar concentration risk)[43] or if the linkages connecting banks become difficult to sort out.[44] Although liquidity and solvency risk can be separated analytically, real market events make it difficult to untangle these risks.[45] Threats to a bank's balance sheet can spook depositors and precipitate a bank run, and, on the flip side, a bad enough run can lead to insolvency.[46] Systemic risk materializes either way.

Anatomy: the instruments of shadow banking

This high level view of shadow banking's economic characteristics provides a context for analyzing the system's component parts. The following financial instruments perform many, if not all, of the eight economic functions of shadow banking:

- *securitization*;
- *asset-backed commercial paper*;
- *credit derivatives*;
- *money market mutual funds*; and
- *repos*.

The mechanics of these instruments are described briefly below. The chapter then examines which of the eight features of shadow banking – credit provision and transfer, intermediation, pooling, structuring, maturity transformation, credit transformation, "money" creation, and opacity – are present in each of these instruments.

Securitization: shadow banking's central artery

The shadow banking system offered to address the liquidity and solvency risks faced by banks by transforming illiquid loans into liquid securities which are sold to investors in capital markets. To understand this alchemy,[47] consider securitization, the central artery of the shadow banking system (introduced in the previous chapter). Securitization allows a lender to sell loans to an investment vehicle (*intermediation*). The bank can thus trade highly illiquid assets for cash.[48] The investment vehicle issues multiple classes of asset-backed securities to investors. The sponsors of these transactions structure the terms of the securities so that the senior classes represent theoretically low-risk assets that can trade on bond markets.[49] The market price of asset-backed securities (together with the imprimatur of credit rating agencies) supposedly reflects the credit and liquidity risk inherent in the instruments.[50]

Figure 10.1 (modified from the previous chapter) explains this process. In stage 1, banks and lenders make (or "originate") loans such as mortgages to consumers or businesses. In stage 2, an investment vehicle buys pools of mortgages using cash paid by investors who bought securities from those vehicles (stage 3). Typically, the last two stages take place more-or-less simultaneously. The securities then pay out to investors based on the cash streams the investment vehicles receive from the underlying mortgages.[51]

Greater demand by investors for the end product (asset-backed securities) funnels more credit back to borrowers (*credit provision*). Banks and other lenders benefit because they have solved the asset–liability mismatch by trading illiquid loans for cash. Unburdened of the risk of loans defaulting, banks can redeploy this cash by making additional loans. Banks can also earn fees at numerous junctures in the securitization process.

Securitization also has much to offer investors in capital markets. By purchasing these asset-backed securities, investors can invest in the lucrative consumer-credit market (including investing in mortgages, credit card debt, and student loans) while holding securities that are theoretically more liquid than the underlying mortgages.[52] This liquidity reflects the effective *liquidity transformation* of securitization, which converts long-term mortgages into theoretically marketable securities.[53]

Moreover, asset-backed securities allow investors to diversify (at least in theory). This diversification occurs in three different ways. First, the pooling of mortgages means that the risk of default on any one mortgage is offset by the fact that other mortgages in the pool will continue to pay out. This risk-spreading through *pooling* is a central benefit of all securitizations. The success of risk-spreading depends on a series of crucial assumptions: losses among mortgages in the pool will not be highly correlated, any correlation can be accurately estimated, and correlation will not suddenly and unexpectedly increase.[54]

Second, securitization facilitates diversification because investors in asset-backed securities are only buying a sliver of the mortgage pool's risk. They can

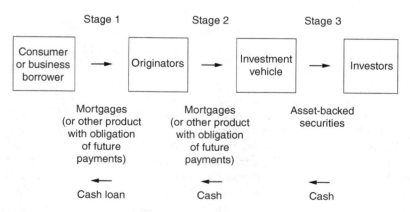

Figure 10.1 Securitization simplified.

diversify away this risk through other investments in their portfolios.[55] This, however, assumes that losses on the mortgage-backed securities that investors purchase are not highly correlated with losses on other assets (including other asset-backed securities) in their portfolios.

Third, investors can achieve diversification through the terms of the securities being issued. Cash payments on the underlying assets need not simply flow to holders of securities pro rata. Instead, the securities can be *structured* to create different classes, or "tranches," of securities, with each class having a different level of risk and a different level of reward.[56]

More senior classes of asset-backed securities – that is those with more senior claims to cash streams on the underlying assets – offer greater safety to investors. In addition, some senior classes of securities may benefit from third-party bond insurance, credit guarantees, or other credit support. Together, these features create *credit transformation*: even risky underlying assets can create a class of high credit quality securities (although this means that other securities issued by securitization vehicle have toxic levels of credit risk).[57]

This safety, when combined with liquidity, means that asset-backed securities replicate many of the features that investors sought in bank deposits. Indeed, for institutional investors, senior asset-backed securities created a substitute for traditional bank accounts.[58] Economist Gary Gorton argues that the supposed liquidity and low risk of senior tranches of asset-backed securities meant that they, like bank deposits, assumed many of the features of "*money.*"[59] As but one example, financial institutions used purchased asset-backed securities as a form of collateral for loans (such as in the repos described below).

Securitization also offers benefits for the economy as a whole, by spreading risk to a wider number of investors, who theoretically can bear that risk more efficiently.[60] Note, however, that both the efficiency of risk-spreading and the economic benefits to investors depend on the accurate pricing of asset-backed securities based on the risk of default on the underlying loans.[61] Risk-spreading also benefits borrowers, who can enjoy lower interest rates from lenders by virtue of those lenders being able to unload their loans onto the capital markets.[62]

The discussion thus far has greatly oversimplified the structure of many asset-backed securities. For example, securitizations can become even more complex when mortgage-backed securities (or other asset-backed securities) are themselves securitized. This occurs when sponsors create a new investment vehicle that purchases mortgage-backed securities and uses them as collateral for another securitization. This re-securitization structure is called a collateralized debt obligation (CDO).[63] Securities issued in CDOs are often re-securitized themselves, creating what is called a "CDO-squared."[64] The iterative layering of securitizations of securitizations of securitizations became wildly popular in financial markets in the pre-crisis years.[65] Re-securitization provides an additional market for asset-backed securities, further increasing their liquidity. The market for asset-backed securities surged up until the Panic of 2007–2008, growing from $168.4 in securities outstanding in 1996 to over $1.2 trillion outstanding in 2006.[66]

Securitization advanced: asset-backed commercial paper

Over time, securitization evolved and generated numerous specialized variants, including asset-backed commercial paper. Asset-backed commercial paper is created when companies seeking financing sell some of their assets to an investment vehicle. The investment vehicle then issues short-term securities with maturities between 90 and 180 days. As with other securitizations, the investment vehicle uses the proceeds from selling securities to investors to purchase the underlying assets. Those assets serve as collateral for the obligations of the investment vehicle to make payments on the commercial paper being issued. Safe, liquid, short-term commercial paper offers investors economic benefits similar to deposit accounts with a bank.[67]

Aside from issuing shorter-term securities, asset-backed commercial paper differs from traditional securitization in several respects. First, the investment vehicle in asset-backed commercial paper (called a "conduit") may purchase a revolving set of assets that may change over time. Second, as the issued commercial paper matures, the conduit will issue new paper to investors (the proceeds of which will be used to purchase fresh assets and pay the fees of the various service providers to the transaction).

These first two features mean that conduits may suffer an asset–liability mismatch of their own. The investment vehicle conduits have short-term obligations to investors yet hold longer-term assets. This mismatch leads to a third feature of ABCP that differs from traditional securitizations: in exchange for a fee, a third party often agrees to provide liquidity support to the vehicle. This third party contracts to provide infusions of cash or liquid assets into the conduit as needed.[68]

Like securitizations, asset-backed commercial paper issuances often include some form of financial guarantee (which comes in several flavors, including a letter of credit, credit derivative, or bond insurance) from another financial institution.[69] Finally, asset-backed commercial paper transactions are created by a "sponsor," which may be either a large corporation that needs to finance its operations or a financial institution. The sponsor develops the structure of the entire transaction and identifies assets (and sellers of assets if the sponsor is not selling them itself) to back the securities. In some circumstances, the sponsor may also contract to provide credit enhancement or liquidity support to the issuing vehicle.[70]

Asset-backed commercial paper enjoyed phenomenal growth in the decade before the crisis. The market doubled in size from January 2001, when approximately $600 billion in these instruments were outstanding in the United States, to the eve of the crisis in January 2007, when over $1.2 trillion was outstanding.[71] At that point in 2007, more asset-backed commercial paper was outstanding than any other short-term debt instrument, including U.S. Treasuries.[72]

Credit derivatives

Credit derivatives formed another important strand in the shadow banking web. As explained in the previous chapter, this type of derivatives represents contracts in which one party (the "credit protection seller") agrees to pay the other party (the "credit protection buyer") a specified amount should a "credit event" occur with respect to certain reference assets. In exchange, the credit protection buyer pays a premium to the seller. In plainer English, the credit protection seller provides a form of "insurance" to the buyer against credit risk on the reference assets. This might mean insurance against either the insolvency of a particularly important commercial counterparty or default on loans, bonds, or other assets in the credit protection buyer's portfolio.[73] Figure 10.2 depicts the basic economics of a credit derivative.

The distillation and insurance of specific credit risks represents another form of the "*structuring*" feature described above, in which rewards and risks of underlying assets are unbundled and re-bundled.[74] Credit derivatives also involve *intermediation*. A credit protection seller can turn around and hedge the risk it assumes under a credit derivative. When the credit protection seller writes numerous credit derivatives it is essentially *pooling* risks. Intermediation and pooling are particularly strong in the case of OTC derivatives dealers, institutions that act as middlemen in the credit derivatives market. The market for OTC credit derivatives has been dominated by just over a dozen such dealers.[75]

Although derivatives can be used for many reasons, they have often been used as tools in connection with securitization. An investor can use credit derivatives to hedge the risk of a default on asset-backed securities in its portfolio.[76] Bond insurance, in which a regulated company provides a guarantee on bond payments, provides this same function. Figure 10.3 sketches out the basic economic bargain of a credit derivative used in this way. It thus depicts how credit derivatives serve as another link in a larger chain of credit risk transfers in the securitization process.

If credit derivatives allow investors to offload credit risk, they also enable them to buy more securities and take on fresh risk by making new loans or investments.[77] As noted in the previous chapter, there is extensive evidence that financial institutions have used credit derivatives in this manner.[78]

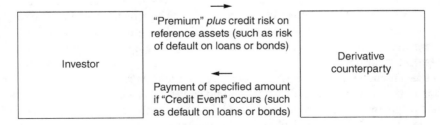

Figure 10.2 The economics of a credit derivative contract.

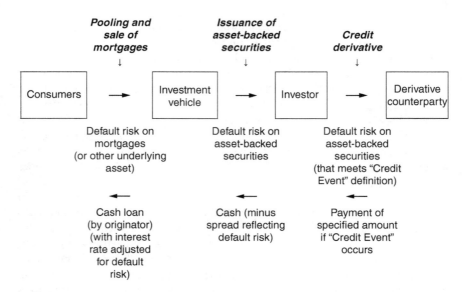

Figure 10.3 Credit derivative and hedging the credit risk of an asset-backed security.

Just as asset-backed securities can themselves be securitized and re-securitized, so too can a credit protection seller hedge its own credit risk under the derivative contract with a second credit derivative. The new credit protection seller under that second derivative can then itself hedge with a third credit derivative. Rinse, lather, repeat, and long, convoluted chains of risk transfers form.[79] Credit derivatives of all types experienced meteoric growth in the first decade of the twenty-first century. From the first half of 2001 to its market peak in the second half of 2007, the notional value of credit default swaps increased over ninety-eight-fold from approximately U.S.$631 billion to $62 trillion.[80]

Money market mutual funds

Money market mutual funds, one of the first pieces of the shadow banking system, were first created in the 1970s. Their creators designed these funds to provide low-risk, highly liquid securities to investors as a substitute for bank deposits but with higher effective interest rates.[81] (The growth of money market mutual funds in response to restrictions on bank deposits is discussed below.) These funds sell shares to investors and use the proceeds to invest in relatively safe debt securities, such as senior asset-backed securities, asset-backed commercial paper, and corporate debt.[82] In doing so, the funds engage in maturity transformation at the margin; even if the fund holds very short-term assets, investors can "withdraw" funds invested on demand.[83] Money market mutual funds enjoyed spectacular growth, expanding from no assets under management in the 1970s (when the funds were created) to U.S.$4 trillion at their peak in 2008.[84]

Repos

Repurchase agreements (commonly known as "repos") represent the final principal strand in the shadow banking web. In a repo transaction (to summarize from the previous chapter), a borrower sells a security at below the current market price and agrees to repurchase it at an agreed-upon, higher price in the future.[85] This sale and repurchase provides the same economics as a secured loan, with the security being sold serving as collateral.[86] The difference between the current market price of the security and the price at which the borrower sells it represents the "haircut."[87] Larger haircuts (when the security is sold to the lender for far below market price) mean more collateral for the lender and lower leverage for the borrower.[88] Smaller haircuts translate into less collateral and more leverage.[89]

Some repo transactions, called tripartite repos, involve a clearing bank that acts as intermediary between the borrower and lender. This institution holds and administers the collateral for the transaction pursuant to a contract among the three parties. A third party holding the collateral reduces the counterparty risk of the lender in the transactions.[90]

The repo market became a significant financing source for corporations and particularly financial institutions.[91] Many financial institutions borrow from the "overnight" repo market – that is repurchase agreements with a term of less than a day – to meet short-term funding needs. This extremely short maturity of the loan has important consequences. There is a possibility that the collateral will become less liquid. Because the collaterol sometimes cannot be sold as soon as the loan matures, the repo transaction effectively represents another example of maturity transformation.[92]

Lenders enter into repo transactions to enjoy a short-term investment opportunity. (Other lenders might want to hold the securities to gain a vote on corporate governance matters of the company that issued the security).[93] Gary Gorton and Andrew Metrick argue that by providing firms with a short-term collateralized investment, repos provide many of the investment features of demand deposits.[94] They argue that exemptions in the Bankruptcy Code that allow repo lenders to seize collateral without being subject to the automatic stay (a topic discussed in Chapters 7 and 9 and analyzed again in the next chapter) make this form of loan much safer.[95]

Official data on the total size of the repo market in the United States has been scant; however, the sums being borrowed are enormous.[96] According to the Federal Reserve, the nineteen primary dealer banks in the United States reported $4.5 trillion in financing through fixed income security repos as of March 2008.[97] Scholars estimate that repo lending in the United States peaked just before the crisis at $10 trillion in gross amount outstanding.[98] The tri-party repo market peaked before the crisis at $2.8 trillion outstanding.[99]

Driving impulse behind shadow banking instruments: credit and leverage

Repos highlight one of the primary reasons financial institutions created the entire shadow banking system – to allow them to borrow funds, which they turn around and use to invest. Leverage allows an investor to increase potential returns on equity beyond what would be possible through a direct investment of its own funds. Leverage comes in three forms. First, balance sheet leverage represents the most visible form of the three and arises when a firm's assets exceed its equity capital. Banks increase balance sheet leverage when they borrow funds to acquire more assets. Second, economic leverage arises when an investor is exposed to a change in value of an investment beyond the amount it paid for that investment. Economic leverage does not necessarily appear on the investor's balance sheet. For example, a loan guarantee may not appear on a firm's balance sheet if it represents a contingent liability that may materialize in the future. Last, embedded leverage describes when a firm's exposure to an investment is larger than the market factor for that investment. Embedded leverage arises when a firm invests in a security or other investment that is itself leveraged.[100]

Per introductory corporate finance, leverage both magnifies potential returns on equity and potential losses for firms that invest with borrowed money.[101] Leverage is the lifeblood of the business of financial institutions.[102] Indeed, it is impossible to understand the evolution of the shadow banking system without considering how it enabled leveraged investments by financial institutions.[103] Shadow banking instruments helped increase leverage in financial markets in three ways: by providing new instruments for borrowing, by increasing economic leverage, and by creating embedded leverage.

Provision of credit

Many of the shadow banking instruments described in Chapter 10 – asset-backed securities, asset-backed commercial paper, and repos – represent effective loans, whether direct or indirect. Asset-backed securities and asset-backed commercial paper funnel money from capital market investors to originating lenders and ultimately to consumer or commercial borrowers. Repurchase agreements represent an economic loan, in which the borrower receives temporary funds from the lender. Even money market mutual funds function as loan conduits, as they sell shares to investors and use the funds to purchase bonds for their portfolio. These devices not only extend credit from investors to borrowers, they also transfer credit risk from borrowers to investors.

Credit derivatives represent another mechanism for transferring credit risk, albeit without the credit protection seller lending any money. However, credit derivatives *can* indirectly increase the supply of loans. Investors can take on more risk and invest more when they offload credit risk via hedging credit derivatives. A number of empirical studies demonstrate that banks increase the supply of credit they provide as they hedge credit risk with credit derivatives.[104]

Economic leverage

Many shadow banking instruments also allow financial firms to increase economic leverage per the example of credit derivatives. Note that the credit protection seller does not have to commit funds up front to cover its expected obligations to the buyer. This frees up capital that the seller can deploy elsewhere, including by underwriting additional credit derivatives.[105] This mirrors the canonical example of economic leverage that does not appear on a balance sheet: a financial guarantee that represents a contingent liability.[106] Chapter 11, "Regulatory capital arbitrage revisited" explains how many shadow banking financial instruments were constructed to move leverage off a financial institution's balance sheet in order to obtain regulatory relief and for other purposes.

Returning to the example above: the credit protection buyer, however, may have concerns about the credit risk of its counterparty. Therefore, credit and other derivative contracts often include a margin feature, by which one party has to post certain collateral to secure its future payment obligations.[107] They also have a functional equivalent in the collateral features of repurchase agreements.[108] Lower collateral or margin requirements – whether in a repo or credit derivative – can result in party with future obligations enjoying higher leverage. Lower collateral means that that party need deploy less of its own capital to cover its future payment obligations. Lower collateral also means that a firm may enter into more transactions (for example, borrowing more money through repos or underwriting more credit protection via derivative contracts). When set too low, collateral requirements allow a firm to increase leverage excessively. This would enable a repo "borrower" to borrow more funds and a credit protection seller to overinvest in underwriting fresh derivative contracts.

Embedded leverage

Shadow banking instruments can also increase embedded leverage. The layering of securitization upon securitization or the hedging and re-hedging of investments with credit derivatives means that the leverage of individual investments can be multiplied many times over. "Putting it all together: from instruments to a system," below, provides other examples of how one shadow banking instrument (for example a repo) can allow a firm to make a leveraged bet in another already leveraged instrument (for example, a subordinated asset-backed security or a credit default swap).

The shadow banking instruments side by side: lumping and splitting

The capacity to provide credit and increase leverage represents one of the common features of the array of shadow banking instruments. It is critical, however, to describe not only the common features of shadow banking instruments, but to highlight their differences as well. Table 10.1 compares the

Table 10.1 Economic features of shadow banking instruments

Instrument	Credit provision	Intermediation provided by	Pooling and structuring	Maturity or liquidity transformation/credit transformation	Resemblance to deposit accounts; economic features of "money"
Asset-backed securities	Yes.	Investment vehicle; government-sponsored entities; originating lenders.	Pooling of underlying loans or other assets; structuring via tranching.	Long-term loans may be converted into securities; even when securities have maturity dates that match the underlying assets, their theoretical liquidity would allow investors to sell quickly. Tranching and credit support creates credit transformation.	Possibly strong for senior securities; senior securities used as collateral for repos.
Asset-backed commercial paper	Yes.	Investment conduit; sponsors.	Same as above.	Significant maturity and liquidity transformation. Credit and liquidity support from providers enable liquidity and credit transformation.	Strong given short maturity, liquidity, and lower risk.
Credit derivatives	To extent that credit protection buyer uses credit transfer to take fresh credit risk.	Intermediation provided by dealers in credit derivatives who offer credit protection and then hedge the assumed risk.	Pooling occurs by credit protection seller "insuring" various risks of different firms; terms of instrument unbundle and isolate financial risks being insured.	No direct maturity or liquidity transformation, but allows long-term credit risk to be offloaded. Strong credit transformation.	No, but to extent enables additional short-term credit, can increase money supply.

Money-market mutual fund shares	Yes.	Money market mutual fund.	Pooling of assets owned by fund; no structuring.	Maturity transformation at margin, by converting short-term investments by fund into even shorter maturity instruments (which are equivalent of demand deposits). Significant liquidity transformation.	Strong (designed to resemble bank deposit accounts).
Repos	Yes.	In tri-party repos, by clearing bank.	Possible indirect pooling in tri-party repos by clearing bank.	Liquidity transformation at margin; even liquidity of highly liquid collateral for these loans may not match intraday maturity of loans.	Strong: short-term investment; collateral (not subject to bankruptcy stay) provides security for loan and can be re-hypothecated; collateral for repo acts as form of money.

various shadow banking instruments according to six of the eight economic features listed in the introduction to this chapter.

1   *Credit provision and credit transfer.* To what extent does the instrument provide increased loans to commercial or consumer borrowers?
2   *Intermediation.* In the market for the instrument, what institution acts as middleman between counterparties, e.g., between borrowers and investors?
3   *Pooling.* Does the instrument bundle together the future cash streams or risks of various assets?
4   *Structuring.* Does the instrument carve up the risks and rewards of various assets into particular investment slices?
5   *Maturity or liquidity transformation.* Does the instrument and relevant intermediary convert long-term assets into short-term investments? Does the transaction convert illiquid assets into assets that can theoretically be sold into liquid markets?
6   *Credit transformation.* Does the transaction create high credit quality assets from the cash streams of low credit quality assets?
7   *"Money."* Do some versions of the instrument offer some of the features of deposit accounts, namely low risk and high liquidity, to investors? Does it thus take on some of the economic features of "money"?

(The eighth feature, opacity, is discussed briefly when the following chapter discusses the crash of the shadow banking system in the Panic of 2007–2008.)

This comparison of the features of shadow banking instruments becomes critical when assessing both the economic risks posed by each category of instrument and the ways in which each category should be regulated to address those risks. Assessing risk and regulation involves the thorny intellectual exercise of lumping versus splitting; to what degree do the various shadow banking instruments perform similar economic functions and pose similar economic risks and to what degree are they different.

Key players

Shadow banking involves not only a series of financial instruments, but a roster of different financial institutions, each playing a different role in the system.

Investment banks. These firms serve as the hubs of the shadow banking web and play the middleman in almost every type of shadow banking transaction thanks to their vast networks of clients. They act as both brokers in the markets for the various shadow banking instruments, which makes them all but indispensable to the functioning of the system.[109] Investment banks may also purchase asset-backed securities for their own accounts. Investment banks buy or sell credit protection in credit derivatives, whether to hedge their own risk, provide a service to clients, or speculate.[110] The 2011 lawsuit by the Securities and Exchange Commission against Goldman Sachs involving a series of securitization and

credit derivatives transactions put together by that firm underscored the central-
ity of investment banks as middlemen or market markers in the shadow banking
system.[111]

Hedge funds. Hedge funds played a vital role of their own in the shadow
banking system; because these funds are essentially unregulated (or were until
Dodd-Frank), they could invest in a much wider array of assets than banks and
other financial institutions.[112] Moreover, their ability to take on leverage was
limited only by the demands of their investors and creditors.[113] Hedge funds
bought some of the riskiest instruments in the shadow banking system, which
law precluded banks and other regulated entities from purchasing.[114] This
freedom allowed hedge funds to earn handsome profits and to inject liquidity
into shadow banking markets.[115] Although hedge funds were competitors for
investment banks, their unregulated capacity for risk-taking also made hedge
funds attractive places for regulated institutions to invest money,[116] ideal counterparties for transferring credit risk (for example, as credit protection sellers in
credit derivatives),[117] and valuable customers (for the broker-dealer services of
investment banks).[118] Some credit hedge funds specialized in making bond and
other credit investments.[119]

Government-sponsored entities (GSEs): Freddie and Fannie. Freddie Mac
and Fannie Mae helped prime the shadow banking pump. These firms (together
with the Government National Mortgage Association) created the mortgage-
backed securities market.[120] Congress chartered Freddie Mac and Fannie Mae as
privately owned companies to create a liquid national market for residential
mortgages to promote increased homeownership.[121] To fulfill their missions,
Freddie and Fannie engaged in two lines of business. First, they pooled and
securitized residential mortgages of certain loan sizes that met certain credit
standards and other criteria ("conforming mortgages").[122] Freddie and Fannie
would then guarantee the asset-backed securities created from these mortgages.[123] Second, the GSEs purchased for their own investment portfolios mortgages and mortgaged-backed securities issued by others.[124] Chapter 6 and
Chapter 11 more fully analyze the role of the government in subsidizing, regulating, and deregulating these two companies. Together, they historically dominated the mortgage-backed securities market. However, in the decade before the
crisis, these institutions faced significant competition as investment banks began
creating "private label" mortgage-backed securities not guaranteed by Freddie or
Fannie (as discussed in Chapter 6).[125]

Less regulated mortgage lenders and other loan originators. These less regulated entities provided the raw material for mortgage-backed securities by
making (or originating) the mortgage loans that would be securitized.[126] These
lenders pioneered many of the exotic mortgages that were ultimately marketed at
less credit-worthy borrowers (the infamous subprime mortgages).[127] These mortgages did not meet the regulatory criteria for securitization by Freddie or Fannie,
but were purchased for the private label securitizations mentioned above.[128] The
high yields on subprime mortgages fueled the profits and growth of the private
label market.[129] Other non-bank lenders, among them credit card, student loan,

and automobile finance companies originated loans for other kinds of asset-backed securities.[130]

Banks and regulated entities. The shadow banking system connected less regulated entities with depository banks and other regulated lenders. The fact that shadow banking represents a bypass of traditional borrow-from-depositors–lend-to-borrowers banking model should not be understood to mean that banks are not players in the shadow banking webs. In fact, banks operate at many different nodes in the web: for example, they originate loans that are securitized,[131] invest in investment grade asset-back securities,[132] and borrow and lend through the repo market.[133] Chapter 11 discusses how regulation changed to enable banks to make these investments. Bank involvement in shadow banking poses of course risks and challenges for regulation, including that banks will abuse the government subsidies they enjoyed, such as deposit insurance, to take investment risk with taxpayer money.[134]

Financial conglomerates. This danger becomes acute because banks now sit under the same corporate umbrella as investment banks, broker dealers, hedge funds, mortgage lenders, insurance companies, and other financial institutions. Indeed, financial conglomerates often house many or all of the categories of shadow banking players under one corporate roof.[135] Conglomerates have the opportunity to transfer subsidies from banks to other affiliates in the corporate group, including via below cost loans or guarantees.[136]

Putting it all together: from instruments to a system

Although the various shadow banking instruments need to be analyzed individually, they also must be viewed together as a system. The various shadow banking markets were developed and function separately. However, over the last several decades financial institutions have increasingly used them in conjunction with one another. Thus, these instruments have formed both chains and webs that connect financial institutions in complex ways. The discussion above of how investors use credit derivatives to hedge risk from asset-backed securities provided a simple example.[137] In addition, money market mutual funds regularly purchase senior asset-backed securities for their bond portfolio.[138] Investors in asset-backed securities often use repos for short-term financing.[139] Any number of financial institutions can act as repo lenders. Figure 10.4 links the foregoing transactions together to provide a simple depiction of a shadow banking web.

Figure 10.5 simplifies the above illustration to show how the various instruments effectively represent both the provision of credit (loans) and the transfer of credit risk. Figure 10.5 also demonstrates how this simple web can ultimately funnel more credit back to household and commercial borrowers, while diffusing the credit risk from those original loans to a wide number of investors and financial institutions. This figure throws into sharp relief the shadow banking system's arteries for providing credit and veins for carrying away credit risk.

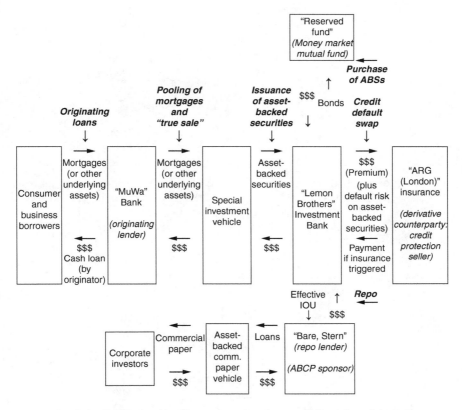

Figure 10.4 The shadow banking instruments together: a small version of the system.

Of course the previous two figures are gross over-simplifications of the complex ways in which the markets for the various shadow banking instruments connect with one another. Shadow banking instruments can be used like demonically complex tinker toys to connect financial institutions in myriad ways and assist them in providing credit, increasing leverage, hedging risk, and speculating. The markets for shadow banking instruments can connect in at least four different ways. First, any asset that generates predictable cash flows can be securitized. For example, credit derivatives can be used to create asset-backed securities in what are called synthetic CDOs.[140] Second, the various shadow banking instruments can serve as investments for key shadow banking institutions. For example, money market mutual funds might purchase not only asset-backed securities, but asset-backed commercial paper or lend in the repo markets.[141] Third, credit derivatives can be used to hedge the risk of any shadow banking instrument or exposure to a counterparty in a shadow banking transaction.[142] Finally, one category of shadow banking instrument can be used as collateral for another shadow banking transaction. Indeed, asset-backed securities

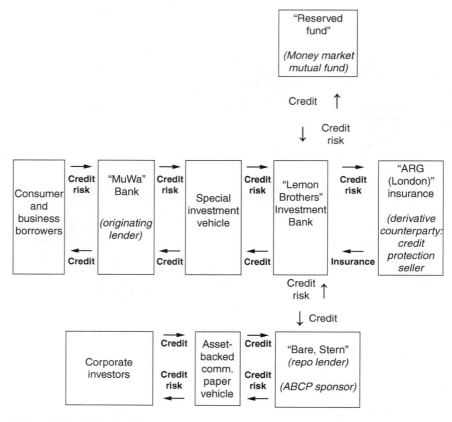

Figure 10.5 Credit provision and credit risk transfer in the shadow banking system.

were an important source of collateral for repo transactions.[143] Some scholars argue that the need for high-quality collateral to support repos increased the market size for asset-backed securities significantly and transformed those securities into a form of money.[144]

Meteoric growth: shadow banking eclipses depository banking

The various institutions involved in shadow banking enjoyed spectacular growth. In the United States by the eve of the crisis, the combined assets of broker dealers, government-sponsored entities, non-bank finance companies, and asset-backed securities issuers surpassed the assets owned by traditional banks, savings institutions, and credit unions.[145] In 1980, the number of mortgages held by banks dwarfed those that were securitized. Over the next twenty-seven years, this situation dramatically reversed as mortgage securitization realized explosive growth.[146]

Notes

1 Gary Gorton defines the shadow banking system through a mixture of specific financial instruments (repos and securitization) and one particular economic function (the creation of information insensitive debt). Gary B. Gorton, *Slapped by the Invisible Hand: The Panic of 2007*, 27 (2010, Oxford University Press).

2 Market risk means the potential losses an individual or firm could suffer (whether from a decrease in the value of assets or an increase in liabilities) due to changes in market price. Hennie van Greuning and Sonja Brajovic Bratanovic, *Analyzing and Managing Banking Risk: Framework for Assessing Corporate Governance and Financial Risk*, 111 (2003, World Bank Publications).

3 Other scholars also focus on intermediation in their definition of shadow banking. Zoltan Poszar, Tobias Adrian, Adam Ashcraft, and Hayley Boesky, Shadow Banking, Federal Reserve Bank of New York, *Staff Report No. 458* (July 2010), 8 available at www.newyorkfed.org/research/staff_reports/sr458.html (last visited July 28, 2013).

4 Erik F. Gerding, Code, Crash, and Open Source: The Outsourcing of Financial Regulation to Risk Models and the Global Financial Crisis, 84 *Washington Law Review* 127, 147–9 (2009) (describing pooling in securitization).

5 Ibid. at 149 (describing structuring or "tranching" in securitizations).

6 This is one of the functions of credit intermediation in the definition of shadow banking by Pozsar *et al.*, *supra* note 3.

7 See Financial Stability Board, Shadow Banking: Strengthening Oversight and Regulation, 11 (October 27, 2011).

8 Pozsar *et al.*, *supra* note 3.

9 Gary Gorton emphasizes this feature in his definition of shadow banking that focuses on "informationally insensitive debt." Gorton, *supra* note 1, at 27.

10 N. Gregory Mankiw, *Macroeconomics*, 75–7 (5th ed. 2003, Worth/Palgrave Macmillan) (listing three features of money).

11 See Gerding, *supra* note 4, at 175 (describing information destruction in securitization).

12 E. Gerald Corrigan, Are Banks Special? in Federal Reserve Bank of Minneapolis, *1982 Annual Report* available at www.minneapolisfed.org/pubs/ar/ar1982a.cfm (last visited July 28, 2013).

13 Ibid.

14 Compare Corrigan, *supra* note 12.

15 Ibid.

16 Financial Stability Board, Shadow Banking: Scoping the Issues, 4 (April 12, 2011) available at www.financialstabilityboard.org/publications/r_110412a.pdf (last visited July 28, 2013).

17 Compare Corrigan, *supra* note 12.

18 Ibid.

19 Financial Stability Board, *supra* note 16, at 4.

20 Corrigan, *supra* note 12.

21 Tobias Adrian and Hyun Song Shin, Money, Liquidity, and Monetary Policy, 99 *American Economic Review* 600, 604 (2009).

22 See, e.g., Morgan Ricks, Regulating Money Creation After the Crisis, 1 *Harvard Business Law Review* 75 (2011).

23 See Margaret M. Blair, Financial Innovation, Leverage, Bubbles, and the Distribution of Income, 30 *Review of Banking and Financial Law* 225, 270–3 (2010).

24 There have been notable exceptions among economists, particularly Adrian and Shin, who have looked at the monetary effects of shadow banking. See Adrian and Shin, *supra* note 21.

25 Aspinwall argued that money market mutual funds, as well as other products and

institutions, had started to provide substitutes for transaction accounts. He noted other non-bank lenders served as sources of back-up liquidity to the market. Aspinwall also pointed out that even then the Federal Reserve also conducted monetary policy by transacting with dealers in government securities, many of which were not banks. Richard Aspinwall, On the "Specialness" of Banking, 7 *Issues in Bank Regulation* 16 (1983).

26 Ibid.
27 See e.g., Mehrsa Baradaran, Reconsidering the Separation of Banking and Commerce after Financial Collapse, 80 *George Washington Law Review* 385 (2012) (arguing that non-banks performing bank functions makes bank holding company regulation obsolete).
28 Aspinwall himself recognized the possibility of non-banks creating similar economic risks to banks, but placed the burden on extending banking regulations to non-banks on finding evidence that these risks would become manifest. *Supra* note 25.
29 Chapter 11, "Runs: the collapse and rescue of shadow banking."
30 Douglas W. Diamond and Raghuram G. Rajan, Liquidity Risk, Liquidity Creation and Financial Fragility: A Theory of Banking, National Bureau of Economic Research, *Working Paper No. 7430*, 1 (December 1999) available at www.nber.org/papers/w7430.pdf?new_window=1.
31 Keith Pond, *Retail Banking*, 24 (2007, Global Professional Publishing).
32 Ibid.
33 Mark J. Flannery, Debt Maturity and the Deadweight Cost of Leverage: Optimally Financing Banking Firms, 84 *American Economic Review* 320, 320 (1994).
34 The classic economic model of a bank run can be found in Douglas W. Diamond and Philip H. Dybvig, Bank Runs, Deposit Insurance, and Liquidity, 91 *Journal of Political Economy* 401 (1983).
35 Gary Gorton, Private Clearinghouses and the Origins of Central Banking, *Federal Reserve Bank of Philadelphia Business Review* 1, 5 (January/February 1984) (describing twelve banking panics in United States between 1800 and 1915 that impacted even solvent banks).
36 Sudipto Bhattacharya, Arnoud Boot, and Anjan V. Thakor, The Economics of Bank Regulation, 30 *Journal of Money, Credit and Banking*, 745, 754 (1998).
37 Charles M. Kahn and João A.C. Santos, Allocating Bank Regulatory Powers: Lender of Last Resort, Deposit Insurance and Supervision, 49 *European Economic Review* 2107 (2005).
38 Viral V. Acharya, Thomas F. Cooley, Matthew Richardson, and Ingo Walter, Capital, Contingent Capital, and Liquidity Requirements, in *Regulating Wall Street: The Dodd-Frank Act and the New Architecture of Global Finance* 145 (Viral V. Acharya, Thomas F. Cooley, Matthew P. Richardson, and Ingo Walter eds., 2011, John Wiley & Sons).
39 Credit risk includes "counterparty risk" in derivative transactions, which means the risk to a firm that its counterparty in a derivative contract will default on its contractual obligations to make future payments to the firm. Joël Bessis, *Risk Management in Banking*, 12–13 (2nd ed. 2002, Wiley).
40 Robert P. Bartlett, III, Making Banks Transparent, 65 *Vanderbilt Law Review* 293 (2012) (describing various forms of risk concentration problems faced by banks).
41 George G. Kaufman and Kenneth E. Scott, What is Systemic Risk, and Do Bank Regulators Retard or Contribute to It? 7 *Independent Review* 371, 373 (2003).
42 Ibid.
43 Ibid.
44 George G. Kaufman, Bank Contagion: A Review of the Theory and Evidence, 8 *Journal of Financial Services Research* 123, 123 (1994).
45 Nathaniel Frank, Brenda González-Hermosillo, and Heiko Hesse, Transmission of Liquidity Shocks: Evidence from the 2007 Subprime Crisis, Oxford-Man Institute of

Quantitative Finance, *Working Paper*, 22 (August 2008) available at www.oxford-man.ox.ac.uk/documents/papers/2008OMI12.pdf (last visited July 28, 2013).

46 François Marini, Bank Insolvency, Deposit Insurance and Capital Adequacy, 24 *Journal of Financial Services Research* 67 (2003).

47 See Steven L. Schwarcz, The Alchemy of Asset Securitization, 1 *Stanford Journal of Law, Business and Finance* 133 (1994).

48 Janet M. Tavakoli, *Collateralized Debt Obligations and Structured Finance: New Developments in Cash and Synthetic Securitization*, 14 (2003, Wiley).

49 See Steven P. Baum, The Securitization of Commercial Property Debt, in *A Primer on Securitization*, 45, 49 (Leon T. Kendall and Michael J. Fishman eds., 1997, MIT Press).

50 Jian Hu, Assessing the Credit Risk of CDOs Backed by Structured Finance Securities: Rating Analysts' Challenges and Solutions, 10, Unpublished manuscript (August 31, 2007) available at http://papers.ssrn.com/sol3/papers.cfm?abstract_id=1011184 (last visited July 28, 2013).

51 See Steven L. Schwarcz, Protecting Financial Markets: Lessons from the Subprime Mortgage Meltdown, 93 *Minnesota Law Review* 373, 376–7 (2008).

52 Leon T. Kendall, Securitization: A New Era in American Finance, in *A Primer on Securitization*, 1, 5, 13 (Leon T. Kendall and Michael J. Fishman eds., 1997, MIT Press).

53 Pozsar *et al.*, *supra* note 3, at 3.

54 Joshua Coval, Jakub Jurek, and Erik Stafford, The Economics of Structured Finance, 23 *Journal of Economic Perspectives* 3, 10, 27–8 (2009).

55 See Kendall, *supra* note 52, at 13–15.

56 To accomplish this, the indenture or other agreement establishing the terms of each tranche often employs a complex "waterfall" rule for payment to different tranches. The waterfall sets the order in which the classes are entitled to receive payments from the underlying assets; in a simple waterfall, holders of senior classes receive amounts due to them in full before holders of junior classes receive anything. Thus, junior classes face a higher risk of not being paid due to defaults on the underlying assets and receive compensation for this risk with a higher interest rate. Different tranches (with different tradeoffs between risk and reward) appeal to different types of investors. More complex waterfall rules than the example above allow securitizations to carve up risk and reward in very finely tuned ways. For an explanation of waterfalls and tranching, see Baum, *supra* note 49, at 45, 49 (describing commercial mortgage-backed securities).

57 Pozsar *et al.*, *supra* note 3 (discussing credit transformation). Chapter 9, "Credit derivatives."

58 Gary Gorton, Slapped in the Face by the Invisible Hand: Banking and the Panic of 2007, National Bureau of Economic Research, *Working Paper*, 8–10 (May 9, 2009) available at http://papers.ssrn.com/sol3/papers.cfm?abstract_id=1401882 (last visited July 28, 2013).

59 Ibid.

60 See Ronald J. Gilson and Charles K. Whitehead, Deconstructing Equity: Public Ownership, Agency Costs, and Complete Capital Markets, 108 *Columbia Law Review* 231, 245–6 (2008).

61 Gerding, *supra* note 4, at 149–50.

62 James W. Kolani, Donald R. Fraser, and Ali Anari, The Effects of Securitization on Mortgage Market Yields: A Cointegration Analysis, 26 *Real Estate Economics* 677, 678 (1998).

63 Kendall, *supra* note 52, at 15.

64 Coval *et al.*, *supra* note 54, at 7.

65 Efraim Benmelech and Jennifer Dlugosz, The Alchemy of CDO Credit Ratings, National Bureau of Economic Research, *Working Paper No. 14878* (April 2009).

66 Gorton, *supra* note 58, at 25.
67 Viral Acharya and Matthew Richardson, Causes of the Financial Crisis, 21 *Critical Review* 195, 201 (2009).
68 Viral V. Acharya, Philipp Schnabl, and Gustavo Suarez, Securitization Without Risk Transfer, National Bureau of Economic Research, *Working Paper No. 15730*, 2 (February 2010) available at www.nber.org/papers/w15730.
69 In addition, some conduits purchase a mix of different assets to diversify the portfolio. Fitch Ratings, Structured Finance: Asset-backed Criteria Report: Asset-backed Commercial Paper Explained (November 8, 2001) available at http://pages.stern.nyu.edu/~igiddy/ABS/fitchabcp.pdf (last visited October 1, 2010).
70 Three common structures of asset-backed commercial paper transactions involve different roles and objectives for the sponsor. In the first structure, called a "single seller," the sponsor is the only originator of the loans or other assets being used as collateral for the ABCP issuance. Single seller transactions can help corporate borrowers use their assets to finance their continued operations. The second type of transaction involves multiple originators of the underlying collateral. In this "multi-seller" transaction, the sponsor is a financial institution that creates the ABCP transaction as a service to help its clients obtain financing. A financial institution also acts as a sponsor in the third type of structure, called a "securities backed" issuance. Financial institutions create this third type of asset-backed commercial paper structure to move assets off their balance sheets and to engage in regulatory arbitrage of capital requirements and other regulations (the role of regulatory arbitrage in driving the creation of the shadow banking web is discussed in Chapter 11). Ibid.
71 Viral V. Acharya and Phillip Schnabl, Do Global Banks Spread Global Imbalances? Asset-Backed Commercial Paper during the Financial Crisis of 2007–09, 58 *IMF Economic Review* 37, 38–9 (2010).
72 Ibid. at 38.
73 Frank Partnoy and David A. Skeel, Jr., The Promise and Perils of Credit Derivatives, 75 *University of Cincinnati Law Review* 1019 (2007) (defining credit derivatives and analyzing their economic functions and risks).
74 See ibid.
75 See ibid.
76 Aaron Unterman, Exporting Risk: Global Implications of the Securitization of U.S. Housing Debt, 4 *Hastings Business Law Journal* 77, 89 (2008).
77 Norvald Instefjord, Risk and Hedging: Do Credit Derivatives Increase Bank Risk? 29 *Journal of Banking and Finance* 333, 334–5 (2005) (positing that credit derivatives make it attractive for financial institutions to take on new risk as existing risk is hedged).
78 Several studies indicate that banks that used credit derivatives to hedge, replaced that credit risk by making fresh loans or investments. E.g., Beverly Hirtle, Credit Derivatives and Bank Credit Supply, 18 *Journal of Financial Intermediation* 125, 126 (2009). See Chapter 9, note 78 and accompanying text.
79 Henry T.C. Hu, Misunderstood Derivatives: The Causes of Informational Failure and the Promise of Regulatory Incrementalism, 102 *Yale Law Journal* 1457, 1502 (1993).
80 International Swaps and Derivatives Association Inc., ISDA Market Survey Historical Data, available at www.isda.org/statistics/index.html (last visited October 1, 2010).
81 William A. Birdthistle, Breaking Bucks in Money Market Mutual Funds, 2010 *Wisconsin Law Review* 1155, 1156–81 (2010) (describing evolution of money market mutual funds).
82 Birdthistle, *supra* note 81.

83 Sandra C. Krieger, Executive Vice President, Federal Reserve Bank of New York, Remarks at the Global Association of Risk Professionals Twelfth Annual Risk Management Convention, New York City "Reducing the Systemic Risk in Shadow Maturity Transformation" (March 8, 2011) available at www.newyorkfed.org/news-events/speeches/2011/kri110308.html (last visited July 28, 2013).

84 Birdthistle, *supra* note 81, at 1176.

85 Adrian and Shin, *supra* note 21, at 602; Gary Gorton and Andrew Metrick, Securitized Banking and the Run on Repo, 104 *Journal of Financial Economics* 425, 427, 431–2 (2012).

86 Gorton and Metrick, *supra* note 85, at 427, 432.

87 Adrian and Shin, *supra* note 21, at 602.

88 Ibid.

89 Ibid.

90 Gary Gorton, Information, Liquidity, and the (Ongoing) Panic of 2007, National Bureau of Economic Research, *Working Paper No. 14649* (January 2009) available at www.nber.org/papers/w14649 (last visited July 28, 2013).

91 For a description of the repo market, its importance as a source of short-term financing for financial institutions, and how the market seized up in the financial crisis, see Gorton and Metrick, *supra* note 85, at 432–3.

92 Krieger, *supra* note 83.

93 Peter Hördahl and Michael R. King, Developments in Repo Markets During the Financial Turmoil, *BIS Quarterly Review* (December 8, 2008), 38 available at http://ssrn.com/abstract=1329903.

94 Gorton and Metrick, *supra* note 85, at 427–8.

95 Ibid.

96 Gorton and Metrick, *supra* note 85, at 433. Studies estimate the size of the repo market in the Eurozone to be similar as of the end of 2007. Ibid.

97 Ibid.

98 Ibid.

99 Ibid.

100 Katia D'Hulster, The Leverage Ratio, World Bank Group Crisis Response Note No. 11 (December 2009), 1 available at http://rru.worldbank.org/documents/CrisisResponse/Note11.pdf (last visited July 28, 2013).

101 William A. Klein, John C. Coffee, Jr., and Frank Partnoy, *Business Organization and Finance: Legal and Economic Principles*, 343–46 (11th ed. 2010, Foundation Press).

102 The focus on leverage endured even as the global financial crisis took hold. Cf. John Garvey and Adam Dener, Maximizing Operating Leverage at Your Bank, *American Banker*, July 13, 2007, at 1.

103 Financial Stability Board, *supra* note 16, at 4.

104 See *supra* note 78 and accompanying text.

105 There is both theoretical and empirical evidence that financial institutions that offload risk with credit derivatives make fresh loans rather than reduce their overall exposure. See *supra* note 78 and accompanying text.

106 Peter Walton and Walter Aerts, *Global Financial Accounting and Reporting: Principles and Analysis*, 172 (2006, Thomson Learning).

107 Sharon Brown-Hruska, The Derivatives Marketplace: Exchanges and the Over-the-Counter Market, in *Financial Derivatives: Pricing and Risk Management*, 21, 29–30 (Robert W. Kolb and James A. Overdahl eds., 2010, John Wiley & Sons) (comparing collateral mechanisms in over-the-counter and centrally cleared derivatives).

108 Cf. Gorton and Metrick, *supra* note 85, at 427–8 (describing these collateral or "haircut" provisions).

109 Investment banks put together and structure asset-backed securities transactions and then underwrite the securities. They thus connect originating lenders to the institutional investor clients of the investment bank's brokerage units. See Hugh Thomas, A Preliminary Look at Gains from Asset Securitization, 9 *Journal of International Financial Markets, Institutions and Money* 321, 328 (1999). Investment banks also securitize the assets on their own balance sheets. James Crotty, Structural Causes of the Global Financial Crisis: A Critical Assessment of the "New Financial Architecture," 33 *Cambridge Journal of Economics* 563, 570 (2009). They sponsor asset-backed commercial paper issuances, whether as a service for clients, to finance their own operations, or to move assets off their balance sheets for regulatory purposes (as described below). See *supra* note 70 (describing types of asset-backed commercial paper transactions). As dealers of OTC derivatives, investment banks would arrange transactions between credit protection buyers and credit protection sellers in credit derivatives. Franklin Edwards and Frederic Mishkin, The Decline of Traditional Banking: Implications for Financial Stability and Regulatory Policy, Federal Reserve Bank of New York, *Economic Policy Review* (July 1995), 27, 35 (early study noting move of financial institutions away from traditional banking activities towards OTC derivatives dealing).

110 Standard & Poor's, Demystifying Banks' Use of Credit Derivatives (December 8, 2003) available at www.alacrastore.com/research/s-and-p-credit-research-S_PCOR-RECT_Demystifying_Banks_Use_of_Credit_Derivatives-348955 (last visited July 28, 2013) (noting, however, that most bank and investment bank positions in credit derivatives are offsetting, indicating that the firm is dealing in derivatives rather than hedging).

111 See SEC Litigation Release No. 21,489 (April 16, 2010) (*Securities and Exchange Commission* v. *Goldman, Sachs & Co. and Fabrice Tourre*, 10 Civ. 3229 (BJ) (S.D.N.Y. filed April 16, 2010)) (describing SEC allegations).

112 Noah L. Wynkoop, Note, The Unregulables? The Perilous Confluence of Hedge Funds and Credit Derivatives, 76 *Fordham Law Review* 3095 (2008).

113 See Sheridan Titman, The Leverage of Hedge Funds, 7 *Finance Research Letters* 2 (2010) (analyzing why certain hedge funds take on high leverage). Some hedge funds use little or no leverage. Stephen Brown, Anthony Lynch and Antti Petajisto, Hedge Funds, Mutual Funds, and ETFs, in *Regulating Wall Street: The Dodd-Frank Act and the New Architecture of Global Finance* 351, 351 (Viral V. Acharya, Thomas F. Cooley, Matthew P. Richardson, and Ingo Walter eds., 2011, John Wiley & Sons).

114 See Pozsar *et al.*, *supra* note 3 (describing how credit hedge funds acted as shadow banks).

115 Some scholars argue that hedge funds may have played a valuable role by injecting liquidity into shadow banking markets as the crisis deepened. See Brown *et al.*, *supra* note 113, at 352.

116 Some scholars have questioned the wide perception that hedge funds earn outsized returns. E.g., William Fung, David A. Hsieh, Narayan Y. Naik, and Tarun Ramadorai, Hedge Funds: Performance, Risk, and Capital Formation, 63 *Journal of Finance* 1777 (2008) (finding only a subset of funds studied deliver above average returns adjusted for risk).

117 For an analysis of the extensive use by hedge funds of credit derivatives, see Wynkoop, *supra* note 112 (arguing that heavy use of lightly regulated credit derivatives by unregulated hedge funds increases systemic risk).

118 Ben S. Bernanke, Remarks at the Federal Reserve Bank of Atlanta's 2006 Financial Markets Conference, Sea Island, Georgia ("Hedge Funds and Systemic Risk") (May 16, 2006) available at www.federalreserve.gov/newsevents/speech/Bernanke 20060516a.htm (last visited July 28, 2013).

119 Pozsar *et al.*, *supra* note 3.

120 David Reiss, The Federal Government's Implied Guarantee of Fannie Mae and Freddie Mac's Obligations: Uncle Sam Will Pick Up the Tab, 42 *Georgia Law Review* 1019, 1028 (2008).

121 Ibid. at 1028–30.

122 Ibid. at 1031–3.

123 Ibid. at 1031.

124 Ibid.

125 Ibid. at 1030–1.

126 Scholars have criticized the Federal Reserve for inadequately supervising non-bank mortgage lenders that were owned by bank holding companies. Patricia A. McCoy, Andrey D. Pavlov, and Susan M. Wachter, Systemic Risk Through Securitization: The Result of Deregulation and Regulatory Failure, 41 *Connecticut Law Review* 493, 511–13. Independent non-bank mortgage lenders enjoyed greater freedom from federal regulation. Ibid. at 515. Federal bank regulators blamed states for inadequately regulating these independent firms. Ibid. at 523.

127 For a description of these mortgages, see Patricia A. McCoy, Rethinking Disclosure in a World of Risk-Based Pricing, 44 *Harvard Journal on Leegislation* 123, 143–7 (2007).

128 McCoy *et al.*, *supra* note 126, at 496–7.

129 See ibid. at 498.

130 Anna J. Schwartz, Origins of the Financial Market Crisis of 2008, 29 *Cato Journal* 19, 21 (2009).

131 Stuart I. Greenbaum and Anjan V. Thakor, Bank Funding Modes: Securitization versus Deposits, 11 *Journal of Banking and Finance* 379 (1987).

132 See Gorton, *supra* note 1, at 100–1 (describing a specialized bank investment strategy in tranches of CDOs).

133 Mark D. Griffiths and Drew B. Winters, On a Preferred Habitat for Liquidity at the Turn-of-the-Year: Evidence from the Term-Repo Market, 12 *Journal of Financial Services Research* 21 (1997).

134 See, e.g., 12 U.S.C. §§ 1831e(a), 1831e(d) (Federal Deposit Insurance Act provisions restricting permissible activities and debt investments by state savings associations). These statutory provisions are explicitly intended to protect the Federal Deposit Insurance Corporation's (FDIC) insurance fund. 12 U.S.C. §§ 1831e(a)(1).

135 For a stringent criticism of deregulation that allowed financial conglomerates composed of banks, investment banks, and various other types of financial services entities, see Arthur E. Wilmarth, Jr., The Dark Side of Universal Banking: Financial Conglomerates and the Origins of the Subprime Financial Crisis, 41 *Connecticut Law Review* 963, 972–94 (2009).

136 This danger, regulatory efforts to address the danger, and attempts to circumvent those regulations are discussed in Chapter 11.

137 See *supra* notes 77–8 and accompanying text. Of course, credit derivatives can be used to hedge the credit risk from any transaction and any counterparty. See *supra* note 73 and accompanying text.

138 Markus K. Brunnermeier, Deciphering the Liquidity and Credit Crunch 2007–2008, 23 *Journal of Economic Perspectives* 77, 79 (2009).

139 Gorton and Metrick, *supra* note 85, at 427–8.

140 Michael S. Gibson, Understanding the Risk of Synthetic CDOs, Federal Reserve System, Finance and Economics Discussion Series, *Working Paper No. 2004-36*, 1–4 (July 2004) available at http://papers.ssrn.com/sol3/papers.cfm?abstractid= 596442 (last visited July 28, 2013).

141 Naohiko Baba, Robert N. McCauley, and Srichander Ramaswamy, U.S. Dollar Money Market Funds and Non-US Banks, *BIS Quarterly Review* 65, 69 (March 2009) available at http://bis.org/publ/qtrpdf/r_qt0903g.pdf (last visited July 28, 2013).

142 Partnoy and Skeel, *supra* note 73, at 1023–4 (describing use of credit derivatives to hedge).
143 Gorton and Metrick, *supra* note 85, at 428.
144 Ibid.
145 Adrian and Shin, *supra* note 21, at 601.
146 Ibid.

11 "Lawyers, runs, and money"

The rise and collapse of shadow banking

The shadow banking system enjoyed meteoric growth not merely because it served the valuable economic functions described in the previous chapter – credit provision and credit risk transfer, maturity and liquidity transformation, credit transformation, and the creation of money instruments. The system flourished, moreover, because the federal government granted each of the shadow banking markets various legal subsidies and preferences to stimulate their growth. Furthermore, financial institutions designed and deployed shadow banking instruments to engage in systematic regulatory arbitrage of banking and other financial regulations. Asset-backed securities, money market funds, repos, and credit derivatives did not gestate in a legal vacuum merely to serve economic needs. Rather, law played a crucial role in the procreation, midwifing, and feeding of the various shadow banking markets. As the previous chapter explained, the urge to use regulatory subsidies and lower regulatory taxes formed part of the system's DNA, molecular structure, and very reason for existence.

These shadow banking markets developed over a period of thirty years. Yet the pace of regulatory stimulus and regulatory arbitrage that fed the shadow banking markets accelerated dramatically in the years before the Panic of 2007–2008. Each of the shadow banking markets, from securitization to repos, contributed enormously to the inflation of the real estate and securities bubbles in the United States and Europe that imploded during the Panic of 2007–2008. Moreover, as the bubble inflated, policymakers supplied more regulatory stimulus to shadow markets. As the bubble inflated, financial institutions appear to have increasingly used shadow banking markets to engage in the arbitrage of bank capital rules. "Regulatory capital arbitrage" (introduced in Chapter 5) became a primary driver for the creation of securitization and other shadow banking transactions. Financial firms used these products to game these legal rules rather than for economic functions, such as transferring credit risk. Even governments joined the regulatory arbitrage games; witness how Greece and Goldman Sachs engaged in a series of transactions (using a cousin of credit derivatives) to mask that nation's true debt.[1] Furthermore, the shadow banking system facilitated not only regulatory arbitrage, but also fraud, as law-bending shaded into law-breaking.

Meanwhile, as the shadow banking system mushroomed, it turbocharged the leverage cycle. Financial institutions took on more leverage, while the system churned out money-like instruments. These twin dynamics led to dramatic monetary expansion. Here, too, law played an outsized role. Financial institutions herded into certain investment classes that enjoyed low-risk weights under bank capital yet offered higher rewards: investment grade asset-backed securities tied to mortgages and the bonds of certain sovereigns. Moreover, some scholars also claim that the Basel I and Basel II rules had procyclical effects.[2]

The metastasizing growth of the shadow banking system before the Panic of 2007–2008 thus presents a master class in the Regulatory Instability Hypothesis. All the dynamics of the Regulatory Instability Hypothesis both accelerated during and, in turn, fed the bubbles in the United States and Europe. The regulatory stimulus cycle, compliance rot, regulatory arbitrage frenzies, and procyclical and herd-promoting regulations set the stage for the global financial crisis.

This chapter outlines the legal origins of the system in regulatory stimulus and regulatory arbitrage ("lawyers"), shows the crash of the system or the consequence of regulation-driven herding ("runs"), and examines the monetary dimension of regulatory change ("money"). The chapter begins ("Lawyers: regulatory stimulus, regulatory arbitrage, and law-breaking in the shadow banking system") with the legal history of the system. It examines the crucial role that regulatory stimulus and regulatory arbitrage played in the origin of each shadow banking market. The chapter describes how regulatory stimulus and arbitrage accelerated as bubbles in the United States and Europe inflated. It also sketches out how regulatory arbitrage shaded into law-breaking.

The chapter then turns (in "Money: the emergence of a shadow monetary transmission belt, financial regulation, and herding") to the monetary dimension of the shadow banking system, as financial institution leverage and the creation of new money-like instruments fueled monetary expansion. It looks at how regulations encouraged financial institution herding into particular shadow banking markets. Unfortunately, the Federal Reserve paid too little heed to the growth of this shadow system and its effects on asset prices and financial stability. This lack of attention stemmed from many causes. It owed, at least in part, to the origins of the system in legal change: regulatory stimulus and regulatory arbitrage. Central bankers and macroeconomists are neither trained nor inclined to follow legal change. Moreover, the formation of dangerous feedback loops – among shadow banking instruments, asset prices, and political markets – obscured the full import of this system's rise, as well as the risks it posed.

When the bubbles burst, the shadow banking sector faced imminent collapse. Cuttingly, those markets designed to sidestep the heavily regulated depository banking system suffered themselves from canonical bank crises. The Panic of 2007–2008 represented a toxic cocktail of liquidity crises – runs on shadow banking markets – and solvency crises triggered by financial institution investments in those markets. In the United States, the government responded to these crises by adapting and deploying the same tools that governments have historically used to combat banking crises. The government effectively:

- provided deposit insurance to investments in shadow banking markets;
- served as lender or liquidity provider of last resort to those markets; and
- resolved institutions that failed because of shadow banking markets, albeit without necessarily replacing their management or wiping out their shareholders.

In "Runs: the collapse and rescue of shadow banking," this chapter then offers a brief sketch of the fall and rescue of the shadow banking sector. It underscores the bitter irony of how a system designed to mimic depository banking – without the associated regulation – ultimately suffered the same crises and required the same government interventions as traditional banks.

The chapter concludes with a very high level overview of the lessons for the shadow banking crises for financial reform, using the Regulatory Instability Hypothesis as the primary lens.

Lawyers: regulatory stimulus, regulatory arbitrage, and law-breaking in the shadow banking system

Regulatory stimulus and the legal origins of the shadow banking system

Regulatory stimulus and regulatory arbitrage helped spawn, midwifed, and suckled the shadow banking system in two ways. First, the government provided legal preferences and subsidies for shadow markets. It repealed or shielded shadow instruments from various financial regulations that applied to other instruments or institutions that provided functionally equivalent economic services, such as depository banks. These legal preferences gave shadow banking instruments crucial competitive advantages.

Second, at the same time, regulatory arbitrage had a massive impact. Financial institutions carefully designed instruments to mimic the core functions of depository banks albeit with lower "regulatory tax rates" (this fits the "investment structuring" definition of Chapter 5). Capital then flowed into shadow banking markets to sidestep the higher regulatory "tax rates" that applied to depository banking (Chapter 5's "investment switching"). Capital hemorrhaging prompted banks to lobby policymakers to reduce or roll back regulations on their own regulatory sector to allow them to compete. This spurred shadow banking institutions to seek further regulatory preferences. The history below of money market mutual funds, one of the first modern shadow banking instruments, provides a case study of this spiral in which regulatory arbitrage begat regulatory stimulus, which begat further regulatory arbitrage.

Banks ultimately decided not to compete with shadow banking markets, but to participate in them. The banking industry lobbied for legal changes, ranging from major statutes to incremental interpretations by U.S. regulators, to allow them to invest in, underwrite, and deal various shadow banking instruments. The entry of banks in shadow banking markets, from mortgage-backed securities to credit and other OTC derivatives, had cascading effects. New capital inflated these markets. Moreover, financial conglomerates grew increasingly large as a result of this new business. In the United States, these mammoth firms then began playing various regulatory arbitrage games to transfer subsidies from their heavily regulated affiliates (such as depository banks and insurance companies) to affiliates in less regulated, shadow sectors (such as mortgage lenders in Long Beach and derivative sellers in London). Furthermore, banks and other financial firms devised ways to use asset-backed securities, repos, and credit derivatives to game regulatory capital requirements.

This use of shadow banking instruments for regulatory capital arbitrage appears to have dramatically increased in the years immediately prior to the Panic of 2007–2008, when the real estate and capital markets bubbles in the United States and Europe inflated. The shadow banking system also enabled both law-bending and law-breaking, as financial institutions used shadow instruments to mask leverage, risk-taking, and, ultimately, their deteriorating financial condition. Meanwhile, fraud spread all along the securitization pipeline from the origination of mortgages to the sale of CDOs.

Shadow banking's origin story: money market mutual funds

Money market funds, one of the first shadow banking instruments, emerged in the United States in the 1970s. The first money market mutual fund, the Reserve Fund, debuted in 1970.[3] Other funds proliferated in that decade, as U.S. banks struggled with the caps that the former Regulation Q placed on the interest rates they could offer depositors.[4] When inflation spiked in the 1970s and eroded the attractiveness of capped bank deposits, customers flocked to money market mutual funds, which offered a new alternative for those seeking relatively safe, liquid investments.[5]

This increased competition led banks to lobby for a roll back of Regulation Q. Congress obliged with the Depository Institutions Deregulation and Monetary Control Act of 1980 (DIDMCA), which mandated the phased elimination of Regulation Q.[6] The act also implemented other reforms to increase the competitiveness of banks, allow them to operate in an inflationary environment, and reduce overall inflation.[7] Many of these additional reforms would ultimately impact the shadow banking system and contribute to the Panic of 2007–2008. For example, the statute also loosened restrictions on the interest rates banks could charge for loans and preempted state usury laws with respect to home mortgages. This deregulation allowed banks to price mortgage interest rates according to risk, which paved the way for subprime mortgages.[8]

Once banks began to compete on a level regulatory playing field, money market mutual funds, in turn, sought the help of regulators to make their products appear safer and more like bank deposits.[9] In particular, the fund industry wanted to price fund shares based on a fixed "net asset value."[10] Net asset value serves as the price of a particular fund and is based on the assets in the fund's portfolio.[11] As the value of the portfolio changes, the net asset value should fluctuate, but a floating net asset value reveals the volatility in this value.[12] By 1983, three years after DIDMCA, the fund industry successfully convinced the SEC to allow funds to change their pricing from a floating net asset value to a fixed net asset value.[13] This allowed mutual funds to convince investors that their product offered safety and liquidity similar to bank accounts. It also sowed the seeds for bank runs on money market funds a quarter century later. This early history of competition between money market mutual funds and banks provides a clear example of the spirals that form between regulatory arbitrage and deregulation, the subject of Chapter 6.

Regulatory preferences and money creation: bankruptcy exemptions for repos and swaps

The regulatory history of money market mutual funds also underscores how lawmakers and regulators can give certain financial instruments regulatory privileges. Moreover, many of these privileges endow those instruments with enough apparent safety and liquidity to make them "money-like." Gary Gorton and Andrew Metrick provide another example from the early 1980s of legal privileges creating money. They point to how, in 1984, the U.S. Congress granted repurchase agreements ("repos") various exemptions from the Bankruptcy Code.[14] These statutory changes meant that lenders/creditors under repos enjoyed various privileges, such as not being subject to the Code's "automatic stay" when the debtor filed for bankruptcy, that lenders under other instruments did not. Gorton and Metrick argue that these bankruptcy exemptions made repos more "informationally insensitive." In other words, repo lenders no longer had to analyze as carefully the creditworthiness and bankruptcy risk of their borrowers. This, according to Gorton and Metrick, enabled repos to take on more of the features of money.[15] After this statutory change, the market for repos enjoyed explosive growth.[16]

In 2005, the U.S. Congress returned to this repo playbook and granted derivatives (or "swaps") similar exemptions from the Bankruptcy Code.[17] Major financial institutions active in the derivatives market lobbied hard for these exemptions.[18] Law professor Mark Roe argues that these changes allow derivative creditors to "jump to the head of the bankruptcy repayment line." As with repos, these exemptions dulled the incentives of those who entered into derivative contracts to monitor the risk-taking of their counterparties.[19] The 2005 bankruptcy exemptions (together with a 2000 federal statute described below that deregulated derivatives markets) turbocharged the growth of the swaps market.[20]

Government-sponsored institutions: Freddie Mac and Fannie Mae

The U.S. government took a more direct route to jumpstarting and subsidizing the mortgage-backed securities market. Chapter 6 described how Congress granted special federal charters to Fannie Mae (in 1938 in the midst of the Great Depression) and Freddie Mac (in 1970, to create a competitor for Fannie) to spur the development of a secondary market for middle-class residential mortgages. The government granted these entities a raft of subsidies, including tax breaks, exemptions from securities laws, and a special status allowing banks to invest in their securities. Moreover, long before the Panic of 2007–2008, many scholars argued that these entities enjoyed an implicit guarantee from the federal government, i.e., that the government would bail their creditors out in the event of the insolvency of these firms.[21] Chapter 6 also described how these two government-sponsored entities spurred copycats in the business of purchasing and pooling residential mortgages, and creating and guaranteeing residential mortgage-backed securities. That chapter examined how these "private label securitizations" generated competition for Freddie and Fannie and also a complex spiral of regulatory arbitrage and regulatory stimulus.[22]

Bank participation in securitization

Mortgage-backed securities markets enjoyed meteoric growth in the 1980s, and securities firms enjoyed the profits from underwriting these products. Jealous banks pushed Congress and their regulators to relax Glass-Steagall era restrictions on their activities to allow them to purchase and deal in mortgage-backed securities.

PERMITTING BANKS TO INVEST IN MORTGAGE-BACKED SECURITIES

A series of statutory changes enabled banks to purchase mortgage-backed securities. Some of these changes occurred before the mortgage-backed securities market took off in the early 1980s. Each time that Congress created a government-sponsored entity that later came to sponsor mortgage-backed securities – Fannie Mae in 1938, GNMA in 1968, and Freddie Mac in 1970 – it soon afterwards amended 12 U.S.C. § 24 (Seventh) to allow national banks to purchase the securities of that entity.[23] The securities of these government-sponsored firms originally consisted of their capital stock. However, when these firms began issuing and guaranteeing mortgage-backed securities, ultimately 12 U.S.C. § 24 (Seventh) allowed banks to purchase those instruments as well.[24]

Regulatory change enabling bank participation in mortgage securitization accelerated in the 1980s. Congress again amended this same statutory provision, 12 U.S.C. § 24 (Seventh), by passing the Secondary Mortgage Market Enhancement Act of 1984 (SMMEA).[25] SMMEA removed Glass-Steagall's quantitative restrictions on the ability of national banks to purchase privately issued mortgage-backed securities (i.e., private-label securities).[26] More precisely, SMMEA removed these restrictions so long as the mortgage-backed securities purchased were "investment grade" (that is, given a high rating, by an SEC-licensed credit rating agency).[27] The statute also allowed thrifts[28] and credit unions[29] to invest in all mortgage-backed securities to the same extent that national banks could.[30] Furthermore, SMMEA preempted state laws that would have imposed restrictions on investing in those same categories of mortgage-backed securities.[31] Congress thus removed any requirement that private label mortgage-backed securities be registered under state blue sky laws.[32]

As amended, 12 U.S.C. § 24 (Seventh) continued to subject purchases by national banks of private mortgage-backed securities to regulations by the Office of the Comptroller of the Currency (OCC).[33] In 1996, the OCC exercised this statutory power to pass a set of rules on the security investments that national banks could make.[34] These rules place mortgage-backed securities in a category that allowed for unlimited purchases.[35] Federal thrifts enjoyed even more freedom than national banks; the Office of Thrift Supervision never passed regulations specifically limiting their ability to invest in mortgage-backed securities.[36]

PERMITTING BANKS TO ISSUE AND DEAL IN MORTGAGE-BACKED SECURITIES

A series of regulatory interpretations by federal bank regulators allowed banks to issue and deal in mortgage-backed securities.[37] One historical obstacle to these operations came from Section 21 of the Glass-Steagall Act, which prevented depository institutions from engaging "in the business of issuing, underwriting, selling, or distributing" securities for their own account.[38] However, beginning in 1977 and throughout the 1980s and 1990s, the OCC issued a series of interpretations that used a proviso to this statutory prohibition to allow national banks to expand incrementally into the issuance, underwriting, and dealing of mortgage-backed securities.[39] One crucial 1987 OCC interpretation withstood court challenges by the Securities Industry of America that sought to protect the turf of securities underwriters, which were then still separated from banks by Glass-Steagall.[40]

The power of national banks to issue and underwrite mortgage-backed securities (and other asset-backed securities) prompted the Federal Reserve Board to issue its own set of regulatory interpretations under the Glass-Steagall Act to permit certain subsidiaries of bank holding companies to conduct the same activities.[41] These interpretations also survived court challenges by the securities industry.[42] The Federal Reserve also issued another series of interpretations permitting these activities under a separate statute, the Bank Holding Company Act.[43]

Bank participation in derivatives markets

Banks became similarly jealous of the profits of securities firms in the new business of derivatives, which also boomed in the 1980s. As with mortgage-backed securities, banks sought from their regulators a series of incremental regulatory interpretations to allow them to deal (and act as intermediary) in derivatives. Law professor Saule Omarova examines how the OCC changed the definition of the "business of banking" incrementally over several years to allow banks to increasingly deal in derivatives.[44] The OCC issued interpretations allowing national banks to enter into certain credit default swaps, one of the core strands in the shadow banking web.[45] This same series of interpretations allowed national banks to hold below-investment grade debt to hedge risks from derivatives activities.[46]

Swaps unbound

Credit derivatives received another, more massive jolt of regulatory stimulus in 2000. In that year, Congress shielded credit derivatives and other OTC derivatives from regulation by the Commodity Futures Trading Commission (CFTC), the SEC, and state regulators when it passed the Commodity Futures Modernization Act.[47] This statute exempted credit derivatives not only from disclosure regulations, but also from regulations under the Commodity Exchange Act and other statutes that could have led to capital requirements applying to counterparties to these contracts.[48] This masterstroke of deregulation stemmed from efforts by then-Federal Reserve Chairman Alan Greenspan, senior Treasury Department officials, OTC derivatives dealers, and their allies in Congress. This coalition sought to head off an attempt by the CFTC, under the leadership of Brooksley Born, to regulate OTC derivatives. Indeed, a decade before the Panic of 2008, Born had warned of the dangers that these derivatives might cause a financial meltdown.[49]

Accounting for derivatives

The "deregulation" of derivatives also occurred in the accounting world. Financial institutions and their derivatives lobbying organization effectively shut down a proposal in the 1980s from the Financial Accounting Standards Board (FASB) that would have required financial institutions to report swaps on their balance sheets. The FASB reasoned that banks already reported loans as assets and deposits as liabilities on their balance sheets. Swaps effectively represented an asset (expected payments a firm would receive from its counterparty under the swap) and a liability (expected payments to a firm's counterparty) bundled together. According to FASB, firms should thus disclose both the asset and liability aspect of each swap on their balance sheets.[50]

However, financial institutions became concerned that the explosive growth in the derivatives markets meant that this treatment would cause their balance sheets to balloon. Thus, major derivatives players and their industry organization, the International Swap Dealers Association (ISDA), lobbied and persuaded FASB to change its stance. After this shift, parties to derivative contracts did not have to count swaps as assets or liabilities on their balance sheets, but merely had to disclose the changes in the "fair value" of these contracts over time.[51] Two scholars compared this rule to "an individual reporting only the change in their debt balances, instead of the debts themselves."[52]

The scuttling of this proposal meant that swaps were in some sense given preferential accounting treatment compared to bank loans and deposits. To this day, this accounting treatment means that bank balance sheets may vastly under-state the actual leverage and risk of major financial institutions. By some 2013 reports, the accounting rules for derivatives may reduce the assets and liabilities on bank financial statements by trillions of dollars each year.[53] The dangers of this disclosure became evident in cases such as the failure of AIG. That firm disclosed the notional amount of credit default swaps, but scant information on the value of liabilities under those contracts, which eventually mushroomed into hundreds of billions of losses.[54]

The demise of Glass-Steagall and subsidy leakage

The repeal of the Glass-Steagall Act represents the granddaddy of regulatory stimulus of the shadow banking sector. This statutory "Big Bang" rendered moot the slow-drip approach by which bank regulators incrementally lowered the ramparts restricting banks from entering the securities business. The demise of the Depression era statute (which occurred in stages throughout the 1980s and 1990s and culminated in the Gramm-Leach-Bliley Act of 1999) allowed banks, investment banks, and other financial institutions to operate under the same corporate umbrella. This allowed investment bank entities to function as true middlemen in the shadow banking web – and put together securitizations and derivative transactions. As the previous chapter explained, large investment bank conglomerates became the hubs of the shadow bank network. The demise of Glass-Steagall also facilitated fuller bank investments in shadow banking instruments.[55]

Several scholars raised early warnings about the risks of repealing the statute. Law professor Arthur Wilmarth and others warned that financial conglomerates would exploit "too-big-to-fail" status.[56] In other words, financial markets would assume that the government could not allow these behemoths to become insolvent for fear of the massive damage to financial markets. The implicit government guarantee gave these firms a lower cost of raising debt.[57]

Other scholars feared that financial conglomerates would exploit the explicit subsidies afforded to depository banks (and regulated insurance companies) and gamble with taxpayer money.[58] Although banking laws contained provisions to prevent this subsidy leakage within conglomerates from banks to non-banks,[59] scholars have questioned their actual effectiveness.[60] Law professor Saule Omarova argues that the demise of Glass-Steagall division placed much of the work for counteracting subsidy leakage on an obscure Depression era statutory provision, Section 23A of the Federal Reserve Act.[61] Section 23A:

- imposes quantitative limitations on certain extensions of credit and other transactions between a bank and its affiliates that would expose a bank to an affiliate's credit or investment risk;
- prohibits banks from purchasing low-quality assets from their non-bank affiliates; and
- imposes strict collateral requirements with respect to extensions of credit to affiliates.[62]

Omarova details how banks sought exemptions from these strictures "to leverage their subsidiary banks' high credit ratings and access to cheap sources of funding to increase profitability of their non-bank subsidiaries."[63] From 1996 to 2010, the Federal Reserve granted numerous exemptions to financial conglomerates that allowed them to use their bank affiliates to support loans by non-banks. These exemptions specifically allowed banks to support shadow banking operations.[64] For example, between 2000 and 2006, the Federal Reserve gave Citigroup multiple exemptions to allow its banking subsidiary to purchase subprime mortgage assets from a series of mortgage lenders that Citigroup acquired.[65] Omarova connects this decision to Citigroup's ability to expand its non-banking mortgage lending operations and its ability to reap profits from securitization.[66] She also details a separate set of Federal Reserve exemptions that allowed conglomerates to use bank affiliates to support securities lending by broker-dealer affiliates.[67] This eased the ability of financial conglomerates to engage in derivatives and repo transactions, among other shadow banking operations.[68]

Regulatory capital arbitrage revisited

Banks and other regulated financial institutions sought to access shadow banking markets not only to earn profits, transfer credit risk, and invest cash in safe and liquid assets. These firms also sought to use shadow banking instruments to game bank capital requirements. Chapter 5 outlined several strategies of banks and other firms that used investments in asset-backed securities and derivatives to lower the amount of capital that regulations require them to hold. For example, sponsors structured securitizations to stuff more risk (whether credit risk, market risk, or liquidity risk) into particular tranches of asset-backed securities. These tranches then bore more risk than assumed by the risk-weights for those securities under bank capital regulations. This allowed investors in those tranches (such as banks and insurance companies) to take on more risk and enjoy more return. It also lowered the effectiveness of bank capital regulations.[69]

Similarly, the sponsors of securities used derivatives to provide credit and liquidity support for securitizations. Creative uses of these economic guarantees ensured that the providers needed to hold little (or sometimes no) capital even though market prices indicated that the guarantee created a higher risk for the guarantor. The guarantees provided by derivatives, at the same time, reduced the risk for investors and allowed regulated entities, like banks and insurance companies to purchase asset-backed securities.[70] (Note: although this chapter uses the past tense to describe these regulatory arbitrage games, there is no indication that the crisis ended these practices completely).

Rating agency games

Chapter 5 also outlined how the sponsors and purchasers of asset-backed securities engaged in regulatory arbitrage with respect to credit rating agencies. In many respects, rating agencies represented the lynchpin of any successful regulatory capital arbitrage strategy. Banks and other regulated financial firms often could purchase asset-backed securities only if these instruments received an "investment grade" stamp of approval from an SEC-licensed credit rating agency. As Chapter 5 noted, however, these rating agencies receive payment for their services from the issuers of securities. This means that the financial firm that sponsors the securitization enjoys significant leverage over rating agencies. The ratings shopping that ensued – in which sponsors pitted one agency against another to lower ratings standards – represents regulatory capital arbitrage by any other name.[71] Lawmakers merely delegated to rating agencies a core regulatory function of policing which investments are safe enough for banks to purchase.[72] Financial firms then played rating agencies off one another just as they would when faced with the choice of any other regulators with overlapping jurisdictions. Chapter 5 also highlighted reports that some investment banks were able to reverse engineer the formulas rating agencies used to assign ratings to complex asset-backed securities. This enabled those firms to stuff even more risk into certain securitization tranches and to lower the effectiveness of bank capital rules even further.[73]

Securitization and accounting gamesmanship

Banks engaged in other regulatory capital arbitrage strategies beyond those listed in Chapter 5. One of the principal purposes of securitization vehicles has been to allow financial institutions to move assets off their balance sheets. Under the relevant accounting standard, if a firm disposes of assets to a securitization vehicle in a "true sale" for bankruptcy purposes and the firm retains only minimal control over the securitization vehicle, then it no longer must count those assets on its balance sheet.[74] Accounting standards, however, are built to be gamed, and the Panic of 2007–2008 revealed the dangers of the games that financial institutions played.[75] Many financial institutions continued to bear the risk of loans and securities that had been moved off their balance sheet.[76] Financial disclosure thus provided little warning of the risk to firms from these phantom assets, which risk suddenly re-materialized.[77]

Three accounting games that firms played with securitization merit special attention.

NON-CONSOLIDATION

First, firms could avoid "consolidating" certain securitization vehicles (called "variable interest entities" or "VIEs" in the accounting literature) on their balance sheet despite being under obligations to backstop losses for securities issued by those vehicles. For example, a financial institution that sponsored an asset-backed commercial paper vehicle might provide liquidity or credit support for that vehicle, which means it would incur liabilities if securities issued by that vehicle declined in value. Financial institutions took the position that the probability of making payments under these guarantees was sufficiently small so that they did not have to treat these obligations as a balance sheet liability.[78]

In addition, financial institutions may have been subject to "moral recourse" to cover losses on these securities being issued; although the firm would have no contractual obligation to pay investors, the marketplace expected that the firm would step in should extreme losses occur. Again, because financial institutions judged that the probability of liability was low, indeterminate, or non-existent, they decided that they did not need to treat these moral recourse obligations as a balance sheet liability.[79] However, these supposedly low probability events materialized during the Panic of 2008.[80]

VALUING OF RESIDUAL INTERESTS

Financial institutions used securitization for accounting games in a second way. In many securitizations, the financial institution that sold assets to a securitization vehicle would also purchase some of the resultant asset-backed securities. So long as this retained interest was sufficiently small, the seller would also not have to consolidate the securitization vehicle on its balance sheet. (Otherwise, the seller might have to count the securities issued in the securitization that were purchased by other parties on its balance sheet.) Of course the retained interests would be an asset for the seller, but the seller often had considerable discretion in valuing this retained interest – particularly in the absence of market prices for the asset-backed securities. Empirical research indicates that financial institutions often used discretion to overvalue these retained interests and inflate the gains from the sale of the assets.[81]

TIMING AND "WINDOW DRESSING"

The third accounting game involved financial institutions playing with the timing of transactions. Empirical studies show that financial institutions timed various shadow banking transactions to move assets and liabilities off their balance sheets just before the end of financial quarters, when the balance sheet snapshot would be taken.[82] This presents two problems. First, their snapshot nature means that balance sheets would not reflect the risk that existed on an institution's books for most of a quarter but that vanished only a few days before quarter's end. At first blush, this might not seem to be a disclosure problem, assuming firms appropriately and permanently moved assets off balance sheet via a securitization. However, if in any particular quarter the institution was unable to dispose of assets – for example, because the securitization market dried up – balance sheets would suddenly balloon.[83]

Even worse, many firms were not appropriately and permanently disposing of assets, but instead agreed to repurchase the assets at a future date. The sole purpose of these transactions was to "window dress" the financial statements to remove assets temporarily just before a quarter's end. This practice achieved notoriety in the wake of Lehman Brothers' collapse. An investigation of the investment bank's accounting uncovered an elaborate scheme in which Lehman Brothers management used repos to move assets off the firm's balance sheet just before quarterly reports. The assets would then reappear on the firm's balance sheet just after the quarter. The firm used creative accounting to book these repos as sales to mask its leverage just as the global financial crisis hit.[84]

The bubble accelerator: Regulatory Instability Hypothesis redux

Spirals of regulatory stimulus and regulatory arbitrage fueled the growth of the component markets of the shadow banking system and then fused them together. The legal history of shadow banking stretches back into the 1970s. Yet, these spirals appear to have started to spin with increased velocity in the decade before the Panic of 2007–2008. As the Regulatory Instability Hypothesis would predict, regulatory stimulus, regulatory arbitrage, and booming asset markets appear to have generated strong feedback effects.

Many of the most prominent statutory events in shadow banking "deregulation" or regulatory stimulus occurred either in the years just before or as the U.S. real estate bubble formed. Consider how the following congressional statutes, impacted the growth of shadow banking markets:

> *1999: the Gramm-Leach Bliley Act repealed the Glass-Steagall wall;*
> *2000: Congress enacts the Commodity Futures Modernization Act and exempts OTC derivatives from various state and federal laws;*
> *2005: Congress exempts swaps from various provisions of Bankruptcy Code.*

Arthur Wilmarth attributes much of the meteoric growth in securitization markets from 1990 through the Panic of 2007–2008 to the erosion and eventual collapse of Glass-Steagall and the rise of large financial conglomerates. He cites the raw data from the United States:

- total amounts of outstanding residential mortgage-backed securities rose from $1.13 trillion to $4.3 trillion from 1991 to 2007;
- private label residential mortgage-backed securities and asset-backed securities backed by consumer debt increased from $300 billion to $3.2 trillion over this same time period; and
- outstanding commercial mortgage-backed securities rose from $100 billion in 1996 to $360 billion in 2003 to $780 billion in 2007 (while the total amount of commercial mortgages over this eleven year window went from $1.05 trillion to $3.3 trillion).[85]

He then underscores the crucial role that large complex financial conglomerates, which formed as Glass-Steagall deteriorated, played in the expansion of these securitization markets.[86]

All three statutes in this Deregulatory Big Bang contributed to the growth of the OTC derivative market, and credit derivatives in general. Figure 11.1 displays the meteoric growth of credit default swaps (measured by notional amount), with a marked rise after the 2005 Bankruptcy Code changes.

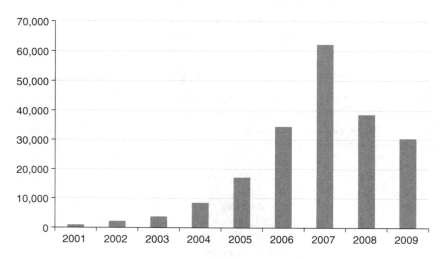

Figure 11.1 Notional amount of credit default swaps outstanding (in U.S.$ billions).[87]

During this same time period, other major episodes of regulatory stimulus jolted shadow banking markets. As Chapter 5 outlined, Basel II and its "do it yourself" capital regulations for certain large banks came into effect in various European countries. This allowed some of the largest banks in the world to set their capital requirements according to their proprietary risk models. This permitted European banks to make riskier investments, including in derivatives tied to U.S. real estate markets, while flaws in the models hid the latent risks.[88]

Basel II did not come into effect for U.S. banks until after the crisis. However, in 2004, the U.S. SEC chose to apply this same internal models approach to the capital rules for large financial conglomerates in the United States as part of its new "Consolidated Supervised Entity" program. The conglomerates promptly increased their leverage by substantial amounts. Moreover, they used the same computer based risk models both to set capital requirements and to price asset-backed securities and derivatives products.[89] Shadow banking instruments, particularly repos, served as principal tools by which these megafirms levered up.[90]

Meanwhile, in the decade before the crisis, U.S. legislators and regulators ignored warning signs of overheating housing markets and excessive household and financial institution leverage.[91] Efforts to regulate complex mortgage products resulted only in weak and belated interagency guidance, issued just as the crisis materialized.[92] Senior regulators, such as Federal Reserve Chairman Alan Greenspan, stymied efforts to regulate subprime mortgage lending, asset-backed securities, and derivatives markets.[93]

Legislators and regulators not only ignored overheating housing markets and household and financial institution borrowing, they actively facilitated and encouraged it. Consider the incremental regulatory interpretations outlined above, by which the Federal Reserve allowed conglomerates to cause their bank affiliates to extend credit to subprime mortgage affiliates. Moreover, Chapter 6 detailed how in 2004 regulators and members of Congress pushed Freddie and Fannie (while executives at those firms pulled) to invest in subprime mortgages and derivatives based on those mortgages.[94] Figure 6.1 in Chapter 6 shows a marked uptick in the total volume of subprime mortgages in this same time period.

Several scholars argue that securitization during this same time period became less a tool for transferring risk and much more a device for regulatory capital arbitrage. One 2008 study (described in Chapter 5) points to how much risk from securitization stayed within the financial system. Close to 50 percent of the senior and a majority of the subordinated tranches of CDOs were owned by banks, thrifts, government-sponsored entities, broker-dealers, and other regulated entities.[95]

A 2009 study looks at the $1.25 trillion ABCP market at the time of the crisis. The study notes that, due to the guarantees provided to ABCP investment vehicles by financial institution sponsors, investors suffered less than 5 percent of the losses, with the balance of the risk remaining with sponsors.[96] Recall, however, that these sponsors held little to no regulatory capital against these guarantees.[97]

A granular look at particular financial firms yields an even more troubling picture. In its 2007 Annual Report, AIG disclosed that $379 billion of its $527 billion exposure on credit default swaps on AAA-rated asset-backed securities written by its Financial Products unit (the business which ultimately brought this insurance conglomerate to its knees in the crisis) stemmed from derivatives written to provide financial institutions with capital relief and not for hedging.[98] This capital relief business was primarily for European firms.[99] In essence, AIG's credit derivative unit was a merchant of regulatory capital arbitrage – with disastrous consequences. Meanwhile, in 2008, the IMF documented a doubling in the size of the balance sheets of ten very large financial institutions from 2004 to 2007. Yet the IMF noted that, over the same period, the risk on the balance sheet of these firms increased only slightly.[100]

Scholars argue that all these data indicate that the shadow banking system did not transfer or spread risk, but instead recycled, concentrated, and concealed it within financial institutions. Firms passed risk back and forth to one another via long daisy chains of shadow banking instruments.[101] Two business school professors thus conclude that regulatory capital arbitrage, not credit risk transfer, was the primary driver of securitization in the four years before the Panic of 2007–2008.[102]

Law-bending and breaking along the securitization pipeline

In several cases, regulatory capital arbitrage enabled by shadow banking instruments shaded into efforts to deceive regulators and investors. Exhibit A takes the form of Lehman Brothers' use of the now infamous "Repo 105" transaction to cloak risky assets on its balance sheet.[103] Note, however, that the government has yet to prosecute any Lehman employee for this transaction. This presents the legal aftermath of the Panic of 2007–2008 in microcosm. The massive financial losses during the crisis generated a widespread belief shared by policymakers, scholars, journalists, and the general public that financial institutions engaged in systematic deception of individual mortgage borrowers and institutional investors all across the shadow banking network. Yet, the aftermath of the crisis has witnessed few criminal prosecutions of financial institutions and their employees.[104] Explanations for this disconnect between public perception and the criminal docket include the following:

- excessive risk-taking by financial institutions may have been stupid, but not necessarily illegal;[105]
- prosecutors face daunting standards of proof in criminal cases;[106]
- government officials fear the negative economic consequences of seeking severe penalties against financial institutions during a credit crunch (a phenomenon now labeled as "too-big-to-prosecute" or "too-big-to-jail");[107] and
- government officials may have been reluctant to provoke politically powerful Wall Street firms.[108]

Despite the lack of criminal prosecutions, public civil suits by U.S. federal and state governments against large financial institutions have proliferated. Many of these suits have ended in settlement purgatory, in which a financial institution agrees to pay fines in the hundreds of millions or even billions of U.S. dollars, but refuses to admit any wrongdoing. These unsettling settlements mean that questions on private and public culpability for losses in shadow banking markets may never be officially answered.[109] Even so, these numerous public civil suits, together with journalist accounts, provide disturbing evidence of massive deception by financial institutions throughout the shadow banking network. The following provides a thumbnail sketch of alleged fraud and law breaking at every node of the securitization pipeline.

Deception in the origination of mortgages. Both prosecutors and scholars have accused the brokers and mortgage lenders who originated the mortgages fed into the securitization pipeline of deceiving mortgage borrowers,[110] discriminating against minorities by offering them higher risk loan products,[111] and other illegal predatory lending.[112] Public civil fraud suits against mortgage originators have thus far resulted in settlements totaling hundreds of millions of dollars.[113] Moreover, a large portion of the settlements between federal bank regulators with respect to abuses in mortgage markets during the bubble years may remain obscured because of "no press release clauses" contained in the settlement agreements. Critics charge that this lack of candor by the FDIC may stem from the agency's desire to hide settlements favorable to industry.[114]

Deception of investors and guarantors of mortgage-backed securities. Another wave of public civil fraud suits has focused on how mortgage lenders and investment banks deceived investors who purchased mortgage-backed securities regarding the quality of the underlying mortgages. For example, in October 2012, the New York State Attorney General sued J.P. Morgan (as successor to

Bear Stearns) under the Martin Act alleging deception of investors in residential mortgage-backed securities.[115] Federal prosecutors brought multiple suits on behalf of government entities (including Freddie Mac and Fannie Mae after the government assumed control of those two firms) that purchased or issued guarantees for these mortgages.[116] This latter category of lawsuit has targeted major banks, including Bank of America (which had purchased the mortgage lender Countrywide)[117] and Wells Fargo.[118] Bank of America later agreed to settle with Fannie Mae for almost $11 billion.[119]

Deception of CDO investors and derivative counterparties. The government has brought more complex cases alleging misconduct even further down the securitization pipeline. These public civil suits allege that financial conglomerates deceived investors purchasing CDOs and other credit derivatives based on mortgage-backed securities. Until 2013, the SEC's 2010 litigation against Goldman Sachs over the ABACUS transactions (first described in Chapter 4)[120] represented one of the few examples of this category of lawsuit.[121] Then, in February 2013, the U.S. Department of Justice launched a civil suit against the rating agency Standard & Poors alleging that it defrauded investors by knowingly giving unwarranted high ratings to mortgage-related CDOs. Several state attorneys general joined this suit.[122]

Financial institution liability for private lawsuits alleging fraud and deception in shadow banking markets may ultimately dwarf liability to the government.[123] The full scope of this liability may take years more to assess, as litigations wind their way through U.S. courts. Yet early evidence produced by these lawsuits indicates that financial firms may have known of fraudulent or deceptive conduct in selling shadow banking instruments.[124]

Compliance rot

From one vantage point, the waves of law-bending and law-breaking during the bubbles preceding the Panic of 2007–2008 stem from unique characteristics of the shadow banking markets. For example, scholars have argued that mortgage lenders became increasingly willing to deceive borrowers when they sold those mortgages to securitization vehicles. When lenders no longer bore the risk of borrower default, they cared less about inducing borrowers to assume the risk of exotic mortgages they could not afford to repay.[125] Similarly, the trading of many shadow banking instruments, such as asset-backed securities and credit derivatives, in thin, opaque markets frustrated price discovery. This, in turn, provided camouflage for fraud and deception, as fewer investor "eyes" watched these markets.[126]

Yet taking a step back reveals that the recent outbreaks fit the historical pattern of epidemics of fraud and regulatory arbitrage frenzies during bubble periods. Shadow banking markets served as Twenty-first Century instruments on which very old bubble themes played. Consider the three lenses from Chapter 4 that explain compliance rot during bubble periods:

Undermining rational deterrence. Chapter 4 analyzed how the dynamics of a bubble provide immediate benefits to breaking the law, but push expected liability further into the future. On one side of the ledger, individuals at financial firms enjoyed immediate and substantial financial rewards for taking excessive risk or inappropriately peddling shadow banking products to customers. For example, recent college graduates brokering subprime loans for mortgage lenders received extraordinary commissions and bonuses based on the yield and volume of loans they produced. They faced incredible incentives to cheat borrowers and fabricate loan documents, with some of these young Turks earning $30,000 to $40,000 per month.[127]

At the other end of the financial food chain are traders at investment funds and large financial conglomerates. Here, too, compensation and bubbling markets created unhealthy incentives for risk-taking.[128] Margaret Blair provocatively argues that compensation packages drove individuals at financial institutions to increase their firms' leverage and intentionally to inflate a bubble.[129] Of course, part of the risks that firms and traders assume is legal risk. The massive returns made possible by a bubble skewed the incentives of individuals to bend and break the law.

At the same time, the prospect of getting caught receded into the future. As Chapter 4 noted, a rising tide of prices tends to cover up excessive risk-taking and even fraud. Rising prices in the shadow banking bubble delayed the moment in which investors and regulators could detect excessive risk or misconduct. When regulators' examination and enforcement resources fail to keep pace with the growth of financial firms and transactions, enforcement becomes diluted. Financial firms and their employees recognize this and potential lawbreakers adjust their calculations on whether to comply with legal rules accordingly.[130]

Behavioral biases. Rising prices may have also triggered behavioral biases. Continued investment returns may have caused market participants to discount excessively the risk of getting caught, just as it may have caused regulators to underestimate the risk of fraud and law-breaking.

Norms. Chapter 4 also explored how changing norms in the financial community may undermine legal compliance. The latest round of bubbles shared with previous bubbles some of the same dynamics that weaken compliance norms. These included a youth movement in the financial industry (from mortgage lenders to Fab Tourre at Goldman Sachs).[131] These bubbles also witnessed an influx of first time mortgage borrowers that created norm asymmetries between these investors and the financial firms with whom they transacted. Many borrowers had different expectations about trust than the financial professionals on the other side of the table.[132] Chapter 4 also discussed how norm asymmetries existed even among sophisticated institutional investors. It gave the example of German banks having different norms of fair dealing from the Wall Street banks that sold CDOs to them.[133]

In short, although it is tempting to see law-bending and breaking in the current age as a product of the unique markets and instruments of our day, deeper dynamics also helped undermine obedience to the law.

Money: the emergence of a shadow monetary transmission belt, financial regulation, and herding

All of this regulatory stimulus, regulatory arbitrage, and even law-breaking had three dramatic effects. First, regulatory stimulus and regulatory arbitrage triggered explosive growth in the various markets for shadow banking instruments. The sheer magnitude of this growth, already described in this chapter and the preceding one, will become even more apparent in the illustrations that follow.

Second, regulatory stimulus and regulatory arbitrage caused these markets to fuse together into a complex system for pumping high octane credit into the economy. Figure 10.5 from the previous chapter (which will be reproduced in a moment) diagrams how the various shadow banking markets and intermediaries fit together like a giant web or tinker toy set. This funneled credit in one direction – to financial institutions and ultimately to individual and commercial borrowers in real estate and other asset markets – and credit risk in the other.

Third, by creating a new means to pump credit into the economy, the shadow banking system exerted dramatic macroeconomic effects. By creating and fostering this system, regulatory stimulus, regulatory arbitrage, and even law-breaking transformed the monetary environment and supercharged monetary expansion. However, policymakers dimly understood the extent of this monetary expansion, let alone the role that regulatory change played in it.

Financial institutions and the leverage cycle

Shadow banking and leverage

The shadow banking expanded the money supply in the two related ways – which were previewed in Chapter 9's discussion of how financial regulation can have monetary effects. In the first pathway, shadow banking markets allowed financial institutions to dramatically increase their leverage. Increased financial leverage, as Chapter 9 explains, can supercharge monetary expansion. By borrowing and re-lending to one another, financial institutions create long credit chains. As the leverage of each institution along the chain increases, the supply of money increases geometrically.

Chapter 9 explained this through the simple example of lower reserve requirements along a chain of deposit-taking banks (see Figure 11.2). With a 10 percent reserve requirement, an initial central bank loan ultimately generates $10,000 of money. With a 5 percent reserve requirement, an initial central bank loan generates $20,000 of money.

The same effect occurs when leverage increases along chains of shadow banking intermediaries. Chapters 9 and 10 detailed how financial institutions borrow and thus increase their leverage not only through issuing deposits and borrowing through standard loan agreements, but also via shadow banking instruments such as short-term repo agreements. Moreover, these firms can effectively borrow by selling assets to securitization vehicles, such as asset-backed

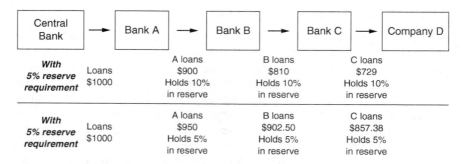

		A loans	B loans	C loans
With 5% reserve requirement	Loans $1000	$900 Holds 10% in reserve	$810 Holds 10% in reserve	$729 Holds 10% in reserve
With 5% reserve requirement	Loans $1000	$950 Holds 5% in reserve	$902.50 Holds 5% in reserve	$857.38 Holds 5% in reserve

Figure 11.2 Money creation via a central bank loan.

commercial paper conduits (while retaining contingent liabilities under those "sales"). At the same time, financial firms lend through repos and by purchasing bonds, including asset-backed securities. Hedging and offloading credit risk with credit derivatives allows financial firms to lend further.

Chapter 9 also unpacked how lowered margin or collateral requirements for instruments such as repo agreements and credit derivatives increase both:

- the effective "carrying capacity" of these instruments in terms of extending credit and transferring credit risk; and
- the effective leverage of the financial institutions borrowing through these instruments.

By increasing financial leverage, these shadow banking instruments can fuel monetary expansion in much the same way that intra-bank lending does in the traditional depository banking sector. Compare now side by side the chain of depository banks with the chain (or web) of shadow banking intermediaries depicted below (originally Figure 10.5) (see Figure 11.3).

The leverage cycle

Not only did the shadow banking system facilitate financial institution leverage, it also provided a new mechanism on which the leverage cycle could gyrate. Recall that Chapter 9 discussed theoretical macroeconomic research that posited that leverage in the economy moves through cycles. This work by Geanakopolos, Kiyotaki, and Moore, and others implies that the external shocks to the financial system would be amplified by this cyclical behavior.

Leverage cycles are no longer theoretical constructs. Looking at data over the last two decades, economists Tobias Adrian and Hyun Song Shin have found evidence of large U.S. investment banks increasing their leverage during asset price booms and deleveraging during price busts.[134] For example, their diagram (Figure 11.4) represents the mean leverage of eighteen large financial institutions

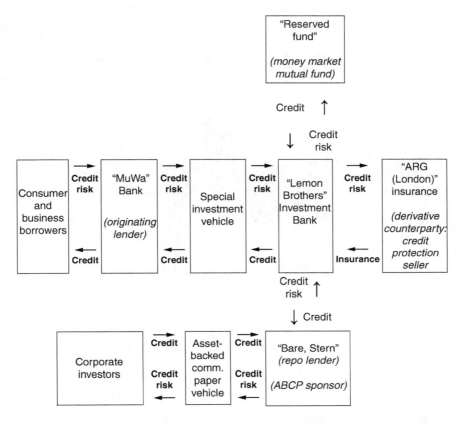

Figure 11.3 Credit risk transfer and credit provision in the shadow banking network.

(the "dealers" who have a daily trading relationship with the Federal Reserve) from 1986 to 2007.

The data depict a clear trend: these large institutions supersize their leverage as markets boom and then dramatically shed leverage when debt-fueled crises hit (the U.S. Savings & Loan crisis in 1987, the Asian crisis in 1998, and the Panic of 2007–2008).

Regulation may have exacerbated in this procyclicality. Chapter 7 outlined scholarship that contends that the Basel I and Basel II capital regimes have been inherently procyclical and encouraged financial institutions to increase their balance sheets during booms and to shrink them during busts.[135]

The creation of money instruments

The growth shadow banking system promoted monetary expansion in a second way, by creating more instruments with money-like features. Law professor

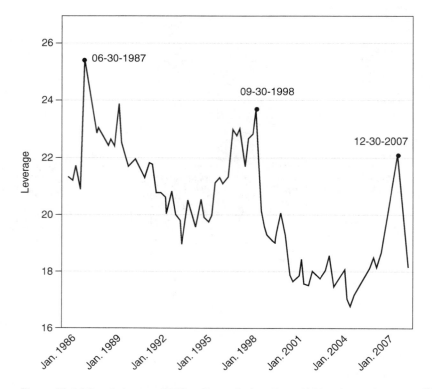

Figure 11.4 Mean leverage of U.S. primary dealers (June 1986 to September 2008).[136]

Morgan Ricks collected data on the gross amounts of various money instruments ("money claims") from 1991 through 2010. His data include both traditional money instruments, such as currency, Treasury bills, and government-insured bank deposits. The data also include "private" money claims, which consist primarily of shadow banking instruments, such as primary dealer repos, asset-backed commercial paper, and money market mutual funds. His results, shown in Figure 11.5, reveal startling growth of these money-like shadow banking instruments starting in 1993. The rate of growth accelerated further between 2002 and 2003.

This data does not even include senior asset-backed securities (other than asset-backed commercial paper), which also offered money-like features by virtue of theoretically low credit risk and high liquidity. Asset-backed securities themselves experienced an explosive growth spurt between 2000 and the onset of the Panic of 2007–2008, as indicated in Figure 11.6, created by Adrian and Shin.

The preceding two figures provide evidence consistent with massive financial industry leveraging during the bubble years in the first decade of this century followed by massive deleveraging when the Panic of 2007–2008 struck.

The figures are also consistent with financial institutions herding into particular asset classes, such as asset-backed securities, money market funds, and

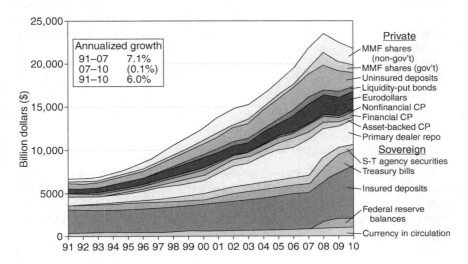

Figure 11.5 Gross money-claims outstanding.[137]

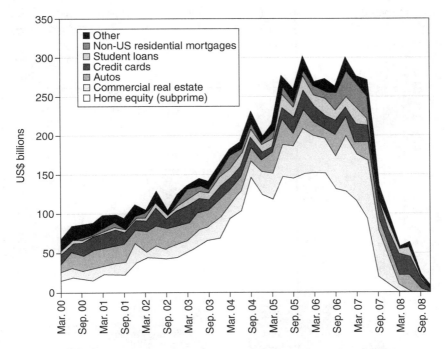

Figure 11.6 New issuances of asset-backed securities by type, 2000–2009.[138]

repos, creating liquidity. Chapter 7 described how various financial regulations can promote investor and financial institution herding into liquidity. These herd promoting legal rules included: capital requirements, legal preferences for certain instruments (such as the Bankruptcy Code exemptions for repos and swaps), deposit insurance, and other explicit and implicit government guarantees. Many of these regulations likely contributed to the dramatic stampede into "liquid" shadow banking markets. Chapter 7 also argued that herding into asset classes can promote the twin effects of bubbles and bank-runs-in-reverse.

A shadow monetary transmission belt

Fitting all this data together clarifies how the shadow banking system can have the same macroeconomic impact as depository banks. The previous chapter highlighted Gerald Corrigan's claim that banking was special because it performed three unique functions.[139] This chapter fleshes out how shadow banking came to perform the third function: serving as a transmission belt for monetary policy. By the eve of the global financial crisis, this new transmission belt came to rival that of traditional depository banking. Adrian and Shin used Federal Reserve data to show that in the United States, by the second quarter of 2007, the assets held by "market based intermediaries" (including the government-sponsored entities Freddie Mac and Fannie, broker dealers, and issuers of asset-backed securities) exceeded the assets of traditional depository banks (see Figure 11.7).

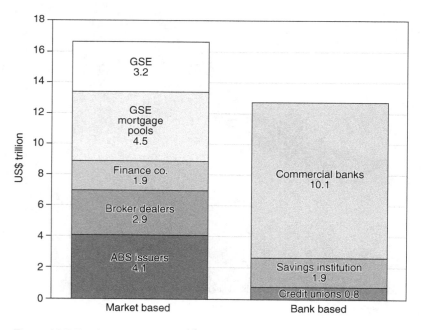

Figure 11.7 Total assets as of 2007.[140]

The rapid growth of this shadow transmission belt does not mean, unfortunately, that central banks paid careful heed. As Margaret Blair notes, in the years
before the 2008 financial crisis the Federal Reserve moved in the opposite direction. Instead of seeking more inclusive metrics of the money supply, in 2006 the
Federal Reserve stopped tracking M3, a broader measure of the money supply in
the United States. Even M3 measures some – but not all – of the liquidity
injected by the shadow banking system.[141] Blair then cites estimates by other
economists that indicate that, at roughly this moment, M3 began to radically
diverge from, and shoot above, narrower measures of the money supply. Figure
11.8 shows Federal Reserve data on changes in M1 and M2 from 2004 to 2013,
the Federal Reserve data in M3 until 2006 (when it stopped tracking this figure),
and one economist's estimate of M3 since that period ("M3 shadow stats").

What this means is that the Federal Reserve stopped tracking broader measures of the money supply (which would have themselves underestimated the
effects of shadow banking) just as the shadow banking was about to fuel dramatic monetary expansion. As Chapter 9 concluded, the central bank pilots
decided to turn off some of their instruments just as their plane entered a gathering storm. Moreover, they missed how the plane suddenly accelerated and
pitched skyward thanks to new turbocharged engines.

Why did the Federal Reserve turn off the instruments? Part of the reason lies
in the fact that broader measures of the money supply are harder to count (for
example, M3 includes Eurodollars held overseas).[143] Part of the reason might be
that M3 appears historically to have moved reasonably parallel to narrower
measures of the money supply.[144] In a masterstroke of bad luck, it was only when
the central bank stopped watching that the divergence began and the bubble
started to metastasize.

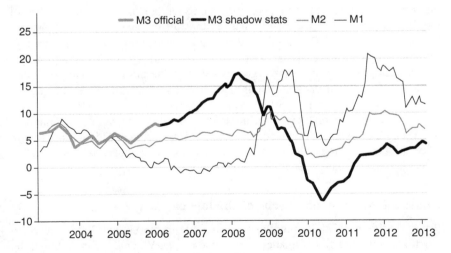

Figure 11.8 M1, M2, M3, and estimated M3.[142]

Yet there is perhaps a more fundamentally troubling reason that the Federal Reserve missed understanding and measuring the full effects of the shadow banking system. Shadow banking had its origins in regulatory change. It was birthed and suckled by regulatory stimulus and regulatory arbitrage. Both of these dynamics unfolded both incrementally (for example, the slow drip of interpretative changes that allowed banks to participate in asset-backed securities markets) and in Big Bangs (the federal statutes that repealed Glass-Steagall and stimulated derivative markets from 1999 to 2005). As noted before in Chapter 9, macroeconomists tend to pay little heed to legal change. This time that proved catastrophic.

The Regulatory Instability Hypothesis and a perfect storm

Ignorance of the shadow banking sector proved perilous because of the potential for awesome feedback loops. The rise of the shadow banking system provides a master class in the Regulatory Instability Hypothesis. Regulatory stimulus, regulatory arbitrage, and law-breaking fueled the growth of an alternate credit system. In turn (as Chapter 9 underscored), the expansion of credit fueled the growth of a bubble in real estate and shadow banking instruments tied to real estate. The inflating bubble promoted more regulatory stimulus (for example, the 2005 bankruptcy exemptions for derivatives and the political pressure on Freddie and Fannie to invest in subprime mortgages and subprime-mortgage-backed securities). It also appears to have fueled more regulatory arbitrage, as financial firms increasingly used asset-backed securities, derivatives, and repos to game capital regulations and increase and mask their leverage.

Increased financial institution leverage simultaneously left those firms exposed to an economic downturn. Meanwhile, the opaque nature of shadow banking and the fact that regulatory arbitrage cloaked much of its leverage meant that both regulators and the marketplace dimly understood the vulnerability of the financial system. This opacity masked the full monetary effects of shadow banking. The growth of a partially hidden banking system meant it was harder to see how the surge in real estate prices was driven not by fundamentals, but by credit. Rising asset prices submerged mistakes in the pricing of real estate and shadow banking instruments. Rising asset prices made further leverage, regulatory stimulus, and regulatory arbitrage appear safe.

At the same time, financial firms herded into investments in the same markets: real estate and real estate-related securities and derivatives. This herding drove prices higher. Herding, in turn, made these asset classes appear safer and instruments in these markets appear more liquid.

Runs: the collapse and rescue of shadow banking

It was a mirage. In 2006, the real estate bubble in the United States started to burst. By 2007, the global financial crisis had begun. When the bubble burst, the crisis spread along the nodes of the shadow banking web – from initial defaults on exotic mortgages, to losses on asset-backed securities, to losses on CDOs and credit derivatives. The full story of the financial crisis will engage scholars for decades. For purposes of this book, it suffices to note how the shadow banking system mirrored a traditional banking crisis. A system created largely to sidestep bank regulations, and which benefitted from the loosening of those regulations, ultimately suffered from the same historical fate as traditional depository banks.

Indeed, the losses on subprime mortgages and mortgage-backed securities triggered intertwined solvency and liquidity crises for financial institutions throughout the shadow banking web. A number of large U.S. financial institutions in every corner of the shadow system either became insolvent or would have become insolvent but for federal intervention. It is difficult to untangle where solvency crises ended and liquidity crises began. Many of the insolvent firms suffered liquidity problems as short-term financing dried up. At the same time, the failure or looming failure of these firms triggered liquidity crises.[145]

Shadow bank runs

As the subprime mortgage crisis intensified, the markets for shadow banking began to freeze. Economists Gary Gorton and Andrew Metrick describe the freeze in the market for asset-backed securities and repos as "shadow banking runs." As the value of asset-backed securities and the creditworthiness of repo borrowers became harder to measure, investors started withdrawing funds from these markets. In the case of repos, lenders demanded much larger haircuts (essentially more collateral) from borrowers or refused to lend altogether.[146]

Other shadow banking instruments suffered similar fates. Many hedge funds that heavily invested in asset-backed securities hemorrhaged capital, as investors made redemption requests. UBS closed its internal hedge fund. Bear Stearns all but collapsed because of losses suffered by two hedge funds that it sponsored. Bear Stearns provided a textbook case of moral recourse when the investment bank pumped funds into these "independent" entities. Other hedge funds foundered.[147] Investors also began a massive sell-off of money market mutual funds, once thought to be as safe and liquid as bank deposit accounts. Two money market mutual funds "broke the buck" (including the Reserve Fund, the first ever money market mutual fund, which suffered massive losses due to the collapse of Lehman Brothers).[148]

Gorton and Metrick point out that this dynamic of investor withdrawal from markets mirrored the logic of a traditional bank run. The same asset–liability mismatch that afflicts depository banks now came to haunt shadow banking markets. Many institutional investors sought to withdraw funds either to keep their own operations afloat in a credit storm or because they feared that if they did not withdraw before other investors, the cupboard would be stripped bare. The long chains of shadow banking instruments made it next to impossible to sort which instruments were affected by subprime mortgage defaults. Asset-backed securities and other shadow banking products thus became difficult to value. Fire sales began, demand in these markets dried up, and the shadow banking system froze.[149]

The crisis was not merely a liquidity crisis. Investment banks, regulated banks and insurance companies, and government-sponsored entities suffered debilitating losses on their investments in asset-backed securities and credit derivatives. They also lost vast sums in their investments in one another.[150] One can get a very rough sense of the extent of the solvency dimension of the crisis (as opposed to the liquidity aspect) by counting those firms that required not short-term government loans or guarantees, but rather longer-term government equity injections. Moreover, many firms still remain under government control (like Freddie and Fannie) or remain financially sick long after the bank run phase of the crisis ended.

Shadow bank bailouts

The government interventions not only provide a window into how the shadow banking system suffered bank-style liquidity and solvency crises. Moreover, these federal interventions represented adaptations of the same tools used to address traditional bank failures. The Federal government invested in, and effectively assumed control of, financial institutions that failed because of shadow banking instruments. This is eerily similar to how the FDIC resolves failing banks. At the same time, the Federal Reserve provided the equivalent of deposit insurance for shadow banking instruments and acted as lender/liquidity provider-of-last resort, which are the traditional policy tools for managing a bank run.[151] An examination of the various components of the federal intervention reveals that government interventions reached into every cranny of the shadow banking system. A list of the markets targeted by the various Treasury Department and Federal Reserve interventions reads like a genealogy of shadow banking instruments and institutions: asset-backed securities, asset-backed commercial paper, credit derivatives, money market mutual funds, and repos.

Indeed, interventions to rescue depository banks were eclipsed by actions taken to support non-depository institutions. Some of the largest and most salient of Federal interventions involved non-depository institutions and thus required either emergency statutory authorization from Congress or creative interpretations by Federal agencies of their statutory authority. Tables 11.1 and 11.2 (below) summarize various Federal Reserve interventions to support non-depository institutions. Taking a step back from the details reveals a striking image; tracing these interventions provides a virtual map of the entire shadow banking system.

Treasury Department investments: "resolving" shadow banks?

The actions of the U.S. Treasury in support of non-depository institutions have been more politically controversial because they are simpler to understand and involve a direct use of taxpayer funds. Indeed the political maelstrom in the wake of the bailouts centers on the Troubled-Asset-Relief Program (TARP), a $700 billion fund created by the Emergency Economic Stability Act of 2008.[152] The U.S. Treasury used the TARP fund to make loans to, and equity investments in, non-depository institutions, such as AIG,[153] Freddie Mac, and Fannie Mae[154] (not to mention several automotive companies). These equity investments and the subsequent control exercised by the government over failing institutions roughly resemble the process that bank regulators (such as the FDIC) take to "resolve" failing depository institutions. The principal difference is that the FDIC has clear statutory authority, a formal process, and experience assuming control of failing banks. By contrast, the TARP actions and pre-TARP interventions were much more ad hoc; law professors Steven Davidoff and David Zaring labeled them "regulation by deal."[155]

The Treasury Department also used TARP funds for the "Public Private Investment Program for Legacy Assets," a program as convoluted as its name suggests. Under this program, the FDIC conducted auctions of illiquid asset-backed securities on the books of depository institutions, and then issued a guarantee on those securities to purchasers. Meanwhile, the Treasury Department used TARP funds to make "co-investments" with private sector purchasers of these asset-backed securities.[156] The mix of loans and guarantees are akin to deposit insurance for asset-backed securities.

Federal Reserve actions: deposit insurance and liquidity provider of last resort for shadow banking markets

The Federal Reserve also provided loans and credit support resembling deposit insurance, while also playing the role of liquidity provider of last resort for shadow banking markets. It undertook a series of obscure and convoluted but far-reaching and extraordinary interventions, relying on its emergency powers under Section 13(3) of the Federal Reserve Act. The Federal Reserve's support of non-depository institutions has been no less significant than that of the U.S. Treasury, but came in much more complex and esoteric packages. The alphabet soup of labels of the Federal Reserve initiatives during the crisis should not obscure the fact that these programs too reached into every corner of the shadow banking system. The Federal Reserve's actions came in two waves: first a series of customized loans and guarantees to financial conglomerates and then a series of complex facilities.

TARGETED INTERVENTIONS: CUSTOMIZED LENDING AND GUARANTEE
FACILITIES

The Federal Reserve's support of the shadow banking system began in March 2008, when its Board of Governors, for the first time since the Great Depression, exercised its 13(3) powers and authorized emergency loans to a non-depository institution, Bear Stearns. The Bear Stearns intervention set a precedent. Table 11.1 lists the bespoke loans and investments that the Federal Reserve made pursuant to its emergency authority under Section 13(3) of the Federal Reserve Act.

Table 11.1 Federal Reserve "bespoke" crisis interventions under Section 13(3) of the Federal Reserve Act[157]

Program name (date)	Description of government action	Highest balance
Bear Stearns Loan (March 14, 2008)	Emergency loan to Bear Stearns from the Federal Reserve's discount window.	U.S.$12.9 billion
Maiden Lane (SPV) (March 2008)	Non-recourse loan that facilitated J.P. Morgan's acquisition of Bear Stearns. Loan was made to a special purpose vehicle that acquired various Bear Stearns assets, primarily asset-backed securities, to guarantee a floor on the losses J.P. Morgan would take on those assets.	U.S.$30 billion
AIG Revolving Credit Facility (September 16, 2008)	Revolving loan to AIG.	U.S.$89.5 billion
AIG Secured Borrowing Facility (October 8, 2008)	Secured loan to AIG.	U.S.$20 billion
Maiden Lane II (SPV) (December 12, 2008)	Funding of special purpose vehicle to purchase residential mortgage-backed securities from AIG.	U.S.$20 billion
Maiden Lane III (SPV) (November 25, 2008)	Funding of special purpose vehicle to purchase the CDOs that received credit protection from credit derivatives provided by AIG Financial Products.	U.S.$28 billion
AIA Aurora LLC and ALICO Holdings LLC (March 2, 2009)	Refinancing and restructuring of previous loans to AIG. Federal Reserve reduced previous loans in exchange for securities in two special purpose vehicles that held all of the common stock of AIG life insurance subsidiaries.	U.S.$25 billion
Citigroup Loss Sharing Facility (November 25, 2008)	Agreement to provide non-recourse loan to backstop $300 billion pool of asset-backed securities that had suffered $50 billion in losses.	U.S.$0
Bank of America Corp. Loss Sharing Facility (January 15, 2009)	Agreement to provide non-recourse loan to backstop $300 billion pool of asset-backed securities owned by Merrill Lynch investment bank that had suffered $50 billion in losses. Bank of America made an emergency acquisition of Merrill Lynch in September 2008.	U.S.$0

If Table 11.1 seems as hard to understand as the description of the various shadow banking instruments in the previous chapter, that is not accidental. In bailing out financial institutions from losses on securitizations, the Federal Reserve in essence became a shadow banker and created a set of loan and guarantee vehicles of its very own. These Rube Goldberg devices represent an attempt to minimize the permanent disruption to the private shadow banking system from government intrusion. Rather than purchase shadow banking instruments directly, the Federal Reserve loaned or issued guarantees to private sector entities. The loans effectively transformed the Federal Reserve into a lender-of-last-resort to participants stuck in frozen markets in shadow banking instruments. These loans also sought to keep key institutions involved in asset-backed securities and credit derivatives afloat. Guarantees of losses on asset-backed securities again represent quasi-deposit insurance for once highly liquid assets. The extensive use of complex securitization vehicles may have reflected a belief among the policymakers that the shadow banking system would have to survive for financial markets to remain intact.[158]

BROADER FACILITIES TO ENTIRE SHADOW BANKING MARKETS

The complexity and opacity of these one-off programs paled in comparison to the series of alphabet soup facilities that the Federal Reserve created to provide loans and guarantees to still broader swaths of the shadow banking sector. Table 11.2 lists the complex loan facilities the Federal Reserve created pursuant to its Section 13(3) powers. As with the one-off programs listed above, many of these facilities essentially created a government-subsidized securitization-style vehicle to provide loans or guarantees to private investors. These actions were taken to encourage investors to continue to extend credit or invest in various shadow banking instruments, including money market mutual funds, asset-backed securities, asset-backed commercial paper, and repos.

The divide between banking and shadow banking further blurred in September 2008, when the remaining U.S. large investment banking firms, Goldman Sachs and Morgan Stanley, began the process to convert into bank holding companies. These firms were thus able to borrow from the Federal Reserve more directly and more cleanly.[159]

The perversity of it all

Behind all the acronyms and fancy structures of the federal interventions lies a stark reality: these federal interventions completed a perverse cycle that should haunt economists and legal scholars. The shadow banking system, which promised to address the economic limitations of banking ended up the victim of the same plagues that have afflicted banks for centuries – bank runs and solvency crises. The perversity becomes apparent when one considers the legal history of shadow banking: this system, created and nurtured by the arbitrage of banking laws and deregulation, ultimately received the same forms of governmental support as regulated banks. This raises not only the specter of moral hazard, but

Table 11.2 Federal Reserve crisis facilities under Section 13(3) of the Federal Reserve Act[160]

Date	13(3) facility (and authorized amount of facility)	Institutions eligible for loans or liquidity support: description of government support	Shadow banking segment directly supported
Spring 2008	Primary Dealer Credit Facility	*Primary dealers in U.S. Treasury securities.* Lending through repurchase transactions, in which primary dealers sell securities to government in exchange for loans from Federal Reserve discount window. Collateral for repos was initially limited to investment grade debt, but was later expanded to include other securities including non-investment grade mortgage-backed securities.[161]	Investment banks
Spring 2008	Term Securities Lending Facility[162]	*Primary dealers in U.S. Treasury securities.* Lending liquid government securities to primary dealers in exchange for certain less liquid securities, including asset-backed securities.[163]	Investment banks
September 2008	Asset-backed Commercial Paper Money Market Mutual Fund Liquidity Facility	*Money market mutual funds (and, indirectly, issuers of asset-backed commercial paper).* Lending to certain bank investors to fund the purchase of asset-backed commercial paper from money market mutual funds.[164]	Money market mutual funds; asset-backed commercial paper issuers
October 2008	Commercial Paper Funding Facility	*Issuers of commercial paper including asset-backed commercial paper.* Providing a liquidity backstop to U.S. issuers of commercial paper through a special purpose vehicle to purchase eligible three-month unsecured and asset-backed commercial paper from eligible issuers.[165]	Asset-backed commercial paper issuers
October 2008	Money Market Investor Funding Facility	*Money market funds.* Extending senior secured loans to special purpose vehicles established by the private sector to purchase money market instruments from investors.[166]	Money market mutual funds
November 2008	Term Asset-backed Securities Loan Facility (U.S.$1 trillion)	*Holders of certain asset-backed securities.* Extending non-recourse loans to holders of asset-backed securities with loans secured only by those securities. New York Federal Reserve to transfer those securities held as collateral to special purpose vehicle.[167]	Issuers and investors in asset-backed securities

creates significant competitive distortions in the marketplace. Shadow banking institutions enjoy all the benefits of banks, but escape most of the regulation. This may afford them a lower cost of capital than entities that provide the same functional economic services.

Lessons

The rise and fall and rise again of banking by any other name have permanently destabilized the architecture of financial regulation both in the United States and abroad. Institutions and markets that perform the same functions, and moreover pose the same severe spillover threats, as banks must be regulated in a similar fashion as banks. If the government safety net is extended, so too must the government regulatory net. The core concerns of banking law – excessive leverage, liquidity crises, and correlated risk-taking – apply equally to the depository and shadow banking sectors. Thus regulators should bring to bear the tools of the banking law trade on the shadow banking system to address these problems: leverage limits and capital requirements, requirements for liquid investments, risk-adjusted premia for "deposit insurance"...

Of course, the rub lies in how to adapt tools from the depository banking world to market based intermediaries. Although the economic risks posed by depository banks and shadow banks are similar they are not the same. Imposing restrictions on the shadow banks that are not reasonably calibrated to counter the spillover costs – whether making them too heavy or too light – creates market distortions and invites regulatory arbitrage.

Furthermore, regulating shadow banking markets will create incentives to push capital deeper into the shadows. The potential negative externalities created whenever financial firms engage in core "banking" functions – credit provision, maturity/liquidity transformation, "money" creation – mean that regulation may be inherently unstable. The managers and creditors of those firms will always have an incentive to externalize the cost of the "bank" failures on the wider economy and taxpayers.

In addition, the prospect of regulated entities participating in shadow bank sectors raises the risk of government subsidies leaking. The government safety net can be extended by banks investing in shadow instruments. This conjures up the usual demons: moral hazard and market distortions. It also creates potential transmission lines for financial crisis contagion.

But this book is not about the last crisis only; it is about how the last crisis replayed the themes of earlier bubbles. The Regulatory Instability Hypothesis came back with a vengeance, with all its elements contributing to destructive bubbles on both sides of the Atlantic. The regulatory stimulus cycle, compliance rot, regulatory arbitrage frenzies, procyclical regulations, and herd-promoting legal rules blazed with particular fury because they worked to create and turbo-charge a parallel credit system. Credit and leverage blew the bubbles larger. The bubbles, in turn, generated more regulatory stimulus, law-breaking, regulatory arbitrage, and herd behavior.

So the question is not how to tinker with financial regulation to re-fight the last war, but how to design legal institutions that can withstand these perennial dynamics that destabilize financial markets and laws.

Notes

1 Beat Balzli, Greek Debt Crisis: How Goldman Sachs Helped Greece to Mask its True Debt, *Der Spiegel Online International*, February 8, 2010, available at www.spiegel.de/international/europe/greek-debt-crisis-how-goldman-sachs-helped-greece-to-mask-its-true-debt-a-676634.html (last visited July 28, 2013).
2 Chapter 7, "Capital requirements."
3 Basil Katz, Money Market Pioneer Bent Cleared of SEC Fraud Charges, Reuters, (November 12, 2012) available at www.reuters.com/article/2012/11/12/us-bent-sec-trial-idUSBRE8AB15F20121112 (last visited July 28, 2013).
4 Regulation Q was found at 12 CFR Pt. 217 (1979).
5 The first money market mutual fund was created in the early 1970s. William A. Birdthistle, Breaking Bucks in Money Market Mutual Funds, 2010 *Wisconsin Law Review* 1155, 1164 (2010).
6 Pub. L. No. 96-221, 94 Stat. 132 (codified as amended in scattered sections of 12 U.S.C.). See R. Alton Gilbert, Requiem for Regulation Q: What It Did and Why It Passed Away, *Federal Reserve Bank St. Louis Review*, 22 (February 1986).
7 Marc Alan Eisner, *The American Political Economy: Institutional Evolution of Market and State*, 183 (2010, Routledge).
8 Patricia A. McCoy, Andrey D. Pavlov, and Susan M. Wachter, Systemic Risk through Securitization: The Result of Deregulation and Regulatory Failure, 41 *Connecticut Law Review* 493, 499 (2009). See also Patricia A. McCoy, Rethinking Disclosure in a World of Risk-Based Pricing, 44 *Harvard Journal on Legislation* 123, 125 (2007).
9 Birdthistle, *supra* note 5, at 1160.
10 Ibid.
11 Ibid.
12 Ibid.
13 Ibid. Valuation of Debt Instruments and Computation of Current Price by Certain Open-End Investment Companies (Money Market Funds), 48 *Federal Register* 32, 555 (July 18, 1983).
14 Bankruptcy Amendments and Federal Judgeship Act of 1984, Pub. L. No. 98-353 (98 Stat. 333).
15 Gary Gorton and Andrew Metrick, Securitized Banking and the Run on Repo, 104 *Journal of Financial Economics* 425 (2012).
16 See Chapter 10, notes 96–9 and accompanying text.
17 Bankruptcy Abuse and Consumer Protection Act of 2005, Pub. L. 109-8 (2005). After the 2005 amendments, a party to one of these derivative contracts is no longer subject to the automatic stay and voidable preferences provisions of the bankruptcy code that would restrict their remedies as a creditor should their counterparty enter bankruptcy. This means that should the counterparty file for bankruptcy, the creditor party in a derivative contract does not face the normal legal restrictions on terminating the derivative contract, accelerating the debtor's obligations, foreclosing on collateral, and exercising set-off rights. Nor is the creditor subject to potential claw-back of pre-bankruptcy payments from the debtor. For a summary of these provisions, See Mark J. Roe, The Derivatives Market's Payment Priorities as Financial Crisis Accelerator, 63 *Stanford Law Review* 539 (2011).
18 David A. Skeel, Jr., Bankruptcy Boundary Games, 4 *Brooklyn Journal of Corporate, Financial and Commercial Law* 1, 10 (2009).

19 Roe, *supra* note 17. This dulling of incentives, he writes, acted as a "financial crisis accelerator" and contributed to the failures of AIG, Bear Stearns, and Lehman Brothers in the Panic of 2008. Roe argues that repeal of these amendments would force the derivatives markets to police counterparty risk and would lower the risk of recurrence of major financial institution failures from derivatives. Ibid.

20 Chapter 10, note 80 (statistics on credit default swap market).

21 Chapter 6, notes 127–8 and accompanying text.

22 Chapter 6, "Securitization and the U.S. subprime crisis – two categories of financial institutions."

23 When Congress created the National Mortgage Association of Washington, the predecessor of GNMA and Fannie Mae in 1938 as a wholly owned corporate instrument of the federal government, it added "the obligations of national mortgage associations" to the list of permissible investments by national banks. National Housing Act Amendments of 1938, Pub. L. 75-424, Ch. 13 §13, 52 Stat. 8, 26 (February 3, 1938).

In 1954, Congress re-chartered the firm to conduct secondary mortgage market operations. Housing Act of 1954, Pub. L. 83-560, Title II, § 201 et seq. 68 Stat 590, 612 (August 2, 1954). With that same act, Congress changed 12 U.S.C. § 24 (Seventh) to allow national banks to invest in "obligations of the Federal National Mortgage Association" instead of "obligations of national mortgage associations." Housing Act of 1954 § 203, 68 Stat. at 622.

In 1968, Congress split the entity into Fannie Mae and Ginnie Mae. Housing and Urban Development Act of 1968, Pub. L. 90-448, Title VIII, 82 Stat. 476, 536. 12 U.S.C. § 24 (Seventh) was again amended to allow national banks in invest in the obligations of both entities. Housing and Urban Development Act of 1968, § 807(j), 82 Stat. at 545.

In 1974, Congress amended 12 U.S.C. § 24 (Seventh) again to permit national banks to invest in obligations of the Federal Home Loan Mortgage Corporation (or Freddie Mac). Housing and Community Development Act of 1974, Pub. L. 93-383, § 805(c)(1), 88 Stat. 633, 726.

24 Steven L. Schwarcz, *Securitization, Structured Finance, and Capital Markets*, §7.04 (2004, LexisNexis).

25 Pub. L. 98-440, Title I, 98 Stat. 1691 (1984). For history and analysis of the statute as it relates to investments by depository institutions in mortgage-backed securities, see David Abelman, The Secondary Mortgage Market Enhancement Act, 14 *Real Estate Law Journal* 136, 142–4 (1985).

26 SMMEA § 105(c), 98 Stat. at 1691 (codified as amended at 12 U.S.C. § 24 (Seventh)). For a discussion of the development of private label mortgage-backed securities, see David Reiss, The Federal Government's Implied Guarantee of Fannie Mae and Freddie Mac's Obligations: Uncle Sam Will Pick Up the Tab, 42 *Georgia Law Review* 1019, 1030–3 (2008).

27 SMMEA allowed investments in "mortgage related securities" as that term is defined in Section 3(a)(41) of the Securities Exchange Act of 1934 (15 U.S.C. § 78c(a)(41)) SMMEA § 105, 98 Stat. at 1691. The statute also allowed investments in securities sold to "accredited investors" under the Securities Exchange Act. SMMEA § 105, 98 Stat. at 1690 (permitting investments by thrifts, credit unions, and national banks in securities "offered and sold pursuant to section 4(5) of the Securities Act of 1933 (15 U.S.C. 77d(5))").

28 SMMEA § 105 (a), 98 Stat. at 1691 (codified as amended at 12 U.S.C. § 1464(c) (1)).

29 SMMEA § 105 (a)–(b), 98 Stat. at 1691 (codified as amended at 12 U.S.C. § 1757).

30 SMMEA § 105 (c), 98 Stat. at 1691 (codified as amended at 12 U.S.C. § 24 (Seventh)).

31 SMMEA § 106, 98 Stat. at 1691–2 (codified as amended at 15 U.S.C. §§ 77r-1, 77d).

32 Patricia A. McCoy and Elizabeth Renuart, The Legal Infrastructure of Subprime and Nontraditional Home Mortgages, Joint Center for Housing Studies, Harvard University Paper UCC08-5, 8, n.40 (February 2008) available at http://jchs.harvard.edu/sites/jchs.harvard.edu/files/ucc08-5_mccoy_renuart.pdf (last visited July 29, 2013).

33 Melanie L. Fein, *Securities Activities of Banks*, § 13.02[A] (3rd ed. 2010 Suppl., Aspen Publishers).

34 Investment Securities, 61 *Federal Register* 63,972 (December 2, 1996) (codified at 12 C.F.R. pt. 1, pt. 7).

35 Eric Smalley, Kristin A. Fisher, Karin R. Jagger, Eliot J. Katz, Kathleen A. Roman, Donald C. Pingleton III, and Tyesha Witcher eds., *Mortgage-Backed Securities: Developments and Trends in the Secondary Mortgage Market 2009–2010*, § 10.8, 747–8 (2009, West Publishing Group). See 12 C.F.R. § 1.3 (e)(20[11]).

36 Smalley *et al.*, *supra* note 35, at 741 (§10:4).

37 Fein, *supra* note 33, at § 13.02[A]; Smalley *et al.*, *supra* note 35, at 748 (§10.8).

38 See 12 U.S.C. § 378(a)(1); 73 Pub. L. 66; 73 Cong. Ch. 89; 48 Stat. 162, 189 (June 15–16, 1933); see Smalley *et al.*, *supra* note 35, at 748–9 (§10.8).

39 Smalley *et al.*, *supra* note 35, at 748–9 (§10.8). In 1935, Congress added the following proviso to this Glass-Steagall Act prohibition:

> nothing in this paragraph shall be construed as affecting in any way such right as any bank, banking association, savings bank, trust company, or other banking institution, may otherwise possess to sell, without recourse or agreement to repurchase, obligations evidencing loans on real estate.
>
> 12 U.S.C. § 378(a)(1), 74 Pub. L. 305; 74 Cong. Ch. 614; 49 Stat. 684, 707
> (August 23, 1935)

For a description of the series of OCC interpretations that allowed banks to issue and sell mortgage-backed securities (and other asset-backed securities), see Fein, *supra* note 33, at § 13.02[A]; Smalley *et al.*, *supra* note 35, at 748–51 (§ 10:8).

40 *Securities Industry Association* v. *Clarke*, 885 F.2d 1034 (2d Cir. 1989) *cert. denied*, 110 S. Ct. 1113 (1990). For analysis of the case, see Fein, *supra* note 33, at §§ 4.05[C][6], 13.02[A].

41 Fein, *supra* note 33, at § 13.02[B].

42 *Securities Industry Association* v. *Board of Governors*, 839 F.2d 47 (2d Cir. 1988), *cert. denied*, 486 U.S. 1059 (1988).

43 Fein, *supra* note 33, at § 13.02[B].

44 Saule T. Omarova, The Quiet Metamorphosis: How Derivatives Changed the "Business of Banking", 63 *Miami Law Review* 1041 (2009).

45 Fein, *supra* note 33, at § 14.05[G] citing OCC Interpretative Letter No. 1051 (February 15, 2006).

46 Ibid.

47 Pub. L. No. 106-554, 114 Stat. 2763.

48 Michael Greenberger, Out of the Black Hole: Regulatory Reform of the Over-The-Counter Derivatives Market, in *Make Markets Be Markets* (Robert Johnson and Erica Payne eds., 2009, Roosevelt Institute).

49 For a gripping account of how Greenspan and Treasury Secretaries Rubin and Summers shut down Born's attempts to regulate OTC derivatives, see The Warning, *PBS Frontline* (October 20, 2009) available at www.pbs.org/wgbh/pages/frontline/warning/view/ (last viewed September 30, 2010).

50 Frank Partnoy and Lynn Turner, Bring Transparency to Off-Balance Sheet Accounting, in *Make Markets Be Markets*, 85, 87–8 (Robert Johnson and Erica Payne eds., 2009, Roosevelt Institute).

51 Ibid.

52 Ibid.

53 Floyd Norris, Hidden Numbers Make Banks Even Bigger, *New York Times*, March 15, 2013, at B1.
54 Partnoy and Turner, *supra* note 50, at 88.
55 Professor Arthur Wilmarth describes how the repeal of the Glass-Steagall Act's division between commercial and investment banking (together with the loosening of other financial regulations) stimulated the growth of securitization, OTC derivatives, and other elements of shadow banking. Arthur E. Wilmarth, Jr., The Dark Side of Universal Banking: Financial Conglomerates and the Origins of the Subprime Financial Crisis, 41 *Connecticut Law Review* 963, 972–94 (2009).
56 Arthur E. Wilmarth, The Transformation of the U.S. Financial Services Industry, 1975–2000: Competition, Consolidation, and Increased Risks, 2002 *University of Illinois Law Review* 215, 300 (2002).
57 Howard Davies, *The Financial Crisis: Who is to Blame?* 40 (2010, Polity).
58 Ibid.
59 Saule T. Omarova, From Gramm-Leach-Bliley to Dodd-Frank: The Unfulfilled Promise of Section 23A of the Federal Reserve Act, 89 *North Carolina Law Review* 101, 109–11 (2011) (discussing Section 23A of the Federal Reserve Act).
60 Ibid.
61 Ibid. at 123.
62 Ibid. at 109–11.
63 Ibid. at 124.
64 Ibid. at 124–5 (describing exemptions to allow bank affiliates to purchase assets such as mortgage and hedge fund loans).
65 Ibid. at 126–30.
66 Ibid. at 130–2.
67 Ibid. at 134–40.
68 Ibid. at 132–4, 141–2.
69 Chapter 5, "Six strategies for regulatory capital arbitrage – Concentrate credit risk and cherry pick," "The crisis and the effects of regulatory capital arbitrage." See also Chapter 5, note 168 and accompanying text.
70 Chapter 5, "Six strategies for regulatory capital arbitrage – Indirect credit enhancements and creative guarantees."
71 Chapter 5, "Regulatory capital arbitrage as compound arbitrage."
72 Erik F. Gerding, Code, Crash, and Open Source: The Outsourcing of Financial Regulation to Risk Models and the Global Financial Crisis, 84 *Washington Law Review* 127, 151–3 (2009).
73 Chapter 5, note 200 and accompanying text.
74 See generally Statement of Financial Accounting Standards No. 140. For a lengthy critique of bankruptcy standards as they were applied to accounting, see Kenneth C. Kettering, Securitization and Its Discontents: The Dynamics of Financial Product Development, 29 *Cardozo Law Review* 1553 (2008).
75 Partnoy and Turner, *supra* note 50.
76 Ibid. at 86–7.
77 Ibid.
78 Ibid. at 89–90. See also Stephen G. Ryan, Accounting In and For the Subprime Crisis, 83 *Accounting Review* 1605 (2008).
79 Ryan, *supra* note 78, at 1632.
80 Cf. ibid. (describing probability of moral recourse to the issuer rising with liquidity events).
81 N. Emre Karaoglu, Regulatory Capital and Earnings Management in Banks: the Case of Loan Sales and Securitizations, FDIC Center for Financial Research, *Working Paper No. 2005-05* (May 2005) available at http://papers.ssrn.com/sol3/papers.cfm?abstract_id=722982 (last visited October 13, 2010).

82 Patricia M. Dechow and Catherine Shakespeare, Do Managers Time Securitization Transactions to Obtain Accounting Benefits? 84 *Accounting Review* 1 (2009).

83 The possibility that originating lenders will be stuck with assets if the securitization pipeline backs up is known as "warehouse risk." Adrian D'Silva and Brian Gordon, Hedges in the Warehouse: The Banks Get Trimmed, Federal Reserve Bank of Chicago Policy Paper Discussion Series (April 1, 2008) available at http://qa.chicagofed.org/digital_assets/publications/policy_discussion_papers/2008/PDP2008-5.pdf (last visited July 29, 2013) (discussing inadequate hedging of this risk by institutions).

84 Report of Anton R. Valukas, Examiner, Vol. 3, Section III.A.4, "Repo 105," *In re* Lehman Brothers Holdings Inc., et al. (Bankr. S.D.N.Y. 2010) (08-13555 (JMP)) available at http://lehmanreport.jenner.com/VOLUME%203.pdf (last visited July 29, 2013).

85 Wilmarth, *supra* note 55, at 988–91.

86 Ibid. at 988–91, 1008–39.

87 International Swaps and Derivatives Association, 2010 Market Survey, available at www2.isda.org/functional-areas/research/surveys/market-surveys/ (last visited July 29, 2013).

88 Jack Ewing, A Fight to Make Banks More Prudent, *New York Times*, December 20, 2011 (focusing on Basel II and risk-taking at Swiss banks).

89 Gerding, *supra* note 72, at 154–9, 161–4.

90 Tobias Adrian and Hyun Song Shin, The Shadow Banking System: Implications for Financial Regulation, Federal Reserve Bank of New York, *Staff Report No. 382* (July 2009) available at http://data.newyorkfed.org/research/staff_reports/sr382.pdf (last visited July 29, 2013).

91 See generally, Wilmarth, *supra* note 55, at 1008–23.

92 Office of the Comptroller of the Currency, Board of Governors of the Federal Reserve System, Federal Deposit Insurance Corporation, Office of Thrift Supervision, and National Credit Union Administration, Interagency Guidance on Nontraditional Mortgage Product Risks (September 29, 2006) available at www.federalreserve.gov/board-docs/srletters/2006/SR0615a2.pdf (last visited July 29, 2013).

93 Kathleen C. Engel and Patricia A. McCoy, *The Subprime Virus: Reckless Credit, Regulatory Failure, and Next Steps*, 189–205 (2011, Oxford University Press); Bethany McLean and Joe Nocera, *All the Devils Are Here: The Hidden History of the Financial Crisis*, 85–95, 97, 103, 106, 243 (2010, Portfolio/Penguin); Gerding, *supra* note 72, at 133–4. See also Edmund Andrews, Greenspan Concedes Error on Regulation, *New York Times*, October 24, 2008, at B1 (reporting that Federal Reserve Chairman dismissed concerns about permissive financial regulation because "housing prices had never endured a nationwide decline and that a bust was highly unlikely").

94 Chapter 6, "Securitization and the U.S. subprime crisis – Deregulation."

95 Viral V. Acharya, Thomas F. Cooley, Matthew Richardson, and Ingo Walter, Capital, Contingent Capital, and Liquidity Requirements, in *Regulating Wall Street: The Dodd-Frank Act and the New Architecture of Global Finance*, 143, 149 (Viral V. Acharya, Thomas F. Cooley, Matthew P. Richardson, and Ingo Walter eds., 2011, John Wiley & Sons).

96 Ibid.; Viral V. Acharya, Philipp Schnabl, and Gustavo Suarez, Securitization without Risk Transfer, 107 *Journal of Financial Economics* 515, 532 (2013).

97 Acharya *et al.*, *supra* note 95, at 148.

98 Acharya *et al.*, *supra* note 95, at 150 citing American International Group Inc. Form 10-K for the fiscal year ended December 31, 2007, at 33, available at www.aig.com/Chartis/internet/US/en/2007-10k_tcm3171-440886.pdf (last visited July 29, 2013).

99 Ibid.

100 Acharya *et al.*, *supra* note 95, at 150 citing International Monetary Fund, *Global*

Financial Stability Report: Containing Systemic Risks and Restoring Financial Soundness, 31 (April 2008, IMF) available at www.imf.org/external/pubs/ft/gfsr/2008/01/pdf/text.pdf.

101 See Hyun Song Shin, Securitisation and Financial Stability, 119 *Economic Journal* 309 (2009).

102 Viral Acharya and Matthew Richardson, Causes of the Financial Crisis, 21 *Critical Review* 195, 196–7 (2009).

103 *Supra* note 84 and accompanying text.

104 Gretchen Morgenson and Louise Story, In Financial Crisis, No Prosecutions of Top Figures, *New York Times*, April 14, 2011, at A1.

105 M.C.K., Prosecuting the Financial Crisis: Just Who Should We be Blaming Anyway? *Economist Blog*, January 25, 2013, available at www.economist.com/blogs/freeexchange/2013/01/prosecuting-financial-crisis (last visited July 29, 2013). Cf. Financial Crisis: Maybe It Was Fraud After All, *The Economist*, October 13, 2010 (describing hypothesis that crisis was "unfortunate catastrophe" and had systemic causes).

106 See Jean Eaglesham, Financial Crisis Bedevils Prosecutors, *Wall Street Journal*, December 6, 2011, available at http://online.wsj.com/article/SB10001424052970204083204577080792356961440.html (last visited July 29, 2013).

107 In March 2013, the U.S. Attorney General indicated that the size and systemic importance of some financial institutions indeed complicates decisions to bring criminal charges against those firms. See, e.g., Daniel Gross, Why Do Banks Get Away with Murder? *Daily Beast*, February 17, 2013, available at www.thedailybeast.com/articles/2013/02/07/why-do-banks-get-away-with-murder.html (last visited July 29, 2013); Peter Schroeder, Holder: Big Banks' Size Complicates Prosecution Efforts, *The Hill*, March 6, 2013, available at http://thehill.com/blogs/on-the-money/banking-financial-institutions/286583-holder-big-banks-size-complicates-prosecution-efforts (last visited July 29, 2013); Peter J. Henning, After Financial Crisis, Prosecutors Navigate Tricky Waters, *New York Times* DealBook Blog, March 13, 2013, available at http://dealbook.nytimes.com/2013/03/13/after-financial-crisis-prosecutors-navigate-tricky-waters/ (last visited July 29, 2013).

108 The Untouchables, *PBS Frontline* (January 22, 2013) available at www.pbs.org/wgbh/pages/frontline/untouchables/ (last visited July 29, 2013).

109 One federal judge, Jed Rakoff, questioned whether this practice serves the public interest. He refused to agree to a settlement between the SEC and Citigroup in a lawsuit in which the agency alleged fraud in selling mortgage-related asset-backed securities. Edward Wyatt, Judge Blocks Citigroup Settlement with S.E.C., *New York Times*, November 29, 2011, at A1. However, the Second Circuit may overturn Judge Rakoff's decision. Peter Lattman, Court Hears Arguments on Judge's Rejection of S.E.C.–Citigroup Deal, *New York Times*, February 9, 2013, at B2. See *SEC* v. *Citigroup Global Markets Inc.*, No. 11 Civ. 7387(JSR), 2011 WL 5903733 (S.D.N.Y. November 28, 2011), *order stayed SEC* v. *Citigroup Global Markets Inc.*, 673 F.3d 158 (2d Cir. 2012).

110 Engel and McCoy, *supra* note 93, at 30–2.

111 Charlie Savage, Countrywide Will Settle a Bias Suit, *New York Times*, December 22, 2011, at B1 (announcing $335 million settlement with Department of Justice of federal discrimination claims). See also Charlie Savage, Wells Fargo Will Settle Mortgage Bias Charges, *New York Times*, July 13, 2012, at B3 (detailing settlement by bank of antidiscrimination charges for at least $175 million).

112 See generally Kathleen C. Engel and Patricia A. McCoy, Turning a Blind Eye: Wall Street Finance of Predatory Lending, 75 *Fordham Law Review* 101 (2007) (arguing that securitization created perverse incentives for lax screening of credit quality of mortgages, which fueled predatory lending in subprime markets).

113 *Supra* note 104.

114 See E. Scott Reckard, *In Major Policy Shift, Scores of FDIC Settlements Go Unannounced*, Los Angeles Times, March 11, 2013, available at www.latimes.com/business/la-fi-fdic-settlements-20130311,0,5882355,full.story (last visited July 29, 2013); Halah Touryalai, Is the FDIC Protecting Banks from Bad Press? *Forbes Blog*, March 12, 2013, available at www.forbes.com/sites/halahtouryalai/2013/03/12/is-the-fdic-protecting-banks-from-bad-press/ (last visited July 29, 2013).

115 Complaint, *People* v. *J.P. Morgan Securities LLC* (October 2, 2012) available at www.ag.ny.gov/sites/default/files/press-releases/2012/jpmcomplaint.pdf (last visited July 29, 2013).

116 See, e.g., Nelson D. Schwartz and Kevin Roose, Federal Regulators Sue Big Banks Over Mortgages, *New York Times*, September 2, 2011, at B1.

117 Ben Protess, U.S. Accuses Bank of America Of a "Brazen" Mortgage Fraud, *New York Times*, October 25, 2012, at A1. See Complaint-in-Intervention, *U.S.* v. *Bank of America successor to Countrywide Financial Corporation et al.*, No. 77 Civ. 1422 (JSR) (S.D.N.Y.) (October 24, 2012) available at www.justice.gov/usao/nys/pressreleases/October12/BankofAmericanSuit/BofA%20Complaint.pdf (last visited July 29, 2013) (alleging fraud in origination and sale of mortgages by Countrywide to Freddie Mac and Fannie Mae).

118 In this suit, federal prosecutors alleged that Wells Fargo originated hundreds of millions of dollars of low-quality residential mortgages, which were then guaranteed by the Federal Housing Administration. U.S. Att'y Off. S.D.N.Y. Press Release: Manhattan U.S. Attorney Files Mortgage Fraud Lawsuit Against Wells Fargo Bank, N.A. Seeking Hundreds of Millions of Dollars in Damages for Fraudulently Certified Loans (October 9, 2012) available at www.justice.gov/usao/nys/pressreleases/October12/WellsFargoLawsuitPR.html (last visited July 29, 2013).

119 Jessica Silver-Greenberg and Peter Eavis, In Deal, Big Bank Extends Retreat From Mortgages, *New York Times*, January 8, 2013, at A1.

120 Chapter 4, notes 121–4 and accompanying text. Louise Story and Gretchen Morgenson, S.E.C. Case Stands Out Because It Stands Alone, *New York Times*, June 1, 2011, at A1.

121 Ibid.

122 Andrew Ross Sorkin and Mary Williams Walsh, U.S. Accuses S. & P. of Fraud in Suit on Loan Bundles, *New York Times*, February 5, 2013, at A1.

123 Jessica Silver-Greenberg, Mortgage Crisis Presents a New Reckoning to Banks, *New York Times*, December 10, 2012, at A1 (outlining potential liability for financial institutions for public and private civil litigation stemming from mortgage and securitization market practices).

124 E.g., Jessica Silver-Greenberg, E-Mails Imply JPMorgan Knew Some Mortgage Deals Were Bad, *New York Times*, February 7, 2013, at B1 (suit by Dexia against J.P. Morgan alleging multibillion losses from fraud in connection with mortgage-related CDOs); Jesse Eisinger, Financial Crisis Suit Suggests Bad Behavior at Morgan Stanley, *New York Times*, January 24, 2013, at B1 (suit by Taiwanese banks against Wall Street firm regarding CDO investment).

125 See Engel and McCoy, *supra* note 93.

126 See generally Dan Awrey, Complexity, Innovation and the Regulation of Modern Financial Markets, 2 *Harvard Business Law Review* 235, 275 (2012).

127 McLean and Nocera, *supra* note 93, at 125–37.

128 Even as the crisis brewed, Rahuram Rajan warned that the compensation of investment managers could have perverse results:

   [T]he incentive structure of investment managers today differs from the incentive structure of bank managers of the past in two important ways. First, the way compensation relates to returns implies there is typically less downside and more upside from generating investment returns. Managers therefore have greater incentive to take risk. Second, their performance relative to other peer managers matters, either because it is directly embedded in their compensation, or because investors exit or enter funds on that basis.

The knowledge that managers are being evaluated against others can induce superior performance, but also a variety of perverse behavior. One is the incentive to take risk that is concealed from investors – since risk and return are related, the manager then looks as if he outperforms peers given the risk he takes. Typically, the kinds of risks that can most easily be concealed, given the requirement of periodic reporting, are risks that generate severe adverse consequences with small probability but, in return, offer generous compensation the rest of the time. These risks are known as tail risks.

Raghuram G. Rajan, Has Financial Development Made the World Riskier, *Proceedings Federal Reserve Bank of Kansas City* 313, 316 (August 2005) available at www.kansascityfed.org/publicat/sympos/2005/pdf/rajan2005.pdf (last visited July 29, 2013)

129 Margaret M. Blair, Financial Innovation, Leverage, Bubbles and the Distribution of Income, 30 *Review of Banking and Financial Law* 225 (2010–2011).

130 Chapter 4, "The probability of detection: swimming naked while the tide rolls in," "The probability of enforcement: causes of action and diluted enforcement."

131 Chapter 4, "Sell side norms: new financial industry participants." See *supra* note 127 and accompanying text (discussing culture of young mortgage brokers).

132 Chapter 4, "Buy side changes: new investors, norms of reciprocity, and norm asymmetries."

133 Chapter 4, Notes 121–4 and accompanying text.

134 Tobias Adrian and Hyun Song Shin, Money, Liquidity, and Monetary Policy, 99 *American Economic Review* 600 (2009).

135 Chapter 7, "Capital requirements." Cf. Joe Peek and Eric Rosengren, Bank Regulation and the Credit Crunch, 19 *Journal of Banking and Finance* 679 (1995) (banks undergoing enforcement proceedings shrinking lending faster than other banks).

136 Ibid. at 604.

137 Morgan Ricks, A Regulatory Design for Monetary Stability, 65 *Vanderbilt Law Review* 1289, 1296 (2012).

138 Adrian and Shin, *supra* note 134, at 601 (using data from J.P. Morgan).

139 Chapter 10, "Shadow banking compared to depository banking: revisiting the 'specialness' of banks."

140 Adrian and Shin, *supra* note 134, at 601 (using Federal Reserve Flow of Funds data).

141 Blair, *supra* note 129, at 270–3.

142 John William's Shadow Government Statistics, Money Supply Charts, available at www.shadowstats.com/alternate_data/money-supply-charts (last visited July 29, 2013) earlier version cited by Blair, *supra* note 129, at 272.

143 Cf. Dean Croushore, *Money and Banking: A Policy-oriented Approach*, 61 (2006, Cengage Learning).

144 Cf. ibid. at 62 (comparing M2 and M3).

145 These included Bear Stearns (brought down by mortgage-related investments by two of its affiliated hedge funds); the government-sponsored entities Freddie Mac and Fannie Mae; major credit protection sellers in credit derivatives (such as AIG); monoline bond insurers who insured ABSs (such as MBIA), mortgage lenders, numerous regulated bank lenders caught up in subprime mortgage lending or investing (such as IndyMac and Washington Mutual), and large financial conglomerates (such as Citigroup). For a high-level overview of how contagion spread throughout the shadow banking system, see Nouriel Roubini and Stephen Mihm, *Crisis*

Economics: a Crash Course in the Future of Finance, 34–6, 89–94, 98–100, 104–14 (2010, Penguin).

146 Gorton and Metrick, *supra* note 15.

147 For an account of run behavior afflicting hedge funds, see Markus K. Brunnermeier, Deciphering the Liquidity and Credit Crunch 2007–2008, 23 *Journal of Economic Perspectives* 77 (2009).

148 Birdthistle, *supra* note 5.

149 Gorton and Metrick, *supra* note 15. See also Gary Gorton, Slapped in the Face by the Invisible Hand: Banking and the Panic of 2007, National Bureau of Economic Research, *Working Paper* (May 9, 2009) available at http://papers.ssrn.com/sol3/papers.cfm?abstract_id=1401882 (last visited July 29, 2013).

150 See generally Acharya *et al.*, *supra* note 95, at 145 (discussing links between solvency and liquidity aspects of crisis).

151 For a summary of Federal Reserve emergency actions during the crisis, see Christian A. Johnson, Exigent and Unusual Circumstances: The Federal Reserve and the US Financial Crisis, in *Law Reform and Financial Markets*, 269 (Kern Alexander and Niamh Moloney eds., 2011, Edward Elgar).

152 Pub. L. 110-343, 122 Stat. 3765.

153 As noted above, AIG received government support after its London affiliate incurred huge losses writing credit derivatives for CDOs and other asset-backed securities. For a critique of this bailout, see William K. Sjostrom, Jr., The AIG Bailout, 66 *Washington and Lee Law Review* 943 (2009).

154 Freddie Mac and Fannie Mae foundered as their capital proved woefully insufficient for the wave of losses they experienced in both the mortgages and mortgage-backed securities in their investment portfolio and their guarantees of their own mortgage-backed securities. These twin mortgage giants have received U.S.\$154 billion in federal money from November 2008 through March 2011. The Budgetary Cost of Fannie Mae and Freddie Mac and Options for the Future Federal Role in the Secondary Mortgage Market Before the House Comm. on the Budget, 112th Congress, 2 (June 2, 2011) (Statement of Deborah Lucas, Assistant Director for Financial Analysis, Congressional Budget Office) available at www.cbo.gov/ftpdocs/122xx/doc12213/06-02-GSEs_Testimony.pdf (last visited July 29, 2013).

In July of 2008, Congress passed and President Bush signed the Housing and Economic Recovery Act of 2008, which provided for the first time a blueprint for how federal law would handle the insolvency of these government-sponsored entities. Pub. L. 110-289, 122 Stat. 265. See Richard Scott Carnell, Handing the Failure of a Government-Sponsored Enterprise, 80 *Washington Law Review* 565 (2005) (providing an early alarm that the government lacked a legal framework for handling the insolvency of these two firms).

155 Steven M. Davidoff and David Zaring, Regulation by Deal: The Government's Response to the Financial Crisis, 61 *Administrative Law Review* 463 (2009).

156 Timothy Geithner, My Plan for Bad Bank Assets, *Wall Street Journal*, March 23, 2009.

157 Table 11.1 originates from Johnson, *supra* note 151, but includes additional detail.

158 More specifically, these structures may have reflected a belief that, rather than nationalize entities, it was better to subsidize private sector investment in these institutions given concerns over the limits of government expertise, the potential for prolonged government ownership of key financial institutions, and the risk that nationalizing entities would discourage investors from providing support to other tottering institutions. For Federal Reserve Chairman Bernanke's account of the reasons for the structure of these interventions, see Ben S. Bernanke, *The Federal Reserve and the Financial Crisis*, 77–86, 97–100 (2013, Princeton University Press).

Other interpretations may be less charitable and include that these opaque transactional structures were designed to mask government subsidies to financial institutions and investors, or that government officials responsible for creating these structures accepted uncritically the technological potential of securitization.

159 Roubini and Mihm, *supra* note 145, at 112.
160 Table 11.2 is also modeled after the chart in Johnson, *supra* note 151, but includes additional detail.
161 See Federal Reserve Bank of New York: Primary Dealer Credit Facility: Frequently Asked Questions (June 25, 2009) available at www.newyorkfed.org/markets/pdcf_faq.html (last visited October 1, 2010).
162 The Federal Reserve did not create this facility using its authority under Section 13(3), but instead treated it as an extension of its powers under its securities lending programs. Johnson, *supra* note 151. This facility allowed primary dealers of U.S. Treasury securities to swap less liquid securities to the Federal Reserve for U.S. Treasury securities for twenty-eight day periods. Ibid.
163 See Federal Reserve Bank of New York: Term Securities Lending Facility: Frequently Asked Questions (June 25, 2009) available at www.newyorkfed.org/markets/tslf_faq.html (last visited October 1, 2010).
164 See Federal Reserve Bank of New York: Asset-backed Commercial Paper Money Market Mutual Fund Liquidity Facility: Frequently Asked Questions (February 5, 2010) available at www.frbdiscountwindow.org/mmmf.cfm?hdrID=14#f3 (last visited October 1, 2010).
165 See Federal Reserve Bank of New York: Commercial Paper Funding Facility: Frequently Asked Questions (October 19, 2009) available at www.newyorkfed.org/markets/cpff_faq.html (last visited October 1, 2010).
166 See Federal Reserve Bank of New York: Money Market Investor Funding Facility: Frequently Asked Questions (June 25, 2009) available at www.newyorkfed.org/markets/mmiff_faq.html (last visited October 1, 2010).
167 See Federal Reserve Bank of New York: Term Asset-Backed Securities Loan Facility: Frequently Asked Questions (July 21, 2010) available at www.newyorkfed.org/markets/talf_faq.html (last visited October 1, 2010).

Part V

Lessons and solutions

Conclusion

Adaptive laws and channeling politics: designing robust regulations and institutions

Eyes on the prize

The bulk of this book has described the ways in which asset price bubbles and financial laws interact to exacerbate bubbles and destabilize financial laws. Historically, the consequences of destabilized financial laws have been severe. Chapter 2 detailed how the history of bubbles has been marred by epidemics of financial fraud and law-breaking. During bubbles, the legitimacy of law erodes when the regulation of financial markets devolves into crony capitalism and individuals in both marketplace and government join in a Saturnalia of law-breaking. In the worst of cases, the collapse of bubbles and the failure of financial laws resulted in the widespread economic devastation and social dislocation of depressions, both Great and forgotten. The collapse of the worst bubbles lays waste to institutions both private and public.

What, then, is to be done? Thus far, this book may leave the reader with a profound sense of fatalism. Laws tend to fail during asset price bubbles – whether because they are rolled back, because they are neither adequately enforced nor obeyed, because the market will find ways to game them, or because they can add fuel to the bubble's fire and render financial markets more vulnerable to its torch. Would not these same dynamics also plague any legal fixes? Why would attempts to address regulatory instability during bubbles not fall victim to these same dynamics? How could we ensure that legal rules designed to prevent the roll back of law will not themselves be rolled back when the next bubble begins? Or that rules designed to promote enforcement and compliance will not themselves be flouted? If law is inherently incomplete and subject to jurisdictional bounds, would not market participants find ways around any attempts to dampen regulatory arbitrage when booms sharpen their appetite for risk and their creativity with law? How do we ensure that policymakers exercise judgment to adapt financial laws to new contexts and new financial threats?

These profound challenges are not easily met. They, like asset price bubbles, have been recurrent and robust features of the financial markets. For all the toil and trouble of financial reform, these destabilizing dynamics will return like a witch's curse the next time that investors burn and markets bubble. Although, these dynamics are not iron historical laws, they are strong forces nonetheless. Lawmakers ignore this gravitational pull at their peril.

Lawmakers often react to collapsed bubbles with moralistic zeal. Yet seeing financial crises in purely moral or even quasi-religious terms of sin and villainy seems suspect. Does human nature really change from one market cycle to another? In the wake of some bubbles, moralistic responses have also devolved into ugly bouts of scapegoating minorities. Moralism also distracts from recognizing the underlying forces that create disequilibrium in financial markets and financial laws. It blinds policymakers to the presence of regulatory cycles. It obscures fluctuating levels of legal compliance and regulatory arbitrage in financial markets. It overshadows regulations that operate to exacerbate booms and busts or promote investor herding. Moralism distracts from the importance of financial institution leverage and legal changes that affect that leverage.

This concluding chapter departs from the convention of many recent books on the financial crisis. It seeks not to provide a white-paper-style list of thirty different solutions to the current global financial crisis. Instead, it proposes solutions to ensure that financial laws remain robust in the face of booming markets. These solutions blend the pragmatic with the provocative, yet emphasize the modest. This concluding chapter stresses that the overarching objective should not be to eliminate asset price bubbles: the laboratories of history and of economists have shown bubbles to be a remarkably robust phenomenon, perhaps embedded within the DNA of financial markets and economic growth. Nor should financial laws aim to smooth out business cycles.

Instead, the objectives should be fourfold: first, to reinforce financial laws so that they can continue to perform their original objectives (such as deterring financial fraud or ensuring the safety and soundness of financial institutions) even in the harsh conditions of boom times. Second, financial regulations must do less to exacerbate bubbles or worsen market mispricings. Third, regulations should lower the risk of the worst-of-the-worst financial crises, by making financial markets and institutions, as well as households and public institutions, more resilient to bubbles and crashes. Fourth and finally, resilience entails more than just economic security. It also means ensuring that the laws governing markets retain their legitimacy. Any policy solution must construct, apply, and maintain financial regulation consistent with the deep values a society holds, including democratic decision-making and respect for legal rights and the rule of law.

These objectives do not seem so modest after all. Consider also that attempts at ensuring the stability of markets and institutions must balance against other values, such as promoting economic growth and investment. For all the economic destruction wrought by Britain's nineteenth century bubbles, that nation did experience profound industrialization and economic growth, as railways proliferated and trade expanded. Other bubbles, of course, have left their countries with a less welcome or productive patrimony. Witness the detritus of the U.S. "subprime crisis": desolate and now moldering tracts of homes stretching from California to Ohio and down to Florida. That is the mere physical evidence of the waste. It does not capture the human cost. Not all destructive gales are also creative.[1]

If these goals are formidable, they are not impossible to achieve. They do not require policymakers to identify bubbles with precision. After all, the dynamics of the Regulatory Instability Hypothesis do not depend on whether market prices have exceeded some fundamental value. Instead, these dynamics grow out of the changes that market booms cause in the resources and incentives of the regulators and the regulated, their cognitive processes and biases, and their norms and ideologies. Measuring these changes may also present no easy feat. However, many of the proposals considered in this chapter – such as creating counter-cyclical regulator budgets – depend on much simpler metrics such as comparing the volume of transactions in a given financial market to the resources of regulators overseeing that market.

Moreover, since mitigating the worst-of-the-worst results of bubbles – lasting financial crisis – is an imperative, policymakers should spend less time fretting about whether market prices have or have not exceeded fundamental value and look instead to the recurrent harbingers of market booms and financial crises in history. These include: a persistent low interest rate environment,[2] increases in the effective money supply,[3] dramatic increases in the leverage of consumers, financial institutions, or the economy as a whole,[4] or the influx of first-time investors in an asset market.[5]

At the same time these guideposts force us to remember that, in pursuing the objectives of making financial regulation more stable, robust, and resilient, some financial regulations are much more important than others. Laws that govern the lending and leverage of financial institutions do double and triple duty. Excessive credit and leverage fuel bubbles, while rendering financial institutions more susceptible to their collapse. Many of these leverage laws, by promoting the safety and soundness of individual financial institutions and mitigating the likelihood of their mass failure, work to dampen systemic risk.

Re-thinking institutional design

Working towards the four objectives above requires not so much a focus on the substance of specific legal rules as a broader re-thinking of the design of regulatory institutions. How can the architecture of legal rules and the public and private bodies that apply those rules be refashioned so that financial laws do not buckle at the most critical moments? The question is not only what substantive powers do regulators need, but, moreover, how do we ensure that regulators will use the powers and do the jobs they already have? How do we ensure that regulators function even when it is Mardi Gras in financial markets, so that *laissez les bon temps rouler* does not create a crisis cocktail when mixed with laissez faire?

Beyond technocratic fantasies and buzzwords

Financial laws operate in the most political of environments, and regulatory design must grapple with the potent political forces that work against effective regulation. Policymakers and scholars must resist indulging in assorted techno-cratic fantasies that regularly wash over financial reform. Financial regulation will never exist on an elevated technical plane removed from the rough-and-tumble of politics. A belief that it can represents mere illusion, and a deeply anti-democratic one at that. Reform should not seek to escape politics altogether, but to design institutions that channel political forces.

At the same time, simple calls for more "accountability" by government offi-cials offer little intellectual nutrition. This buzzword not only clouds clear think-ing on regulatory designs, it may in some cases be counterproductive. Creating institutions that are simply more "accountable" may make them more responsive to the financial institutions and noise traders who call for regulatory roll back at precisely the worst moment – when markets begin to overheat. The better ques-tions to ask are "to whom should lawmakers and regulators be accountable?" "when should they be held to account?" and "how?"

Moreover, who will make use of this accountability? If financial regulation cannot be removed from politics, it also cannot be removed from its extremely technical nature. Studies of recent financial reforms reveal the sadly unsurprising fact that financial industry groups have been far more active than the public in the nitty-gritty "sausage-making" of U.S. federal rule-making.[6] Although polit-ical entrepreneurs[7] and civil society[8] might play vital roles, will they have suffi-cient resources and incentives? Moreover, who will watch those watchers? Consider that financial industry has dominated participation in the agency rule-making process for the Volcker Rule. Yet the Volcker Rule represents the piece of current U.S. financial reform with the most prominent participation by polit-ical entrepreneurs (including the two U.S. Senators that pushed for the statutory provision), policy and academic entrepreneurs (including former Federal Reserve Chairman Paul Volcker and prominent academics such as economist Simon Johnson), and citizen groups (such as Americans for Financial Reform).[9]

If "accountability" provides no panacea, neither does "transparency." To whom should the architecture of financial regulation be transparent and when? There are moments in which greater transparency may prove dicey. For example, financial regulators examining a teetering financial firm might well take care not to provoke a bank run needlessly.[10] Even when information on the guts of the regulatory process should be and are disclosed, could the public make use of them? Could they process the sheer technicality and volume of information gen-erated by the modern apparatus of financial regulation?

If simple calls for accountability and transparency do not provide a solid foundation for financial reform, neither does "leadership" or "political will." Angels do not govern and the "great woman" or "great man" may not be in office when we need him or her. Indeed, men who are great in one period, look far shab-bier in others. The repute of Alan Greenspan, the Federal Reserve Chairman who was once held in high regard for rescuing the U.S. economy from a crisis in Asia and the failure of a prominent hedge fund, lost its luster after the Panic of 2007–2008. Commentators faulted Greenspan not only for this monetary policy, but for his active resistance to strong regulation of financial markets.[11] The arc of his story mirrors those of policymakers and academics in prior bubble periods starting with John Law in the French eighteenth century Mississippi bubble. Political resolve also ebbs and flows. Its tide often rushes against the levees of financial regulation just as bubbles gain strength and financial and political cyclones begin to spin together in the warming waters off-shore.

Leavening economics: more realism about legal rules

As the focus shifts to designing regulation and regulatory institutions and to channeling politics, economists have contributed much. Some economists have made sensible calls to focus financial reforms on simple rules that address the overall incentives of market participants.[12] Other economists have advocated various forms of countercyclical regulations – that is regulations that would automatically adjust to market cycles. These regulations would, for example, require financial institutions to build up more buffers or curtail lending as markets boom.[13] One of the advantages of *countercyclical* rules is that making the regulatory process more automatic would insulate it from political pressure to regulate markets and firms lightly at inopportune times.[14] This call to cyclically increase capital comes on top of sensible proposals by economists for policymakers to dramatically increase the base level of capital that financial institutions, particularly large financial institutions, must hold. As noted throughout this book, increased capital serves as a vital safety net against financial institution failure and the systemic risk that goes along with that failure.[15] Increased capital plays a duel function. First, it reduces financial institution leverage that may fuel a bubble. Second, it makes financial institutions and markets more resilient to the bursting of a bubble and the onslaught of a financial crisis.

Both of these strands of advice display much insight and promise. Yet these hard, mechanical views of incentives and rules need to be leavened by a strong dose of legal realism. Legal practitioners and scholars know that translating simple designs to realign incentives into workable legal rules is a most challenging endeavor. For example, consider proposals to levy a "tax" on bank leverage.[16] How would the tax be measured? Would it be based on debt to equity ratios? How would those ratios be computed? If they are computed by reference to accounting rules, how would regulators address the strong incentives of financial firms to game those accounting rules – whether through off-balance sheet transactions or otherwise? Chapter 5 described how bank capital requirements started out as simple, workable rules. Yet they were subject to gamesmanship. Efforts to revise the rules resulted in new approaches (Basel II's internal models approach) that were themselves gamed. Financial markets evolve around efforts to regulate them. Because of regulatory capital arbitrage, Chapter 5 concluded, financial markets and bank regulation have evolved in almost dialectical fashion – as a kind of complex adaptive system. However, the neat label should not obscure the messy end results.[17]

Chapter 5 also argued that government guarantees and bailouts provide one explanation for what drives financial institutions to seek leverage and to engage in this regulatory capital arbitrage.[18] Accordingly, many economists recommend removing this incentive by foreclosing government bailouts of financial institutions.[19] This view found its way into numerous provisions in the Dodd-Frank Act[20] that forbid government assistance to various financial institutions.[21]

Putting aside whether it is wise to tie the government's hands in a financial crisis, these restrictions have less force than their proponents claim.[22] First, these restrictions are subject to removal by later lawmakers. As described in more detail below, Anglo-American courts look harshly on "legislative entrenchment," or attempts by legislators to hardwire laws that bind their future counterparts.[23] Second, legislators game the rules they place on themselves. Witness the accounting and procedural absurdities in which the U.S. Congress has engaged in order to appear to comply with balanced budget requirements and debt ceilings.[24] And who could stop these legislatures? As law students are taught to ask: where is the remedy? In the United States, court challenges by private plaintiffs against government bailouts would face a gauntlet of challenges. These include the following: whether plaintiffs have standing and whether the matter is a political controversy and is "justiciable," as well as a thicket of separation of powers problems.

In short, even simple legal rules that shape incentives of market participants in sensible ways remain subject to revision and gamesmanship. This underscores the need for a nuanced view of legal rules. Legal rules are by nature "incomplete," that is, they cannot specify commands for every eventuality and state of the world.[25] Laws also have jurisdictional boundaries. Furthermore, they are not self-executing computer codes, but rather operate only through human agents interpreting and applying them. This means that issues of deregulation, enforcement, compliance, and regulatory arbitrage represent permanent features of the institutional landscape.

History rhymes, judgment remains

It also means that judgment remains an inescapable part of financial regulation. Both policymakers and financial market participants must exercise judgment in interpreting and applying the law's commands. We ignore the importance of judgment at great peril. Economist Amar Bhidé places much blame for the Panic of 2007–2008 on financial institutions that made key investment and risk decisions based on computerized models. Bankers took human judgment out of the equation and ignored the signs of impending crisis.[26] If investment decisions should not be placed on auto-pilot, neither should legal rules. Regulators must exercise judgment in applying laws, just as market participants exercise judgment in interpreting and obeying them. Both regulators and the regulated must use discretion in identifying looming risks that laws or markets will fail.

History provides a guide, but an imperfect and oracular one. Financial history does not repeat. It rhymes. The hallmarks of bubbles and the signposts for financial crises may recur – booming asset prices, increases in credit and leverage, and influxes of first-time investors – yet they do so only on an abstract level;

their exact forms vary from era to era. The long history of bubbles has witnessed different forms of regulatory stimulus (Chapters 2 and 3) and different schemes for law-breaking and regulatory arbitrage (Chapters 2, 4, and 5). If this book's efforts to model these legal dynamics seemed mechanical, then context and nuance have their revenge. Differing legal, political, social, and cultural environments mean that the problems of the Regulatory Instability Hypothesis are shape-shifters.

On the other hand, the various dynamics that destabilize law also frustrate the sound application of judgment. Strong forces work against the wise application of laws during bubble times. Political forces array against vigorous regulation. The information available to policymakers and market participants can be at once both limited and overwhelming. Meanwhile, cognitive limitations distort the perception and assessment of risk. Moreover, law operates in a social context. Market booms can reinforce changing beliefs – including ideologies or social norms – that may tilt against prudent long-term decisions.

Models of human behavior matter

Part II of this book, which laid out the Regulatory Instability Hypothesis, created different families of models to explain how bubbles destabilize law. Each family had markedly different assumptions about the determinants of human behavior: rational costs and benefits; cognitive processes, limitations, and heuristics; or political ideologies and norms. It is hard to untangle and assess the explanatory power of these three models during bubble times, as market booms cause law to deteriorate under each model. The various dynamics of the different models reinforce one another in powerful ways. Rational decisions to violate the law may undermine social norms. Political beliefs that the markets can self-govern may feed disaster myopia by bankers and their regulators.

However, the choice of model for explaining human behavior can have significant consequences for the design of institutions to change that behavior. Rational actor models counsel for changing incentives with more carrots and sticks. Policymakers should accordingly meet an increased risk of legal violations with increased deterrence.

Scholars who use behavioral economic models advocate policies to "de-bias" decision-makers[27] or to change the order or framing of the decisions they must make so as to "nudge" them to better outcomes.[28] For example, behavioral economists and social psychologists propose warnings for dangerous products that include graphic labels of the potential harms (rather than simple text disclosures).[29] They recommend addressing the fact that consumers save too little for retirement by creating "opt-out" rather than "opt-in" savings programs.[30]

Finally, models that emphasize ideologies or social norms might argue in favor of policies that counteract groupthink.[31] At the same time, these models might argue for creating communities that foster the development of socially beneficial norms. For example, a sense of common purpose might induce a group of regulators to take enforcement seriously. Or legal rules might even strengthen the ability of financial markets to self-govern, as financial firms responsible for each other's failure would see themselves as a "community of fate."[32]

The proposals below borrow from each of these camps. Often a single design feature may work under more than one model. However, not everything is a "win/win." Some efforts that work well under one view of human behavior may work to undermine policies that assume another set of motivations. Many scholars question whether an excessive focus on carrot and stick incentives may undermine efforts to cultivate norms and intrinsic motivation.[33] For example, research has shown that efforts to pay students for grades may undermine their motivation to learn on their own in the absence of monetary incentives.[34] Policies based on instrumental views of human nature may conflict with those based on softer, but no less important determinants of behavior.

Disequilibrium in law: decoupling cycles

The most promising institutional designs would address incentives, cognitive processes, and beliefs at the same time. One key to finding these levers is to look for mechanisms that dampen the feedback mechanisms that destabilize financial regulation. When economic, political, and regulatory cycles meet, they gather destructive force, like cyclones combining out at sea.

Decoupling political cycles from financial cycles

The Regulatory Instability Hypothesis includes an array of feedback loops between financial markets and political markets. Chapter 3 detailed how booming markets interact with any tectonic shifts in political coalitions to generate ideal conditions for regulatory stimulus. Financial reforms should look to decouple the political cycle from market cycles. Yet achieving this decoupling would require overcoming daunting challenges.

Chapter 3 argued that the rise of the corporate form such as in nineteenth century Britain helped promote regulatory stimulus. Company promoters could use other people's money to push for legal changes. Furthermore, the centralization of authority that comes with the corporation allows interest groups to overcome collective action challenges in organizing for political change.[35] Fast-forward to the early twenty-first century, when the U.S. Supreme Court issued its landmark opinion in *Citizens United.* The Court struck down campaign finance laws that prohibited corporate entities and unions from making independent expenditures on "electioneering communications."[36] Strong corporate free speech rights complicate efforts to restrict political influence over financial regulation. *Citizens United* also underscores that regulatory and institutional design confront unique problems in every country. The different constitutional and legal environments mean that, to a large extent, all regulatory design solutions must be local.

Independence is not enough

For both central banks and financial regulators, the classical response to the problem of perverse political incentives is to house authority within an independent agency. Insulation from political pressures allows central banks to remove the punchbowl, as William McChesney Martin once supposedly said, just as the party gets starting.[37] Without this independence, central banks would face pressure from politicians seeking reelection to juice the economy every electoral cycle.

Independence has several cornerstones, including ensuring that the policymakers at an agency cannot be removed at the whim of the elected branches of government and providing agencies with autonomous sources of funds. However, these forms of insulation are by no means complete. The heads of regulatory agencies must have some political accountability in a democratic society and are at some point appointed and re-appointed by elected officials. Moreover, the heads of agencies may still seek to curry favor with the political branches to gain additional funding or to protect or expand their regulatory turf. Legal scholars Lisa Schultz Bressman and Robert Thompson detail the less-visible levers that U.S. presidents have used to influence and shape independent federal agencies.[38]

Regulators may also seek to accommodate industry for various reasons ranging from benign (improving the effectiveness of regulation) to malignant (increasing their own private sector employment prospects as the "revolving door" between government and industry spins). As noted in Chapters 3 and 6, all of these political pressures on regulators – including at independent agencies – increase during market booms.

Agency independence offers no protection from other subtler forces that can weaken effective financial regulation during booms and bubbles. Regulators have strong disincentives to take actions that might cool investment or lending for fear of being blamed for upsetting the economic applecart.[39] Apart from political pressure, regulators at independent agencies may also have ideological blind spots that make them reluctant to question whether there is excessive risk-taking in financial markets.[40] Furthermore, regulators may suffer the same cognitive biases and limitations that afflict investors.[41]

The U.S. Federal Reserve's performance leading up to the 2008 financial crisis provides a case study in the limitations of regulator independence in combating a financial bubble. As the United States implements financial reform in the wake of that crisis and gives regulatory agencies powerful new policy tools, the open secret is that the Federal Reserve, one of the most independent bodies in the U.S. federal government, *had* broad powers to regulate the institutions and financial instruments at the heart of the later crisis.[42] The Federal Reserve had the power to regulate so-called "exotic" mortgages – but delayed taking any regulatory action until 2006. At that point, it only issued non-binding guidance together with other financial regulators.[43] The Federal Reserve had the power to regulate lending practices and the leverage of bank holding companies and their affiliates. Yet it failed to take adequate steps to curb subprime lending and risk-taking by institutions large and small.[44] In fact, under Alan Greenspan's tenure, the Federal Reserve actively resisted new regulations. For example, Greenspan helped orchestrate passage of a 2000 statute that exempted over-the-counter derivatives from various regulations.[45] Greenspan repeatedly cited a deep belief that financial markets self-regulate as the basis for his laissez faire approach.[46] After the U.S. reaped the whirlwind, the Federal Reserve sought new regulatory powers. This led some critics, including some in the U.S. Congress, to question whether this would be akin to giving a teenager a faster car after he crashed the family station wagon.[47]

The government as investor

The political cycle becomes more closely joined to market cycles when the government invests directly in financial institutions to spur investment. This form of regulatory stimulus can have the most potent effects on financial markets and the most corrosive effects on political governance.

Consider the deep parallels among the histories of the Mississippi, South Sea, and U.S. subprime bubbles. In each case the government sought to spur investment in particular markets by chartering corporations with special government privileges: the *Banque Générale* and *Compagnie d'Occident* in the Mississippi bubble, the South Sea Company in England, and the government-sponsored entities Freddie Mac and Fannie Mae in the United States. The social goals may have differed (reducing the national debt and expanding colonial trade in France and England versus promoting home-ownership in the United States). However, the political and market pathologies bear striking similarities. In each case, the government-sponsored entity enjoyed monopoly or oligopoly power over a particular investment market and zealously defended this position in the political arena. In each case, the private entity wielded outsized influence over government officials.

In each case, government officials chose not to rein in the risky investments of the entity, but, on the contrary to spur them further. The motivations of officials were a thick stew of self-interest (bribes or campaign contributions) and furthering government policies (lowering the national debt, building the Empire, or making housing more affordable). Each government's role as investor undermined its role as regulator and guardian of financial stability.

This does not imply that all government-owned corporations in financial markets would pose the same risks. The problem in these three examples stemmed from the sheer size of these entities. Their metastasizing size distorted financial markets and dwarfed the resources of regulators charged with overseeing them. The government-as-investor in financial markets removes the discipline of competition from markets and the discipline of law from politics. It creates the risk that the private sector will be coopted and the public sector captured.

If the government choses to create, invest in, or guarantee entities in order to spur investment in financial markets, it must therefore impose severe disciplining rules on itself. The entities in which it invests or subsidizes must have a limited mandate to increase financial market investment. Success in spurring investment should lead to a government exit and not to attempts to expand the scope of the government-supported entities' activities. The size of the government-supported entities should be proportional to the size of the financial market in which they operate; the entities should never dominate the market. Finally, there should be a large number of smaller entities supported by the government, such that no one entity can distort the economic or political marketplace.

Industry segmentation and engineering interest group competition

Indeed, competition in financial markets and competition in political markets reinforce one another in positive ways. When financial institutions have differing interests and relatively equal political power, they will work to ensure that their competitors do not obtain unduly favorable treatment from regulators. Chapter 3 described how the U.S. securities industry fought in both the regulatory arena and in courts to prevent bank regulators from allowing U.S. banks to underwrite and deal in mortgage-backed securities.[48] Even though the securities industry lost, they displayed the power of interest group pluralism. Chapter 3 also noted that, as the U.S. financial industry consolidated and legal divisions among investment banking, commercial bank, and insurance began to dissolve, pluralism's power decayed. Chapter 11 explained the policy consequences: greater bank involvement in mortgage-backed securities fed the growth of the shadow banking system. This involvement also provided transmission lines for the transfer of destabilizing government subsidies and, ultimately, for crisis contagion as well.[49]

Segmentation of the financial services sector yields political benefits. Competing financial industry sectors may work to ensure that rivals cannot abuse government subsidies or benefit from lax government regulation or enforcement. Indeed, economists are now awakening to this political economy dimension of industry segmentation. For example, Luigi Zingales now cites political competition as a justification for Glass-Steagall type divisions between investment and commercial banking.[50] Regulatory scholars seem to be rediscovering the wisdom if not the text of Federalist Number 10.[51]

Of course, there are risks. One industry segment may begin a race to the bottom in which every faction receives laxer treatment. Indeed, Chapter 6 modeled a particularly vicious feedback mechanism, as industry segmentation can beget regulatory arbitrage, which can beget cascades of deregulation. Industry segmentation remains stable until severe market or political displacements shatter the political and market equilibria.

Cultivating civil society

At some future point in time, civil society may develop enough to prove a more effective counterbalance to industry interest groups. As Chapter 3 noted, in environmental issues, there is at least a semblance of interest group pluralism because environmental groups are deeply and ideologically committed to defending wildlife, protecting natural spaces, and fighting pollution.[52] A comparable civil society does not yet exist in the world of financial regulation, although scholars like Claire Kelly have written creatively about the possibility of one developing.[53]

It may prove easier to mobilize a public in support of consumer financial protection regulation than in other areas of financial regulation. Witness the recent grassroots movement to convince U.S. customers to "Dump Your Bank" because of the hidden fees banks charged their depositors.[54] Although, citizen rage also flared over government bailouts of financial institutions, little of this rage translated into sustained engagement in the hyper-technical financial rule-making process.[55] As memories of the current financial crisis fade, so too will engagement of civil society with financial regulation.

Several factors, however, may leaven this pessimism. The "Dump Your Bank" protest demonstrated the power of policy entrepreneurs to use new social media technologies to mobilize for issues of financial regulation. New technology can foster a civil society in the financial regulatory realm. But can it sustain this engagement? Unlike the environmental movement, there is little romance in financial regulation. In contrast to the environmental movement, financial reform offers fewer psychic and social rewards to individuals who mobilize for political change.

Decoupling stock market, real estate, and banking cycles

Bank participation in mortgage-backed securities presented other dangers beyond growing the shadow banking system. The regulatory changes that enabled banks to invest in mortgage-backed securities created a coupling rod between banking, securities, and real estate markets. Unfortunately, at least two of these markets can be plagued by cycles. Economic research suggests that banks have been caught up in a leverage cycle.[56] Meanwhile, residential real estate prices evidence positive serial correlation. In other words, when prices rise, they continue to rise, and, when they fall, they continue to fall.[57] Positive serial correlation can translate into boom and bust cycles in real estate markets.[58]

When bank and real estate cycles become joined, it can create economic havoc. Surveys of financial crises across countries and over history reveal a close correlation between real estate crises, on the one hand, and banking crises, on the other.[59] Allowing banks to invest in real estate markets, even indirectly via purchasing asset-backed securities, provides one mechanism that joins these cycles. This creates potential feedback loops among booming markets and provides yet another transmission line for crisis contagion when one market starts to crash.

Restricting bank investments in securities and real estate can dampen this feedback and decouple these cycles. Yet this too offers no silver bullet. If banks cannot invest in real estate or securities, other financial institutions will spring up to fill the gap. Regulatory divisions between banking and real estate finance companies may disadvantage the latter. If restricted from financing themselves by accepting deposits, these non-bank finance companies may prove particularly fragile. Moreover, a lack of access to government deposit insurance and other explicit and implicit government subsidies can raise their cost of funding.

Conversely, when real estate or securities markets boom, banks will press governments to allow them to enter restricted markets and compete with these alternative finance companies. Yet they will also seek to keep their deposit insurance and government subsidies. This all should sound familiar; it is in essence a summary of what transpired in Sweden and Japan in the 1980s as described in Chapter 6. Regulations that restrict bank investments in certain markets are particularly prone to roll back and dilution when those markets begin to bubble.

Finance companies (or any class of financial institutions) that invest in real estate markets should be subject to strong countercyclical regulations (which are explained below) to force them to build up buffers as real estate markets boom. If those regulations restricting banks from real estate markets are loosened, deregulation must be done with great care. Governments must counteract residual subsidies enjoyed by banks that would distort competition. Moreover, a quick bout of deregulation may cause a market boom as real estate or other markets are flooded with new credit. This boom may trigger or inflame a bubble when investors begin to chase higher prices.[60] This book has argued that the problem is often not deregulation, but deregulation done wrong. Both investors and regulators may mistake higher prices in the wake of a post-deregulation credit boom as evidence of changed market fundamentals rather than an unsustainable, temporary condition brought about by regulatory change.

When the levee breaks: separate pools of capital and social security

Restrictions on bank investments point to the benefits of segregating certain pools of investment capital from cyclical markets. This provides another perspective on proposals to privatize social security accounts. Imagine how much more pronounced the recent twinned real estate and capital markets bubbles might have been had Congress enacted George W. Bush administration proposals to privatize social security. Imagine how much more devastating the Panic of 2007–2008 would have been had citizens lost social security savings in the crash. Keeping social security funds separate from capital markets provides macroeconomic stability in several ways. It keeps additional liquidity out of booming and cyclical markets. It also protects retiree nest eggs, however modest they may be. Collectively, this guaranteed income to senior citizens ensures a minimum level of spending that prevents economic downturns from deepening. It goes without saying that this income also mitigates the human cost of collapsed bubbles.

The levees that keep this reservoir of capital separate from the stock market are, however, unstable. During boom times retirees and other citizens may join the political pressure to weaken these walls and let individuals invest their social security savings in the market. This political pressure dissipated with the Panic of 2007–2008, but will return. After all, the Social Security Trust Fund continues to face long-term challenges to its solvency.[61]

An academic point: disequilibrium in law

Indeed, all of these policies to decouple market and political cycles from one another would face enormous political stress as bubbles inflate. However, there is great value in merely realizing that these cycles exist and that they generate feedback for one another. Allow a momentary digression from policy analysis to consider a more academic point: legal policymakers and scholars must pay greater heed to feedback mechanisms that alter the effectiveness of regulations. They need to understand cycles that shape the content and application of legal rules. They also need to appreciate the radical disequilibrium that can afflict financial regulation, as well as other areas of law.

Economists have long studied and debated the prevalence of disequilibria in financial markets and economies. This includes not only the older, heterodox research of Hyman Minsky and Charles Kindleberger,[62] but also the more cutting edge behavioral finance research on noise trading and positive feedback investment strategies.[63] Some strands of economic research have been informed by research from other disciplines, including mathematics and physics, that argues that financial markets behave in inherently nonlinear ways.[64] Even in more orthodox economic circles, disequilibrium and nonlinearity have gained important footholds. Cutting edge macroeconomic research has investigated the workings of the leverage cycle.[65] Canonical macroeconomic works, such as those authored by Kiyotaki, Moore, Bernanke, and others create sophisticated models of cycles and amplification or "accelerator" feedback mechanisms.[66] A handful of legal scholars have begun teasing out the implications of economic research on the nonlinearity of markets for financial regulation.[67]

Much more study is needed on potential nonlinearity affecting legal rules. The Regulatory Instability Hypothesis created a set of theories that suggests financial laws suffer bouts of profound disequilibrium. These laws may suffer severe and even cyclical changes. The interaction of financial markets, political markets, and legal rules may result in nonlinear changes in the production, enforcement, interpretation, violation, and gamesmanship of legal rules. In other words, the passage and repeal of legal rules, the intensity of enforcement, the levels of legal compliance and regulatory arbitrage, and herd behaviour induced by regulation each may change abruptly and even cyclically from one market period to another. This feedback among markets, the political environment, and legal rules can result in sudden and significant swings in the effectiveness of financial regulation. The potential of feedback mechanisms to affect law poses severe challenges to creating "optimal" legal rules.

The instability of financial regulation may have parallels in other areas of law. A handful of legal scholars have begun to explore nonlinear behavior and feedback mechanisms in various legal regimes in areas such as tort law,[68] administrative law,[69] international law,[70] communications law,[71] and tax law.[72] Environmental law scholars, by contrast, have examined the ways in which legal regimes have struggled to keep pace with feedback mechanisms that can result in abrupt, nonlinear changes in the natural environment, such as climate change.[73] Some environmental law scholars have advocated various institutional design measures to help environmental law regimes adapt to and intervene in these nonlinear and potentially catastrophic environmental processes.[74] Parallels between environmental and financial crises abound, and many of the institutional design recommendations in this chapter resonate with this environmental law literature. Yet environmental and financial regulatory scholarship could benefit from much more cross-pollination, as regulatory institutions in both fields grapple with similar challenges of complexity, nonlinearity, and potentially destructive feedback mechanisms.

Integrating macroeconomic policy and financial regulation

Legal scholarship must also make deeper forays into and connections with macroeconomics. Chapter 11 explained how financial regulation has a monetary dimension; changes to financial regulations that affect financial institution leverage or endow certain financial instruments with more of the economic characteristics of "money" can affect the effective supply of money in financial markets. Increases in this "liquidity," in turn, can fuel asset price bubbles. Chapter 11 also argued that, even if financial regulations are not used as monetary policy tools (whether to combat bubbles or otherwise), central banks still need a sophisticated sense of how significant changes in financial regulations would impact monetary conditions. Changes in the *effective strength* of financial regulations, whether through changes in levels of enforcement, compliance, or regulatory arbitrage, could have just as significant or an even greater impact than deregulation or the roll back of regulations.

This nexus between the monetary environment and prudential regulations highlights a deep need to coordinate macroeconomic and regulatory policy. This insight represents one of the central contributions of the macroprudential literature.[75] These calls for integration have historic precedent, as previous financial crises have led to similar calls for integrating macroeconomic policy and traditional financial regulation. For example, in the wake of financial crises in Sweden, Norway, and Finland in the early 1990s, scholars made this same call for integration.[76]

These scholars were driven by a concern that sudden and massive deregulation of financial institutions in those countries in the 1980s created destabilizing credit booms. These booms contributed to bubbles, which popped and triggered severe financial crises. The cocktail of deregulation of financial institutions and monetary growth could create dangerous feedback loops.[77] Australian scholars have reached the same conclusion on integrating regulatory and monetary policy after studying the history of financial crises in their nation.[78]

If macroeconomic policy is to be better integrated with prudential regulation, then academics must build bridges to span the yawning gulf between macro- and microeconomics.[79] This gulf creates a spot in which the macroeconomic consequences of aggregated microeconomic phenomena – such as regulatory changes – can escape attention. In this sweet spot, crises incubate. In the legal academy, there is only a nascent movement to integrate macroeconomics into the study of law.[80]

What lawyers add

A larger question looms: what can lawyers and legal scholars contribute to integrating monetary and regulatory policy? They can and must engage in at least three different ways.

First, lawyers can give monetary policymakers a more nuanced sense of the forms that regulatory change can take and when they are taking place. After all, the rise of the shadow banking system, which had tremendous but underappreciated monetary and regulatory consequences, grew because of an accretion of small regulatory changes. Chapter 11 explained how various legislative and regulatory decisions fueled the growth of markets for shadow banking instruments, and allowed these markets to fuse together into a parallel banking system. These decisions included more than just sweeping legislative changes (such as the repeal of Glass-Steagall or the statute exempting over-the-counter derivatives from a raft of state and federal regulations). They also included less show-stopping or controversial regulatory changes such as the granting of legal preferences to certain instruments (such as bankruptcy exemptions for repos and swaps)[81] and gradual changes in regulatory interpretations (such as those that allowed banks to participate in mortgage-backed securities and derivatives markets or to extend credit to non-banking affiliates).[82] Many changes in the *effective strength* of financial regulations came not from government officials, but from the actions of market participants engaging in sophisticated regulatory capital arbitrage. Regulatory capital arbitrage allowed financial institutions to game capital requirements and thus to dramatically increase and cloak their effective leverage.[83]

Lawyers and legal scholars need to equip central banks and regulators with a sense of how legal change can assume different shapes. At the same time, macroeconomists need to work with regulators and lawyers to understand the monetary and other macroeconomic impacts of these changes. Historically, two dynamics have thwarted this understanding. On the one hand, "Big Bang" legal changes (such as the repeal of major statutes) are easy to recognize. Yet their potentially massive economic effects – by unleashing a tidal wave of credit – may actually mask their risks. Investors, regulators, and central banks, can mistake the resultant rise in prices for improving fundamentals rather than as a temporary and perhaps unsustainable bubble caused by regulatory change. In other words, regulatory change may serve as the "displacement" in behavioral economic models of how bubbles form. Rising prices cloak imprudent lending and unstable financial institutions. Again, the problem is not in deregulation per se, but in deregulation done in an ill-conceived or improperly monitored manner.

On the other hand, small incremental changes can cause similar long-term effects. However, piecemeal changes can fly under the radar of central banks and scholars. The cumulative risks they pose can be hard to discern. For example, a decade-long series of regulatory interpretations that increasingly allowed banks to participate in mortgage-backed securities or derivatives markets may pose greater microeconomic risks for the stability of banks. They may also trigger increasing macroeconomic effects by increasing the supply of credit. Lawyers, microeconomists, macroeconomists, and regulators need to take a sustained look at the interaction of financial regulation and monetary conditions to understand the effects of legal changes and to identify potential tipping points.

Legal scholars can make a second contribution by identifying more laws, regulations, and policies that have the types of procyclical effects described in Chapter 7. Which legal rules operate to exacerbate the boom bust cycle? Chapter 7 gave an example of a nuanced study by the late legal scholar Sarah Woo that looked how the policies of bank regulators during firm bankruptcies triggered fire sale feedback loops.[84] Legal scholars can bring to the table this kind of thicker knowledge of how legal rules, relationships, and institutions interact.

Third, lawyers can use this specialized knowledge to think through the bramble bush of institutional design issues that come with integrating monetary policymaking and financial regulation. Should the connected but different functions of monetary and regulatory policy be housed within the same government body? That runs the risk of one of those duties being relatively neglected in terms of resources and institutional mission and worldview. If the experience of the Federal Reserve in the waning years of Alan Greenspan's Chairmanship provides any indication, a focus on the "hard" economics of central banking would overshadow prudential regulation (with consumer protection suffering as forgotten stepchild).

Assigning monetary and financial regulatory policies to separate bodies, however, requires extensive efforts to cultivate policy coordination and information sharing. The Dodd-Frank Act created a number of new bodies, including the Financial Stability Oversight Council to look at systemic risk threats.[85] It established the Office of Financial Research to track information on those threats.[86] However, merely creating or rearranging boxes on a governmental organizational chart obviously does not guarantee cooperation. Legislators and regulators must pay close attention to more finely grained questions such as creating clear mandates to integrate monetary and financial regulatory policy, specifying how to resolve conflicts between monetary and regulatory objectives, and institutionalizing relationships among lower-level staff members at different bodies. Financial reform faces the vexing challenge of changing the mindsets and norms of those individuals working at central banks and regulatory agencies. These officials must appreciate both the deep connections and tensions between their respective missions.

Gathering information; the serendipitous benefits of regulatory reform

On a more prosaic level, central banks and regulators should use the various tools already at their disposal to measure changes in financial institution leverage. Indeed, various provisions in the current rounds of financial reform designed to mitigate that leverage have a monetary dimension, Moreover, these provisions can be used to provide information to central bankers and regulators on changes in leverage, whether in shadow banking markets or otherwise.

Consider the difficulty of measuring the monetary effects of over-the-counter credit derivatives with the public information currently unavailable.[87] The need to develop better measures of liquidity in financial markets reveals a collateral benefit of Dodd-Franks' credit derivative regulations. Moving credit derivatives to exchanges and setting collateral requirements for other credit derivatives would allow central bankers to gather vital data on credit derivatives, the asset markets they affect, and the leverage they create. Indeed, knowing is half the battle.[88]

The need for more information on credit derivatives and the leverage they create makes some of the more obscure and less sexy provisions of the Dodd-Frank Act particularly vital. Various sections in Title VII of the statute give the Commodity Futures Trading Commission (CFTC) the authority to pass new regulations to gather information from swap counterparties and clearing organizations.[89] The CFTC should use this authority to create systems to gather crucial information on the macroeconomic impact of credit derivatives. These systems could track not only the volume of credit derivatives generally. They could also gauge the pricing of those derivatives and, most importantly, changes in the overall collateral that counterparties require under credit derivative contracts (above and beyond any collateral required by regulators pursuant to Dodd-Frank). Indications of whether leverage requirements are tightening or loosening in the aggregate can provide a sense of changes in overall market liquidity. Moreover, if regulators could gather more finely grained information on credit derivatives that relate to particular asset classes, they could then track changes in leverage and liquidity in particular asset markets, and not just on an aggregate level.

Adaptive institutions

Although some existing regulatory tools can be put to better uses, other institutions may have to be created or renovated to counteract the forces that destabilize financial regulation during boom times. The remainder of this chapter provides sketches of institutional structures that can help regulators and regulations adapt to changing market conditions, rising political pressures, cognitive limitations, and shifting norms. Although these proposals aim to provoke, the discussion below also considers their limitations.

Countercyclical rules

Instead of relying on agency independence, a radically different approach to insulating regulation from political pressure would lessen the need for human discretion by making regulation more automatic. More automatic regulations would reduce the ability of regulators to forbear from regulating during boom times. They would simultaneously provide regulators with some cover with politicians and industry groups: "I'd love to help, but my hands are tied." The benefits of more automatic regulations can be expressed in more formal terms of game theory. By binding their own hands with automatic regulation, policymakers send a signal of their commitment to industry and can thus bargain harder. This roughly parallels the winning strategy for the classic game of "chicken," as described by Thomas Schelling.[90]

At the same time, automatic regulations could adjust to economic cycles. Regulations begin to clamp down on financial institution lending and leverage as markets begin to overheat. In other words, regulations could be designed to adapt automatically to counteract the procyclical effects identified in Chapter 7. That chapter described these "procyclical" regulations with the example of loan loss reserve requirements. Many loan loss reserve regulations operate to require banks to hold fewer reserves as cyclical markets boom, and increased reserves after markets crash. This translates into a surfeit of bank credit that fuels market booms and a drought of credit that deepens a bust. Lower reserves on the cusp of a crash also render banks dangerously exposed to failure.[91]

Economists devised a solution to this problem by restructuring these rules to work *countercyclically*. Spain pioneered countercyclical loan loss reserve regulations or what it called "dynamic loan loss provisioning." Using economic data on bank losses during real estate cycles, Spanish regulators devised regulations that require banks to hold increased reserves as real estate cycles begin to heat up, but lower reserves after the cycle turns and the market dips.[92]

These regulations would have the double benefit of making booms and busts less severe, but also making banks more robust to economic downturns. To reiterate an earlier point, the objective is not, however, to smooth out the business cycle. Setting more modest goals means that countercyclical regulations need not be finely calibrated to adjust to every macroeconomic shift and every financial boom. Countercyclical regulations can serve as dampeners that allow financial architecture to survive major earthquakes. They should not attempt to quiet every tremor. This means that, although countercyclical regulations require good economic data and good macroeconomic and microeconomic models, the models do not have to be perfect.

This countercyclical idea caught fire in macroprudential scholarship.[93] This idea has also shaped brand new laws and policies. The Basel III Accord among international bank regulators is chocked full of provisions that make regulations countercyclical, including countercyclical capital requirements.[94] In the United States, the Dodd-Frank Act seeks to introduce countercyclical regulations to the United States. One set of provisions in the statute requires the Federal Reserve and other federal banking regulators to seek to make their capital requirements countercyclical.[95]

Regulatory arbitrage and the need for networked regulations

The Spanish example of countercyclical regulations, however, should temper any view that countercyclical regulations represent a panacea. Even with dynamic loan loss provisioning, Spain experienced a real estate bubble, the collapse of which crippled Spanish financial institutions.[96] Economists have argued that countercyclical regulations spared Spain's larger banks from the brunt of the financial crisis experienced by financial institutions in other European countries.[97] However, the Spanish experience suggests that the countercyclical approach does not represent a cure-all. The Spanish rules applied only to certain banks (*bancos*) and not to *cajas* (called *caixas* in some regions), which are a type of savings bank.[98] It was lending by the *cajas* that drove Spain's real estate bubble. The mass collapse of *cajas* after the bubble burst dragged that country into the maelstrom of Europe's financial crisis, a crisis that has ultimately not spared Spain's more heavily regulated *bancos*.[99]

This progression of events underscores a profound challenge to countercyclical regulations; like any more stringent financial regulation, legal arbitrage could swiftly render countercyclical regulations ineffective should they be applied only to one class of financial institution. Capital may flow around the regulation, as less regulated lenders attract more loan business and more investment from shareholders. Moreover, more capital may flow around the regulation just when an asset market begins to overheat and the countercyclical provisions begin to bite harder.

Chapter 5 described the effects of legal arbitrage on certain regulations that directly or indirectly restrict the flow of credit to financial markets. The capacity of investors and financial institutions to engage in *investment switching* (i.e., turning to alternative, less regulated investment opportunities or sources of credit) or *investment structuring* (i.e., crafting legal devices to exploit loopholes in regulations that restrict credit or investment) means that one countercyclical regulation in isolation may have little effect.

This arbitrage may work within a country (when there are markets or institutions subject to different regulatory regimes) and certainly across borders as well. For example, the effects of a countercyclical reserve or capital requirement on Italian banks may be thwarted by legal arbitrage. When these regulations tighten during boom times, borrowers may seek funds from (and investors may seek to invest capital in) the Italian banks' French, Swiss, or Austrian competitors. Higher capital requirements in Italy would also encourage Italian bankers to engage in the type of regulatory capital arbitrage strategies described in Chapter 5.

Addressing legal arbitrage requires that regulations of different financial institutions within a country and across borders be coordinated or even networked. Countercyclical mechanisms must be built into a range of regulations that cover different categories of financial institutions that serve the same markets. Countercyclical regulations should apply across economic substitutes for credit and investment products. If reserve requirements increase during a boom for Italian banks, so must collateral requirements for repos or other instruments that might serve as a substitute source of credit.

Similarly, capital requirements should ideally increase in other jurisdictions in a countercyclical fashion. Again, in the face of tighter restrictions in Italy, investors may flock to credit and investment opportunities in France, Switzerland, or Austria. This raises a number of challenges. Regulations must be coordinated across borders so that borrowers cannot use loans obtained in France to invest in an overheated Italian property market and thus make an end run around even well-designed countercyclical Italian regulations. Setting up the regulatory defense to this end run is by no means easy.

Solutions that work technically still must run a second gauntlet of political resistance. In the long run, the interests of French and Italian regulators in the above example converge to a degree. The French regulators have an interest in limiting the exposure of its financial institutions to an Italian real estate bubble, and their Italian counterparts have an interest in containing the damage from the collapse of a bubble.

That is not to say, however, that everyone in those two countries will share this long-term outlook. French financial institutions will salivate over the possibility of investing in booming Italian financial markets. Italian borrowers and real estate developers may lobby either to loosen Italian regulations on bank lending or seek a Gallic credit substitute. Furthermore, there will be enormous political pressure on Italian regulators to dilute countercyclical regulations should they actually work and investors begin to abandon an overheating Italian market for opportunities elsewhere (say in Slovenia). Although, the free flow of capital to other markets may be economically desirable, the bitter taste of capital flight requires plenty of grappa to wash down.

In addition, other countries would need their own countercyclical regulations to prevent a game of "whack-a-bubble." If Italian financial regulations tighten and cause investors to move to Slovenia, Slovenia needs its own countercyclical regulations to prevent its own real estate bubble. Slovenian countercyclical regulations that dampen booms would have the collateral benefit of reducing the political pressure on regulators in Italy and other neighboring jurisdictions.

What is needed then is a network of countercyclical regulations within and across countries. Building such a network would require more than close bilateral relations, but, moreover, an effective network of regulators and strong multilateral coordination. The Basel Committee and other multilateral financial regulatory organizations would serve as the natural incubators for these networks. This coordination problem is not unique to countercyclical regulations. It applies equally to all financial regulations. Legal arbitrage means that any enhanced financial regulation that affects a particular category of financial institution may simply drive activity to less regulated categories.

Countercyclical cousins: contingent capital and the search for
appropriate regulatory triggers

Countercyclical regulations have close cousins in other regulatory proposals that
have been floating around the financial regulation world for years. Scholars have
also proposed replacing standard bank capital regulations with requirements
that banks hold certain types of hybrid financial instruments. The theory is that
these financial instruments would reinforce market discipline, while providing
an extra cushion for banks in case their risk of failure spikes. One set of proposals would require banks to issue and maintain contingent convertible bonds,
that is debt that would automatically convert into equity should the bank's
financial health deteriorate. This conversion to equity would give troubled financial institutions greater buffers, provide a systemic risk bulwark against banks
falling like dominoes, and alert regulators.[100] This contingent capital approach
builds off earlier policy proposals that would have required banks to issue subordinated debt.[101]

The thorniest question is how to set the automatic triggers for when this debt
would convert into capital.[102] Setting the trigger according to market prices –
such as changes in the value of a bank's equity, credit spreads for a bank's debt
over a certain benchmark, or the price of credit derivatives protecting against the
bank's default – poses a severe risk that the alarm may go off too late. Each of
these approaches assumes that the markets will accurately price risk. To price
risk, investors would need accurate information on a company (which underscores the need for securities disclosure). Even accurate disclosure, however,
may not short circuit the types of market bubbles discussed throughout this
book.[103] To put it bluntly, if we are looking to counteract the effects of "irrational" markets, we should be circumspect in relying on market prices to sound
the klaxon early.

The dangers of dead-hand control

Overreliance on countercyclical rules might place crucial regulations on a disastrous autopilot. A dead hand might steer the economic ship onto the rocks. In
addition, the models or triggers behind countercyclical regulations might work at
one point, but later fail. For example, if models are built on ten years of historic
data, they might miss financial crises that last occurred twenty years ago.[104]
Models built on historic data would miss the "black swan" events popularized by
Nassim Taleb, i.e., those rare hundred year financial storms.[105]

Moreover, models and countercyclical regulations operate best in a static
environment. Financial markets, however, never stop evolving. They generate
new types of instruments and institutions and thus new risks. Automatic regulations, again, may fall victim to regulatory arbitrage.

Regulation-on-autopilot also increases the danger of regulators falling
asleep at the wheel. Scholars describe this as "automation bias." This describes
how various engineering solutions that automate safety decisions may lead to

catastrophic failure when the humans who serve as the last line of defense rely excessively on technology.[106] Some scholars attribute part of the blame for several subway and railway accidents to this bias, as train operators deferred too much to computerized safety systems.[107] Addressing automation bias requires that technology be designed not only with fail-safes that allow humans to override automated decisions. Moreover, human pilots must retain the "feel" of control to keep them alert. The pilot metaphor is not accidental. When designing airplanes with "fly-by-wire" controls (in which computers make continual adjustments to airplane controls like flaps, rudder, ailerons, and engine speed), aerospace engineers have learned to ensure that the airplane pilots continue to experience enough difficulty in controlling the plane so that they feel responsible for the plane's flight.[108] Of course, allowing regulators to override automatic regulations leaves them susceptible to political pressure and errors in judgment.

Countercyclical regulator budgets

An excessive focus on making regulations countercyclical should not obscure the need to make sure regulations are adequately enforced and obeyed. Recall the discussion in Chapters 3 and 4 of how a market boom can leave financial regulators with flat budgets vastly outgunned. As noted above, budgets that come from the largesse of political branches make regulators more susceptible to political pressure. This pressure may increase as extended market booms create strong disincentives for regulators to take actions that might stem the flow of punch to the party.

To address these problems, policymakers should make regulator budgets more countercyclical. The budgets of financial regulators, particularly those with examination and enforcement responsibilities, should automatically increase during booms as transaction volume in the markets they oversee spikes or the size of the institutions that they regulate mushrooms. Increased budgets will allow regulators to keep pace with a vastly expanded workload.

The devil, as always, is in the details. One alternative to increasing regulator budgets to keep up with market booms is to allow regulatory agencies to fund themselves through transaction taxes or licensing fees. Many bank regulators currently receive much of their funding through one of these sources.[109] Yet some kinds of transaction and licensing fees may themselves create perverse incentives for regulators. If individual fees represent a significant source of revenue for a regulatory body and the regulated entities have a choice of regulators, the regulated possess a large degree of bargaining leverage over the regulators. Regulators may be then reluctant to revoke a license or challenge a transaction. Scholars have expressed concern, for example, that the U.S. Office of the Comptroller of the Currency may be compromised in regulating banks for fear of losing licensing revenue should banks choose to switch to an alternative state charter.[110] Even small, broad based transaction taxes may raise similar concerns. For example, the SEC receives funds (albeit only after Congress releases these funds) from a fraction-of-a-penny transaction tax on each trade on the New York Stock Exchange and NASDAQ.[111] This may create a disincentive for securities regulators to pass regulations that might drive significant trading volume to less transparent trading platforms or offshore exchanges.[112]

A better approach would be to automatically increase regulator budgets during market booms without requiring them to fund themselves through taxes or fees. For example, the budget of securities regulators should automatically increase according to several metrics of the SEC's workload. Budget benchmarks might include overall stock market capitalization, the volume of market transactions, or the number of new securities filings. Regulator budgets should not, however, be strictly countercyclical. After a severe market downturn, a regulatory agency's workload may actually increase, when it is called upon to clean up the mess after the party has ended (such as by resolving failed institutions and prosecuting newly uncovered fraud). Thus, instead of a strict countercyclical budgeting process, policymakers should build automatic "kickers" into regulator budgets during booms.

This, of course, may still skew regulator incentives towards actions that promote boom times. This makes even clearer the imperative to ensure that financial regulators vigorously perform their functions – from addressing excessive leverage and risk-taking by banks to combatting financial fraud – during bubble times.

Only human

To ensure that regulators have the incentives and capacities to regulate effectively during bubble times, lawmakers must address the core human variables in the financial regulation equation. Here, again, the models of what drives human behavior matter intensely. Determining whether regulators make decisions according to rational cost–benefit calculations, cognitive heuristics, or norms and ideologies determines what sorts of legal institutions should be created to counteract bubble dynamics. The view of regulator-as-rational-maximizer would suggest changing the mix of carrots and sticks for government officials. Behavioral economic models might argue in favor of de-biasing or "nudging" regulators to make better decisions during bubbles. Addressing the norms and ideologies of regulators, by contrast, might require a more far-reaching redesign of regulatory institutions.

To some extent, a pragmatic mix of different solutions from different models could reinforce one another in positive ways. However, a deep yearning for "win/win" policies cannot hide the tectonic tensions between these models. Specifically, an excessive focus on carrots and sticks may undermine other intrinsic and social motivations of regulators. The discussion below focuses on two sets of proposals:

- reforming the ways in which regulatory staff are compensated and promoted to align their incentives with their long-term regulatory mission; *versus*

- enhancing the intellectual capital of, and fostering professional norms among, regulators by borrowing from the examples of successful regulatory bodies, as well as foreign and military services.

Other institutional proposals, discussed later in the chapter, seek to leverage insights from behavioral economics via debiasing and nudging.

Carrots and sticks: regulator compensation, promotion, and retention

One way to address the skewed incentives of financial regulators during bubbles is to overhaul the compensation, hiring, and promotion policies of financial regulators. Compensation is a logical place to start. The challenge is not solely to raise compensation to a level to ensure that the government can attract and retain talent in the face of competition from financial and legal sectors. It is also to design a compensation scheme that better aligns the incentives of regulators with their statutory mission. Executive compensation offers valuable lessons. In the 1980s and 1990s, business school academics started a revolution by arguing that executive compensation could be redesigned to align the interests of corporate management with shareholders.[113] "Pay for performance" took many forms including performance bonuses, and corporate grants of stock or options to management.[114] If the corporation did well, the theory went, so would executives.[115]

Some scholars have argued for transplanting this model to the public sector by paying regulators with the financial instruments of the banks they oversee. For example, legal scholars Todd Henderson and Fred Tung have proposed a scheme to pay bank regulators with subordinated debt issued by, or "phantom" securities linked to, the banking companies they oversee. If banks fail, regulators would suffer a blow to their personal wealth.[116] These proposals also include payments to the regulators of restricted bank stock to ensure that regulators do not become too conservative.[117]

This model could be adapted for other types of financial regulators whose job entails more than preventing bank failure by tying regulator compensation to various performance metrics. For example, a small portion of the compensation of securities regulators could be decreased by the number of financial frauds or restatements that occur on their watch. Models for this new approach to compensation already exist. In the United States, many federal employees receive modest performance bonuses.[118]

However, the devil, as always, is in the details. Executive compensation is again instructive. The "pay for performance" revolution may have led to perverse results; as executive compensation ballooned, academics questioned whether corporate governance or the marketplace provided an adequate check to ensure that pay did in fact reflect performance.[119] Poorly designed compensation devices and performance metrics created incentives for corporate management to engage in accounting games, investment decisions that increased short-term profits but entailed long-term risk, and even fraud, in each case to gin up stock prices to maximize compensation.[120] One lesson: the recipients of performance based compensation will pay close attention to the minutiae of rules to maximize their pay.

Thus policymakers need to ensure that the compensation metrics create proper and not perverse incentives that further the true long-term mission of the agencies. It is by no means straightforward to translate many of the generalized statutory mandates of regulators – such as "protect investors" – into concrete performance goals. Moreover, regulator performance is seldom measured along one axis only. If the only goal of securities regulation was to protect investors, more regulation would always be better and investors would be discouraged from taking any risk. The real regulatory goal must thus be rephrased as "to protect investors while allowing them to earn returns and allowing markets to provide capital to the private sector."

There is a very grave danger, however, with taking the carrot-and-stick approach with regulator pay too far. Many of the individuals who enter public service may have been motivated to do so not by compensation or job security. Instead, idealism, and ideology may have moved them. Those same factors may shape their decision-making while on the job by reinforcing intrinsic motivations and social norms within a community of regulators. A laser focus on compensation and carrot-and-stick incentives may not only then fail to change the behavior of regulators, it may undermine crucial pillars of regulatory institutions.

Cultivating regulator norms and developing intellectual capital

Reinforcing these pillars, however, is much less straightforward than changing economic incentives. Cultivating norms within communities and regulators requires greater attention to "soft" factors. The squishiness of the inquiry does not mean that it is any less critical. Furthermore, a number of useful precedents can serve as models for fostering norms and developing the intellectual capital of regulators at the same time.

Some scholars studying the Federal Deposit Insurance Corporation attribute a strong institutional culture in that agency to a key institutional factor. The FDIC is charged statutorily with protecting "the fund," that is the pool of cash that the agency safeguards to insure FDIC member banks. The fund has become more than just a mission printed on the paper of a statute, but, moreover, a focal point for instilling a sense of purpose among the agency's staff.[121] Note that this same dynamic may work to promote norms within the private sector financial community. In the wake of the financial crisis, a handful of economists and legal scholars have argued for strengthening the ability of financial markets to self-regulate and discipline one another.[122]

Other government branches have found creative ways to cultivate norms and develop intellectual capital. The military and foreign services have created numerous institutions designed to train officers and encourage farsighted planning. These institutions include in-house graduate schools (such as war colleges), policy planning arms, and think tanks.[123] Both militaries and foreign services also have nurtured relationships with external academic institutions and think tanks. These relationships develop through fellowships that enable academics to spend short stints in government service or public officials to enjoy research leaves. Some agencies also sponsor academic research grants.

The overarching goal of these programs is to encourage innovative thought about future diplomatic and military threats and opportunities. These programs seek to meet this goal by removing talented officers from everyday work responsibilities and exposing them to thinkers from outside the organization. This helps to counteract groupthink, often a noxious byproduct of strong, but insular institutional cultures.

Both foreign services and the militaries also spend considerable resources to expose their officers to their counterparts in other countries and to develop cross-border diplomatic and security networks. Obviously, overseas postings are a way of life for foreign service and military officers. Often these postings, involve the officers acting as liaisons to, and being housed in, other governments or intergovernmental organizations.[124] This idea is not completely foreign to financial regulation, as national regulators have liaisons to international regulatory organizations (such as the International Organization of Securities Commissions). Moreover, in the European Union, "supervisory colleges" of regulators from different nations have been charged with overseeing financial institutions.[125]

Applying these various initiatives to financial regulatory bodies would not only foster learning and research, but would also nurture the development of professional norms among regulatory staff. These norms could provide a bulwark against political pressure to deregulate at inopportune moments. Norms might also serve as a counterweight to any tendency of regulators to identify too much with private industry.

Some financial regulators – notably central banks – have already made significant steps in these directions. Central banks have large research arms staffed by economists hired from premier graduate programs.[126] The Dodd-Frank Act creates a new Office of Financial Research whose principal task is to collect data from financial companies to assist the Financial Stability Oversight Council. However, this Office of Financial Research also may pursue "applied research" and "essential long term research."[127]

More can be done along all these fronts. These research programs can be expanded to include more economists working on regulatory questions not just macroeconomists. These programs should also welcome non-economists, including lawyers and accountants. Other regulatory bodies – including securities and consumer finance agencies – need robust research and planning arms. Regulators from these agencies should be regularly seconded to the fledgling international organizations for regulatory cooperation, such as IOSCO for securities regulators. Moreover, agencies should second staff to counterparts in other countries in regular rotations. For example, regulators from Britain's Financial Services Authority could be assigned to a tour of duty with its counterpart in Japan.

There are risks even with fostering professional norms among regulators. Should regulators develop an "elite" mentality, they become either too antagonistic to industry or too removed from their sense of public duty. As in reforming regulator compensation, when developing an identity for regulators, policy-makers need to consider the multiple policy objectives that financial regulators are charged with meeting. More regulation is not always better. The overarching idea is to resist the tendency for perverse regulatory cycles, not to contribute to them, or to replace them with bureaucratic agglomeration. Nevertheless, recognizing that financial regulators are members of a profession that requires intellectual resources and strategic foresight – and not a mere bureaucracy that demands the occasional stick or carrot – can do much to ensure that regulators faithfully and competently execute their responsibilities even during bubble times.

Resetting the rules of the game

Realigned incentives and strong norms can only do so much to counteract political pressure during bubble periods. Moreover, these measures alone cannot address another persistent challenge to financial regulators, namely keeping up with the pace of private sector financial innovation. The rapid development of new financial instruments, transactions, and markets confounds the ability of regulators to understand the true purpose behind these inventions (i.e., to ask whether instruments have an economic purpose beyond arbitraging regulation), let alone to spot systemic and other risks. Both of these problems, political pressure and regulators falling behind in an intellectual arms race, underscore the need to change some of the structural ground rules of financial regulation.

The licensing of financial instruments and "shell games"

A large number of policymakers and scholars have made compelling arguments for changing the licensing and approval process. They contend that financial institutions should not be able to offer new financial products without the written approval of regulators. Many of these proposals aim to correct the asymmetry of information between the financial industry and government watchdogs to allow regulators to protect consumers or mitigate systemic risk.[128] A key feature of these proposals is specifying who – the regulator or the private sector financial innovator – has the burden of proving that a transaction is "safe," legitimate, efficient, or in the public interest.

This licensing approach could be extended quite a bit further to allow regulators to identify abusive regulatory arbitrage transactions. Here is a general rule of thumb to spot regulatory arbitrage: look for shell companies with few or no employees or operations. Shell companies serve a lighthouses (to create a nautical theme), often located offshore on distant islands in the English Channel or the Caribbean, that would send a beacon to passing ships that some form of regulatory arbitrage – tax, banking, accounting – is taking place. Except of course the signal is not sent, as the lighthouse keeper sees no profit in warning authorities. To continue the metaphor (perhaps past the shoal of absurdity): consider how many financial shipwrecks – Enron in 2011, special purpose vehicles in the

Panic of 2007–2008, and even the 1873 *Gründerkrach* in Germany – occur in the immediate vicinity of shell companies.

Reengineering legal architecture could at least begin to level the playing field and allow regulators to identify and invalidate improper shell companies. Lawmakers could implement a rule that any contracts with a company with no employees or operations are presumed unenforceable in that jurisdiction unless the shell company provides a notice to certain regulators of the company's economic purpose. A tougher version of the rule could ratchet up from a disclosure requirement to requiring regulatory approval for contracts to be enforceable.

Regulator licensing schemes are generally criticized for stifling financial innovation. Yet too often "innovation" is used as a rhetorical cudgel rather than as a delicate scalpel. It is important to ask piercing questions about the purposes for which an innovation is being used. If financial firms developed an instrument for economic objectives (such as transferring or spreading risk), regulators should approve an instrument. However, if the instrument has no purpose other than to arbitrage a financial law, then it should be invalidated.

Even so, it may be no mean feat to divine the purpose of complex financial products. Moreover, financial firms may have incentives to mask the purposes of products or to adapt some legitimate innovations for new and untoward purposes. The history of asset-backed securities demonstrates that products ostensibly designed for economic purposes can be transformed into instruments of regulatory arbitrage.[129] The potential for devolution suggests a strong need for placing the burden of proof on the financial industry in licensing decisions. It also argues for other procedural mechanisms to force ongoing regulatory review of financial products, including the following proposal of sunsets for certain regulatory decisions.

Sunsetting deregulation

In the wake of financial reform following the Panic of 2007–2008, some scholars have worried about the wisdom of regulating without fully understanding the causes of the crisis or the consequences of financial reform. Some have advocated an incremental approach to regulation to allow policymakers to judge the consequences of their actions.[130] Other scholars propose sunset provisions to manage this uncertainty and remove failed regulatory experiments well before they become entrenched by bureaucratic and political inertia.[131]

These proposals discount, however, the political dynamics that promote deregulation as memories of a crisis dim and frustrate effective regulatory responses to new threats as they emerge. Chapter 3 described how a variety of forces undermine the production of new regulations during bubble periods. It examined how market booms and the lapse of time from previous crises both invigorate interest groups pushing for regulatory stimulus and contribute to "disaster myopia." Although political inertia and the excessive government intrusion represent legitimate concerns, it is important to remember the interest group imbalance that pervades financial regulation. Absent interest group competition created by financial industry segmentation, there may be few parties to resist regulatory changes that allow financial institutions to increase systemic risk and externalize the cost of their risk-taking onto taxpayers or entire economies.

Deregulation and regulatory stimulus, on the other hand, can add fuel to over-heating markets, and weaken the stability of regulation and markets. Often, law-makers and regulators do not fully understand the consequences of deregulatory changes. Too seldom are deregulatory changes fully studied after the fact. Consider the wealth of scholarly articles during the debate over whether the Glass-Steagall Act should be rolled back, but the relative dearth of articles (at least until recently) studying the consequences after the statute's repeal. That imbalance may suggest the extent to which interest group politics, directly or indirectly, sets not only the media agenda, but the academic one as well. Even clear *post hoc* analysis of deregulation would be complicated by the tendency, explained above, for deregulation to cloak the risks it creates when it fuels market bubbles.

The potential hidden risks of massive deregulation suggest borrowing several pages from the book of reform skeptics. First, regulatory changes that unleash financial institution leverage should proceed incrementally. This would allow markets and regulators to understand better the effects of deregulation on market prices, financial institution behavior, and policy objectives. Nevertheless, incremental change must still be carefully monitored for its aggregate effects. Small regulatory changes can fly under the radar of public scrutiny. Moreover, policy-makers and scholars can miss the dangers of incremental regulatory changes and not see when law has passed critical tipping points.

Second, policymakers should consider imposing sunset provisions on more dramatic instances of various forms of regulatory stimulus – including the repeal of regulations, looser interpretations of legal rules, and certainly government subsidies to particular markets. These sunset provisions would provide an institutional mechanism to counteract some of the political pressure to deregulate during bubbles. It would reset the rules of the "precedent games" described in Chapter 3, in which financial industry groups use legal precedent when requesting regulatory interpretations in order to ratchet down the intensity of legal rules. If no interest group opposes this devolution, sunset provisions would provide some tonic to political imbalances. Sunsets would push the regulatory needle back in the direction of greater control of financial institution risk-taking and leverage.

Putting a shelf-life on a limited set of legal rule changes may frustrate the creation of expectations in financial markets. There is little doubt that industry groups will push to reinstall sunsetting deregulatory changes. Yet, there is great value in merely forcing the financial industry to justify the continuation of a deregulatory action. Deregulatory sunsets would provide at least some semblance of a check on poorly considered regulatory stimulus.

Double key deregulation

Law can also address the problem of overly strong incentives to deregulate during boom times by creating other institutional checks on deregulation. The repeal of certain critical regulations should include a fail-safe device that would require the consent of multiple institutions before the regulations can be repealed or loosened. This "double key" deregulation could, for example, take the form of two or more separate regulatory agencies needing to provide written consent before a regulation could be repealed. Double key sign-off could also be required before a regulator disengages the autopilot on the types of countercyclical regulations described above. For example, if a countercyclical regulation would require capital requirements to increase, but a regulator believes that would be unwise, she could maintain the current regulatory level only if she received approval from policymakers in another agency.

The Dodd-Frank Act contains several analogous mechanisms to this double key fail-safe. A number of provisions in the law require one agency to approve another's granting of exemptions to crucial provisions. For example, the Federal Reserve must agree to an exemption granted by the Office of the Comptroller of the Currency that would ease restrictions on the ability of a national bank to engage in transactions with affiliates.[132] This double key device addresses the troubling pre-crisis history of a series of incremental regulatory exemptions that allowed national banks to transfer government subsidies to subprime mortgage affiliates and other related companies active in shadow banking markets.[133] The Dodd-Frank statute also creates elaborate systems, in which multiple regulatory bodies must consent to the designation of certain non-bank financial institutions as subject to enhanced regulation.[134] Yet these types of provisions are designed to ensure due process and to restrict agency action, not to spur it. The double key design could also require that regulatory agencies receive legislative approval before deregulating. A legislature might also tie its own hands in its ability to repeal certain important financial regulations or laws by requiring supermajority votes or joint approval with other branches of government.

Implementing any of these double key solutions requires attention to the architecture of public law in a given country. Many solutions might need to be structured carefully to comply with the dictates of local constitutional and administrative law. To take the United States as an example, various features of U.S. law might limit some of the proposals above. For example, in *U.S.* v. *Winstar*,[135] the Supreme Court looked at the issue of whether certain contracts between the federal government, on the one hand, and private savings and loan institutions, on the other, remained enforceable despite subsequent congressional legislation that would have invalidated the contracts. The Court ruled that the contracts were indeed enforceable, but there was no majority opinion. Writing for a plurality, Justice Souter engaged in a long analysis of whether honoring these contracts would have unconstitutionally impeded the sovereign powers of Congress and the government. Justice Souter noted the ancient common law presumption in England against legislative entrenchment, i.e., the ability of a legislature to bind future legislatures.[136] The fact that this case resulted in no clear majority (but instead a plurality opinion, two concurrences, and a dissent) signals that attempts in the United States to hardwire laws or regulations and thus bind legislators or presidents to previous sovereign decisions will meet serious and sometimes fatal constitutional challenges.

The U.S. Supreme Court has also been skeptical of creative devices to hard-wire budget deficit reduction.[137] The Supreme Court would likely be much more deferential to the House and Senate in their ability to set internal procedural rules that might tie their own legislative hands.[138] For example, existing Senate rules require the vote of sixty senators to end a filibuster.[139] Senate custom gives individual Senators the right to place a "secret hold" on certain legislation and on a President's nominee to an executive position that requires Senate confirmation.[140] Similar internal procedures might be used to restrict the Senate or House from easily repealing a particular category of statute.

The double key check on deregulation has more practical limitations too. The approach works best when it is clear what constitutes "deregulation" – for example repeal of an entire statute, or lowering a capital requirement from one numerical standard to another. The double key device functions less well when deregulation or regulatory subsidies take other forms – such as subtler modifications to a law or regulation or changes to the interpretation or enforcement of a legal rule.[141]

The architecture of administrative law

Moreover, the double key can only block actions; it does not encourage policy-makers to take active steps, such as addressing new threats to financial stability. This underscores a larger challenge: the structure of U.S. administrative law is designed to cabin and control regulatory discretion. Working to ensure that regulators use their powers has not been central to its design. New rules and institutions designed to encourage effective regulation face an ancient tension between limiting government discretion and power and ensuring its efficacious use.

Yet, at least in the United States, some less radical tweaks to the existing architecture of administrative law may start to rebalance the playing field of deregulation given the lineup of interest groups and the dynamics of financial booms. For example, Carolyn Sissoko argues that U.S. administrative law may be structurally biased in favor of financial deregulation. She writes that the doctrine of standing limits the ability of many groups affected by deregulation, such as consumers, to challenge deregulatory efforts. The doctrine of standing in some cases may prevent these groups from even getting through the courthouse door to challenge an agency action. Her arguments may be extended to taxpayers who have to fund the bailouts of failed financial institutions. To remedy this, Sissoko resuscitates an older concept and recommends creating "citizen standing" in order to challenge certain deregulatory actions.[142] Michael Livermore and Richard Revesz propose another solution to address agency inaction. They argue that a central regulatory body (in this case, the Office of Information and

Regulatory Affairs (OIRA) within the White House Office of Management and Budget (OMB)) should review rejected petitions filed with federal agencies that call for new regulations.[143]

Legal requirements that financial regulators justify new rules in terms of economic costs and benefits pose another structural challenge to effective regulation during bubble times. The U.S. Court of Appeals for the D.C. Circuit, the most important appellate court in the United States for administrative law matters below the Supreme Court, has made this cost–benefit analysis a formidable obstacle for financial regulators. In several high-profile cases in the last decade, this court has invalidated new SEC regulations, ruling that that agency had not conducted a sufficient cost–benefit analysis.[144]

As Chapter 3 notes, prophylactic legal rules, such as regulations designed to mitigate systemic risk may fare particularly poorly in running this gauntlet. Legal scholars have noted that, under many variants of cost–benefit analysis, hard economic costs tend to crowd out softer social benefits.[145] The benefits of prophylactic financial rules may be similarly hard to see. After all, no one sees the crises that do not happen. Moreover, industry groups have both the incentives and resources to produce data on the possible costs. There are fewer comparable groups with the practical ability to present evidence on the other side of the benefits of prophylactic regulation. If courts do not adjust their rulings to recognize this imbalance, Congress should intervene to ensure that prophylactic systemic risk regulations are not subject to cramped interpretations of cost–benefit analysis requirements.[146]

Waking the watchers

Harnessing competition

Solving the problem of agency inaction requires the creation of new institutions whose task is to sound the alarm about bubbles, poorly conceived deregulation, excessive regulatory stimulus, or metastasizing systemic risks. Greater disclosure of the actions of financial regulators and policymakers can help. Indeed, the chapter discusses below various proposals, including "radical regulatory transparency." However, greater regulatory transparency is of little use unless there are persons or institutions that can process the revealed information and use it to discipline regulators.

The financial universe does contain some parties that have a keen interest in ensuring that national financial regulators do not shirk their duties as well as possess the analytical capacity to perform this policing. These watchdogs include other financial institutions that may fear their competitors are receiving sweetheart treatment. An agency's public sector competitors (rival agencies within the same country or in other nations) may serve a similar oversight function. These public sector rivals may be motivated to monitor their counterparts because of either fear of losing regulatory turf or a desire to protect their own "client" financial institutions from losing a competitive position due to unfair regulatory treatment.

Legal structures to employ these two types of watchdogs must be skillfully designed. First, each type of competitors, financial institutions, and regulators, may respond to lax regulation by demanding the same lowering of standards in their own jurisdiction. This creates the specter of a classic regulatory race to the bottom. Second, even where competition among regulators does not lead to a race to the bottom, it may interfere with the necessary collaboration of regulators across jurisdictions. Therefore, mechanisms that grant these watchdogs the power to oversee and discipline financial regulators must be structured to ensure that the floor does not drop out of regulatory standards.

Much scholarly work remains to be done to support regulatory design. We still have an impoverished understanding of the effects of competition among regulatory agencies, particularly in the financial realm. Without better theoretical frameworks and empirical data, it is extremely risky to recommend a sweeping redesign of national regulatory architecture. Consider that before the crisis many scholars and some policymakers in the United States advocated a unified financial regulator, along the lines of the U.K. Financial Services Authority.[147] The performance of that regulator in the years leading up the Panic of 2007–2008 dimmed that enthusiasm and prompted British lawmakers to break up the FSA.[148] Meanwhile, U.S. lawmakers have looked to cabin the regulatory powers of the Federal Reserve.[149] At the same time, German lawmakers have moved to let the *Bundesbank* assume responsibilities from Germany's financial regulator.[150] This scramble suggests not so much the cultural and contextual differences between financial regulation in different nations as the intellectual muddle caused by a lack of theory and evidence about regulatory design, regulatory competition, and the allocation of regulatory responsibilities among multiple financial regulators.

New watchdogs: institutionalizing dissent

Instead of grand designs, perhaps the more pragmatic course would be to create new institutions within the existing regulatory architecture of any country. Lawmakers should consider creating regulatory bodies whose only task would be to hold other financial regulators' feet to the fire. These watchdogs would fight against deteriorating regulation, ill-conceived interpretative changes, and lax enforcement. These watchdogs would ensure that financial regulators faithfully enforce the laws.

The U.S. Financial Stability Oversight Council (with the assistance of the Office of Financial Research) might play some of these roles to an extent.[151] However, this super-council of regulators may be better suited to spotting macro-risks. Without a large staff and a clear legal and cultural mandate, this super-regulator may struggle to attend to the incredibly important technical details of rule-making and interpretation by regulatory agencies in the ordinary course. The incremental agglomeration of small-scale rule changes and enforcement actions matters intensely.

Macro-regulators need to work alongside smaller institutional bodies whose job is to check poorly conceived small-scale regulatory stimulus – whether it takes the form of a roll back of a regulation, questionable agency interpretations of a legal rule, or lax enforcement actions. The inspector general office in many U.S. regulatory agencies serves as a useful template.[152] Here the role of the watchdog would not be to serve as a general ombudsman. Instead, the watchdog would function as a catalyst for vigorous regulation during boom times and as a sentry watching for regulatory overreaction during busts. This role meshes with calls for an independent regulatory agency to serve as the financial sector equivalent of a National Transportation Safety Board. Under those proposals, an independent body would conduct an inquiry – akin to a coroner's inquest – to determine the causes of either a particular financial institution's failure or a larger financial crisis. The public body would then issue recommendations for regulatory reform.[153]

Law professors Brett McDonnell and Daniel Schwarcz have made a compelling proposal for deploying "regulatory contrarians" within financial regulators. McDonnell and Schwarcz argue that certain types of existing officials or bodies within regulatory agencies – such as inspector generals and ombudsmen – work to counteract group-think and make agencies more responsive to certain risks and policy considerations. They categorize these existing contrarians into four categories: ombudsmen, consumer representatives, investigative contrarians, and research contrarians. According to McDonnell and Schwarcz, the first two categories generally operate to promote consumer financial protection. The latter two types either investigate alleged agency mistakes or conduct general research. McDonnell and Schwarcz argue for adapting these contrarians to give them a broader mandate of ensuring that financial regulators respond to emerging financial risks, whether by passing new rules or adapting and enforcing existing rules. These contrarians could also provide a check against the wanton repeal of rules.[154]

This type of body could also be tasked with prospective duties of identifying crises before they happen. For example, some scholars have called for a National Institute of Finance that would be given broad power to collect from regulators data on financial institutions in order to identify emerging systemic risks.[155] This idea influenced the creation of the Office of Financial Research described above. Separating out the identification of systemic threats from the power to regulate them would address concerns that a central "systemic risk regulator" would concentrate too much power in one place.[156] Having separate watchdog institutions creates a healthy dose of checks and balances. These would guard against abuse of power and mistakes arising from overreliance on one set of decision-makers.

Policy entrepreneurs and the cursus honorum

Once new watchdog bodies are created, the question remains: would talented individuals enlist? Would these watchdog agencies attract capable staff? The public sector will never be able to match the compensation of Wall Street or Fleet Street. Yet the discussion of norms above underlined how other motivations can inspire individuals to work for regulatory agencies and regulatory contrarians. Prestige and power can mingle with idealism to recruit the brightest and best.

The prospect of career enhancement in the public and private sectors may prove particularly attractive. Consider the political rise of Eliot Spitzer as he took on Wall Street practices as New York's Attorney General in the aftermath of the dot-com bubble. His subsequent fall from grace in a sex scandal should not detract from the potential rewards to being a vigorous regulator. The private sector may also offer rewards to vigorous regulators. Although many bemoan the revolving door, there is both anecdotal and empirical evidence that more *aggressive* rather than lax regulators receive the best job opportunities in law firms and financial institutions.[157]

The types of institutions that cultivate norms among regulators may also add to their prestige. The ancient Romans created a *cursus honorum* that created the steps for political leaders to rise to power. Modern France has the *École normale supérieure* and other selective and prestigious *grande écoles* to train young people for the highest positions in government. Associates often trade their lucrative positions at U.S. law firms for stints in the offices of a U.S. Attorney. Other associates leave to take positions in the federal government, including the U.S. Departments of Treasury or Justice, the Federal Reserve, or the Securities and Exchange Commission. Elitism, however much derided, can cultivate better regulators. Moreover, the names we call regulators have a powerful valence. Earlier versions of this manuscript were changed to replace "bureaucrat" with a less loaded nomenclature for public servants.

Regulatory peer review

Another way to harness regulatory competition would be to graft the concept of peer review from the academic world to the regulatory one. Under this approach, one financial regulator would retain primary responsibility for inspecting a given class of financial institutions and enforcing a set of substantive laws. Teams from other regulators would then audit the work of the primary regulator by re-inspecting randomly chosen financial institutions. The potential for having embarrassing mistakes brought to light would make the primary regulator more diligent. This approach could be expanded so that foreign regulators might also have the periodic ability to audit their counterparts' work. A foundation for this cross-border peer review already exists in the "supervisory colleges" developed by the European Union and proposed by the G-20.[158] Other international bodies have begun to use different programs to monitor the implementation of financial regulation by national regulators. These include the Basel Committee's Consistency Assessment Program[159] and the International Monetary Fund's Financial Sector Assessment Program (FSAP).[160]

This peer review represents a significant extension of the concept of "back-up authority." Back-up authority gives a second regulatory body the power to regulate the financial institutions, products, and markets of a primary regulator.[161] It provides a check should the primary regulator fail to take action.

Lessons from international trade law

Developing other legal mechanisms can afford financial institutions a means to express concerns about the under-regulation or deregulation of their cross-border competitors. International trade law might be instructive. Regimes like the World Trade Organization allow member nations to bring formal complaints on behalf of industries within their borders against other countries for imposing trade barriers or granting illegal subsidies to their home country firms.[162] There are powerful parallels to the regulation of financial markets. Deregulation, under-regulation, and under-enforcement of financial regulation by one country may represent a form of either unfair competition or cheating on obligations contained in agreements such as the Basel Accords.

Creating a mechanism for international trade-style dispute resolution would require, however, significant changes not only to the substance of the Basel Accords but to their legal status as well. The Basel Accords are not binding treaties among nations, but are recommendations from an international organization to bank regulators in member countries. This is "soft law" that aims to set common international standards.[163]

Moreover, not all trade regimes are equally effective. Many critics consider the North American Free Trade Agreement to be much less effective at economic integration and curtailing protectionism than the World Trade Organization.[164] Part of the success of applying the trade model to financial regulation will depend on whether remedies are well conceived. A country with a successful complaint should be allowed to impose some level of sanctions. Its remedies should not include, however, being allowed to reduce its own level of regulation, lest a complaint spur a race to the bottom. Policymakers should also consider giving private firms or industry standing in these new dispute resolution forums to complain about lax regulations or enforcement.[165] Here, too, financial regulation might borrow from international trade law; many bilateral investment treaties endow private parties with rights to force a sovereign nation into arbitration.[166]

Radical transparency

One necessary element of checking regulatory action or inaction is ensuring that regulatory action is transparent. This chapter has already skewered the loose usage of this buzzword. High level, abstract annual reports by a regulatory agency are of little use. What is needed are gritty details. It bears repeating that much of regulation occurs not in high level decisions on the content of legal rules – such as, whether to pass or repeal a regulation – but rather in how the rubber meets the road when regulations are enforced. Double keys and other policy devices may do little to affect the decisions that regulators in the field must make in their examination and enforcement roles. A regulatory staffer responsible for inspecting the safety and soundness of a particular bank makes thousands of decisions in deciding whether that institution's finances and practices meet any number of legal standards.

There is a large potential for that staffer to make mistakes or to engage in regulatory forbearance, i.e., the tendency to relax enforcement against financial institutions because of the many potential career ramifications for the regulator. This book has noted several times the problem of regulator forbearance and the strong disincentives regulators have to discipline financial institutions with excessive leverage and shaky finances. Moreover, more senior and political policymakers can frustrate effective regulation by instructing or interfering with examination and enforcement in the field.

To make the regulatory process transparent, the following discussion focuses on making enforcement, examination, and regulatory models transparent, as well as the limits that regulatory transparency should respect.

Transparency of enforcement

One tool to address inadequate examination, inspection, and enforcement is to make the enforcement activities of regulators more transparent and open to public scrutiny. As a term, "transparency" has lost much of its currency through overuse. It is thus critical to articulate concrete proposals. At a minimum, regulatory agencies should disclose which individuals were responsible for examinations, inspections, and enforcement of which financial institutions. This promotes accountability in the same way as inspection certificates in elevators. This accountability would also ensure the integrity of the compensation systems discussed above that might create performance incentives for regulators.

In addition, agencies should disclose other key pieces of information, such as logs of their examinations at various financial institutions, to allow the public to assess regulatory performance. The logs would reveal when an agency inspected a given financial institution, what the agency staff evaluated, and what problems they uncovered. Some regulatory agencies, such as the FDIC, already provide some of this enforcement information in their "call reports" on banks they have examined. However, these call reports omit crucial regulatory and supervisory ratings and other information, treating this data as confidential.[167]

The provision of raw regulatory information is, however, not enough. This disclosure should be directed to the regulatory contrarians and other watchdogs proposed above. Close attention must be paid to the format and design of disclosure so that the most critical facts – including financial institution leverage – can be easily understood by the reader.

Outsourcing regulation to models

Many regulatory agencies now rely on sophisticated computer based models and other technologies to evaluate the complex financial risks faced by financial institutions (including credit, market, operational, and liquidity risk).[168] Like every model, however, those used by regulators are only as good as their simplifying assumptions. Moreover, models do not forecast risks adequately when the data on financial institutions being inputted are shoddy. This is encapsulated by the old phrase "garbage in, garbage out." Obscured regulatory models prevent the public from assessing the full effectiveness of regulations.[169]

This problem is compounded when agencies outsource regulatory responsibilities to the proprietary models of financial institutions. For example, many banking, securities, and insurance regulations delegate responsibility for regulating the investment risk-taking of financial institutions to credit rating agencies.[170] These institutions are allowed to invest in debt securities that have been rated "investment grade" by a rating agency that in turn has been licensed by the government.[171] Rating agencies thus received government-granted oligopoly power and assumed the role of evaluating the safety of financial institution investments.[172]

This trend of regulatory outsourcing to private sector risk models accelerated in recent years. The Basel II Accord permits national bank regulators to allow certain large banks in their jurisdiction to set their own regulatory capital using their own internal proprietary models.[173] In the United States, the SEC chose to adopt this Basel II approach in 2004 when it allowed large investment bank-centered financial conglomerates to set their regulatory capital according to their proprietary risk models.[174] This switch – part of the SEC's Consolidated Supervised Entity Program – enabled investment banks to dramatically increase their leverage in the run-up to the current financial crisis.[175] The SEC's own Inspector General lambasted this program and found that the SEC's failure to audit the investment bank models contributed to the collapse of the Bear Stearns investment bank.[176] At the same time, policymakers and economists faulted the internal models approach of Basel II for leaving banks in Europe dangerously exposed in the financial crisis.[177]

These experiences draw into question whether bank regulators have the resources and expertise to audit private sector risk models in a meaningful way. The audit process also remains hidden from public view, increasing the risk not only of mistake but of regulatory forbearance, as well. Forbearance can translate into allowing financial institutions to use "loose" models to take on more risk and gain a competitive advantage.[178]

One response to these failures of private sector risk models would be to delegate less regulatory responsibility to them. This, however, may not be so easy. The role of rating agencies is now fairly deeply embedded in both law and regulation.[179] Many of the alternatives to evaluating the safety of financial institution investments have their own flaws. Chapter 5 summarized the failures of risk-bucket approaches to setting capital requirements. It examined how these types of regulations spurred regulatory arbitrage. Gauging the risk of financial instruments based on spreads or other market measures, as noted above, entrusts markets with pricing risk correctly. When markets are least likely to do so – when bubbles begin – is unfortunately when this market discipline would be most needed.

If regulation through private sector models is here to stay, then we need to dramatically improve the ability of the public and the marketplace to police both these models and the regulators auditing them. Fairly radical transparency is needed. Use of private sector models – whether rating agency models or internal bank models used to set capital – for key regulatory functions should be conditioned on disclosing in detail the key assumptions and structure of those models.

This crowdsources the policing of the models. It permits more technologically sophisticated members of the public to audit the models for critical flaws. Requiring disclosure of risk models builds off lessons from the "open source" movement in software; in open source software, the underlying code is disclosed and users may freely copy and adapt it. The regulatory functions of risk models also function as a kind of financial "code." As with open source software, disclosure might allow the "many minds" in the public to collaborate in "debugging" this financial code.[180]

To back-test the models (and to ensure that they are actually being used faithfully), the public would also need disclosure of the performance of financial assets. For example, evaluating risk models used to set bank regulatory capital would require detailed information on bank balance sheets as they change over time.

Limitations of transparency

Regulatory transparency must have some limits. There is some risk that disclosure of information uncovered in a regulator's examination of a bank might trigger a run on that firm.[181] Nevertheless, transparency with a time delay – that is later disclosure of the results of an examination – greatly lessens this risk. There are fewer concerns with *post hoc* disclosure of examination and enforcement actions by bank regulators.

Financial institutions have a legitimate proprietary interest in their models, which might be undermined by too much disclosure. We do want to encourage firms to invest more to create better risk models. Moreover, full disclosure of risk models might create more copycatting, and thus dangerously increase the homogeneity of risk models in the private sector. On the other hand, dangerous homogeneity may exist now. At least with greater disclosure it could be more easily identified.

We should also be circumspect about full public disclosure of many of the algorithms that regulators use to enforce the law. Disclosing, for example, the algorithms used by stock exchanges and securities regulators to detect insider trading would only enable evasion of the law. Similarly, there have been recent reports that fuller disclosure by rating agencies of their models allowed investment banks to reverse engineer and game the models. According to these reports, investment banks were thus able to stuff more risk into highly rated asset-backed securities.[182] Investment banks could thus arbitrage bank capital regulations and, possibly, deceive investors in those securities. Yet this investment bank gamesmanship might have been addressed by fuller discloser of the models the banks themselves used to structure those securities.

Memento mori *devices and "soft" countercyclical regulation*

This book ends with a final proposal that splices together some of the DNA of the preceding institutional proposals. It borrows from countercyclical regulations, but does not seek to impose substantive rules. Instead, this final proposal represents a "soft" form of countercyclical regulation. This proposal, which I call a *memento mori* device, would confront policymakers with the consequences of deregulating or failing to regulate. This device would force policymakers to explain publicly in a detailed report their reasons for failing to regulate a financial market aggressively. This reporting requirement would be triggered by either the repeal of a regulation or deviation from a countercyclical regulation (i.e., taking a countercyclical regulation off autopilot). The legislature or agency that takes this action would be required to state its detailed reasons, including why the historical reasons for a particular legal rule no longer apply. For example, to loosen a limitation on the loan-to-value ratios of bank loans, a regulator may need to issue findings why this action would not spur risky lending and fuel an asset boom.

The *memento mori* report could not only seek to force consideration of deregulation. It could also serve as a prompt to explain regulatory *inaction* in the face of growing threats to financial markets. Even if we cannot identify bubbles with precision, we know many of the warning signs: a persistent low interest rate environment,[183] increases in the effective money supply,[184] dramatic increases in leverage of consumers, financial institutions, or the economy as a whole,[185] or the influx of first-time investors in an asset market.[186] These harbingers of a financial crisis could serve as triggers for a *memento mori* report. In this report a legislature or regulator must issue findings as to whether there is increased risk to the financial system. For example, the triggers for countercyclical regulation described above could prompt regulators to report on potential threats from a bubble, an epidemic of fraud, or a chain of financial institution failures.

Moreover, the reports would require that regulators detail their concrete plans for addressing these threats. This soft countercyclical regulation would help keep regulators vigilant against new threats to financial stability. It would also require them to address the ways in which the Regulatory Instability Hypothesis suggests that financial law deteriorates during bubbles:

- *Is the government providing excessive regulatory stimulus to financial markets?*
- *Is the government subsidizing, or investing in, overheating markets?*
- *Is it enforcing laws adequately?*
- *Is the level of compliance with laws deteriorating?*
- *How and to what extent are financial institutions using financial products as instruments of regulatory arbitrage?*
- *More particularly, how are these firms using these instruments to hide increases in their leverage?*

- *To what extent are regulations having procyclical effects, i.e., exacerbating the boom?*
- *To what extent are regulations promoting herding by financial institutions into liquidity or particular types of investments and risks?*

Precedents

In pressing regulators to think about threats to financial stability, *memento mori* reports resemble the strategic reviews that defense departments and ministries routinely conduct. In the United States, for example, military planners must engage in Quadrennial Defense Reviews that outline the short- and long-run threats to national security and the measures that country's military must take to address those threats.[187]

One key element of any *memento mori* report is that the policymakers responsible for a decision must identify themselves by name. For legislative actions, this might require a roll call vote. This would both hold the decision makers accountable for their decisions, and should provide a sobering tonic for regulators immersed in a market boom with its attendant deregulatory pressures. It would also remove the protective cloak of anonymity, which allows policymakers in the aftermath of a crisis to shift blame easily.

One can see perhaps the kernel of a *memento mori* device in the Dodd-Frank Act provisions that require that each voting member of the Financial Stability Oversight Council, which would include heads of federal financial regulatory agencies, to submit together with the Council's annual report to Congress a signed certification that, "such member believes that the Council, the Government, and the private sector are taking all reasonable steps to ensure financial stability and to mitigate systemic risk that would negatively affect the economy."[188] If the member believes that not all reasonable steps are being taken, the member must submit a statement outlining which steps she believes are required.[189]

This provision differs from the *memento mori* concept in one key respect: it is annual and not triggered by certain economic conditions. The routinization of an annual report creates the risk that this Dodd-Frank certification will become rote and a makeweight. By contrast, the advantages of a *memento mori* triggered events, such as a dramatic boom in asset prices or in an increase in financial institution leverage, are that it would be more out of the ordinary, more newsworthy, and thus potentially more sobering for policymakers.

Encouraging thought, mobilizing engagement

Memento mori requirements are of course no panacea. Policymakers hell-bent on taking a course of action may treat these reports as no more than a speed bump. We should be humble about our ability to humble policymakers in the midst of boom times. Nevertheless, these reports would have great value if they provide an impetus for other political actors to mobilize support for more active financial regulation. This function of *memento mori* devices thus closely resembles the role that Environmental Impact Statements play in U.S. environmental law. Under the National Environmental Policy Act, federal agencies must conduct a detailed review of the possible environmental impacts of many projects receiving federal funds. The issuance of these reports is designed to inform the public of projects with potentially significant environmental repercussions. In theory, this also allows political groups, like environmental NGOs, to mobilize to attempt to block troubling projects. Environmental law scholars argue that the true success of the environmental impact statement, however, is not in bad projects that were blocked by protest. Instead, the value of this device is in those bad projects that never saw the light of day, but instead died in the bowels of the federal bureaucracy because of fear of public resistance should an impact statement be issued.[190]

This analogy to environmental law begs the question, though, of who would mobilize for active financial regulation. There are far fewer NGOs who support financial regulation in the same way that Greenpeace, the World Wildlife Fund, and other environmental groups advocate for stringent environmental regulation. Political entrepreneurs, such as individual legislators and political candidates, might take advantage of *memento mori* reports. However, their voices may be drowned out by the thunder of a financial boom.

Final remarks: the limitations of the law and moral instruction

How indeed will those voices be heard? Part of the answer to this question comes in providing some historical memory of bubbles and the ways in which they have caused the periodic deterioration and decay of financial regulation.

This chapter has offered various solutions to make financial regulation more adaptive[191] and to channel political forces so as to counter the perverse cycle of regulatory stimulus and reregulation. It has left for later the difficult labor of crafting concrete substantive regulations and sifting through empirical and experimental evidence to evaluate the need for particular regulations in particular contexts. Empirical and experimental evidence should also be used to evaluate the success of many of the proposals suggested above.

This is also no mean task. It is particularly difficult to evaluate regulations designed to prevent crisis since it is difficult to see the catastrophes that were averted. This creates a particular trap for financial regulations, namely that they may become victims of their own success. This trap may explain part of the periodic roll back of financial regulations as memories of a previous crisis wane, which roll back then prompts the cycle to restart.

Ultimately, we should be modest in our expectations of the law to escape this cycle completely, just as we should not expect to prevent all bubbles from occurring. We might also consider whether there are tools other than law that may be brought to bear on the problems described in this book. In examining financial laws, when looking to other disciplines, I have relied principally on economics and, to a lesser extent, history, psychology, and political science. Other social sciences or disciplines may also have much to say about bubbles and regulation.

We might even examine what morality and culture – areas of human inquiry not easily quantified and thus less discussed in law and economics – have to contribute. Both regulate human behavior, even in markets. Both undoubtedly play a role in the development of bubbles and in their aftermath.[192] I called those proposed regulatory mechanisms that force policymakers to confront publicly the possibility of a destructive bubble a *memento mori* device. These devices seek to remind policymakers of financial crises past and of the cyclic nature of financial markets and financial regulation.

The incantation *memento mori* – Latin for "remember, you will die" – was integral to the tradition in ancient Rome when a general or emperor was accorded a triumphal procession through the streets of the capital. The honoree was accompanied in his chariot by a slave, who held above the head of the triumphant one a laurel wreath, while whispering in his ear "memento mori, memento mori..." Venerated as a god for that day, the general was reminded by this spoken rite of the limits of his "immortality" and the boundaries of his power.

Western European art uses this same term to describe a still life painting that incorporated symbols of death to instruct the viewer about the vanity and fleetingness of life. The *memento mori* (or *vanitas*) motif featured prominently, for example, in Dutch painting since the seventeenth century. Dutch paintings in this style often included, alongside skulls and hourglasses, tulips. These flowers had increased cultural and moral resonance in that country after the Tulipomania of 1637 – which was perhaps history's first bubble.[193] Their association with that speculative mania made tulips a lasting symbol of the recurrence of human folly, financial and otherwise.

Indeed, slaves whispering *memento mori* and paintings of tulips may not have humbled every Roman emperor or Dutch burgher. Art like law may do little to abolish bubbles or other human follies. Yet the fact that those details from the images of Roman triumphs and Dutch still lifes speak to us still suggests that it is our calling to strive nonetheless.

Notes

1 Joseph Schumpeter gave the classic economic description of the creative destruction in market economies introduced by innovation, even as he expressed skepticism on the prospects for survival of capitalism. Joseph Schumpeter, *Capitalism, Socialism and Democracy* (1942, Harper & Brothers). For a recent book highlighting the positive roles bubbles have in stimulating innovation and economic growth and building infrastructure, see Daniel Gross, *Pop! Why Bubbles are Great for the Economy* (2007, Harper Business).
2 Chapter 1, "The role of credit in bubbles: the dangers of debt-fueled bubbles," "Rigor and pragmatism in identifying bubbles."
3 Chapter 1, "Rigor and pragmatism in identifying bubbles."
4 Chapter 1, "Rigor and pragmatism in identifying bubbles."
5 Chapter 1, "Rigor and pragmatism in identifying bubbles."

6 See Kimberly D. Krawiec, Don't "Screw Joe The Plummer": The Sausage-Making of Financial Reform, Duke Law Faculty Scholarship Paper 2445 (November 11, 2011) available at http://papers.ssrn.com/sol3/papers.cfm?abstract_id=1925431 (last visited July 31, 2013).

7 E.g., Justin O'Brien, The Politics of Enforcement: Eliot Spitzer, State–Federal Relations, and the Redesign of Financial Regulation, 35 *Publius* 449 (2005).

8 Claire Kelly, Financial Crises and Civil Society, 11 *Chicago Journal of International Law* 505 (2011).

9 Krawiec, *supra* note 6.

10 Heidi Mandanis Schooner, The Secrets of Bank Regulation, 6 *Green Bag* 389 (2003).

11 For an early article summarizing growing criticism of Greenspan's positions on financial regulation, see Edmund L. Andrews, Greenspan Concedes Error on Regulation, *New York Times*, October 24, 2008, at B1.

12 For example, Raghuram Rajan presents an incisive list of policy proposals to change the incentives for risk-taking by executives at financial firms. Raghuram G. Rajan, *Fault Lines: How Hidden Fractures Still Threaten the World Economy*, 160–8 (2010, Princeton University Press).

13 Markus K. Brunnermeier, Andrew Crockett, Charles Goodhart, Avinash D. Persaud, and Hyun Song Shin, *The Fundamental Principles of Financial Regulation*, 29–34 (2009, Centre for Economic Policy Research).

14 See ibid. at 36 ("regulation should be based on pre-set rules; otherwise, few regulator/supervisors will actually dare to face odium of tightening in boom conditions").

15 E.g., Anat Admati and Martin F. Hellwig, *The Bankers' New Clothes: What's Wrong with Banking and What to Do about It* (2012, Princeton University Press).

16 Simon, Johnson, Could Tax Reform Make the Financial System Safer? *New York Times* Economix Blog, July 21, 2011, available at http://economix.blogs.nytimes.com/2011/07/21/could-tax-reform-make-the-financial-system-safer/ (last visited July 30, 2013) (proposing tax on "excessive leverage").

17 Chapter 5, "The Basel Accords: the dialectics of capital requirements and regulatory capital arbitrage," and "Conclusion and complex adaptive systems."

18 Chapter 5, "Cheap debt: government guarantees, systemic risk, and the instability of regulatory capital requirements."

19 E.g., Rajan, *supra* note 12, at 160–1.

20 Dodd-Frank Wall Street Reform and Consumer Protection Act (Pub. L. No. 111–205).

21 E.g., Dodd-Frank Act § 716, 124 Stat. 1648 (codified at 15 U.S.C. § 8305) (prohibiting "federal assistance" to certain entities engaged in the derivatives business ("swaps entities")); § 1101, 124 Stat. 2113 (codified at 12 U.S.C. § 343) (restricting emergency lending powers of Federal Reserve).

22 For a compelling argument that bailouts are inevitable, see Adam J. Levitin, In Defense of Bailouts, 99 *Georgetown Law Journal* 435 (2011).

23 *Infra* notes 136 and 137.

24 Joseph White, What Not to Ask of Budget Processes: Lessons from George W. Bush's Years, 69 *Public Administration Review* 224 (2009) (providing short summary of U.S. federal budget laws and processes, as well as the way in which these rules and processes were manipulated by political branches).

25 See Katharina Pistor and Chenggang Xu, Incomplete Law, 35 *New York University Journal of International Law and Politics* 931 (2003).

26 Amar Bhidé, *A Call for Judgment: Sensible Finance for a Dynamic Economy*, 104–30 (2010, Oxford University Press).

27 Christine Jolls and Cass R. Sunstein, Debiasing through Law, 35, *Journal of Legal Studies* 199 (2006).

28 Richard H. Thaler and Cass R. Sunstein, *Nudge: Improving Decisions About Health, Wealth, and Happiness* (2008, Yale University Press).

29 Cf. Jolls and Sunstein, *supra* note 27, at 214–15 (surveying policies that require graphic labels of health risks on cigarette packages (such as pictures of tumors) based on behavioral economic research, but cautioning against "extreme" measures). See also David Hammond, Geoffrey T. Fong, Ron Borland, K. Michael Cummings, Ann McNeill, and Pete Driezen, Text and Graphic Warnings on Cigarette Packages: Findings from the International Tobacco Control Four Country Study, 32 *American Journal of Preventive Medicine* 202 (2007) (testing and finding evidence that graphic warnings of cigarette health risks led to greater consumer understanding roughly consistent with behavioral economic literature).

30 See Thaler and Sunstein, *supra* note 28, at 109–10 (discussing opt-in versus opt-out savings plans for individuals).

31 Michael E. Murphy, Assuring Responsible Risk Management in Banking: The Corporate Governance Dimension, 36 *Delaware Journal of Corporate Law* 121, 154–5 (discussing norms promoting or countering groupthink in corporate governance); cf. Brett McDonnell and Daniel Schwarcz, Regulatory Contrarians, 89 *North Carolina Law Review* 1629, 1639–40 (2011) (discussing groupthink in regulatory agencies).

32 Saule T. Omarova, Wall Street as Community of Fate: Toward Financial Industry Self-Regulation, 159 *University of Pennsylvania Law Review* 411 (2011).

33 See, e.g., Dan M. Kahan, The Logic of Reciprocity: Trust, Collective Action, and Law, 102 *Michigan Law Review* 71, 80–5 (2003) (discussing tension between deterrence and social-norm based explanations of tax compliance and evidence that norm of reciprocity provides better explanation for compliance). See generally Ruth W. Grant, *Strings Attached: Untangling the Ethics of Incentives* (2011, Princeton University Press).

34 Grant, *supra* 33, at 111–21.

35 Chapter 3, "The corporate form in the political marketplace."

36 *Citizens United* v. *Federal Election Comm'n*, 558 U.S. 50 (2010).

37 This quote has been attributed to former Federal Reserve Chairman William McChesney Martin. Robert J. Barbera, *The Cost of Capitalism: Understanding Market Mayhem and Stabilizing Our Economic Future*, 74 (2009, McGraw-Hill).

38 Lisa Schultz Bressman and Robert B. Thompson, The Future of Agency Independence, 63 *Vanderbilt Law Review* 599 (2010).

39 Geoffrey Miller describes how this same political pressure prevented central bankers in Japan from taking steps to address the real estate bubble as it developed in that country in the 1980s. Geoffrey P. Miller, The Role of a Central Bank in a Bubble Economy, 18 *Cardozo Law Review* 1053, 1055 (1996).

40 Chapter 3, "Revolving doors and expanding the concept of capture."

41 Chapter 3, "Behaviorally biased regulators."

42 E.g., Andrews, *supra* note 11.

43 See Office of the Comptroller of the Currency, Board of Governors of the Federal Reserve System, Federal Deposit Insurance Corporation, Office of Thrift Supervision, and National Credit Union Administration, Interagency Guidance on Nontraditional Mortgage Product Risks, 71 *Federal Register* 58, 609 (October 4, 2006). See Alex Binkley, Regulation of Exotic and Nontraditional Mortgages, in Developments in Banking and Financial Law: 2006–2007, 26 *Annual Review of Banking and Financial Law* 1 (2007) (detailing interagency guidance and criticisms of it).

44 E.g., Andrews, *supra* note 11.

45 Peter S. Goodman, The Reckoning: Taking Hard New Look at a Greenspan Legacy, *New York Times*, October 8, 2008, at A1.

46 Ibid. See also Erik F. Gerding, Code, Crash, and Open Source: The Outsourcing of Financial Regulation to Risk Models and the Global Financial Crisis, 84 *Washington Law Review* 127, 133–4 n.17, 18, 21 (2009).

47 *CBS News*, Geithner Defends Plan to Step Up Oversight: Senators Question Giving Federal Reserve More Regulatory Power Over Banks (June 18, 2009) available at www.cbsnews.com/stories/2009/06/18/business/main5095594.shtml (last visited July 31, 2013).

48 Chapter 3, "If you can't beat 'em: financial industry consolidation and liberalization." See also Chapter 11, "Bank participation in securitization."

49 Chapter 11, "Bank participation in securitization." See also Chapter 11, "Bank participation in derivatives markets," "The demise of Glass-Steagall and subsidy leakage," and "Lessons."

50 Luigi Zingales, Why I Was Won Over by Glass-Steagall, *Financial Times*, June 10, 2012, available at www.ft.com/cms/s/0/cb3e52be-b08d-11e1-8b36-00144feabdc0. html#axzz229LjcO25 (last visited July 31, 2013).

51 The Federalist No. 10 (James Madison) (concerning "factions").

52 Jeffrey M. Berry, *The Interest Group Society*, 31–4 (3rd ed. 1997, Longman Publishing Group) (describing rise of citizen interest groups, including environmental groups, in U.S. politics).

53 Kelly, *supra* note 8.

54 John Diaz, The Rise of Consumer Clout; Impact of Social Networking, *San Francisco Chronicle*, January 8, 2012, at E3.

55 Cf. Krawiec, *supra* note 6 (documenting massive participation in rule-making process of Volcker Rule of financial industry groups compared to much less extensive participation of organized citizen groups despite the public salience of the financial crisis and this regulation in particular).

56 Chapter 9, "Leverage cycles." See also Chapter 11, "Financial institutions and the leverage cycle."

57 For studies that show this positive serial correlation, see Karl E. Case and Robert J. Shiller, The Efficiency of the Market for Single-Family Homes, 79 *American Economic Review* 125 (1989); Peter Englund and Yannis M. Ioannides, House Price Dynamics: An International Empirical Perspective, 6 *Journal of Housing Economics* 119 (1997) (finding correlation of house prices within fifteen OECD countries); Peter Englund, John M. Quigley, and Christian L. Redfearn, Improved Price Indexes for Real Estate: Measuring the Course of Swedish Housing Prices, 44 *Journal of Urban Economics* 171, 195 (1998) (finding positive serial correlation in Swedish residential real estate); Edward L. Glaeser and Joseph Gyourko, Housing Dynamics, Unpublished Manuscript (April 21, 2007) available at http://realestate.wharton. upenn.edu/news/newsletter/pdf/may07.pdf (last visited July 31, 2013).

58 Franklin Allen and Elena Carletti, Systemic Risk from Real Estate and Macroprudential Regulation, Unpublished manuscript (August 22, 2011) available at www. federalreserve.gov/events/conferences/2011/rsr/papers/AllenCarletti.pdf (last visited July 31, 2013).

59 Carmen Reinhart and Kenneth Rogoff document a post-World War II pattern of real estate prices booming before major banking crises then declining in the year a banking crisis hits and continuing to decline for a period of several years afterwards. Carmen M. Reinhart and Kenneth S. Rogoff, *This Time is Different: Eight Centuries of Financial Folly*, 159 (2009, Princeton University Press) (hereinafter, Reinhart and Rogoff, *This Time is Different*). See also Carmen M. Reinhart and Kenneth S. Rogoff, Is the 2007 U.S. Subprime Crisis So Different? An International Historical Comparison, 98 *American Economic Review* 339 (2008). Their dataset shows that this pattern holds in both developed and emerging market countries. Reinhart and Rogoff, *This Time is Different*, *supra*, at 159–61.

In looking at developed countries in the period from 1970 to 2001, Michael Bordo and Olivier Jeanne found a pattern of many banking crises occurring either at the height of a real estate boom or immediately following a crash. Michael Bordo and Olivier Jeanne, Boom-Busts in Asset Prices, Economic Instability, and Monetary

Policy, National Bureau of Economic Research *Working Paper No. 8966*, 9–10 (2002) available at www.nber.org/papers/w8966 (last visited July 31, 2013).

In another study that looked at housing price data before forty-six banking crises, a boom and bust in real estate prices preceded over two-thirds of those crises. In that same study, banking crises followed thirty-five out of fifty-one real estate boom and bust cycles. Christopher Crowe, Giovanni Dell'Ariccia, Deniz Igan, and Pau Rabanal, How to Deal with Real Estate Booms: Lessons from Country Experiences, *IMF Working Paper 11/91* (April 2011) available at www.imf.org/external/pubs/cat/longres.aspx?sk=24812 (last visited July 31, 2013). See also Allen and Carletti *supra* note 57.

Other economists have documented links between specific banking crises (or series of banking crises in specific countries) and real estate boom and bust periods. Richard J. Herring and Susan Wachter, Real Estate Booms and Banking Busts: An International Perspective, Wharton Financial Institutions Center, *Working Paper No. 99-27* (1999) available at http://fic.wharton.upenn.edu/fic/papers/99/9927.pdf (last visited July 31, 2013). For a discussion of the links between the three banking crises in Norway from the 1890s to the 1990s and real estate booms and busts in that country, see Karsten Gerdrup, Three Episodes of Financial Fragility in Norway since the 1890's, *BIS Working Paper 142* (October 2003) available at www.bis.org/publ/work142.htm (last visited July 31, 2013).

60 Erik F. Gerding, Deregulation Pas de Deux: Dual Regulatory Classes of Financial Institutions and the Path to Financial Crisis in Sweden and the United States, 15 *NeXuS* 135, 145, 149–50 (2010).

61 Robert Pear, Social Security's Financial Health Worsens, *New York Times*, April 24, 2012, at A13.

62 Chapter 1, "Outside the mainstream: Minsky, leverage, and cycles."

63 Chapter 1, "Behavioral finance models of bubbles."

64 E.g., Benoit Mandelbrot and Richard L. Hudson, *The Misbehavior of Markets: A Fractal View of Financial Turbulence* (2006, Basic Books); Didier Sornette, *Why Stock Markets Crash: Critical Events in Complex Financial Systems* (2004, Princeton University Press).

65 Chapter 11, "Financial institutions and the leverage cycle," Chapter 9, "Leverage cycles."

66 E.g., Nobuhiro Kiyotaki and John Moore, Credit Cycles, 105 *Journal of Political Economy* 211 (1997); Ben Bernanke, Mark Gertler, and Simon gilchrist, The Financial Accelerator and the Flight to Quality, 78 *Review of Economics and Statistics* 1 (1996).

67 See, e.g., Lawrence A. Cunningham, From Random Walks to Chaotic Crashes: The Linear Genealogy of the Efficient Capital Market Hypothesis, 62 *George Washington Law Review* 546 (1994) (applying insights from chaos theory to understand stock market crashes); Katharina Pistor, On the Theoretical Foundations for Regulating Financial Markets, Columbia Law School, *Public Law and Legal Theory Working Paper No. 12-304* (June 28, 2012) available at http://papers.ssrn.com/sol3/papers.cfm?abstract_id=2113675 (last visited July 31, 2013) (examining implications of Hyman Minsky's work as well as "imperfect knowledge economics" and liquidity constraints for periodic financial market instability and financial regulation); José Gabilondo, Dodd-Frank, Liability Structure, and Financial Instability Cycles: Neither a (Ponzi) Borrower Nor a Lender Be, 46 *Wake Forest Law Review* 469 (2011) (examining implications of Minsky's work of financial instability for modern financial regulation); Kathryn Judge, Fragmentation Nodes: A Study in Financial Innovation, Complexity, and Systemic Risk, 64 *Stanford Law Review* 657 (2012) (exploring feedback mechanisms in securitization and real estate markets and effects on financial crisis).

68 E.g., Jason Scott Johnston, Uncertainty, Chaos, and the Torts Process: An Economic Analysis of Legal Form, 76 *Cornell Law Review* 341 (1991).

69 Donald T. Hornstein, Complexity Theory, Adaptation, and Administrative Law, 54 *Duke Law Journal* 913 (2005); J.B. Ruhl, Complexity Theory as a Paradigm for the Dynamical Law-and-Society System: A Wake-up Call for Legal Reductionism and the Modern Administrative State, 45 *Duke Law Journal* 849 (1996). J.B. Ruhl and James Salzman, Mozart and the Red Queen: The Problem of Regulatory Accretion in the Administrative State, 91 *Georgetown Law Journal* 757 (2003).

70 Yuval Shany, Assessing the Effectiveness of International Courts: A Goal-based Approach, 106 *American Journal of International Law* 225, 257 (2012) (discussing feedback loops in international courts); Alec Stone Sweet, *The Judicial Construction of Europe*, 55 (2004, Oxford University Press) (same).

71 Barbara A. Cherry, The Telecommunications Economy and Regulation as Coevolving Complex Adaptive Systems: Implications for Federalism, 59 *Federal Communications Law Journal* 369 (2007).

72 Michael A. Johnson, A Gap in the Analysis: Income Tax and Gender-Based Wage Differentials, 85 *Georgetown Law Journal* 2287 (1997).

73 E.g., David E. Adelman, The Challenge of Abrupt Climate Change for U.S. Environmental Regulation, 58 *Emory Law Journal* 379 (2008).

74 E.g., Alejandro E. Camacho, Adapting Governance to Climate Change: Managing Uncertainty through a Learning Infrastructure, 59 *Emory Law Journal* 1 (2009); J.B. Ruhl and Robert L. Fischman, Adaptive Management in the Courts, 95 *Minnesota Law Review* 424 (2010); J.B. Ruhl, General Design Principles for Resilience and Adaptive Capacity in Legal Systems with Applications to Climate Change Adaptation, 89 *North Carolina Law Review* 1373 (2011); Alejandro E. Camacho, Transforming the Means and Ends of Natural Resources Management, 89 *North Carolina Law Review* 1405 (2011).

75 Gabriele Galati and Ricchild Moessner, Macroprudential Policy: A Literature Review, *BIS Working Paper No. 337* (2011) available at www.bis.org/publ/work337.pdf (last visited July 31, 2013).

76 See Bent Sofus Trano̷y, The Swedish Financial Sector 1985–92: Policy-assisted Boom, Bust and Crash, in *Success and Failure in Public Governance: A Comparative Analysis*, 401, 409–11, 415–16 (Mark Bovens, Paul 't Hart, and B. Guy Peters eds., 2001, Edward Elgar).

77 See Erik F. Gerding, Deregulation Pas de Deux: Dual Regulatory Classes of Financial Institutions and the Path to Financial Crisis in Sweden and the United States, 15 *NeXuS* 135, 149–50 (2010). See also E. Philip Davis, *Debt, Financial Fragility and Systemic Risk*, 256 (1995, Oxford University Press); Peter Englund, The Swedish Banking Crisis: Roots and Consequences, 15 *Oxford Review of Economic Policy* 80, 88–9, 95–6 (1999); Lars Jonung, Lessons from Financial Liberalisation in Scandinavia, 50 *Comparative Economic Studies* 564, 577 (2008) (describing general trend of financial deregulation in Scandinavian countries in 1980s triggering asset price booms); Urban Bäckström, What Lessons Can be Learned from Recent Financial Crises? The Swedish Experience, 1997 *Federal Reserve Bank of Kansas City Proceedings* 129, 130 (1997) ("Credit market deregulation in 1985 … meant that the monetary conditions became more expansionary").

78 Jeffrey Carmichael and Neil Esho, Asset Price Bubbles and Prudential Regulation, in *Asset-Price Bubbles: The Implications for Monetary, Regulatory, and International Policies*, 481 (William C. Hunter, George G. Kaufman, and Michael Pomerleano, eds., 2003, MIT Press).

79 See Richard A. Posner, *A Failure of Capitalism: The Crisis of '08 and the Descent into Depression*, 231–2 (2009, Harvard University Press) (arguing that the crisis provided a "wake-up call to the economics profession" and underscored the need to integrate macroeconomics with research in finance theory on the operation of financial markets).

80 Legal scholarship has not been devoid of research on the nexus between legal rules
    and macroeconomic conditions. This research, still nascent, has broken into several
    lines of inquiry:
      Liquidity, leverage, and financial regulation. A handful of legal scholars have
    studied post-crisis, the nexus between monetary conditions, financial institution
    leverage, and financial regulation (which was the focus of Chapter 9). See, e.g., Mar-
    garet M. Blair, Financial Innovation, Leverage, Bubbles, and the Distribution of
    Income, 30 *Review of Banking and Financial Law* 225, 229–32 (2010); Margaret M.
    Blair and Erik F. Gerding, Sometimes Too Great a Notional: Measuring the "Sys-
    temic Significance" of OTC Credit Derivatives, 1 Lombard Street (August 31, 2009)
    available at http://papers.ssrn.com/sol3/papers.cfm?abstract_id=1475366 (last visited
    July 31, 2013); José M. Gabilondo, Leveraged Liquidity: Bear Raids and Junk Loans
    in the New Credit Market, 34 *Journal of Corporation Law* 447 (2009); José M.
    Gabilondo, So Now Who is Special? Business Model Shifts Among Firms that
    Borrow to Lend, 4 *Journal of Business and Technology Law* 261 (2009); Erik F.
    Gerding, Credit Derivatives, Leverage, and Financial Regulation's Missing Macro-
    economic Dimension, 8 *Berkeley Business Law Journal* 29 (2011).
      Law and asset price bubbles. A number of legal scholars have focused on how
    financial regulation can contribute to or retard asset price bubbles. See Adam J.
    Levitin and Susan Wachter, Explaining the Housing Bubble, *Georgetown Law and
    Economics Research Paper No. 10-16* (April 12, 2012), available at http://papers.
    ssrn.com/sol3/papers.cfm?abstract_id=1669401 (last visited July 31, 2013); Erik F.
    Gerding, Laws Against Bubbles: An Experimental-Asset-Market Approach to Ana-
    lyzing Financial Regulation, 2007 *Wisconsin Law Review* 977 (examining whether
    categories of financial regulation can dampen asset price bubbles). Other scholars
    have recently looked at whether the formation of a bubble should render some con-
    tracts unenforceable. See John Patrick Hunt, Taking Bubbles Seriously in Contract
    Law, 61 *Case Western Reserve Law Review* 681 (2010).
      Legal institutions and macroeconomic stability and sustainability. Professor
    Steven Ramirez has argued that financial regulation plays a vital role in macro-
    economic stability by promoting investor confidence. Steven A. Ramirez, Fear and
    Social Capitalism: the Law and Macroeconomics of Investor Confidence, 42 *Wash-
    burn Law Journal* 31 (2002). He has also examined how the New Deal introduced
    various legal institutions that were designed to bolster, directly or indirectly, national
    economic output and other macroeconomic goals. Steven A. Ramirez, The Law and
    Macroeconomics of the New Deal at 70, 62 *Maryland Law Review* 515 (2003). A
    number of other legal scholars have shared Professor Ramirez's vision of a macro-
    economic approach to law as an antidote to the perceived orthodoxy of microeco-
    nomic approaches to law. These scholars often write in a more philosophical and
    idealistic vein, finding in a macroeconomic approach to law and regulation a vehicle
    to achieve broader social goals. See, e.g., Mark Kelman, Could Lawyers Stop Reces-
    sions? Speculations on Law and Macroeconomics, 45 *Stanford Law Review* 1215
    (1993) (positing that law and legal interventions might provide a corrective to reces-
    sions and the resulting higher unemployment and economic misallocation); Douglas
    A. Kysar, Sustainability, Distribution, and the Macroeconomic Analysis of Law, 43
    Boston College Law Review 1 (2001) (framing the macroeconomic approach in
    terms of promoting environmental sustainability).
      Institutions of macroeconomic policymaking. Other legal scholars have written on
    more concrete topics involving the legal institutions involved in macroeconomic
    policymaking. For example, a number of scholars have written on the laws affecting
    central banks, bank regulators, and monetary policy generally. See, e.g., Heidi Man-
    danis Schooner, Comparative Analysis of Consolidated and Functional Regulation:
    Super Regulator: The Role of Central Banks in Bank Supervision in the United
    States and the United Kingdom, 28 *Brooklyn Journal of International Law* 411

(2003) (analyzing the compatibility of monetary policy and prudential supervision roles of central banks, and the legal structures supporting these twin roles). Some of this scholarship on macroeconomic (and particularly monetary) legal actors adopts a more critical perspective. See, e.g., Timothy A. Canova, Financial Market Failure as a Crisis in the Rule of Law: From Market Fundamentalism to a New Keynesian Regulatory Model, 12 *Harvard Law and Policy Review* 369 (2009) (arguing for greater popular control of macroeconomic policy to reverse capture of the Federal Reserve by the financial industry). Another strand of scholarship on monetary policy looks at the architecture of the international financial system, such as the International Monetary Fund. See, e.g., Rosa M. Lastra, *Legal Foundations of International Monetary Stability* (2006, Oxford University Press).

Legal architecture of fiscal policy. Still other scholars have written about the macroeconomic dimension of law while analyzing the legal architecture of fiscal policy. See, e.g., Kate Stith, Rewriting the Fiscal Constitution: The Case of Gramm-Rudman-Hollings, 76 *California Law Review* 595 (1988) (examining statutory regime designed to constrain federal spending); Neil H. Buchanan, Social Security, Generational Justice, and Long-Term Deficits, 58 *Tax Law Review* 275 (2005) (analyzing shortfalls in Social Security, effects of federal budget deficits, and tax policies); David A. Super, Rethinking Fiscal Federalism, 118 *Harvard Law Review* 2544 (2005).

Macroeconomic effects on legal decision-makers. Another line of inquiry focuses on how macroeconomic conditions can affect legal decision-makers. See, e.g., Nancy C. Staudt and Yilei He, The Macroeconomic Court: Rhetoric and Implications of New Deal Decision-Making, 5 *Northwestern Journal of Law and Social Policy* 87 (2010) (arguing that macroeconomic conditions influenced statutory interpretation by judges in the New Deal Supreme Court).

Legal institutions and growth. A number of legal scholars have examined how the development of legal institutions can promote economic growth. E.g., Adam Feibelman, Consumer Bankruptcy as Development Policy, 39 *Seton Hall Law Review* 63 (2009). Still other scholars have focused on regulatory change as a means to stimulate innovation and thus macroeconomic growth. See, e.g., John E. Tyler and Peter H. Schuck, U.S. Policy Regarding Highly Skilled Immigrants: Change Whose Time Has Come, in *The Kauffman Task Force on Law, Innovation, and Growth, Rules for Growth: Promoting Innovation and Growth Through Legal Reform*, 83 (2011, Ewing Marion Kauffman Foundation) available at www.kauffman.org/uploadedfiles/Rules-for-Growth.pdf (last visited July 31, 2013).

81 Chapter 11, "Regulatory preferences and money creation: bankruptcy exemptions for repos and swaps."
82 Chapter 11, "Bank participation in securitization," "Bank participation in derivatives markets," and "The demise of Glass-Steagall and subsidy leakage."
83 Chapter 5, "A case study: regulatory capital arbitrage," and "The crisis and the effects of regulatory capital arbitrage." See also Chapter 11, "Regulatory capital arbitrage revisited."
84 Sarah Pei Woo, Regulatory Bankruptcy: How Bank Regulation Causes Fire Sales, 99 *Georgetown Law Journal* 1615 (2011).
85 Dodd-Frank Act §§ 111–12, 124 Stat. 1392–8 (codified at 12 U.S.C. §§ 5321, 5322) (establishing the Financial Stability Oversight Council (FSOC) and its authority).
86 Dodd-Frank Act §§ 151–4, 124 Stat. 1412–18 (codified at 12 U.S.C. §§ 5341–4).
87 Gerding, Credit Derivatives, Leverage, and Financial Regulation's Missing Macroeconomic Dimension, *supra* note 80, at 70.
88 Ibid. at 70–1.
89 See, e.g., Dodd-Frank Act §§ 727, 124 Stat. 1696 (codified at 7 U.S.C.§ 2(a)(13)-(14) (requiring public reporting of certain swap transaction data); § 728, 124 Stat. 1697 (codified at 7 U.S.C. §24a) (authorizing CFTC to pass regulations to govern

swap data repositories); § 729 124 Stat. 1701 (codified at 7 U.S.C. § 6r) (authorizing CFTC to pass regulations to add additional reporting and recordkeeping requirements for uncleared swaps); § 730, 124 Stat. 1702 (codified at 7 U.S.C. § 6t) (authorizing CFTC to pass rules requiring additional reports from large swap traders).

90 Thomas C. Schelling, *Arms and Influence*, 116–25 (1966, Yale University Press). In Schelling's classic formulation of the game, two cars race towards one another. The first driver to swerve to avoid a crash loses. Under one winning strategy, a driver should remove the steering wheel (this was back when steering wheels were detachable) and throw it out the window to signal to the opponent that now his only sensible choice is to veer from an impending crash. Ibid.

91 For a sample of earlier economic research on this form of procyclicality, see Charles A.E. Goodhart, The Historical Pattern of Economic Cycles and Their Interaction with Asset Prices and Financial Regulation, in *Asset-Price Bubbles: The Implications for Monetary, Regulatory, and International Policies*, 467 (William C. Hunter, George G. Kaufman, and Michael Pomerleano, eds., 2003, MIT Press); Claudio Borio, Craig Furfine, and Philip Lowe, Procyclicality of the Financial System and Financial Stability: Issues and Policy Options, *BIS Papers No. 1* (2001) available at www.oenb.at/en/img/bispap01a_tcm16-15484.pdf (last visited February 26, 2010); Jeffrey Carmichael and Neil Esho, Asset Price Bubbles and Prudential Regulation, in *Asset-Price Bubbles: The Implications for Monetary, Regulatory, and International Policies*, 481 (William C. Hunter, George G. Kaufman, and Michael Pomerleano, eds., 2003, MIT Press).

92 Spanish regulations, which first took effect in 2000, used historical data on bank loan losses compared to the country's GDP to construct an additional loan loss provision that banks would have to take in good years to compensate for future loan losses during later economic downturns. Spanish banks had the option of using this government-calculated dynamic provision or using their own internal statistical models to calculate a more appropriate provision for credit risk. Jaime Caruana, Banking Provisions and Asset Price Bubbles, in *Asset-Price Bubbles: The Implications for Monetary, Regulatory, and International Policies*, 537 (William C. Hunter, George G. Kaufman, and Michael Pomerleano, eds., 2003, MIT Press).

93 E.g., Brunnermeier *et al.*, *supra* note 13.

94 Basel Committee on Banking Supervision, Basel III: A Global Regulatory Framework for More Resilient Banks and Banking Systems Part A.4. (December 2010, rev'd June 2011).

95 Dodd-Frank Act § 616, 124 Stat. 1615 (codified at 12 U.S.C. §§ 1844(b), 1467a(g) (1), 3907(a)(1)).

96 See generally Julio Ramos-Tallada, Financial Distress and Banking Regulation: What is Different about Spain? 6 *Journal of Innovation Economics* 49 (2010).

97 Franklin Allen and Elena Carletti, Financial Regulation Going Forward, Institute of Monetary and Economic Studies, Bank of Japan *Discussion Paper No. 10-E-18*, 11 (May 6, 2010) available at www.imes.boj.or.jp/english/publication/conf/2010/Session5.pdf (last visited July 31, 2013).

98 Douglas J. Elliott, An Overview of Macroprudential Policy and Countercyclical Capital Requirements, Brookings Institute, *Working Paper 40* (March 10, 2011) available   at   www.brookings.edu/~/media/research/files/papers/2011/3/11%20 capital%20elliott/0311_capital_elliott.pdf (last visited July 31, 2013).

99 See generally Larry Neal and María Concepción García-Iglesias, The Economy of Spain in the Eurozone Before and After the Crisis of 2008, Unpublished manuscript (February 20, 2012) available at http://mpra.ub.uni-muenchen.de/37008/1/SpainEuroExperienceFeb20_2012.pdf (last visited July 31, 2013); Carrie Harrington, The Spanish Financial Crisis, Unpublished manuscript (April 2011) available at http://ebook.law.uiowa.edu/ebook/content/spanish-financial-crisis (last visited July 31, 2013).

100 Boris Albul, Dwight M. Jaffee, and Alexei Tchistyi, Contingent Convertible Bonds and Capital Structure Decisions, Coleman Fung Risk Management Research Center, Institute of Business and Economic Research, *UC Berkeley Working Paper 2010-01* (March 26, 2010) available at www.escholarship.org/uc/item/95821712?display=all (last visited May 10, 2010); John C. Coffee, Jr., Systemic Risk After Dodd-Frank: Contingent Capital and the Need for Regulatory Strategies Beyond Oversight, 111 *Columbia Law Review* 795 (2011).

101 Scholars at the American Enterprise Institute's Shadow Financial Regulation Committee have recommended replacing capital requirements on banks with requirements that banks issue and maintain subordinated debt. Shadow Financial Regulatory Committee, Reforming Bank Capital Regulation, *Statement 160* (March 2, 2000) available at www.aei.org/article/16542 (last visited July 31, 2013). See also Mark E. Van Der Weide and Satish M. Kini, Subordinated Debt: A Capital Markets Approach to Bank Regulation, 41 *Boston College Law Review* 195 (2000). The theory of this proposal is that holders of subordinated debt would be particularly exposed should a company fail. Accordingly, steep drops in the values of subordinated debt would sound the alarm. Holders of subordinated debt might also play a valuable corporate governance role in disciplining management not to take excessive risks.

102 See Wulf A. Kaal and Christoph K. Henkel, Contingent Capital with Sequential Triggers, 49 *San Diego Law Review* 221 (2012) (proposing one set of trigger mechanisms).

103 Chapter 8, "Improving fundamental information to investors and information processing of investors."

104 Gerding, *supra* note 46, at 171.

105 Nassim Nicholas Taleb, *The Black Swan: The Impact of the Highly Improbable* (2007, Random House). See also Nicholas Taleb and Avital Pilpel, Epistemology and Risk Management, *Risk and Regulation* (Summer 2007), available at www.fooledbyrandomness.com/LSE-Taleb-Pilpel.pdf (last visited July 31, 2013).

106 Linda J. Skitka, Kathleen L. Mosier, Mark Burdick, and Bonnie Rosenblatt, Automation Bias and Errors: Are Crews Better Than Individuals? 10 *International Journal of Aviation Psychology* 85 (2000) (analyzing bias in context of automated systems in airline cockpits); Linda J. Skitka, Kathleen L. Mosier, and Mark Burdick, Does Automation Bias Decision-making? 51 *International Journal of Human–Computer Studies* 991 (1999) (same). See also Mary L. Cummings, Automation and Accountability in Decision Support System Interface Design, 32 *Journal of Technology Studies* 23 (2006).

Other scholars describe the risks of automating safety decisions as leading to an "automation paradox." One engineering scholar describes this paradox thus: "The better you make the automation, the more difficult it is to guard against these catastrophic failures in the future, because the automation becomes more and more powerful, and you rely on it more and more." Shankar Vedantam, Metrorail Crash May Exemplify Automation Paradox, *Washington Post*, June 29, 2009, at A9.

107 Vedantam, *supra* note 106; Mary T. Dzindolet, Hall P. Beck, and Linda G. Pierce, Adaptive Automation: Building Flexibility into Human-Machine Systems, 6 *Advances in Human Performance and Cognitive Engineering Research* 213 (2006). See also Robert N. Charette, Automated to Death, *IEEE Spectrum*, December 2009, available at http://spectrum.ieee.org/computing/software/automated-to-death/0 (last visited July 31, 2013).

108 Vedantam, *supra* note 106.

109 Christine E. Blair and Rose M. Kushmeider, Challenges to the Dual Banking System: The Funding of Bank Supervision, 18 *FDIC Banking Review* 1 (2006).

110 E.g., Arthur E. Wilmarth, Jr., The Financial Services Industry's Misguided Quest to Undermine the Consumer Financial Protection Bureau, 31 *Review of Banking and*

Financial Law 881, 912–13 (2012). Cf. Binyamin Appelbaum, By Switching Their Charters, Banks Skirt Supervision, *Washington Post*, January 22, 2009, at A1. For another analysis of banks switching between OCC and state charters, see Blair and Kushmeider, *supra* note 109.

111 The SEC collects these transaction fees pursuant to Section 31 of the Securities Exchange Act of 1934 (15 U.S.C. 78ee)(2009). See also Section 31 Transaction Fees, 17 C.F.R. § 240.31 (2009).

112 The SEC turns over a large portion of the fees it receives to the Treasury. Notably, the Dodd-Frank Act did not incorporate controversial proposals to allow the SEC to retain more of these fees or to become self-funding. Edward Wyatt, S.E.C. Hurt by Disarray in Its Books, *New York Times*, February 3, 2011, at B1.

   By contrast, the statute provided for self-funding of the new Office for Financial Research and the Financial Stability Oversight Council. Those two agencies will be funded by assessments levied on large bank holding companies and systemically significant non-bank financial companies. Dodd-Frank §§ 118, 124 Stat. 1408 (codified at 12 U.S.C. § 5328) § 155, 124 Stat. 1418 (codified at 12 U.S.C. § 5345). The Council, again, determines which non-bank financial companies qualify as systemically significant, and thus has some incentive to make a broad determination to secure funding. However, the Secretary of the Treasury sets the actual assessment schedule subject to the approval of the Council. Dodd-Frank § 155(d), 124 Stat. 1419 (codified at 12 U.S.C. § 5345(d)).

113 See e.g., Michael C. Jensen and Kevin J. Murphy, CEO Incentives: It's Not How Much You Pay, But How, 3 *Harvard Business Review* 138 (May–June 1990); Michael C. Jensen and Kevin J. Murphy, Performance Pay and Top-Management Incentives, 98 *Journal of Political Economy* 225 (1990).

114 Michael C. Jensen, Kevin J. Murphy, and Eric Wruck, Remuneration: Where We've Been, How We Got to Here, What are the Problems, and How to Fix Them, *Harvard Negotiations, Organizations, and Markets Working Paper No. 04-28* (2004); European Corporate Governance Institute, *Finance Working Paper No. 44/2004*, 23–43 (July 24, 2004) available at http://papers.ssrn.com/sol3/papers.cfm?abstract_id= 561305&rec=1&srcabs=537783 (last visited April 15, 2011).

115 See *supra* note 112.

116 Frederick Tung and M. Todd Henderson, Pay for Regulator Performance, University of Chicago Law and Economics, *Olin Working Paper No. 574* (August 24, 2011) available at http://papers.ssrn.com/sol3/papers.cfm?abstract_id=1916310 (last visited July 31, 2013).

117 Ibid.

118 Christopher Lee and Hal Straus, Two-Thirds Of Federal Workers Get a Bonus, *Washington Post*, May 17, 2004, at A1.

119 For critical appraisals of the results of the pay for performance revolution, see Lucian Bebchuk and Jesse Fried, *Pay Without Performance: The Unfulfilled Promise of Executive Compensation* (2004, Harvard University Press) (arguing that corporate governance does not effectively check executive compensation). See also Randall S. Thomas, Should Directors Reduce Executive Pay? 54 *Hastings Law Journal* 437 (2003) (arguing many boards are unaware of important details of executive compensation).

120 Some of the intellectual architects of pay for performance found executive compensation for performance to have been flawed and to have contributed to a wave of corporate scandals in the last decade. They even liken poorly designed compensation schemes to "organizational heroin." They attribute this flaw to the overvaluation of equity (a bubble in other words) during this period. See Jensen *et al.*, *supra* note 114, at 44–9.

121 See Wilmarth, *supra* note 110, at 947–50.

122 Omarova, *supra* note 32.

123 For a comparative analysis of think tanks, see James G. McGann and R. Kent Weaver, eds., *Think Tanks and Civil Societies: Catalysts for Ideas and Action* (2002, Transaction Publishers). For a history of the U.S. Army War College, see Judith Stiehm, *The U.S. Army War College: Military Education in a Democracy* (2002, Temple University Press). For an analysis of the past and future roles of the Policy Planning Staff of the U.S. State Department, see Richard N. Haass, Planning for Policy Planning, in *Avoiding Trivia: The Role of Strategic Planning in American Foreign Policy*, 23 (Daniel W. Drezner ed., 2009, Brookings Institution Press).

124 The development of similar networks among national regulators has sparked a debate on their potential lack of democratic accountability. See Anne-Marie Slaughter, Global Government Networks, Global Information Agencies, and Disaggregated Democracy, 4 *Michigan Journal of International Law* 1041 (2003).

125 For an analysis of different forms of international cooperation in financial regulation and a policy blueprint for effective institutional design to promote further cooperation, see Eric J. Pan, The Challenge of International Cooperation and Institutional Design in Financial Supervision: Beyond Transgovernmental Networks, 11 *Chicago Journal of International Law* 243 (2010).

126 Stephen G. Cecchetti, Research in Central Banks, *Newsletter Studienzentrum Gerzensee* (September 2002) available at www.szgerzensee.ch/fileadmin/Dateien_ Anwender/Dokumente/newsletter/September02.pdf (last visited July 31, 2013) (describing elements of effective central bank research programs).

127 Dodd-Frank § 153(a), 124 Stat. 1415 (codified at 12 U.S.C. § 5343(a)).

128 These licensing proposals have come from scholars who occupy different points on the ideological spectrum and express differing policy concerns (for example, consumer protection versus overall economic efficiency and systemic risk). Compare Oren Bar-Gill and Elizabeth Warren, Making Credit Safer, 157 *University of Pennsylvania Law Review* 101 (2008) (proposing federal regulator to oversee financial products to protect consumers). Compare with Eric A. Posner and E. Glen Weyl, An FDA for Financial Innovation: Applying the Insurable Interest Doctrine to 21st-Century Financial Markets, 107 *Northwestern Law Review* 1307 (2013) (arguing for financial agency that would screen derivative products and only approve those used for hedging rather than speculation); Eric A. Posner and E. Glen Weyl, A Proposal for Limiting Speculation on Derivatives: An FDA for Financial Innovation, University of Chicago Institute for Law and Economics, *Olin Research Paper No. 594* (January 29, 2012), available at http://papers.ssrn.com/sol3/papers.cfm?abstract_id=1995077 (last visited July 31, 2013) (same).

129 Chapter 5, "An overview of how regulatory capital arbitrage works." See also Chapter 11, "Regulatory capital arbitrage revisited."

130 Lawrence A. Cunningham and David Zaring, The Three or Four Approaches to Financial Regulation: A Cautionary Analysis Against Exuberance in Crisis Response, 78 *George Washington Law Review* 39 (2009).

131 Charles K. Whitehead, The Goldilocks Approach: Financial Risk and Staged Regulation, 97 *Cornell Law Review* 1267 (2012); Roberta Romano, Regulating in the Dark, in *Regulatory Breakdown: The Crisis of Confidence in U.S. Regulation* (Cary Coglianese ed., 2012, University of Pennsylvania Press).

132 E.g., Dodd-Frank § 608(a), 124 Stat. 1609, (codified at 12 U.S.C. § 371c(f)).

133 Saule T. Omarova, From Gramm-Leach-Bliley to Dodd-Frank: The Unfulfilled Promise of Section 23A of the Federal Reserve Act, 89 *North Carolina Law Review* 101 (2011).

134 For example, the statute creates a "triple-key" system for designating certain non-banks as subject to the FDIC's "Orderly Liquidation Authority." Under the statute, certain non-depository financial institutions may be designated as "covered financial companies" and thus subject to liquidation by the Federal Depository Insurance Corporation upon insolvency instead of the U.S. Bankruptcy Code. To be designated as a "covered financial company," the statute creates a "three-key" system: generally,

the Treasury Secretary can make the designation only after making certain findings, obtaining the recommendation of two-thirds of the Federal Reserve Board of Governors, obtaining the recommendation of two-thirds of the FDIC Board, and consulting with the President. Dodd-Frank § 203(a)-(b), 124 Stat. 1450 (codified at 12 U.S.C. § 5383(a)-(b)). This process (together with a judicial review mechanism prescribed by the statute for this determination) is intended to check agency action and not to remedy agency inaction.

135 See 518 U.S. 839 (1996).

136 Ibid. at 871–3. The Court cited the following commentary from Blackstone:

> Acts of parliament derogatory from the power of subsequent parliaments bind not…. Because the legislature, being in truth the sovereign power, is always of equal, always of absolute authority: it acknowledges no superior upon earth, which the prior legislature must have been, if it's [*sic*] ordinances could bind the present parliament.
>
> Ibid. at 872 citing W. Blackstone, 1 *Commentaries on the Laws of England*, 90 (1765, Clarendon Press/University of Oxford)

The plurality opinion, however, noted that the presence of a written Constitution meant that Blackstone's rational for legislative entrenchment does not necessarily apply in the United States. 518 U.S. at 872–3 citing Julian N. Eule, Temporal Limits on the Legislative Mandate: Entrenchment and Retroactivity, 1987 *American Bar Foundation Research Journal* 379, 392–3. Justice Souter's opinion then looked at whether a number of constitutional provisions, including the Contracts Clause, would weigh in favor of honoring the government's contracts in the case at the expense of the ability of future legislatures and administrations from exercising their powers. 518 U.S. at 873–910.

137 In the case of *Bowsher* v. *Synar*, 478 U.S. 714 (1986), the U.S. Supreme Court ruled that provisions of a statute designed to limit the federal budget deficit were unconstitutional. That statute had assigned to the Comptroller General, an agent of Congress, certain functions that the court found lay solely within the province of the executive branch.

138 For a case in which the Supreme Court deferred to internal Senate rules on the Senate's internal procedure for impeaching a federal judge see *Nixon* v. *United States*, 506 U.S. 224 (1993).

139 U.S. Senate, Rules of the Senate, Precedence of Motions (Rule XXII).

140 The ability of a senator to place a secret hold originates from the unanimity requirement in the Morning Business rule of the Senate. See U.S. Senate, Rules of the Senate, Morning Business (Rule VII). Carl Hulse, Democrats Try to Break Grip of the Senate's Dr. No, *New York Times*, July 28, 2008, at A1.

141 For an account of deregulation that took place through changing agency interpretations of a statute, see Saule T. Omarova, The Quiet Metamorphosis: How Derivatives Changed the "Business of Banking," 63 *Miami Law Review* 1041 (2009).

142 Carolyn Sissoko, Is Financial Regulation Structurally Biased to Favor Deregulation? 86 *Southern California Law Review* 365 (2013).

143 Michael A. Livermore and Richard L. Revesz, Regulatory Review, Capture, and Agency Inaction, *New York University Law and Economics Working Paper 309* (2012) available at http://lsr.nellco.org/nyu_lewp/309 (last visited July 29, 2013).

144 *Chamber of Commerce of the U.S.* v. *SEC*, 412 F.3d 133 (D.C. Cir. 2005) (invalidating for failure to perform requisite cost–benefit analysis an SEC rule governing independent directors on mutual fund boards); *Business Roundtable* v. *SEC*, 647 F.3d 1144 (D.C. Cir. 2011) (ruling that SEC rule requiring proxy access was arbitrary and capricious because of failure of agency to perform appropriate cost–benefit analysis). Cf. *Goldstein* v. *SEC*, 451 F.3d 873 (D.C. Cir. 2006) (striking down hedge fund registration rule as arbitrary).

For a sampling of academic commentary on the SEC's struggles in the D.C. Circuit, see, e.g., Troy A. Paredes, On the Decision to Regulate Hedge Funds: The SEC's Regulatory Philosophy, Style, and Mission, 2006 *University of Illinois Law Review* 975 (2006); Donald C. Langevoort, The SEC as a Lawmaker: Choices about Investor Protection in the Face of Uncertainty, 84 *Washington University Law Review* 1591 (2006) (discussing case in which D.C. Circuit struck down SEC rule on mutual funds for failure to perform cost–benefit analysis); Edward Sherwin, The Cost-Benefit Analysis of Financial Regulation: Lessons from the SEC's Stalled Mutual Fund Reform Effort, 12 *Stanford Journal of Law, Business and Finance* 1 (2006) (arguing financial regulators need to justify regulation according to federal rules requiring cost–benefit analysis).

145 For a detailed analysis of the ways in which cost–benefit analysis has been misused in environmental regulation, see Richard L. Revesz and Michael A. Livermore, *Retaking Rationality: How Cost–Benefit Analysis Can Better Protect the Environment and Our Health* (2008, Oxford University Press).

146 For a sketch proposal of how to conduct cost–benefit analysis in the realm of financial regulation, see Eric Posner and E. Glen Weyl, Benefit–Cost Analysis for Financial Regulation, 103 *American Economic Review* 393 (2013).

147 For one critical examination during this period of calls for a single financial regulator, see Joseph J. Norton, Global Financial Sector Reform: The Single Financial Regulator Model Based on the United Kingdom FSA Experiences – A Critical Reevaluation, 39 *International Law* 15 (2005).

148 Cf. Eilís Ferran, The Break-up of the Financial Services Authority, 31 *Oxford Journal of Legal Studies* 455 (2011) (criticizing breakup of the FSA and analyzing its consequences).

149 *Supra* note 47.

150 Klaus C. Engelen, Germany's Fight over BaFin: The Ramifications of a Bundesbank Takeover, *International Economy* 54 (Winter 2010).

151 The FSOC enjoys a broad mandate to identify risks to financial stability, monitor financial regulatory developments, and make recommendations to various federal regulators. Dodd-Frank § 112(a), 124 Stat. 1393 (codified at 12 U.S.C. § 5322(a)).

152 The Dodd-Frank Act makes liberal use of Inspector Generals to police the behavior of financial regulatory agencies. See e.g., Dodd-Frank § 211(d), 124 Stat. 1514 (codified at 12 U.S.C. §5391(d)) (requiring review of FDIC by Inspector General of that agency).

153 Eric Fielding, Andrew W. Lo, and Jian Helen Yang, The National Transportation Safety Board: A Model for Systemic Risk Management, 9 *Journal of Investment Management* 17 (2011).

154 McDonnell and Schwarcz, *supra* note 31.

155 Committee to Establish the National Institute of Finance, www.ce-nif.org/ (last visited June 1, 2012); S. 3005, 111th Congress (2010).

156 The Dodd-Frank Act reflects these concerns. It gives one agency, the FSOC, the power to designate which non-bank financial companies are systemically significant, while other agencies take the lead in developing and enforcing the regulations that would apply to those designated companies. Dodd-Frank § 113, 124 Stat. 1398 (codified at 12 U.S.C. § 5323).

Of course any division of labor and the creation of checks and balance create coordination problems.

157 Ed deHaan, Kevin Koh, Simi Kedia, and Shivaram Rajgopal, Does the Revolving Door Affect the SEC's Enforcement Outcomes? American Accounting Association, Annual Meeting Presentation (July 2012) available at http://aaahq.org/newsroom/RajgopalDeHaanKediaKoh.pdf (last visited July 31, 2013); Edward Wyatt, Study Questions Risk of S.E.C. Revolving Door, *New York Times*, August 5, 2012, at B2.

158 Duncan Alford, Supervisory Colleges: The Global Financial Crisis and Improving International Supervisory Coordination, 24 *Emory International Law Review* 57 (2010).

159 Basel Committee on Banking Supervision, Basel III Regulatory Consistency Assessment Programme 5–7 (April 2012) available at www.bis.org/publ/bcbs216.pdf (last visited July 27, 2013).

160 Chris Brummer, How International Financial Law Works (and How It Doesn't), 99 *Georgetown Law Journal* 257, 280–1 (2011).

161 This is analogous to provisions in the Dodd-Frank Act that give certain financial regulators "back-up" authority to examine institutions subject to primary regulation by another agency. E.g., Dodd-Frank Act § 172, 124 Stat. 1438 (codified at 12 U.S.C. §1820(b)(3)) (giving FDIC back-up authority to examine certain non-bank financial companies supervised by Federal Reserve Board in connection with power of FDIC to take non-bank financial companies into receivership).

162 For a summary of dispute settlement mechanisms under the WTO and other important international regimes such as NAFTA, see Michael Trebilcock, Robert Howse, and Antonia Eliason, *The Regulation of International Trade*, 49–90 (5th ed. 2012, Routledge).

163 For a scholarly analysis of soft law in international financial regulation, see Chris Brummer, *Soft Law and the Global Financial System: Rule Making in the 21st Century* (2012).

164 See generally Stephen Clarkson, Integration and Disintegration in North America: The Rise and Fall of International Economic Law in One Region, 2 *European Yearbook of International Economic Law* 327 (2011).

165 Policymakers and scholars have considered various proposals to give private firms standing in WTO dispute settlement mechanisms as well. E.g., Thomas J. Schoenbaum, WTO Dispute Settlement: Praise and Suggestions for Reform, 47 *International and Comparative Law Quarterly* 647 (1998).

166 Jason Webb Yackee, Pacta Sunt Servanda and State Promises to Foreign Investors Before Bilateral Investment Treaties: Myth and Reality, 32 *Fordham International Law Journal* 1550 (2008).

167 Federal Financial Institutions Examination Council Central Data Repository (CDR) Public Data Distribution (PDD) Frequently Asked Questions, available at https://cdr.ffiec.gov/public/HelpFileContainers/FAQ.aspx (last visited July 15, 2012).

168 Gerding, *supra* note 46.

169 Ibid.

170 Ibid. at 151 citing Kenneth C. Kettering, Securitization and Its Discontents: The Dynamics of Financial Product Development, 29 *Cardozo Law Review* 1553, 1674–6 (describing rating agencies as "de facto lawmakers").

171 Gerding, *supra* note 46, at 153.

172 Frank Partnoy, The Siskel and Ebert of Financial Markets? Two Thumbs Down for the Credit Rating Agencies, 77 *Washington University Law Quarterly* 619, 681 (1999).

173 Gerding, *supra* note 46, at 154–7.

174 Gerding, *supra* note 46, at 158–9. Alternative Net Capital Requirements for Broker-Dealers That Are Part of Consolidated Supervised Entities, Exchange Act Release No. 34–49, 830, 69 *Federal Register* 34,428 (June 21, 2004) (codified at 17 C.F.R. pts. 200 and 240).

175 Gerding, *supra* note 46, at 158–9.

176 Office of Inspector General, SEC's Oversight of Bear Stearns and Related Entities: The Consolidated Supervised Entity Program 4 (2008), *Report No. 446-B* (September 25, 2008) available at www.sec-oig.gov/Reports/AuditsInspections/2008/446-a.pdf (last visited July 31, 2013).

177 Conrad de Aenlle, When Crisis Hit, a Global Framework for Limiting Risk Proved Ineffective, *New York Times*, October 19, 2008, available at www.nytimes.

com/2008/11/20/business/worldbusiness/20iht-rriskbis.1.17962169.html?pagewanted=
all (last visited July 31, 2013); Jack Ewing, A Fight to Make Banks More Prudent, *New
York Times*, December 21, 2011, at B1; Sins of the Few, *World Finance* (December 12,
2008) (online edition) available at www.worldfinance.com/home/final-bell/sins-of-the-
few (last visited July 31, 2013).

178 Gerding, *supra* note 46, at 185, 188.
179 Partnoy, *supra* note 172.
180 Gerding, *supra* note 46, at 129–34 (analogizing the delegation of regulatory responsibility to models as creating a "new financial code"), 190–1 (outlining benefits of
"open source" risk models).
181 Schooner, *supra* note 10.
182 Gretchen Morgenson and Louise Story, Rating Agency Data Aided Wall Street in
Deals, *New York Times*, April 24, 2010, at A1.
183 Chapter 1, "Rigor and pragmatism in identifying bubbles."
184 Chapter 1, "Rigor and pragmatism in identifying bubbles."
185 Chapter 1, "Rigor and pragmatism in identifying bubbles."
186 Chapter 1, "Rigor and pragmatism in identifying bubbles."
187 This review is required by statute. 10 U.S.C § 118 (2009).
188 Dodd-Frank § 112(b)(1), 124 Stat. 1396 (codified at 12 U.S.C. § 5322(b)(1)).
189 Dodd-Frank § 112(b)(2) 124 Stat. 1396 (codified at 12 U.S.C. § 5322(b)(2)).
190 For a somewhat dated but still insightful analysis of the theory and practice of the
National Environmental Policy Act, see Serge Taylor, *Making Bureaucracies Think:
The Environmental Impact Statement Strategy of Administrative Reform* (1985, Stanford University Press).
191 This chapter uses the term "adaptive" to mean flexible regulations that policymakers
adjust to economic or political conditions. Other legal scholars have used the term
"adaptive regulations" to describe regulations formulated together by public and
private sector actors. For a small sample of the literature in this vein, see Lawrence
G. Baxter, Adaptive Regulation in the Amoral Bazaar, 128 *South African Law
Journal* 253–72 (2011) (arguing that this type of regulation must be grounded in
morality); Philip J. Weiser, The Future of Internet Regulation, 43 *UC Davis Law
Review* 529 (2009); Gideon Parchomovsky and Philip J. Weiser, Beyond Fair Use,
96 *Cornell Law Review* 91 (2010).
192 For a cultural study of the securities regulation created in the wake of certain English
bubbles that examines the role of morality in passing these new rules, see Stuart
Banner, *Anglo-American Securities Regulation* (1998, Cambridge University Press).
193 Tulips were used for their symbolic value as *memento mori* and *vanitas* devices. Ann
Goldgar, *Tulipmania: Money, Honor, and Knowledge in the Dutch Golden Age*,
90–2 (2007, University of Chicago Press). Art historians have noted that painters
and patrons valued this flower for a number of reasons, not least because of their
exotic beauty and their role as status symbol in seventeenth century Holland. For
histories of the tulip motif in Dutch and European painting, see Celia Fisher, *Flowers
of the Renaissance*, 79–86 (2011, J. Paul Getty Museum). See also Simon Schama,
*The Embarrassment of Riches: An Interpretation of Dutch Culture in the Golden
Age*, 162 (1991, Harper Perennial) (discussing *vanitas* and *memento mori* paintings
in the Netherlands, including in responses French Mississippi bubble); ibid. at
359–71 (analyzing other Dutch art motifs that responded to Tulipomania). Examples
of the tulip in *vanitas* paintings also date to before the 1637 Tulipomania. Cf. Benjamin R. Bennett-Carpenter, *Moving Memento Mori Pictures: Documentary, Mor-
tality, and Transformation in Three Films*, 63 n. 14 (2008, ProQuest) (describing
1603 painting). But see Fred G. Meijer, *Dutch and Flemish Still-life Paintings*, 25–6
(2003, Ashmolean Museum) (rejecting claims that tulips in paintings after Tulipomania referenced that financial crisis and arguing these flowers were inherently
popular painting subjects because of their beauty).

Index

Page numbers in *italics* denote tables, those in **bold** denote figures.

CPSIA information can be obtained
at www.ICGtesting.com
Printed in the USA
BVHW04s2143200718
522131BV00002B/16/P

9 781138 674394